MAGILL'S
SURVEY
OF
SCIENCE

MAGILL'S
SURVEY
OF
SCIENCE

EARTH SCIENCE SERIES

Volume 4
1681-2224
Physical Properties of Minerals—Rock Magnetism

Edited by
FRANK N. MAGILL

Consulting Editor
Dr. James A. Woodhead

SALEM PRESS
Pasadena, California   Englewood Cliffs, New Jersey

∞ The paper used in these volumes conforms to the
American National Standard for Permanence of Paper
for Printed Library Materials, Z39.48-1984.

Library of Congress Cataloging-in-Publication Data
Magill's survey of science. Earth science series/edited
by Frank N. Magill.
    p. cm.
    Includes bibliographical references.
    1. Earth sciences. I. Magill, Frank Northen,
1907-
QE28.M33   1990   89-10923
550—dc20   CIP
ISBN 0-89356-606-3 (set)
ISBN 0-89356-610-1 (volume 4)

PRINTED IN THE UNITED STATES OF AMERICA

CONTENTS

EARTH SCIENCE

MAGILL'S
SURVEY
OF
SCIENCE

PHYSICAL PROPERTIES OF MINERALS

Type of earth science: Geology
Field of study: Mineralogy and crystallography

Minerals are naturally occurring, inorganic solids with a definite chemical composition and a definite crystal structure. Many minerals are readily identified by their physical properties, but identification of other minerals may require instruments designed to examine details of their chemical composition or crystal structure. The characteristic physical properties of some minerals, such as hardness, malleability, ductility, and electrical properties, make them commercially useful and economically valuable.

Principal terms

CLEAVAGE: the tendency for minerals to break in smooth, flat planes along zones of weaker bonds in their crystal structure

CRYSTAL: a solid bounded by smooth planar surfaces that are the outward expression of the internal arrangement of atoms; crystal faces on a mineral result from precipitation in a favorable environment

CRYSTALLINE: a characteristic of a solid, indicating that it has a regular periodic arrangement of atoms in a three-dimensional framework

DENSITY: in an informal sense, the relative weight of mineral samples of equal size; it is defined as mass per unit volume

LUMINESCENCE: the emission of light by a mineral

LUSTER: the reflectivity of the mineral surface; there are two major categories of luster: metallic and nonmetallic

MINERAL: a naturally occurring, inorganic, homogeneous solid with a definite chemical composition and a definite crystal structure

MOHS HARDNESS SCALE: a series of ten minerals arranged in order of increasing hardness, with talc as the softest mineral known (1) and diamond as the hardest (10)

ROCK: an aggregate of one or more minerals

TENACITY: the resistance of a mineral to bending, breakage, crushing, or tearing

Summary of the Phenomenon

Minerals are the building blocks of rocks. A mineral is a naturally occurring, inorganic, homogeneous solid with a definite chemical composition (or definite range of compositions), which can be expressed by a chemical formula, and a definite atomic crystal structure, which is reflected in its crystal shape and other physical properties. By definition, man-made materials cannot be minerals and, therefore, synthetic gemstones produced in the laboratory are not considered minerals. Also, minerals are inorganic, meaning that they are not produced by organisms and are not composed of organic (carbon-based) molecules. As a result, pearls are not minerals. Coal and hydrocarbons are not minerals because they are not homogeneous and because they contain organic molecules. Minerals must be solids, which means that liquids are not minerals (although liquid mercury is sometimes considered to be a mineral; mercury is a solid at temperatures below -40 degrees Celsius).

The chemistry of some minerals varies within a particular range because of substitution of one element for another in the crystal structure (ionic substitution). For example, iron (Fe^{2+}) and magnesium (Mg^{2+}) may substitute for each other in the olivine minerals. In the plagioclase feldspars, calcium (Ca^{2+}) may substitute for sodium (Na^{1+}), with a concomitant substitution of aluminum (Al^{3+}) for silicon (Si^{4+}) so that the mineral remains electrically neutral.

Crystal structure is the internal ordering of atoms in a specific three-dimensional geometric framework, called a crystal lattice. Crystal faces are the outward expression of this internal ordering. All specimens of a particular mineral have the same internal crystal structure and are referred to as crystalline, regardless of whether crystal faces are present. Volcanic glass is not a mineral, because it lacks an orderly internal atomic crystal structure; it is a noncrystalline, amorphous material.

Minerals have diagnostic physical properties resulting from their chemistry and crystal structure. Physical properties of minerals include color, hardness, streak, luster, crystal shape, cleavage, fracture, and density, or specific gravity. Several minerals have additional diagnostic physical properties, including tenacity, magnetism, taste, reaction to hydrochloric acid, luminescence, and radioactivity.

Color is an obvious physical property, but it is one of the least diagnostic for mineral identification. In some minerals, color results from the presence of major elements in the chemical formula; in these minerals, color is a diagnostic property. For example, malachite is always green, azurite is always blue, and rhodochrosite and rhodonite are always pink. In other minerals, color is the result of trace amounts of chemical impurities or of defects in the crystal lattice structure. Depending on the impurities, a particular species of mineral can have many different colors. For example, pure quartz is colorless, but quartz may be white (milky quartz), pink (rose quartz), purple (amethyst), yellow (citrine), brown (smoky quartz), green, blue, or black. Similarly, fluorite may be colorless, white, pink, purple, blue, brown, green, or yellow. The following is a partial list of colors and trace chemical impurities which may cause them: Pink coloration may be caused by iron or titanium; green coloration may be caused by iron, chromium, or vanadium; blue coloration may be caused by titanium, titanium and iron, or a combination of iron with different valences; yellow coloration may be caused by nickel, and greenish yellow coloration may be caused by iron. The color of sphalerite varies from white to yellow to brown to black, with increasing amounts of iron substituting for zinc. Defects in the crystal lattice structure can also cause color. For example, the purple color of fluorite and amethyst and the brown color of smoky quartz result from defects in the crystal structure. Some structural effects (and colors) can be caused by exposing minerals to radiation. Some minerals have different colors depending on the direction in which the mineral is oriented as light passes through it. This property is known as pleochroism and is best seen in thin sections or small mineral grains using a petrographic microscope. Hornblende, hypersthene, tourmaline, and staurolite are pleochroic.

Hardness is the resistance of a mineral to scratching or abrasion. Hardness is a result of crystal structure; the stronger the bonding forces between the atoms, the harder the mineral. The Mohs hardness scale, devised by a German mineralogist, Friedrich Mohs, in 1822, is a series of ten minerals arranged in order of increasing hardness. The minerals on the Mohs hardness scale are talc (the softest mineral known), gypsum, calcite, fluorite, apatite, potassium feldspar (orthoclase), quartz, topaz, corundum, and diamond (the hardest mineral known). A mineral with higher hardness number can scratch any mineral of equal or lower hardness number. The relative hardness of a mineral is easily tested using a number of common materials, including the fingernail (a little over 2), a copper coin (about 3), a steel nail or pocket knife (a little over 5), a piece of glass (about 5.5), and a steel file (6.5). The hardness of some minerals varies with crystallographic direction. For example, kyanite can be scratched with a knife parallel to the direction of elongation, but it cannot be scratched perpendicular to the elongation.

Streak is the color of the mineral in powdered form. Streak is more definitive than mineral color, because although a mineral may have several color varieties, the streak will be the same for all. Streak is best viewed after rubbing the mineral across an unglazed porcelain tile. The tile has a hardness of approximately 7, so minerals with a hardness of greater than 7 will not leave a streak, although their powdered color may be studied by crushing a small piece.

Luster refers to the reflectivity of the mineral surface. There are two major categories of luster: metallic and nonmetallic. Metallic minerals include metals (such as native copper and gold), as well as many metal sulfides, such as pyrite and galena. Another metal sulfide, sphalerite, commonly has a submetallic luster, although in some samples, its luster is nonmetallic. Nonmetallic lusters can be described as vitreous or glassy (characteristic of quartz and olivine), resinous (resembling resin or amber, characteristic of sulfur and some samples of sphalerite), adamantine or brilliant (diamond), greasy (appearing as if covered by a thin film of oil, including nepheline and some samples of massive quartz), silky (in minerals with parallel fibers, such as malachite, chrysotile asbestos, or fibrous gypsum), pearly (similar to an iridescent pearl-like shell, such as talc), and earthy or dull (as in clays).

Crystal shape is the outward expression of the internal three-dimensional arrangement of atoms in the crystal lattice. Crystals are formed in a cooling or evaporating fluid as atoms begin to slow down, move closer, and bond together in a particular geometric gridwork. If minerals are unconfined and free to grow, they will form well-shaped, regular crystals. On the other hand, if growing minerals are confined by other, surrounding minerals, they may have irregular shapes. Because crystal faces are related to the internal structure of a mineral, the crystal faces of several specimens of the same mineral will be similar. This fact was observed as early as 1669 by Nicolaus Steno, who observed that "the angles between equivalent faces of crystals of the same substance, measured at the same temperature, are constant," which is commonly referred to as the Law of Constancy of Interfacial Angles. Although different crystals of the same mineral may be different sizes, the angles between corresponding crystal faces are always the same. Some of the common shapes or growth habits of crystals include acicular (or needlelike, such as natrolite), bladed (elongated and flat like a knife blade, such as kyanite), blocky (equidimensional and cubelike, such as galena and fluorite), and columnar or prismatic (elongated or pencil-like, such as quartz and tourmaline). Other crystal shapes are described as pyramidal, stubby, tabular, barrel-shaped, or capillary.

Cleavage is the tendency for minerals to break in smooth, flat planes along zones of weaker bonds in their crystal structure. Cleavage is one of the most important physical properties in identifying minerals because it is so closely related to the internal crystal structure. Cleavage is best developed in minerals that have particularly weak chemical bonds in a given direction. In other minerals, differences in bond strength are less pronounced, so cleavage is less well developed. Some minerals have no planes of weakness in their crystal structure; they lack cleavage and do not break along planes. Cleavage can occur in one direction (as in the micas, muscovite, and biotite) or in more than one direction. The number and orientation of the cleavage planes are always the same for a particular mineral. For example, orthoclase feldspar has two directions of cleavage at right angles to each other. The amphiboles (hornblende, tremolite, actinolite, and the like) also have two directions of cleavage, but at angles of approximately 56 and 124 degrees. Cubic cleavage (three directions at right angles) is a characteristic feature of halite (table salt) and galena. Rhombohedral cleavage (three directions not at right angles) is characteristic of calcite. Fluorite has four directions of cleavage, which produces octahedral (eight-sided) cleavage fragments with triangular cleavage faces. Sphalerite has six directions of cleavage (dodecahedral cleavage). Cleavage is an outstanding criterion for identification of minerals in which it is well developed.

Fracture is irregular breakage that is not controlled by planes of weakness in minerals. Conchoidal fracture is a smooth, curved breakage surface, commonly marked by fine concentric lines, resembling the surface of a shell. Conchoidal fracture is common in broken glass and quartz. Fibrous or splintery fracture occurs in asbestos and sometimes in gypsum. Hackly facture is jagged with sharp edges and occurs in native copper. Uneven or irregular fracture produces rough, irregular breakage surfaces.

Density is defined as mass per unit volume (typically measured in terms of grams per cubic centimeter). In a very informal sense, density refers to the relative weight of samples of equal size. Quartz has a density of 2.6 grams per cubic centimeter, whereas a "heavy" mineral such as galena has a density of 7.4 grams per cubic centimeter (about three times as heavy). Specific gravity (or relative density) is the ratio of the weight of a substance to the weight of an equal volume of water at 4 degrees Celsius. The terms "density" and "specific gravity" are sometimes used interchangeably, but density requires the use of units of measure (such as grams per cubic centimeter), whereas specific gravity is unitless. Specific gravity is an important aid in mineral identification, particularly when studying valuable minerals or gemstones, which might be damaged by other tests of physical properties. The specific gravity of a mineral depends on the chemical composition (type and weight of atoms) as well as the manner in which the atoms are packed together.

Tenacity is the resistance of a mineral to bending, breakage, crushing, or tearing. A mineral may be brittle (breaks or powders easily), malleable (may be hammered out into thin sheets), ductile (may be drawn out into a thin wire), sectile (may be cut into thin shavings with a knife), flexible (bendable, and stays bent), and elastic (bendable, but returns to its original form). Minerals with ionic bonding, such as halite, tend to be brittle. Malleability, ductility, and sectility are diagnostic of minerals with metallic bonding, such as gold. Chlorite and talc are flexible, and muscovite is elastic.

Magnetism causes minerals to be attracted to magnets. Magnetite and pyrrhotite are the only common magnetic minerals, and they are called ferromagnetic. Lodestone, a type of magnetite, is a natural magnet. When in a strong magnetic field, some minerals become weakly magnetic and are attracted to the magnet; these minerals are called paramagnetic. Examples of paramagnetic minerals include garnet, biotite, and tourmaline. Other minerals are repelled by a magnetic field and are called diamagnetic minerals. Examples of diamagnetic minerals include gypsum, halite, and quartz.

Some minerals are easily identified by their taste. Most notable is halite, or common table salt. Another mineral with a distinctive taste is sylvite, which is distinguished from halite by its more bitter taste. Some minerals, such as calcite, effervesce or fizz when they come into contact with hydrochloric acid; the bubbles of gas released are carbon dioxide. Other minerals that effervesce in hydrochloric acid include aragonite, dolomite if powdered, and malachite. Most of the carbonate minerals will react with hydrochloric acid, although some will not react unless the acid is heated.

Luminescence is the term for emission of light by a mineral. Minerals that glow or luminesce in ultraviolet light, X rays, or cathode rays are fluorescent minerals. The glow is the result of the mineral changing invisible radiation to visible light, which happens when the radiation is absorbed by the crystal lattice and then reemitted by the mineral at lower energy and longer wavelength. Fluorescence occurs in some specimens of a mineral but not all. Examples of minerals which may fluoresce include fluorite, calcite, diamond, scheelite, willemite, and scapolite. Some minerals will continue to glow or emit light after the radiation source is turned off; these minerals are phosphorescent. Some minerals glow when heated, a property called thermoluminescence, present in some specimens of fluorite, calcite, apatite, scapolite, lepidolite, and feldspar. Other minerals luminesce when crushed, scratched, or rubbed, a property called triboluminescence, present in some specimens of sphalerite, corundum, fluorite, and lepidolite and, less commonly, in feldspar and calcite. Luminescence is generally caused by the presence of certain rare earth or lanthanide elements, or uranium or thorium. The fluorescence of specimens of calcite and willemite from Franklin, New Jersey, is attributed to the presence of manganese.

Radioactive minerals contain unstable elements that alter spontaneously to other kinds of elements, releasing subatomic particles and energy. Some elements come in several different forms, differing by the number of neutrons present in the nucleus. These different forms are called isotopes, and one isotope of an element may be unstable (radioactive), whereas another isotope may be stable (not radioactive). Radioactive isotopes include potassium 40, rubidium 87, thorium 232, uranium 235, and uranium 238. Examples of radioactive minerals include urananite and thorianite.

Some minerals also have interesting electrical characteristics. Quartz is a piezoelectric mineral, meaning that when squeezed, it produces electrical charges. Conversely, if an electrical charge is applied to a quartz crystal, it will change shape and vibrate as internal stresses develop. The oscillation of quartz is the basis for its use in digital quartz watches.

Methods of Study

In many cases, the physical properties of minerals can be studied using relatively common, inexpensive tools. For example, hardness may be determined by attempting to scratch the mineral in question with a number of common objects, including a fingernail, copper coin, pocket knife or nail, piece of glass, or steel file. The relative hardness of a mineral may also be determined by attempting to scratch one mineral with another, thereby bracketing the unknown mineral's hardness between that of other minerals on the Mohs hardness scale. Streak may be determined by rubbing the mineral across an unglazed porcelain tile to observe the color (and sometimes odor) of the streak, if any. Color and luster are determined simply by observing the mineral.

The angles between adjacent crystal faces may be measured using a goniometer. There are several types of goniometers, but the simplest is a protractor with a pivoting bar, which is held against a large crystal so that the angles between faces can be measured. There are also reflecting goniometers, which operate by measuring the angles between light beams reflected from crystal faces.

Density can be determined by measuring the mass of a mineral and determining its volume (perhaps by measuring the amount of water it displaces in a graduated cylinder), then dividing these two measurements. In order to determine the specific gravity (SG) of a mineral, it is necessary to have a specimen that is homogeneous, without cracks, and without bits of other minerals attached. Mineral specimens with a volume of about 1 cubic centimeter are most useful. Specific gravity is usually determined by first weighing the mineral in air and then weighing it while it is immersed in water. When immersed in water, it weighs less because it is buoyed up by a force equivalent to the weight of the water displaced. A Jolly balance, which works by stretching a spiral spring, can measure specific gravity. For tiny mineral specimens weighing less than 25 milligrams, a torsion balance (or Berman balance) is useful for accurate determinations. Heavy liquids, such as bromoform (SG = 2.89) and methylene iodide (SG = 3.33), are also used to determine the specific gravity of small mineral grains. In heavy liquids, grains of quartz (SG = 2.65) will float, whereas heavy minerals, such as zircon (SG = 4.68) or garnet (SG = 3.5 to 4.3), will sink. The mineral grain is placed into the heavy liquid and then acetone is added to the liquid until the mineral grain neither floats nor sinks (that is, until the specific gravity of the mineral and the liquid are the same). Then, the specific gravity of the liquid is determined using a Westphal balance.

An ultraviolet light source (with both long and short wavelengths) is used to determine whether minerals are fluorescent or phosphorescent. A portable ultraviolet light can be used to prospect for fluorescent minerals. Thermoluminescence can be triggered by heating a mineral to 50-100 degrees Celsius. Radioactivity is measured using a Geiger counter or scintillometer.

Minerals may be identified using a number of techniques and instruments, including X-ray diffraction, differential thermal analysis, thermogravimetric analysis, the electron microscope, and the petrographic microscope. X-ray diffraction works by bombarding a crystal or powdered mineral with X rays. When the X rays strike the mineral, they are scattered or diffracted; the X rays penetrate below the mineral surface and are reflected from layers of atoms in the crystal lattice. Minerals can then be identified by comparing the positions and intensities of the reflections produced with those listed in standard tables of mineral data. Differential thermal analysis (DTA) identifies temperatures at which one mineral is transformed into another; it is used primarily to identify clay minerals. Thermogravimetric analysis, which is commonly used in conjunction with DTA, measures the change in weight of minerals as they are heated. The electron microscope allows the mineralogist to study extremely small minerals. The transmission electron microscope is used to gain insights into the structure of minerals. The scanning electron microscope is primarily used to examine surface details of minerals. The energy dispersive analyzer can be used in conjunction with both types of electron microscope and can provide semiquantitative chemical analyses of selected mineral particles.

A petrographic microscope with a polarized light source is required for studying optical properties of minerals, which can be extremely useful in identification. Optical properties can be studied using crushed or powdered samples of minerals (called grain mounts) or with thin sections of rocks. The optical properties are determined by observing changes in polarized light passing through the mineral. Optical properties include index of refraction, birefringence, relief, pleochroism, extinction angle, and interference figures. A universal stage may be used to change the orientation of the mineral for more accurate measurements of optical properties. Index of refraction refers to the ratio between the velocity of light in a vacuum and to the velocity of light in the mineral. In general, high refractive index is related to high specific gravity. Index of refraction is commonly measured by placing crushed grains of an unknown mineral in oils of known refractive index for comparison. Birefringence, which is present in minerals that have more than one index of refraction, splits a beam of light passing through the mineral into two beams of unequal velocities. Birefringence is studied by its color in crossed polarized light on minerals of known thickness. Relief is the difference between the refractive index of the mineral and the refractive index of the surrounding material (usually a mounting medium such as Canada balsam or epoxy); it is studied by observing how clearly the mineral stands out from the mounting medium. Pleochroism is a difference in the color of a mineral as it is rotated on the microscope stage in plane polarized light.

Chemical analyses of minerals may be performed using wet chemistry (which requires dissolution of mineral specimens), blowpipe analysis (an old technique for studying the behavior of a mineral in a flame), neutron activation analysis (usually performed in a nuclear reactor, with neutrons bombarding the mineral, producing characteristic radioisotopes that are studied with gamma-ray spectroscopy), atomic absorption spectrometry (which involves dissolution of the mineral and studying how light emitted by a cathode-ray tube is absorbed by a flame produced by burning the liquid sample), X-ray fluorescence spectrometry (XRF, which bombards a mineral with X rays and examines the wavelengths of radiation emitted from the mineral), the electron microprobe (which works like XRF—but with an electron beam to bombard the atoms in the mineral—and can be used to study the chemical composition of very small areas of minerals), and cathodoluminescence (which activates minerals using an electron beam, thus exciting certain ions and producing luminescence).

Context

The physical properties of minerals affect their usefulness for commercial applications. Minerals with great hardness, such as diamonds, corundum (sapphire and ruby), garnets, and quartz, are useful as abrasives and in cutting and drilling equipment. Other minerals are useful because of their softness, such as calcite (hardness 3), which is used in cleansers because it will not scratch the surface being cleaned. Also, calcite in the form of marble is commonly used for sculpture because it is relatively soft and easy to carve. Alabaster, a form of gypsum (hardness 2), is also commonly carved and used for decorative purposes. Soapstone, made of the mineral talc (hardness 1), was quarried and carved by American Indians in eastern North America. Talc is also used in talcum powder because of its softness.

Some metals, such as copper, are ductile, which makes them useful for the manufacture of wire. Copper is one of the best electrical conductors. Copper is also a good conductor of heat and is often used in cookware. Gold is the most malleable and ductile mineral. Because of its malleability, gold can be hammered into sheets so thin that 300,000 of them would be required to make a stack 1 inch high.

Because of its ductility, 1 gram of gold (about the weight of a raisin) can be drawn into a wire more than a mile and a half long. Pure gold is too soft to be used in coins or jewelry and is almost always alloyed with other metals (such as silver, or copper) to harden it. Because of its high specific gravity (SG = 19.3 when pure), gold can be collected by panning in streams. Gold is the best conductor of heat and electricity known, but it is generally too expensive to use as a conductor.

Other minerals are valuable because they do not conduct heat or electricity. They are used as electrical insulators or for products subjected to high temperatures. For example, kyanite, andalusite, and sillimanite are used in the manufacture of spark plugs and other high-temperature porcelains. Muscovite is also useful because of its electrical and heat-insulating properties; sheets of muscovite are often used as an insulating material in electrical devices. The "isinglass" used in furnace and stove doors is muscovite. Sheets of muscovite were used as windowpanes in medieval Europe because of the mineral's cleavage, transparency, near absence of color, and glassy luster. Because of its glassy luster, ground muscovite is commonly used to give wallpaper a shiny finish.

The fibrous cleavage, flexibility, incombustibility (flame resistance), and low conductivity of heat that are characteristic of asbestos (chrysotile, crocidolite, and other asbestos minerals) make it ideally suited for fireproofing, heat and electrical insulation, roofing materials, and brake linings. Asbestos can also be woven into fireproof fabrics because of its flexible fibers. The use of asbestos is declining, however, because of health concerns; the tiny, needlelike fibers may become lodged in the lungs, leading to various asbestos-related diseases.

Cleavage is the property responsible for the use of graphite as a dry lubricant and in pencils. Graphite has perfect cleavage in one direction, and is slippery because microscopic sheets of graphite slide easily over one another. A "lead" pencil is actually a mixture of graphite and clay; it writes by leaving tiny cleavage flakes of graphite on the paper. Conchoidal fracture is the property which permits arrow-heads and stone tools to be made from quartz, cryptocrystalline quartz (flint and chert), and obsidian (volcanic glass). The sharp edges are produced where many conchoidal fractures merge.

The color of the streak (or crushed powder) of many minerals makes them valuable as pigments. Hematite has a red streak and is used in paints and cosmetics. Lazurite has a blue powder and was once used as the paint pigment ultramarine blue (now produced artificially). Silver is commonly used in photographic films and papers because in the form of silver halide, it is light-sensitive and turns black. After developing and fixing, metallic silver remains on the film to form the negative. Silver is also one of the best conductors of heat and electricity and is often used in electronics.

The uranium-bearing minerals (urananite, carnotite, torbernite, and autunite) are used as sources of uranium, which is important because its nucleus is susceptible to fission (splitting or radioactive disintegration), producing tremendous amounts of energy. This energy is used in nuclear power plants for generating electricity and in atom bombs. Pitchblende, a variety of urananite, is a source of radium, which is used as a source of radioactivity in industry and medicine. The high specific gravity of barite makes it a useful additive to drilling muds to prevent oil well gushers or blowouts. It is also opaque to X rays and is used in medicine for "barium milk-shakes" before patients are X-rayed so that the digestive tract will show up clearly.

Many minerals are economically valuable because of their unique physical properties. Others are useful as a result of their chemical properties. These include halite, or table salt; sylvite, which is used as a salt substitute for persons with high blood pressure and as a source of potassium for fertilizers; apatite, which is used as a source of phosphate for fertilizers; borax minerals, which are used in the manufacture of boric acid and detergents; gypsum, which is used in plaster of paris and wallboard; and numerous minerals that are ores for iron, lead, copper and zinc, and other metals.

Bibliography

Blackburn, W. H., and W. H. Dennen. *Principles of Mineralogy.* Dubuque, Iowa: Wm. C. Brown, 1988. This book is divided into three parts: The first part is theoretical and includes crystallography and crystal chemistry, along with a section on the mineralogy of major types of rocks. The second part is practical and includes chapters on physical properties of minerals, crystal geometry, optical properties, and methods of analysis. The third part contains systematic mineral descriptions. Designed for an introductory college course in mineralogy, but should be useful for amateurs as well.

Bloss, F. D. *An Introduction to the Methods of Optical Crystallography.* New York: Holt, Rinehart and Winston, 1961. This book is for the advanced student of mineralogy who is interested in the ways in which the crystal structure of a mineral changes the characteristics of a beam of light passing through it, as studied with the petrographic microscope. Theoretical, it may be of interest to persons with a background in physics or geology.

Chesterman, C. W., and K. E. Lowe. *The Audubon Society Field Guide to North American Rocks and Minerals.* New York: Alfred A. Knopf, 1988. This book contains 702 color photographs of minerals, grouped by color, as well as nearly a hundred color photographs of rocks. All the mineral photographs are placed at the beginning of the book, and descriptive information follows, with the minerals grouped by chemistry. Distinctive features and physical properties are listed for each of the minerals, and information on collecting localities is also given. A section at the back of the book discusses various types of rocks. A glossary is also included. Suitable for the layperson.

Desautels, P. E. *The Mineral Kingdom.* New York: Ridge Press, 1968. An oversize, lavishly illustrated coffee-table book with useful text supplementing the color photographs. It covers how minerals are formed, found, and used and includes legends about minerals and gems as well as scientific data. Provides a broad introduction to the field of mineralogy. Intended for the amateur, it also makes fascinating reading for the professional geologist.

Frye, Keith. *Modern Mineralogy.* Englewood Cliffs, N.J.: Prentice-Hall, 1974. This book addresses minerals from a chemical standpoint and includes chapters on crystal chemistry, structure, symmetry, physical properties, radiant energy and crystalline matter, the phase rule, and mineral genesis. Designed as an advanced college textbook for a student who already has some familiarity with mineralogy. Includes short descriptions of minerals in a table in the appendix.

Kerr, P. F. *Optical Mineralogy.* New York: McGraw-Hill, 1977. This book is designed to instruct advanced mineralogy students in the study and identification of minerals using a petrographic microscope. The first part concerns the basic principles of optical mineralogy, and the second part details the optical properties of a long list of minerals.

Klein, C., and C. S. Hurlbut, Jr. *Manual of Mineralogy.* 20th ed. New York: John Wiley & Sons, 1985. One of a series of revisions of the original mineralogy textbook written by James D. Dana in 1848. The first part of the book is dedicated to crystallography and crystal chemistry, with shorter chapters on the physical and optical properties of minerals. The second part of the book provides a classification and detailed, systematic description of various types of minerals, with sections on gem minerals and mineral associations. Considered to be the premier mineralogy textbook for college-level geology students; many parts of it will be useful for amateurs.

Mottana, A., R. Crespi, and G. Liborio. *Simon & Schuster's Guide to Rocks and Minerals.* New York: Simon & Schuster, 1978. This book is fully illustrated with color photographs of 276 minerals. It provides background information on physical properties, environment of formation, occurrences, and uses of each mineral. A sixty-page introduction to minerals provides sophisticated technical coverage that will be of interest to both mineralogy students and amateurs. The last part of the book illustrates and describes one hundred types of rocks. A glossary is also included.

Pough, F. H. *A Field Guide to Rocks and Minerals.* Boston: Houghton Mifflin, 1976. This well-written and well-illustrated book is suitable for readers of nearly any age and background. One of the most readable and accessible sources, it provides a fairly complete coverage of the minerals. Designed for amateurs.

Zussman, J., ed. *Physical Methods in Determinative Mineralogy.* New York: Academic Press, 1967. A reference book that describes technical methods used in the study of rocks and minerals, including transmitted and reflected light microscopy, electron microscopy, X-ray fluorescence spectroscopy, X-ray diffraction, electron microprobe microanalysis, and atomic absorption spectroscopy. Written for the professional geologist or advanced student.

Pamela J. W. Gore

Cross-References

THE STRUCTURE OF MINERALS

Type of earth science: Geology
Field of study: Mineralogy and crystallography

The discovery of the internal structures of minerals by the use of X-ray diffraction was pivotal in the history of mineralogy and crystallography. X-ray analysis revealed that the physical properties and chemical behavior of minerals are directly related to the highly organized arrangements of their atoms, and this knowledge has had important scientific and industrial applications.

Principal terms

CLEAVAGE: the capacity of crystals to split readily in certain directions; in well-defined structures, cleavage planes pass between sheets of atoms

CRYSTAL: externally, a solid material of regular form bounded by flat surfaces called faces; internally, a substance whose orderly structure results from a periodic three-dimensional arrangement of atoms

ION: an electrically charged atom or group of atoms

IONIC BOND: the strong electrical forces holding together positively and negatively charged ions (for example, sodium and chloride ions in common salt)

MINERAL: a naturally formed inorganic substance with characteristic physical properties, a definite chemical composition, and, in most cases, a regular crystal structure

X RAY: radiation interpretable in terms of either very short electromagnetic waves or highly energetic photons (light particles)

Summary of the Phenomenon

From earliest times, people have been fascinated by distinctively formed and attractively colored crystals conspicuously embedded in drab rocks. These striking minerals, with their flat faces meeting in straight edges, stimulated the human imagination and challenged the intellect. Primitive humans saw these patterned stones, despite their flaws, as special, and they used them as decorations, talismans, and medical aids. Ancient natural philosophers reasoned that minerals were imperfect realizations of some ideal geometric shape; they also accepted the idea that minerals were alive and grew in caves, as if they were a kind of plant. This animistic idea of minerals lasted into the Renaissance, but by the sixteenth century, the new mechanical philosophy that undergirded the scientific revolution caused certain scientists to think of crystals in terms of the arrangements of material particles. Atomism began to rival animism in the explanation of mineral structure. For example, Thomas Harriot, an English mathematician, proposed that the densest minerals were those in which every atom touched its twelve nearest "neighbors" (today, scientists would say that this structure represents the closest packing of uniform spheres). In the early seventeenth century, Johannes Kepler, best known for his work in astronomy, explained the myriad patterns of snowflakes by the association of spherical particles.

Although students of crystals had long surmised that crystals possessed regular internal structures, it was not until late in the seventeenth century that some scientists began to formulate specific theories. In 1678, Christiaan Huygens, the Dutch physicist and astronomer, became interested in calcite, a transparent mineral that exhibited an extraordinary property: An object viewed through this mineral appeared as a double image. By assuming calcite to be made up of small ellipsoidal particles packed in a regular array, Huygens used his wave theory of light to show how these particles caused the formation of double rays of light.

Important steps toward the understanding of mineral structure occurred through the work of Nicolaus Steno, a Danish physician at the court of the Medicis in Florence. He helped to discredit the idea of the vegetative growth of minerals by showing how a tiny seed crystal could grow by the superimposition of particles on its faces. In 1669, he noted that quartz crystals, whatever their size and origin, had constant angles between corresponding faces. Despite this important discovery, Steno did not generalize his observations, and it was not until a century later that the law of constancy of angles for all crystals of a given substance was established.

During the seventeenth and eighteenth centuries, natural philosophers used two basic ideas to explain the external structures of minerals: particles, in the form of spheres, ellipsoids, or various polyhedra; and an innate attractive force, or the emanating "glue" needed to hold particles together. These attempts to rationalize mineral structures still left a basic problem unanswered: How does one explain the heterogeneous physical and chemical properties of minerals with homogeneous particles? This problem was not answered satisfactorily until the twentieth century, but the modern answer grew out of the work of scientists in the eighteenth and nineteenth centuries. The most important of these scientists was René-Just Haüy, often called the "Father of Crystallography."

Haüy, a priest who worked at the Museum of Natural History in Paris, helped to make crystallography a science. Before Haüy, the science of crystals had been a part of biology, geology, or chemistry; after Haüy, the science of crystals was an independent discipline. His speculations on the nature of the crystalline state were stimulated when he accidentally dropped a calcite specimen, which shattered into fragments. He noticed that the fragments split along straight planes that met at constant angles. No matter what the shape of the original piece of calcite, he found that broken fragments were rhombohedra (slanted cubes). He reasoned that a rhombohedron, similar to the ones he obtained by cleaving the crystal, must be preformed in the inner structure of the crystal. For Haüy, then, the cleavage planes existed in the crystal like the mortar joints in a brick wall. When he discovered similar types of cleavage in a variety of substances, he proposed that all crystal forms could be constructed from submicroscopic building blocks. He showed that there were several basic building blocks, which he called primitive forms or "integral molecules," and they represented the last term in the mechanical division of a crystal. With these uniform polyhedra, he could rationalize the many mineral forms observed in nature. Haüy's building block was not, however, the same as what later crystallographers came to call the unit cell, the smallest group of atoms in a mineral that can be repeated in three directions to form a crystal. The unit cell is not a physically separable entity, such as a molecule; it simply describes the repeat pattern of the structure. On the other hand, for Haüy, the crystal was a periodic arrangement of equal molecular polyhedra, each of which might have an independent existence.

In the nineteenth century, Haüy's ideas had many perceptive critics. For example, Eilhardt Mitscherlich, a German chemist, discovered in 1819 that different mineral substances could have the same crystal form, whereas Haüy insisted that each substance had a specific crystal structure. As Haüy's system came under attack, scientists suggested new models of crystal structure, and as these models met with difficulties, the theories that took their place became increasingly abstract and idealized. Some crystallographers shunned the concrete study of crystals (leaving it to mineralogists), and they defined their science as the study of ordered space. This mathematical analysis bore fruit, for crystallographers were able to show that, despite great variety of possible mineral structures, all forms could be classified into six crystal systems on the basis of certain geometrical features, usually axes. The cube is the basis of one of these systems, the isometric, in which three identical axes intersect at right angles. Symmetry was another factor in describing these crystal systems. For example, a cube has fourfold symmetry around an axis passing at right angles through the center of any of its faces. As some crystallographers were establishing the symmetry relationships in crystal systems, others were working on a way to describe the position of crystal faces. In 1839, William H. Miller, a professor of mineralogy at the University of Cambridge, found a way of describing how faces were oriented about a crystal, similar to the way a navigator uses latitude and longitude to tell where his ship is on the earth. Using numbers derived from axial proportions, Miller was able to characterize the position of any crystal face.

Friedrich Mohs, a German mineralogist best remembered for his scale of the hardness of minerals, was famous in his lifetime for his system of mineral classification, in which he divided minerals into genera and species, similar to the way biologists organized living things. His system was based on geometrical relationships that he derived from natural mineral forms. He wanted to transform crystallography into a purely geometrical science, and he showed that crystal analysis involved establishing certain symmetrical groups of points by the rotation of axes. When these point groups were enclosed by plane surfaces, crystal forms were generated. The crystallographer's task, then, was to analyze the symmetry operations characterizing the various classes of a crystal system.

Beginning in 1848, Auguste Bravais, a French physicist, took the same sort of mathematical approach in a series of papers dealing with the kinds of geometric figures formed by the regular grouping of points in space, called lattices. Bravais applied the results of his geometric analysis to crystals, with the points interpreted either as the centers of gravity of the chemical molecules or as the poles of interatomic electrical forces. With this approach, he demonstrated that there is a maximum of fourteen kinds of lattices, which differ in symmetry and geometry, such that the environment around any one point is the same as that around every other point. These fourteen Bravais lattices are distributed among the six crystal systems. For example, the three isometric Bravais lattices are the simple (with points at the vertices of a cube), body-centered (with points at the corners along with a point at the center of a cube), and face-centered (with corner points and points at the centers of the faces of the cube). With the work of Bravais, the external symmetry of a mineral became firmly grounded on the idea of the space lattice, but just how actual atoms or molecules were arranged within unit cells remained a matter of speculation.

In the latter part of the nineteenth century, various European scientists independently advanced crystallography beyond the point groups of the Bravais lattices by recognizing that the condition of translational equivalence was a restriction justified only by an external consideration of points. The condition of translational equivalence means that if one found oneself within a lattice and could move from point to point, one would find the same view of one's surroundings from each position. Leonhard Sohncke in Germany recognized that other symmetry elements could bring about equivalence. For example, he introduced the screw axis, in which a rotation around an axis is combined with a translation along it. In the late 1880's, the Russian mineralogist Evgraf Federov introduced another symmetry element, the glide plane, in which a reflection in a mirror plan is combined with a translation without rotation along an axis. Using various symmetry elements, Federov derived the 230 space groups, which represent all possible distributions that atoms can assume in minerals. Shortly after the work of Federov, William Barlow, an English chemist, began to consider the problem of crystal symmetry from a more concrete point of view. He visualized crystals not in terms of points but in terms of closely packed spherical atoms with characteristic diameters. In considering atoms to be specifically sized spheres, he found that there are certain geometric arrangements for packing them efficiently. One can appreciate his insight by thinking about arranging coins in two dimensions. For example, six quarters will fit around a central quarter, but only five quarters will fit around a dime (illustrating the importance of size in determining coordination number). Barlow showed that similar constraints hold for the three-dimensional packing of spherical atoms of different diameters.

The most revolutionary breakthrough with regard to mineral structure occurred in 1912, when Max von Laue, a German theoretical physicist working with two experimentalists, discovered that X rays passing through a crystal produced a diffraction pattern on a photographic plate. Before 1912, scientists had little genuine knowledge of the internal structure of minerals, but after 1912, scientists used X rays scattered from crystals to determine the precise arrangement of atoms in even extremely complicated minerals. The scientists principally responsible for extending the technique of X-ray diffraction to minerals were the British father-and-son team of William Henry Bragg and William Lawrence Bragg. Most notably, Lawrence Bragg interpreted the spots on diffraction photographs as reflections of the X rays from the planes of atoms in the crystal, and he derived a famous equation based on this understanding of X-ray diffraction. During the years 1913 and 1914, the Braggs worked assiduously in determining the structures of many minerals, for example, diamond (carbon), fluorite (calcium fluoride), pyrite (iron disulfide), and calcite (calcium carbonate), as well as sphalerite and wurzite (two forms of zinc sulfide). World War I delayed the spread of the X-ray diffraction technique, but after the war, the number of research workers increased, first in the United States, then in the Scandinavian countries.

As scientists determined more and more mineral structures, they became convinced that minerals are basically composed of spherical atoms or ions, each of characteristic size, packed closely together. For example, the silicate minerals were of central concern to William Lawrence Bragg in England and Linus Pauling in the United States. The basic unit in these minerals is the tetrahedral arrangement of four oxygen atoms around a central silicon atom. Each tetrahedral unit has four negative charges, and so one would expect that electric repulsion would force these tetrahedral building blocks to fly apart. In actual silicate minerals, however, these units are linked, in chains or rings or sheets, in ways that bring about charge neutralization and stability. These tetrahedra may also be held together by such positively charged metal ions as aluminum, magnesium, and iron. These constraints lead to a fascinating series of structures. Pauling devised an enlightening and useful way of thinking both about these silicate structures and about complex inorganic substances in general. In the late 1920's, he proposed a set of principles (now known as Pauling's Rules) that govern the structures of ionic crystals, that is, crystals in which ionic bonding predominates. The silicate minerals provide striking examples of his principles. One of his rules deals with how a positive ion's electrical influence is spread among neighboring negative ions; another rule states that highly charged positive ions tend to be as far apart as possible in a structure. Pauling's Rules allowed him to explain why certain silicate minerals exist in nature and why others do not.

During the 1930's, the X-ray analysis of minerals was largely the province of physicists in Europe and chemists in the United States. Very few mineralogists, with their lack of advanced training in physics and mathematics, were equipped to make contributions in this new field. It was not until the 1960's that the structure determination of minerals became an important activity in some large geology departments. By this time, the slow and cumbersome early methods of working out mineral structures had been surpassed by computerized X-ray crystallography, through which it was possible to determine, quickly and elegantly, the exact atomic positions of highly complex minerals. In the 1970's and 1980's, scientific interest shifted to the study of minerals at elevated temperatures and pressures. These studies often showed that temperature and pressure changes cause complex internal structural modifications of the mineral, including shifts in distances between certain ions and in their orientation to others. New minerals continue to be discovered and their structures determined. Structural chemistry has played an important role in deepening understanding both of these new minerals and of old minerals under stressful conditions. This knowledge of mineral structure has benefited not only mineralogists, crystallographers, and structural chemists, but also inorganic chemists, solid-state physicists, and many earth scientists.

Methods of Study

Early scientists identified minerals by such readily observable physical properties as hardness, density, cleavage, and crystal form. In the seventeenth and eighteenth centuries, chemists were able to determine the chemical compositions of various minerals by gravimetric methods, which involved dissolving samples in appropriate solvents and then precipitating and weighing individual constituents. In this way, they found that such metals as cobalt, nickel, and manganese were part of the fabric of certain minerals. The first methods of examining the external structure of minerals were quite primitive. In the seventeenth century, Nicolaus Steno cut sections from crystals and traced their outlines on paper. A century later, Arnould Carangeot invented the contact goniometer. This device, which enabled crystallographers to make systematic measurements of interfacial crystal angles, was basically a flat, pivoted metal arm with a pointer that could move over a semicircular protractor. William Hyde Wollaston, an English metallurgist, invented a more precise instrument, the reflecting goniometer, in 1809. This device used a narrow beam of light reflected from a mirror and directed against a crystal to make very accurate measurements of the angles between crystal faces. The reflecting goniometer ushered in a period of quantitative mineralogy that led to the multiplication of vast amounts of information about the external structure of minerals.

The discovery of the polarization of light in the nineteenth century led to another method of mineral investigation. Ordinary light consists of electromagnetic waves oscillating in all directions at right angles to the direction of travel, but a suitable material can split such light into two rays, each vibrating in a single direction (this light is then said to be plane polarized). Various inventors, mainly in England, perfected the polarizing microscope, a versatile instrument using plane-polarized light to identify minerals and to study their fine structure. Even the darkest minerals could be made transparent if sliced thin enough. These transparent slices produced complex but characteristic colors because of absorption and interference when polarized light passed through them.

In the twentieth century, X-ray diffraction provided scientists with a tool vastly more powerful than anything previously available for the investigation of internal mineral structures. Before the development of X-ray methods, the internal structure of a mineral could be deduced only by reasoning from its physical and chemical properties. After X-ray analysis, the determination of the detailed internal structures of minerals moved from speculation to precise measurement. The phenomenon of diffraction had been known since the seventeenth century. It can be readily observed when a distant street light is viewed through the regularly spaced threads of a nylon umbrella, causing spots of light to be seen. In a similar way, Max von Laue reasoned that the closely spaced sheets of atoms in a crystal should diffract X rays, with closely spaced sheets diffracting X rays at larger angles than more widely spaced ones. William Lawrence Bragg then showed how this technique could be used to provide detailed information about the atomic structure of minerals. In terms of determinations done and papers produced, X ray methods have continued to outnumber other techniques that later proliferated for studying mineral structure.

The powder method of X-ray diffraction proved to be a useful and easy way to identify minerals and to obtain structural information. Albert W. Hull at General Electric and Peter Debye and Paul Scherrer at Göttingen University independently discovered this method, which consists of grinding a mineral specimen into a powder that is then formed into a rod by gluing it to a thin glass fiber. As X rays impinge on it, this rod is rotated in the center of a cylindrical photographic film. The diffraction pattern on the film can then be interpreted in terms of the arrangement of atoms in the mineral's unit cell.

Although X rays have been the most important type of radiation used in determining mineral structures, other types of radiation, in particular infrared (with wavelengths greater than those of visible light), have also been effective. Infrared radiation causes vibrational changes in the ions or molecules of a particular mineral structure, and that permits scientists to map its very detailed atomic arrangement. The technique of neutron diffraction makes use of relatively slow neutrons from reactors to determine the locations of the light elements in mineral structures (the efficiency of light elements in scattering neutrons is generally quite high).

In recent decades, scientists have continued to develop sophisticated techniques for exploring the structure of minerals. Each of these methods has its strengths and limitations. For example, the electron microprobe employs a high-energy beam of electrons to study the microstructure of minerals. This technique can be used to study very small amounts of minerals as well as minerals in situ, but the strong interaction between the electron beam and the crystalline material produces anomalous intensities, and thus electron-microprobe studies are seldom used for a complete structure determination. Many new techniques have helped scientists to perform structural studies of minerals in special states—for example, at high pressures or at temperatures near the melting point—but the most substantial advancements in determining mineral structures continue to involve X-ray analysis.

Context

A central theme of modern mineralogy has been the dependence of a mineral's external form and basic properties on its internal structure. Because the arrangement of atoms in a mineral provides a deeper understanding of its mechanical, thermal, optical, electrical, and chemical properties, scientists have determined the atomic arrangements of many hundreds of minerals by using the X-ray diffraction technique. This great amount of structural information has proved to be extremely valuable to mineralogists, geologists, physicists, and chemists. Through this information, mineralogists have gained an understanding of the forces that hold minerals together and have even used crystal-structure data to verify and correct the formulas of some minerals. Geologists have been able to use the knowledge of mineral structures at high temperatures and pressures to gain a better understanding of the eruption of volcanoes and other geologic processes. Physicists have used this structural information to deepen their knowledge of the solid state. Through crystal-structure data, chemists have been able to expand their understanding of the chemical bond, the structures of molecules, and the chemical behavior of a variety of substances.

Because minerals often have economic importance, many people besides scientists have been interested in their structures. Rocks, bricks, concrete, plaster, ceramics, and many other materials contain minerals. In fact, almost all solids except glass and organic materials are crystalline. That is why a knowledge of the structure and behavior of crystals is important in nearly all industrial, technical, and scientific enterprises. This knowledge has, in turn, enabled scientists to synthesize crystalline compounds to fill special needs: for example, high-temperature ceramics, electrical insulators, semiconductors, and many other materials.

Bibliography

Bragg, William Lawrence. *Atomic Structure of Minerals*. Ithaca, N.Y.: Cornell University Press, 1937. Bragg wrote this book while he was Baker Professor at Cornell University in the spring semester of 1934. Primarily a discussion of mineralogy from the perspective of the vast amount of new data generated by the successful application of X-ray diffraction analysis to crystalline minerals. Because of its provenance in a series of general lectures, the text is highly readable, though a knowledge of elementary physics and chemistry is presupposed. Of use to mineralogists, physicists, chemists, and all other scientists interested in the physical and chemical properties of minerals.

Bragg, William Lawrence, G. F. Claringbull, and W. H. Taylor. *The Crystalline State*. Vol. 4, *The Crystal Structures of Minerals*. Ithaca, N.Y.: Cornell University Press, 1965. The X-ray analysis of crystals generated so much data that proved to be of interest to workers in so many branches of science that Bragg needed several collaborators and volumes to survey the subject; this volume is a comprehensive compilation of crystal-structure information on minerals. Because each collaborator wrote on that aspect of the subject of which he had expert knowledge, the analyses of structures are authoritative. Can be appreciated and used by anyone with a basic knowledge of minerals, as crystallographic notation is kept to a minimum and the actual structures take center stage.

Evans, Robert Crispin. *An Introduction to Crystal Chemistry.* 2d ed. New York: Cambridge University Press, 1964. In this book, Evans, a Cambridge chemist, analyzes crystal structures in terms of their correlation with physical and chemical properties. His approach is not comprehensive; rather, he discusses only those structures that are capable of illustrating basic principles that govern the behavior of these crystals. Though the author's approach demands some knowledge of elementary chemistry and physics on the part of the reader, there is no need for detailed crystallographic knowledge.

Lipson, Henry S. *Crystals and X-Rays.* New York: Springer-Verlag, 1970. Lipson wrote this book, which is part of the Wykeham Science series, to give advanced high school students and college undergraduates an inspiring introduction to the present state of X-ray crystallography. Though many scientists treat crystallography as a mathematical subject, Lipson stresses the observational and experimental, for example, by showing how the X-ray diffraction technique was used to determine the structures of some simple minerals.

Pauling, Linus. *The Nature of the Chemical Bond and the Structure of Molecules and Crystals: An Introduction to Modern Structural Chemistry.* 3d ed. Ithaca, N.Y.: Cornell University Press, 1960. Pauling's first scientific paper was the X-ray analysis of a mineral, molybdenite, and he went on to determine many other mineral structures. He used both crystal structures and quantum mechanics to develop a classic theory of the chemical bond. This book grew out of his own work and his tenure as Baker Professor at Cornell University during the fall semester of 1937. The beginner will encounter difficulties, but readers with a good knowledge of chemistry will find this book informative and inspiring.

Sinkankas, John. *Mineralogy for Amateurs.* New York: Van Nostrand Reinhold, 1966. As the title suggests, Sinkankas intended his book primarily for the amateur mineralogist. Because of its simplified presentation of many complex ideas, it has become popular with nonprofessionals. Includes a good chapter on the geometry of crystals, in which the basic ideas of mineral structure are cogently explained. Very well illustrated with photographs and drawings (many of the latter done by the author).

Smith, David G., ed. *The Cambridge Encyclopedia of Earth Sciences.* New York: Crown, 1981. This volume is part of a Cambridge series of reference works dedicated to the sciences. The various sections of this encyclopedia (on geology, mineralogy, oceanography, seismology, and the physics and chemistry of the earth) were written by authorities from England and the United States. Though primarily a reference work, this book is both readable and informative in most sections; for example, part 2 contains a good analysis of the internal structure of minerals. Some knowledge of elementary physics and chemistry is needed for a full understanding of most sections. Profusely illustrated with helpful diagrams and photographs.

Robert J. Paradowski

Cross-References

Biopyriboles, 164; Electron Microprobes, 596; Electron Microscopy, 601; Gem Minerals, 802; Infrared Spectra, 1232; Ionic Substitution in Minerals, 1245; Mass Spectrometry, 1521; Metamictization, 1545; Physical Properties of Minerals, 1681; Neutron Activation Analysis, 1734; Orthosilicates, 1969; Radioactive Minerals, 2143; X-Ray Powder Diffraction, 2751.

SURFACE MINING TECHNIQUES

Type of earth science: Engineering geology

Surface mining techniques are methods whereby ore is extracted from the earth. Much of humankind's general quality of life is determined by ores that are recovered in these mines. Surface mining techniques are employed when ore is found close to the surface of the earth.

Principal terms

DRAGLINE: a large excavating machine that casts a rope-hung bucket, collects the dug material by dragging the bucket toward itself, elevates the bucket, and dumps the material on a spoil bank, or pile

GRADE: the classification of an ore according to the desired or worthless material in it or according to value

HIGHWALL: an unexcavated face or bank of exposed overburden and ore in a surface mine

ORE: any rock or material that can be mined at a profit

OVERBURDEN: the material overlying the ore in a surface mine

SCRAPER: a digging, hauling, and grading machine having a cutting edge, a carrying bowl, a movable front wall, and a dumping or ejecting mechanism

STRATIFIED: a term used to describe material formed or lying in beds, layers, or strata

Summary of the Methodology

Before mining can be attempted, a fair amount of geologic assessment must be completed regarding quality and quantity of ore. In many countries, no permits are required, but where they are required, these documents can become quite lengthy and extensive indeed. This premining assessment can range anywhere from simple outcrop, or surface, mapping in the case of some sand and gravel deposits to extensive core drilling and geochemical sampling programs for gold and silver, industrial minerals, and others. Generally, without a clear understanding of strike and dip (angles at which the strata meet the horizontal plane) of the ore body, surface terrain, grade and quantity of ore reserves, depth and characteristics of overburden, and precise location of the ore, detailed mine planning can scarcely be attempted. Once these factors are known, equipment can be selected.

The permitting process in the United States is the most extensive in the world. It is to everyone's benefit to restore the mined lands to near premining conditions, but this benefit does not come without added cost to mining. Permitting ensures that an adequate amount of environmental monitoring, sampling, and analysis takes place before, during, and after mining to assess environmental damage and to promote effective mitigation of this damage. For extensive mining operations, this process can involve many person-hours of concentrated effort and coordination between geologists, hydrologists, soil scientists, wildlife specialists, engineers, and other support staff.

Once all the permits are approved and in place, mining can begin. Surface mines can be as simple as a small sand and gravel operation often seen adjacent to streams with only a scraper fleet or as complex as an open-pit or multiseam coal mine with draglines, shovels, and blasthole drills. Topsoil removal is the first procedure generally undertaken in surface mining. In areas where overburden is shallow, this operation may be as simple as dozing the topsoil into piles, exposing the ore, as in sand and gravel. In larger operations, however, scrapers are found to be more common as the primary topsoil-stripping device.

Once topsoil has been removed, the overburden may be prepared for drill benches if the material is too hard to be removed without blasting. Overburden drilling is accomplished by mobile truck- or track-mounted drills; the larger equipment is designed to drill deeper holes. Patterns and rows may be square or offset slightly depending upon objectives and the type of material being shot. Bulk powder or bagged blasting compound is then loaded into each hole and surface, and sometimes downhole delays (time-delay devices) are wired in, depending upon the effect desired. Ammonium nitrate and fuel oil (ANFO) is the most common blasting compound used. One of the most interesting aspects of blasting, developed since the late 1970's, is called cast blasting, the objective being to cast, or throw by blasting, overburden material into adjacent empty pits, thereby avoiding removal of this material by generally more expensive means. Although initial results were less than satisfactory, trial and error, along with established applied science, produced a greatly improved technique. This method of blasting is used extensively throughout the world, although its use is not common in very shallow surface mines. It is, however, ideal for many stratified deposits where there may be thick (greater than 36 meters) zones of overburden, or waste, rock.

The stripping sequence can begin after the overburden has been shot. In relatively shallow cover or bench height (less than about 18 meters) truck/loader operations are fairly common. Large stripping shovels load rock into haulage trucks for removal. Haulage distances are kept short to maximize efficiency and productivity. Overburden thicknesses greater than about 6 meters may require removal in benches or lifts, depending on equipment design, until the ore is exposed.

Where overburden thicknesses exceed about 18 meters, stripping can often be best accomplished by dragline methods. Draglines are the largest mobile units of equipment made by humans. Large walking draglines possess 40- to 120-meter booms, weigh up to 12 million kilograms (working weight), and move from 10 to 170 cubic meters of material with a single bucket. The walking mechanism is designed to provide the machine greater maneuverability than crawler-mounted stripping shovels possess. Draglines operate from the top of the highwall instead of the pit floor and can thus move more and deeper amounts of overburden cheaper and faster. A bulldozer is sometimes used to refine the dragline bench, often referred to as a pad. Stripping may also be accomplished with a truck/shovel fleet, scrapers, or a variety of other innovative equipment, such as the bucket-wheel excavator. Bucket-wheel excavators equipped with special booms and belt conveyors have proven effective in Germany and other parts of Europe.

Ore removal is fairly simplistic, as the name implies, but may involve some type of special handling, as for separating ore from waste rock, or gangue, in the pit; removal of thin (less than 0.3 meter thick) partings within coal or other stratified ores; or simply leaving blocks of material unmined because of poor grade, or quality. Ore can be removed by truck fleet, conveyor, or a combination. Frequently, the ore must be treated at a preparation plant (reduced, crushed, concentrated, washed, and so on) prior to delivery to the customer.

There is also a fairly unique "auger-miner," which can be used to extract ore (usually coal) from underneath final mine highwalls, situations where the edge of permit or economic surface mining limit has been reached. This technology is at the far end of surface mining and is really a subsurface technique. The mining sequence is completed after the backfilling, regrading, and reclamation is finished.

There are eleven varieties of surface mining methods: open-pit, mountaintop removal, conventional contour, boxcut contour, longwall strip, multiseam, block-cut, area, block-area, multiseam scraper, and terrace mining. Open-pit mining involves removing overburden and ore in a series of benches from near surface to pit floor. Expansion can occur outward and downward from the initial dig-in point. Many metallic deposits and industrial minerals are mined by this method; an example is the Bingham Canyon mine in Utah. The chief disadvantage of this method is the near impossibility of reclaiming large pits such as at Bingham, where nearly all the extracted material has been processed or transported away.

Mountaintop removal mining was popularized in eastern Kentucky. It involves removing—in boxcut fashion spoiling (dumping the overburden) in valleys on the first cut—an entire mountaintop, leaving a fairly flat pit floor upon which to reclaim overburden from succeeding cuts. A postmining surface of gently rolling terrain will replace the rugged premine surface. Disadvantages of this method are limited valley fill material, increased capital costs for additional equipment, and a need for extensive mine planning so as to ensure maximum productivity at minimum cost. It is, however, more effective than is contour mining.

In conventional contour mining, material is spoiled downslope from the active pit, often resulting in toxic material resting on native ground causing erosion, poor vegetative reestablishment, and potential acid mine drainage. This type of mining results in a long striplike band running around the hillside and has been discouraged by stricter environmental laws in Kentucky and West Virginia. It is generally favored by smaller operators because expenses are lower and premine and reclamation planning efforts are reduced, but the method disturbs much more acreage than do other steep slope methods. A method similar to conventional contour mining, but with somewhat improved environmental impacts, is boxcut contour mining. Spoil segregation and terrace regrading help to inhibit toxic downslope material and to aid revegetation. The low wall of the boxcut helps to support most of the spoil.

Longwall strip mining has been attempted in some parts of West Virginia. This innovative method involves removing a small pit by conventional stripping methods, followed by the set up of continuous miner (or excavator), chocks (blocks or wedges), and conveyor. After a pass by the continuous miner, the chocks are advanced, allowing the roof to fail, similar in fashion to underground longwall mining. Although production costs are higher, land restoration may be more easily achieved. This benefit may extend to groundwater (preventing acid mine drainage) when geology is favorable.

Multiseam mining is done in many locations throughout the world. Frequently, a bottom and top split are separated by about 6-18 feet or more. This distance means that this "interburden" material must also be removed and often drilled and shot as well. Yet, even though the overall stripping ratio may be higher, it may be beneficial and economical to extract both seams. Permitting and assessment costs are lower, as well. Block-cut mining is also suitable in areas of moderate to steep topography. A single box- or block-cut is excavated, and mining progresses outward in two directions from the initial cut. Environmental disturbances are minimized as regrading and revegetation of the first cut are accomplished during mining of subsequent cuts.

Large areas of flat or gently rolling terrain are ideal for area mining, in which draglines or large stripping shovels remove overburden. Succeeding pits are dug normal or parallel to the strata-bound ore body. This method is the most common type of mining attempted in the major lignite and subbituminous coal fields of western North Dakota, Montana, and northeastern Wyoming.

Block-area mining is similar in many respects to both area and block-cut methods. It is designed to recover seams as thin as 0.3 meter. Capital requirements are less than in some methods, and overburden removal can be sequenced with reclamation regrading.

Multiseam scraper mining involves uncovering large blocks of coal (up to 122 meters wide by 305 meters long) by scraper. After the coal is removed, scrapers again remove the parting between succeeding seams until all the coal is mined. This method is ideal for the coal and thin parting sequences found in the upper Midwest.

Terrace mining involves overburden and ore removal in a series of benches, or terraces. These benches may follow natural features, as in stream or lake terraces. This type of mining has been effective in recovery of diamonds and sand and gravel.

Applications of the Method

The role of surface mining techniques in society is primarily one of extraction. It has been known since the Bronze Age that materials taken from the earth and mixed in appropriate amounts can yield products, or alloys, superior to an equivalent amount of their elemental counterparts. As society progressed from its early days, so have its surface mining techniques. Humankind has cleverly devised an ever-increasing diversity of equipment and methods to remove ore from geologically complex and technologically difficult conditions. Ultimately, the polar regions and other planets could be "final frontiers" to the mining industry.

Surface mining brings the coal that is burned in large power plants to heat homes. It provides the phosphates to fertilize crops. It produces the limestone, marble, iron, and other types of building materials used in construction of bridges, roads, and homes. It also is responsible for the gold, silver, diamonds, and other gems that are found in jewelry and electronics. In short, surface mining is a prelude to refining, distribution, and construction of civilized society.

An example of how surface mining techniques are employed in ore production can be found at the Jim Bridger surface coal mine in southwestern Wyoming. Both conventional and cast blasting are used to fracture overburden, which is removed by four large draglines. Track-mounted shovels and loaders dump the coal into 85-ton end-dump trucks. The trucks then travel to conveyor dump sites that feed directly into the Jim Bridger Power Plant, one of the largest steam electric plants in the United States. In 1988, the Jim Bridger mine moved more than 38 million cubic meters of material and mined more than 6 million tons of coal.

In order to make the Jim Bridger mine possible, the synthesis and application of a number of important earth science disciplines were required. The initial phase of the project involved a number of exploration core holes to determine the extent and thickness of both the overburden and coal seams. In 1977, after development of the first pit, geochemical analysis of the overburden, coal, and reclaimed spoil became important to ensure that proper mining, ore blending, and reclamation procedures were on track. A number of geotechnical and structural geology problems have developed in the mature mining phase, as the active pit has approached a length of nearly 16 kilometers. These problems have been addressed, and solutions to high-wall development and potential auger mining have been proposed at least initially. Thus, the evolution and development of surface mining techniques at only one mine take on a uniquely personalized role.

Context

Surface mining does not come without its price and, in many cases, is far from easy. Surface mines are frequently located far from populated areas. In some of the Arctic regions, operations may be inhibited for much of the year by unfavorable weather. Some surface mines experience difficult mining conditions year-round. It is important to realize how important proper equipment selection is with respect to a particular mine's success or failure. Also, in order to select appropriate equipment for the mining task at hand, it is equally important to have a good idea of precisely where the ore body is located. Waste rock is nearly always handled differently from the ore itself. It should be fairly easy to distinguish coal from its usually light-colored overburden, but it becomes quite difficult to differentiate dilute metallic ore from its associated waste rock without an assay. One-tenth of a percent difference in grade can be significant in these cases.

Surface mining techniques have evolved through the ages from simply scratching at the surface with a crude pick and scraping material into a cup to the highly sophisticated tandem dragline and deep open-pit operations found in nearly every major country in the world. It is this experimentation and evolution that keeps pushing back the economic limit into deeper cover or lower grade ores that will continually expand world ore reserves. Yet many of these reserves are finite from a surface mining perspective. Ultimately, reserves will be exhausted, and people will be forced into developing more expensive underground mines for many commodities.

Ugly scars from surface mining left on the landscape in many developing countries and in some parts of the eastern United States has prompted the need for tougher environmental legislation. In the United States since the 1950's, toxic materials have been specially handled and surface and groundwater problems are being seriously addressed.

Bibliography

Chironis, N. P., ed. *Coal Age Operating Handbook of Coal Surface Mining and Reclamation*. New York: McGraw-Hill, 1978. An excellent, nontechnical introduction to surface coal mining techniques. Well illustrated, and the photographic reproductions are of high quality. Many site-specific case studies, which make this volume particularly interesting to all levels.

Crawford, J. T., III, and W. A. Hustrulid, eds. *Open Pit Mine Planning and Design*. New York: American Institute of Mining, Metallurgical, and Petroleum Engineers, 1979. This volume is the product of a workshop and contains much valuable information on geology, economics, pit design, and production planning. Profusely illustrated with photographs, graphs, and charts. Some of the mathematics is cumbersome, but, overall, a good reference. Suitable for college-level students.

Cummins, A. B., and I. A. Given, eds. *SME Mining Engineering Handbook*. Vol. 1. New York: Society of Mining Engineers of the American Institute of Mining, Metallurgical, and Petroleum Engineers, 1973. Often used as a college-level textbook, this reference was the standard of the industry and is still quite valuable for many aspects of mining. The mining law and health and safety sections are highlights. Many illustrations, charts, and tables, but this volume is not easily read by the general reader.

Fung, R., ed. *Surface Coal Mining Technology, Engineering, and Environmental Aspects*. Park Ridge, N.J.: Noyes, 1981. This book is a summary volume compiled from two symposium volumes and two users manuals on premine planning. Many illustrations and graphs. The section on fragmentation practices is very good. Although some of the sections are somewhat technical, the mathematics is, for the most part, not overbearing. Suitable for the college-level student, but anyone can gain some overall knowledge of the developing technologies.

Institution of Mining and Metallurgy. *Surface Mining and Quarrying*. Brookfield, Vt.: IMM/North American Publications Center, 1983. This symposium volume contains thirty-eight papers on a variety of topics related to surface mining. Many of the papers are illustrated, but some are quite technical. The illustrations and photographs vary somewhat in quality, but it is a good reference overall and very good on specific topics. Good for college-level students.

Stefanko, Robert. *Coal Mining Technology Theory and Practice*. New York: Society of Mining Engineers, 1983. Although this book is geared to underground coal mining, there are many excellent sketches illustrating the basics behind most of the different types of surface mining. The language is for the most part non-technical. Suitable for high-school-level readers.

Paul S. Maywood

Cross-References
Underground Mining Techniques, 1710; Mining Wastes and Reclamation, 1718; Earth Resources, 2175; Future Resources, 2182.

UNDERGROUND MINING TECHNIQUES

Type of earth science: Engineering geology

Underground mining techniques are among the methods used to extract minerals from the earth. Whenever valuable solid minerals occur at depths beneath the land surface too great to be recovered at a profit using other techniques, underground methods are employed.

Principal terms

DRIFT: a horizontal passageway driven along the course of a vein or bed; in coal mining, it is also called an entry

LEVEL: all connected horizontal mine openings at a given elevation; generally, levels are 30-60 meters apart and are designated by their vertical distance below the top of the shaft

MINABLE COAL BED: a layer of coal of such quality and thickness (at least 30 centimeters) that it can be mined at a profit

ORE: a mineral aggregate of sufficient value, both in quantity and quality, to be mined at a profit

PANEL: an area of underground coal excavation for production rather than development; the coal mine equivalent of a stope

PILLAR: ore, coal, rock, or waste left in place underground to support the wall or roof of a mined opening

RAISE: vertical or steeply inclined excavation of narrow dimensions compared to length connecting subsurface levels; unlike a winze, it is bored upward rather than sunk

SHAFT or WINZE: vertical or steeply inclined excavation of narrow dimensions compared to length; shafts are sunk from the surface, and winzes are sunk from one subsurface level to another

STOPE: an excavation underground to remove ore, other than for development work; the outlines of a stope are determined either by the limits of the ore body or by raises and levels

VEIN: a well-defined, tabular mineralized zone, which may or may not contain ore bodies

Summary of the Methodology

Underground mining methods are applied to extracting numerous solid minerals, including such metallic minerals as the ores of gold, silver, copper, lead, zinc, and iron; such fuels as coal, oil shale, and tar sands; and such nonmetallic minerals as limestone, sulfur, rock salt, and potash. When the valuable mineral to be extracted occurs at a depth too great to allow surface mining at a profit, underground mining methods are used. The depth at which profitability decreases depends on the value of the mineral deposit to be mined. Thus, some metallic minerals have been surface (open-pit) mined to depths equaling or exceeding the maximum depths at which coal has been mined by underground methods. A number of physical factors influence the underground mining method to be chosen, including size, shape, continuity, and depth of the mineral deposit; range and pattern of ore quality; strength, hardness, and structural characteristics of the deposit and the surrounding and overlying rock; groundwater conditions; subsurface temperatures (some mines are so hot they must be air-conditioned); local topography and climate; and environmental protection considerations. If solution mining (flooding the pit) is being considered, the chemical composition of the ore mineral also will be an important consideration. Additionally, technologic and economic factors must be considered, such as availability of workers and worker safety; availability of water, power, and transportation; and, most important, a market for the mineral.

Once a decision has been made to develop an underground mining operation, a method is chosen from one of the following four categories: a method involving predominantly self-supporting openings, a method predominantly dependent on artificial supports, a caving method, or a solution mining method. Methods involving predominantly self-supporting openings are open stoping, sublevel stoping, shrinkage stoping, and room-and-pillar mining. Prior to production of the mineral in marketable quantities, the mine must be developed. Development work begins with gaining access to the mineral deposit by sinking a shaft, driving a horizontal tunnel-like excavation (adit) into a hillside, or driving a sloping tunnel-like excavation (decline) from the surface. Once accessed, portions of the deposit to be mined are blocked out by bounding them with a three-dimensional network of horizontal tunnel-like excavations (levels) and vertical shaftlike excavations (raises or winzes). Each of these blocked out areas defines a stope to be mined by the stoping method selected for the particular mine.

Open stoping is any mining method in which a stope is created by the removal of a valuable mineral without the use of timber, or other artificial supports, as the predominant means of supporting the overburden. Open stopes include both isolated single openings, from which pockets of ore have been extracted, and pillared open stopes, where a deposit of considerable lateral extent has been mined with ore pillars left for support. In sublevel stoping, large blocks of ore between the levels and raises that bound the stope are partitioned into a series of smaller slices or blocks by driving sublevels. The ore is then drilled and blasted by miners in the sublevels in a sequence that causes the sublevels to retreat *en echelon* (in step formation) with each successively lower sublevel being mined slightly ahead of the one immediately above it. This process allows all the broken ore to fall directly to the bottom of the stope, where it passes through funnel-like openings (called draw points) to the haulage level below for transport out of the mine.

In shrinkage stoping, the ore in the stope is mined from the bottom upward, with the broken ore allowed to accumulate above the draw points to provide a floor from which blasting operations can be conducted. The broken ore is periodically drawn down from below (shrunk) to maintain the proper headroom for blasting. Room-and-pillar mining is a form of pillared open stoping employed where the mineral deposit is relatively thin, flat-lying, and of great lateral extent. It is employed most commonly in the mining of coal but is also used to mine other nonmetals such as rock salt, potash, trona, and limestone.

Stull stoping, cut-and-fill stoping, square-set stoping, longwall mining, and top slicing are among the methods predominantly dependent on artificial support. Stull stoping is a method that can be considered transitionary between those methods involving predominantly self-supporting openings and those involving predominantly artificially supported openings. It is used chiefly in narrow, steeply sloping (dipping) vein deposits. Timbers (called stulls) are placed for support between the lower side wall (called the footwall) and the upper side wall (called the hanging wall) of the vein.

The cut-and-fill stoping method, like shrinkage stoping, has a working level floor of broken rock; however, in this case, the broken rock is waste rather than ore. Instead of draw points, heavily timbered ore chutes are constructed through the waste rock to pass the broken ore to the haulage level for transport from the mine. The solid ore is fragmented by blasting so that it falls on top of the waste rock floor, where it is collected and dumped down the ore chutes. Waste rock, often from development work elsewhere in the mine, is placed in the stope to build up the floor and maintain the desired headroom for blasting.

Square-set stoping is a method employing extensive artificial support. "Square sets" (interlocking cube-shaped wooden frames of approximately 2.5-3 meters on a side) are constructed to form a network resembling a playground's "monkey bars" to provide support for the stope. As mining progresses, the square sets are immediately filled with waste rock—except for those sets kept open for ventilation, ore passes, or passageways for miners (called manways). In the longwall method, a massive system of props or hydraulic supports is used to support the roof over a relatively long, continuous exposure of solid mineral to be mined. Virtually complete extraction results, and the overlying roof behind the line of support collapses into the mined void as the mining advances. A method similar to longwall is top slicing, in which ore is extracted in horizontal timbered slices starting at the top of the ore deposit and working downward. A timbered mat is placed in the first cut, and the overburden is caved. As subsequent cuts are advanced, caving is induced by blasting out props (timbers) behind the face, while working room under the mat is continuously maintained. It differs from longwall mining in that several levels are developed *en echelon* rather than mining progressing on a single level.

There are two caving methods commonly used in underground mining: sublevel caving and block caving. In sublevel caving, work begins in the uppermost sublevel of the stope and progresses downward. As the ore is blasted and collapses onto the sublevel floor for removal, the wall rock of the stope immediately caves behind the ore. The broken ore is removed through the sublevels. In block caving operations, the ore body is induced to cave downward because of gravity for the entire height of the stope (usually more than 30 meters). The process is initiated by undercutting the block of ore and allowing it to collapse. The collapsed ore is removed through draw points at the bottom of the stope.

In addition to these methods, minerals can be extracted from the earth by solution mining. Solution mining differs from all the methods discussed above in one important aspect. In solution mining, men do not work underground to mine the valuable mineral. Instead, wells are drilled and liquid flows or is pumped down the wells and through the deposit to dissolve the mineral. The mineral is later recovered by processing the pregnant solution (liquid containing the dissolved mineral) after it has been pumped to the surface.

Applications of the Method

The particular underground mining method chosen for a mining operation is the one best suited to the nature and occurrence of the mineral to be mined; it is the one that is the most practical and economical when all the characteristics of the particular mineral deposit are considered. A number of physical factors must be considered when selecting a mining method. The strength of the ore body and the hardness of the ore will dictate the method that must be used to break the mineral from the solid. If the ore body is extremely hard, explosives will generally be required. If the ore is relatively soft, mechanical cutting machines can be used more efficiently and economically to remove the ore from the solid. The shape, depth, and orientation with respect to the horizontal of the ore body will influence how access to the ore body will be made and how the underground openings in, around, and through the ore body will be arranged. The chemical composition will influence whether the ore can be readily dissolved if solution mining is being considered.

Open stoping is possible only in strong rock and ores. A small ore body can be open stoped by hand drilling and blasting. When ore bodies become flatter, then the open stope method, in effect, becomes the room-and-pillar method, unless the ore body is thick enough to block into vertical stopes. The room-and-pillar method may be employed in thin or thick flat-lying ore bodies with strong ore and strong walls. Minerals typically mined using the room-and-pillar method include coal, the evaporite minerals rock salt and potash, trona, borax, and limestone. Of these, coal is by far the most common and commercially important.

Sublevel stoping is suitable for thick and massive flat-lying ore bodies with strong ore and strong walls. It may also be employed in such ore bodies when the ore is weak but the walls are strong. It is essentially a method, however, for steeply dipping ore bodies because it relies on gravity to bring ore down to the loading level. Shrinkage stoping is best suited to veins and beds dipping at 60 degrees or more, with walls that would sluff-off (slough) if left unsupported but that are still strong enough not to squeeze or collapse. Shrinkage stoping cannot be used in weak rock because the sides of the stope would squeeze together and trap the broken ore so that it would not flow when drawn (shrunk) from below.

Stull stoping is suited for mining narrow, steeply dipping veins of fairly strong ore. The stulls provide the only means of artificial support and usually require that the rock of the vein's hanging wall and footwall be moderately strong. The method is used primarily in small mines, preferably with rich ore to cover the high cost of the method. Cut-and-fill stoping is a very versatile method, on the other hand, applicable under a wide range of conditions: from small to large deposits of irregular shape and from flat-lying deposits to deposits standing vertically. Massive ore bodies can be blocked into stopes and mined by this method; yet, veins as narrow as 3 meters have been mined at depths of 2,700 meters using the method. Its best application is in steeply dipping deposits where filling operations are easiest and the ore to be mined is of moderate strength and confined between weak walls, which require permanent support. In addition, for the method to be practical, the ore must be strong enough to support itself in the roof of the stope.

Square-set stoping is most often used in any type of thick ore deposits where the ore is structurally very weak. Because it is labor-intensive and requires large quantities of timber, it is used only when it is the sole way to extract an ore of sufficient value to justify the expense. Longwall mining is best suited to mining thin, flat-lying mineral deposits with relatively weak walls and roof. In the most common application, the mining of bedded coal, the longwall face is mined using a machine called a shearer (a rotating spiked drum), which moves back and forth across the longwall face cutting the coal. Usually, coal extraction in the panel (the coal mining equivalent of a stope) approaches 100 percent. Typical longwall faces in American coal mines range from 125 to more than 200 meters in width.

Top slicing is a method best suited for mining massive, thick-bedded, or wide-veined deposits (for example, large horizontal deposits) containing weak ore and walls that will not stand unsupported over short spans. It is also adaptable to many other sets of conditions. Like square-set stoping, it is labor-intensive and requires a plentiful supply of timbers. Sublevel caving allows selective mining of weak or medium-strength ore bodies in weak rock. Small ore bodies can be mined as the method is extremely flexible. Extraction is high, but dilution of the ore by mixing with the collapsing waste rock from the walls of the caved-out stope can be a problem.

Although salt, potash, sulfur, copper, and uranium are usually mined by underground methods such as those described above, they also are mined using solution-mining methods. For example, rock salt can be extracted by pumping hot water underground through wells to dissolve the salt. The resulting saltwater solution is pumped to the surface, where the salt is recovered through evaporation. A similar process, called the Frasch process, is used to extract sulfur. In this process, water above the boiling point that is prevented from becoming steam by being kept under pressure (called superheated water) is pumped underground, where it melts the sulfur. The molten sulfur is then pumped to the surface.

Copper, uranium, and gold are sometimes recovered by a different, and slower, process called leaching. Leaching is accomplished by passing a solution through pore spaces and fractures in the ore deposit, which acts chemically with the minerals to dissolve them. The solution containing the dissolved minerals is pumped back to the surface, where it is processed to remove the minerals.

Context

From prehistoric times on, mining has provided humans with materials for fuel, shelter, and the acquisition of food. In fact, the various stages in humankind's culture are described by anthropologists in these terms. Thus, there is the paleolithic period (old stone age), the neolithic period (new stone age), the bronze age, and the iron age. It was mining that produced the materials needed for developing implements, building, trade, and jewelry. Therefore, without mining in general, and underground mining in particular, civilization would be without most of the necessities and conveniences that humankind takes for granted. There would be no television, refrigerators, automobiles, airplanes, electric power, telephones, water from a tap, or gas heating, to mention only a few of these things.

Transportation, communications, and construction have been revolutionized, in part, because of the materials made available through mining. Mining has produced titanium for high-performance aircraft and space vehicles, rare earth elements for color television picture tubes, and alloy steels for implements, tools, bridges, and high-rise building frames. Agriculture has also been changed dramatically through the use of mined mineral fertilizers such as phosphates, potash, and nitrates to produce greater crop yields. The salt used by highway crews to melt snow from roads in the winter is also a mining product. Many common household products also are mined, including trona for baking soda, borax for laundry use, and abrasives for use in kitchen cleansers. In fact, one cannot catalog the materials and products in a home without compiling an extensive list of mined products.

Mining has also had a significant political effect on humankind. Witness the early Spanish explorers' quest for gold and silver in the New World and the impetus given to the development of western North America by the gold rushes to California, the Black Hills of South Dakota, Alaska, and the Canadian Yukon. In later history, as a prelude to World War II, Germany invaded the Ruhr to obtain coal, and Japan invaded Manchuria to acquire coal and iron.

The relevance of underground mining methods to society is not limited simply to the production of useful and valuable minerals. The ideas and concepts developed for underground mining also have been applied and adapted to other uses. Techniques used in underground mining are used in the construction industry, especially on projects involving underground openings for transportation, electric power generation, fuel storage, and military purposes. The construction of highway, railroad, and subway tunnels can be cited as examples of transportation applications. Large hydroelectric dams and similar projects utilize rock tunnels and chambers to channel the falling water used to turn the turbines that generate the electricity. Underground caverns created using underground mining technology are being utilized for petroleum and liquefied natural gas storage, and minelike underground excavations in rock also are being investigated for use as deep underground storage, or disposal, facilities for nuclear wastes. Military applications include underground chambers for housing intercontinental ballistic missiles and for nuclear weaponproof command facilities.

Bibliography

Crickmer, D. F., and D. A. Zegeer, eds. *Elements of Practical Coal Mining*. 2d ed. New York: Society of Mining Engineers of the American Institute of Mining, Metallurgical, and Petroleum Engineers, 1981. This book is intended to be a beginner's book and will give the reader an overview of the fundamentals of coal mining. Appropriate for use in vocational schools, high schools, community colleges libraries, and by those persons in or expecting to enter the coal mining industry.

Cummins, A. B., and Ivan A. Given, eds. *SME Mining Engineering Handbook*. New York: Society of Mining Engineers of the American Institute of Mining, Metallurgical, and Petroleum Engineers, 1973. Principles, essential information, and data are provided primarily for use by mining engineers and practical operators. An authoritative reference book for anyone interested in mining technology and the mining industry.

Kauffmann, P. W., S. A. Hawkins, and R. R. Thompson. *Room and Pillar Retreat Mining: A Manual for the Coal Industry*. U.S. Bureau of Mines Information Circular 8849. Washington, D.C.: Government Printing Office, 1981. Designed to provide coal mine engineers and managers practical technical information for conducting room-and-pillar retreat mining operations, this Bureau of Mines publication provides a very thorough description of a common variation on the room-and-pillar method of mining coal.

Peters, W. C. *Exploration and Mining Geology*. 2d ed. New York: John Wiley & Sons, 1987. Chapter 6 of this book, "Approaches to Mining," provides a short, but thorough, summary of surface and underground mining methods. The remainder of the book provides an overview of the geologist's work in mineral discovery and mineral production.

Stout, K. S. *Mining Methods and Equipment*. New York: McGraw-Hill, 1980. Profusely illustrated with sketches, drawings, and photographs, this book provides a thorough introduction to the fundamental concepts of mining and their applications in producing ore and coal. The technical detail presented makes it suitable as a text for an entry-level course in mining engineering and for persons with more than a casual interest in mining. The number and quality of the illustrations make the technical detail less daunting to the layperson.

Thomas, L. J. *An Introduction to Mining: Exploration, Feasibility, Extraction, Rock Mechanics*. New York: Halsted Press, 1973. An introductory text written for students of mining and mining engineering, this book covers the entire mining process, from initial exploration to mine operation. Chapter 6, entitled "Underground Metalliferous Mining," and chapter 7, entitled "Underground Mining of Bedded Deposits," provide lucid descriptions of the principal underground mining methods.

Dermot M. Winters

Cross-References

Building Stone, 178; Coal, 232; Evaporites, 631; Fertilizers, 706; Hydrothermal Mineralization, 1108; Industrial Metals, 1216; Industrial Nonmetals, 1225; Iron Deposits, 1254; Surface Mining Techniques, 1703; Nuclear Waste Disposal, 1758; Oil Shale and Tar Sands, 1939; Earth Resources, 2175; Strategic Resources, 2188; Sedimentary Mineral Deposits, 2296; Uranium Deposits, 2580.

MINING WASTES AND RECLAMATION

Type of earth science: Engineering geology

Mining has produced vast areas of disturbed land and disrupted ecosystems. The magnitude of extraction activities, combined with inadequate responses by mining companies, has inspired reclamation laws and research.

Principal terms

ECOLOGICAL SUCCESSION: the process of plant and animal changes from simple pioneers such as grasses to stable, mature species such as shrubs or trees

ECOSYSTEM: a self-regulating, natural community of plants and animals interacting with one another and with their nonliving environment

EROSION: the movement of soil and rock by natural agents such as water, wind, and ice, including chemicals carried away in solution

LANDFORMS: surface features formed by natural forces or human activity, normally classified as constructional, erosional, or depositional

MINING WASTES: soil and rock removed in the process of extracting minerals, primarily overburden and unusable earth

ORPHAN LANDS: unreclaimed strip mines created prior to the passage of state or federal reclamation laws

RECLAMATION: all human efforts to improve conditions produced by mining wastes, mainly slope reshaping, revegetation, and erosion control

TOPSOIL: in reclamation, all soil which will support plant growth, but normally the 20-30 centimeters of the organically rich top layer

Summary of the Methodology

Over the years, humankind has found more and more uses for the minerals within the earth and has been able to develop deposits of lower and lower quality. Miners remove 15 meters or more of overburden (soil and rock) to obtain 30 centimeters of coal; some copper mines process ores as low as 0.5 percent. These endeavors produce literally mountains of waste, often referred to as spoil; all human exploitation of earth resources produces waste as a by-product, but none more than the mining of coal. Another inevitable by-product is ecosystem disruption—the alteration of plant and animal habitat—and changes in hydrology, which includes all aspects of water. Reclamation is the effort to heal the altered environment through landform modification, revegetation, and erosion control.

Mining can be categorized as underground or surface. Underground mining, although it generally produces far less environmental disruption, is declining relative to surface mining because of its greater danger and expense. The main safety problem comes from the underground presence of heavier-than-air methane, the major component of natural gas. Surface mining offers the advantages of safety and the use of large, labor-saving equipment. Types of surface mining include open pit, area and contour stripping, dredging, and hydraulic operations. Open-pit mining is used for the extraction of metallic ores, sand, and building stone, including limestone for cement and aggregate (the term for crushed rock used in concrete, asphalt, and road base material). Area and contour strip mining is used where the resource is in sedimentary layers, such as phosphate (fertilizer), gypsum (wallboard), and coal; coal strip mining constitutes about half of all surface mining. The difference between area and contour strip mining is essentially the number of rows, or strips, made by the shovel, with contour strip mining in hilly terrain involving fewer rows. Dredging is used to obtain river sand and valuable heavy metals such as gold and tin. Hydraulic mining involves the use of high-pressure water to tear down a mountain and wash away all but the heavy gold or tin. Effects of this devastating technique are still visible, more than a century later, in the Gold Country of California.

Mining differs from other types of land disturbance in that it is a onetime effort to obtain a mineral, with waste as a by-product and reclamation a human response to its negative impact. By contrast, construction involves relatively permanent structures, and agriculture produces continual harvests of food and other raw materials. Mining activity, and subsequent waste, began at least as early as the first extraction of pottery clay and metallic ores. What has changed since then is the scale of operations—especially since the Industrial Revolution, when the steam engine was invented as a mobile power source, and abundant coal became a substitute for scarce charcoal in the manufacture of iron and steel. As a result, humankind now has the ability literally to move mountains. With modern machinery, the Panama Canal could have been dug in one month, rather than the years it in fact took. Big Muskie, a power shovel used for coal strip mining, is a $25-million, 32-story behemoth as big as a football field; it can remove 150 cubic meters of earth per minute.

Until the mid-twentieth century, a "use it" ethic of land use was dominant. Nature was all too often seen as an enemy to be conquered. Since World War II, however, with the rise of environmental concerns, the United States has recognized the need to restore these disturbed lands. Nevertheless, coal strip mining has increased with the growing demand for energy. Between the 1930's and early 1970's, electrical demand doubled every decade. When the 1973 energy crisis hit, the huge deposits of western coal were seen as one pathway to energy independence. Additionally, the abrupt halt in orders for new nuclear power plants meant that almost all new electrical power plants since 1973 have been fueled by coal.

Reclamation efforts in the past have been slight because of apathy, the relatively small areas involved, and cost. Current efforts are directly linked to the growth of conservation and environmental movements in response to population growth and the development of available lands. In the United States, population and economic growth following World War II resulted in pollution conditions that shocked the nation. The first large-scale environmental conference was held at Princeton University in June, 1955. Entitled "The International Symposium on Man's Role in Changing the Face of the Earth," it set the agenda for the coming national concern for the environment. Steward Udall, Secretary of the Interior, was instrumental in the 1967 publication of *Surface Mining and Our Environment: A Special Report to the Nation.* It was a clear call to attack the growing problem of unreclaimed coal strip mines, described as "orphan" lands.

The creation in 1970 of the Environmental Protection Agency led the way to what came to be called "the environmental decade." The Surface Mining Control and Reclamation Act of 1977, though covering only coal mining, was landmark legislation. It requires revegetating and restoring the land to its approximate original contour; bans mining of prime agricultural land in the West and where owners of surface rights object; requires operators to minimize the impact on local watersheds and water quality; establishes a fee on each ton of coal to help reclaim orphan lands; and delegates enforcement responsibility to the states, except where they fail to act or where federal land is involved. Major efforts are under way to correct the land disruptions associated with coal mining, including research which may apply to other mining operations. Although mining has become more expensive, reclamation gives substantial hope for restoring the land.

Applications of the Method

The 1950's were a period of growing concern for land disrupted by human activity. Some of the most important research was conducted by the U.S. Geological Survey and the U.S. Department of Agriculture through its Forest Service. The Geological Survey studied watershed effects, mainly water quality, runoff, and erosion. Forest Service research concentrated on the revegetation problem; by 1983, enough progress had been made to shift the emphasis from research and development to dissemination of reclamation technology to users. Results have been applied to existing mines in cooperation with mining companies.

In response to the rapid expansion of subbituminous coal mining for electrical power production, research attention has shifted from the Appalachian region to the western states, where the largest deposits are found. Subbituminous coal not only occurs in 10- to 15-meter-thick layers in the West, but also is more workable for blowing into the furnaces of power plants; its relative energy value is lower, however, so even more coal is required. Research issues involving mine waste include the impact on landforms, water quality, and hydrology and the potential uses of mine waste. Early research on mining waste involved description of the new landforms created by human activity. The unreclaimed landforms produced by strip mining, still visible in orphan lands, are spoil banks, final-cut canyons (which are often filled with ponds), headwalls (above the final cuts), and transport roads.

Important research on water quality dates from the 1950's and was focused on acid mine-drainage problems in Appalachia, where it has long been recognized as a problem from underground mines. Acid is produced in any type of earth movement where iron pyrite and other sulfides are removed from a reducing environment to an oxidizing one. Within the earth these sulfides are stable, but when exposed to oxygen and water they readily oxidize, producing sulfuric acid, the main ingredient in acid mine drainage. Coal strip mines can produce acid when the sulfide-rich layers above and below the coal (often called fire clay) are scattered on the surface or left exposed in the final cut. A major reclamation need is to identify these acid-producing materials and bury them. Acids speed up the release of dangerous metals such as aluminum and manganese, which can be toxic to vegetation; they also cause deformities in fish.

Hydrologic impacts mainly involve changes in runoff and sediment. A major study was conducted by the U.S. Geological Survey in Beaver Creek basin, Kentucky. This area was selected because mining operations were just beginning there under typical Appalachian conditions. Data collected from 1955 to 1963 revealed large increases in runoff and sediment. By contrast, another study in Indiana demonstrated the tremendous water-holding capacities of the disturbed lands. The surface topography had much to do with the different results because a more level condition existed in Indiana. Another study was conducted at a basin in northeastern Oklahoma while it was being subjected to both contour and area strip mining. After initial increases in runoff and erosion, huge decreases occurred as much of the drainage became internalized. When reclamation began under a new state law, however, erosion rates comparable to unprotected construction sites were measured (up to 13 percent sediment by weight). Clearly, slopes lacking a protective vegetation cover will produce much more runoff, which in turn will carry enormous sediment loads. Nevertheless, in several orphan lands, water and sediment are trapped internally because of the drainage obstacles and depressions created by the mining operation.

Mining waste landforms have some interesting uses. Perhaps most important is recreation, especially fishing in final-cut ponds. In some North Dakota mines, natural revegetation has formed refuges for deer and other wildlife. One site in northeastern Oklahoma, given to the local Boy Scouts, now supports a dense population of trees and birds and is a wonderful small wilderness. Other uses include forestry in the East and sanitary landfills near urban areas. Most softwoods, such as pine, prefer more acidic soils, which are common in eastern strip mines. Use in sanitary landfills is aided by the already disturbed condition of the land and by the fact that the clays and shales commonly found in coal strip mines provide relatively impermeable conditions.

The linkage between mining waste landforms, vegetation/soil conditions, and erosion was recognized early. One study in Great Britain found that even in successfully revegetated strip mines, erosion rates were 50-200 times that of undisturbed areas. Revegetation is the key to reclamation; it, in turn, is heavily dependent upon the quality of the soil. Because of the diverse nature of soil and local ecosystems, a specific reclamation plan is never made easily.

Effective reclamation plans require sufficient data on soil pH (a measure of acidity or alkalinity), soil chemistry for fertility and toxicity problems, water retention capability, soil organisms, and useful native plants, especially perennials. The best way to provide the needed soil conditions is to save and rapidly replace the topsoil and to establish a vegetation cover quickly in order to protect the soil from rain and gully erosion. Even thin layers of good topsoil are a major improvement over the deeper subsoils, which tend to be low in organic matter and rich in acid-producing sulfides.

Detailed planning is now an integral part of the reclamation process. When planning is completed before mining begins, some of the impact can be minimized; reclamation can proceed in concert with mining to shorten the interval before replanting. Since erosion is highly destructive to revegetation efforts, erosion control systems are vital. They are designed to direct the flow of water and to dissipate its energy, enhancing soil moisture for vegetation.

Also vital to a good reclamation plan is a thorough understanding of local ecosystems and the potential success or failure of restoration efforts. Revegetation is mainly an exercise in ecological succession. Once an ecosystem is disrupted, it is difficult to reestablish. In some cases, it may be wiser to pursue a different course. Furthermore, because ecological succession is slow, fifty years or more may be needed to gauge success or failure accurately.

Western lands have received special attention because of their more fragile ecosystems. The major problem is lack of water, which not only limits plant growth but also results in thin topsoil and soil chemistry problems, such as salinity. Revegetation is much slower in the West, and seed for many of the most useful species is normally not available. Still, impressive gains have been made through the combined efforts of government agencies and mining companies. It is unlikely that this level of cooperation would have occurred without the legal requirements of the 1977 Surface Mining Control and Reclamation Act.

Context

The key issues with respect to mining waste and reclamation involve time and values. While pursuing matter and energy resources, humans often face the dilemma of immediate, short-term gains at the expense of long-term losses. For this reason, prime western agricultural land is protected by the 1977 Surface Mining Control and Reclamation Act. The value of food during famine or siege, when bread is literally more valuable than gold, is a vital lesson about the importance of productive land.

The need for conservation and recycling is supported by the ecological axiom that, in nature, matter cycles but energy flows; by recycling matter, large energy savings result from reusing materials such as steel, aluminum, and glass. Since energy flows, and so cannot be recycled, conservation is the best source of additional energy. These savings reduce the pressure to disturb more land in order to extract energy-producing coal. A key factor in the environmental impact of mining is the adaptability of natural ecosystems. How much stress can they tolerate, and what kind of conditions can be expected from the consequent ecological succession?

Ecosystems are remarkably resilient and adaptable. Still, the pace of human activity is so rapid and the recovery of ecosystems so slow that the human race would be wise to err on the side of conservation.

Questions are currently being raised about the impact of coal burning on potential atmospheric heating. Because coal is nearly pure carbon and because carbon dioxide (produced when carbon is burned) is a major greenhouse gas (one that absorbs and thus traps heat radiating from the earth's surface), the world's increasing dependence on coal for electrical power production could lead to climatic changes that could affect agriculture. Revegetation efforts can help in this area because growing plants remove carbon dioxide from the atmosphere. One suggested replacement for coal, nuclear power, has its own set of mining waste problems, along with a need for long-term storage of radioactive wastes.

Two opposing land-use viewpoints provide a framework for discussion: the historic "use it" ethic and the growing "preserve it" ethic. Many, however, prefer a middle road of scientific conservation or sustainable earth practices, both of which include reclamation. From a political perspective arise the issues of tolerance levels and affordability. Government has a responsibility to protect the health and welfare of its citizens. Where clear dangers exist, government has a responsibility to act. Many pollution issues, however, are controversial. How much is too much, and at what level does the cost of abatement become so high as to be unaffordable? Human use of the earth without pollution is impossible, and there are limits to what can be done to abate it. Still, public support remains strong for pollution control, cleanup of past pollution problems, and reclamation of disturbed land.

Bibliography

Collier, C. R., et al., eds. *Influences of Strip Mining on the Hydrologic Environment of Parts of Beaver Creek Basin, Kentucky, 1955-66*. U.S. Geological Survey Professional Paper 427-C. Washington, D.C.: Government Printing Office, 1970. One of the first basinwide studies over an extended period of time, it attempted to cover all aspects of hydrologic impacts. A fundamental reference for any serious student of strip mining. Parts 427-A (basin description) and 427-B (covering 1955-59) were published in 1964.

Law, Dennis L. *Mined-Land Rehabilitation*. New York: Van Nostrand Reinhold, 1984. A heavily illustrated hardback with an attractive layout and print style. Provides extensive coverage of reclamation issues, which sometimes seems simplistic and sometimes overly complex but is thorough. Heavily footnoted and contains useful references and tables. Intended as an introduction to the topics involved in rehabilitation, sections include mining procedures, environmental impacts, surface rehabilitation, revegetation, and planning.

Miller, G. Tyler, Jr. *Living in the Environment*. 5th ed. Belmont, Calif.: Wadsworth, 1988. The dominant textbook in environmental science for college students, it is also suitable for use by any serious high school student or adult. Its strength is the diversity of topics covered, ranging from ecosystems to politics. Contains a useful glossary, an extensive bibliography, and an index. An excellent primer on ecosystems, land use, and energy. Contains much information about environmental legislation.

Narten, Perry F., et al. *Reclamation of Mined Lands in the Western Coal Region.* U.S. Geological Survey Circular 872. Alexandria, Va.: U.S. Geological Survey, 1983. Free and highly useful, this source has sixty pages filled with photos and detailed information about the current status of reclamation research and know-how. Well written, informative, and thorough; a must for anyone interested in reclamation, especially revegetation.

Thomas, William L., Jr., ed. *Man's Role in Changing the Face of the Earth.* Chicago: University of Chicago Press, 1956. These are proceedings of the international symposium by the same name, with contributions by many well-known scientists of the period. Divided into sections entitled "Retrospect" (past), "Process" (present), and "Prospect" (future), the book concludes with summary remarks by the conference cochairmen. A classic in the environmental literature. Topical coverage is extensive. Few illustrations, but a thorough index.

U.S. Department of the Interior. *Surface Mining and Our Environment: A Special Report to the Nation.* Washington, D.C.: Government Printing Office, 1967. This exquisitely illustrated, full-color, oversized paperback is now a classic for those interested in surface mining. Telling much of its story in vivid photo-essays and striking illustrations, it alerted the nation to the problems of surface mining and appealed for action. Topics include the nature and extent of surface mining, its environmental impact and related problems, past achievements and future goals, existing laws, and recommendations for action.

U.S. Environmental Protection Agency. *Erosion and Sediment Control: Surface Mining in the Eastern U.S.* EPA Technology Transfer Seminar Publication. Washington, D.C.: Government Printing Office, 1976. This two-part paperback manual ("Planning" and "Design") was written for technicians, professionals, and laypersons. Includes a useful glossary, but lacks a bibliography. Provides an understanding of the underlying mechanics and rationale of erosion control and basic information on procedures and design. Illustrated with photos and diagrams.

Vogel, Willis G. *A Guide for Revegetating Coal Minesoils in the Eastern United States.* USDA Forest Service General Technical Report NE-68. Broomall, Pa.: Northeast Forest Experiment Station, 1981. With much useful information about revegetation under humid conditions, this publication is a must for anyone interested in revegetation of mining waste.

Nathan H. Meleen

Cross-References

Coal, 232; Land Management, 1327; Land-Use Planning, 1335; Surface Mining Techniques, 1703; Underground Mining Techniques, 1710; Earth Resources, 2175; Sedimentary Mineral Deposits, 2296; Surface Water, 2504; Weathering and Erosion, 2723.

MOUNTAIN BELTS

Type of earth science: Geology
Field of study: Tectonics

Mountain belts are products of plate tectonics, produced by the convergence of crustal plates. Topographic mountains are only the surficial expression of processes that profoundly deform and modify the crust. Long after the mountains themselves have been worn away, their former existence is recognizable from the structures that mountain building forms within the rocks of the crust.

Principal terms

CONTINENTAL SHELF: the submerged offshore portion of a continent, ending where water depths increase rapidly from a few hundred to thousands of meters

EPEIROGENY: uplift or subsidence of the crust within a region, without the internal disturbances characteristic of orogeny

GABBRO: a silica-poor intrusive igneous rock consisting mostly of calcium-rich feldspar and iron and magnesium silicates; its volcanic equivalent is basalt

GRANITE: a silica-rich intrusive igneous rock consisting mostly of quartz, potassium- and sodium-bearing feldspar, and biotite or hornblende

IGNEOUS: from the Latin *ignis* (fire), a term referring to rocks formed from the molten state or to processes that form such rocks

METAMORPHISM: the change in the mineral composition or texture of a rock because of heat, pressure, or the chemical action of fluids in the earth

OROGENY: the profound disturbance of the earth's crust, characterized by crustal compression, metamorphism, volcanism, intrusions, and mountain formation

PLATE TECTONICS: the theory that the crust of the earth consists of large moving plates; orogeny occurs where plates converge and one plate overrides the other

SEDIMENTARY ROCKS: rocks that form by surface transport and deposition of mineral grains or chemicals

SUBDUCTION: the sinking of a crustal plate into the interior of the earth; subduction occurs at subduction zones, where plates converge

Summary of the Phenomenon

Mountains have many origins. They can be volcanic, like Mount Vesuvius, or they can be formed by vertical movements along faults, as the Sierra Nevada or the Ruwenzori of central Africa were. Some mountains are the result of relatively gentle epeirogenic (deformational) uplift of the crust—for example, the Black Hills or the

Adirondack Mountains. The causes of epeirogeny, however, are poorly understood. The great mountain chains of the earth, such as the Andes, the Rocky Mountains, or the Himalaya, however, formed not only from uplift but also from internal deformation of the crust, volcanic activity, metamorphism, and the intrusion of vast quantities of molten rock into the crust, especially granite and related rocks. These processes are collectively called orogeny, and mountain chains that form from such processes are called orogenic belts. Orogeny is one of the most important consequences of plate tectonics. It occurs when plates collide and one plate overrides the other—a process known as subduction—in response to compressional forces and heating generated by the plate collision.

The earth's crust consists of two types, called continental and oceanic by geologists. The continents and the adjacent continental shelves are underlain by granitic crust, averaging about 40 kilometers thick. The ocean floors are made of gabbro and basalt, averaging about 5 kilometers thick. The true edge of a continent is not the shoreline, which is constantly changing, but the boundary between continental and oceanic crust. The edge of the continental shelf coincides closely with this boundary.

Many mountain belts form at subduction zones with a continental overriding plate and an oceanic descending plate. The downward bending of the plate creates a deep, narrow trench on the ocean floor, sometimes more than 10 kilometers below sea level. The descending oceanic plate sinks into the earth's interior, eventually to be reabsorbed. The overriding plate experiences orogeny. All orogenic belts differ in detail, but most have certain major features in common. A typical orogenic belt consists of parallel zones, which may be defined by distinctive rock type, type of metamorphism, level of igneous activity, or type of deformation of the rocks. The zones, generally parallel to the boundary where the two plates collide, are the result of different crustal conditions and processes at different distances from the plate boundary. It is useful to regard orogenic belts as having an "outer" side, adjacent to the plate boundary, and an "inner" side within the overriding plate.

The first zones recognized in orogenic belts were those defined by environment of deposition: an outer zone of thick, deep-water sedimentary rocks and volcanic rocks and an inner zone of thinner, shallow-water sedimentary rocks without abundant volcanic rocks. The nineteenth century American geologist James Hall first described these zones, which he envisioned as parallel troughs formed by downward folding of the crust. Because these troughs were viewed as immense versions of ordinary downward folds, or synclines, James Dana later called the troughs geosynclines. The outer trough was called eugeosyncline, and the inner trough was called miogeosyncline.

The original concept of the geosyncline disturbed many geologists, because it did not quite match the structure of active mountain belts. In 1964, Robert Dietz reexamined the geosyncline concept and showed that the rocks need not have accumulated in troughs. With this insight, it became clear that the rocks of miogeosynclines corresponded closely to those of the continental shelves, while eugeosynclines were a good match to the rocks of many volcanic island chains. Later, it became clear that the rocks of the eugeosyncline often formed separately from the miogeosyncline and were later juxtaposed by plate motions.

Because of these revisions of the original geosyncline concept, many geologists have abandoned the original terms and prefer the terms "geocline," "eugeocline," and "miogeocline" instead. The eugeocline is the outer belt of deep-water sedimentary rocks and volcanic rocks. The miogeocline is the inner belt of shallow-water sedimentary rocks. Beyond the miogeocline is the platform, where thin shallow-water or terrestrial rocks were deposited on the stable interior of the overriding plate. In addition, most orogenic belts have an inner belt of coarse sedimentary rocks deposited late in the history of the orogenic belt. This belt, called the molasse basin, consists of debris eroded from the mountains and deposited at their base. Molasse basins consist mostly of rocks deposited in shallow-water or land environments.

Much of the structure of a mountain belt is related to processes in the descending plate. As the descending plate reaches a depth of about 100 kilometers, it begins to melt, and molten rock, or magma, invades the overriding plate. In general, volcanic rocks in orogenic belts become progressively richer in silica with increasing distance from the plate boundary, because the rising magma has more time to react with silica-rich continental crust. Also, volcanic and intrusive rocks in mountain belts tend to become more silica-rich over time. Most orogenic belts have a main axis of igneous activity, the igneous arc, where volcanic and intrusive activity are concentrated. The igneous arc is generally on the inner side of the eugeocline. In deeply eroded orogenic belts, intrusive rocks of the igneous arc, usually granitic in composition, are exposed as great masses known as batholiths.

Different thermal conditions in different parts of the overriding plate give rise to two distinct zones of metamorphism. Adjacent to the descending plate, rocks are carried downward to great depths, often 20 kilometers or more, but because the rocks are in contact with the still-cool descending plate, they remain unusually cool. Temperatures in this zone generally average 200-300 degrees Celsius, instead of the 500-600 degrees Celsius that might be expected at 20 kilometers depth. This low-temperature, high-pressure metamorphism is known as blueschist metamorphism, because many of the minerals that form often impart a bluish color to the rocks.

Generally coinciding with the igneous arc is an inner belt of metamorphism where temperatures are high but pressures are moderate. Peak temperatures commonly exceed 600 degrees Celsius, with pressures typically reflecting depths of 5-10 kilometers. Such conditions are called amphibolite metamorphism. Adjacent to the region of highest temperature is a region of lower-temperature metamorphism, where temperatures of 400-500 degrees Celsius prevail. This type of metamorphism is called greenschist metamorphism, from the greenish color of many of the minerals formed. The outer zone of blueschist metamorphism generally occupies the outer part of the geocline. Amphibolite metamorphism generally coincides with the igneous arc and the inner part of the eugeocline. Greenschist metamorphism commonly extends into the miogeocline.

The deformation of rocks in the overriding plate depends on the nature of the rocks, stress, temperature, and confining presure. Orogenic belts display several zones of distinctive structures. The most important of these belts are the accretionary prism, zone of basement mobilization, and the foreland fold-and-thrust belt. The eugeocline in general is a region of intense deformation; deformation in the miogeocline is less intense. The outermost edge of the orogenic belt is occupied by the accretionary prism, and it often forms much of the eugeocline. Where the colliding plates meet, sediment is scraped off the descending plate. Other sediment is eroded from the continent and pours into the trench. The sediment from the continent is deposited rapidly, with little weathering or sorting, to form impure sandstone called graywacke. Submarine landslides and slumps are common in the unstable setting of the trench; the resulting complex of chaotically deposited graywacke is called flysch. A wedge of intensely deformed sediment accumulates on the edge of the continent, much the way a wedge of snow accumulates ahead of a snowplow. This wedge of sediment is the accretionary prism. Frequently, fragments of oceanic crust break off the descending plate and are incorporated into the accretionary prism. These slices of oceanic crust, called ophiolites, are of enormous geologic value. Not only do they mark the location of former subduction zones, but they also provide otherwise unobtainable cross sections of oceanic crust exposed on dry land. The actual contact between the two plates is marked by mélange, a chaotic mixture of broken rock with fragments ranging from microscopic to kilometers in size.

The high temperatures in the igneous arc and amphibolite zone of metamorphism can make the rocks of the crust plastic. That is, the rocks flow like stiff fluids, even though they do not melt. Because the hot rocks are less dense than the cooler crust around them, they rise upward. A mass of rock that flows upward in this manner is called a diapir. The process of heating deep crust (or "basement") so that it rises is called basement mobilization, and evidence of it occurs in many mountain belts. The mobilized crust appears as intensely deformed and highly metamorphosed rock called gneiss. Often the rising mass of gneiss appears to have shouldered the overlying rocks aside, so that the rocks are arched upward with a central core of gneiss. Such a structure is called a gneiss dome.

Compressional forces arising from plate convergence thicken the crust of the overriding plate in a number of ways. Within the accretionary prism, sheets of sedimentary rock are thrust downward beneath the overriding plate, resulting in a stack of faulted slices of rock. These slices may thicken internally by fracturing along small faults and stacking the resulting small slices one above the other, a process called duplexing. Within the igneous arc, crustal thickening occurs when magma invades the crust, increasing its volume. Magma can also be added to the base of the crust, a process called underplating. Heating of the crust within the igneous arc makes much of the lower crust plastic, permitting the plastic crust to be squeezed upward by compression. This process probably assists the upward movement of gneiss domes.

The thickening of the crust results in the uplift of the surface and the formation of topographic mountains. In the foreland, which basically coincides with the miogeocline, deformation is largely a response to events in the active core of the mountain belt. Some of the deformation in the foreland seems to be driven by rising masses of mobilized basement. Rocks of the miogeocline and some of the underlying crust fracture into sheets that are shoved over the rocks beneath. Fractures or faults where one mass of rock overrides another are called thrust faults. These rocks may also be buckled into folds by compressive forces. Rocks nearer the surface often slide off the rising mountain belt. The rocks may break into thin sheets called nappes that stack one atop the other or may crumple into folds. Often the folded rocks have detached from the rocks beneath, much like a carpet slides and folds when a piece of furniture is pushed over it. This process of detachment is called décollement. Because this deformation involves only the surface layers of rock and not the underlying basement rocks, it is called thin-skinned deformation.

Other kinds of plate collisions result in different combinations of structures. Oceanic-oceanic subduction zones have somewhat simpler orogenic belts. When the descending plate begins to melt, magma rises and breaks through the surface to create a volcanic island arc such as is found in the Aleutian Islands or the Lesser Antilles. Since both plates are oceanic crust, made largely of basalt, the magma also is basalt. Erosion strips sediment off the volcanic islands and dumps much of it in the trench to form an accretionary prism. Over a very long time, the island arc may be built up into a continuous belt of intensely deformed volcanic rocks and sedimentary rocks derived from them. The Greater Antilles and the Isthmus of Panama probably formed this way. Such orogenic belts consist essentially of a eugeocline and igneous arc, with the associated metamorphic zones and deformation structures.

Continent-continent collisions start out as continent-ocean subduction zones, but eventually the convergence of plates brings two continents together, one of which is pushed beneath the other. Continent-continent collisions include the Himalaya, where India is being pushed beneath Tibet, and the Persian Gulf, where the Arabian Peninsula is being pushed beneath Iran. Because continental crust is thick and relatively light, the descending plate cannot be subducted. Instead, one continent rides onto the other, creating a double thickness of crust. Eventually, resistance to further movement may cause plate motions to change on a regional or even global scale.

Usually the overriding continent has had a long history of orogeny before the collision, whereas the other continent may have had none. Orogeny results in such a wide range of structures that it is usually immediately obvious which of the continents is or was the overriding plate. The collision boundary between the two continents, called a suture, may display relics of the former accretionary prism, including melange, fragments of ophiolites, or evidence of blueschist metamorphism.

Often a small block of crust, called a terrane, collides with a larger plate. The terrane may be a volcanic island chain or a small fragment of continental crust. The northern coast of New Guinea is an area where terranes (in this case volcanic island chains) are colliding with a continent. The addition of terranes to a larger plate is called accretion. Terranes are recognizable as distinct blocks of crust separated from adjacent rocks by major faults. In many cases, eugeoclines did not form near their corresponding miogeoclines but as separate terranes. Repeated accretion of terranes can add large areas to a continent. Roughly 1,000 kilometers of the western United States was accreted to North America in the last 500 million years.

After orogeny ceases, it is common for mountain belts to experience a period of crustal extension and faulting. Once the compressional forces that uplifted the mountains subside, many mountain ranges simply cannot support their own mass and begin to spread under their own weight. It requires about 20 million years for erosion to level a mountain range. Nevertheless, long after the topographic mountains are gone, the structures created by orogeny remain. The most conspicuous markers of ancient orogenies are usually the eugeocline and miogeocline, igneous arc, and molasse deposits.

If mountains are worn away within a few tens of millions of years, it follows that the present Urals and Appalachians, the products of continental collisions more than 200 million years ago, cannot be remains of the original mountains. In the case of the Appalachians, this point is clear because rivers such as the Potomac flow across the structures in the mountain belt. Clearly, the Appalachians were once level enough (or buried) that rivers could flow across them. The Appalachians, the Urals, and even the Alps are the result of recent epeirogenic uplift after erosion had largely, or entirely, leveled the original mountains. Why mountain belts sometimes experience renewed periods of uplift long after orogeny ceases is unknown.

Methods of Study

Since the earliest days of geology, the formation of mountain belts has been regarded as one of the central problems of geology. Interpreting the structure and origin of mountain belts makes use of virtually every methodology used in the earth sciences. One of the most conspicuous features of geology as a science is its emphasis on spatial and temporal relationships. The relationships in space and time between rock units are the key pieces of information required to interpret the history of the earth. The task facing the geologist on the small scale is to integrate hundreds of local observations into a coherent picture that describes the distribution and history of the rocks in a small region. The task facing the geologist on the large scale is to integrate many local studies into a coherent history of a large region (possibly the entire earth).

Geologic mapping is the major tool for summarizing the spatial relationships of rock units. In modern geologic mapping, the geologist in the field plots observations on a base map or aerial photograph, using various symbols for rock type and orientation of bedding or other structures. Time and sequence relationships can be determined at contacts between different rock units, using methods that are essentially common sense. The fundamental principle is that later events are overprinted on earlier ones. The principle of superposition, for example, holds that the lowest layers in a series were deposited before the higher layers. Observations at rock contacts allow the geologist to piece together the sequence of events in an area.

Geologic mapping in orogenic belts presents particular problems. Rocks are often folded or tilted, displaced by faults, and shuffled out of their normal sequence by thrust faults. The fundamental principles described above still apply. Folded rocks must have been folded after the youngest rocks in the fold were deposited, faults must be younger than the rocks they displace, and so on. Additional geologic methods can provide further information. Many structures in sedimentary rocks, such as ripple marks formed by gentle wave action, are all essentially governed by gravity and have a distinct "right way up." They help the geologist determine the original orientation of tilted rocks. Fossils can be used to correlate rock layers and determine that rocks have been faulted out of their normal order. Radiometric dating can provide additional information on the sequence and timing of events.

Comparisons between regions are invaluable in working out the history of an orogenic belt. Processes that are hard to recognize in some regions may be very obvious in others. Thrust faults and exotic terranes are major features of the Appalachians, for example, but both types of structures were first recognized in rugged mountain ranges where the rocks are much better exposed than in the low and forested Appalachians.

The internal structure of mountain ranges can be studied by a variety of methods. In ranges such as the Alps or the Himalaya, several kilometers of internal structure may be directly exposed in deep valleys, yet even this much relief amounts to less than a tenth of the thickness of the crust. Drilling, usually for petroleum, also provides direct access to the interior of orogenic belts. Seismic studies, where natural or artificial seismic waves are detected after traveling through the earth's crust, are an additional means of probing deep beneath mountain ranges. Gravity and magnetic studies, in which buried rock masses can be detected by their gravitational attractions or magnetic fields, provide indirect access to the deep interior of mountain ranges.

Context

To preindustrial ages, mountains were places of danger filled with natural hazards, wild animals, and possibly hostile peoples. To a technological age with a vastly greater command of nature, mountains are places of beauty that generate income. Switzerland is the supreme example of a land where mountains yield wealth for human beings. Apart from their value as centers for recreation, mountains are economically valuable as sources of mineral wealth. The geologic processes that create mountains also concentrate mineral deposits. The Andes of Chile contain some of the world's largest copper deposits, the Andes of Colombia produce emeralds, and the foothills of the Sierra Nevada are famous for their gold. Understanding the processes that create mountains also improves understanding of how mineral resources form and where to seek them.

Yet mountains can be actively dangerous. The processes that create them also result in earthquakes and volcanic eruptions, while the processes that erode them create floods and landslides. Many of the most mountainous nations, where mountain building is a continuing process, are also underdeveloped nations with vulnerable, rapidly expanding populations.

Bibliography

Cook, Frederick A., L. D. Brown, and J. E. Oliver. "The Southern Appalachians and the Growth of Continents." *Scientific American* 243 (October, 1980): 156-168. Seismic probing has revealed the fault where ancient Africa rode onto North America to create the southern Appalachians. *Scientific American*, which is aimed at the scientifically informed but nonspecialist reader, roughly at college level, is probably the best source of information on recent advances in science for nonspecialists. Its coverage of advances in the earth sciences since 1970 has been especially thorough.

Dietz, Robert S. "Geosynclines, Mountains, and Continent-Building." *Scientific American* 226 (March, 1972): 30-38. Dietz's reanalysis of the traditional geosyncline concept bridged the conceptual gap between modern concepts of plate tectonics and the evolution of ancient mountain belts.

Howell, David G. "Terranes." *Scientific American* 253 (November, 1985): 116-125. Terranes are small blocks of crust added to a mountain belt by plate collisions. This article describes types of terranes and what happens when they collide.

James, David E. "The Evolution of the Andes." *Scientific American* 229 (August, 1973): 60-69. A summary of a relatively simple mountain chain whose formation is related to the continuing convergence of the Pacific and South American plates. Such mountain belts are a good starting point for understanding more complex mountains.

Jones, David L., A. Cox, P. Coney, and Myrl Beck. "The Growth of Western North America." *Scientific American* 247 (November, 1982): 70-84. The westernmost 1,000 kilometers of North America are a mosaic of at least 200 small blocks added by plate collision in the last 500 million years. This article was written by some of the scientists who were most influential in discovering this process.

Molnar, Peter. "The Structure of Mountain Ranges." *Scientific American* 255 (July, 1986): 70-79. A summary of discoveries about the internal structure of mountain ranges. The apparently solid crust of a mountain range is actually brittle and unable to support its own weight without external compressive forces.

Molnar, Peter, and P. Tapponier. "The Collision Between India and Eurasia." *Scientific American* 236 (April, 1977): 30-41. The mechanical paradox of plate tectonics driving India northward into Eurasia has been resolved by the deformation of the Eurasian crust far beyond the immediate collision zone. This article illustrates one way that continental collisions can result in large-scale changes in crustal behavior.

Spencer, Edgar W. *Introduction to the Structure of the Earth*. 3d ed. New York: McGraw-Hill, 1988. A college-level textbook on structural geology. Chapters 1-3 survey plate tectonics and its role in deforming the crust. Chapter 19 describes mountain ranges that form from continent-ocean plate collision, particularly the structure of western North America. Chapter 20 describes mountains that form by continent-continent collision, with emphasis on the Appalachians and Alps.

Suppe, John. *Principles of Structural Geology*. Englewood Cliffs, N.J.: Prentice-Hall, 1985. A college-level textbook on the structures that form when rocks deform. Chapter 1 is a survey of plate tectonics and its role in deforming the crust. Chapter 12 describes the structure of the Appalachians, and Chapter 13 describes the structure of western North America.

Steven I. Dutch

Cross-References

Continental Crust, 261; Continental Growth, 268; Continental Structures, 290; Displaced Terranes, 377; Fold Belts, 734; Folds, 739; Geosynclines, 898; Island Arcs, 1261; Lithospheric Plates, 1387; Plate Margins, 2063; Plate Tectonics, 2079; Stress and Strain, 2490; Subduction and Orogeny, 2497; Thrust Belts, 2519; The Transverse Ranges, 2542.

NEUTRON ACTIVATION ANALYSIS

Type of earth science: Geochemistry
Field of study: Analytical techniques

Neutron activation analysis uses a flux of neutrons to excite the nuclei of chemical elements in samples, thus causing the excited nuclei to emit characteristic gamma radiation. The technique provides a sensitive method for measuring the amount of chemical elements contained in geological samples, particularly when there is only a small amount of the element in the sample.

Principal terms

CROSS SECTION: the effective area that a nucleus presents to an oncoming nuclear particle, which determines the chance that the particle will strike the nucleus, causing a nuclear reaction

GAMMA DECAY: the emission of high-energy electromagnetic radiation as a nucleus loses excess energy

GAMMA SPECTRUM: the unique pattern of discrete gamma energies emitted by each specific type of nucleus; it identifies that nucleus

HALF-LIFE: the time during which half the atoms in a sample of radioactive material will decay

ISOTOPE: atoms of the same chemical element containing equal numbers of protons whose nuclei have different masses because they contain different numbers of neutrons

NEUTRON: an uncharged particle that is one of the two major nuclear constituents having nearly equal masses and different electric charges

NUCLEAR REACTION: a change in the structure of an atomic nucleus brought about by a collision of the nucleus with another nuclear particle such as a neutron

NUCLEUS: the tiny central portion of an atom that contains all the positive charge and nearly all the mass of the atom

PROTON: a particle that carries a single unit of positive charge equal in size to that of the electron; one of the two major nuclear constituents having nearly equal masses and different electric charges

Summary of the Methodology

In neutron activation analysis, a sample of interest to the scientist is placed in a beam of neutrons produced by a radioactive source, such as an accelerator or a nuclear reactor. The neutrons interact with nuclei contained in the sample and alter their structures, frequently leaving the nuclei of the sample with excess energy. After a predetermined time, the sample is taken out of the beam of neutrons. The altered nuclei in the sample lose their excess energy by emitting nuclear radiation that is characteristic of each individual type of nucleus. The radiation is detected and allows identification of the nucleus that emitted it. The intensity of a particular characteristic radiation is directly related to the number of nuclei of that species in the sample. Usually, the radiation studied in neutron activation analysis is gamma radiation, that is, high-energy electromagnetic radiation emitted by nuclei without altering their chemical nature. The gammas emitted by the sample are directly related to the abundance of a particular chemical element in the sample.

Neutron activation analysis grew out of the systematic study of the interaction of neutrons and nuclei conducted by nuclear physicists in order to understand the structure of the nucleus. Interpretation of the patterns of gammas emitted by a sample following irradiation by neutrons requires several types of background information. First, not all types of nuclei react in the same way with a neutron beam. The cross section for the nuclear reaction, which measures the chance that a particular nuclear species will be produced, depends not only on the structure of the nucleus involved but also on the energy of the neutrons used for bombardment of the sample. The reaction cross section must be measured in a separate experiment as the energy of the neutrons is varied. Many reaction cross sections have been measured and are tabulated in the scientific literature.

Second, the gamma radiation from a particular nuclear species has characteristic energies which can be precisely and conveniently measured using germanium-based detectors. The pattern of energies of gammas emitted by a particlar type of nucleus identifies that nucleus just as the pattern of visible light emitted by an atom—its spectrum—identifies that atom. Tables of the gamma spectra of nuclei are an important input to neutron activation analysis. Such tables, along with the cross sections for nuclear reactions, are frequently stored in the memory of a computer and automatically recalled during analysis of the gamma spectra from neutron activation analysis.

Third, emission of nuclear radiation occurs gradually in time at a rate characterized by the half-life of the given decay, that is, the time for half the nuclei in a sample to emit their gamma radiation. Half-lives for nuclear species vary from picoseconds to millions of years. Nuclear species of interest for neutron activation analysis generally have half-lives ranging from seconds to days, as the species must live long enough for the sample to be transported to the detector and must decay quickly enough so that they can be detected in a reasonable amount of time. As the neutrons interact with the sample nuclei, producing new energetic nuclei, the energetic nuclei decay with their characteristic half-lives. Thus, the number of excited nuclei in a sample depends on the half-life of the nucleus as well as on the time it has spent in the neutron beam. Half-lives of nuclear radiation are measured in separate experiments and are tabulated; the analyst keeps careful record of the exposure of the sample to neutrons.

The variations in the half-lives of excited nuclei can be used to identify nuclei present in the sample. Decays with short half-lives happen very rapidly so that the first gammas obtained from the sample are mostly those with half-lives less than about five minutes. If the sample then sits for half an hour, the short-lived nuclear species will have decayed, and the gammas from the sample will be those from nuclei with longer half-lives. Thus, in neutron activation analysis, gammas from the sample are measured at a series of carefully planned time intervals. Modern laboratories use computers to calculate the effect of half-lives on the gamma spectra that have been recorded.

Fourth, the number of excited nuclei produced during neutron irradiation (and thus the intensity of a particular gamma emission) depends on the concentration of a particular nuclear species in the sample. Because the chemical nature of an atom is not affected by the number of neutrons in its nucleus, most chemical elements are characterized by more than one type of nucleus or isotope, that is, nuclei with the same number of protons in them and thus belonging to the same element but with different numbers of neutrons. Different isotopes have different reaction cross sections and different gamma spectra. Thus, the analyst must know the relative amounts of each isotope of a given element in order to relate the intensity of a gamma emission to the abundance of a particular element in the sample. These data are well known and readily available.

Finally, the number of gammas at a particular energy depends on the number of neutrons that are aimed at the sample. If the neutrons are produced by a radioactive source or an accelerator, they form a beam and are described as a particular number of particles per area per time. If the sample is placed inside a nuclear reactor, the neutrons bombard it from all directions, and the irradiation is described in terms of a neutron flux, or the number of neutrons crossing a square centimeter of the sample each second. The energy distribution of the neutrons that strike the sample must also be recorded because reaction cross sections depend on energy. In an accelerator or a radioactive source, the neutrons produced usually have a well-defined single energy. In a reactor, they will have a distribution of energies that must be measured for an individual reactor and for a particular location in the core of that reactor.

Applications of the Method

Neutron activation analysis has found wide application in the earth sciences; it has been used not only in traditional pursuits such as analysis of ores during prospecting and the study of the distribution of rare elements in the earth's crust but also in more exotic studies of the distribution of rare chemical elements in rock samples from the moon and of the transport of pollutants in the environment.

Neutron activation analysis is expensive because it requires a neutron source and specialized detectors and counting systems, all of which are run by a computer in modern labs. The technique is not sensitive to the chemical state of an atom but merely determines the number of atoms of a particular element to be found in the sample; therefore, it is not suitable for determining the chemical state in which elements are present. On the other hand, neutron activation analysis is very fast compared to standard quantitative analysis, thus compensating for the expense when fast results are needed. For example, neutron activation analysis using a radioactive source to produce the neutrons has been conducted in the field to determine the copper and manganese content of ores. The technique is advantageous in that samples did not have to be transported to a lab for analysis, and results of the analysis could be used to guide drilling operations.

Neutron activation analysis cannot detect every chemical element in the sample, as not all chemical elements produce gammas with suitable half-lives or have large cross sections for nuclear reactions. In some cases, strong gammas from abundant elements may mask the weaker signals from less abundant species. The technique for producing neutrons may strongly influence the elements that are detected. For example, the high-energy or fast neutrons produced in accelerators using tritium targets interact strongly with oxygen and silicon, while lower-energy neutrons characteristic of nuclear reactors interact very little with these elements. Thus, fast neutrons are characteristically used for rapid determinations of the silicon and oxygen content of minerals. Frequently, samples are subjected to analysis using more than one sort of neutron source to detect different elements. Rock samples will first be subjected to fast neutron analysis to determine their content of silicon and oxygen and then to analysis using a reactor to detect about twenty-five other elements. Finally, neutron activation analysis may be supplemented by chemical separation of elements for the detection of very rare elements.

Neutron activation analysis is ideally suited for the study of trace elements, that is, relatively rare elements present in samples in small quantities. Because neutrons easily penetrate geological materials, samples for neutron activation analysis require little preparation, and the technique does not destroy the sample, which can thus be saved for display or subjected to further analysis. Therefore, the technique is often applied to samples of archaeological importance in which samples are too precious to destroy in analysis. It offers the researcher the further advantage that many elements in the same data can be identified, and thus elements may be found whose presence in the sample was not initially expected. This scanning for many elements at once is an advantage in problems such as the search for pollutants in river water. For example, extensive studies of environmental mercury in Sweden have been conducted using neutron activation analysis of minerals, coal, and plant and animal tissues.

A particular application of neutron activation analysis is autoradiography. In this case, the sample is irradiated and then placed in contact with a piece of film. The film is developed and records concentrations of radioactivity, showing how particular chemical elements, for example uranium and thorium, are distributed within the sample.

Probably the most famous example of the use of neutron activation analysis in earth science is the study of the lunar rocks brought back to earth by the Apollo astronauts. Scientists wished to know the chemical composition of these rocks in order to obtain clues as to their history and to learn whether the moon formed from the same original material as did the earth. At the same time, only relatively small samples were available, as the lunar rocks had to be carried back from the moon in circumstances where the amount of weight was critical; in addition, scientists wanted to save the lunar rocks for future analysis and for public display. Neutron activation analysis does not damage the sample it studies. Even when combined with chemical separation techniques to aid analysis for very scarce elements, the samples needed are very small—on the order of milligrams—as opposed to the gram-sized samples needed for standard chemical analysis. Thus, the lunar rock samples could be subjected to neutron activation analysis to determine their basic elemental composition and still be left intact for display or analysis by other methods. Some of the surprising results from neutron activation analysis of the lunar rock samples include the fact that lunar rocks and soils are very low in oxygen compared to their terrestrial counterparts.

One of the problems in studying the lunar samples was to determine their content of rare earth elements such as europium, neodymium, or gadolinium. These elements are chemically very similar and thus difficult to separate by quantitative chemical analysis. On the other hand, their nuclear structures are very different; therefore, neutron activation analysis is an ideal tool for distinguishing among them. Results of the analysis showed that overall abundances of the rare earth elements in lunar rocks were fifty to a hundred times greater than is standard for chondritic meteorites, which are meteorites believed to represent the primordial composition of the material from which the solar system formed. At the same time, lunar rocks were depleted in the element europium compared to chondritic meteorites and terrestrial rocks. Explanation of these strange patterns of elemental abundances uncovered by neutron activation analysis supports the theory that the moon formed from a disk of material spun off from the very early earth by a collision with a very large planetesimal.

Context

Neutron activation analysis provides a powerful technique for simultaneously determining the amounts of many chemical elements in a geological sample without destroying the sample. Although it requires a source of neutrons and fairly complex instrumentation, it is much faster than conventional chemical analysis and can analyze a sample for several elements at the same time with little sample preparation. This technique is also uniquely sensitive to very small amounts of particular elements and thus can often detect minute amounts of such elements present in samples that would escape all but extremely detailed and time-consuming chemical analyses using atomic spectroscopic techniques designed to search for that element.

Applications of neutron activation analysis to earth science fall into two broad categories. The first consists of cases in which researchers take advantage of the speed of neutron activation analysis to obtain immediate results on the elemental compositions of their samples. Such work is often done in the field, using a radioactive source to produce the neutrons, and the results of the analysis guide field operations. Similarly, neutron activation analysis may be used to screen a very large number of samples rapidly on a production basis.

The second category of applications of neutron activation analysis utilizes the ability of the technique to determine rapidly very small concentrations of certain chemical elements. One example of this application has been the systematic study of trace elements in rocks of various ages. In the energy industry, neutron activation analysis has been applied to the study of trace elements in coals, thereby providing clues to the origin of particular coal beds. The quality of coal as a heat source varies widely from bed to bed. An understanding of why this variation occurs might lead to new methods of treating coals before burning them in order to reduce pollution. Finally, the ability of neutron activation analysis to scan large numbers of samples for minute quantities of chemical elements has been put to use in the study of sources of pollution, particularly by metals, in the environment. Large numbers of samples of river water or runoff near landfills can be checked for the presence of a wide variety of metals quickly and efficiently using neutron activation analysis.

The advent of computer-based systems has automated much of the tedious calculation needed to analyze data from neutron activation analysis. The technique is thus accessible to a much wider variety of researchers than was previously the case and promises to find increasing use as a probe of the elemental composition samples of interest to earth scientists.

Bibliography

Fite, L. E., E. A. Schweikert, R. E. Wainerdi, and E. A. Uken. "Nuclear Activation Analysis." In *Modern Methods of Geochemical Analysis*, edited by Richard E. Wainerdi and Ernst A. Uken. New York: Plenum Press, 1971. A comparatively brief summary of the technique of neutron activation analysis, designed for geologists who are not familiar with nuclear physics. While not terribly difficult to read, the chapter stresses the equipment required for use of neutron activation analysis and provides examples from geology.

Keller, C. *Radiochemistry*. New York: John Wiley & Sons, 1988. A general text on the use of radionuclides, both naturally occurring and artificially formed, as in the case of neutron activation analysis. Although the section on neutron activation analysis is brief, the text provides a thorough treatment of the background material needed to understand this relatively complex analytical technique.

Kruger, Paul. *Principles of Activation Analysis*. New York: Wiley-Interscience, 1971. This volume concentrates on the experimental details and on the instrumentation needed to carry out neutron activation analysis. Written as a textbook for the scientist planning to use neutron activation analysis, who is not a specialist in the field. The details of the technique are thoroughly discussed.

Lenihan, J. M. A., S. J. Thomson, and V. P. Guinn. *Advances in Activation Analysis*. Vol. 2. New York: Academic Press, 1972. Although slightly old, this volume provides an excellent series of examples of the use of neutron activation analysis to study a variety of problems not only in the earth sciences but also in the arts and in archaeology. It discusses some of the varied results that can be obtained by using a variety of neutron sources.

Rakovic, Miloslav. *Activation Analysis*. London: Iliffe Books, 1970. A good introduction to the field, including details of chemical preparations and sample-
handling skills. Organized by the chemical element that is being studied rather
than by the technique being used. A good source for a person interested in
studying a particular chemical element.

Ruth H. Howes

Cross-References

Elemental Distribution in the Earth, 391; Groundwater Pollution, 1028; Landfills,
1351; Lunar Rocks, 1414; Meteorites: Carbonaceous Chondrites, 1638; The Structure
of Minerals, 1693; Elemental Distribution in the Solar System, 2434.

NON-SILICATES OTHER THAN OXIDES AND CARBONATES

Type of earth science: Geology
Field of study: Mineralogy and crystallography

Non-silicate minerals (exclusive of the carbonates and oxides), although not as abundant as the silicates in the part of the earth that is accessible to humankind, are important because they are the major sources of many of the critical elements and compounds upon which civilized society is based.

Principal terms

CRYSTALLINE: a property of a chemical compound to have an orderly internal atomic arrangement that may or may not have well-developed external faces

ION: an atom that has a positive or negative charge

IONIC BONDING: the means by which two or more atoms of different elements combine to form a compound because electrons are transferred from one atom to another

METAL: an element with a metallic luster, high electrical and thermal conductivity, ductility, malleability, and high density

MINERAL: a naturally occurring, solid chemical compound with a definite composition and an orderly internal atomic arrangement

ORE: a mineral or minerals present in large enough amounts in a given deposit to be profitably mined for the metal(s)

ROCK-FORMING MINERAL: the common minerals that comprise the bulk of the earth's crust (outer layer)

SEMIMETAL: elements that have some properties of metals but are distinct because they are not malleable or ductile

Summary of the Phenomenon

The earth is composed of a great diversity of rock types. Each rock is typically made up of one or more minerals, and each mineral is, in turn, composed of one or more of the eighty-eight naturally occurring elements found in the earth. One of the most important elements is silicon; geologists commonly divide minerals into two broad categories, silicates and non-silicates. Silicates are those minerals that contain silicon as an essential part of the composition. The non-silicates lack silicon in their formulas.

Silicon, like every element, has unique properties that distinguish it from all others. The smallest physically separable part of the element that retains the properties of that element is the atom. The atom, which can be considered a spherical body, is made up of three basic parts: Protons (with positive charges) and neutrons (with no charge) make up the core, or nucleus, and electrons (with negative charges) surround the nucleus. Each individual element is identified by a unique number of protons in the nucleus of the atom, called the atomic number. For example, oxygen has an atomic number 8, because it contains eight protons, and uranium has an atomic number of 92, because it contains ninety-two protons. Most elements also contain neutrons, but that number varies. Most oxygens contain eight neutrons and, therefore, have a mass number (the sum of protons and neutrons) of sixteen. This can be represented at $_8O^{16}$, where the subscript eight is the atomic number and the superscript sixteen is the mass number. Other atoms of oxygen may contain nine or ten neutrons, and in those cases the mass numbers are seventeen and eighteen, respectively. The number of positively charged protons in the atom dictates that a like number of negatively charged electrons must surround the nucleus in a neutral atom. How elements combine to form minerals depends on how electrons are transferred or shared. Atoms that readily give up one or more electrons develop positive charges and are referred to as positive ions or cations. Sodium is a common cation; it readily gives up one electron and develops a $+1$ charge because it has one more proton than it has electrons. Atoms that gain electrons develop negative charges and are called anions. Cl^{-1} and O^{-2} are examples of anions that have gained one and two electrons, respectively. Na^{+1} and Cl^{-1} are two ions that are mutually attractive, because one electron is transferred from each sodium to each chlorine. As a result, a stable chemical compound, NaCl, the common mineral halite, is formed. The means of transferring electrons to form chemical compounds is referred to as ionic bonding. Although other types of bonding exist, ionic bonding is the type that forms most minerals. In some cases, a strongly bound cation and anion grouping, called an anionic complex, will take on a negative charge and will attract more weakly bound cations; phosphate, $(PO_4)^{-4}$, and borate, $(BO_3)^{-2}$, are examples.

The earth is divided into several distinct layers (crust, mantle, and core), each with unique physical and chemical properties. Since only the crust is readily accessible to scientists, this discussion is largely restricted to this outermost layer. Estimates suggest that the crust is dominated by only eight elements (oxygen, silicon, aluminum, iron, magnesium, calcium, sodium, and potassium). Data also indicate that the large atoms of oxygen make up in volume almost 94 percent of the crust. What this means is that the crust on average can be thought of as made up of large spheres of oxygen, with all of the other common elements as smaller spheres filling in the 6 percent of the space among these oxygens.

There are very specific geochemical rules that dictate how ions of different sizes can fit in orderly ways within these oxygens. In most general terms, the smaller the cation, the fewer the oxygens that can surround it, and oxygens (and other large anions) can only form around cations in groups of three, four, six, eight, or twelve. B^{+3} (ionic radius = 0.23 angstrom, 1 angstrom = 10^{-8} centimeters) is very small and combines with only three oxygens. Si^{+4} (0.42 angstrom), which is slightly larger, surrounds itself with four oxygens.

One of the more common classification schemes for minerals is based on the composition of the anion or anionic complex, with the following eleven mineral classes recognized: the native elements; sulfides and sulfosalts; oxides and hydroxides; carbonates; halides; nitrates; borates; phosphates, arsenates, and vanadates; sulfates and chromates; tungstates and molybdates; and silicates. The silicates make up the vast majority of the minerals in the crust, with all the other classes accounting for only 3 percent of the total.

Of all the elements, only 20, the native elements, are known to occur in the earth in the free state. These elements can be separated into metals, semimetals, and nonmetals. Within the metals, based on atomic structure, three groups are recognized: the gold group (gold, silver, copper, and lead), the platinum group (platinum, palladium, iridium, and osmium), and the iron group (iron and nickel-iron). Mercury, tantalum, tin, and zinc are metals that have also been identified. Within the semimetals, two groups are commonly recognized: the arsenic group (arsenic, antimony, and bismuth) and the tellurium group (selenium and tellurium). Sulfur and two forms of carbon (graphite and diamond) are the nonmetal minerals.

The sulfides include a great number of minerals, many of which are important economically as sources of metals. Although sulfur is the dominant anion, this group also includes compounds with arsenic (arsenides), tellurium (tellurides), selenium (selenides), antimony, and bismuth as the anion. Commonly included with the sulfides are the sulfosalts. These sulfosalts are generally distinct because they contain the semimetals arsenic (As) and antimony (Sb) in the metal site. Only four sulfides are considered to be rock-forming minerals: pyrite (FeS_2), marcasite (FeS_2), chalcopyrite ($CuFeS_2$), and pyrrhotite (FeS to Fe_7S_8).

The halides are minerals that contain one of four anions—fluorine (F), chlorine (Cl), bromine (Br), and iodine (I). The Cl-bearing chlorides are the most abundant halides, with the fluorides second in abundance, but the bromides and iodides are very rare. The only two halides that are considered to be rock-forming minerals are halite (NaCl) and fluorite (CaF_2).

The nitrates are minerals that include the $(NO_3)^{-1}$ anionic group, which is made up of one nitrogen ion (N^{+4}) surrounded by three oxygen ions (O^{-2}). None of the nitrates is considered common, and they are relatively few in number. Most occur only in deposits in very arid regions.

The borates are minerals that have boron (B) strongly bound to either three or four oxygen ions with $(BO_3)^{-3}$ or $(BO_4)^{-4}$ as the anionic complex. All the borates are restricted to dry lake deposits in extremely arid regions. None is considered a common rock-forming mineral, but borax ($Na_2B_4O_7 \cdot 10H_2O$) is probably the most readily recognized.

In the phosphate class (which includes the arsenates and vanadates), the phosphorus cation (P^{+5}) is surrounded by four oxygens to form a $(PO_4)^{-3}$ anionic complex. Arsenic (As^{+5}) and vanadium (V^{+5}) cations are almost identical in size to P^{+5} and therefore substitute for each other and form their own respective anionic complexes: $(AsO_4)^{-4}$ and $(VO_4)^{-4}$. Although this class includes many minerals, most are extremely rare; only one, apatite ($Ca_5(PO_4)_3(F,Cl,OH)$), is common.

The sulfate minerals are another large class built around the anionic complex $(SO_4)^{-2}$. The sulfur cation (S^{+6}) is surrounded by four oxygens. The chromates are included with the sulfates because Cr^{+6} and S^{+6} are similar in size, and both have very similar structures. Two main subgroups of sulfates are recognized: the anhydrous sulfates and the hydrous sulfates. Although this class includes many minerals, very few are considered to be common. Examples of anhydrous sulfates are barite $(BaSO_4)$ and anhydrite $(CaSO_4)$. The most common hydrous sulfate is gypsum $(CaSO_4 \cdot 2H_2O)$. In the chromates, the chromium cation Cr^{+6} combines with four oxygens to form $(CrO_4)^{-2}$.

The tungstate and molybdate minerals are very similar to the sulfates, with either the tungsten (W^{+6}) or molybdenum (Mo^{+6}) cations surrounded by four oxygens in a pattern slightly different from that in the sulfates. None of the tungstates or molybdates is a common rock-forming mineral, and all are relatively rare.

Methods of Study

The study of the chemical and physical properties of these non-silicate minerals can be approached from many different perspectives. It can be accomplished with varying degrees of sophistication and may or may not require expensive or complicated instrumentation. A number of physical properties are studied not only because they help identify particular minerals but also because the physical properties dictate whether minerals have any commercial use.

Several properties that are related to how light affects minerals include color, streak (color of the powdered form of the mineral), luster (appearance of the surface of the mineral in reflected light), diaphaneity (capacity of a mineral to transmit or absorb light), and luminescence (emission of light, by a mineral, that is not caused by incandescence). Although color is easily recognized, the causes of color in minerals are diverse, but color generally results from the interaction of light waves and electrons.

The study of the shape (or habit) of minerals may include simply the description of the general shape of crystals or a very careful analysis of the external morphology of minerals that have well-developed crystal faces. Measurement of the angular relationships between faces with the optical goniometer is helpful in describing minerals. The systematic study of the external form of minerals is commonly called morphological crystallography. Other properties that are studied include the tendency of minerals to fracture (break along irregular surfaces) or to cleave (break along straight planar surfaces that represent planes of internal weakness) and tenacity (resistance or response to attempts to break, bend, or cut). Hardness, another essential property, refers to the resistance of a substance to abrasion. Hardness is commonly evaluated on a scale of relative hardness, called Mohs scale, which uses a set of common minerals of different hardnesses for comparison. Other properties that may have industrial applications include magnetism and electrical properties. Minerals containing uranium and thorium exhibit another property, radioactivity, that is measurable with a Geiger counter or scintillation counter.

A variety of thermal properties are commonly determined. Differential thermal analysis (DTA) measures the temperatures at which compositional and structural changes take place in minerals. The DTA curve, which is a graphic recording of the thermal changes in a mineral, is a characteristic of many minerals. Density (mass per unit of volume) is another key property. Density is normally determined as specific gravity (the ratio of the density of the substance to that of an equal volume of water at 4 degrees Celsius and 1 atmosphere of pressure). Depending on the amount and size of the mineral sample available, three methods may be used to determine density: Jolly Balance, Berman Balance, or pycnometer.

The petrographic microscope is an important analytical tool used to study the optical properties of minerals in polarized light transmitted through the specimen. Both crushed samples and thin sections (0.030 millimeter thick) are commonly utilized. Many of the metal-bearing minerals, particularly the native metals and sulfides, do not readily allow polarized light to pass through them, so microscopic analysis is conducted on highly polished samples in reflected light.

The study of the orderly internal atomic arrangement within minerals is commonly called structural crystallography. The most common method used to study this internal morphology is the X-ray diffraction powder method, in which a small, finely powdered sample is bombarded with X rays. Like the human fingerprint, every mineral has unique diffraction patterns (caused by X rays interacting with atomic planes). Several other important X-ray diffraction methods involve single crystals (oscillations, rotation, Weissenberg, and precession methods) and are primarily used, not for identification purposes, but for refining the complex internal geometries of minerals.

In addition to the physical properties of minerals, a variety of chemical methods can be used to identify and study non-silicate minerals. Until the 1960's, quantitative chemical analysis methods such as colorimetric tests, X-ray fluorescence spectrography, and atomic absorption spectrography were commonly used for mineral analysis. Since that time, however, most mineral analyses have been produced by electron microprobe analysis.

Context

A great number of the non-silicates under consideration touch people's lives in a multitude of ways. A brief sampling of how products are derived from each of these classes is worthy of some mention. Of the native elements, one only needs to look over the commodity reports in the daily newspaper to understand the importance of the likes of gold, silver, and platinum to world economies. Most of the gold in the world is owned by national governments, which commonly use it to settle international monetary disputes. It, like silver and platinum, is also becoming increasingly popular as a form of investment. In addition, gold is used in jewelry, scientific instruments, and electroplating. Silver is used in the photographic, electronics, refrigeration, jewelry, and tableware industries. Most copper is used in the production of electrical wire and in a variety of alloys, brass (copper and zinc) and bronze (copper, tin, and zinc) being the most common. Platinum is a very important metal because of its high melting point, hardness, and chemical inertness. It is primarily used by the chemical industry as a catalyst in the production of chemicals but is also used in jewelry and surgical and dental tools. Sulfur has a wide variety of uses in the chemical industry (production of insecticides, fertilizers, fabrics, paper, and soaps). In addition to their use as gems, diamonds are used in a variety of ways as cutting, grinding, and drilling agents.

Like the native elements, the sulfides are also the source of a number of metals. The most important ores of silver, copper, lead, zinc, nickel, mercury, arsenic, antimony, molybdenum, and arsenic are sulfides. All these metals play an important but usually obscure role in every technological society. The government of the United States considers most of these commodities to be critical in time of war and has huge stockpiles of them in reserve throughout the country, since most are mined in other countries.

The two most important halides, halite and fluorite, are widely used. Halite, or ordinary table salt, is a source of sodium and sodium compounds, chlorine, and hydrochloric acid, which are all important in the chemical industry. It is also used as a de-icing compound, in fertilizers, in livestock feeds, and in the processing of hides. Most fluorite is used to make hydrofluoric acid for the chemical industry or as a flux in the production of steel and aluminum.

In the borates, borax is used to produce glass, insulation, and fabrics. It is also used in medicines, in detergents, in soaps, and as a preservative.

Of the phosphates, only apatite is a common mineral, but at least three others are important for the elements that they contain. Monazite ($(Ce,La,Y,Th)PO_4$) is the primary source of thorium, which is a radioactive element with considerable potential as a source of nuclear energy. Autunite, a complex phosphate, and carnotite, a complex vanadate, are both important sources of uranium. Apatite, which is a source of phosphorus, is most widely used in fertilizers and detergents.

Of the sulfates, barite, anhydrite, and gypsum are the three most commonly used. The bulk of the barite is used as a drilling mud in the minerals and energy exploration industry. Anhydrite and gypsum occur in similar geological conditions and have similar compositions and uses. Both are used as soil conditioners. Gypsum is mainly used for the manufacture of plaster of Paris, which is used in wallboard.

In the tungstates, wolframite ($(Fe,Mn)WO_4$) and scheelite ($CaWO_4$) are the main ores of tungsten, which is used as a hardening alloy, in lamp filaments, and in tungsten carbide for cutting tools.

The natural beauty of the crystals of many of these minerals graces museums and collections throughout the world. In addition, a number of these minerals are cut or polished and used as gems. Far fewer than one hundred minerals are referred to as gems, and of the approximately fifteen important gem minerals, two are among the classes discussed here: diamond and turquoise. Other minerals that are considered gems of lesser importance are the sulfides sphalerite and pyrite, fluorite, the sulfates gypsum and barite, the phosphates apatite and amblygonite, and the tungstate scheelite.

Bibliography

Berry, L. G., B. Mason, and R. V. Dietrich. *Mineralogy—Concepts, Descriptions, Determinations*. 2d ed. San Francisco: W. H. Freeman, 1983. A college-level introduction to the study of minerals that focuses on the traditional themes necessary to understand minerals: how they are formed and what makes each chemically, crystallographically, and physically distinct from others. Descriptions and determinative tables include almost two hundred minerals (more than one-half of which are non-silicates).

Dietrich, Richard V., and B. J. Skinner. *Rocks and Rock Minerals*. New York: John Wiley & Sons, 1979. This short, readable college-level text provides a relatively brief but excellent treatment of crystallography and the properties of minerals. Although the descriptions of minerals focus on the silicates, the important rock-forming non-silicates are also considered. The book is very well illustrated and includes a subject index and modest bibliography.

Ernst, W. G. *Earth Materials*. Englewood Cliffs, N.J.: Prentice-Hall, 1969. The first four chapters of this compact introductory text deal with minerals and the principles necessary to understand their physical and chemical properties, as well as with their origins. Chapter 3 specifically deals with a number of the important rock-forming non-silicate minerals. The text includes a subject index and short bibliography.

Hurlbut, C. S., Jr., and G. S. Switzer. *Gemology*. New York: John Wiley & Sons, 1979. A well-illustrated introductory textbook for the reader with little scientific background. Its coverage includes the physical and chemical properties of gems, their origins, and the instruments used to study them. Later chapters treat methods of synthesis, cutting and polishing, and descriptions of gemstones.

Klein, C., and C. S. Hurlbut, Jr. *Manual of Mineralogy*. 20th ed. New York: John Wiley & Sons, 1985. An excellent second-year college-level text for use as an introduction to the study of minerals. The topics discussed include external and internal crystallography, crystal chemistry, properties of minerals, X-ray crystallography, and optical properties. The book also systematically describes more than one hundred non-silicate minerals.

Pough, Frederick H. *A Field Guide to Rocks and Minerals*. 4th ed. Boston: Houghton Mifflin, 1976. One of the most popular and easily accessible books dealing with non-silicate minerals. Intended for the reader with no scientific background, it includes chapters on collecting and testing minerals, descriptions of environments of formation, physical properties, classification schemes, and mineral descriptions.

Tennissen, A. C. *Nature of Earth Materials*. 2d ed. Englewood Cliffs, N.J.: Prentice-Hall, 1983. This text is written for the non-science student and treats minerals from the perspective of both the internal relationships (atomic structure, size, and bonding) and external crystallography. It includes an excellent overview of the physical properties of minerals and classification and description of 110 important minerals.

Ronald D. Tyler

Cross-References

Carbonates, 190; Gem Minerals, 802; Ionic Substitution in Minerals, 1245; Physical Properties of Minerals, 1681; The Structure of Minerals, 1693; Oxides, 1976; Radioactive Minerals, 2143.

NUCLEAR POWER

Type of earth science: Economic geology

Nuclear power obtained from the fission of uranium and plutonium nuclei represents a significant percentage of world energy resources. Its production in appropriately designed nuclear fission reactors is especially important as a low-pollution supplement to fossil fuels.

Principal terms

HALF-LIFE: the time required for half of the atoms in a given amount of a radioactive isotope to disintegrate

ISOTOPES: an element's different forms whose atoms have the same number of protons but different numbers of neutrons

MODERATOR: a material used in a nuclear reactor for slowing neutrons to increase their probability of causing fission

NUCLEAR FISSION: the splitting of an atomic nucleus into two lighter nuclei, resulting in the release of neutrons and some of the binding energy that held the nucleus together

NUCLEAR FUSION: the collision and combining of two nuclei to form a single nucleus with less mass than the original nuclei, with a release of energy equivalent to the mass reduction

NUCLEUS: the central part of an atom, containing roughly equal numbers of protons (positive particles) and neutrons (uncharged particles with slightly more mass than protons)

RADIOACTIVITY: the spontaneous emission from unstable atomic nuclei of alpha particles (helium nuclei), beta particles (electrons), and gamma rays (electromagnetic radiation)

Summary of the Phenomenon

The idea of the atom as a source of energy developed near the beginning of the twentieth century following the discovery of radioactivity by Antoine-Henri Becquerel. The energy of this spontaneous emission, first measured by Pierre and Marie Curie, was found to be far greater than ordinary chemical energies. The origin of the energy was identified with the atom itself, and the work of Albert Einstein in 1905 suggested that its explanation lay in the transportation of a tiny amount of mass m into energy E proportional to the square of the speed of light c ($E = mc^2$). This hypothesis was confirmed in the 1920's by the accurate determination of atomic masses, showing that the loss of mass of the products of radioactive decay is proportional to their energies and, as predicted, about 1 million times greater than chemical energies.

In 1911, Ernest Rutherford presented a nuclear model of the atom. Using data from the scattering of alpha particles (high-speed helium nuclei from radioactive emissions) by atoms, he showed that most of the mass of the atom (99.95 percent) is concentrated in a positively charged nucleus about 100,000 times smaller than the radius of its orbiting electrons. The discovery of the neutron by James Chadwick in 1932 confirmed that the number of protons in the nucleus of an atom is the same as the number of its electrons. The electrons are bound to the atom by their electric force of attraction to the protons. Electric repulsion between the much closer protons requires a much stronger nuclear force to hold them together in the nucleus. In 1935, Hideki Yukawa showed that the strong nuclear force binding nucleons (protons and neutrons) has a short range about the size of the nucleus. If protons escape this range, they are repelled by electric forces to exceedingly large energies. Chemical binding energies are a few electron volts per atom (an electron volt is the energy required to move an electron through one volt); nuclear energies are several million electron volts per nucleon.

Nuclear fission was discovered in 1939 after Otto Hahn and Fritz Strassmann had bombarded uranium with neutrons at their laboratory in Berlin, leaving traces of radioactive barium. When these results were sent to their former colleague Lise Meitner, who had left Germany because of increasing Nazi persecution, she recognized the possibility that neutrons had split uranium atoms (which have 92 protons) into two nearly equal parts, yielding barium (56 protons) and krypton (36 protons). She and her nephew Otto Frisch calculated the enormous energy—about 200 million electron volts—that would be released in reactions of this type, producing lighter atoms, such as barium, strontium, and cesium, and excess neutrons with a combined mass smaller than that of the original uranium atom. These results were reported to Niels Bohr and quickly verified in several laboratories in 1939. Soon Bohr developed a theory of fission showing that the rare isotope uranium 235 (uranium with 235 nucleons: 92 protons and 143 neutrons) is far more likely to produce fission, especially with slow neutrons, than the common isotope uranium 238, which makes up 99.3 percent of natural uranium. It was also recognized that if a sufficient number of neutrons were emitted in fission, they could produce new fissions with even more neutrons, resulting in a self-sustaining chain reaction. In this process, the fissioning of one gram of uranium 235 would release energy equivalent to burning about three million tons of coal.

The first nuclear reactor to achieve a controlled, self-sustaining chain reaction was developed under the leadership of the Italian physicist Enrico Fermi in 1942 at the University of Chicago. To increase the probability of fission in natural uranium, only 0.7 percent of which is uranium 235, and to prevent any chance of explosion, the neutrons were slowed down by collisions with carbon atoms in a graphite "moderator." It was necessary to assemble a large enough lattice of graphite (385 tons) and uranium (40 tons) to achieve a "critical mass" of fissile material in which the number of neutrons not escaping from the "pile" would be sufficient to sustain a chain reaction. Cadmium "control rods" were inserted to absorb neutrons during construction so that the chain reaction would not begin the instant the critical size was reached. On December 2, 1942, the rods were slowly withdrawn; the neutron intensity suddenly increased, as predicted, creating a chain reaction.

The uranium 235 isotope is the only natural material that can be used to produce nuclear energy directly. By early 1941, however, it was known that uranium 238 captures fast neutrons to produce the new element plutonium. Plutonium has a 24,000-year half-life and is fissile, so it can be used as a nuclear fuel. Plutonium can be "bred" in a uranium reactor from uranium 238 with excess neutrons from the fissioning of uranium 235. One other fissionable isotope, uranium 233, can be obtained by neutron capture from the thorium isotope thorium 232. Uranium 233 is a possible future nuclear fuel. The two basic types of reactor in use are thermal reactors, which use slow neutrons, and fast breeder reactors, which use fast neutrons to breed plutonium. Plutonium can be separated by chemical methods, but very expensive physical methods are necessary to separate uranium 235 from uranium 238, involving many stages of gaseous diffusion or centrifuge processes that can distinguish between their slightly different masses. Most thermal reactors use about 2 or 3 percent enriched uranium; fast breeder reactors use about 20 percent, and weapons require more than 90 percent.

Thermal reactors for generating useful power consist of a core containing a critical assembly of fissionable fuel elements surrounded by a moderator to slow the neutrons, a coolant to transfer heat, and movable control rods to absorb neutrons and establish the desired fission rate. Reactor fuel elements are made of natural or enriched uranium metal or oxide in the form of thin rods clad with a corrosion-resistant alloy of magnesium, zirconium, or stainless steel. Moderator materials must be low neutron absorbers with atomic mass close to the mass of neutrons so that they can slow them down by repeated collisions. Most reactors use moderators made of graphite, water, or heavy water, which contains the hydrogen isotope deuterium. Ordinary water is low in cost and doubles as a coolant, but it absorbs neutrons about one hundred times more than graphite and about one thousand times more than heavy water. Coolants such as water, carbon dioxide, and helium transfer heat liberated by fission from the core, producing steam or hot gas to drive a turbine for generating electricity in the conventional manner. Control rods are made of high neutron absorbers, such as cadmium or boron, and can be adjusted for any desired power output.

Most British and French reactors are gas-cooled with graphite moderators. The first reactor to supply public electricity was the Calder Hall station in England, which began operation in 1956 and still produces about 200 megawatts of power. It uses natural uranium in a graphite moderator with a high-pressure carbon dioxide coolant. The second-generation British "advanced gas-cooled graphite reactors" (AGRs) use about 100 tons of 2 percent enriched uranium dioxide to produce about 1,000 megawatts, with a high output of plutonium for possible future use. The "high temperature gas-cooled reactor" (HTGR) at Fort St. Vrain, Colorado, uses pellets containing 93 percent enriched uranium dioxide and thorium in order to breed uranium 233 dispersed in a graphite moderator, with helium as a coolant. It operates at about 300 megawatts with less than a ton of uranium.

Most reactors in the United States are "light water reactors" (LWRs); they use ordinary water as both moderator and coolant and require some fuel enrichment. About seventy are "pressurized water reactors" (PWRs), and about thirty are "boiling water reactors" (BWRs). The first commercial PWR began producing 100 megawatts of power in 1957 at Shippingport, Pennsylvania. The first privately financed reactor, a 200-megawatt BWR, started in 1960 at Dresden, Illinois, with 58 tons of uranium. Most LWRs use 2 to 3 percent enriched uranium dioxide fuel elements clad in a zirconium alloy, although the PWR was first developed with much higher fuel enrichments for compact shipboard use. In a PWR, water is circulated at high pressure through the reactor core at above 300 degrees Celsius and then through a heat exchanger, where steam is produced in a secondary loop. In a BWR, the water is boiled in the core at about 280 degrees, eliminating the high cost of an external heat exchanger and highly pressurized containment vessel. LWRs have the fail-safe feature: If the temperature increases fast enough to expel water from the core, neutrons will be slowed less effectively and the fission rate will decrease.

Canada has specialized in heavy water reactors, since they can use natural uranium with no need for fuel enrichment. In the Canadian deuterium-uranium system (CANDU), the heavy water coolant is circulated past fuel elements inside pressure tubes, which are surrounded by a heavy water moderator in a low-pressure tank. The coolant is pumped through a heat exchanger to boil ordinary water for driving steam turbines. Since 1968, twenty-three CANDU plants in the 200 to 700 megawatt range have been built in Canada, Argentina, India, Pakistan, and South Korea. Variants of this system employ light water or gas as a coolant to reduce the high cost of heavy water, but they may require enriched fuel.

The main alternative to thermal reactors are fast breeder reactors, which can obtain about fifty times as much energy from natural uranium by producing more plutonium from uranium 238 than the uranium 235 they use. Since neutron capture by uranium 238 requires fast neutrons (about one thousand times faster than thermal neutrons), no moderator can be used, and a 15 to 30 percent fuel enrichment is needed to sustain the chain reaction. A typical breeder core consists of a compact assembly of fuel rods with 20 percent plutonium and 80 percent depleted uranium (most uranium 235 is removed) oxides surrounded by a "blanket" of depleted uranium carbide to absorb neutrons and yield more plutonium. The "liquid metal fast breeder reactor" (LMFBR) uses sodium in liquid form (above 99 degrees Celsius) as a coolant, since water would slow the neutrons. Loss or interruption of sodium can lead to meltdown of the core, so some designs seal the core in a pool of sodium. The first commercial fast breeder reactor began in the Soviet Union in 1972, producing 350 megawatts. France has the most advanced fast breeder reactor program, with its 1,200-megawatt Super Phénix breeder reactor.

Most of the problems associated with fission power could be eliminated with nuclear fusion reactors. These problems include the handling, storage, and reprocessing of highly radioactive materials such as plutonium, the possible theft of such materials by terrorists, the disposal of radioactive waste products, the dangers of a reactor accident, and the limited availability of fission fuels. The fusion of hydrogen isotopes to produce helium releases energy comparable to fission but requires no critical mass of fuel that might cause meltdown, has many fewer radioactive products with no storage or disposal problems, and uses a fuel of almost unlimited supply. About 0.01 percent of the hydrogen in ocean water is in the form of deuterium. To overcome electrical repulsion and bring deuterium atoms close enough to cause a fusion reaction, an ignition temperature of about 100 million degrees is required. Ignition and isolation of such reactions require some kind of magnetic confinement of a plasma (ionized gas) or inertial confinement of deuterium pellets. Energy would be extracted by nuclear reactions in a surrounding lithium blanket caused by neutrons emitted during fusion. Some progress has been made in achieving these requirements, but a practical source of fusion power is many years away.

Experiments at several laboratories have suggested the possibility of room-temperature fusion by using electrolysis to draw deuterium ions into the crystal lattice of hydrogen-absorbing materials such as palladium or titanium. Because electrical repulsion between charged nuclei increases greatly as they approach each other, it is difficult to understand how this process could bring deuterium ions close enough for fusion to occur. Even if such experiments are confirmed and explained, the development of a reactor to produce electrical power with this technique may be difficult if not impossible. Hydrogen absorption declines sharply with increasing temperature, decreasing by a factor of at least ten as the temperature approaches the boiling point of water. Much higher temperatures would have to be produced for an efficient steam-driven electrical generator.

Methods of Study

A variety of methods are used to study the basic physics, operational characteristics, and safety requirements of nuclear reactors. Energies available from nuclear reactions are determined from accurate atomic mass measurements in a mass spectrograph performed by comparing the deflections of ions (charged atoms) in a magnetic field. Ions of different isotopes are separated and brought to a focus at different positions on a photographic film, and the intensities of these lines indicate their relative abundance. In 1935, Arthur Dempster used this technique at the University of Chicago to discover and measure the rare uranium 235 isotope. Charged particles and gamma rays are usually detected from the ionization they produce in a Geiger counter or a gas-filled proportional counter. In these devices, a high voltage separates electrons and ions, causing further ionization that results in an electrical pulse. In the proportional counter, the pulse size is proportional to the initial ionization, so particle energies can be discriminated.

Neutron absorption and scattering characteristics at different energies are measured for the materials used in various reactor components by several methods. Neutron detectors usually depend on reactions that produce ionizing particles, such as neutron capture by boron, which yields lithium and helium ions. A thin layer of boron on the walls of a proportional counter makes neutron detection possible from the resulting ions. Both the magnitude and energy spectrum of neutrons in a reactor can be measured by the foil activation method, in which thin foils are exposed to the reactor flux and the induced radioactivity is then measured. Fission rates can be measured with a fission counter by placing a thin layer of fissile material on one electrode of a proportional counter, yielding high-energy fission fragments that produce distinctive pulses. Other aspects of reactor operation and safety are studied by means of various sizes and types of research reactors.

The study of reactor safety involves estimating the biological effects of radiation and analyzing the risk factors in possible reactor accidents. Information on the effects of large doses of radiation is based on medical X rays, animal experiments, and studies of Japanese atomic bomb survivors. Radiation doses are monitored by photographic film dosimeters and simple ionization chambers. Normal background radiation from radioactivity in the earth, radon gas, and cosmic radiation is about double the average dose received by a person for medical purposes annually. The radioactivity from normal reactor operation is considerably less than background radiation, leading to an estimated risk of about three additional cancer deaths per year in the United States as compared with about three thousand per year from medical X rays. Whole-body doses over the complete reactor fuel cycle (mining, operation, and reprocessing) were estimated by the American Physical Society in 1978 at a maximum of one hundred times less than the annual background radiation received by plant workers. The major public concern focuses on accidental releases of large amounts of radioactivity. The Nuclear Regulatory Commission estimates the risk from a reactor accident at less than one death over its service lifetime.

The risks of a nuclear accident can be studied when one actually occurs. The most serious commercial reactor accident in the United States occurred in 1979 at the Three Mile Island power station in Pennsylvania; the loss of some coolant led to the shutdown of one reactor, as designed, but resulted in costly damage to the core. Because of containment structures, including a thick steel vessel around the core and a reinforced concrete building with walls several feet thick, the highest average dose released was about ten times less than the annual background radiation. A much more serious accident occurred at Chernobyl in the Soviet Union in 1986; a loss of coolant in a graphite reactor led to increased power followed by explosions and fire, killing thirty-one men. Because of a lack of containment, radioactive material was spread over much of Europe. Nine thousand excess cancer deaths were predicted, a figure roughly equal to the number of deaths from coal-burning-related air pollution in the United States each year. The long-range effect of this accident, however, has yet to be determined.

The disposal of radioactive wastes is another area of concern and continuing study. Methods of solidifying such waste in glass or other materials for confinement in metal canisters and burial are being studied. The solid waste projected through the year 2010 would cover about 40,000 square meters (10 acres). Of several disposal sites under study, the most likely is deep underground burial in formations of salt or rock.

Context

Nuclear power is an important source of low-pollution energy in spite of serious problems that have emerged since 1980. By the end of the 1980's, 17 percent of electrical energy in the United States was generated by about one hundred nuclear reactors producing about 60,000 megawatts of power. Domestic uranium supplies can support about five times the total amount of installed capacity until the year 2025. More than three hundred reactors in twenty-five countries provide about 200,000 megawatts of the world's power. Known reserves of uranium in high-grade ores total several million tons. The noncommunist world consumes about 36 million kilograms a year, so there is enough high-grade ore to supply a nuclear power program at ten times its present level for about fifty years. That is a huge energy resource, roughly comparable with the remaining reserves of oil. The use of fast breeder reactors rather than thermal reactors would extend this resource by a factor of fifty or sixty, far beyond current planning horizons.

The future of conventional nuclear power is uncertain. Since the Three Mile Island accident in 1979, public distrust of nuclear power has increased. The concern about reactor safety has led to new requirements that have increased the cost of nuclear power plants by a factor of five above inflation. Bankers and investors have become increasingly cautious about financing new plant construction. The high rate of government subsidies has complicated the evaluation of real dollar costs of nuclear power, but estimates indicate that the profit potential of conventional nuclear power is about half that of coal power. As a result, no new plants have been ordered in the United States since 1979, despite large subsidies, and several have been postponed or canceled while under construction. The total U.S. nuclear power capacity, operational and planned, slipped from 236 reactors in 1976 to 128 in 1983.

Although coal supplies more than 50 percent of electrical energy in the United States and is in plentiful supply, there are serious problems associated with its use. Uranium mining does not carry the risks of fire, explosion, black lung disease, or other hazards of coal mining. The risk to uranium miners, mainly from radon gas, is about ten times less than that faced by coal miners for the same energy content of fuel produced. Approximately one hundred coal miners are killed every year in the United States. Air pollution from a coal-fired plant is estimated to cause at least one thousand deaths over its operating lifetime, compared with one death estimated for a nuclear plant. Other serious problems associated with the burning of fossil fuels include acid rain, the greenhouse effect (the trapping of solar radiation by increased carbon dioxide), and continued dependence on foreign sources of oil.

One promising approach to the safer production of nuclear fission power is the development of small-scale modular reactors that use tiny ceramic-coated fuel pellets in small enough quantities in their cores that meltdown is impossible. Although initially expensive, such units would not require expensive safety systems and could be built on an assembly line, producing one module at a time to match operating capacity with the demand for power.

Bibliography

Blair, Ian. *Taming the Atom: Facing the Future with Nuclear Power*. Bristol, England: Adam Hilger, 1983. This book gives a very readable account of the development and use of nuclear power from a British perspective. The basic physical principles of nuclear power are covered, along with a good survey of the nuclear industry. An appendix on world nuclear reactors includes diagrams and data.

Cameron, I. R. *Nuclear Fission Reactors*. New York: Plenum Press, 1983. The first half of this book is a technical treatment of nuclear fission and reactor theory. The second half is a more readable survey of reactor types and a good discussion of safety and environmental aspects of reactors. The bibliography lists about 150 references to books and technical articles.

Cohen, Bernard L. *Before It's Too Late: A Scientist's Case for Nuclear Energy*. New York: Plenum Press, 1982. Aimed at the general reader, this book discusses problems in the public understanding of nuclear power. It covers the danger of radiation, the possibility and results of a meltdown accident, the problem of radioactive waste, and the assessment of risks. Each chapter lists many references.

Craig, J. R., D. J. Vaughan, and B. J. Skinner. *Resources of the Earth*. Englewood Cliffs, N.J.: Prentice-Hall, 1988. This introductory college textbook contains a chapter on nuclear power, the nuclear fuel cycle, reactor safety, and uranium mining. Other chapters on fossil fuels and environmental problems give useful comparative information.

Inglis, David R. *Nuclear Energy: Its Physics and Its Social Challenge*. Reading, Mass.: Addison-Wesley, 1973. This book is based on an introductory college course for general students. It explains the basic principles of nuclear energy and describes reactors and their radioactive products. Technical details and historic documents are given in several appendices.

Marion, J. B., and M. L. Roush. *Energy in Perspective*. New York: Academic Press, 1982. Written for a college survey course, this book has chapters on energy consumption, energy sources, nuclear power, and the effects of nuclear radiations. Contains many good diagrams, tables, and photographs.

Priest, Joseph. *Energy: Principles, Problems, Alternatives*. Reading, Mass.: Addison-Wesley, 1984. This textbook is designed for a college survey course on energy. It has chapters on nuclear fission power, breeder reactors, and fusion reactors. Contains interesting illustrations and tables, an appendix giving energy and consumption comparisons, and a glossary of terms.

Joseph L. Spradley

Cross-References

Mass Spectrometry, 1521; Underground Mining Techniques, 1710; Mining Wastes and Reclamation, 1718; Nuclear Waste Disposal, 1758; Radioactive Decay, 2136; Radioactive Minerals, 2143; Earth Resources, 2175; Future Resources, 2182; Strategic Resources, 2188; Uranium Deposits, 2580.

NUCLEAR WASTE DISPOSAL

Field of study: Urban geology and geologic hazards

Nuclear waste disposal in a geologic repository is considered the safest and surest way to achieve isolation of the wastes from the surface environment. No one can guarantee that a repository will last forever, but its combined geologic characteristics will minimize damage in the event of failure.

Principal terms

HALF-LIFE: the time required for one-half the radioactive isotopes in a sample to decay

HIGH-LEVEL WASTES: wastes containing large amounts of dangerous radioactivity

ISOTOPES: atoms of the same element that differ in the number of uncharged neutrons in their nuclei

LEACHATE: water that has come into contact with waste and, as a result, is transporting some of the water-soluble parts of the waste

LOW-LEVEL WASTES: wastes that are much less radioactive than high-level wastes and thus less likely to cause harm

PERMEABILITY: a measure of the ease of flow of a fluid through a porous rock or sediment

POROSITY: a measure of the amount of open spaces capable of holding water or air in a rock or sediment

RADIOACTIVITY: the spontaneous release of energy accompanying the decay of a nucleus

SOLUBILITY: the tendency for a solid to dissolve

SORPTION: the process of removing a chemical from a fluid by either physical or chemical means

TRANSURANIC: an isotope of an element that is heavier than uranium and that is formed in the processing and use of nuclear fuel and plutonium

Summary of the Methodology

Nuclear waste disposal is a necessary evil in a world where radioactive isotopes and the energy produced by their decay are used, among other things, for generating electricity, diagnosing and treating diseases, and making nuclear weapons. Nuclear wastes are not all the same. Some wastes, because of their composition, are more dangerous than others, and some are more dangerous for longer periods of time. When evaluating a geologic site for disposal of nuclear wastes, the characteristics of the site must be identified so that the waste will be isolated from the earth surface environment for a minimally acceptable period of time. Ensuring the minimal length of isolation is most important for those wastes that are dangerous for a long time and those that contain large concentrations of dangerous isotopes. Such wastes, usually called high-level wastes, consist of isotopes of uranium and plutonium produced in the use and processing of nuclear fuel. The length of isolation is not so important for those wastes that are dangerous for shorter times and are less concentrated. These wastes are called low-level wastes and may include some long-lasting wastes but in lower concentrations. An example of a low-level waste is slightly contaminated garbage, such as disposable laboratory equipment, disposable medical equipment, and disposable gloves and overalls (which are used in the handling of radioactive materials). The length of time that a particular waste is dangerous depends on which radioactive isotopes are in the waste and on the half-life of each isotope. The half-life is the time required for one-half of the radioactive isotopes in a sample to decay.

During the natural process of radioactive decay, the nucleus of a radioactive isotope, the "parent," is changed into that of another isotope, the "daughter," and energy is released. This radioactive decay from parent to daughter is usually one step in a series of many, as the original parent isotope changes into a nonradioactive, stable isotope. At each step, energy is released in the form of energetic particles or energetic rays. Thus, in a sample of uranium, the parent uranium isotopes are constantly decaying in a series of steps through various daughter isotopes until the sample consists of pure lead, the ultimate daughter isotope in the uranium decay series. It takes a long time for all the uranium to decay completely to lead. The half-life of one uranium isotope, uranium 238, is 4.5 billion years. The long half-life of uranium suggests that the half-lives for some of the daughter isotopes in the decay series are also long.

Exposure to radiation is never without risk. The problem with a long half-life is that the isotope is giving off energetic particles or rays that are dangerous to plants and animals for an extended period. Thus, high-level wastes, where the isotopes are in concentrated form, must be isolated from the surface environment for a long time. Low-level wastes are less dangerous only because the concentrations of radioactive isotopes are lower. While they need to be isolated from the surface environment, they are not as destructive to life as are high-level wastes.

Plants and animals are exposed to radiation through air, water, and food. Naturally occurring radioactive isotopes may be in the air (in the form of radon, for example) and taken into the lungs. Some radioactive isotopes are dissolved in the water we drink (potassium 40) and in the food we eat (carbon 14). To minimize excessive exposure to radiation, a geologic repository must isolate radioactive waste from the surface environment. A geologic repository is any structure in either rock or soil which uses, in part, the natural abilities of these materials to isolate the wastes from the surface environment. A geologic repository may be a shallow trench dug in the soil, partially filled with low-level waste and covered with the excavated soil, or it may be a cavern constructed deep underground in hard rock. Regardless, the purpose of the repository is to isolate the waste in such a way that there is no excess exposure of organisms to radiation as a result of the presence of the repository. In this sense, isolation means that the waste must be kept from contaminating the surrounding air, water, and food.

The rocks or soil of a geologic repository must have certain characteristics to isolate wastes properly. Some of the more important characteristics are porosity, permeability, mineral solubility, and sorption capacity. Porosity and permeability are related but are not the same. Porosity is a measure of the ability of a rock or soil to hold a fluid, either liquid or gas. Expressed as a percentage of the volume of the sample, porosity is the volume of open, or pore, space in the rock or soil. If the soil or rocks of a geologic repository have high porosity, then large amounts of water or air may contact the waste; however, contact with the waste does not necessarily mean that the contaminated water or air will reach the surface environment. If the rock or soil is also permeable—that is, if the pores are interconnected enough so that the water or air can flow from the repository to the surface—then the repository is not likely to provide adequate isolation. Porosity can exist without permeability when many small pores contain a large volume of fluid, but the connections between pores are too small to allow fluid flow. Permeability can exist with small porosity when a few penetrating cracks in an otherwise solid rock allow easy fluid flow.

Mineral solubility is an important characteristic in cases where water may contact the waste. Soluble minerals, those that tend to dissolve in water, may be removed from the surrounding rock or soil by moving water. When minerals dissolve, a space is left behind that adds to the porosity, and may increase the permeability, of the repository.

The sorption capacity of a mineral is the ability of that mineral to remove a dissolved molecule or ion from a fluid. Sorption may occur by either chemical or physical means. A type of chemical sorption is the ion exchange that takes place in a home water-softening unit. Water containing problem ions (in the case of a repository, radioactive ions) flows over the exchanging minerals. The problem ions attach to the mineral and, in the process, force the ion that was attached originally into the solution. The water is thus cleansed of problem ions. In physical sorption, the water and the contaminant are attached to the mineral by the force of friction, which results in a thin layer of water attached to the mineral surface. The attached, or physically sorbed, water and any material dissolved in it are not moving.

All these characteristics of rock and soil are related in some way to the possibility that the waste will escape from the repository and be transported by a fluid to the surface. It is unlikely that any repository will be a perfect candidate to provide isolation when all the characteristics are considered. Some characteristics, however, may be more important than others, and weakness in one may be offset by strength in another.

Applications of the Method

Shallow burial of low-level wastes and deep burial of high-level wastes are preceded by careful description of the strengths and weaknesses of the geologic material of the repository. In the case of shallow burial, the repository material is usually soil or saprolite (near-surface rock that has been partially turned to soil by the actions of water). To determine the strengths and weaknesses of a particular soil for containing low-level waste, the earth scientist must study the structure, hydrology, mineralogy, and chemistry of that soil.

When water, in the form of rain or snowmelt, enters a soil, in most cases it does not flow through the soil uniformly. Water tends to flow more easily through the soil along certain permeable paths. In nearly every soil there are preferred flow paths and isolated areas. Sometimes the structure is inherited from the original rock that broke down to soil. Fractures and other cracks contained in the original rock may be preserved as cracks in the soil. Structures inherited from the parent rock are especially evident in saprolite, which exists in a stage between rock and true soil.

Other soil structures are the products of soil processes. Such structures include the cracks developed when a soil dries out, the tunnels formed by burrowing organisms such as worms and ants, and the openings left when the roots of dead plants decay. All these structures are important because they determine how and how fast water will flow through a soil.

The means and speed of water flow through soil are important aspects of its hydrology. The flow of water into a shallow burial trench is usually restricted by engineered, low-permeability barriers such as compacted clay or plastic liners. If the liners fail and water flows through and out of the wastes, the surrounding soil should slow the flow of contaminants in two ways: physically and chemically. Physically impeding, or retarding, the flow of contaminated water from the waste trench means that the soil structure does not provide permeable flow paths; the water is forced to flow through many small, interconnected pores. As a result, the waste-transporting water contacts more of the mineral material in the soil. Chemical retardation of wastes occurs when the contaminants in the slowly moving fluid interact with the minerals of the soil. Some of those minerals have the capacity to sorb contaminants, thereby further slowing their migration. Other reactions between the minerals and the wastewater result in the chemistry of the water changing in such a way that the contaminants may become insoluble and form new solids in the soil. The effect is the same: The flow of contaminants from the burial trench is slowed or stopped.

Disposal of high-level wastes in a geologic repository requires that many of the same characteristics of the host rock be determined. In addition to having the appropriate hydrological, mineralogical, and chemical characteristics, the host rock is required to be reasonably stable for ten thousand years. For example, the modern hydrological characteristics of the proposed Yucca Mountain repository site in Nevada are ideal. The proposed repository will be located below the desert surface, out of the reach of downward-percolating rainwater and well above the nearest fresh groundwater. In the desert environment, rainfall is so infrequent that it cannot reach the repository from above, nor can the infrequent rainfalls raise the groundwater level to flood the repository.

The problem is that climates have changed in the past—the desert Southwest of the United States used to be much wetter—and climates will undoubtedly change in the future. In addition, the repository may be disturbed, whether inadvertently or purposely, by human activities. The most likely inadvertent disturbance is that created by future generations, who, in a search for mineral deposits, will puncture the repository with drilling equipment. To avoid this scenario, the repository must be located in an area unlikely to yield mineral wealth. Deeply buried layers of rock salt, thought to be ideal repositories because of their stability and their resistance to water flow, are no longer being considered. Many of the rock salt deposits are already being mined for the salt, and future generations may mine the remaining ones. In addition, some of these deposits are associated with oil and natural gas. The likelihood of near- and distant-future mineral exploration in the vicinity of salt beds makes them unlikely hosts for a high-level repository.

Context

Nuclear waste disposal, whether of low-level or high-level wastes, is a problem that will remain. More waste is being created every day. A geologic repository and its host rock or soil must safely isolate the wastes from the surface environment for a specified period of time. Should the repository and host material fail, plants and animals will be exposed to radioactive elements. The risk of exposure to radiation can never be eliminated, but careful design of the repository and careful determination of the host material's strengths and weaknesses can result in a disposal site that minimizes the risk.

Ultimately, the siting of a nuclear waste disposal facility will be a political decision. That political decision must be based on sound technical information and judgments. As nuclear wastes accumulate in temporary holding facilities (for example, spent fuel elements from nuclear reactor power generators are stored in large water-filled pools near the reactor), political pressures build to solve the disposal problem. An informed public, while pressing for a solution, will understand delays necessitated by the need to gather and interpret the data. It must also be understood that risk can be minimized but never eliminated.

Bibliography

Bartlett, Donald L., and James B. Steele. *Forevermore: Nuclear Waste in America*. New York: W. W. Norton, 1985. Written by two reporters, this book looks at the history and future of nuclear waste disposal in the United States. The strength of the book is in tracing the political aspects of decision making in a technical field. Accessible to any reader with an interest in the subject, regardless of technical background.

Burns, Michael E., ed. *Low-Level Radioactive Waste Regulation: Science, Politics, and Fear*. Chelsea, Mich.: Lewis, 1987. One of the few books available for the general reader that deals exclusively with the problems of low-level wastes. Individual articles by groups of authors cover a range of issues from technical aspects of exposure risks to the politics among states when deciding where to locate a repository. Some of the articles may be too technical for the lay reader, but there is a wealth of data contained in tables throughout. Contains extensive references for further reading and an adequate glossary.

Carter, Luther J. *Nuclear Imperatives and Public Trust: Dealing with Radioactive Waste*. Washington, D.C.: Resources for the Future, 1987. Carter provides a detailed but not overly technical history of the radioactive waste repository story. The book details the political and bureaucratic decision-making processes and shows how ill-informed decisions led to early disasters. Contains a good glossary of terms and extensive footnotes.

Grossman, Dan, and Seth Shulman. "A Nuclear Dump: The Experiment Begins (Beneath Yucca Mountain, Nevada)." *Discover* 10 (March, 1989): 48. A newsy, nontechnical article on the proposed Yucca Mountain, Nevada, high-level waste repository. A very accessible, if brief, discussion of some of the tests needed to characterize the rocks and their history. The authors point out areas of disagreement on technical questions and indicate the complexity of such problems. There are a few good illustrations of what the repository will look like. In general, a good introductory article for anyone with no background in the subject.

League of Women Voters Educational Fund Staff. *The Nuclear Waste Primer: A Handbook for Citizens*. New York: Lyons, 1987. A very compact (ninety-page) introduction to the nuclear waste problem. After a quick introduction to some of the technical jargon used in radiation chemistry, the book describes the magnitude of the problems of dealing with low- and high-level wastes, concluding with suggestions for citizen action. The glossary is brief but comprehensive.

Richard W. Arnseth

Cross-References

NUCLEOSYNTHESIS

Type of earth science: Geochemistry

Nucleosynthesis is the process by which the elements are formed in the interior of stars during the course of their normal evolution. Hydrogen and helium are thought for the most part to have been generated at the origin of the universe itself (nucleogenesis) while all other heavier elements are synthesized via nuclear reactions in stellar cores. The heaviest elements are created in the death throes of massive stars.

Principal terms

BIG BANG THEORY: the theory that the universe was created via an initial explosion that resulted in the formation of hydrogen and helium

CHARGED-PARTICLE REACTION: a nuclear reaction involving the addition of a charged particle, proton or electron, to a nucleus

DEUTERIUM: an atom built of one proton and one neutron; an essential stepping-stone in the proton-proton cycle in solar-type stars

ISOTOPE: an atom with the same number of protons as another but differing in the number of neutrons and the total weight

NEUTRON REACTION: a nuclear reaction in which a neutron is added to increase the atomic mass of the nucleus, forming isotopes

NUCLEONS: positively charged protons and neutral neutrons; large particles that occupy the atomic nucleus

NUCLEOSYNTHESIS: the building up of the chemical elements from preexisting hydrogen by nuclear reaction processes

SUPERNOVA: a massive star that explodes after available energy in the interior is used up and the star collapses

Summary of the Phenomenon

Two of the most fundamental questions of modern astrophysics have to do with the origin and composition of the universe's primordial matter: when it came into existence and how it relates to the Einsteinian space-time structure of the present universe. With developments in twentieth century physics, the problems have resolved themselves essentially into two parts: the origin of the simplest elements, hydrogen and helium, during the initial formation of the present universe and the subsequent nucleosynthesis of the other elements in the pressure cookers known as stars.

To understand elemental synthesis, one must rely on experimental observations interpreted in the light of current theory. Such data principally have to do with abundances of nuclear species now and in the past. This data set is provided from composition studies of the earth, meteorites, and other planets, and from stellar spectra. The distribution of hydrogen and heavier elements in stars throughout the galaxy, particularly in what are referred to as population I and II stars (younger and older, respectively), indicates how the chemical composition of the Milky Way galaxy has changed over time. From these studies, most theorists conclude that the galaxy has synthesized 99 percent of its own heavy elements and thus that nucleosynthesis occurs during the natural evolution of stars. In the light of variations observed in stars of diverse ages, scientists have formulated theories regarding the formation of elements within stellar structures. A dramatic piece of evidence along that line, for example, was the discovery of technetium, all of whose isotopes, being radioactive, are short-lived, indicating that the star in which it is found must be currently producing the element. The study of of naturally occurring radioactive isotopes, long- and short-lived, not only allows for measuring the time of galactic and stellar nucleosynthesis but also provides evidence that synthesis of elements heavier than hydrogen must be occurring continuously throughout the universe.

Starting with the simplest element, hydrogen, which possesses one proton and one electron and is by far the predominant element in the universe, the study of nucleogenesis has progressed to a consideration of the origin of the universe. Beginning in 1946, George Gamow and others presented the theory that the entire structure started as a gigantic explosion of an extremely dense, hot "singularity," or infinitesimally small object. The explosion would have been so intense as to provide the propellant for all subsequent motion of the outwardly expanding matter and for the creation of the elements. Such a "big bang" concept has come to be accepted almost unanimously, with certain modifications. The discovery of an isotropic microwave background radiation, corresponding to a 3-Kelvin temperature residual from the original fireball, lent support to the theory, along with the 1970's through the use of gigantic accelerators, which permit examination of the formation and interactions of the basic constituents and forces of nature. Such physics have determined that element synthesis, via nuclear reactions, combining protons, electrons, and neutrons, could have occurred only when the temperature dropped to below 1 billion Kelvins about three minutes after the explosion. Before that point, the energy of motion would have been too great either to form those particles or to let them cling together in electromagnetic interactions. That period of element synthesis probably lasted about one hour; eventually the temperature and pressure would have dropped too low to sustain any further reactions. Because of the instability of particles with atomic masses of 5 to 8, no particle combinations beyond a mass of 4 would have been formed; thus the universe was probably composed of about 75 percent hydrogen and 25 percent helium. The formation of the helium nucleus, with a mass of 4, would have used up all the available neutrons. The reactions would have progressed in a certain order. First, neutrons and protons would combine to produce deuterium; deuterium and protons would then give helium 3; the collision of two helium 3 nuclei would produce a helium 4 nucleus and two protons, releasing energy in the process as gamma rays. This postulated process seems to be in excellent agreement with observational data and theoretical calculations.

For roughly a million years, radiation was so intense that larger particular bodies could not form. Only after the radiation pressure became low enough would such inhomogeneities as galaxies and stars solidify. At that state, the dominating force in the universe became gravity, the galaxies and stars forming as a result of gravitational contraction. Scientists' understanding of galactic formation remains sketchy, but stellar evolution—from birth in dust-cloud nurseries to death—is well understood through a combination of observational data, laboratory measurements of nuclear reactions and their rates, and copious amounts of theoretical work. As stated best by Subrahmanyan Chandrasekhar, the working hypothesis generally accepted by astrophysicists is that the stars are the places where the transmutation of elements occurs, all the elements beyond hydrogen being synthesized there. All the energy available to a star throughout its life span, with minor exceptions, is derived from such transformations.

As the original gas and dust in a nebula collapse and contract, they heat up enormously, until the temperature in the core reaches some 10 million Kelvins, at which point thermonuclear proton-proton reactions occur, to form deuterium and give off positrons and radiant energy. Further reactions occur, increasing the helium formed, decreasing hydrogen, and producing energy sufficient to halt the gravitational collapse of the star. For most stars, this stage probably occupies the greater part of their lifetime. The more massive the star is, however, the faster it will exhaust the hydrogen supply at the core and the shorter its time of stability will be. Stars such as the Sun are in the range for forming helium. Some interesting side reactions occur also. Some 5 percent of the helium reacts to make beryllium, boron, and lithium; in an even rarer occurrence, proton capture produces the isotope boron 8. The latter is important because it is very sensitive to temperature and therefore acts as a good test of stellar theories; the reaction produces neutrinos, which earthbound astronomers can then study.

In older stars, formed as second, third, or later generations, some heavier elements are present. In these, the so-called carbon-nitrogen-oxygen cycle proposed by Hans Albrecht Bethe works, again turning four protons to helium. Because a higher temperature is necessary to overcome the electrostatic (Coulomb) repulsion barrier, this cycle takes place only in larger stars. In either case, when a significant amount of core hydrogen is used up, with helium ash left, the star will contract. Meanwhile, the hydrogen-containing outer area expands, causing the star to become a red giant; its central temperature rises to 100 million Kelvins. At this stage, helium burns to form beryllium, forming one beryllium atom per billion helium atoms. Also produced are carbon, oxygen, and neon, the principal source of energy being the conversion of three heliums to carbon 12 plus gamma radiation. This burn, however, is short-lived, lasting only 10 to 100 million years, as compared to more than 5 billion years for the present sun. Any further synthesis requires much higher thermal energy input than can ever occur.

Beyond this stage, in larger stars, the processes become more complex. When helium is exhausted, contraction starts again. For objects such as the Sun, this shrinkage will continue until it is halted by electron degeneracy (a mutual repulsion of tightly squeezed electrons) to form white dwarfs, small and intensely radiative bodies losing their heat into space, with no further nuclear energy available. Many become surrounded by a halo of expanding gases, the so-called planetary nebula; material from the star flows into space as a last gasp of the red giant stage. In larger stars the temperature continues to climb, to 70 million Kelvins, eventually causing new sets of elements to form, including magnesium 24, sodium 23, neon 20, silicon 28, and sulfur 32. With further contraction, until the temperature reaches 1 billion Kelvins, elements up to and including iron are created. Synthesis stops here, however, because of the energy required to form more stable nucleons bound together.

Additional synthesis does not involve charged-particle reactions but rather neutron-induced reactions, which tie up neutrons and produce energy. Such reactions are called s-processes because they proceed very slowly, taking from 100 to 100,000 years per capture step. This process accounts for the heavier isotopes on even atomic number elements and the distribution of nuclides up to bismuth. This reaction, in conjunction with a p-process involving successful proton reactions, can account for all the stable isotopes up to bismuth. For higher elements, however, a more rapid neutron-capture chain called the r-process is required; it takes place when there is an enormous neutron flux so that many captures can take place in milliseconds. Conditions perfect for such acts occur in supernovae, or stars that explode with some of the greatest violence seen in the universe. Type I supernovae are from old, small stars, with masses of 1.2 to 1.5 times that of the Sun; in such an explosion the entire star is destroyed, pushing the temperature to 10 billon Kelvins, Type II supernovae occur in stars with masses greater than ten times that of the Sun. Under contraction, the temperature in the nucleus of the star rises to 5 billion Kelvins, iron and nickel nuclei photodissociate to helium and neutron particles, the helium present dissociates into nucleons, and the resulting protons capture any available electrons, forming new neutrons. The collapse, which takes one second, results in a core mass of neutrons, with explosive ejection of the outer layer and all the elements into the intersteller regions. Such explosions, which occur perhaps once in a hundred years in a galaxy, contribute all the material from which other stars, clouds, and planets such as Earth are formed.

Methods of Study

Since the first theories of the processes of elemental origins were proposed, scientific understanding of nucleosynthesis has progressed greatly, thanks principally to an improved ability to determine abundances of elements particularly in stars and nebulae, and to better understanding of transformation conditions during synthesis. Nuclear physics data on reaction rates, particle formation, and interactions at diverse temperatures and energies, along with clearer notions of strong and weak force interactions, have contributed vital knowledge on both the universe's origin and the generation of elements in stellar bodies during and at the end of a star's life cycle.

Isotopic abundances can be determined from meteorites by the use of mass spectroscopy. In this experimental technique, particles are heated until they break apart into ionic forms; the bodies are then propelled, under the influence of electric and magnetic fields, through a vacuum chamber. The curved path followed depends on the mass and the charge on the elements. Collection at the end of the path allows detailed comparisons to be made, with particular attention to the anomalies that are critical to theories of nucleosynthesis.

Spectral analysis has been the principal tool for studying extraterrestrial abundances. In such analysis, light from the observed object is passed through a prism or diffraction grating so that it is broken into all of its component colors; the resulting spectrum ranges from the blue to the red region of the visible section of the spectrum. Invariably, the background will be crossed by dark or bright lines, depending on whether it is an emission or absorption spectrum. These lines, identifiable in the physics laboratory, act as fingerprints, quickly showing such information as what elements are present and their abundances. Observation of material emitted by supernovae, for example, not only shows how heavy elements are enriched in space but also contributes greatly to theories of explosive charged-particle nucleosynthesis.

Similar analyses, using spectroscopes, telescopes, and various light-intensity enhancing instruments such as charge-coupled devices (CCDs), have been done of other objects, including medium-mass stars with s-process element formation, novae explosions, and mass flows from solar-type stars. The latter can be studied best in the Sun, by analyzing the composition of the solar wind with data returned by meteorological and scientific satellites. Detectors placed above the atmosphere can be equipped to detect charged particles such as protons or electrons. Experiments to view the universe in some region of the electromagnetic spectrum besides visible light, such as radio, gamma, infrared, or ultraviolet, also must be placed beyond the disturbing influence of the atmosphere.

Much of the information usable for the theoretical study of nucleosynthesis comes from two terrestrial sources. First, experimental studies using nuclear reactors and particle accelerator machines have provided comprehensive measurements of reaction rates and of the actions of the weak force in nature. Increasingly reliable determinations of critical cross sections, representing the space in which reaction occurs between two particles, and of the neutron-capture process, which is responsible for the bulk of nuclei more massive than iron, have become possible with highly refined accelerators and electrical detectors. Theoretical predictions and experimental results are thus more in harmony than ever before.

The second important advance has been in computer technology, which has made possible greatly increased numerical calculations of structures and the evolution of astrophysical objects. The advent of high-speed computers has allowed much greater predictive ability for the standard model of the big bang and regarding the formation of elements at various stages in the stars. Such detailed models, particularly of massive stars, in terms of hydrodynamic phases, have shown, for example, that supernovae are immensely important in the synthesis of heavy elements. Models for actions at extreme temperature and density conditions are very close to what is observed during the expansion, cooling, and mass ejection processes of the dying stars. Computer technology has helped identify further problems through capture modeling, such as the sites necessary for r-process neutron-capture nucleosynthesis.

Context

Nucleogenesis and nucleosynthesis are two of the most important topics of current research in astronomy, the ultimate origin of the universe, and the evolution of stars from beginning to end. The understanding of origins has been advanced greatly by the advent of particle accelerators of remarkably high energies. These instruments provide physicists with clearer pictures of the elementary particle structures of the universe and of their interaction under the four forces controlling them. During the creative process of the big bang, these four forces—strong and weak nuclear, electromagnetic, and gravitational—were unified as one, separating only as initial conditions of temperature, pressure, and density changed. Under their actions, radiation and particles ultimately formed, with radiation finally dispersing enough that combinations of protons and electrons, then neutrons, could arise.

Although the modern understanding of nucleosynthesis is thought to be quite satisfactory, there are still problems unsolved. Certain elemental anomalies have not been explained by either experiments or theory; neither has the shortage of neutrinos from the Sun. Predictions of energy fluxes and solar winds from other stars, particularly red giants, represent other unsolved problems. The answer to what causes a dust cloud to begin to contract to form a star is unknown; a widely accepted notion is that the contraction is prompted by the shock wave of a supernova. Problems remain with the big bang theory itself, so that alternative theories, such as the "inflationary universe," have been proposed. The investigation of such problems of modern physics and astronomy has led to numerous insights, including the possibility that planets may be by-products of stellar formation; in such a scenario, the galaxy may be filled with planets and, possibly, life forms. Further fine-tuning of reaction rates, mechanisms, and such experimental topics as element reactions may solve some of the deepest philosophical and scientific mysteries of modern science.

Bibliography

Abell, George O. *Exploration of the Universe*. 4th ed. New York: Holt, Rinehart and Winston, 1982. One of the best standard textbooks on astronomy available. Covers in detail the life history of stars, particularly those in which heavy elements are formed. Separate sections on white dwarfs, neutron stars, black holes, and supernovae. Glossary and references. Excellent diagrams and pictures.

Arnett, W. David, and James W. Truran, eds. *Nucleosynthesis: Challenges and New Developments*. Chicago: University of Chicago Press, 1985. This collection of papers sheds light on discoveries having to do with the origin of hydrogen and other elements through the actions of stars. Deals extensively with reaction rates, various processes, primordial hydrogen, galactic chemical composition, massive stars, and supernovae. Extensive bibliography. For the advanced layperson.

Bowers, Richard, and Terry Deeming. *Astrophysics*. Vol. 1, *Stars*. Boston: Jones and Bartlett, 1984. A detailed exposition on the characteristics of stars. The writer extends basic data into an understanding of how stars evolve differently depending on their original mass and brightness. Extensive sections on formation of elements during diverse stages of life cycles. Difficult reading unless one ignores the mathematics.

Clayton, Donald D. *Principles of Stellar Evolution and Nucleosynthesis*. Chicago: University of Chicago Press, 1984. Arguably one of the best, most complete works on the evolution of stars, tracing the life histories of different-sized objects. Extensive dicussion of element formation and of unsolved problems in the field. Mathematics spread throughout the work, but the advanced layperson should find it understandable. Additional references.

Hartmann, William, Pamela Lee, and Tom Miller. *Cycles of Fire: Stars, Galaxies, and the Wonder of Deep Space*. New York: Workman Publishing, 1988. A delightful work encompassing the history of stars from birth to death. Touches on a multitude of topics, including black holes, white dwarfs, binary stars, and the origin of the universe and planets. Attractive illustrations complement the well-written text. Glossary and some references.

Henbest, Nigel. *The Exploding Universe*. New York: Macmillan, 1979. An overview of the violent nature of the universe, this book deals with how atoms, elements, stars, planets, and other objects are formed and die. Detailed sections on the fundamental forces and particles of nature and their relationships to the formation of the elements. Glossary. Fairly easy reading.

Ozima, Minoru. *Geohistory: Global Evolution of the Earth*. New York: Springer-Verlag, 1987. A well-written book deals with the origin of the earth, its waters, atmosphere, and rocks. Addresses the issue of the internal structure of the earth as it has changed over time. Abundant diagrams. Bibliography. For the more advanced layperson.

Rolfs, Claus E., and William S. Rodney. *Cauldrons in the Cosmos: Nuclear Astrophysics*. Chicago: University of Chicago Press, 1988. This book represents the then-current state of knowledge on the stars, pertaining to the synthesis of the elements. Starting with basic data, it tracks the lives of stars of varying masses, detailing the elements created at each step. Good pictures and diagrams; extensive bibliography. Although there is some mathematics, the text is quite clear.

Schramm, David, ed. *Supernovae*. Dordrecht, Netherlands: Reidel Press, 1977. A detailed work on supernovae, particularly the Crab Nebula. Traces how stars explode and how elements are formed in the final death throes. Presents a good overview of theories with a minimum of mathematics. Contains helpful illustrations and bibliography.

Shklovskii, Iosif S. *Stars*. San Francisco: W. H. Freeman, 1978. A basic review of stars—how they work and why they exist and die. Extensive sections on origins of elements at various stages in stellar life, focusing on the production of heavy elements in star deaths. Well written. Numerous line drawings provide clarity. Bibliography.

Arthur L. Alt

Cross-References

Elemental Distribution in the Earth, 391; The Evolution of Earth's Composition, 496; Geochronology: Radiocarbon Dating, 840; Meteorites: Carbonaceous Chondrites, 1638; Elemental Distribution in the Solar System, 2434; The Origin of the Solar System, 2442.

NUMERICAL MODELING

Type of earth science: Geology
Field of study: Mathematical geology

Numerical modeling is the use of computers to simulate nature. It is the most efficient and accurate way of visualizing natural systems and predicting their behavior. In the geosciences, numerical modeling has become a major research tool.

Principal terms
CATASTROPHE THEORY: a branch of mathematics applied to physical systems characterized by discontinuous jumps in behavior
CHAOTIC DYNAMICS: a mathematical theory that deals with the irregular behavior of unpredictable natural systems
COMPUTER EXPERIMENTS: numerical modeling performed with large computers, the result of which is quantitatively equivalent to laboratory-controlled, physical experimentation
FRACTALS: geometrical-numerical constructions that resemble the irregular and intricate shapes and forms of natural objects
MODEL: a mathematically described representation of a phenomenon or object used to subject either to quantitative analysis
NONUNIQUENESS: the quality of several different models that can equally well reproduce, simulate, or satisfy a set of observations

Summary of the Methodology

To use a computer to perform numerical modeling, one must first have a model. A model is a quantitative description of natural phenomena in the form of mathematical formulas, sets of equations, or computer codes. A model may also be the numerical description of a natural object, such as the earth or the hydrogen atom. Numerical modeling can be described as a set of computer-based methodologies used to construct, use, and test models. Through numerical modeling, models may be used to build other models or to improve existing ones.

A model may be constructed with very few elements yet describe a wide variety of phenomena of relevance to science. The Newtonian formula $F = Ma$, or force equals mass times acceleration (Isaac Newton's second law of motion for a particle), is a numerical model of enormous importance in science and technology because it describes the dynamics of the (nonrelativistic) world with astonishing accuracy. Newton's formula is a mathematical description of experience, a model which agrees with existing measurements to within a specified accuracy and which can be used with confidence to predict the behavior of some mechanical systems.

Some corrections to the Newtonian model were made by Albert Einstein's theory of relativity. For example, $F = Ma$ predicts that for a particle of constant mass, a constant force applied to it produces a constant acceleration; that is, the speed of the particle will constantly increase as long as the force is acting. It is not difficult to realize that the particle would eventually acquire an arbitrarily large speed, and such is the formula's prediction. Einstein's model, however, asserts that that prediction is erroneous and that the particle will never reach the speed of light, regardless of the size and constancy of the force. Einstein's model correctly predicts what has been verified by careful experimentation on the behavior of subatomic particles and at the same time reproduces Newton's formulas in the realm of low velocities. That means not that Newton's laws are wrong but only that they are limited in scope and applicability—as all models are—and that more than one model may exist that explains the same data equally well. "Force equals mass times acceleration" will continue to be used to build airplanes, bridges, and automobiles and to model seismic waves, fluid motions in the earth's core, the growth and decay of mountains, and the deformation of rocks.

With the advent of computers came the possibility of evaluating the models of nature fast and accurately. Numerical manipulations only dreamed of a few decades before became routine. This increased ability permitted the construction and testing of highly complex models; it became possible to simulate nature with a level of detail never achieved before. Numerical modeling became the most popular and effective method of model creation, manipulation, and testing.

It is, however, very important to recognize that there is nothing in the process of numerical modeling that guarantees that the model one selects is unique. In other words, other, different models may exist that can reproduce the observations equally well. Moreover, there is no guarantee that any of these models is correct, if by "correct" is understood a model that represents reality. Unfortunately, there are no general rules to search for uniqueness other than to hope that the phenomena being modeled contain easily identified, unique characteristics. Consequently, every model must be tested with all the data available, including observations that are independent of the phenomena under investigation.

For example, solid-earth geophysicists interested in exploring the earth's interior rely on seismic wave observations, which provide the most relevant data. Yet, in their search for a model of the earth's interior, they must also incorporate measurements of the earth's gravity and magnetic fields, experimental results on the effects of high pressures and temperatures on minerals and rocks, measurements of the earth's tides, calculations of the amount of heat reaching the surface from the earth's interior, and as many other measurements as possible to set strong constraints on any possible choice of a model. The selection of one model or of a certain set of models over others depends directly on how well the model fits all the observations. The construction of a realistic model of the earth's interior is a constantly evolving numerical modeling process, an endeavor in which most geophysicists participate by adding their findings to the ever-growing mass of data. New findings are used to refine previous models; the refinements will result in new predictions that require confirmation through new and better data; and the process will continue.

   Besides the advances in large-scale computing, developments in mathematics, geometry, and classical mechanics are revolutionizing the way in which geoscientists numerically construct their models. Traditional mathematics, from which the majority of conventional numerical models are derived, is strongly based on concepts of the continuity and smoothness of functions. Many natural events in the geosciences, however, involve sudden or discontinuous change, and geologic objects have rough contours. There exist, in fact, so many irregular phenomena that conventional mathematics is unusable. For some geoscientists, this argument alone is enough to make them reluctant to incorporate more quantification into the earth sciences. It turns out, however, that many geologic phenomena can be modeled, thanks to catastrophe theory, the geometry of fractals, and the mathematics of chaos—all relatively new developments.

   Catastrophe theory is a branch of mathematics that can deal in an organized way with systems that change suddenly, or jump. The term "catastrophe" is used in its sense of unexpected, sudden change, not cataclysmic disaster. The sudden boiling of slowly heated water, the abrupt onset of turbulence in a river flow, and the generation of an earthquake by the unexpected rupture of strained rocks are examples of catastrophes in this sense. Catastrophe theory deals with these and other, similar phenomena by using a geometrical representation of the behavior of the system under study. The representation consists of folded and cusped surfaces and hypersurfaces (surfaces of more than two dimensions) that show the places where there is critical behavior and how the system reaches them. Interestingly, many totally independent phenomena show identical behavior surfaces. Important examples of catastrophe models in the geosciences are the fold catastrophe, which describes the optical focusing of seismic waves; the cusp catastrophe, which describes the behavior of earthquake-generating faults or the sudden changes in the otherwise slowly evolving fossil record; and the parabolic umbilic catastrophe, which describes the morphogenesis of a salt dome.

   Fractals and fractal geometry are popular tools for handling the complex reality of forms and shapes that geologists cannot describe with traditional Euclidean geometry. Natural objects such as mountains and coastlines have complicated, irregular shapes without smooth surfaces or straight lines. Fractals were developed to describe the shape of objects irregular at any scale—that is, irregular no matter how much they are magnified. As magnification of a fractal object increases, more detail may appear, but the basic irregular shape remains. This property is shared by many geologic or geologically controlled phenomena. With fractals, such objects can be described numerically.

   Some natural phenomena are chaotic: Their behavior is unpredictably random, stochastic, or intrinsically turbulent. Mathematically, chaotic behavior is identified with extreme sensitivity to the most minute changes in the initial conditions that started the time evolution of the system. Weather systems have this property, which is why it is impossible to produce an accurate weather forecast more than a few days in advance. If two slightly different sets of initial values of temperature, moisture, and wind velocity, for example, have been used to predict the weather, the predictions will totally diverge from each other after a few simulated days—even if the initial data are identical except for an amount equivalent to the least possible difference between numbers that the computer can register. The computer has not modeled more than a few days ahead, and yet the two slightly different initial conditions have produced unrelated—in fact, unpredictably random—outcomes. The mathematical models that simulate these chaotic systems, however, do not contain a single random component. On close scrutiny, the reason for the apparent randomness becomes clear: A well-organized, though highly irregular, fractal object lurks in the background of most chaotic systems. It is beginning to be recognized that many geosystems, such as the fluid flows in the earth's core that produce the random reversals of the geomagnetic field, are in fact only apparently random, or chaotically random. That implies that it is possible to simulate those phenomena through a deterministic and therefore understandable mathematical model.

The next few decades will probably see a widespread reassessment of many of the most firmly established theories of the earth. Many old models will have to be abandoned because catastrophe theory, fractal geometry, and chaotic dynamics will have found a way into both the descriptive and the quantitative aspects of geology.

Applications of the Method

The extent to which numerical modeling is used depends on the nature of the area of geology being studied. In structural geology, which is concerned with modeling intensely deformed rocks, simulations require computer programs similar in many ways to those used to model complex fluid flows. Geochemistry's interaction with physical chemistry and thermodynamics results in a highly mathematical subject, so numerical modeling is commonplace. In hydrogeology, modeling the flow of underground water is one of the most dynamic areas of research; in sedimentology, modeling helps scientists to understand stratigraphic sequences and the evolution of sedimentary deposits through time.

Less traditional methods that involve catastrophe theory are used to model the behavior of geologic faults, while fractals are used to computer-generate images of landscapes that closely resemble the shapes of topographic accidents, the forms of mountains, the textures of soils, or the fragmentation of rocks. These simulations have become routine in many areas of applied geology, cartography, and flight.

Numerical modeling is most commonly practiced in all areas of geophysics. It is used in the study of global systems, such as atmospheric and oceanic circulation, which are simulated routinely to produce weather forecasts; in exploration geophysics, where numerical modeling of seismic, gravitational, electric, or other geophysical observations is the most common method of data interpretation; and in earthquake seismology, where earthquake forecasting is attempted by modeling the slow deformation of rocks and the motion of the tectonic plates. It is also used in the determination of the earth's internal structure, which is revealed through the modeling of its elastic response to large earthquakes; in the study of the earth's magnetic field; and in the study of earthquake mechanisms, as determined by modeling the ground motions that would be recorded on seismograms.

This last example can provide an illustration of numerical modeling. One purpose of modeling the ground motion produced by earthquakes is to study their mechanisms. This study sheds light on the forces that produce earthquakes, which in turn leads to an understanding of how mountains grow, how ocean basins subside, how continents have drifted in the past, and how they will drift in the future. To model an unknown earthquake mechanism, a computer is programmed to produce a theoretical, or synthetic, seismogram that calculates how a seismic wave generated by a suspected mechanism would look. Comparing the synthetic seismogram with observed seismograms from the studied event provides clues as to how the first guess can be modified to improve the fit with the data. A new computation provides a new synthetic that, it is hoped, will simulate the data better. The original model is refined until a final model is found that satisfactorily reproduces all the available seismograms. The more observations can be matched with the synthetics, the closer one should be to a correct model of the earthquake source.

This methodology is not uniquely seismological; it is, in fact, the most common form of numerical modeling in geophysical research. The normal procedure can be summarized as follows. First, a model of a phenomenon or its causes is developed based on available observations, experience, and intuition. Second, a mathematical theory is formed that allows the numerical evaluation of the observable aspects of the phenomenon. Third, a satisfactory agreement is sought between what is numerically calculated and what is observed. Finally, a new model is proposed that explains the phenomenon and its causes. If that is not possible, the entire process is repeated.

Context

Numerical modeling is one of the most commonly used techniques to perform scientific research, to develop new technologies, and to solve some of the problems that both science and technology generate. Numerical modeling is the art of simulating nature using mathematics and a large computer. In the geosciences, numerical modeling is used extensively by petroleum engineers to simulate the flow of fluids in a reservoir; by geologists, who model the paths of elastic waves to determine the geometry of a potential oil trap; by seismological engineers, who need to design buildings to withstand earthquakes without waiting for them to occur; and, in general, by geoscientists who want to simulate processes that cannot be reproduced in the laboratory or that cannot be resolved through analytic mathematical methods.

Numerical modeling is performed with large-capacity, high-speed computers or supercomputers, helped usually by high-resolution color displays, computerized animation, and many other display systems. The general use of computer-aided modeling and design has meant some decreased interest in traditional laboratory experimentation, which is generally costly and more difficult to control than a simpler, equally valid, computer experiment. Nevertheless, there remain many laboratory tasks that can be performed only by direct manipulation of the subject matter.

In many branches of the geosciences, discoveries are made with numerical modeling that may affect everyone's lives, because the geosciences deal largely with the prospecting, extraction, and exploitation of the world's mineral resources. Many future scenarios are numerically modeled that produce hints of what life will be like on earth in twenty or two hundred years, as the availability of energy sources changes.

Besides predictions of the world reserves of oil and minerals, numerical modeling has been used to simulate the effects of a nuclear war. Some results have indicated the possibility that a nuclear war would cause the total extinction of life on earth, which would occur after a period of cold climate and dust-darkened skies known as nuclear winter.

Numerical modeling of a cataclysmic fall of a gigantic meteorite has convinced some geoscientists that such an event was responsible for the extinction of the dinosaurs, 65 million years ago. The disappearance of the dinosaurs is not an unimportant event for the human species; once the dinosaurs became extinct, mammals, which until then had barely developed, began to spread and freely evolve, resulting in the emergence of humans some 3 million years ago.

Bibliography

Arnold, V. I. *Catastrophe Theory*. 2d rev. ed. Berlin: Springer-Verlag, 1986. A fascinating journey through the physics of catastrophe theory by one of its originators and most prolific contributors. The book provides a concise, nonmathematical view of the applications of the theory in optics and wave propagation, the development of forms (including geoforms), and the distribution of matter in the universe. Some good illustrations are included.

Conlan, R., ed. *Understanding Computers: Software*. Alexandria, Va.: Time-Life Books, 1985. A very readable account of the art of computer programming and its uses in numerical modeling. Provides superb diagrams and color photographs of actual computer output of flight simulations, global weather, astrophysics, and planetary physics. Suitable for high school readers.

Gleick, James. *Chaos: Making a New Science*. New York: Viking Penguin, 1987. The most informative and accurate account of the new science of chaos, its birth, its development, and its future. Written for the nonscientist, the book is designed to convey the major points of the new science in an entertaining, anecdotal style. The ideas of chaos, universality, and fractal geometry are described clearly, with complementary graphics and color pictures taken from actual research papers.

Hofstadter, Douglas R. *Metamagical Themas: Questing for the Essence of Mind and Pattern*. New York: Basic Books, 1985. Reprints of the most important articles the author wrote for *Scientific American*. The interested reader can find long and varied explanations of the power of computers and the beauty of mathematics. A certain level of sophistication in science helps one to understand the finer points.

Stewart, Ian. *The Problems of Mathematics*, New York: Oxford University Press, 1987. A well-known mathematician describes the most central problems of modern mathematics in nonmathematical terms. The book explores the theory of numbers, the limits of computability, chaos, catastrophe theory, and fractal geometry. Includes extensive bibliographic citations of other nontechnical books and articles on the subjects.

Weiner, Jonathan. *Planet Earth*. Toronto: Bantam Books, 1986. For anyone interested in the earth sciences, this book should be a source of continuous delight. It was written as a companion to the PBS television series. Fully illustrated, it contains detailed descriptions of many of the models with which geoscientists study the earth, from the magnetosphere to the inner core. Contains an extensive bibliography on works of science for the nonspecialist.

J. A. Rial

Cross-References

The Atmosphere's Global Circulation, 121; Earthquake Engineering, 430; Earthquake Hazards, 437; Earthquake Locating, 445; Earthquake Prediction, 461; Secular Variation of Earth's Magnetic Field, 540; Earth's Magnetic Field at Present, 548; Oil and Gas Exploration, 1878; Oil and Gas: Petroleum Reservoirs, 1909; Plate Motions, 2071; Plate Tectonics, 2079; Future Resources, 2182; Seismic Reflection Profiling, 2333; Volcanoes: Eruption Forecasting, 2622; Weather Forecasting, 2717.

OCEAN-ATMOSPHERE INTERACTIONS

Type of earth science: Oceanography

The interactions between the oceans and the atmosphere are basic to the understanding of oceanography and meteorology. The two largest masses of matter on the earth, one a liquid and the other a gaseous envelope, have a powerful effect on weather and climate on a global scale.

Principal terms

ATMOSPHERE: five clearly defined regions above the earth's surface, composed of layers of gases and mixtures of gases, water vapor, and liquid particles

CORIOLIS EFFECT: the movement of any moving body to the west or east, depending on whether the latitude is north or south, respectively; this effect is the result of the earth's rotation

EL NIÑO: part of a gigantic meteorological system called the Southern Oscillation that links the ocean and atmosphere in the Pacific

GYRES: the major wind systems responsible for broadly symmetrical patterns of surface-water transport

KUROSHIO: the current, also known as the Japan Current, where cold continental air flows over warm ocean currents moving toward the poles

LA NIÑA: the part of the Southern Oscillation that brings cold water to the South American coasts, which makes easterly trade winds stronger, the waters of the Pacific off South America colder, and ocean temperatures in the western equatorial Pacific warmer than normal

Summary of the Phenomenon

The largest fraction of the heat energy the atmosphere receives for maintaining its circulation is derived from the condensation of water vapor originating mainly from marine evaporation. Therefore, fundamental to the understanding of atmospheric behavior and oceanic behavior is an understanding of the processes occurring at the air-sea boundary. The interactions between the marine and atmospheric environments involve constant interchanges between moisture, heat, momentum, and gases.

The study of oceanic and atmospheric interactions is the examination of a huge gaseous body and a massive liquid body, neither of which is ever homogeneous in content. As the makeup of the atmosphere varies, dependent on the areas over which it flows, so the content of the oceans varies in density, temperature, salinity, rate of movement by regular currents, and surface movement under the influence of winds. As a consequence, this interaction is very complex and not entirely understood. Certain conditions, however, that are regularly met can act as a general guide to understanding ocean-atmosphere interactions.

Atmospheric circulations depend on heat rising from below. Because of the large area of the earth covered by oceans, the main source of heat in the atmosphere is reflected from the sea surface. In the oceans, the heat supply is primarily from the atmosphere and the sun. Heat-supply processes are important to the development of convection currents in the surface layer of the ocean, to the local exchange of energy with the atmosphere, and to slower, deep-water circulation. The heat exchange between the ocean and atmosphere has a pattern similar to evaporation. Wherever the surface of the ocean is warmer than the atmosphere, heat is transferred from the ocean to the air and is moved to great heights by eddies and convection currents in the air.

The range of weather extremes is smaller over the ocean than over land. Because of the enormous heat-storage capacity of the ocean, it tends to stabilize atmospheric conditions and qualities. The upper layer of the oceans (approximately 70 meters in depth) can store approximately thirty times more heat than the atmosphere. Ocean climates, therefore, are mostly determined by the atmospheric circulation and latitude. Ocean climate and atmospheric circulation are both affected by the solar distribution over the earth's surface, which is a function of the latitude and the season of the year. Northern latitudes receive proportionately less solar radiation than do latitudes at the equator; in winter, some northern latitudes receive very little solar radiation. Because of the greater capacity of the oceans to store heat, for a given change in heat content, the temperature change in the atmosphere will be around thirty times greater than in the ocean. Therefore, the ocean will lose its heat by radiation much more slowly than will the air. Land, which is intermediate with regard to heat storage and heat loss, will be modified by the effect of heat storage and heat loss of the ocean.

The atmosphere adjacent to the oceans is constantly interacting with the oceans. Air does not simply flow along the surface of the sea but has a frictional effect or wind stress, which causes the surface water to be carried along with the wind. Wind stresses on the surface of the sea produce ocean waves, storm surges, and shallow ocean currents. Pure wind-driven currents are the result of frictional wind surface stresses and the earth's rotational motion. This rotational motion can be seen in the Coriolis effect, which causes a deflection of air currents and ocean currents to the east or west, depending on the hemisphere. Because the sea is continually in contact with the atmosphere, the gases that occur in the atmosphere are also found in seawater. The concentration of the gases depends on their solubilities and on the chemical reactions in which they are involved. These concentrations are affected by temperature, which is determined by many factors, and by wind and wave actions.

The sea also has a large storage and regulating capacity with respect to processes involving carbon dioxide in the atmosphere and in the sea, including those processes relevant to plant life and photosynthesis. This whole group of reactions concerning carbon dioxide is extremely complex. Carbon dioxide, a powerful reflector of heat, forms a heat-conserving umbrella in the atmosphere that reflects heat back to the earth's surface. This "greenhouse effect" acts much like a horticultural greenhouse, which traps heat and raises the temperature of the air inside the greenhouse.

The largest fraction of radiant energy absorbed by the oceans is used in evaporation. The maximum evaporation and heat exchange between the sea and the atmosphere occur where cold continental air flows over warm ocean currents moving toward the poles. Examples of this phenomenon are the Kuroshio (Japan Current) and the Gulf Stream. The radiant energy that is absorbed and stored by the oceans at lower latitudes is given off to the atmosphere at places and during seasons of lower solar energy. This process is important to understand in terms of the Southern Oscillation and the effect of El Niño and La Niña.

The major wind systems are responsible for broadly symmetrical patterns of surface-water transport known as gyres, which rotate clockwise around the North Pacific and North Atlantic and counterclockwise around the South Pacific and South Atlantic oceans. Their tropical segments are the North and South Equatorial currents, which are driven westward by trade winds. The Equatorial Countercurrent, a compensating flow, travels west to east in the Pacific between the North and South Equatorial currents along a course that averages a few degrees north of the equator. At times, it spreads along the South American coast to form the warm El Niño.

Marked by warm water and high winds from the western pacific, El Niño typically brings heavy winter rains to Peruvian deserts and warm weather to the west coast of the United States. El Niño is probably caused by interaction between the oceanic and atmospheric systems. During El Niño, the southeast trade winds over the equatorial Pacific collapse, allowing warm water from the western Pacific to flow eastward along the equator. This warm-water flow suppresses the normal upwelling of cold, nutrient-rich water and leads to the absence of fish normally feeding on the nutrient-laden cold water.

El Niño is part of a gigantic meteorological system, called the Southern Oscillation, that links the ocean and atmosphere in the Pacific. This system normally functions as a kind of huge heat pump, distributing energy from the tropics at the equator to the higher latitudes through storms that develop over the warm western Pacific. Another part of the Southern Oscillation has been dubbed La Niña, which brings cold water to the South American coasts. La Niña exaggerates the normal conditions of the system. During this activity, easterly trade winds are stronger, the waters of the eastern Pacific off South America are colder, and ocean temperatures in the western equatorial Pacific are warmer. This rather narrow band of atmosphere and ocean can generate powerful effects on both global weather and global climate. Therefore, the study of this interaction is essential to the understanding of all natural activity.

Methods of Study

Because the study of the ocean-atmosphere interactions is concerned with the boundary between marine and air masses, it is of necessity an interdisciplinary type of study. The data used are gathered by oceanographers and meteorologists who have made this interaction the area of their research. The same instruments are used, drawing heavily upon the type of data collected, that are employed in oceanographic and meteorologic research, with a shift in emphasis. Because gathering the data is expensive and utilizes costly, specialized kinds of equipment, nearly all studies are conducted by government scientists or are sponsored by government grants.

Scientists who study ocean-atmosphere interactions are interested in seeing how these huge bodies of matter affect each other and how these effects influence the weather and climate in the rest of the world. They are also interested in the ability to predict weather and climate changes more accurately. Each element researched, such as salinity, is compared with some other element, such as temperature, to see what relationship may exist. Air temperature and air movement are compared with wave movement, changing ocean currents, and water temperature. Each of a vast number of data is examined for possible interrelations and interactions. When interrelations are found, the data are fed into a computer model for correlation with other data. Computer models have been effective to some extent in predicting the results of interactions between marine and atmospheric environments. Separate computer models are used with the output aimed at the interactions between these forces.

Scientists do not fully understand all the mechanisms that link certain phenomena of the ocean and atmosphere interactions, such as El Niño and La Niña. It is their hope that in studying and understanding the mechanisms involved, they may be able to predict, for example, the amount and area of precipitation in a certain region, such as the American Midwest, by measuring the snowfall of another region, such as the Himalaya.

Context

The interaction between the oceans and the atmosphere can cause immense problems on a global scale. An example of this interaction and its consequences is seen in the phenomenon known as El Niño. Every three to five years, the surface waters of the central and eastern Pacific Ocean become unusually warm at the equator. Warm currents and torrential rains are brought to the normally dry desert area of central Peru, and nutrient supplies for marine life along the west coast of South America are disrupted. Hardship can occur as a result, such as the demise of the anchovy fishing industry in Peru. El Niño is also credited with the extreme drought conditions that upset the United States Midwest in the mid-1980's and for the torrential rains in the Himalaya, India, and Bangladesh.

La Niña brings an effect opposite to that of El Niño; easterly trade winds are stronger, the waters of the eastern Pacific off South America are colder, and ocean temperatures in the western equatorial Pacific are warmer than normal. As a result, the deserts in Peru and Chile become drier than normal, and the Indian subcontinent is inundated by heavier-than-usual rainfall and flooding. In Bangladesh in late

1988, heavy rains and flooding killed more than one thousand people, destroyed the homes of twenty-five million people, inundated 5 million acres of rice land, and damaged 43,000 miles of roads. While the storms were generated by the La Niña phenomenon, much of the flooding was the result of massive deforestation in the Himalaya and foothills, which allowed water to rush down from the barren, eroded hills onto Bangladesh near sea level.

There has been great international concern about the temperature buildup referred to as the greenhouse effect. Many scientists believe the cooling effect of La Niña will tend to counteract the greenhouse effect of increasing temperature, at least temporarily. International cooperation is encouraged by the United Nations Environmental Program (UNEP), which works with governments, international organizations, and industry to develop a framework within which the international community can make decisions to minimize atmospheric changes and the effects they could have on the earth.

Bibliography

Glantz, Michael H., and J. Dana Thompson. *Resource Management and Environmental Uncertainty: Lessons from Coastal Upwelling Fisheries*. New York: John Wiley & Sons, 1981. Excellent information on and discussions of El Niño. Considers social, economic, and political values in terms of the effects from the ocean-atmosphere interactions and the weather and climate changes they produce. Not a difficult reading level.

Kerr, R. A. "La Niña's Big Chill Replaces El Niño." *Science* 241 (August 26, 1988): 1077-1078. An excellent source, although *Science* magazine is not available in all libraries. Illustrated. For advanced high school science majors and college students.

Knox, C. E. "Hot and Cold Pacific Fed Midwest Drought." *Science News* (October 15, 1988): 247. Describes the influence of El Niño on the mid-1980's drought suffered by the midwestern United States. Includes map. *Science News* gives accurate summaries of articles appearing in less accessible publications.

Linden, E. "Big Chill for the Greenhouse." *Time* 132 (October 31, 1988). Similar to the Kerr article (above) but at an easier reading level. *Time* magazine frequently offers brief but accurate coverage of new scientific research and discoveries.

Thurman, Harold V. *Introductory Oceanography*. 5th ed. Columbus, Ohio: Merrill, 1975. An introductory college-level text. Chapter 7, "Air-Sea Interactions," describes the Coriolis effect, the "heat budget" of the world ocean, and weather and climate. Chapter 8, "Ocean Circulation," describes currents. Includes glossary and index. Well illustrated.

George K. Attwood

Cross-References

The Atmosphere's Global Circulation, 121; The Atmosphere's Structure and Com-

OCEAN BASINS

Type of earth science: Geology
Field of study: Tectonics

Ocean basins contain basaltic crust produced by sea-floor spreading at mid-ocean ridges, which may be covered with a thin layer of oceanic sediments. Sea-floor sediments and rocks in the oceans may contain a record of the history of the development of ocean basins. Ocean basin deposits have provided evidence supporting the theories of sea-floor spreading and plate tectonics.

Principal terms

BASALT: a dark-colored, fine-grained rock erupted by volcanoes, which tends to be the basement rock underneath sediments in the ocean basins

BIOGENIC SEDIMENTS: the sediment particles formed from skeletons or shells of microscopic plants and animals living in seawater

DEPOSITION: the process by which loose sediment grains fall out of seawater to accumulate as layers of sediment on the the sea floor

LITHOSPHERE: the outermost layers (the crust and outer mantle) of the earth, which are arranged in distinct rigid plates that may be moved across the earth's surface by sea-floor spreading and plate tectonics

MAGNETIC ANOMALIES: linear areas of ocean crust that have unusually high or low magnetic field strength; magnetic anomalies are parallel to the crest of the mid-ocean ridges

MID-OCEAN RIDGE: a continuous mountain range of underwater volcanoes, located along the center of most ocean basins; volcanic eruptions along these ridges drive sea-floor spreading

RIFTING: the splitting of continents into separate blocks, which move away from one another across the earth's surface

SEA-FLOOR SPREADING: a theory that the continents of the earth move apart from one another by rifting of continental blocks, driven by the eruption of new ocean crust in the rift

SEISMIC REFLECTION: study of the layered sediments in ocean basins by bouncing sound waves sent into the sea floor off the different rock layers

SEISMIC REFRACTION: examination of the deep structure of the ocean crust, using powerful sound waves that are bent into the crustal layers rather than being immediately reflected back to the ocean surface

Summary of the Phenomenon

Ocean basins make up one-third of the earth's surface, and the rocks and sediments in these basins may preserve an important record of the past history of the oceans. Earth materials in the ocean basins consist of a layer of volcanic basalts produced by sea-floor volcanic eruptions at the mid-ocean ridges, which may be covered by layers of marine sediments and sedimentary rocks. The shape of individual ocean basins may be changed as a result of the interactions of lithospheric plates, such as plate collisions, plate accretion, and plate destruction. Ocean basin rocks and sediments may contain valuable deposits of metals and other economic minerals, which may represent important natural resources that could be extracted by humans at some time in the future.

Eruption of volcanic basalts in ocean basins makes up an important part of sea-floor spreading. The creation of new oceanic crust by volcanic eruptions along the mid-ocean ridges provides the driving force to move blocks of continental lithosphere across the earth's surface. For example, the separation of South America from Africa during the past 200 million years has been driven by the creation of the South Atlantic Ocean by sea-floor spreading along the Mid-Atlantic Ridge between these two continents.

Ocean basin shapes may be altered by plate interactions. As lithospheric plates are rifted and move apart from one another, new ocean basins are created between the continental landmasses. In contrast, lithospheric plates may run into one another, and plate collisions cause the ocean basin between continents to be destroyed by subduction, in which crustal slabs are forced downward into the mantle and are remelted. An example is seen in southern Europe, where the collision of the northward-moving African plate with the Eurasian plate has caused the Mediterranean Sea to become shallower and narrower at the same time that crumpling of the edges of the continents has caused mountain building of the Alps in Europe and the Atlas Mountains in northern Africa.

The volcanic basement rocks in ocean basins may preserve a record of the earth's magnetic field during the past, through the record of oriented magnetic minerals contained within basalts. When basalt erupted at mid-ocean ridges cools as a result of exposure to cold seawater, magnetic minerals within the igneous rock are aligned with the earth's magnetic field and are "locked" into position by the crystallization of adjacent mineral grains. Thus, the alignment of magnetic minerals within sea-floor basalts in the ocean basins acts as an enormous magnetic tape recorder, which preserves a record of the alternating reversals of the magnetic field of the earth. Oceanographers investigating the magnetism of the sea floor during the 1950's discovered the existence of long, straight areas of ocean crust with unusual magnetic properties. These linear magnetic anomalies were parallel to the mid-ocean ridges but offset from the ridge crests. The anomalies are symmetrical about the mid-ocean ridges: Anomaly records on both sides form identical "mirror images" of each other. This finding supports the theory of sea-floor spreading, which predicted that creation of new oceanic crust at mid-ocean ridges would cause rifting and separation of previously cooled basalts to either side of the ridge.

Sea-floor spreading theory further predicted that the older the anomaly, the farther it has been pushed away from the ridge crest. This prediction was proved by deep-ocean drilling, which drilled into and determined the age of sediments immediately atop specific magnetic anomalies in the ocean crust. Estimates of the rate of creation of new oceanic crust along the ridges may be calculated from the distance between the crest of the mid-ocean ridge and specific magnetic anomalies whose age has been determined. These calculations have proven that creation of new oceanic crust does not occur at a constant rate through time and that there have been episodes of rapid sea-floor spreading and of slower spreading during the past.

Examination of the chemistry and mineral composition of the volcanic rocks of an ocean basin may provide a record of the history of volcanic eruptions at the mid-ocean ridges and help geologists to determine the chemistry and type of igneous rocks being erupted at any point in the past. Understanding the mineral content of sea-floor crust erupted at specific times in the past allows geochemists to make predictions about the nature of the deeper portions of the earth's crust. Chemical changes in sea-floor basalts may reflect similar changes occurring in the lower crust or upper mantle of the planet.

In addition to preserving historical information in the harder igneous rock basement, ocean basins provide a record of sediment deposition during the past. These regions of the ocean floor are among the flattest areas on the surface of the planet and have minimal relief: Most ocean basins are smooth and nearly flat, with less than 1 meter of vertical altitude change in 1 kilometer of horizontal distance. Their smoothness is the result of burial of the blocky, irregularly faulted volcanic basement rocks beneath layers of slowly accumulating mixtures of biogenic sediments, turbidites, and other sediment particles derived from continental sources. Newly erupted basement rocks are gradually covered by oceanic sediments, so there is an overall correlation between crustal age and total sediment thickness within an ocean basin. Verification of this relationship by deep-ocean drilling provided further support for sea-floor spreading.

Sedimentary rock layers provide information on the history of deposition in the ocean basins by their structure and by the fossils preserved in sediment layers. Marine geologists examine the types, sizes, and sorting of the individual grains that compose sea-floor sediments. Geologists attempt to determine the sources of sediment particles deposited in ocean basins and to analyze both the changes in sediment particles as they fall through the water column and changes occurring on the sea floor after the sediments are deposited. Fine-grained particles derived from continental sources may be carried far out to sea by the winds to be deposited in the deep ocean basins. Also, biogenic particles either may dissolve as they sink through the oceans or may be dissolved on the sea floor by deep-ocean water masses.

Paleontologists study the fossils buried within layers of sedimentary rock. Marine sediments deposited in water depths shallower than the carbonate compensation depth have abundant microscopic fossil remains of ancient one-celled plants and animals (plankton) that lived in the shallow water of the oceans during past geologic time. As these organisms died, their remains sank to the sea floor, to become an important part of the sedimentary rock layers. Examining the record of fossils preserved in sea-floor sediments is like reading the pages of a book containing the history of the ocean basin: Changes in the type and number of ancient fossil organisms and fossil assemblages may be preserved in the microfossils contained in sea-floor sediment layers.

Perhaps one of the most fascinating aspects of the study of sea-floor sediments in the deep-ocean basins is that these materials contain significant amounts of micrometeorites and extraterrestrial material. Micrometeorites may fall on the continents, but their scarcity and small size make them difficult to identify. In deep-ocean basins far from the continents, however, sediment accumulates at a much slower rate as a result of a combination of the distance from continental sediment sources and the dissolution of biogenic sediment particles by corrosive bottom waters. As a result, deep-ocean sediments tend to be fine-grained red clays, which have few to no fossils and which may be deposited at rates as slow as 1 millimeter per million years. In these red clays, extraterrestrial materials may make up a significant portion of the sediment particles because of the extremely slow sediment deposition rates.

Methods of Study

Because the ocean basins contain a variety of geologic materials, including igneous, sedimentary, and metamorphic rocks, a number of different techniques are used in the study of ocean basins, depending upon the specific feature of interest. Methods that are suitable for the study of one aspect of the ocean basins may be completely useless for obtaining information about other features of the basin. Some of the methods used include acoustic profiling, seismic reflection and refraction studies, dredging, sediment coring, and deep-ocean drilling. In addition, information on ocean basins may be derived from ancient sea-floor deposits that have been uplifted and are presently found above sea level on the continents.

The overall shape of the ocean basin and the water depths of individual parts of the basin may be studied by acoustic profiling, or echo sounding. This technique uses an acoustic transponder (a sound source) mounted on the hull of an oceanographic vessel to emit sound waves, which travel down through the water until they are reflected back by the sea floor up to a shipboard recorder, which measures the total time between emission of the sound pulse and its return. The water depth is equal to one-half the total time (sound must go down, then up again), multiplied by the speed of sound in seawater. Profiles of the ocean basin's shape are obtained by continuously running the echo sounder while the ship is sailing across the basin.

While acoustic profiling gives the water depth of the ocean basin, the energies of the sound waves are insufficient to provide information about the buried structure of the ocean floor. The shape and thickness of the basement rocks and the sediment cover on the floor of an ocean basin may be examined by seismic reflection profiling, which is somewhat similar to echo sounding. In seismic reflection studies, a large energy source (such as the explosion of a dynamite charge) is released in seawater to create high-energy sound waves, which move down through the ocean with sufficient energy to penetrate the sediment layers of the sea floor before they are reflected back up to the vessel by the different sub-bottom layers. Reflection profiling is also made by continuously producing these high-energy sound waves while sailing across a basin, to obtain a record of the thickness and geometry of the sediment layers and the harder basement rocks of the sea floor.

The deep structure of basement rocks is investigated by seismic refraction studies, which may be made by one oceanographic vessel and a stationary floating recorder (sonobuoy) or by two vessels. In seismic refraction studies, extremely large energy sources are released in the ocean to create powerful sound waves, which have the ability to penetrate through sea-floor sediment layers into the deeper layers of igneous basement rocks. Sound waves penetrating layers in the sea floor are bent (refracted) into the layer and travel through it for a certain distance before they are refracted back up to the ocean surface. An acoustic recorder at the surface measures the depth of sound penetration below the sea floor and the time elapsed since the explosion. Refraction profiles may be done by exploding charges off the stern of a moving vessel, using a stationary sonobuoy as the recording device, or refraction profiles may be made in a "two-ship" experiment, where one vessel acts as the "shooter" and the second vessel is the stationary recorder. By alternately "leap-frogging" past each other, two ships may make a much longer continuous reflection profile than is possible with only one vessel and a sonobuoy.

The history of sediment deposition preserved by marine sediments in ocean basins may be studied by obtaining long cores of sea-floor sediments, either by sediment coring or by ocean-floor drilling programs. Once a long sediment core is obtained from the ocean floor, the sediment particles and fossils within the sediments are studied layer by layer in order to examine the sedimentation history of the basin. Younger sediments are placed atop older layers, so by beginning with the uppermost layers of the sediment core and continuing into deeper layers, the geologist can examine the record of progressively older deposits in the ocean basin.

Direct examination of the basement rocks of the ocean basins may be made by dredging rocks from the mid-ocean ridges, by drilling through the sediment cover to take cores of the volcanic basalts, or by studying portions of the ocean floor that have been uplifted above sea level by tectonic activity. Dredging uses a wire mesh bag attached to a rigid iron frame, which is towed on a long cable behind a vessel to obtain rock samples from the sea floor. As the ship moves across the surface, it drags the dredge along the bottom, and sea-floor rocks are broken off by the frame and caught in the wire mesh bag attached to the rear of the dredge.

Deep-ocean drilling programs have provided long basalt cores that have been drilled from the sea floor in different ocean basins. The deepest sea-floor borehole drilled in the oceans by the Deep Sea Drilling Project, site 504B, located near the Galápagos Islands in the eastern Equatorial Pacific, has been extended to a depth of 1,350 meters below the surface of the sea floor. Drilling at this location recovered 275 meters of sea-floor sediments, and more than a kilometer of sea-floor basalts have been penetrated, with the possibility of further deepening of this hole into the ocean crust by later drilling operations at this location.

Information about the ocean basins has also been provided by uplifted sections of sea floor, located in areas of plate collisions. These ancient sea-floor deposits, or ophiolite sequences, are found on the island of Newfoundland in eastern Canada, on the island of Cyprus in the eastern Mediterranean Sea, and on the island of Oman in the Persian Gulf, among other locations. Rocks in the ophiolite sequences are an important natural resource, because they contain copper and many other valuable metals interspersed between basalts and igneous rocks. These ancient ocean-floor deposits, which have been uplifted above sea level by the collision of two lithospheric plates, may contain enormous reserves of rare metallic minerals. The metallic deposits in ophiolites were originally deposited as vein minerals between the volcanic basalts in the deeper portions of ocean crust. By understanding the factors controlling the formation of ophiolites, scientists may be able to predict other locations where these rocks may be found, and humans will be better able to utilize these valuable minerals in the future.

Context

Volcanic basement rocks and sedimentary rock layers in the ocean basins have provided evidence supporting the theories of sea-floor spreading and plate tectonics, and these geologic materials have preserved a record of earth history. Evidence for sea-floor spreading derives from the linear magnetic anomaly patterns of ocean crust and from the symmetry of features about the mid-ocean ridges. Sea-floor sediment thicknesses increase with greater distance from the ridge crest, and both the sediment thickness patterns and the magnetic anomaly patterns are symmetrical about the mid-ocean ridges, as predicted by the spreading hypothesis. Eruption of sea-floor basalts at the mid-ocean ridges provides the driving mechanism to move blocks of lithosphere around the surface of the earth.

A history of the chemistry and mineral content of volcanic rocks erupted along the mid-ocean ridges is preserved in sea-floor basement rocks, and magnetic minerals in these igneous rocks preserve a record of past reversals of the magnetic field of the earth. Sedimentary rocks and the fossils contained within them provide a history of the ancient organisms which were alive in past oceans, and marine sediment particles preserve a record of ancient sources of particles deposited in the oceans far from land and also may contain the history of the effects of differing ocean chemistry on sea-floor deposits.

Finally, rocks and sediments in the ocean basins may represent an untapped resource of economic mineral deposits, based on the wealth of minerals that have been found in ophiolite sequences, sections of ancient sea floor that have been uplifted above sea level by the interactions of moving lithospheric plates. These sea-floor mineral deposits may provide future economic resources, which may be exploited after all the continental mineral deposits are exhausted.

Bibliography

Anderson, Roger N. *Marine Geology: A Planet Earth Perspective*. New York: John

Wiley & Sons, 1986. A textbook discussing various aspects of oceanography, whose content is aimed at readers with minimal scientific background.

Cox, Allan, comp. *Plate Tectonics and Geomagnetic Reversals*. San Francisco, Calif.: W. H. Freeman, 1973. A compilation of the important scientific papers discussing the discovery of linear sea-floor magnetic anomalies and the development of the hypotheses of sea-floor spreading and plate tectonics.

Glen, William. *The Road to Jaramillo: Critical Years of the Revolution in Earth Science*. Stanford, Calif.: Stanford University Press, 1982. This volume covers the history of the examination of the magnetic record of the continents, the discovery of linear sea-floor magnetic anomalies, and their role in the development of the hypotheses of sea-floor spreading and plate tectonics.

LeGrand, H. E. *Drifting Continents and Shifting Theories*. New York: Cambridge University Press, 1988. A review of the history of the "modern revolution in geology," which culminated in the development of the theory of global plate tectonics.

Seibold, Eugen, and Wolfgang H. Berger. *The Sea Floor: An Introduction to Marine Geology*. New York: Springer-Verlag, 1982. A textbook covering geological oceanography, designed for freshman-level college courses for students with minimal backgrounds in science, which covers all the information attainable by studying ocean basins.

Van Andel, Tjeerd H. *New Views on an Old Planet: Continental Drift and the History of Earth*. New York: Cambridge University Press, 1985. A survey of the theories of continental drift and plate tectonics, written for an educated lay audience.

_____. *Science at Sea: Tales of an Old Ocean*. San Francisco, Calif.: W. H. Freeman, 1981. A general-audience book discussing some of the methods used by seagoing oceanographers to study the sediments and rocks of the oceanic crust. It also describes some of the hazards and problems inherent in oceanography at sea.

Dean A. Dunn

Cross-References

DEEP OCEAN CURRENTS

Type of earth science: Oceanography

Deep ocean currents involve significant vertical and horizontal movements of seawater. They distribute oxygen- and nutrient-rich waters throughout the world's oceans, thereby enhancing biological productivity.

Principal terms

BATHYMETRIC CONTOUR: a line on a map of the ocean floor that connects points of equal depth

BOTTOM CURRENT: a deep-sea current that flows parallel to bathymetric contours

BOTTOM-WATER MASS: a body of water at the deepest part of the ocean identified by similar patterns of salinity and temperature

CONTINENTAL MARGIN: that part of the earth's surface the separates the emergent continents from the deep-sea floor

CORIOLIS EFFECT: an apparent force, acting on a body in motion, caused by the rotation of the earth

SALINITY: a measure of the quantity of dissolved solids in ocean water

SURFACE WATER: relatively warm seawater between the ocean suface and that depth marked by a rapid reduction in temperature

THERMOHALINE CIRCULATION: vertical circulation of seawater caused by density variations related to changes in salinity and temperature

TURBIDITY CURRENT: a turbid, relatively dense mixture of seawater and sediment that flows downslope under the influence of gravity through less dense water

UPWELLING: the process by which bottom water rich in nutrients rises to the surface of the ocean

Summary of the Phenomenon

Deep-sea currents, ocean currents that involve vertical as well as horizontal movements of seawater, are generated by density differences in water masses that result in the sinking of cold, dense water to the bottom of the ocean. For many years, however, most oceanographers refused to accept the presence of these currents. Even when the Deep Sea Drilling Project, an international effort to drill numerous holes into the ocean floor, was initiated, most researchers envisioned the deep sea as a tranquil environment characterized by sluggish, even stationary, water. More recently, however, oceanographers and marine geologists have accumulated abundant evidence to suggest the opposite: that the deep sea can be a very active area in which currents sweep parts of the ocean floor to the extent that they affect the indigenous marine life and even physically modify the sea floor.

In the 1930's, Georg Wust argued for the likelihood that the ocean floor is swept by currents. Furthermore, he suggested that these currents play an important role in the transport of deep-sea sediment. Wust's ideas were not widely accepted; in the 1960's, however, strong evidence for the existence of deep-sea currents began to accumulate. In 1961, for example, oceanographers detected deep-sea currents moving from 5 to 10 centimeters per second in the western North Atlantic Ocean. These researchers also determined that the currents changed direction over a period of one month. In 1962, Charles Hollister, while examining cores of deep-sea sediment drilled from the continental margin off Greenland and Labrador, noted numerous sand beds that showed evidence of transport by currents. The nature of these deposits suggested to Hollister that they did not accumulate from turbidity currents, dense sediment-water clouds that periodically flow downslope from nearshore areas. Moreover, it appeared to Hollister that the sand was transported parallel to the continental margin rather than perpendicular to it, as might be expected of sediment transported by a turbidity current. He argued that the sand beds in the cores were transported by, and deposited from, deep-sea currents moving along the bottom of the ocean parallel to the continental margin. Since then, extensive photography of the ocean floor has provided direct evidence for the existence of deep-sea currents. Such evidence includes smoothing of the sea floor; gentle deflection, or bending, of marine organisms attached to the sea floor, as though they were standing in the wind; sediment piled into small ripples; and local scouring of the sea floor.

Essentially all earth scientists now agree that the deep-sea floor is swept by rather slow-moving (less than 2-centimeter-per-second) currents. The driving force behind these currents, and all oceanic currents for that matter, is energy derived from the sun. Differential heating of the air drives global wind circulation, which ultimately induces surface ocean currents. The vertical circulation of seawater, and thus the generation of deep-sea currents, is controlled by the amount of solar radiation received at a point on the earth's surface. This value is greatest in equatorial regions; there, the radiation heats the surface water, the seawater that lies within the upper 300 to 1,000 meters of the ocean. As this water is heated, it begins to move toward the poles along paths of wind-generated surface circulation, such as the Gulf Stream current of the northwestern Atlantic Ocean.

The cold waters that compose the deep-sea currents originate in polar regions. There, minimal solar radiation levels produce cold, dense surface waters. The density of this water may also be increased by the seasonal formation of sea ice, ice formed by the freezing of surface water in polar regions. When sea ice forms, only about 30 percent of the salt in the freezing water becomes incorporated into the ice. The salinity and density of the nearly freezing water beneath the ice are therefore elevated. This cold, saline seawater eventually sinks under the influence of gravity to the bottom of the ocean, where it moves slowly toward the equator. Deep-sea circulation driven by temperature and salinity variations in seawater is termed "thermohaline circulation" and is much slower than surface circulation; the cold, dense water generated at the poles moves only a few kilometers per year. After moving along the bottom of the ocean for anywhere from 750 to 1,500 years, the cold seawater rises to the surface in low-latitude regions to replace the warm surface water, which, as noted above, moves as part of the global surface circulation system back to the polar regions.

Thermohaline circulation and related deep-sea currents are commonly affected by the shape of the ocean floor. Although sinking cold seawater seeks the deepest route along the sea floor, deep-sea currents may be blocked by barriers. The Mid-Atlantic Ridge, the large volcanic ridge running down the middle of the Atlantic Ocean, may prevent the movement of water from the bottom of the western Atlantic to the eastern Alantic. On the other hand, the funneling of deep-sea currents through narrow passages or gaps in sea-floor barriers will lead to an increase in the velocity of the current. Once beyond the passage, however, the current spreads and velocity is reduced.

The circulation pattern of deep-sea currents is controlled to a large extent by the earth's rotation. The Coriolis effect, the frictional force achieved by the earth's rotation that causes particles in motion to be deflected to the right in the Northern Hemisphere and to the left in the Southern Hemisphere, induces deep-sea currents to trend along the western margins of the major oceans. Thus, water sinking from sources in the North Atlantic Ocean and moving south toward the equator will be deflected to the right, causing it to run along the western side of the North Atlantic. Similarly, north-directed deep-sea currents generated by the sinking of cold water from the Antarctic region will also be deflected to the western margin of the Atlantic. The Coriolis effect guides deep-sea currents along bathymetric contour lines, lines on a map of the ocean floor that connect points of equal depth. Deep-sea currents that have a tendency to move parallel to the bathymetric contours are known as bottom currents. Barriers to flow may locally deflect deep-sea currents from the bathymetric contours; nevertheless, bottom currents are most conspicuous along the western margins of the major oceans.

The formation of the cold seawater required to set deep-sea currents in motion can itself be considered in terms of short- and long-term controls. Seasonal sea ice formation is probably the most important process in the production of the north-flowing water generated at the south polar region, or the Antarctic bottom water (AABW). Velocities of the AABW are highest in March and April, that period of the year when sea ice production in the ocean surrounding Antarctica is greatest. During Southern Hemisphere summers, however, the sea ice melts and there is an increase in the freshwater flux to the ocean from the continent, both of which actions reduce the salinity and therefore the density of the seawater, thereby decreasing AABW production.

Many oceanographers and marine geologists have argued that long-term variations in the production of the cold, dense bottom water required to generate deep-sea currents may be related to global climatic changes. More specifically, deep-sea currents appear to be most vigorous during glacial periods, when sea ice production is enhanced and the sea ice remains on the ocean surface for a greater proportion of the year. Nevertheless, there is also evidence to suggest that the velocities of deep-sea currents in the North Atlantic Ocean were much lower during the most recent glacial periods than they were during the times between glacial phases. Much more work is required to gain a more complete understanding of long-term controls on deep-sea currents.

Methods of Study

The most common methods of study of deep-sea currents include direct measurement of current velocities, bottom photography, echo sounding, and the sampling of ocean-floor sediment. The speed and direction of deep-sea currents have been determined by the use of free-fall instruments, such as the free-instrument Savonics rotor current meter. This device, dropped unattached into the ocean, is capable of recording current velocities and directions over a period of several days. It returns automatically to the surface of the ocean, at which time a radio transmitter directs a ship to its position. Other current-measuring devices can be suspended at various depths in the ocean from fixed objects, such as buoys or light ships, to monitor currents for long periods. One such anchored meter measures the flow of water past a fixed point. Flowing water causes impeller blades, similar to the blades of a fan, to rotate at a rate proportional to the current's speed. In addition, the blades cause the meter to align with the current's direction. Electrical signals indicating the direction and speed of the current are transmitted by radio or cable to a recording vessel. Current velocities of less than 1 centimeter per second can be detected by this meter.

To get the most complete picture of the variability of the ocean, a combination of various measurement techniques with remote sensing may be employed. Such a multidimensional approach may involve the measurement of current velocity, pressure (a measure of depth), water temperature, and water conductivity (a measure of salinity). These data can be transmitted via satellite to a land station or even directly to a computer.

Perhaps the most persuasive evidence for the existence of deep-sea currents and their influence on the ocean bottom has been gained through bottom photography. Sediment waves, or ripples, apparently formed from sediment carried by deep-sea currents, along with evidence of current-induced scour of the ocean floor, were first photographed in the Atlantic Ocean in the late 1940's. Since then, the technology of bottom photography has advanced greatly. This advancement became most apparent with the exploration, in the late 1980's, of the wreck of the SS *Titanic* in the northwestern Atlantic. Bottom photography permits detailed study of some of the smaller features on the ocean floor apparently formed by deep-sea currents. Benthonic organisms, marine organisms that live attached to the ocean floor, bending in the flow of the current, are a particularly intriguing example of the phenomena recorded by this technique.

Echo-sounding studies of the sea floor have yielded abundant information on ocean-floor features that are either formed or modified by deep-sea currents. Notable among these are very long ridges in the North Atlantic evidently constructed from sediment carried by deep-sea currents. In echo sounding, a narrow sound beam is directed from a ship vertically to the sea bottom, where it is reflected back to a recorder on the ship. The depth to the sea floor is determined by multiplying the velocity of the sound pulse by one-half the amount of time it takes for the sound to return to the ship. The depths to the ocean floor are recorded on a chart by a precision depth recorder, which produces a continuous profile of the shape of the sea floor as the ship moves across the ocean.

Sediment transported by and deposited from deep-sea currents can be studied directly by actually sampling the ocean floor. Sampling of these deposits is best accomplished by the use of various coring devices capable of recovering long vertical sections, or cores, of sea-floor sediment. Sediment recovery is achieved by forcing the corer, a long pipe usually with an inner plastic liner, vertically into the sediment. The simplest coring device, the gravity corer, consists of a pipe with a heavy weight at one end. This type of corer will penetrate only 2-3 meters into the sea floor. The piston corer, used to obtain longer cores, is fitted with a piston inside the core tube that reduces friction during coring, thereby permitting the recovery of 18-meter or longer cores. Analysis of the sediment recovered from the ocean floor by these and other coring devices reveals much information about small-scale features formed by deep-sea currents.

Context

Because cold bottom-water masses often are nutrient-rich and contain elevated abundances of dissolved oxygen, deep-sea currents are extremely important to biological productivity. There are areas of the earth's surface where nutrient-rich cold bottom waters rise to the ocean surface. These locations, known as areas of upwelling, are generally biologically productive and therefore are important food sources. Especially pronounced upwelling occurs around Antarctica. Bottom waters from the North Atlantic upwell near Antarctica and replace the cold, dense, sinking waters of the Antarctic.

The great amount of time required for seawater to circulate from the surface of the ocean to the bottom and back again to the surface has become an important practical matter. If pollutants are introduced into high-latitude surface waters, they will not resurface in the low latitudes for hundreds of years. This delay is particularly important if the material is rapidly decaying radioactive waste that may lose much of its dangerous radiation by the time it resurfaces with the current. The introduction of toxic pollutants into a system as sluggish as the deep-sea circulation system, however, means that they will remain in that system for prolonged periods. Nations must, therefore, be concerned with the rate at which material is added to this system relative to that at which it might be redistributed at the surface of the ocean by wind-induced surface circulation. The multinational Geochemical Ocean Sections (GEOSECS) program, introduced as part of the International Decade of Ocean Exploration, attempted to assess better the problem of how natural and synthetic chemical substances are distributed throughout the world's oceans. The GEOSECS program, carried out from 1970 to 1980, yielded abundant information regarding the movement of various water masses and, among other things, the distribution of radioactive material in the oceans. For example, GEOSECS demonstrated that tritium produced in the late 1950's and early 1960's by atmospheric testing of nuclear weapons had been carried to depths approaching 5 kilometers in the North Atlantic Ocean by 1973.

Bibliography

Baker, D. J. "Models of Oceanic Circulation." *Scientific American* 222 (January, 1970): 114. A somewhat complex discussion of surface circulation in the world's oceans. Generally suitable for college-level readers.

Hollister, C. D., A. Nowell, and P. A. Jumar. "The Dynamic Abyss." *Scientific American* 250 (March, 1984): 42. This excellent article addresses the formation of bottom waters that flow away from the polar regions toward the equator. Suitable for high school students.

Kennett, James P. *Marine Geology.* Englewood Cliffs, N.J.: Prentice-Hall, 1982. This book contains an excellent discussion of deep-sea currents and thermohaline circulation. The major methods of study of deep-sea currents, including bottom photography (there are two pages of black-and-white bottom photographs), are discussed in detail. Best suited to the college student.

Ross, David A. *Introduction to Oceanography.* Englewood Cliffs, N.J.: Prentice-Hall, 1988. A fine introductory oceanography textbook with an informative discussion of deep-sea currents and their mechanisms of generation. There is also a section on oceanographic instrumentation. Suitable for high school students.

Shepard, Francis P. *Submarine Geology.* 3d ed. New York: Harper & Row, 1973. An excellent, if somewhat dated, text on marine geology. The section on methods and instrumentation employed in the study of the oceans is particularly good. Suitable for general audiences.

Smith, F. G. "Measuring Ocean Currents." *Sea Frontiers* 18 (May, 1972): 166. This article discusses methods used to determine the speed and direction of ocean currents.

Steward, R. W. "The Atmosphere and the Oceans." *Scientific American* 221 (September, 1969): 76. A good discussion of the energy exchange between the atmosphere and the ocean and the resulting phenomena. For all readers.

Gary G. Lash

Cross-References

SURFACE OCEAN CURRENTS

Type of earth science: Oceanography

Ocean currents represent a dynamic earth system that, along with atmospheric circulation, helps to distribute heat evenly over the earth. Responding to the seasons, the currents play important roles in earth climates, marine life, and ocean transportation.

Principal terms

CORE RING or CORE EDDY: a mass of water that is spun off of an ocean current by the current's meandering motion

CORIOLIS EFFECT: the apparent deflection of any moving body or object from its usual course, caused by the rotation of the earth

CURRENT: a sustained movement of seawater in the horizontal plane, usually wind-driven

DRIFT: a movement similar to a current but more widespread, less distinct, slower, more shallow, and less easily delineated

EARTH'S HEAT BUDGET: the balance between the incoming solar radiation and the outgoing terrestrial reradiation

GYRE or GYRAL: the very large, semiclosed circulation patterns of ocean currents in each of the major ocean basins

PLANETARY WINDS: the large, relatively constant prevailing wind systems that result from the earth's absorption of solar energy and that are affected by the earth's rotation

THERMOHALINE CIRCULATION: any circulation of ocean waters that is caused by variations in the density of seawater resulting from differences in the temperature and/or salinity of the water

Summary of the Phenomenon

The "heat budget" of the earth results in temperatures that make possible life on the planet. The ocean currents play a vital role in the heat budget. The currents are major determinants of climates and strongly influence the distribution of marine life. Ocean currents must be studied in relation to other aspects of the environment, with which they are interwoven. The currents are, for example, closely associated with atmospheric circulation. The planetary winds are the prime movers of the currents. The friction of the wind blowing over the ocean surface establishes the slow movements in the shallow surface waters that become a global circulation of immense volumes of seawater. There are deeper ocean currents that are much slower-moving and difficult to monitor, whose significance, therefore, is less well understood. The deep currents are primarily caused by thermohaline circulation. They are driven by slowly responding to slight differences in the densities of the water resulting from differences in temperature and salinities. This study concerns the shallow, wind-driven currents, the ones affecting the surface waters, although they may be hundreds of feet deep.

Most significant about ocean currents are their geographic locations and their directions of flow. It is helpful to recognize overall patterns. There are large-circulation gyres in each of the major ocean basins. These gyres, or gyrals, move clockwise in the Northern Hemisphere and counterclockwise in the Southern Hemisphere. The North Central Atlantic gyre, for example, located east of the United States, is one of the best known and most studied. The Florida Current (part of the Gulf Stream system) is on the west side of the gyre and is a warm current flowing poleward (northward). The Canaries Current, on the east side of the gyre, is a cold current and is flowing equatorward (southward). The North Atlantic Drift and the North Equatorial Current form the eastward and westward components of the gyre, respectively. The result of the circulation in the gyre is that warm water from the equatorial region is transported poleward to the heat-deficient areas. Simultaneously, the Canaries Current is transporting colder water back toward the equator. The ocean currents thus help to distribute heat more evenly over the earth's surface. In the Atlantic Ocean south of the equator, the large gyre is counterclockwise. The warm Brazil Current on the west side of the gyre is flowing poleward (southward), transporting heat away from the equator. The Benguela Current on the east side of the gyre is moving colder water toward the equator.

In the Pacific Ocean, similar patterns of clockwise and counterclockwise gyres are apparent. North of the equator, the Japan Current (also known as Kuroshio) is transporting the warm water poleward, and the California Current is moving the colder water equatorward. In the Pacific Ocean south of the equator, the cold, equatorward-flowing, nutrient-rich Humboldt Current lies off the west coast of South America and is renowned as one of the most fertile commercial marine fishery areas on earth. The Indian Ocean possesses similar gyres, although the attenuated portion north of the equator presents some special circumstances.

The forces that drive the oceanic current circulations are the planetary winds. The planetary winds are in turn driven by solar energy. The ocean currents, therefore, are in fact "sun-driven." It is sunshine that energizes the Gulf Stream and the other currents. Some general principles about the earth's heat budget can be stated. The sun heats the earth—its atmosphere, oceans, and land—but each portion heats differently. The atmosphere, the most fluid and most responsive of the three, has developed large planetary bands of alternating pressure belts and wind belts, such as the Northeast Trade Winds and the Prevailing Westerlies. The Northeast Trade Winds lie between 5 and 25 degrees north latitude. The winds are predominantly from the northeast and form one of the most constant of the wind belts. The friction of the wind moving over the ocean surface causes the surface waters to move with the wind, but because of the Coriolis effect, caused by the earth's rotation, the movement of the water current in the Northern Hemisphere tends to be about 45 degrees to the right of the winds that cause the current. The resultant current, the North Equatorial Current, is fragmented into different oceans because of the inter-

vening continents. Largely as a result of the Coriolis effect, the current deflects to
its right and in the Atlantic Ocean eventually becomes the Gulf Stream. In the
Pacific Ocean, the comparable current is the Japan Current. One can thus see the
origins of the clockwise gyrals in the Northern Hemisphere. Another wind belt in
the Northern Hemisphere, the Prevailing Westerlies, is located between 35 and
55 degrees north latitude. The winds are not as constant as the Northeast Trade
Winds, and they prevail from the west. The correlation of the latitudes of the
Westerlies and the west-to-east moving currents of the gyres is apparent. The
currents slow down and become more widespread, shallower, and less distinguishable but are urged on toward the east by the Westerlies. The North Atlantic Drift
and the North Pacific Current are the results.

Again analyzing the North Central Atlantic gyre, the blocking positions of the
continents cause the North Atlantic Drift to split, part moving southward toward the
equator as the cold Canaries Current and part moving poleward into the Arctic
Ocean as the warm Norwegian Current. The Canaries Current merges into the
North Equatorial Current to complete the gyre. The temperature characterizations
of currents and drifts as "warm" or "cold" are relative. There are no absolute
temperature divisions. Some warm currents are actually lower in temperature than
some cold currents. For example, the Norwegian Current is considered a warm
current only because it is warmer than the Arctic water into which it is entering.
Itself only a few degrees above freezing in winter, it nevertheless transfers significant amounts of heat into these high latitudes and moderates the winter temperatures in Western and Northern Europe. A compensating movement of cold water out
of the Arctic is accomplished by the southward flowing Labrador Current between
Greenland and North America.

The Gulf Stream is the world's greatest ocean current; however, there is some
confusion about what comprises the Gulf Stream. The Gulf Stream is generally
taken to include the entire warm-water transport system from Florida to the point at
which the warm water is lost by diffusion into the Arctic Ocean. It would include
the North Atlantic Drift and the Norwegian Current. To the professional oceanographer, the Gulf Stream is a smaller segment of that transport system—that portion
off the northeast coast of the United States. The Gulf Stream system thus includes
the Florida Current, the Gulf Stream, the North Atlantic Drift, and the Norwegian
Current.

Ocean current patterns in the Southern Hemisphere are almost a mirror image of
those in the Northern Hemisphere, adjusted for differences in continent configurations. The Southeast Trade Winds drive the South Equatorial Current. The Coriolis
effect causes deflections to the left. Resultant gyres are counterclockwise, but again,
the poleward-moving currents transfer the heat away from the equator, and the
equatorward-moving currents return colder water. In general, cold currents are
richer in nutrients, have a higher oxygen content, and support a greater amount of
life than warm currents. Most products of the world's commerical fisheries are
yielded by these cold waters. On the other hand, cold currents offshore are associ-

ated with desert climates onshore. The atmospheric circulations that drive the ocean currents also create conditions that are not conducive to precipitation in the latitudes of these cold currents. Examples are the Sahara Desert adjacent to the Canaries Current, the Peru-Chile Desert adjacent to the Humboldt Current, the Sonoran Desert adjacent to the California Current, and the Kalahari Desert adjacent to the Benguela Current.

There are other currents that are less permanent, and even erratic, in occurrence, such as the warm El Niño Current that periodically develops off the west coast of northwestern South America for reasons that are not well understood. It is believed to trigger widespread climate aberrations and is the subject of much study. Still other currents are caused by tides, storms, and local weather conditions, but they are local in nature, of limited duration, and less important in affecting the earth's environment than the great ocean currents that are driven by the planetary winds.

Methods of Study

The study of ocean currents has acquired new significance as scientists have learned of the role of currents in earth climates and marine life. Information comes from many sources. One of the earliest attempts to identify and chart an ocean current was by Benjamin Franklin when he was postmaster general of colonial America. His map of the Gulf Stream was published in 1770 and has proven to be remarkably accurate when one considers his sources of information. Franklin had noted that vessels sailing westward from England to America in the midlatitudes of the Atlantic Ocean were taking longer than ships moving eastward and longer than ships moving westward but in lower latitudes. He correctly concluded that the vessels were moving against a slow, eastward-moving current.

Since that time, vast amounts of data have been acquired to detect, measure, and chart the currents. One of the early methods still employed is the use of drift bottles. Sealed bottles are introduced into the sea at various locations and dates and are allowed to float with the currents. Finders are requested to note the date and location of the bottle-find and to return the data to the address in the bottle. Various types of current meters are used. Some are moored to the bottom and can transmit results by means of radiowaves. Others are retrieved and serviced periodically. It is difficult for a ship at sea to measure currents, because the ship itself is drifting with the current and the meter would indicate no relative motion between the ship and the water. Currents are generally very slow and difficult to measure. A few currents may be measured at 6 to 8 kilometers per hour, but much more common are those less than 1 kilometer per hour. The average surface velocity of the North Atlantic Drift is about 1.3 kilometers per hour. The currents also vary in width and depth. The Florida Current off Miami is about 32 kilometers wide, 300 meters deep, and moving at about 5 to 8 kilometers per hour. It is transporting more than 4 billion tons of water per minute. The volume of flow is more than one hundred times that of the Mississippi River. As the flow proceeds north and then east as the North Atlantic Drift, it spreads, thins, slows, and splits into individual meandering flows that are difficult to follow. Spin-off eddies, or "core rings," occur that can persist for months.

One very useful method of tracking ocean currents is to be able to identify water of slight temperature variations and salinity differences. When the flow movement is so slow as to be practically undetectable with current meters, the slight temperature and salinity differences can be used as "tracers" to identify current movements. This method is also used in identifying the even slower-moving deep ocean water currents. A new technique is the use of satellite imagery and high-altitude aerial photography. Using sensors that detect radiation at selected bands of the electromagnetic spectrum, satellites collect data on broad patterns of seawater temperatures and thus help scientists to understand the movements and extent of the currents. This type of sea monitoring will be useful in detecting any changes that might occur in the oceans in the future and in alerting scientists to possible changes in the earth's overall heat budget.

Context

Ocean currents play a vital role in the environment. The earth is at a fine-balanced temperature. Energy from the sun is absorbed by the earth and especially by the oceans. Along with atmospheric circulation, the ocean currents serve to distribute the absorbed heat more evenly over the earth's surface. Immense volumes of warm seawater are slowly moving poleward, transporting heat from the heat-surplus equatorial regions of the earth to the heat-deficient regions nearer the poles. Cold water currents in turn move chilled water back toward the equator. Although neither solar energy nor rainfall is evenly distributed over the earth, the mixing actions of the ocean currents keep the earth environment from being uninhabitable. Perhaps the most notable examples of these moderating effects of the ocean currents are the climates of the west coasts of the continents in the middle and high latitudes, especially in Europe. The densely populated nations of northwestern Europe experience much milder winters than would otherwise be expected for such high latitudes. Northwestern North America is similarly benefited.

Life in the sea is also aided by these ocean-water mixings. In addition to heat, ocean currents distribute oxygen and nutrients, the result being certain areas in the oceans where very favorable life-supporting conditions occur. These fertile areas of mixing are concentrated sources of commercial marine fishery products. Where mixing is limited, virtual deserts arise in the ocean such as the Sargasso Sea, located in the center of the North Central Atlantic gyre. Seasonal shiftings of the currents are being studied. The global warming caused by the greenhouse effect is expected to alter ocean currents, creating a further need to study these currents and their effects on climate and marine life.

Bibliography

Duxbury, Alyn C., and Alison B. Duxbury. *An Introduction to the World's Oceans.* 2d ed. Dubuque, Iowa: Wm. C. Brown, 1989. This book includes a clearly written section on the earth's planetary winds and their effects on the ocean currents. The general patterns of ocean-current circulation are mapped, and diagrams are used to explain the Coriolis effect. Suggested readings are listed.

Gaskell, T. F. *The Gulf Stream*. New York: New American Library, 1972. Following a general discussion of ocean currents, a more detailed description of the Gulf Stream is given. Life in the current, its meanderings, and its effects on climate are discussed. This book is informative and easy to read. A brief bibliography is included.

Gross, M. Grant. *Oceanography: A View of the Earth*. 4th ed. Englewood Cliffs, N.J.: Prentice-Hall, 1987. This is a general introductory text for oceanography. It is well illustrated in all aspects of the study of the oceans. Ocean currents are explained and mapped. Both horizontal and vertical aspects of oceanic circulation are related to winds, temperatures, and salinities. Comprehensive and easy to read. Contains a glossary and an index.

Ingmanson, Dale E., and William J. Wallace. *Oceanography: An Introduction*. 4th ed. Belmont, Calif.: Wadsworth, 1989. A general introduction to oceanography. Written as an introductory college text but can be read by the high school student who is interested. The text is well illustrated, and important terms are in bold print. Includes a glossary, and each chapter contains a list of further readings.

Pickard, George L., and William J. Emery. *Descriptive Physical Oceanography: An Introduction*. 4th ed. Elmsford, N.Y.: Pergamon Press, 1982. This book covers only the physical aspects of oceanography, in a less comprehensive and more technical manner than general-introduction oceanography texts. It presents a detailed description of ocean circulation, both surface currents and deep currents. Includes details on the types of current meters and the methods of current measurements. An extensive bibliography is provided.

Stowe, Keith. *Ocean Science*. 2d ed. New York: John Wiley & Sons, 1983. An introductory text for college students who have little background in the sciences. Three chapters discuss oceanic and atmospheric circulation; one deals specifically with surface ocean currents. All chapters include review questions and suggestions for further reading. A glossary is included.

Thurman, Harold V. *Introductory Oceanography*. 5th ed. Columbus, Ohio: Merrill, 1988. This is an introductory text to oceanography. It is comprehensive but not too technical for the general reader. It is very well illustrated and includes some high-quality color maps and diagrams. Each chapter includes questions and exercises and also lists references and suggested readings. The circulations of the ocean currents are addressed according to the major ocean basins, with maps and diagrams for each basin.

John H. Corbet

Cross-References

The Atmosphere's Global Circulation, 121; The Atmosphere's Structure and Com-

OCEAN-FLOOR DRILLING PROGRAMS

Type of earth science: Oceanography

Ocean-floor drilling programs have allowed geologists and oceanographers to extend their knowledge of the earth's history by analyzing long marine sediment cores and basement rock cores recovered from the sea floor. Data from ocean-floor drilling have provided evidence supporting the theories of sea-floor spreading and plate tectonics and have permitted the investigation of the paleoclimatic and paleoceanographic history of the earth.

Principal terms

ABYSSAL PLAINS: flat-lying areas of the sea floor, located in the ocean areas far from continents; they cover more than half the total surface area of the earth

BASALT: a dark-colored, fine-grained rock erupted by volcanoes, which tends to be the basement rock underneath sediments in the abyssal plains

CHERT: a hard, well-cemented sedimentary rock that is produced by recrystallization of siliceous marine sediments buried in the sea floor

CORRELATION: the demonstration that two rocks in different areas were deposited at the same time in the geologic past

DEPOSITION: the process by which loose sediment grains fall out of seawater to accumulate as layers of sediment on the sea floor

MID-OCEAN RIDGE: a continuous mountain range of underwater volcanoes located along the center of most ocean basins; volcanic eruptions along these ridges drive sea-floor spreading

PALEOCEANOGRAPHY: the study of the history of the oceans of the earth, ancient sediment deposition patterns, and ocean current positions compared to ancient climates

PLATE TECTONICS: a theory that the earth's crust consists of individual, shifting plates that are formed at oceanic ridges and destroyed along ocean trenches

SEA-FLOOR SPREADING: a theory that the continents of the earth move apart from each other by splitting of continental blocks, driven by the eruption of new ocean floor in the rift

Summary of the Methodology

Most of our knowledge of the history of the earth comes from the study of sedimentary rocks, as sediments may contain the preserved fossil remains of ancient plants and animals, while sedimentary structures record the processes of deposition. Sedimentary rocks exposed on land tend to have an incomplete record because they may be deformed by folding and faulting, which may destroy both the fossils and the sedimentary structures and may be eroded by wind, water, and ice moving across the surface. In contrast, marine sedimentary sequences contain a more complete record of accumulation because they accumulate in a lower-energy environment, which is not as affected by folding, faulting, erosion, and post-depositional alteration as are terrestrial sediments. As a result, the deep-sea sediments tend to preserve a continuous record of sediment deposition in the ocean basins.

Ocean drilling techniques were originally developed in the 1950's by petroleum exploration companies searching for shallow-water hydrocarbon and petroleum deposits located on the continental shelves. These industrial exploration methods were adapted in the 1960's to obtain long sediment cores from the sea floor in deep-water areas on the continental slopes and abyssal plains. By drilling through the entire sediment record into the harder basement rocks below marine sediments, geologists hoped to acquire the complete history of sediment deposition within an ocean basin from the time that sediments were first deposited atop volcanic basalts.

Preliminary attempts to drill the ocean floor included engineering tests for Project Mohole by the drilling barge *CUSS I*, which in 1961 drilled marine sediments off La Jolla, California, and at the deep-water Experimental Mohole Site east of Guadalupe Island, off Baja California, Mexico, in a water depth of 3,566 meters. Although further Project Mohole development was not undertaken because of a combination of political conflicts and increasing cost estimates for the project, in 1964 four American universities formed a consortium to initiate a program of scientific deep-sea drilling. JOIDES, the Joint Oceanographic Institutions for Deep Earth Sampling, successfully operated a drilling program in April-May, 1965, using the vessel *Caldrill I* to drill six holes on the Blake Plateau off Florida to sub-bottom depths of more than 1,000 meters, with continuous core recovery.

Following these successful trials, JOIDES proposed an eighteen-month program of scientific drilling in the Atlantic and Pacific oceans, to be called the Deep Sea Drilling Project (DSDP), operated by the Scripps Institution of Oceanography of La Jolla, California, using the drilling vessel *Glomar Challenger*. *Glomar Challenger* left Orange, Texas, on July 20, 1968, on Leg 1 of the Deep Sea Drilling Project. The results of DSDP drilling on the first nine cruises in the Atlantic and Pacific oceans caused the National Science Foundation to extend the drilling program beyond the initial eighteen-month period, with further drilling in the Indian Ocean and in the seas surrounding Antarctica.

When DSDP began operations, many other American oceanographic institutions joined JOIDES in support of the drilling program, and the success of DSDP also attracted scientific participation and financial support from foreign countries. The International Program of Ocean Drilling (IPOD) started in 1975 when the Soviet Union, the Federal Republic of Germany, France, the United Kingdom, and Japan joined JOIDES, with each country providing $1 million yearly to support drilling programs. DSDP/IPOD drilling activities continued through the early 1980's, leading to international scientific exchange of information between oceanographers.

Because the initial JOIDES proposal was only for eighteen months, it was never expected that ocean drilling would continue for fifteen years. Because of demands for ocean drilling in deeper waters and in high-latitude polar areas, JOIDES proposed in the early 1980's that a larger drilling vessel be acquired for continued drilling. The last cruise of the *Glomar Challenger*, DSDP Leg 96, ended in Mobile, Alabama, on November 8, 1983, with the retirement of the drilling vessel from service. In 1983, responsibility for scientific supervision of the international project, now called the Ocean Drilling Program (ODP), passed from the Scripps Institution to Texas A&M University, and the drilling vessel *Sedco/BP 471* replaced *Glomar Challenger*. The first cruise of a ten-year ODP drilling program began on March 20, 1985, when the *Sedco/BP 471*, informally called the *JOIDES Resolution*, left port to begin drilling on ODP Leg 101.

In shallow water, drilling is accomplished either by building a drilling platform directly atop the sea floor or by firmly anchoring a drilling vessel to the bottom. In deep-water ocean drilling, however, it is not possible to anchor the drilling vessel to the bottom, so the technique of dynamic positioning is used to maintain the position of the vessel above the hole being drilled. In dynamic positioning, an acoustic beacon emitting sounds at either 12.5 kilohertz or 16 kilohertz is dropped to the sea floor. Four hydrophones, located at different points on the hull of the drillship, receive the signal from the acoustic beacon at slightly different times, depending on the position of the hull relative to the beacon. The position of the ship is maintained by a shipboard computer, which interprets the information from the hull hydrophones and controls the position of the ship by driving both the main propellers and two laterally oriented propellers, or hull thrusters. If the vessel is pushed off location by waves or surface currents, the shipboard computer attempts to compensate by using the propellers and hull thrusters to maintain the ship's location relative to the sea-floor beacon.

In order to drill sediment and rock samples from the sea floor, a drill bit is attached to the bottom of a 9.5-meter-long piece of hollow cylindrical stainless steel drill pipe. More individual lengths of pipe are connected on the rig floor of the drillship to make a "drill string," which extends from the vessel through the water down to the sea floor, where coring may begin. Usually, about 450-510 lengths of drill pipe are required simply to reach the bottom, and the assembly of this drill string may take twelve hours before bottom drilling may be started. Once the string reaches the sea floor, the drill pipe is rotated by hydraulic motors on the rig floor, and the rotary action combined with the weight of the drill string causes the drill bit to spiral down into the sea floor. Sharp iron carbide or diamond cutting teeth on the drill bit assist the penetration of the drill string into the sediment and the rock on the ocean bottom.

Samples of sediment and rock are retrieved from the sea floor by drilling a hole about 25 centimeters in diameter, using a drill bit with a 7.5-centimeter hole in its center. In effect, sediment is cored by "drilling the doughnut and saving the doughnut hole": Rotating the drill string grinds the outer ring of sediment to small pieces against the diamond teeth of the drill bit, while the material in the center of the drill hole is saved as a core of drilled sediment 6.6 centimeters in diameter. As the drill string is lowered deeper into the drilled hole, the core is pushed up into a plastic core liner in a steel "core barrel" within the lowest stand of drill pipe. After 9.5 meters of the sea floor has been drilled, the core barrel is pulled up to the rig floor by a cable lowered through the drill string.

The results of each cruise, or leg, have been published in a series of books, entitled *Initial Reports of the Deep Sea Drilling Project*, which are published by the U.S. Government Printing Office. The cores recovered from the DSDP and ODP holes represent an invaluable record of the history of ocean sediment deposition around the globe. These recovered sediment cores are studied by a variety of scientists, who are interested in the sediment type, fossil content, geochemistry, magnetic orientation and strength, shear strength, and other sedimentary properties of the samples.

Applications of the Method

The first three cruises of the *Glomar Challenger* provided information proving that sea-floor spreading had occurred in the Atlantic Ocean: A series of DSDP holes across the Mid-Atlantic Ridge showed that the age of bottom sediments increased with distance from the ridge crest and indicated that the ages of sediments with depth correlate from one hole to the next. The total thickness of sediment atop basaltic basement also increased with greater distance from the ridge crest, on both the east and west sides of the Mid-Atlantic Ridge. Further DSDP and ODP drilling has provided evidence that sea-floor spreading has occurred in all the earth's ocean basins. In addition, ocean drilling has confirmed the relative youth of the ocean basins, as predicted by plate tectonics; the oldest sea floor yet discovered is Early Jurassic in age (160 million years old), compared to continental rocks, which may be as old as 4.5 billion years.

Glomar Challenger and *JOIDES Resolution* have operated from the Norwegian Sea to the Ross Sea off Antarctica and have drilled holes in water depths from 193 meters on the Oregon continental shelf to 7,050 meters in the Marianas Trench off Guam, in the western Pacific Ocean. The deepest hole through sea-floor sediment deposits is more than 1,750 meters below the sea floor, and one site in the equatorial Pacific Ocean west of South America (DSDP Hole 504B) has been drilled through 300 meters of sediment and 1,500 meters of volcanic basement rock.

Sea-floor drilling has indicated that deep-sea sediments contain long sequences of well-preserved microfossils, which may be used for global stratigraphic correlation, in contrast to the fragmentary record preserved on land, where structural deformation of sediment deposits may complicate the problem of correlating different sedimentary sequences. Analyses of these sediments has revealed the history of deposition in the different ocean basins and has provided information on ancient climates and oceanographic conditions (such as the position, strength, and temperature of past ocean currents).

Sediment cores have indicated the presence of great shifts in oceanic climate conditions during the geologic past and have demonstrated that the Antarctic continent has been covered by glacial ice caps for at least 40-50 million years, rather than the 5 million years accepted prior to DSDP drilling near Antarctica. Another startling result of ocean drilling has been the discovery that the Mediterranean Sea dried up between 12 and 5 million years ago: Massive salt and evaporite mineral deposits below the Mediterranean basin indicate that the Strait of Gibraltar connection to the Atlantic Ocean was blocked during this time. Blockage of the Gibraltar connection allowed the water in the basin to evaporate, causing the deposition of vast salt and evaporite mineral deposits as the Mediterranean dried up.

Ocean drilling has also provided evidence for the existence of deep-water hydrocarbon accumulations: Drilling in the cap of the Sigsbee Knolls at a water depth of 3,400 meters in the Gulf of Mexico revealed traces of oil in these sea-floor sediments. If future technology is developed, humankind may be able to exploit these deep-water petroleum resources. Furthermore, scientific ocean drilling has enabled geologists to understand the processes controlling the deposition of "black shale" deposits and other high-productivity sea-floor sediments, which may be altered by burial into source beds for the generation of petroleum hydrocarbons. Understanding of the processes affecting the formation and distribution of these sediments may assist in future exploration for fossil fuel resources.

Not all the information provided by ocean drilling has been concerned with the sediment column. Drilling into basement rocks has allowed geophysicists to compare the structure of sea-floor basement to that of layered igneous-rock deposits that have been uplifted above sea level on the edges of certain continents. Similarly, direct drilling through these basalt and gabbro layers has allowed a comparison of the rock type to sound velocities measured by marine geophysicists. Some other results of hard-rock sea-floor drilling have been the investigation of sediment and mineral deposition by hydrothermal processes at rapidly opening mid-ocean ridge segments, such as the sulfides deposited by high-temperature fluids emitted by "black smoker" and "white smoker" structures near the Galápagos Islands west of South America. Drilling of bare basement rocks along mid-ocean ridges in the Atlantic, Pacific, and Indian oceans has enabled geochemists and igneous petrologists to study the frequency at which sea-floor volcanic rocks are produced at individual ridge segments and to determine whether temporal changes occur in the chemistry of basalts erupted from one location on the ridge. These studies of sea-floor basement rocks may be applied to mineral exploration of marine rocks that have been uplifted above sea level and exposed on continents.

In addition to scientific results, DSDP and ODP operations have resulted in improvements in drilling technology by developing the ability to reenter sea-floor boreholes, by devising techniques for "bare-rock" drilling on the sea-floor, and through the development of new coring bits. During DSDP Leg 1, it was discovered that existing drill bits could not penetrate hard chert beds; thus, they also would not be able to penetrate through deeper igneous rocks below sea-floor sediments.

The drag bits were solid, consisting of a central opening and radial curved ridges of steel or tungsten carbide, capped with industrial diamonds and designed to churn through soft sediments. As a result, DSDP began a drill-bit design program, which led to the development of roller bits capable of penetrating both chert layers and sea-floor basalts. These bits consist of four conical cutting heads studded with tungsten carbide or diamond cutting teeth, situated around the central core opening in the bit.

Another important technical development of DSDP, first successfully accomplished on Leg 15, was the ability to reenter a drilled borehole on the sea floor. Even with roller bit designs, drill bits wear out from the stresses of rotary coring through sea-floor sediments and rocks. When a bit fails, the entire drill string has to be "tripped," or pulled up to the vessel to replace the bit at the lower end of the string, which in most deep-ocean drilling sites requires pulling the string up not only several hundred meters from below the sea floor but also through 2,000-5,000 meters of seawater. During early DSDP legs, bit failure forced the abandonment of a hole because after the fatigued bit was replaced, it was impossible to reenter the original borehole. Successful reentry techniques were facilitated by the development of a steel reentry cone 6 meters in diameter, topped with three sonar reflectors and a rotating sonar scanner that can be lowered through the drill string. In areas where hardened sediment layers are anticipated, requiring bit replacement to complete drilling, the reentry cone is placed on the sea floor prior to drilling the initial borehole. As bits become worn, they may be replaced and the hole reentered by using the sonar scanner to locate the reentry cone (and thus the original hole).

DSDP and ODP drilling specialists have also devised methods to enable drilling in hard sea-floor areas, such as mid-ocean ridges, which were not previously drillable by existing techniques. Development of a sea-floor "guide base" for drilling has allowed successful drilling and reentry of boreholes in these areas and has permitted the implantation of sea-floor sensing devices, such as earthquake-measuring seismometers, in these holes.

Context

Ocean-floor drilling programs have enabled scientists to correlate apparently unconnected phenomena into the theory of plate tectonics, a global synthesis of geology and oceanography. Ocean drilling has provided verification of the sea-floor spreading hypothesis as it applies to plate tectonics and has indicated that sea-floor spreading has occurred in all the earth's ocean basins.

Before long sediment cores could be acquired from the sea floor, scientists' knowledge of sea-floor geology was sparse, based on limited samples available from dredging and shallow coring of the sea floor by oceanographic vessels. Prior to the Deep Sea Drilling Project, global stratigraphic correlation was based on a fragmentary record preserved on land, where structural deformation of sediment deposits may complicate the problem of correlating different sedimentary sequences; DSDP drilling, however, has revealed that deep-sea sediments contain long sequences of well-preserved microfossils. Furthermore, sea-floor sediment cores have revealed the history of the ocean basins and have provided information on ancient climates and oceanographic conditions (such as the position, strength, and temperature of past ocean currents). A new science, paleoceanography, has been developed based on this information from DSDP and ODP drilling. Analysis of the earth's ancient climates may provide information to predict future shifts in the biosphere.

Ocean drilling has also provided evidence for the existence of deep-water hydro-carbon accumulations, which has enabled petroleum exploration companies to drill petroleum deposits on the continental slopes and may eventually lead to the discovery of significant hydrocarbon deposits in ocean basins. If future technology is developed, humans may be able to exploit these deep-water petroleum resources. Furthermore, scientific ocean drilling has enabled geologists to understand the processes controlling the deposition of high-productivity sea-floor sediments, which form the source materials for the generation of petroleum hydrocarbons and coal deposits. In addition, studies of sea-floor basement rocks may lead to a more complete understanding of the nature of mineral deposition at mid-ocean ridges, which may be applied to mineral exploration of similar marine rocks that have been uplifted above sea level and exposed on continents.

Finally, deep-ocean drilling has led to technological innovations in the tools and techniques used to sample the sea floor. These methods have been adapted by industrial companies exploring for hydrocarbons buried beneath marine sediments and for mineral deposits on the sea floor.

Bibliography

Bascom, Willard. *A Hole in the Bottom of the Sea*. Garden City, N.Y.: Doubleday, 1961. A history of the Mohole Project, which planned to drill through oceanic rocks down to the crust-mantle boundary.

Hsu, Kenneth J. *The Mediterranean Was a Desert*. Princeton, N.J.: Princeton University Press, 1983. A personal account of DSDP Leg 13 drilling in the Mediterranean Sea basin during 1970, as written by one of the two chief scientists on the drilling vessel *Glomar Challenger*.

Nierenberg, William A. "The Deep Sea Drilling Project After Ten Years." *American Scientist* 66 (January/February, 1978): 20-29. A review of the significant technical and scientific developments of the DSDP, written by the director of Scripps Institution of Oceanography.

Peterson, M. N. A., and F. C. MacTernan. "A Ship for Scientific Drilling." *Oceanus* 25 (Spring, 1982): 72-79. Summary of the technical aspects of ocean drilling on *Glomar Challenger*, written for a nonscientific audience by the director of the DSDP.

Shor, Elizabeth Noble. *Scripps Institution of Oceanography: Probing the Oceans, 1936 to 1976*. San Diego, Calif.: Tofua Press, 1978. The book recounts the formation of the Scripps Institution of Oceanography and provides a history of the oceanographic research performed by its scientists. Chapter 12 covers the history of the Deep Sea Drilling Project.

Van Andel, Tjeerd H. "Deep-Sea Drilling for Scientific Purposes: A Decade of Dreams." *Science* 160 (June 28, 1968): 1419-1424. A summary of the results of scientific ocean drilling up to the start of the Deep Sea Drilling Project.

Warme, John E., Robert G. Douglas, and Edward L. Winterer, eds. *The Deep Sea Drilling Project: A Decade of Progress*. Tulsa, Okla.: Society of Economic Paleontologists and Mineralogists, 1981. A volume of scientific papers discussing the results of oceanographic research based on sediments and rocks recovered by DSDP. Best suited to those with some scientific background.

West, Susan. "Diary of a Drilling Ship." *Science News* 119 (January 24, 1981): 60-63.

_____. "Log of Leg 76." *Science News* 119 (February 21, 1981): 124-127. These articles tell a reporter's story of seven days aboard *Glomar Challenger* during Leg 76 drilling operations in the Atlantic Ocean off Florida.

_____. "DSDP: Ten Years After." *Science News* 113 (June 24, 1978). Summarizes the choices facing the DSDP in 1978: whether to continue ocean drilling with *Glomar Challenger* or to seek a larger and more sophisticated drilling vessel.

Dean A. Dunn

Cross-References

The Abyssal Sea Floor, 1; Biostratigraphy, 173; Deep-Sea Sedimentation, 325; Micropaleontology: Microfossils, 1674; Ocean Basins, 1785; Deep Ocean Currents, 1792; Oceans: Carbonate Compensation Depths, 1855; Oil and Gas Exploration, 1878; Paleobiogeography, 1984; Paleoclimatology, 1993; Plate Tectonics, 2079; Sedimentary Mineral Deposits, 2296; Stratigraphic Correlation, 2485; Transgression and Regression, 2534.

OCEAN-FLOOR EXPLORATION

Field of study: Remote sensing

The exploration of the ocean floor by probes, submersibles, and remote-operated vehicles is a relatively recent human enterprise. Much of what is known about the floor of the oceans from its geography, the details of its geology, and its unique biology has been discovered since 1960.

Principal terms

ACOUSTIC ECHO SOUNDING: a method of determining the depth of the ocean floor; it measures the time of a reflected sound wave and relates that to distance

CARTOGRAPHY: the science of mapmaking; developing a map or chart of the ocean floor by linking the individual points of ocean-floor depths

CHEMOSYNTHESIS: the synthesis of organic substances by living organisms through the energy of chemical reactions

CORING DEVICES: devices that core into ocean-floor sediments to provide scientists with information on the composition of the seabed

FRACTURE ZONES: areas defining the edges between the continents on the sea floor

GEOMORPHIC DOMAIN: major underwater features that define the appearance of a sea-floor area

HYDROTHERMAL VENTS: vents of very hot water expelled from a volcanically active vent on the sea floor

REMOTELY OPERATED VEHICLE (ROV): a submersible operated from a remote location; for example, a robot that explores the sea floor while operated by tether from a surface ship

SOUNDING: the measurement of depth; a sounding line is a line used for the measurement of depth

TELEPRESENCE: the ability of a human to explore an area remotely by live television

Summary of the Phenomenon

Scientists know more about the surface of the moon than about the floor of the earth's oceans. The reason for this surprising lack of knowledge is twofold. First, more than half the planet lies at depths of more than 3 kilometers, greater than humans can explore at first hand. Second, engineering devices (manned or unmanned) that can travel to such great depths under positive control became technologically possible only relatively recently. Yet, from these remotely operated devices, scientists are discovering an often alien environment in a vast and unexplored landscape that covers three-quarters of the earth.

The first explorers of the ocean floor charted harbor basins by the topography they could actually see or from soundings taken with weighted lines—which represented only a tiny fraction of the earth's ocean bottom. The first recorded midocean sounding was accomplished by the Spanish explorer Ferdinand Magellan in 1521. He spliced two sounding lines together and lowered them over the side of his ship in the Tuamotu Archipelago until they ran out. Although the 365 meters of line did not reach bottom, Magellan immodestly declared that he had discovered the deepest part of the ocean. The first modern sounding was taken in 1840 in the South Atlantic, measuring a depth of 4,434 meters. The first map of the ocean floor was constructed using approximately 7,000 soundings in 1895. All these soundings were taken with line and weight, which was the only method available at that time to explore the ocean floor.

The first comprehensive ocean-floor soundings were made possible with the advent of acoustic echo sounding in 1920, but the method was not widely used until the 1940's. Considering every recorded sounding prior to World War II, there was, on the average, only one sounding per 2,500 square kilometers of ocean bottom. The use of submarines became widespread with the widening war in the 1940's; they had specific requirements to find out the exact extent of the ocean-floor topography. With the subsequent vast improvement of echo sounding and sonar technologies, a new age of exploration was engendered. By the early 1970's, a combination of satellite navigation (which enabled accurate geographical positioning of soundings) and precise echo sounders enabled a rapid charting of the ocean floor using a science called cartography. Sunlight does not penetrate to depths greater than about 100 meters under the very best of circumstances. Hence, for scientists to chart the geography of the sea floor, they must combine individual soundings to form sea-floor charts, ultimately covering vast, global areas.

A picture has developed of the sea floor that has revealed a widely variable seascape, at least as mutable as the continents but quite unlike above-water, continent-born landscapes. The underwater topography is unaffected by the powerful erosional forces found about the surface; the submarine world is shaped by forces that are unique to the oceans. The major submarine features (called the geomorphic domain) are deep-sea trenches, rifts (deep valleys with steep sides), flat-topped undersea volcanic cones, and fracture zones of very long linear cracks and fissures.

Oceanographic research ships have prowled the oceans for the past two centuries. Such ships as *Challenger*, *Discovery*, and *Endeavor* used lines and weights to determine depths. With a slight modification, they used the same lines and weights to carry sampling devices to the ocean floor to obtain specimens for later examination on the surface. Such remote-sensing devices were called coring devices, and some were complex enough to carry several types of sampling equipment, from water to temperature probes and even sea-life traps of various kinds. Nevertheless, all these sampling devices were not usually a part of a single probe and, more often than not, were sent down independently.

Humans have also studied the ocean floor personally, first as free divers, then using the breathing apparatus invented in the 1940's. Oxygen and nitrogen are toxic and dangerous even at 100 meters, however, thus limiting a diver with a self-contained breathing apparatus to above this level. Thus, it became necessary to invent manned submarines that could dive to deeper depths. These submarines are a form of remote-sensing device in that they shield the people within them from the tremendous ocean pressures by thick hulls.

Such a submarine capable of deep dives (as deep as 6,100 meters) is the *Alvin*. Like most submersibles of this type, *Alvin* has a robot hand that extends from the body to enable the operators inside to perform work outside the submarine. This famous submersible has also allowed investigators to observe life forms around submerged volcanic vents on the ocean floor. One of *Alvin*'s most famous dives was on the sunken hull of the *Titanic* in 4,000 meters of water in the North Atlantic. It was on this dive, however, that the limitations of such a manned submersible became apparent. The trip from the surface to the ocean floor alone required more than two hours and the same time to return. That limited the amount of time *Alvin* had to work on the ocean floor to merely a few hours.

Oceanographers and other scientists have thus been led to invent devices called remotely operated vehicles (ROVs). These devices perform work on the ocean floor with as much dexterity as a human inside a submersible. ROVs carry cameras with capabilities from still photo to live television. Some maneuver independently on tethers and have remotely operated arms. One inventor of such devices, and discoverer of the *Titanic*'s final resting place, is Robert Ballard of Woods Hole Oceanograhic Institution in Massachusetts. Ballard, with funding from the U.S. Navy and the National Geographic Society, invented three different types of remote-sensing ROVs for exploring the ocean floor. Ballard's ROVs include the *Argo*, a camera sled equipped with still and live cameras, mounted on a platform towed behind a surface ship. Others are the *Jason* and *Jason Junior*; *Jason Junior* rides to the ocean floor on *Jason*, then detaches and is capable of a wide range of movement. According to Ballard, such devices free humans from the inherent dangers of piloting manned submersibles to great depths, eliminate the excessive travel time from and to the surface, obviate the need for a complex manned vehicle, and give surface operators a "telepresence" on the ocean floor.

Applications of the Method

Undersea remote-sensing devices have revealed that the ocean floors are complex, distinctive, active landscapes with vast mountain ranges, plains, highlands, valleys, and active volcanic vents. Far from being a static, quiescent place, the ocean floor is a dynamic, constantly active geologic area of considerable interest to geologists.

The earth's continents drift across the planet in a slow, never-ending flux measured in billions of years; vital information describing this process may be found at the fracture zones that mark the boundaries between the earth's continental plates. On such fracture zones, most of the earth's earthquakes are centered. In addition, most of the planet's active volcanoes lie on the ocean floor. Only by extensive on-site study of these regions will scientists fully understand what they seek to know about the planet's earthquakes and volcanoes. Because the very character of the earth's crust is different at these continental boundaries (as opposed to the upper, higher regions of crust on the continents' surface levels), scientists need to study the nature of the active regions far below sea level.

At the fracture zones, magma from deep inside the earth wells up to near the surface, heating the cold seawater to very high temperatures (hot enough, in some cases, to melt lead) and spewing forth mineral-rich deposits from hydrothermal vents into the water. At these places, strange life forms have been discovered that do not rely on sunlight (photosynthesis) for their survival. They are entirely dependent on the minerals from the vents, surviving in a metabolic state called chemosynthesis. One of these creatures, called a tube worm, was discovered by Ballard in 1977 onboard the *Alvin* at a depth of 6,100 meters near hydrothermal vents off the Galápagos Islands. Such astonishing discoveries give rise to questions that challenge fundamental biological assumptions. For example, did the life forms evolve independently from surface, photosynthetically supported plants, and if so, what does that portend for the possibility of chemosynthetically evolved life throughout the universe? If such development is possible, then there may be vast reservoirs of life in the universe that have evolved in the absence of a neighbor star, long considered the most basic requirement for the development of life forms.

Exploration of the ocean floor has applications for the economies and energy needs of modern civilization. On the vast ocean-floor regions lie metal ores (such as manganese nodules) that may one day supply a significant percentage of industrial requirements for this resource. Also, a blanket of very cold water (near or slightly below freezing) lies on much of the ocean floor, which may one day be exploited for its energy transfer capacity in ocean thermal energy power plants.

Context

As spectacular as is the emergent image of the ocean floor derived from the millions of soundings taken thus far, it remains merely a coarse outline of the total picture of the underwater domain. As remote-sensing devices improve, five fundamental goals in addition to basic soundings will be accomplished: a more complete understanding of the extent and details of available resources on the ocean floor; an expansion of humankind's telepresence on the deep frontiers of the ocean floor effected from remote locations; continued exploitation of the available resources on the ocean floor, such as petroleum, mineral, and food resources; collection and categorization of a vast amount of basic scientific information on the geology, available energy, and biology of the sea floor; and ongoing exploration to discover and investigate life forms previously unknown or entirely unsuspected.

These discoveries will both enrich science's base of knowledge about the earth and make the ocean's resources available to the world's peoples. The technology developed to explore the ocean floor will also be employed in other scientific endeavors. For example, such remote-sensing capabilities will probably be adapted for use in space exploration.

Bibliography

Ballard, Robert D. *The Discovery of the Titanic*. New York: Warner Books, 1987. Ballard, as the world's leading expert on sea-floor ROVs and telepresence, describes the expedition that discovered the *Titanic*. The remote sensing of the ocean floor is discussed in detail, along with its future potential. A beautiful and important photographic work.

Busby, R. Frank. *Manned Submersibles*. Washington, D.C.: Office of the Oceanographer of the United States Navy, 1976. A detailed catalog of the world's submersibles and habitats. Describes all the deep-ocean vehicles and discusses their remote manipulating capabilities as well as other capabilities.

Dugan, James. *World Beneath the Sea*. Washington, D.C.: National Geographic Society, 1967. This colorful and well-illustrated text discusses the promise of exploring the oceans, from manned habitats to the oceans' deepest regions. Illustrates graphically the difficulties involved in ocean exploration.

Koblick, Ian G., and James W. Miller. *Living and Working in the Sea*. New York: Van Nostrand Reinhold, 1984. Although this work is primarily directed to sea-floor habitats, it offers a valuable discussion of the rigors of ocean floor exploration. Also discusses a wide range of ocean-floor exploration techniques and equipment. Of textbook quality, well indexed and illustrated.

O'Neill, Gerard K. *2081: A Hopeful View of the Human Future*. New York: Simon & Schuster, 1981. This work is normally associated with space exploration, but when referencing the potential of the world's oceans for energy and resource production, it emerges as a more well-rounded view of the future. An excellent and well-thought-out scenario of what the future will be like as shaped by technology, including what humankind will reap from the oceans.

Weiner, Jonathan Weiner. *Planet Earth*. New York: Bantam Books, 1986. This work gives an excellent accounting of historical sea-floor exploration, from the earliest voyages of *Challenger* and the first soundings that revealed the vast seascape below. A beautifully illustrated and well-indexed volume for all readers interested in the human exploration of planet Earth.

Wertenbaker, William. *The Floor of the Sea*. Boston: Little, Brown, 1974. This book gives an insightful and personal accounting of oceanographer Maurice Ewing and his search to understand the fundamental shape of the vast underwater regions of this planet. Discusses the great oceanographic vessels of history, their crews, and how they pieced together the geography and geology of the ocean floor.

Dennis Chamberland

Cross-References

OCEAN POWER

Type of earth science: Economic geology

Ocean power encompasses several distinctly different approaches to power generation which, if developed properly, promise potentially large amounts of clean, renewable energy. The importance of developing such alternate energy sources for a world largely dependent on fossil fuels possessing the drawbacks of escalating cost, ultimate exhaustibility, and environmental pollution cannot be overstressed.

Principal terms

MARINE BIOMASS ENERGY CONVERSION: the cultivation of marine plants such as algaes for conversion of the harvest into synthetic natural gas and other end products

MARINE CURRENT ENERGY CONVERSION: power from the transfer of kinetic energy in major ocean currents into usable forms, such as electricity

OCEAN THERMAL ENERGY CONVERSION: power derived from taking advantage of the significant temperature differences found in some tropical seas between the surface and deeper waters

OCEAN WAVE POWER: the use of wind-generated ocean surface waves to propel various mechanical devices incorporated as an electrical generating system

SALINITY GRADIENT ENERGY CONVERSION: power generated by the passage of water masses having different salinities through a special, semipermeable membrane, taking advantage of osmotic pressure to operate turbines

TIDAL FLOW POWER: power from turbines sited in coastal areas to take advantage of the daily rising and ebbing tidal flow

Summary of the Methodology

Attempts at harnessing ocean power involve the use of specialized technologies developed to exploit natural flows of energy within the marine environment. These energy flows are generated by the interaction of the ocean's waters with the effects of the sun's energy; the gravitational pull of other celestial bodies, such as the moon; and, to a much lesser extent, such influences as geothermal activity occurring on the sea bottom. Many engineering schemes have been devised to try to tap into each of these natural energy flows. All recognize the fact that the earth's surface is mostly ocean—71 percent of it is covered by the sea—and that this immense fluid environment is always in motion in response to an interplay of natural processes.

The most ambitious, and at the time of this writing most productive, ocean power schemes have been tidal power projects. The efficacy of these projects is dependent on how well engineered they are to take advantage of the key factors involved. These factors include the character of a tide at a particular coastal locale as determined by local bottom topography, surface coastline geography, and the orientation of the coast to the open sea. Submarine topographic influences can accentuate the rise of an incoming tide, acting like a wedge to lift the oncoming bulge of tidal water. Thus, tides can reach up to 15 meters on coasts having the right tide-enhancing topography and orientation. The maximum rise and fall of a tide as experienced in a particular location is important in tidal power, as it represents the amount of usable head; "head" is a term used in hydraulic engineering to describe the difference in elevation existing between the level at which water can flow by gravity down from an upper to a lower level, thus making itself available to do work. Unfortunately, only some one hundred coastal sites worldwide are classified as having significant head and thus are optimal candidates for tidal power installations. Scientists conservatively estimate that the global, dissipated tidal power amounts to 3 terawatts per year, or 3 trillion watts. Of this amount, perhaps only 0.04 terawatt would ever be exploitable from feasible tidal power sites.

All the other forms of ocean power are ultimately dependent, in one way or another, on the effect of the sun. The daily influx of solar energy makes the earth an immense heat engine. This engine is a closed system, with the sun being the primary, exterior input source. Scientists estimate that the potential energy in one day's quota of sunshine falling on the earth is equivalent to 100,000 times more energy than is presently produced by all electricity-generating plants now operating. On a yearly basis, this huge energy input is calculated to be roughly 178,000 terawatts. Much of this input is retained as heat energy in the world's oceans, estimated to be in the neighborhood of 3,000 terawatts per year. The oceans thus act as tremendous storage basins or heat sinks of solar energy, with the tropical seas significantly warmer than those at higher latitudes. Because of the process of convection at work within the oceans, water masses of varying temperatures and salinities are set in motion as they attempt to come into equilibrium. Large-scale ocean currents are products of huge convective cells circulating in the seas, guided by the rotation of the earth. Heat transfer of the absorbed solar energy proceeds on a global scale, with the cold, dense polar waters slowly sinking and traveling along the ocean bottoms toward the equator. Simultaneously, the warm, tropical surface waters flow in an opposite direction above, as demonstrated by such familiar, major flows as the Florida Current. The heat flow is interrupted and modified in various ways by the presence of continents, island chains, and extremes of ocean bottom topography.

This global pattern of heat transfer between the equatorial and polar regions also occurs, but at much faster rates, in the atmosphere and is the motive force behind the major, planetary wind patterns. The interaction of these wind patterns with the ocean's surface is the source of most surface ocean wave propagation, as well as a factor in surface water current creation and maintenance. In addition to the effects of wind generation, the global convective patterns also create, as mentioned, water masses possessing different salinities, which, in turn, are another factor determining the flow and mixing properties of ocean waters. Finally, the sum total of all the life forms inhabiting the seas, termed the marine biomass, also participate in the energy flow patterns. Various marine ecologies act as vectors or transient reservoirs of stored and processed solar energy. All of the above-described marine energy flow patterns, including the living component, have figured in various schemes to extract for human use some of the vast amounts of energy passing through these natural systems.

Applications of the Method

The French government has been the world pioneer in transforming tidal flow power engineering schemes into reality by constructing a large, functioning tidal energy station at the estuary of the La Rance River in Brittany in northern France. At this site, the government corporation Électricité de France has continually operated a 240-megawatt (240-million-watt) installation since 1967. The large tidal range of the estuary reaches a maximum of slightly more than 13 meters, which affects a large body of water comprising 23 square kilometers. This water is controlled through a dam built at a narrow point only 762 meters wide. At La Rance, a combination of factors produces a useful hydraulic head and has proven itself economically profitable for several decades. Twenty-four 10,000-kilowatt turbine generators operate within conduits inside the tidal dam, turning at the low speed of 94 revolutions per minute. The turbine blades are designed to operate bidirectionally, in response to either an incoming or an outgoing tide. Thus the French plant exploits the free tidal water movement almost continuously. Other nations, notably the Soviet Union, also have operational tidal flow generator stations. In 1968, the Soviet Union built a 0.04-megawatt installation in the northern region of the country at Kislaya Guba. Plans for installations far larger than La Rance exist, most as feasibility studies, in many other countries. One of the more significant plans, looked into by both Canada and the United States, is one designed to exploit the large tidal difference found in the Bay of Fundy in the Nova Scotia, Canada, area. Such a project is estimated to be able to supply the electrical needs of all of the cities of the United States' New England region.

Ranking next to tidal flow power in nearness to economic feasibility and actual, implementable technology is the ocean thermal energy conversion, or OTEC, approach. This method could ultimately be a very large-scale global operation, as many more sites exist that are usable for OTEC than are available for tidal power. Projected, theoretical limits to this energy source are in the neighborhood of 1 terawatt per year. OTEC involves either the construction of floating, open-ocean plants or coastal, land-based plants that exploit the temperature differences existing between water masses at varying depths in the tropical seas. Only small pilot plants have thus far been built, and they have never been run for more than short periods. A major project in Indonesia, however, involves the construction of a complex of four 100-megawatt plants that belong to the open-ocean, floating-plant category.

Calculations indicate that this plant, when completed, would produce electricity at a cost of only 8.2 cents per kilowatt hour. That compares very favorably with the cost breakdown of 11.7 cents per kilowatt hour for nuclear fission plants and 10.7 cents per kilowatt hour for coal-burning plants.

The optimal conditions for the most efficient OTEC sites have been calculated to be those where an 18-degree Celsius temperature difference exists between the surface and depths in the range of 600 to 1,000 meters. Regions of the ocean that meet or approach these thermal conditions have been identified as being, among others: Puerto Rico and the West Indies, the Gulf of Guinea, the Coral Sea, many of the Polynesian island groups, and the northwest African island groups. The actual process of converting the thermal difference found in such areas involves a system in which a turbine is turned by heat from the warm, surface water layer. The heat is transferred through devices termed heat exchangers, which introduce the thermal energy into a closed system. A working fluid such as ammonia, contained in sealed pipes, propels the system through the process of controlled convection. The warmed ammonia is heated to a vapor in an evaporator unit that drives the turbine. The used vapor is then conducted through a condenser unit where cold water drawn from below cools it down to a liquid state for another usage cycle. The cool water is brought into contact with the system by the deployment of a very long pipe, hundreds of meters in length, which projects down through the thermocline, or boundary, between the upper and lower water masses. Although the efficiency of the system is typically low, only 2-3 percent, the thermal reservoir is immense and is constantly replenished by the sun. To make such projects attractive economically, they need only be built on a sufficiently large scale.

Similar to OTEC in its use of the major oceanic flows of thermal energy are plans to exploit large-scale currents. One such current, the Gulf Stream—often called the Florida Current—constantly conveys many millions of gallons past a given point. One plan is a direct approach involving placing large turbines within the main flow of the current. Ideally, the generating site would be close to major electrical consumers such as coastal cities. A good case can be made for implementing marine current energy conversion along the eastern coast of Florida. The city of Miami, a very large consumer of electrical power, is washed on its doorstep by the Florida Current. This current is estimated to carry approximately 30 million cubic meters of water per second past the city at a rate sometimes reaching 2.5 meters per second. One scheme would involve anchoring a large cluster of special, very slow-speed turbines or water windmills to the bottom that would ride midwater in controlled buoyancy. This complex would function at a depth ranging from 30 to 130 meters and stretch some 20 kilometers across the flow of the Florida Current directly adjacent to Miami. Estimates of the power output of this array are on the order of 1,000 megawatts, provided constantly on a 24-hour, year-round basis. It would extract roughly 4 percent of the usable kinetic energy of the Florida Current at this point in its flow, which is calculated to be in the range of 25,000 megawatts. In addition to the Florida Current, other strong currents exist worldwide that may also be good potential sites for future turbine arrays.

Another way to take advantage of oceanic thermal flow is to utilize the kinetic energy of surface waves directly to power mechanical devices used to generate electricity. Unfortunately, until recently, all ocean surface wave power devices had been generally designed to deal with wave heights and strengths within a certain energy range. Beyond this range, the device, unless retrieved to shore, invariably suffered storm wave damage or destruction. A new approach to wave power device design has solved the drawbacks that have hitherto hindered practical surface wave energy application. It capitalizes on the fact that waves raise and lower buoyant objects. If the floating object is also long and perpendicular to the ocean surface, with most of its mass below the waterline, it is inherently stable and less subject to damage. Such a device is embodied in several variations of a wave-powered pump that is beginning to see practical economic applications. In one form, a large, vertical cylinder floats in the waves. Inside, the lower end is open to the lifting and sinking of the water level in unison with the wave motion. Because of its great length (tens of meters or more), it amplifies the wave motion in the column of air resting above the water. This motion propels air up and down through a double-flow electrical air turbine. As long as it remains in sufficiently deep water, it receives very little damage, no matter the magnitude of wave energy. A buoylike device floats at the cylinder top, keeping out wave splash and snugly maintaining inside air pressure. The cylinder can be anchored by flexible moorings to the sea bottom, and electrical cables can feed the power output to shore. Coastal-based variants have also been built solidly into rocky cliffs; they respond to wave-driven air pressure that enters from a conduit at its base. An example of the coastal-based type is now operating as a 500-kilowatt plant at Tostestallen in Norway. Numerous rocky coasts worldwide could be similarly utilized for wave power generation.

Yet another form of ocean power currently in use today is marine biomass energy conversion. This method involves the harvesting of large tracts of plants such as marine algaes. Like other plants, algaes use the process of photosynthesis to convert the sun's radiant energy into usable chemical energy. In the process, they manufacture various plant tissues that can be processed to yield useful compounds either for manufacturing ingredients or as fuel. In the case of algaes, the fuel would be in the form of methane. Estimates suggest that 10,000 kilowatts of electrical energy could be recoverable as methane from 2.6 square kilometers of a marine alga known as kelp. Up to a million dollars of other useful products can be extracted from the same amount of kelp. In addition to kelp farming for fuel, shallow, coastal basins can also be constructed or modified from natural sites to serve as depositories for sewage waste. Seawater could be introduced to the wastes along with special algaes that would use the sewage as food. The end product would be similar, after harvesting, to the kelp-methane fuel. Thus, sewage would become a recycled fuel instead of an eyesore and a marine pollutant.

A form of ocean power that has been envisioned but not implemented is the use of salinity gradients within the sea. This idea is still in the theoretical stage, because of the lack of key materials necessary for the effective technologies to work. A major drawback at this point is the lack of appropriately tough and efficient synthetic membranes necessary for this energy to be economically practical. Salinity gradient energy works on the principle of extracting energy from osmotic pressure by the use of semipermeable membranes. Such membranes would most likely be fabricated from some type of plastic possessing the correct, chemical properties and would take advantage of osmotic pressure between water masses having different percentages of dissolved salts. Influenced by osmotic pressure, less salty water will naturally flow through a semipermeable membrane to the side of greater salinity. The membrane would therefore be designed to be permeable to the fresher water but impermeable to the saltier water. Osmotic pressure would therefore propel a controlled, one-way flow that could be employed to propel water-driven turbines for electricity.

Context

Global human population growth is still explosively on the rise, especially in the Third World countries. In hand with population growth is increasing, worldwide urbanization and industrialization. Because of these trends, consumption of energy to run manufacturing processes, transportation, food production, climate control, and communication systems has escalated dramatically. The trend has not peaked, and extrapolative studies predict an ever-increasing need for more energy. Coupled with this ravenous energy use are the by-products of mounting energy consumption: widespread pollution and a general degradation of the world environment. Delicate ecosystems are irrevocably altered or even destroyed by the direct or indirect effects of rising energy usage. The greenhouse effect and the destruction of the life-protecting ozone layer may be directly attributable to rising energy needs and associated chemical pollutants. The world industrial society already faces the specter of diminishing energy sources and the eventual, ultimate exhaustion of all fossil fuels. New energy sources, such as the nuclear option, seem to possess, so far, many drawbacks to widespread usage.

Renewable energy sources that are clean and have a low impact on the quality of the environment are the ideal long-term solutions. Some alternate energy forms fitting this description are either technically feasible today or almost so. The various forms of ocean power that have been actually developed or are in theoretical stages are excellent candidates for helping to alleviate some of the world's more pressing energy-related problems. For at least some geographic areas, ocean power is not only an efficient, clean power source but also economically competitive with fossil fuels or even nuclear power. Tidal flow power is an excellent example of the increasing viability of some forms of ocean power. Wave flow power and OTEC seem to be on the verge of realistic usage and more widespread acceptance as alternatives. All forms of ocean power represent a way of living in harmony with the environment that still offers the option of maintaining a high level of technical civilization.

Bibliography

Bascom, Willard. *Waves and Beaches: The Dynamics of the Ocean Surface*. Garden City, N.Y.: Anchor Press/Doubleday, 1980. An excellent introduction to the subject of oceanography, this book emphasizes the role of wave and beach processes. A very useful chapter devoted to energy from marine sources is included which objectively presents the pros and cons of ocean power. Well illustrated throughout. Suitable for all readers wishing a working knowledge of the physical oceanographic processes involved.

Carr, Donald E. *Energy and the Earth Machine*. New York: W. W. Norton, 1976. A thorough survey of the primary energy sources that power the industrial world, including the fossil fuels. Ocean power sources are dealt with within the scope of water-derived energy sources in general. Suitable for high school students or anyone wishing a general background on the subject.

Constans, Jacques A. *Marine Sources of Energy*. Elmsford, N.Y.: Pergamon Press, 1980. An excellent treatment of the subject of ocean power, this book dwells on each subcategory in an easy-to-read and enlightening manner. Richly provided with explanatory diagrams, tables, drawings, and maps, which help explain the concepts involved. Appropriate for all readers, high school and above, especially those interested in the technical problems of ocean engineering.

Gage, Thomas E., and Richard Merrill, eds. *Energy Primer, Solar, Water, Wind, and Biofuels*. 2d ed. New York: Dell Publishing, 1978. Similar to hands-on books such as *The Whole Earth Catalog*, this source provides a wealth of information for those interested in the actual "nuts and bolts" involved in implementing alternate energy technologies. Suitable for those with an interest in the subject beyond the theoretical aspect.

Gashus, O. K., and T. J. Gray, eds. *Tidal Power*. New York: Plenum Press, 1972. One of the very best books devoted exclusively to the generation of power through tidal ocean flow, it includes details of the design and operating problems of the large-scale facility at La Rance, France, and the proposed facilities at the Bay of Fundy in Nova Scotia, Canada. Suitable for readers at the college level or above.

Meador, Roy. *Future Energy Alternatives*. Ann Arbor, Mich.: Ann Arbor Science Publishers, 1979. A well-written survey of all the major alternatives to fossil fuels, including the ocean power options. The author assumes no technical background and expertly introduces the general reader to each energy alternative in turn. An excellent book for the high school or college student as well as for the post-academic adult with a curiosity about energy alternatives.

Teller, Edward. *Energy from Heaven and Earth*. San Francisco: W. H. Freeman, 1979. A good comparison of the major forms of energy used by the industrialized world and the social and economic consequences of their use, it also offers extensive discussions of energy-use policies and their bearing on the development of new energy sources. A worthwhile introduction to the overall energy picture for students or interested laypersons.

Wilson, Mitchell, and the editors of *Life*. *Energy*. New York: Time, 1963. A profusely illustrated overview of the subject of energy. An easy-to-read text outlines the history of energy-related physics and the growth of applied technology designed to exploit energy sources. Suitable for any reader at the high school level or beyond.

Frederick M. Surowiec

Cross-References

The Atmosphere's Global Circulation, 121; Climate, 217; Coastal Processes and Beaches, 240; Heat Sources and Heat Flow, 1065; Hydroelectric Power, 1095; Ocean-Atmosphere Interactions, 1779; Deep Ocean Currents, 1792; Surface Ocean Currents, 1798; Ocean Waves, 1839; Earth Resources, 2175; Future Resources, 2182; Sea Level, 2267; Seawater Composition, 2282; Storms, 2477; Wind, 2730.

THE OCEAN RIDGE SYSTEM

Type of earth science: Geology
Field of study: Tectonics

The ocean ridge system is a complex chain of undersea volcanic mountains that are found in all the oceans. These mountains contain rift valleys along their axes, which are believed to be spreading centers from which continental motion takes place. All existing evidence, such as volcanic activity, the flow of heat from within the earth, and various types of faulting and rifting, supports modern theories about sea-floor spreading, tectonic plates, and continental drift.

Principal terms

ASTHENOSPHERE: a zone of rock within the mantle that has plastic flow properties attributable to intense heat
BASALT: a heavy, dark-colored volcanic rock
CONVERGING PLATES: a tectonic plate boundary where two plates are pushing toward each other
DIVERGENT PLATES: a tectonic plate boundary where two plates are moving apart
METALLOGENESIS: the process by which metallic ores are formed
SEDIMENTS: the solid fragments of rock that have been eroded from other rocks and then transported by wind or water and deposited
TECTONIC PLATES: according to theory, the seven major plates into which the earth's crust is divided

Summary of the Phenomenon

The ocean ridge system is a complex chain of mountains about 80,000 kilometers in length that winds through the ocean basins. These mountain ranges vary from a few hundred to a few thousand kilometers in width and have an average relief of 0.6 kilometer. Studies of the sea floor indicate that ocean ridges are found in every major ocean basin. They are composed of basalt and covered by various types of sediments. Many of the ridges have narrow depressions that extend thousands of kilometers along their axes. Heat probes lowered into these rifts indicate much higher temperatures than on the flanks of the ridges. Another very significant finding has been that the rocks that make up the sea floor are much younger than those that make up the continents. This finding countered the pre-1960's belief that the rocks of the ocean basin are more ancient than those of the continents.

In the 1960's, the theory of sea-floor spreading suggested that new sea floor is constantly being added by volcanic activity at the ocean ridges. The theory of plate tectonics proposes that the earth's crust is divided into several major plates. These plates extend down into the earth's mantle to a hot, semimolten zone known as the asthenosphere. Since the rock that composes the tectonic plates is less dense than is the rock that forms the mantle, the plates may be considered to be floating on the asthenosphere. Because the interior of the earth is much hotter than the surface, a flow of heat toward the surface is a constant process. This method of heat transfer, known as convection, is a density type of current. Material such as molten rock or hot air or water is less dense than is the same material in a cooler state. As a result, it flows upward with cooler material filling in below. When the hot material reaches a higher level and releases its heat, it too returns to the depths to be reheated. It is this process, along with the relatively low density of the tectonic plates, which causes the plates to drift apart.

The location and symmetry of the mid-ocean ridges, especially in the Atlantic and Indian oceans, suggests the configuration of the continents before they began to drift apart. The modern theories of plate tectonics and sea-floor spreading are in basic agreement with the theory of continental drift as proposed by Alfred Wegener in 1915; however, modern ideas regarding the mechanics of drift differ. The basic concept of sea-floor spreading at the oceanic ridges proposes that tension cracks form in the crust at these spreading centers. Molten rock from the mantle then flows upward through these fissures forming both the volcanic ridges and creating new sea floor. As the fissures widen, new crustal material moves away on both sides and additional new sea floor is created. It is in this way that the mid-ocean ridges such as the Mid-Atlantic Ridge, the East Pacific Rise, the Antarctic Rise, and the Carlsberg Ridge of the Indian Ocean were formed. The spreading away from the oceanic ridges takes place at a rate of about 2 centimeters per year in the Atlantic and about 5 centimeters per year in the Pacific.

As new sea floor is being created at the ridges, old sea floor is being destroyed at continental margins. Here, old sea floor is subducted beneath continental plates. At these converging plate boundaries, old sea floor is forced downward into the mantle, where it undergoes remelting. This molten rock may then find its way back to the surface through cracks or fissures in the overlying rock. Volcanic action is the result of this material reaching the earth's surface. Because old sea floor is destroyed in this manner, it is now understood why rocks that make up the ocean floor are relatively young. Deep-sea-floor drilling projects in the Atlantic and Indian oceans have failed to find rock or fossil samples that are older than the Jurassic period of earth history, which ended about 140 million years ago.

The present ocean ridges show large offsets in some areas. This phenomenon results from transform faulting. As spreading of the plates took place at divergent boundaries, fracture zones developed at right angles to the axes of the ridges. Displacements of the ridges along these faults produced the observed structure.

The narrow rift valleys are believed to have been caused by downfaulting along divergent plate boundaries. Some rift zones, such as the one associated with the Carlsberg Ridge of the northern Indian Ocean, link up with continental rift zones. This rift has been shown to be connected with the African rift zone. Studies conducted during the 1970's indicate that there exist extensive amounts of volcanism and seismic activity along rift zones. Also found along oceanic ridges are hot-water springs. The existence of these springs, or smokers, had been predicted, but direct evidence for them was not gathered until the early 1960's, when metal-bearing sediments were discovered on the East Pacific Rise. The first actual observation of a smoker took place in 1980 by the crew of the deep-diving research submarine *Alvin*. The *Alvin* was part of an underwater research program being conducted near the Galápagos spreading center in the eastern Pacific. Researchers were surprised to find a rather extensive plant and animal community living near the smoker at a depth too great for photosynthesis to be a factor. Clams as long as 30 centimeters were found, as well as white crabs and tube worms some 3 meters long.

Smokers have been found to emit great quantities of sulfur-enriched waters. Dissolved within the acidic water are various types of metals. These metals are dissolved from the rocks as the superheated water moves toward the surface. Metals such as copper, zinc, iron, silver, and gold are extracted and concentrated into a supersaturated fluid. When this fluid is discharged from a smoker at the sea floor, it will precipitate to form an ore body if cooling takes place rapidly. These massive sulfide deposits are sometimes made permanent when volcanic eruptions cover them with basalt flows.

Although most of the knowledge regarding the nature of the sea bottom has been gained since the 1960's, the Mid-Atlantic Ridge system has been known to exist since echo-sounding studies were done after World War I. By 1960, it had been determined that the Mid-Atlantic Ridge was continuous with other oceanic ridge systems around the world. The same cannot be said of the rift system that was discovered in the Mid-Atlantic Ridge. Profiles taken across ridge systems do not always indicate such rift depressions. This anomaly can probably be explained by considering the possibility that these rifts have been filled with volcanic material and therefore go undetected.

A rather extensive study was made along the Mid-Atlantic Ridge about 200 miles south of the Azores in 1974. It was found that the rift valley is bordered by a series of steep slopes that appear to be high-angle faults. Many open vertical fissures were observed, some of them as much as 8 meters across. Although no active volcanism was observed during this study, mounds of pillow lava along the fissures indicated that volcanism had taken place. The positioning of the faults and fissures indicated that the Mid-Atlantic Ridge is spreading outward east and west from its central axis.

The East Pacific Rise, which is part of the system of mid-ocean ridges, stands some 2 to 3 kilometers above the ocean floor and is thousands of kilometers wide. The slopes in this area are not as great as those of the Mid-Atlantic system, but the mechanism of ridge formation is the same. It has been suggested that part of the East Pacific Rise extends under the North American continent and that the San Andreas fault may be part of this system. Evidence supporting this possibility is that the rate of displacement along the fault is comparable to the rate of ridge spreading on the East Pacific Rise near the Gulf of California.

Methods of Study

The ocean floor has been investigated by the use of sonar since the early 1900's:

Sound waves from a device are sent into the sea in all directions. As these waves strike an object, they are reflected back to the source. By analyzing the reflections, scientists are able to determine the nature of the sea floor. This technique was refined during World War II for the purpose of locating enemy submarines. By the early 1950's, new maps and charts of the sea floor had been made using sonar.

In the 1960's, a plan to drill a deep hole through the crust of the earth to the mantle was proposed. Since this deep hole was to intersect the Mohorovičić discontinuity (named after the Croation geologist who discovered it, Andrija Mohorovičić), the project was called Mohole. Since the crust of the earth is much thinner under the ocean basins than it is under the continents, the ocean was the most logical location in which to drill. Although the 6-kilometer-deep hole was never drilled, several preliminary holes were. Samples taken from this drilling revealed the presence of gray claylike sediments overlying dark heavy basalts. Project Mohole has since been replaced by a plan to drill many holes at various locations into the rock beneath the ocean depths. This project, which is under the direction of various American oceanographic institutes, is known as the Deep Sea Drilling Project. Much of the drilling was done from the deck of the now-retired *Glomar Challenger* of the company Global Marine, Incorporated. More than six hundred holes have been drilled in the Atlantic, Pacific, and Indian oceans and the Mediterranean Sea, revealing a wealth of data on the nature and evolution of the ocean basins.

In the past, ocean researchers have had to gather data from the decks of ships by lowering various tools to the bottom to gather samples—there was a need for direct observation by the oceanographer. In 1948, the first minisubmarine, or bathyscaphe, made an unmanned dive to 759 meters. In 1954, a manned vessel was taken to a depth of 4,050 meters. By 1960, interest in these submersibles grew quickly in the United States. Since that time, submersibles such as the *Aluminaut* and *Alvin* have been used in various deep-sea research projects. Submersibles have been used for on-site studies of the rift zone of the Mid-Atlantic Ridge and of the hot-spring smokers of the East Pacific Rise.

Another technique known as marine seismology has been employed to study the ocean ridges. Because oil companies have used seismic studies for more than half a century in the exploration for oil deposits on continents, it was only a matter of time before this technology would be adapted for study of the ocean depths. The process involves the making of a sound explosion in the sea, which is accomplished by the use of an air gun. The sound waves are produced by the rapid release of compressed air. The waves then travel through the water to the bottom, where they are reflected to seismometers located on the ocean floor. The data are collected and a seismogram is generated by a computer. This technique has been used to locate active magma chambers in rift zone areas.

Context

Studies of submarine rift areas have revealed the hot-water springs that are referred to as smokers. Smokers discharge water that contains sulfur in solution as well as various types of metals such as copper, iron, zinc, silver, and gold. These metals precipitate to the sea bottom and, if they are cooled rapidly enough, form deposits. If the ore bodies are covered with volcanic material shortly after their deposition, they become protected from the erosive processes of seawater. In time, these deposits drift from oceanic spreading centers to become parts of continents. Many mineral deposits formed in just this manner have been mined since ancient times.

In the late 1950's, metal-rich sediments were first found along mid-ocean ridges. By the late 1960's, metalliferous muds were found at the bottom of the Red Sea, the Gulf of California, and the East Pacific Rise near the Galápagos Islands and south of Baja, California. Since 1977, marine geologists have been able actually to observe the formation of metal deposits while observing smokers from the research submarine *Alvin*. Interest in ridge deposition of metals centers on the processes of metallogenesis. Mining of such deposits, however, even with advanced technology, is not profitable. It will no doubt be considered in the future, however, as the copper deposits in the area of the Galápagos spreading center alone are estimated to be worth in excess of $2 billion.

Bibliography

Anderson, Roger N. *Marine Geology: An Adventure into the Unknown*. New York: John Wiley & Sons, 1986. A well-written, somewhat technical volume on the geology of the oceans. Contains excellent chapters on metallogenesis and mineral deposits. This volume is suitable for the college student of geology or the informed layperson.

Compton, R. R. *Interpreting the Earth*. New York: Harcourt Brace Jovanovich, 1977. A volume suitable for the layperson, it covers general topics in geology. Well illustrated.

Dott, Robert H., and Roger L. Batten. *Evolution of the Earth*. 4th ed. New York: McGraw-Hill, 1988. A well-illustrated volume dealing with topics in historical geology. Suitable for the high school or college freshman student of geology.

Edyll, C. P. *Exploring the Ocean World*. New York: Thomas Y. Crowell, 1972. A collection of papers on topics such as chemistry, physics, and biology of the oceans, underwater archaeology, and marine ecology and pollution. Suitable for the general reader.

Shepard, F. P. *Submarine Geology*. New York: Harper & Row, 1973. A technical volume dealing with such topics as methods and instrumentation of oceanic study, sediments and sedimentation, plate tectonics, erosive processes, and sea-bottom topography, stratigraphy, and deposits. Suitable for the college-level student of geology or oceanography.

Skinner, B. J., and S. C. Porter. *The Dynamic Earth*. New York: John Wiley & Sons, 1989. A well-written, well-illustrated volume dealing with general topics in physical geology such as rocks, minerals, erosion, earth resources, sedimentation, and tectonics. Ideal for the college-level introductory physical geology course.

Weiner, Jonathan. *Planet Earth*. New York: Bantam Books, 1986. A well-illustrated volume dealing with general topics in the earth sciences. The companion to the Public Broadcasting Service (PBS) television series of the same name. Suitable for the general reader.

Wicander, R., and J. S. Monroe. *Historical Geology*. New York: West Publishing, 1989. A very well-illustrated volume dealing with such subjects as geologic time, origin and interpretation of sedimentary rocks, and a detailed account of the historical geology of the earth through various time periods. Excellent for a first-year college course in historical geology.

David W. Maguire

Cross-References

Continental Rift Zones, 275; Hydrothermal Mineralization, 1108; Igneous Rock Bodies, 1131; Igneous Rocks: Basaltic, 1158; Lithospheric Plates, 1387; Crystallization of Magmas, 1420; The Origin of Magmas, 1428; Sub-Sea-Floor Metamorphism, 1614; Ocean Basins, 1785; The Oceanic Crust, 1846; Plate Margins, 2063; Plate Motions, 2071; Plate Tectonics, 2079; Subduction and Orogeny, 2497; Volcanism at Spreading Centers, 2607.

OCEAN TIDES

Type of earth science: Oceanography

Tides are the displacements of particles on earth, caused by the differential attraction of the moon and the sun. There are atmospheric tides, land or crustal tides, and ocean tides. Of these, ocean tides are the most apparent, because the ocean, as a fluid, is more easily stretched out of shape by the pull of the moon.

Principal terms

BASINS: container-like places on the ocean floor, usually elliptical, circular, or oval in shape, varying in depth and size

BORE: a wall of incoming tidal waters

DIURNAL TIDE: having only one high tide and one low tide each lunar day; tides on the Gulf of Mexico are diurnal

MIXED TIDE: having the characteristics of diurnal and semidiurnal tidal oscillations; these tides are found on the West Coast of the United States

NEAP TIDE: a tide with the minimum range, or when the level of the high tide is at its lowest

OSCILLATION: an up-and-down or back-and-forth swinging motion

RANGE: the difference between the high-tide water level and the low-tide water level

SEMIDIURNAL: having two high tides and two low tides each lunar day

SPRING TIDE: a tide with the maximum range, occurring when lunar and solar tides reinforce each other, a few days after the full and new moons

Summary of the Phenomenon

Each particle in the ocean moves in response to the force of gravitational attraction exerted on it by both sun and moon. Although the sun is 27 million times the size of the moon, the moon is the primary factor in the ebb and flow of ocean waters. In fact, the moon's power is more than double the periodic tidal-stretching force exerted by the sun, because it is much closer to the earth. This is explained by Sir Isaac Newton's universal law of gravity, which states that a force is proportionate to the mass of the attracting body, but its power of attraction diminishes in proportion to the square of the distance. Thus, nearness counts for more than distant mass in solar and lunar relations with the earth.

In order to explain how tides are caused, tidal scientists use the concept of a theoretical "equilibrium tide." This concept is based on an ideal in which the ocean waters are always in static equilibrium and in which no continents obstruct the flow of water on the earth's surface. When the moon is directly above a particular location, its force of attraction causes water bulges to pile up directly under the moon, and also on the opposite side of the earth, where the bottom of the ocean is pulled closer to the moon than is the surface of that area. Meanwhile, in the opposite quadrants of the globe, two low-water troughs result from the pull of the water away from these areas. Thus, the earth rotates beneath tidal bulges and troughs, which result in high and low tides.

Tides generally follow the lunar day, which is twenty-four hours and fifty minutes, or the time it takes the moon to orbit the earth. Some complex tidal cycles, however, result from the combined influences of sun and moon. If there were no moon, the sun's influence alone would cause tides to occur at the same time each day; however, because the plane of the moon's orbit around the earth is in a different plane from that of the earth's orbit around the sun, mixtures of full diurnal and semidiurnal tides result. In most areas, semidiurnal tides are the rule, with high and low tides occurring twice each lunar day, averaging twelve hours and twenty-five minutes apart. Full diurnal tides occur when only one high tide and one low tide take place in a lunar day, such as in the Gulf of Mexico. Mixed tides result from a combination of both diurnal and semidiurnal tidal oscillations. Such tides are found in the Pacific and Indian oceans.

Other factors which contribute to the variability of ocean tides are the phases of the moon, the position of sun and moon relative to the earth, and the latitude and topography of the tide's location on earth. When the sun, moon, and earth are aligned (in "conjunction" or "opposition"), then the combined gravitational effects of these bodies will exert additional pull on the earth, resulting in increased tidal amplitude. This phenomenon, when lunar and solar tides reinforce each other, is called spring tide and occurs around the full and new moons. In between the spring tides, a neap (from the word "nip") tide takes place when the sun and moon and earth are positioned at the apexes of a triangle. At this time, during the first and third quarters of the moon's phase, solar high tides are superimposed on lunar low tides, so resulting tides are the lowest in the month. In the open ocean, spring tides may be more than 1 meter (approximately 4 feet) high, while neap tides may be less than a meter (only 2 feet). Tidal amplitude will also vary, depending on latitude. Near the poles, tides can range to 15 meters or more in height. Around the equator, however, the difference between high and low tides is generally a matter of centimeters.

Despite the complexity of the many variables which determine tidal behavior, tidal scientists can now predict the time and height of a tide anywhere, on any past or future date, given one condition: that they have sufficient information on how the local topography of the site modifies the tide. Local geographical conditions such as the width of a bay's mouth, the uneven slope of the bottom, the depth of the body of water—these are the features that determine the range, amplitude, and time of the local tide. Why does the island of Nantucket experience a difference of no more than a foot between high and low water, while only a few hundred miles away, the Bay of Fundy has the highest tides in the world, with a rise of 15 meters during spring tides? Scientists have developed a theory of tidal oscillation which holds that the ocean is divided up among a great many basins of water, each with its own depth, length, and resulting period of oscillation. The boundaries of each basin are determined by the surrounding land above and below the ocean, and the influences of gravitational attraction in each are always changing, as are the currents which flow in. Ordinarily, when water rocks up and down in a basin, the water at the rim is most active, while the least amount of motion occurs in the center of the basin, around a tideless node. Thus, the physical dimensions of these basins determine the period of oscillation of the waters throughout the basin.

When the pull of the moon creates a high tide on the side of the earth closest to it, why should a high tide occur simultaneously on the opposite side? Logically, one would not expect this to be the case. To answer that, it is necessary to know that the moon and the earth revolve not only around each other but also around a common center of gravity located 1,600 kilometers below the surface of the earth. As the earth-moon system revolves, the centrifugal force stretches the oceans out into space, but the earth's gravity keeps the oceans from actually flying off. At its center, the earth is not still, but is moving in a circle which is a small fraction of the size of the moon's orbit. This invisible revolution of the earth around the moon produces a centrifugal force throughout the earth, which varies as the moon revolves and pulls the earth's surface out of shape. It is the resulting "prolate," or lemon-shaped, elongations of the earth which are observed as the tides. The tides nearest the moon are caused by gravitational attraction. On the side of the earth farthest from the moon, however, the centrifugal force is greater than the pull of the moon. To compound the complexity of the situation, the moon's gravitational force is also pulling the ocean floor of that area away from the waters there. Thus, high tides are produced on both sides of the earth opposite the moon.

Because tides are actually long waves, an observer on the moon might expect to see the two tidal bulges move around the earth at a speed consistent with the pace of the moon. Instead, he sees the tidal waves moving out of step with the moon. Keeping pace with the moon would be possible on two conditions: if the oceans of the world were 22 kilometers deep (whereas they average a bit more than 3 kilometers deep) and if there were no continents obstructing the movement of tidal waves. Thus, the speed of the movement of the tides is only 1,100 to 1,300 kilometers per hour, and the tides do not keep up with the moon as it travels westward around the terrestrial globe.

The impact of the ocean waters' backlash against the world's coastlines has been shown to cause more than erosion or navigational difficulties. According to the theory of G. H. Darwin, the friction caused by ocean tides actually slows the rotation of the earth. The result of the earth revolving more slowly is that the moon is allowed to recede to a higher orbit, and with the moon gradually growing more distant, at a rate of 4 centimeters a year, the months are getting longer, though not noticeably so. To put this in perspective, researchers say that within the last 120,000 years, the length of a day has increased by one to two seconds. In a million years, the tidal energy produced at the expense of the earth's rotation will have pushed the moon away and made the months on earth much longer. A result of the changing distance between the earth and moon is that tidal potential is also changing. As the moon recedes, it has less influence on the earth, and the tidal range diminishes. In the past and future history of tides, it could be said that during the early days on earth, tides were at their peak in power and range, with mighty deluges barraging places which today experience only a few centimeters of change between high and low waters. When the moon was half the distance from the earth that it is today, it would have wielded eight times the tide-producing force it has today, creating a possible tidal range of several hundred meters. Looking to the distant future, eons of tidal friction will slow the earth's rotation and allow the moon to recede until it takes the moon much longer to complete its orbit. The time will come when the length of a month and the length of a day will be the same. This will mean the end of lunar tides.

Methods of Study

Tides are not simple to predict. Qualitative prediction of the tides has been going on in harbors around the world for centuries, but quantitative prediction began in the past century, when men first designed tide-predicting machines to help forecast the tides. The first such machine was invented in 1872 by Lord Kelvin, who is often referred to as the first electrical engineer. Kelvin's machine was capable of drawing a line picture of the curve of the tide, and for this achievement he was knighted. Soon after this breakthrough, an employee of the United States Coast and Geodetic Survey invented a tide-predicting machine that showed the times and heights of the tides. More recently, the Survey designed a simpler machine which combines the capabilities of both previous inventions: It gives the curve of the tides as well as the times and the heights of the tides. Unfortunately, these machines are not completely reliable because other factors, such as heavy storms, winds, or accumulation of sand as a result of wave action, can have dramatic impact on the water levels. Tide tables can only give the approximate high and low tides.

Today, tide-predicting machines have been replaced by faster digital computers. Nevertheless, tidal analysis still involves long, complex computations, and predictions can be made only for places where a long series of observations are available. For each given spot on earth, and for given time intervals, observations must be made which provide the value of the gravitational acceleration, the deflection of the vertical, and the measurements for the elevation of the water level. With this set of numbers in hand, the matter of prediction becomes one of extrapolating from the past into the future. Thus, around the coasts of the world, in inlets, in tidal rivers, and on islands, the water levels caused by tidal forces are carefully recorded. These measurements are analyzed locally. Once these measurements of the water level of a given place are taken within specified time intervals, the phases and amplitudes of the tide can be determined by a number of mathematical methods. Then, knowing the phases and amplitudes, scientists can reproduce the measurements according to a harmonic series (a series of terms whose reciprocals form an arithmetic progression, 1, $\frac{1}{2}$, $\frac{1}{3}$, . . . $\frac{1}{n}$). This harmonic method is a fairly reliable means of tidal prediction for deep-water ports, but in shallow-water areas, nonharmonic methods may need to be used. Finally, a determination of harmonic constants is made by national authorities, and the resulting data are sent to the International Hydrographic Bureau in Monaco. As a result, hydrographic offices in countries around the globe publish tide tables forecasting the high- and low-water times and water heights for the world's ports.

The problem of the measurement of tidal displacements in the open ocean has yet to be solved. This situation results from the fact that tidal sea-level records pertain primarily to the coastal locations, and there are few or no measurements from the open ocean.

Context

Knowledge of ocean tides serves crucial purposes in the fields of navigation, coastal engineering, and tidal power generation. In addition, it holds a key position in relation to geophysics, marine geodesy, and astronomy.

Tides are of vital importance in navigation. Although the tides have become tamer, they still both help and hinder all mariners. The *Coast Pilots and Sailing Directions* for different parts of the world reveals the menacing possibilities which tides in various places are known to cause. Tidal currents often move violently when opposed by winds or confined in narrow channels. Men have been swept off boats by the onslaught of giant waves when sailing in a flood tide through narrow straits. At certain stages of the tide, the waters can have dangerous eddies, whirlpools, or bores. A bore is created when a large portion of the flood tide enters a channel at once as one wave. Bores are walls of water which can be highly destructive and dangerous. Wherever they occur, they control the schedule of all shipping, as well as the rhythm of harbor life in the area. Even where there are no bores, the largest oceangoing liner must wait for slack water before entering a harbor where rushing tidal currents can fling it against piers. Since it is to the ship's advantage to sail in the direction of the tidal current flow, knowledge of tides is invaluable. All navigators approaching a coast rely on tide tables to supplement the information on depths in their nautical charts.

Coastal-engineering work is dependent on knowledge of the tides for such undertakings as the management of tidal estuaries, construction of harbors, and damming of tidal rivers. Another practical aspect of tide information concerns the handling of problems that arise from the pollution of coastal waters and the ocean.

Tidal power generation is a new field which has gained increasing attention because of the shortage of available energy sources. Humans have long dreamed of harnessing the tidal forces for their energy needs. In 1966, the first tidal power station ever built was completed in the La Rance estuary in France. Construction of the project took place just after the Suez crisis, when France felt uncertain about the future of its oil supply. The half-mile Rance Dam was built to harness energy from the very large tides of the area—with a mean range of nearly 8.5 meters and rising to more than 13 meters at equinoctial spring tides. This power installation transmits electricity to Paris and the surrounding area, producing more than 580 billion watt-hours of energy a year but costing slightly more than the cost of operation of hydroelectric plants. In 1968, the Soviet Union finished construction on a 400-kilowatt tidal plant north of Murmansk, at a site where the maximum tide is less than 4 meters in height. In China, more than forty small tidal plants have been built, according to dated reports. Plans for an additional eighty-eight more include one which will be China's largest and will be sited where a famous bore occurs. In the United States, at Passamaquoddy Bay in Maine, a major tidal power plant project was abandoned, because of the expense of maintaining the pipes and machinery in salt water, and of transmitting the electricity generated to the nearest big users.

Additional areas of practical concern involving tides include the correlation of tides with earthquakes, volcanic eruptions, and geyser activity. Some scientists believe that tides trigger earthquakes. In 1975, one study reported that tidal stresses seem to cause specific kinds of large earthquakes which occur within the top 30 kilometers of the earth's crust. The evidence is as yet inconclusive; however, the correlation of clusters of smaller earthquakes with the force of the ocean tides may prove useful in the prediction of disasters because these smaller earthquakes often occur just before larger ones and could serve as a forewarning of what is to come. Other studies conclude that tides have caused certain volcanic eruptions and have a regulating influence on the fluctuations of geyser activity. Thus, the influence of tides extends not only to these areas yet to be fully researched but also to the future of the earth-moon system and even to the length of the days and months on earth.

Bibliography

Clemons, Elizabeth. *Waves, Tides, and Currents*. New York: Alfred A. Knopf, 1967. Written for young adults, this book will appeal to interested nonscientists of all ages. Complexities of tidal phenomena are lucidly explained and read like a story. Includes photographs and easy-to-understand diagrams, a bibliography, and a glossary.

Freuchen, Peter. *Peter Freuchen's Book of the Seven Seas*. New York: Julian Messner, 1957. A well-written general-interest book which gives a very clear explanation of the tides. It includes scientific explanations for laypersons of all ages, as well as folklore and history as the author imagined it. An entertaining book full of photographs.

Godin, Gabriel. *The Analysis of Tides*. Toronto: University of Toronto Press, 1972. This book is primarily a study of the mathematical principles underlying the analysis of the tides, but it covers the origin of tidal phenomena and the measurement of time, which is intimately related to celestial motion. The book contains an excellent chapter on Newtonian mechanics and celestial motion. Suitable for college-level students who want to gain a more technical knowledge of the tides.

Gregory, R. L., ed. *Tidal Power and Estuary Management*. Dorchester, England:

Henry Ling, 1978. A collection of papers presented at the Symposium on Tidal Energy and Estuary Management, held under the auspices of the Colston Research Society at the University of Bristol in 1978. The papers were written by eminent authorities in the field of estuary management, many of them associated with tidal power production. This text presents a holistic picture of current research and thinking in two of the fields most intensively concerned with the tides. The viewpoints of engineers, botanists, zoologists, mathematicians, and economists make interesting reading.

Melchoir, Paul. *The Tides of the Planet Earth*. Elmsford, N.Y.: Pergamon Press, 1978. Written by the foremost authority on tides, this text is suited for college-level readers who are not intimidated by technical language and who understand some mathematics or are willing to skip through it. The 146-page bibliography covers all papers to 1978 published on the subject of earth tides and related topics. The introduction gives a brief summary of the relation of tidal research to the fields of astronomy, geodesy, geophysics, oceanography, hydrology, and tectonics, as well as a brief history of discoveries made about tides.

Wylie, Francis E. *Tides and the Pull of the Moon*. Brattleboro, Vt.: Stephen Greene Press, 1979. A lucid account of lunar and tidal phenomena and their influences on daily life. This well-written book includes information from science, history, and marine lore. It contains extensive bibliographical notes at the end of each chapter to guide readers to excellent sources on each topic covered. A complete introduction for anyone interested in the subject.

Nan White

Cross-References

OCEAN WAVES

Type of earth science: Oceanography

Waves shape beaches, and wave energy can be harnessed to generate power. Storm waves have inflicted great damage on man-made structures and have killed thousands of people.

Principal terms

DEEP-WATER WAVE: a wave traveling in water with a depth greater than half its wave length

FETCH: the area or length of the sea surface over which waves are generated by a wind having a constant direction and speed

STORM SURGE: a general rise above normal water level resulting from a hurricane or other severe coastal storm

SWELL: ocean waves that have traveled out of their wind-generating area

TSUNAMI: a long-period sea wave produced by a submarine earthquake or volcanic eruption

WAVE HEIGHT: the vertical distance between a wave crest and the adjacent wave trough

WAVE LENGTH: the horizontal distance between two successive wave crests or wave troughs

WAVE ORBIT: the path followed by a water particle affected by wave motion; in deep water, the orbit is nearly circular

WAVE PERIOD: the time (usually measured in seconds) required for two adjacent wave crests to pass a point

WAVE REFRACTION: the process by which a wave crest is bent as it moves toward shore

Summary of the Phenomenon

The waves that agitate a lake or ocean are rhythmic, vertical disturbances of the water's surface. Their appearance may vary from a confused seascape of individual hillocks of water, each with a rounded or peaked top, to long, orderly swell waves with parallel, rounded crests. Waves involve a transfer of energy from place to place on the ocean's surface. The earthquake that jolts the Japanese coast one evening may generate a tsunami that races across the Pacific and destroys a pier in Hawaii the next morning. The water itself, however, does not move; it is the wave form, or the energy impulse, that travels. The water stays where it is but oscillates as the wave form goes past.

Waves can originate in many ways. Tsunamis are shock waves resulting from a sudden disturbance of the water's surface by a submarine earthquake or volcanic eruption. Shock waves can also be generated when a pebble is tossed into a pond or a ship creates a wake. A second type of wave is the type produced by the gravitational pull of the sun and the moon—the tides that raise and lower the ocean's surface. Tide waves are the largest ocean waves of all, stretching halfway around the world as they race along the equator at speeds of up to 1,600 kilometers per hour.

Waves can also originate through the action of the wind. Ordinary waves on the ocean or a lake form in this way. If there is no wind, the water surface is calm. If a slight breeze arises, the water surface is instantly roughened by patches of tiny capillary waves, the smallest waves of all. As the wind continues to blow steadily and in the same direction, ripples will appear because the surface roughness created by the capillary waves has given the wind something to push against. Soon the crests of adjacent ripples are being pushed together to create larger and larger crests. This process continues as the intensity of the wind increases, with small waves steadily giving way to larger and larger ones.

Three factors determine the size of the waves ultimately produced: the wind speed; the duration, or the length of time that the wind blows in a constant direction; and the fetch, or the extent of open water over which the wind blows. A 37-kilometer-per-hour wind blowing for 10 hours along a fetch of 120 kilometers will generate waves 3 meters high, but a 92-kilometer-per-hour wind blowing for three days along a 2,400-kilometer fetch will generate waves 30 meters high. Fortunately, such waves are very rare.

One way to understand the motion of water particles within a wave is to analyze the direction of water movement at various places in the wave. One can do so by sitting in a boat beyond the breakers. As the forward slope of a wave crest approaches, a lifting motion is experienced, followed by a forward push as the crest passes beneath the boat. This forward push is seen when waves break at the beach and their crests are thrown forward in a violent rush of water. Once the crest has passed, the boat is on the back slope of the wave, and now a downward motion is experienced. Next comes a backward motion, as the trough passes beneath the boat. This backward motion is also in a beach's breaker zone; after the crest has crashed forward on the beach, there follows a strong outward surge of water. This outward surge represents the backward water motion in the wave's trough. When all the preceding observations are combined, it can be seen that when a wave passes, the water particles move first up, then forward, then down, and finally back. This circular path is known as the wave orbit.

The term "heavy sea" is often encountered in descriptions of the ocean. A heavy sea results from the prolonged action of strong winds over the open ocean. The waves are large, peaked, and confused, totally lacking in orderly arrangement by size. Frequently, there is much spray in the air as a result of the tops being blown off the waves. A heavy sea is what one would expect to encounter in a hurricane or a violent storm. The term "swell," on the other hand, refers to waves that have moved out of the wind-generating area. As these waves approach the beach, they appear as long rows of smoothly rounded wave crests, evenly spaced at wide intervals and of uniform height. These swells have been produced by a distant storm at sea and have then moved out of the wind-generating area. As they travel outward, their original irregularities are diminished. Very little energy is lost, however, because a wave traveling at the ocean's surface encounters very little friction.

Groups of larger swell waves will be interspersed with groups of smaller ones. Oceanographers believe that such variation is caused by two or more wave patterns traveling together across the ocean's surface. When the crest of the larger wave pattern is superimposed on the crests of the smaller wave pattern, larger swell waves will result. When the trough of the larger pattern is superimposed on the crests of the smaller pattern, the swell waves will be smaller.

Oceanographers also recognize two major categories of wind-generated waves: deep-water and shallow-water waves. Deep-water waves travel in water depths greater than half their wave length, and wind waves in the open ocean are generally in this category. Shallow-water waves, on the other hand, travel in water so shallow that their wave orbits are affected by friction with the bottom. The shallower the water becomes, the slower they go. This reduction in speed as waves approach the shoreline results in a process known as wave refraction, in which apparently straight wave crests approaching a shoreline from an angle are seen to be bent when viewed from above.

Close to the beach is the surf zone. There, the forward speed of waves is slowed and their crests are bunched together. The shape of the crests changes from nearly flat to broadly arched, and there is a conspicuous increase in the height of the wave. In addition, the water in the crest of the wave begins moving faster than the water in the trough because of the friction created by the bottom, and this friction soon causes the crest to collapse in a torrent of water. The wave has "broken." Oceanographers recognize two types of breaker. The first is a plunging breaker, in which the wave crest curls smoothly forward, trapping a tube-shaped pocket of air below. The other type is known as a spilling breaker, in which foaming water spills down the forward slope of the crest as the breaker advances. This type of breaker has no air-filled tube.

The final zone, found between the breakers and the beach, is a narrow strip characterized by the rhythmic alteration of water rushing shoreward on the beach and water sliding back out to sea. The inward rush of water is known as the swash; it is a miniature wall of foaming water filled with air bubbles. The backward flow is a thin, glistening film of water known as the backwash.

Two additional wave types require special mention. The first is a giant ocean wave known as a tsunami, which can be caused by submarine earthquakes, volcanic eruptions, or a landslide's dumping massive amounts of debris into a bay, lake, or reservoir. In the open ocean, tsunamis behave just as any other ocean wave. They have crests and troughs which vary in height by a meter or so while the wave is still at sea. The tsunami wave length is enormously long, however, averaging perhaps 240 kilometers between crests. Tsunamis also have astonishingly high speeds— sometimes 650 kilometers per hour or more. A tsunami does not come ashore as a plunging breaker; rather, the crest rushes in as a surge of foaming water.

The second special wave type is known as a storm surge. Storm surges are drastic rises in sea level accompanying hurricanes or other severe coastal storms. Several factors combine to create such a surge. One factor is the reduced atmospheric pressure that occurs in the eye of a hurricane. This reduction may allow the ocean's surface to rise a meter or more. If, in addition, the sun and moon are aligned in such a way as to produce unusually high tides, the storm surge may rise a meter higher. A third contributing factor is the presence of strong onshore winds. In a major hurricane, these winds will push massive waves against the coast, increasing the impact of the storm surge. Finally, the nature of the offshore bottom plays a role. Shallow offshore bottoms permit wind to get a better "grip" on the water, raising its level higher. As a result, a hurricane that creates a 4-meter storm surge along Florida's east coast, with its deep offshore waters, would be able to raise a 10-meter storm surge on Florida's west coast, where the bottom is flat and shallow for a distance of 160 kilometers offshore.

Methods of Study

Until the early 1940's, the principal method for studying waves was to observe the sea's surface and to record the length, height, speed, and period of individual waves. Based on an analysis of wave period, it was determined that the various types of ocean wave could be arranged in an increasing spectrum of size. Capillary waves were found to be the smallest ocean waves, with periods of less than 0.1 second. Ripples came next, with periods of 0.1 to 1 second. Ordinary wind waves followed, with periods ranging from 1 second to 1.4 minutes. Larger still were tsunamis, with periods averaging 17 minutes, and finally the tides, with periods of 12 or 24 hours.

One basic wave-measuring instrument is the tide gauge, which is used to study tsunamis. The tide gauge is usually mounted on a pier in the quiet waters of a harbor, where it will not be exposed to damaging surf. It consists of a float inside a vertical, hollow pipe. The float is free to rise and fall with the water level, and a continuous record is made of the float's movement. The pipe is sealed at the bottom in such a way that only the long-period waves associated with a tsunami can force the float to rise. In this way, the tide gauge can record the preliminary waves of a tsunami and serve as a warning of the larger waves that follow. After the destruction of Hilo, Hawaii, by a tsunami on April 1, 1946, a seismic sea wave warning system was set up for the Pacific Ocean, utilizing seismograph records and the type of tide gauge just described.

Other instruments measure the impact of storm waves against pilings, piers, and deep-water structures. The measurements obtained from these instruments have enabled engineers to design structures that can better withstand the impact of storm waves. Before the 1950's, lighthouses and breakwaters were the structures most vulnerable to wave attack, but since that time, large oil drilling and production platforms have been built in the open ocean many kilometers from shore. During severe storms, several of these platforms have capsized, causing tragic losses of life.

In laboratory experiments, ocean waves can be simulated in wave tanks. These range from tabletop models with glass sides that look like aquariums to outdoor tanks that can hold large boats and generate breakers several meters in height. The mathematical treatment of waves is facilitated by the regularity of their pattern, and computers are able to predict wave heights and other wave characteristics with a high degree of accuracy.

Beginning with the energy crisis in the late 1970's, intensive consideration has been given to the possibility of harnessing wave energy to generate power. Many systems have been designed, and as of 1990, several were being tested. The fundamental principle on which most wave generators work is that the motion of a passing wave is similar to the rise and fall of a piston.

Context

Beaches owe their origin to wave action. The waves bring in the needed sand to build the beach and then smooth it daily, erasing imprints with their in-and-out motion. Storm waves, however, are capable of great damage. The height of such waves in the open ocean can be dramatic; the USS *Ramapo* measured waves 34 meters high in 1933, for example. When these waves finally reach shore, the destruction can be enormous. Concrete blocks weighing 65 tons or more have been torn loose from breakwaters by such waves. Even sandy coastlines are not immune from attack. A longshore current is set up when the waves reach the shoreline at an angle, and this current can transport vast quantities of sand along a coast. Where this transported sand is trapped by an obstacle, such as a harbor jetty, excessive deposition will take place, perhaps requiring expensive dredging. At other points along the coastline, beach erosion may occur, also causing problems.

One of the most feared wave types is the tsunami. This wave type is most frequently encountered on the shores of the Pacific. Although tsunamis are almost imperceptible in the open ocean, they can engulf boats, buildings, and people when they reach shore. There are records of tsunamis rushing up mountain sides to elevations of 30 meters or more. An added danger is that tsunamis have a series of crests which arrive 20 minutes or so apart, and often the third or fourth to arrive is the largest.

Storm surges are another dangerous wave type. They are commonly encountered along the Atlantic and Gulf coasts of the United States and have been known to carry oceangoing ships a kilometer or more inland. Six thousand people lost their lives in one such storm surge in Galveston, Texas, in 1900, and hundreds of thousands have drowned in a single storm surge on the shores of India's Bay of Bengal. Expensive storm surge barriers now guard Providence, Rhode Island; London; and the Netherlands.

Two other wave types that may present hazards for humans are rogue waves and seiches. Rogue waves are huge, solitary waves occasionally encountered in the ocean. They are particularly associated with the southward-flowing Agulhas current off South Africa and have been credited with sinking or severely damaging several large cargo ships. Seiche waves are oscillations in an enclosed water body such as a lake or bay. One such seiche, created by a hurricane, overflowed the dike surrounding Florida's Lake Okeechobee in 1928 and drowned two thousand persons.

Bibliography

Bascom, Willard. *Waves and Beaches: The Dynamics of the Ocean Surface*. Rev. ed. New York: Anchor Books, 1980. A thorough treatment of the nature of waves and beaches and the principles that govern them. A good introduction for the nonscientist and an excellent source for the professional oceanographer. Contains many helpful diagrams and tables and numerous black-and-white photographs. Suitable for college-level readers.

Bird, Eric C. *Coastline Changes: A Global Review*. New York: John Wiley & Sons, 1985. This book is based on the results of a project conducted by the International Geographical Union's Working Group on the Dynamics of Coastline Erosion. It presents a detailed picture of the effects of wave erosion on the coastlines of 127 countries. Illustrated with numerous photographs and maps. Suitable for college-level readers.

Fairbridge, Rhodes W., ed. *The Encyclopedia of Oceanography*. New York: Reinhold, 1966. An oceanography source book for the student and the professional. It has excellent sections on waves and the related topics of fetch, tsunamis, wave energy, wave refraction, and wave theory. A well-illustrated and carefully cross-referenced volume. The text is aimed at readers with some technical background.

Gross, M. Grant. *Oceanography: A View of the Earth*. 4th ed. Englewood Cliffs, N.J.: Prentice-Hall, 1987. A well-written and well-illustrated text. Chapter 9 provides a comprehensive overview of all aspects of ocean waves, with diagrams, tables, and photographs. The appendix contains a table of conversion factors, and there is an excellent glossary. Suitable for general audiences.

Ingmanson, Dale E., and W. J. Wallace. *Oceanography: An Introduction*. 4th ed. Belmont, Calif.: Wadsworth, 1989. Chapter 11 of this oceanography text provides a comprehensive treatment of all aspects of ocean waves. It includes many fine photographs, particularly of tsunami damage. The appendix contains a table of conversion factors, a complete set of charts of the U.S. coastline, and a glossary. Suitable for college-level readers or the interested layperson.

Murty, T. S. *Storm Surges: Meteorological Ocean Tides*. Ottawa: Department of Fisheries and Oceans, 1984. This book covers storm surges throughout the world. The introductory sections pertaining to the origin of storm surges are too technical for the lay reader, but chapter 7, "Case Studies of Storm Surges on the Globe," gives detailed storm surge data for every coastal zone that is subject to them.

Myles, Douglas. *The Great Waves*. New York: McGraw-Hill, 1985. A book on the subject of tsunamis designed for the lay reader and scientist alike. It gives background information pertaining to the origin of tsunamis and describes major destructive tsunamis throughout world history. Eyewitness accounts are included whenever available. There are no photographs, but the endpapers reproduce a fine etching of the tsunami accompanying the Lisbon earthquake of 1775. Suitable for high school readers.

Tricker, R. A. R. *Bores, Breakers, Waves, and Wakes: An Introduction to the Study of Waves on Water.* New York: Elsevier, 1964. A thorough treatment of water-wave behavior, written with the aim of simplifying the mathematics so as to make the discussion understandable to the general reader. Chapter 17, "Ships' Wakes," provides fine coverage of that topic. There are many black-and-white and color plates illustrating various wave types. Suitable for college-level readers.

Donald W. Lovejoy

Cross-References

Coastal Processes and Beaches, 240; Hurricanes and Monsoons, 1088; Lakes, 1318; Landslides and Slope Stability, 1365; Ocean Power, 1818; Ocean Tides, 1832; Sand, 2253; Sediment Transport and Deposition, 2290; Sedimentary Mineral Deposits, 2296; Storms, 2477; Tsunamis, 2548; Weathering and Erosion, 2723; Wind, 2730.

THE OCEANIC CRUST

Type of earth science: Geology
Field of study: Tectonics

The oceanic crust is that portion of the outer layer of material forming the earth that underlies the world oceans. This crust is a dynamic layer, primarily composed of basalt, where new, submarine mountain ranges are being continuously formed and old ocean floors are being destroyed.

Principal terms

FRACTURE ZONES: large, linear zones of the sea floor characterized by steep cliffs, irregular topography, and faults; such zones commonly cross and displace oceanic ridges by faulting

HYDROTHERMAL VENTS: sea-floor outlets for high-temperature, mineralized springs that are associated with sea-floor spreading centers and which are often the site of deep-sea, chemosynthetic biological communities

OCEAN TRENCHES: long, deep, and narrow depressions in the sea floor (greater than 6,000 meters deep), with relatively steep sides; these features mark the boundary between ocean crust and continental crust and are associated with the subduction of oceanic crust

OCEANIC RIDGES: long, narrow elevations of the sea floor, some 2-3 kilometers higher than the surrounding ocean basins, that are associated with the creation of new sea-floor material

PLATE TECTONICS: the theory of mobility within the earth's crust that accounts for mountain building at ocean ridges, spreading of the sea floor, and subduction at ocean trenches by dividing the crust into a series of plates that interact by colliding, rifting, or sliding past one another

SEA-FLOOR SPREADING: the process whereby crustal plates move away from mid-ocean ridges, creating new crustal material as molten rock moves upward through rifts at the ridge crests

SEAMOUNTS: isolated elevations on the sea floor, usually rising to higher than 1,000 meters, which are commonly the shape of an inverted cone reflecting their volcanic origin; a flat-topped seamount is known as a guyot

SEISMIC ACTIVITY: a disturbance of the crust caused by earthquakes or earth movements, often associated with zones of sea-floor subduction and ocean-ridge formation

SUBDUCTION: the process whereby old sea floor that was produced millions of years earlier at the ocean ridges is forced under continental crust in the vicinity of trenches

Summary of the Phenomenon

The earth is not homogeneous from its center to its surface, but rather it is composed of three concentric layers: the core, the mantle, and the crust. The core of the earth is composed of a dense mixture of nickel and iron, with a solid inner portion and a liquid outer portion. The core is extremely hot, ranging from about 5,000 degrees Celsius at the center to 4,000 degrees Celsius in the outer core. The core extends from a depth of about 2,900 to 6,378 kilometers (center of the earth) and accounts for 31.5 percent of the earth's mass. The next layer, the mantle, consists of less dense rock and holds 68.1 percent of the mass.

The material of the mantle has the properties of iron-magnesium silicate rock rich in olivine and pyroxene minerals. The mantle is about 2,870 kilometers thick and cooler than the core (1,500-3,000 degrees Celsius). The mantle also has two zones. The lower portion is presumed to be essentially rigid, but the upper mantle, or asthenosphere, is more plastic and flows when stressed. The asthenosphere extends to a depth of 700 kilometers and is likely the site of molten magma formation. The outermost layer, the crust, is the less-dense outer shell of the earth. Also known as the lithosphere, this layer consists of granitic continental crust and basaltic oceanic crust. The crust is underlain and likely fused with a layer of heavier mantle rock. The boundary between the crust and mantle is known as the Mohorovičić discontinuity (or Moho); the boundary occurs under continents at depths of 10-70 kilometers but only 5-10 kilometers under the oceans.

Above the Moho, both the oceanic and continental crusts have properties that resemble basalt. Basalt, a common volcanic rock found extensively on the earth's surface, is composed of silicates of calcium, magnesium, and iron. These rocks have an average density of 3 grams per cubic centimeter. Under the continents, but not the oceans, the basalt is overlain by a rock layer with properties similar to those of granite. Granite is a common igneous rock composed of silicates of aluminum and potassium. Such rocks are lighter in color and weight than is basalt, with an average density of 2.8 grams per cubic centimeter. Thus, the continental crust "floats" as massive blocks on a layer of basalt. Because the densities of the continental and oceanic crusts are not greatly different, approximately 93 percent of the continental blocks are submerged in the underlying basaltic crust. Continental blocks are analogous to floating icebergs of various heights in that the Moho is pushed deeper under continental mountain ranges than it is under flat coastal plains. The Moho assumes a shape that reflects the surface of the continent but exaggerated to nine times greater. The bottoms of the continental blocks must rise as material is eroded to the sea thus keeping the exposed-to-submerged ratio constant. This flotation phenomenon is known as isostasy, and the rising process is called isostatic adjustment.

One of the most remarkable characteristics of the oceanic crust is its structural uniformity. Essentially, marine sediments overlie igneous rock, which forms three distinct layers. The sediments vary considerably in thickness and in composition. Shell material and debris from marine plants and animals form dominant sediments around the equator and near the polar seas; detritus from the land and glacial deposits are common near the continents; and chemical precipitates (oozes) are found elsewhere. The oceanic ridge crests are generally free of sediments. From the flanks of the ridges to the continents, the sediments generally increase in thickness to more than 3 kilometers at the continental margins. The three igneous layers are each relatively uniform in composition and thickness. The upper layer has been penetrated by deep ocean drilling and is known to be composed of basaltic lavas, 1-2.5 kilometers thick. The basal layer, directly overlying the mantle, is thin (0.5 kilometer) and presumably formed of layered peridotite. Peridotite is a dense ultrabasic igneous rock consisting mainly of olivine minerals. Similar rocks are thought to be the principal constituent of the mantle. The main (middle) layer is 5 kilometers thick and has properties consistent with a gabbroic composition. Gabbro is a coarse-grained igneous rock consisting mainly of plagioclase feldspar, pyroxene, and olivine minerals. It is the deep-seated equivalent of the overlying, fine-grained basalt. In certain areas, metamorphism and hydrothermal processes have formed other rock and mineral types including amphibolite, greenschists, zeolites, and serpentine. The surface features of the oceanic crust include such interesting and interrelated topographic features as oceanic ridges, fracture zones, seamounts, abyssal plains, deep-sea trenches, and island arcs. The existence of each of these features can be explained by the concepts of plate tectonics and sea-floor spreading.

The oceanic ridge system is the major topographic feature of the ocean basins, extending 80,000 kilometers as a continuous range throughout all the oceans. Ocean ridges generally rise 2-3 kilometers higher than do the bordering ocean basins. The ridge system in the Atlantic and Indian oceans lies equidistant between the adjacent continents, whereas in the Pacific Ocean, the system is highly asymmetric with respect to the continents. Passing out of the Indian Ocean between Antarctica and Australia, the ridge system continues eastward across the southern Pacific then arcs northward well toward the South American continent. Here known as the East Pacific Rise, it eventually passes into the Gulf of California and presumably under the Basin and Range province of the western United States to reemerge in the Pacific Ocean as the Juan de Fuca Ridge off British Columbia. Although almost entirely submarine, the ridges do rise above sea level at a few places in the Atlantic and Pacific oceans where recently active volcanos have formed islands (for example, Iceland, Tristan da Cunha, and the Galápagos Islands). The ridges are also seismically active, with frequent tensional earthquakes of intermediate strength. Such earthquakes are generally restricted to the oceanic crust within a few kilometers of the ridge crest. The crest of the ridges in the Atlantic and Indian oceans are characterized by a central rift valley that is commonly 2-3 kilometers deep and 20-30 kilometers wide. Volcanism occurs along the centerline of the rift valley, which is also the site of most of the seismic activity. In the Pacific Ocean, earthquakes are confined to a similar narrow zone, but volcanism appears to have been much greater. Here, lava flows have filled the central rift valley to a large part so that the ridge crest appears smooth.

The ocean ridge system is clearly a continuous feature on a global scale, but when viewed in detail, the ridge crests are frequently offset by fracture zones. For example, the Mid-Atlantic Ridge has no less than forty such zones. These fracture zones are steeply cliffed features which vary in width from a few to 50 kilometers. They are mainly confined to the oceanic crust and only rarely approach the continental margins. Fracture zones are only seismically active along that portion of the fault line between the offset ridge crests; the segments extending toward the continents are seismically quiet. Earthquakes between the crests are associated with transverse motion, indicating that the fracture zones are the result of faults in which each side moves horizontally but in opposite directions. These displacements of oceanic crust are known as transform faults.

Throughout the world's oceans, beyond the flanks of the ridge systems, numerous irregularities rise from the sea floor. Small volcanic extrusions that rise less than 1 kilometer from the ocean floor are known as abyssal hills. Larger volcanic features that reach 1 kilometer or more are called seamounts. Seamounts that have flat tops are known as guyots. The flattening is thought to have resulted when seamounts were near sea level and subjected to wave attack and erosion. The composition of seamounts is closely related to their proximity to oceanic or continental crust. For example, near the center of the Pacific Ocean, the seamounts (including those that broach the sea surface to become islands) are composed of basaltic-type rock characteristic of oceanic crust, whereas along the margin of the Pacific Ocean the islands are composed of the granitic-type rocks that are found on the continents. The boundary between these two regions has been named the Andesite Line for the type of rocks found in the volcanic mountains of South America. In tropical areas, seamounts often support coralline reefs in the form of atolls. Atolls are generally circular in plan, consisting of a central lagoon surrounded by a narrow carbonate reef dotted with elongated islands. Presumably, atolls form as volcanic islands subside at a rate that is matched by the upward growth of the encircling reef.

The relatively flat surfaces of the ocean floor, which extend from the mid-ocean ridges to either the marginal trenches or the continental slopes, are known as abyssal plains. Excluding the trenches, these plains are the deepest portion of the ocean. Abyssal plains account for nearly 30 percent of the earth's surface, comprising 75 percent of the Pacific Ocean basin and 33 percent of the Atlantic and Indian ocean basins. Oceanic rises are areas of the ocean floor that are elevated above the abyssal plain, distinctly separated from a continental mass, and of greater areal extent than are typical seamounts or abyssal hills. General oceanic rises lie at least 300 meters above the surrounding ocean floor. Rises are not seismically active and are thought to result from the uplifting of oceanic crust associated with volcanic hot spots (source areas for magma in the upper mantle). Examples are the Bermuda Rise in the North Atlantic Ocean and the Chatham Rise in the southwestern Pacific Ocean.

The oceanic trenches are the deepest parts of the oceans. They are elongate, narrow, and commonly arcuate in shape with the convex side facing to sea. With few exceptions, they occur at the margins of ocean basins. By convention, an ocean deep must be at least 6,000 meters below sea level to be considered a trench. Trenches are found in the Atlantic and Indian oceans but are most common in the Pacific. The deepest are found in the western Pacific, where the Mariana trench plunges to a depth of 11,033 meters. The largest, however, is the Peru-Chile trench adjacent to South America; it is 5,900 kilometers long, averages 100 kilometers wide, and extends to depths below 8,000 meters. Most trenches are associated with island arc systems or with volcanic ranges adjacent continents. Examples include the Guam and Saipan islands west of the Mariana trench and the Andes east of the Peru-Chile trench. Island arcs are volcanic belts that parallel the trench on the continental side. The profiles of the trenches are asymmetrical, with steep sides toward the island arcs. Trenches are also areas of high earthquake activity, low gravitational pull, and low heat flow from the earth.

The concepts of plate tectonics and sea-floor spreading provide the mechanisms necessary for creating the features of the ocean floor. Plate tectonics proposes that the earth's lithosphere is composed of several plates of differing shapes and areas that glide over the plastic asthenosphere. Convection cells caused by radioactive decay of isotopes in the molten rocks of the mantle are the driving mechanism for this motion. These cells circulate the heat upward, causing upwelling in the mantle. The movement of the plates results in areas of separation where magma flows to the surface, creating the volcanic mountains of the mid-ocean ridges. Thus, the ocean floor spreads outward from the ridge crest expanding the dimensions of the ocean. This process occurs in the Atlantic Ocean at the expense of the Pacific Ocean. Where plates collide, such as off the coast of Southeast Asia and South America, deep trenches are formed as oceanic crust is forced under (or subducts) the lighter continental crust. The process is associated with volcanism as the oceanic crust is remelted and island arcs are formed by the accompanying submarine eruptions. The rate of spreading affects the form of the ridge system. Rapid spreading (up to 5 centimeters per year) produces a broad, relatively low ridge without a deep central valley, such as that found in the East Pacific Rise, west of South America. Slow spreading (1-3 centimeters per year), on the other hand, results in a high-relief ridge with a deep central rift valley such as that of the Mid-Atlantic Ridge.

Hot waters are discharged by hydrothermal vents at active mid-ocean ridges. The chemical composition of ocean water and deep-ocean sediments is influenced by seawater circulating through hot oceanic crust, formed by volcanic eruptions. Some seawater enters the oceanic crust through faults and eventually reaches the vicinity of the magma chambers below the spreading center where molten rock collects before eruption. Reactions with hot basalt charge the seawater with metallic sulfides and remove magnesium and other elements. The hot water then flows into the ocean through irregular, chimneylike vents up to 10 meters high. The vent mounds are made of silica, native sulfur, and metallic sulfide minerals. The bright-colored chimneys and their surrounding deposits resemble valuable ore deposits of copper, zinc, and other metals which are found on the continents. This phenomenon may also be an important process in regulating the chemical composition of seawater, as well as providing a chemical base for a deep-sea biological community that uses chemical energy rather than sunlight to produce organic compounds (chemosynthesis instead of photosynthesis).

Methods of Study

The oceanic crust covers about 70 percent of the earth's surface, yet it has received relatively little attention. For example, deep-sea drilling and sampling of the crust has been completed at only one site for every 500,000 square kilometers of ocean floor. The great depth of the oceans, the tremendous logistical problems of working on and in the sea, and the high cost of oceanic research have all acted to limit the amount of scientific information that is available. Technological advances in the second half of the twentieth century have permitted researchers to explore the oceanic crust with remote sensing techniques as well as through diving excursions to the ocean floor.

The structure of the earth and particularly the oceanic crust have been investigated indirectly by seismic refraction and reflection methods. Studies in the early 1950's showed that the crust was composed of several layers on the basis of the velocity of sound within each layer. Ocean sediment transmits sound at 2 kilometers per second, basalt transmits at 5.1, gabbro transmits at 6.7, and peridotite transmits at 8.1. Precise measurements of the length of time required for a seismic shock wave to penetrate these layers have permitted the thickness of each layer to be calculated.

Accurate and detailed maps of the ocean floor (bathymetric charts) have been compiled from enormous collections of sounding data. By the early 1900's, electronic devices called precision depth recorders (PDRs) became available for oceanographic surveys. These early surveys gave the first realistic view of the ocean's major surface features. Side-scanning sonar, a later development, has provided three-dimensional illustrations of small-scale features of the sea floor. This type of bathymetric data can be recorded continuously as the research ship is under way, and locations can be determined precisely from navigational satellites.

Ocean crustal rock is an average of 7 kilometers thick. This great thickness, plus the hundreds of meters of sediment and thousands of meters of seawater overlying the crust, have made the direct sampling of this rock very difficult. Deep-ocean drilling has, however, permitted samples to be collected from considerable depths below the ocean floor. Beginning in 1968, the Deep Sea Drilling Project (DSDP) has extensively explored the oceanic crust from the ship *Glomar Challenger*, operated by Global Marine, Incorporated. Sponsored by the National Science Foundation and the Office of Naval Research, this project has drilled a total of 160 kilometers of cores. The deepest penetration into the ocean floor was 1.7 kilometers; the deepest water in which drilling took place was 7,000 meters. More than 840 sites were drilled in all parts of the world oceans. Scientists from all over the world participated in this project, which confirmed much of the theory of how the earth's crust moves. DSDP also provided significant data on the age of the ocean basins and the rates of sea-floor spreading.

Other important deep-sea data have been gathered by research submersibles and airborne remote sensors. Starting in the 1960's, submersibles such as Woods Hole Oceanographic Institution's *Alvin* have made some remarkable oceanographic discoveries, especially along the mid-ocean ridges. Much of the knowledge of hydrothermal vents has been obtained through submersible observations. A submersible possesses numerous advantages over surface vessels, including direct observation and sampling. They are, however, dependent on surface ships for support and transport to the dive sites. Aircraft magnetometer surveys have yielded valuable information on paleomagnetism and the earth's gravitational field. These data showed that the polarity of the earth's magnetic field is recorded in the crustal rocks as the ocean floor is formed. Thus, a record was revealed that demonstrated sea-floor spreading by mirror-image of polar reversal patterns on the east and west sides of the Mid-Atlantic Ridge.

Satellites have also played a part in the exploration of the oceanic crust. The short-lived Seasat satellite carried a sophisticated altimeter that could measure the precise distances between the satellite and the ocean surface. Slight differences in sea level were observed which correspond to ocean deeps and density anomalies (such as accumulations of dense rock). For example, the sea stands higher over mid-ocean ridges and lower over trenches. Satellite images are now being used to map previously unknown topographic features of the ocean floor.

Context

The oceanic crust is not a static feature; rather, it is a dynamic layer that profoundly affects the basic processes of the earth. The fundamental aspect of sea-floor spreading is that new sea floor forms along mid-ocean ridges and slowly moves away from the ridge (a few centimeters per year) to be consumed or subducted in trenches at the edge of continents. This process results in many natural hazards, such as earthquakes and volcanoes, that are catastrophic to human populations. On the positive side, this process also results in the formation of valuable mineral deposits as well as regions of spectacular beauty.

Of all the geological hazards, earthquakes are among the most frequent and most destructive. A plot of worldwide seismic activity shows that most earthquakes are confined to rather narrow but continuous zones that surround large stable plates. Most of these boundaries occur in oceanic crust. The earthquakes are associated with the relative movements of these plates, particularly collisions, rifting, and dragging at the plate boundaries. Knowledge of the mechanisms and rates of sea-floor spreading will permit scientists to predict better when and where a potential catastrophe will occur. One of the ultimate goals of crustal dynamics research is to develop a reliable early warning system in order to allow orderly evacuation of earthquake-prone areas.

For the purpose of hazard assessment, volcanoes can be placed into one of two groups, according to the composition of their magmas. Basaltic volcanoes, associated with oceanic crusts, produce large quantities of lava with minimal explosive activity. The volcanoes of the Mid-Atlantic Ridge and the Hawaiian Islands are examples of this type. In contrast, more acidic volcanoes, normally associated with subductive zones, tend to be more violent and unpredictable. The viscosity of the magmas can lead to a buildup of gas pressure, resulting in massive explosions such as Krakatoa in the East Indies and the volcanoes of the west coast of South America. As a human hazard, basaltic volcanoes are relatively benign and may even serve as a safe tourist attraction. Volcanoes are clearly beyond human control, but prediction and risk assessment can reduce the hazards.

Sea-floor spreading can result in mineralization from rising magma on ocean ridges. Pockets of metal-enriched brines and muds have been found along many of the rift valleys of ocean ridges. These deposits result from interaction of seawater and hot magma. In the Red Sea rift, oceanographers have discovered a single pocket which contains an estimated 200 million tons of metal-rich mud. This mud is a multimetallic resource (including copper, zinc, iron, silver, gold, nickel, vanadium, lead, chromium, cobalt, and manganese), the mining of which could provide several salable products. Much research and development work needs to be undertaken in order to build an economically feasible deep-sea mineral extraction device.

Another metallic resource of the deep-ocean floors is a brownish-black, potato-sized object known as a manganese nodule. Cross-sectional cuts of these nodules show concentric growth rings that require a million years for 1 millimeter to form. Though this may seem exceedingly slow, the nodules are so numerous, particularly in the Pacific Ocean, that the annual growth totals many millions of tons. Magnesium nodules contain many other valuable metals including copper, nickel, and cobalt. They form by precipitation around a small grain from solutions emanating from the oceanic crust and its cover of sediments.

The deep-sea floor is receiving more and more consideration as a place to store nuclear waste. There are certainly many environmental risks involved, but the deep sea option has some advantages over land-based storage. For example, the deep sea is one of the least valuable and most plentiful pieces of real estate on earth. It has no significant fishing or petroleum use; manganese mining is a possibility, but the deep-sea region is so immense that numerous sites are available. Perhaps the most compelling reason favoring the deep sea is that, except at the ridges and trenches, the ocean floor is extremely stable. Earlier suggestions that radioactive material be placed in the ocean trenches have now been disregarded. The trenches are very unstable areas and zones of subduction with a high incidence of faulting and earthquake activity that could damage storage containers, releasing radioactive material into the environment. Many legal and technological questions need to be answered before deep-sea disposal can begin.

Bibliography

Bonati, Enrico. "The Origin of Metal Deposits in the Oceanic Lithosphere." *Scientific American* 238 (February, 1978): 54-61. Describes the geochemical processes occurring at the spreading centers of ocean ridges that produce metal-rich minerals and the implications for such deposits found throughout the earth's crust.

Edmond, John M., and Karen Von Damm. "Hot Springs on the Ocean Floor." *Scientific American* 248 (April, 1983): 78-84. A discussion of the role of deep-ocean hydrothermal springs in depositing metallic ores and sustaining life in the absence of sunlight.

Gross, M. G. "Deep-Sea Hot Springs and Cold Seeps." *Oceanus* 27 (Fall, 1984). An introduction to a special issue devoted to the exploration, geochemistry, chemosynthesis, and biology associated with water discharge on the ocean floor.

Heirtzler, James R., and W. B. Bryan. "The Floor of the Mid-Atlantic Rift." *Scientific American* 233 (August, 1975): 78-90. Data gathered by FAMOUS (French-American Mid-Ocean Undersea Study) are summarized, particularly investigations of the Mid-Atlantic Rift south of the Azore Islands, involving the use of the submersibles *Alvin*, *Archimede*, and *Cyana*.

Kennett, James P. *Marine Geology*. Englewood Cliffs, N.J.: Prentice-Hall, 1982. A comprehensive treatment of the geology of the sea floor, including ocean morphology, geophysics, plate tectonics, oceanic crust, and marine sediments.

Menard, H. W. "The Deep-Ocean Floor." *Scientific American* 221 (September, 1969): 126. A summary of the dynamic effects of sea-floor spreading is presented with description of related topographic features of the ocean bottom.

Ross, D. A. *Introduction to Oceanography*. 4th ed. Englewood Cliffs, N.J.: Prentice-Hall, 1983. Representative of a number of informative introductory textbooks on ocean science, this text provides an overview of plate tectonics and geophysics as these subjects relate to the features and dynamics of the oceanic crust as well as oceanography study methods including deep-sea drilling.

Shepard, F. P. *Geological Oceanography*. New York: Crane, Russak, 1977. Examines the concept of sea-floor spreading, features of the ocean bottom, and findings of deep-sea drilling programs.

Tarling, D. H., and M. Tarling. *Continental Drift: A Study of the Earth's Moving Surface*. Garden City, N.Y.: Doubleday, 1971. A comprehensive discussion of the theory of plate tectonics and its early development.

Tokosoz, M. Nafi. "The Subduction of the Lithosphere." *Scientific American* 233 (November, 1975): 88-98. A discussion of how the subduction of oceanic crust is related to ocean trenches, island arcs, volcanism, and earthquakes.

Charles E. Herdendorf

Cross-References

OCEANS: CARBONATE COMPENSATION DEPTHS

Type of earth science: Oceanography

Carbonate compensation depths are the levels within ocean basins that separate calcium carbonate-containing sea-floor sediments from carbonate-free sediments. The carbonate compensation depth (CCD) may be different in different ocean basins, and it may rise or fall at different times in the same ocean basin as a result of the balance between surface production of carbonate and deep-water carbonate dissolution in the basin.

Principal terms

DEPOSITION: the process by which loose sediment grains fall out of seawater to accumulate as layers of sediment on the sea-floor

PALEODEPTH: an estimate of the water depth at which ancient sea-floor sediments were originally deposited

PLANKTON: microscopic marine plants and animals that live in the surface waters of the oceans; these floating organisms precipitate the particles that sink to form biogenic marine sediments

PRECIPITATION: the formation of solid mineral crystals from chemicals dissolved in water

PRODUCTIVITY: the rate at which plankton reproduces in surface waters, which in turn controls the rate of precipitation of calcareous or siliceous shells or tests by these organisms

RED CLAYS: fine-grained, carbonate-free sediments that accumulate at depths below the CCD in all ocean basins; their red color is caused by the presence of oxidized fine-grained iron particles

TEST: an internal skeleton or shell precipitated by a one-celled planktonic plant or animal

Summary of the Phenomenon

Marine sediments are composed of a variety of materials of biological or terrestrial origin. Individual sediment grains in oceanic deposits may be either clastic or biogenic particles. Clastic sediments are materials derived from the weathering, erosion, and transportation of exposed continental rocks, and these grains are classified by particle diameter into gravels, sands, silts, and clays. Clastic sediment particles become less common with increasing distance from the continental landmasses and are nearly absent from deep-water sediments on the abyssal plains. Biogenic sediment particles are composed of skeletons and tests precipitated by planktonic plants and animals living in the shallowest waters of the ocean. Biogenic particles composed of calcium carbonate or of opaline silica make up the majority of oceanic sediments, which are deposited at great distances from land. Deposition of biogenic sediments is controlled by two factors: the biological productivity of surface waters and the dissolution of biogenic particles by corrosive bottom waters.

Biogenic sediment particles are produced in shallow, well-lighted surface waters as a result of the biochemical activity of microscopic plants and animals, which precipitate solid shells and tests from minerals dissolved in seawater. Biological productivity is a measure of the number of the organisms present and their rate of reproduction. The productivity of planktonic organisms is directly related to chemical and physical conditions in the surface waters. High-productivity waters have abundant supplies of oxygen, with dissolved nutrients and chemicals needed for precipitation of shells and tests and enough light for photosynthesis by plants. Generally, high productivity is found in warm-water areas with abundant dissolved oxygen and nutrients.

When planktonic plants and animals die, their shells fall through the water column to be deposited on the bottom of the ocean. This "planktonic rain" causes deposition of sea-floor sediments by the sinking of biogenic particles produced in the surface waters, and it moves chemicals from surface waters to deep waters. The higher the productivity values in surface waters, the greater will be the supply of biogenic sediment particles to the sea floor. As biogenic particles sink through the water column to the sea floor, they may be dissolved by corrosive seawater. Surface waters are saturated with dissolved calcium carbonate, so most dissolution takes place in deep waters, which are undersaturated with carbonate.

Calcareous sediments are produced by the accumulation of biogenic particles of calcium carbonate that survive the fall through the water and are deposited and buried on the sea floor. Accumulation rates of biogenic sediments are controlled by the balance between surface productivity and deep-water dissolution: The higher the biological productivity in the surface, the greater the number of shells that will sink to the ocean bottom. In certain high-productivity areas associated with upwelling of cold, nutrient-loaded water masses to the surface, sea-floor sediment accumulation rates may be as high as 3-5 centimeters per thousand years. In areas with higher dissolution rates, fewer calcareous particles will survive to be deposited on the ocean floor. In these low-productivity areas, all the carbonate produced at the surface may be dissolved, and sediment accumulation rates may be as low as 1 millimeter per million years.

The carbonate compensation depth (CCD) demarcates the boundary between carbonate-rich sediments (calcareous oozes and chalks) and carbonate-free sediments (red clays) in the oceans; it is the result of deep-water dissolution rates exceeding the rate of supply of calcium carbonate to the deep sea by surface productivity. The depth of the CCD marks the point at which the supply of carbonate sinking in the "planktonic rain" from surface waters is exactly balanced by the rate of removal of carbonate dissolution in deep waters. Calcareous sediments will be deposited on the sea floor in water depths shallower than the CCD, because in these areas, the rate of supply of calcium carbonate is higher than the dissolution rate. In these areas, individual particles of calcium carbonate will survive the trip through the water column and are deposited as biogenic sediments on the sea floor.

Below the compensation depth, dissolution exceeds the rate of supply, so all carbonate particles supplied from the surface are dissolved, and sea-floor sediments are carbonate-free. Surface sediments in water depths below the CCD tend to be red clays, or combinations of fine-grained materials derived from continental sources and carried to the deep sea by wind, mixed with micrometeorites and other particles from extraterrestrial sources. Red clays generally lack fossils, as a result of complete dissolution of carbonate and opaline silica, so only a few solution-resistant fossils, such as phosphatic fish teeth and whale ear bones, are found in these sediments. The reddish-brown color of deep-sea clay deposits is a result of the presence of iron particles, which have reacted with oxygen in seawater to form the rust-brown color.

Much information on the past history of the compensation depth in different ocean basins has been provided by ocean-floor drilling programs. The level of the CCD has changed dramatically throughout geologic history, with fluctuations of up to 2,000 meters being recorded in deep-sea sediments. Changes in the CCD are believed to be caused by changes in either the rate of supply of carbonate to the oceans or the rate of carbonate dissolution in the deep sea, which may be caused by changes in the shape of ocean basins or by changes in the location of carbonate deposition within different ocean basins. Calcium carbonate is delivered to the oceans by rivers draining eroded continental rocks. The oceans are the primary geochemical reservoir for calcium carbonate, so most of the calcium carbonate on the earth remains dissolved in ocean water or in the form of calcareous sediments on the sea floor. The amount of carbonate deposition on the sea floor depends on the input of calcium carbonate derived from continental weathering and delivered to the oceans by rivers. Because oceanic plankton can precipitate solid calcium carbonate at a much faster rate than the rate of input of dissolved carbonate from rivers, most of the calcium carbonate that is deposited in the oceans must dissolve in order to maintain the chemical balance between dissolved carbonate and solid carbonate in oceanic sediments.

Any changes in the locations of carbonate deposition may cause corresponding changes in the level of the CCD as the compensation depths in different oceans change as a result of bathymetric fractionation or basin-basin fractionation. In bathymetric fractionation, a balance is established between the rates of carbonate deposition in shallow-water and in deep-water sedimentary basins. Greater deposition of calcium carbonate in shallow waters atop the continental shelves will cause a shallowing of the CCD as more deep-water carbonate deposits are dissolved so as to balance the shallow-water deposition. Similarly, the level of the compensation depth may vary by basin-basin fractionation of carbonate, which establishes a balance between the compensation depths in different ocean basins. For example, greater deposition of calcium carbonate in the Pacific Ocean will cause the Pacific CCD to become deeper, while at the same time, the Atlantic compensation depth must become shallower, because greater deposition of carbonate in Pacific sediments will leave less dissolved carbonate for precipitation in the Atlantic Ocean.

Even within an ocean basin, the level of the CCD may vary, depending on the balance between carbonate productivity and dissolution in a local area. For example, in the Equatorial Pacific Ocean, the compensation depth is 500-800 meters deeper than in areas immediately to the north and south of this high-productivity area as a result of the greater supply of carbonate in the "planktonic rain" below these high-productivity surface waters. Also, the compensation depth tends to shoal near the edges of ocean basins, because higher biological productivity in shallow water near the continents causes rapid sinking of large amounts of organic carbon produced by planktonic plants and animals. Breakdown of this organic carbon by sea-floor bacteria produces increased amounts of dissolved carbon dioxide gas, which reacts with water molecules to form carbonic acid; carbonic acid is corrosive to solid calcium carbonate. Greater carbonic acid concentrations lead to increased carbonate dissolution in bottom waters and cause upward migration of the CCD into shallower waters.

Methods of Study

Carbonate compensation depths may be studied by obtaining a series of deep-sea sediment samples from different depths within an ocean basin to determine the relationship between sediment type and water depth. In 1891, a study was published describing the global patterns of sea-floor sediment type in each ocean basin, based on sediment samples obtained on the HMS *Challenger* oceanographic expedition. It was discovered that virtually no calcium carbonate was present below depths of 4,500 meters as a result of dissolution of carbonate.

The CCD in the modern ocean was first described in detail in 1935, based on sediment core transects taken across the South Atlantic Ocean by the 1925-1927 German *Meteor* expedition. Similar studies of sediment cores from different depths in the Pacific Ocean revealed that calcareous oozes are common sea-floor sediments in water depths to 4,400 meters, with noncalcareous red clays being found in surface sediments deeper than 4,400 meters. Cores with calcareous oozes underlying red clays were obtained, however, in depths well below the present CCD, indicating that this geochemical boundary has migrated vertically throughout geologic history.

One innovative experiment to measure the rate of calcium carbonate dissolution with increasing water depth involved the placement of a stationary mooring for a period of months in deep water in the Pacific Ocean. Calcite spheres and calcareous microfossils were hung in permeable nylon bags at different water depths on the mooring; the nylon bags allowed seawater to come in contact with the calcium carbonate and thus permitted carbonate dissolution to occur. By measuring the weight loss of spheres suspended for a few weeks to months on the mooring, the rate of dissolution was determined for different water depths. In this experiment, little carbonate dissolution was observed at water depths shallower than 3,700 meters, while a rapid transition from minimal dissolution to extreme dissolution was seen. Rapid loss of carbonate by dissolution occurred in carbonate spheres suspended between the lysocline (the depth at which carbonate dissolution first begins to occur) and the compensation depth. Below 4,500 meters, the carbonate compensation depth, all carbonate was removed within a matter of weeks, demonstrating the ability of bottom waters to dissolve calcium carbonate.

Information on compensation depths may also be provided from microfossils preserved in sea-floor sediments. Calcite dissolution can be measured by enrichment of solution-resistant forms of planktonic organisms, by benthic-planktonic foraminiferal ratios (foraminifera are one-celled animals that secrete a calcium carbonate internal test), by fragmentation indices (the percentage of broken planktonic tests compared to whole tests), or by the coarse-fraction ratios of sea-floor sediments. Different microfossils will have differing susceptibilities to dissolution, depending on the thickness of the walls of the microfossil tests. Thin-walled plankton will be more solution-susceptible, while thicker-walled tests will resist dissolution. Thin-walled planktonic tests in sea-floor sediments deposited in water depths between the lysocline and the CCD will be removed by dissolution more rapidly than thicker-walled tests, leading to greater enrichment of solution-resistant fossils with greater carbonate dissolution. Relative dissolution rates may be measured by the ratio between solution-susceptible and solution-resistant planktonic shells in sea-floor sediments.

Similarly, the deeper-water bottom-dwelling benthonic foraminifera tend to have thicker walls than the tests of planktonic foraminifera, which live floating in the shallow surface waters. Sea-floor sediments may contain both benthic and planktonic varieties of foraminifera. Dissolution of calcium carbonate will preferentially remove the thinner-walled planktonic foraminifera, thus leading to enrichment in the proportion of benthic forms remaining in the sediment. The relative amount of carbonate dissolution in sediments may be determined by measuring the proportion between benthic and planktonic foraminifera in sediment samples.

Finally, fragmentation of planktonic tests may provide an indication of dissolution of carbonate from marine sediments. The percentage of broken tests to whole tests will increase with greater dissolution of carbonate. Also, coarse-fraction percentages of sediments provide information on carbonate dissolution, because unbroken foraminiferal tests are sand-sized, with particle diameters greater than 63 microns in size. (One millimeter is equal to 1,000 microns.) As foraminifera are dissolved, they tend to break into smaller fragments, so dissolution tends to break down sand-sized particles into smaller silt-sized fragments. By measuring the proportion between sand-sized and silt-sized particles (the coarse-fraction percentage) in calcareous sediments, it is possible to obtain an indicator of the relative amount of dissolution that has affected those sediment deposits. The more dissolution that has occurred, the smaller will be the percentage of coarse (sand-sized) sediment particles.

All these methods provide similar depth estimates for the CCD at approximately 4,500 meters below the sea surface, about halfway between the crests of the mid-ocean ridges and the abyssal plains. Individual compensation depths may vary in the different ocean basins of the world, however, as a result of basin-basin fractionation of carbonate. For example, in the Pacific Ocean, the CCD is typically between 4,200 and 4,500 meters, while in the Atlantic and Indian oceans the CCD is deeper, being found near a depth of 5,000 meters. Even within an ocean basin, the level of the CCD may vary, depending on the balance between carbonate productivity and dissolution in a local area. In the centers of the North and South Pacific oceans, the average compensation depth is between 4,200 and 4,500 meters, while near the equator it is found near 5,000 meters because of the higher biological productivity of equatorial surface waters.

Analyses of deep-sea cores drilled by the *Glomar Challenger* have revealed that the level of the carbonate compensation depth has changed by up to 2,000 meters in the South Atlantic, Indian, and Pacific ocean basins. For example, one of the results of Deep Sea Drilling Project Leg 2 was the discovery of significant vertical excursions in the compensation depth of the Atlantic Ocean. In sea-floor boreholes drilled in the North Atlantic, 2-5-million-year-old calcareous ooze sediments were found atop older (5-23-million-year-old) red clays, which in turn were deposited atop carbonate deposits older than 23 million years. In order for these sediments to have accumulated in that order, large vertical changes must have occurred in the compensation depth, starting when the sea floor was shallower than the CCD more than 23 million years ago. Red clays were deposited between 23 and 5 million years ago, when the CCD became shallower. After these red clays accumulated, deepening of the compensation depth allowed the deposition of younger calcareous sediments atop the carbonate-free red clays.

In order to study the past history of the compensation depth within an ocean basin, it is necessary to obtain a series of cores that were deposited at different paleodepths at the same time in the past. (The paleodepth is the depth at which ancient sea-floor sediments were deposited.) Paleodepth estimates for sea-floor sediments are calculated by studying the cooling history of sea-floor basement rocks. After new sea floor is produced by volcanic activity at the mid-ocean ridge system, these rocks cool and contract, thus sinking to greater water depths as they move away from the ridge system. The older the sea floor, the greater its water depth will be, so sediments deposited atop volcanic sea floor will accumulate in progressively deeper water. Once a series of sediment cores deposited at the same time in the past has been obtained, it is possible for the oceanographer to determine the paleodepth of the compensation depth by finding the paleodepth below which no calcium carbonate is present in ancient sediment deposits.

Context

Studying the history of the compensation depths in different ocean basins increases oceanographers' understanding of the relationships between the chemistry of seawater and ocean-sediment deposition patterns and changes in these factors through time. Marine sediments and their accumulation patterns provide information on the interactions between the earth's climate and the physical, chemical, and geological oceanography of the planet through the effects of these interactions on marine planktonic organisms. By understanding the factors that control deep-sea sediment deposition, oceanographers may better understand the relationships between ocean chemistry and sediment accumulation patterns throughout the history of the earth. This knowledge may allow scientists to forecast potential future changes in ocean chemistry that may affect marine life, which depends upon the chemical balance of oceans to survive.

In addition, humans extract many natural resources from the ocean, including fish and other marine life, marine minerals, and oceanic sediment deposits. In particular, because all petroleum and natural gas deposits accumulate in marine sediments, it is necessary for marine geologists to obtain a thorough understanding of ocean sedimentation processes in order to explain the factors influencing the accumulation of petroleum deposits. Finally, because sea-floor sediment deposits accumulate at very slow rates by human standards of measurement, by understanding the factors that control deep-sea sediment deposition, humans will be able to make informed decisions concerning the rates at which these geological materials are extracted from the sea floor.

Bibliography

Berger, Wolfgang H. "Sedimentation of Deep-Sea Carbonate: Maps and Models of Variations and Fluctuations." *Journal of Foraminiferal Research* 8 (October, 1978): 286-302. A summary of the oceanographic influences on carbonate dissolution and carbonate sediment deposition patterns, with abundant illustrations.

Berger, Wolfgang H., and E. L. Winterer. "Plate Stratigraphy and the Fluctuating Carbonate Line." In *Pelagic Sediments: On Land and Under the Sea*, edited by Kenneth J. Hsü and Hugh C. Jenkyns. Oxford, England: Blackwell Scientific, 1974. A thorough review of the factors that may cause vertical migrations of the compensation depth through time. The text is suitable for college-level readers and contains many explanatory figures.

Hay, William A. "Paleoceanography: A Review for the GSA Centennial." *Geological Society of America Bulletin* 100 (December, 1988): 1934-1956. This review of all aspects of the study of ancient oceans, from the work of the first geologists to current research, covers the history of oceanographic examination of sea-floor sediments, the development of deep-sea sediment sampling, and the history of research on the lysocline and the CCD.

Kennett, James P. *Marine Geology*. Englewood Cliffs, N.J.: Prentice-Hall, 1982. A college-level textbook on all aspects of marine geology and geological oceanography. Chapter 14, "Biogenic and Authigenic Oceanic Sediments," describes the deposition of sea-floor sediments and the factors influencing the positions of the lysocline and the CCD, as well as changes in these depths through time.

Sliter, William V., Allan W. H. Be, and Wolfgang H. Berger, eds. *Dissolution of Deep-Sea Carbonates*. Washington, D.C.: Cushman Foundation for Foraminiferal Research, 1975. This book contains a number of research papers analyzing the dissolution of carbonates in the water column and on the sea floor, along with studies of the factors influencing the position of the lysocline and the compensation depth in ocean basins. Suitable for college-level readers.

Dean A. Dunn

Cross-References

Biostratigraphy, 173; Deep-Sea Sedimentation, 325; Micropaleontology: Microfossils, 1674; Ocean Basins, 1785; Ocean-Floor Drilling Programs, 1805; Oil and Gas Exploration, 1878; Paleobiogeography, 1984; Paleontology: Systematics and Classification, 2001; Sedimentary Mineral Deposits, 2296; Stratigraphic Correlation, 2485; Transgression and Regression, 2534.

THE ORIGIN OF THE OCEANS

Type of earth science: Oceanography

Oceanic waters are derived from the outgassing of hydrated minerals bound up during the formation of the earth. Subsequent evolution of the waters involves primarily ions dissolving in the fluid medium by interactions with the continental and oceanic bottom sediments to give the basic saltiness characteristic of earth's oceans.

Principal terms

CARBONACEOUS CHONDRITES: a class of meteoritic bodies found to contain large amounts of carbon in conjunction with other elements; used to date the solar system and provide chemical composition of original solar nebula

GEOCHEMICAL SINKS: the means by which elements and compounds are removed from the crustal area and oceans to be recycled in active chemical cycles

OUTGASSING: the process by which trapped volatiles in the earth leak out gradually over time to form the terrestrial atmosphere and oceans

PRIMORDIAL SOLAR NEBULA: the original collection of dust and gases that comprised the basic cloud from which the solar system was formed

SMOKERS: undersea vents on the active rift areas, emitting large amounts of superheated water and dissolved minerals from deep inside the earth

SOLAR WIND: the particles being ejected from the sun's surface as a result of the action of solar flares of great energy stripping away the original atmosphere of the earth

VOLATILES: chemical elements and compounds that become gaseous at fairly low temperatures, allowing them to be released from solids easily

WATER OF HYDRATION: water that is bound up loosely to minerals present in the rocks, much of which went to form the oceans

Summary of the Phenomenon

Of all the planets in the solar system, the earth stands out as basically a watery world, distinguished from its peers by excessive quantities of liquid water. Covering more than 1.35 billion cubic kilometers, the earth's seas contain enough salt to cover all Europe to a depth of 5 kilometers. This salty solution is composed primarily of sodium chloride, some 86 percent of the ions by weight, in association with other ions of magnesium, calcium, potassium, sulfate, and carbonate groups, providing a salinity of 35,000 parts per million with pH 8 for the hydrogen-ion concentration, or slightly basic in nature. Of all the water on earth, 97 percent of it is salty, the remainder being proportioned among ice (77 percent of total fresh water) and continental and atmospheric waters. The ice itself, principally in the Arctic-Greenland area (1.72 million square kilometers, 3,200 meters thick) and the Antarctic area (12 million square kilometers, 4,000 meters thick), provides effects ranging from climatic control to habitats for living organisms, to sources of new seawater that, in the past, have caused sea levels to rise more than 100 meters.

The problem of the oceans' origin is twofold: the primordial origin of the water itself and the origin and rate of addition of the salt-inducing ions present in the past and contemporary waters. The data base for solving the problems includes chemistry of water, the amounts and types of runoffs delivered by rivers into the sea, and the composition of volcanic gases, geysers, and other vents opening to the surface. In addition, most researchers find the oceans and atmosphere to be linked in origin, providing additional data for analysis.

Numerous sources for the earth's water have been proposed, although the problem has not been resolved completely. Sources include the primordial solar nebula, the solar wind acting over time, bodies colliding with the earth, impact degassing, and outgassing from the planetary interior. A final solution involves the investigation of factors controlling water on earth, particularly rates, amounts, and types of outgassing, modes of planetary formation, possible chemical reactions providing water, loss rates of gases to space, and, finally, internal feedback mechanisms such as changes in earth's albedo (reflective power), temperature, alteration of mass, and other factors not clearly understood.

The solar wind as a primary source can be eliminated for several reasons. The basic constituents, charged protons, may help formulate water in the atmosphere by reactions with oxygen, but all evidence points to no free oxygen in the primordial atmosphere. The geologic record shows the presence of liquid water at least 4 billion years ago, substantially devoid of free oxygen. Astrophysical evidence suggests that the solar flux of energy, associated with the solar wind, was such that, early in the earth's history, water on earth should have been frozen, not liquid, if that was the primary source. The presence of liquid through at least 80 percent of earth's history, however, has been established.

Colliding bodies would be from two primary sources: meteorites and comets. The presence of cometary bodies striking the earth has yet to be documented; however, the basic chemical makeup, consisting of water, various ions, metals, organic molecules, and dust grains, would supply enough water, providing gigantic numbers of cometary objects struck the earth during the first half-billion years of history. No evidence for such happenings is available at present, although a theory of the earth still being bombarded incessantly by small comets containing large quantities of water has been fiercely debated.

Meteoritic impact, particularly during the earlier stages after final planetary accretion, would definitely add water to the crust via two mechanisms. Through the study of carbonaceous chondrites, the oldest and most primitive meteorites, abundant volatiles, such as water, are found to be bound chemically to minerals such as serpentine. Additional waters, trapped in crustal and mantle rocks, would have been released during impact, quite justifiably in terms of large meteoritic rocks. It has been calculated that such impact degassing should have released 10^{22} kilograms of volatiles, quite close to the currently estimated value of 4×10^{21} kilograms for the earth as a whole. Remnants of such ancient astroblemes are lacking, however, because of subsequent erosion, filling in by molten magma, or shifting of the continental masses over 4 billion years.

The most widely accepted origin for the oceans and atmosphere combines the features of the primordial solar nebula and slow outgassing from within the solidifying earth. Original water would have been combined, under gravitational collapse, with silicates and metallic materials during the planetary accretion process, the hydration of minerals assisted by the heating of the earth by infalling bodies and radioactive elemental decay. Such wet silicates appear to hold large quantities of bound water for indefinitely long periods of time. The primordial earth, believed to have accreted cold, trapped the water molecules; if it had started too hot, all the minerals would have been dehydrated, and if too cold, no water would have been released. A delicate balance of temperature must have been achieved. Further, the volatiles forming the atmosphere must have outgassed first, since water must be insulated from solar radiation in order to form a liquid phase.

A secondary problem deals with how swiftly the fluids outgassed, either all at once, as individual events, or in a continuous fashion. Most data suggest the continuous mode of emission, with greatest reliance on data from still active sources, mainly volcanoes, undersea vents, and associated structures. Fumaroles, at temperatures of 500-600 degrees Celsius, emit copious quantities of water, sulfur gases, and other molecules. These bodies grade gradually into hot spots and geysers, areas where water is moved crustward from great depths. Magmatic melts rising in volcanoes release water and other gases directly to the surface. In Hawaii, for example, the Halemaumau Pit, the volcano Kilauea's most active vent, emits, in terms of material, 68 percent water, 13 percent carbon dioxide, and 8 percent nitrogen, with the rest mostly sulfurous gases. Similar types of values are found in ridge-axis black and white smokers, where hydrothermal accretions result in spectacular deposits of minerals falling out of solution from the emerging hot mantle waters. Detailed studies show water trapped in the structures of altered minerals within basaltic crust of the oceanic plates, 5 percent of the rocks, by weight, in the upper 2-3 kilometers being water and hydroxide ions. Free water is known to be extremely buoyant, rising in the crust along shallow dipping faults. Bound water, subducted to great depths, would be expected to cook, moving upward as the rock density lessens, then acting as a further catalyst for melting the surrounding rocks.

In the earth's earliest stages, the primordial atmosphere was released, to vanish from the earth's gravitational pull because of overheating. In the second phase, gases are released from molten rocks, with a surface temperature of 300 degrees Celsius, providing 70 percent water and large quantities of carbon dioxide and nitrogen. In stage three, the atmosphere and oceans gradually change, with gases and liquid water from volcanoes and weathering action, more and more water deposited as liquid as the temperature falls. The rest of the atmosphere added oxygen either by thermal dissociation of water molecules, photochemical breakdown of high-altitude water, or photosynthetic alteration of carbon dioxide to oxygen in plants.

The saltiness of the oceans can be accounted for by the extreme dielectric constant of water, essentially ensuring that it does not remain chemically pure. Geologic evidence shows the general composition to be similar over time, the stability of water content attributable to the continuous seawater-sediment interface. John Verhoogen has shown that only 0.7 percent of the ocean has been added since the Paleozoic era, primarily from lava materials. The salty quality is a product of acidic gases from the volcanoes (hydrochloric, sulfuric, and carbonic acids) acting to leach out the common silicate rocks. Paleontological studies indicate the change in ions must have been extremely slow, as demonstrated by the narrow tolerance of organisms then alive, such as corals, echinoderms, brachiopods, and radiolarians. Present river ion concentrations differ drastically from the ocean's values, however, indicating a different atmospheric environment in the past. Robert M. Garrels and Fred T. Mackenzie have divided the oceans into three historical periods: earliest, with water and volcanic acidic emissions actively attacking the crust, leaching out ions, leaving residues of alumina and silicates; the next period, from 1.5 to 3.5 billion years ago, slow continuous chemical action would go on attacking the sedimentary rocks, adding silica and ferrous ions; and period three, from 1.5 billion years onward, adding ions to the modern concentrations, until the composition is in apparent equilibrium with a mixture of calcite, potassium-feldspars, illite-montmorillonite clays, and chlorite.

Because it is known that output equals input of ions, a new problem, that of geochemical "sinks," has been identified. Calcium carbonate (limestone) is removed by living organisms to form skeletons, as is silica for opaline skeletons. Metals are dropped from seawater as newly formed mineral clays, oxides, sulfides, zeolites, and as alteration products at the hot-water basaltic ridges. Sulfur is removed as heavy-metal sulfides precipitating in anaerobic environments, while salts are moved in pore waters trapped in sediments. Residence times for many of the ions have been determined: for example, sodium cycles in 210 million years, magnesium in 22 million, calcium in 1 million, and silicon in 40,000. With such effective removal systems, it is truly a measure of the geochemical resistivity of the earth's oceans to change that allows the composition to remain so stable for 4 billion years.

Methods of Study

Numerous avenues of approach have been used to investigate the ocean and its ions, including geological, chemical, and physical means. Geology has supplied basic data on the types and makeup of rocks from the earliest solidified materials to present depositional formations. Use of the petrographic microscope, involving thin sections of rocks seen under polarized light, allows the identification of minerals, providing quantity measurements of water attached to the minerals themselves. Paleontological studies of fossil organisms and paleosoils indicate the range of ions in the sea at diverse geologic periods, both by the ions themselves left in the deposited soils and rocks and through studies of the tolerance ranges for similar, twentieth century organisms. Such studies, along with sedimentology investigations of rates and types of river depositions, dissolved ion concentrations, and runoff rates for falling rain, provide determinants for comparing ion concentrations with those in the past for continentally derived materials.

Chemical analysis reveals the various ions present in seawater and rocks, via two principal methods. Use of the mass spectrometer identifies types and quantities of ions present by use of a magnetic field to accelerate the charged ions along a curved path, the size of the path based on the weight and charge of the ions. Collection at the end of the path provides a pure sample of the different ions present. For solid samples, electron beam probe studies provide analysis from an area only one micron in diameter. The electrons, fired at the sample, cause characteristic X rays to arise from the point. Each type of X ray, energywise, is affixed to a specific element or compound. By use of various optics to focus the X rays, identification of even minute variations in concentration is possible.

Solubility studies provide residence times as a means of geochemical analysis for cyclical research. Similar laboratory projects, testing the ability of water to dissolve and hold ions in solution, argue for a primordial earth atmosphere being essentially neutral, or mildly reducing in nature. Such reduction characteristics are based on the study of planetary composition for earth and, presently, for other planets as supplemented by the various "lander missions," such as Vikings 1 and 2 and the Soviet Venera series. Chemical analysis from such missions in interplanetary space has also determined compositions for meteoritic gases, cometary tails and nuclei, and the mixing ratios for noble gases, important for determining the origin of the solar system. The latter study, involving physics in analyzing radioactive isotopes such as helium 3, an isotope of mantle origin, has allowed geophysicists to consider the earth's mantle as a major elemental source and sink for the various geochemical cycles.

Laboratory analysis reaches two other areas. Petrographic studies of returned lunar rocks reveal that the moon is empty of water, lacking even hydroxyl ions. This discovery helps eliminate the solar wind, and meteoritic impact, as major factors in forming oceans. Furthermore, high-temperature/high-pressure metallurgical and chemical studies indicate molten granite, at temperatures of 900 degrees Celsius and under 1,000 atmospheres of pressure, will hold 6 percent water by weight, while basalt holds 4 percent. Based on geochemical calculations of the amounts of magma in the planet and lavas extruded over the first billion years, all the ocean's waters can be accounted for, particularly if parts of the fluid, as steam under pressure, are a result of oxidation of deep-seated hydrogen deposits trapped within or combined with mantle rocks. This supposition is considered an excellent likelihood from evidence gathered on radioactive decay inside the earth.

Context

Water is, by far, a ubiquitous and most important molecule on the earth. All organisms require it as a basic component of cellular structure and for numerous functions inside the body. The origin of earth's water is highly significant, because the very presence of water may have set the scheme for all subsequent evolution, both geological and biological, on the planet. During the formation of the solar system, the accretion of materials trapped water as molecules of hydration, tied to the minerals, which were released later, some 4 billion years ago, through outgassing by volcanoes and other vents acting as pressure escape valves for the molten interior of the earth. This released water, and other volatile gases, formed the atmosphere and subsequent oceans. A vital interchange was established between the ground and atmosphere, one replenishing elements and compounds as they were lost through geochemical sinks in the normal course of history. Water, at first in the atmosphere, then as liquid seas, apparently helped to mediate the greenhouse effect, a mechanism through which, if allowed to act unhindered, would have accumulated large amounts of heat in the atmosphere, trapping infrared radiation from the sun in carbon dioxide molecules, overheating the early earth. Such actions would have given the earth the characteristics of the planet Venus: enormously hot and totally inhospitable for life's occurrence.

The outgassed fluid, settling as rain, also played the dominant role in shaping the landforms of earth. As a mechanism for fluidization of rocks, it controls the motions to a large extent of magmas and lavas, helping them rise to the surface. As a weathering agent, water, in the forms of rain, snow, and ice, carves away the landscape, removing elements, as ions, to the sea. In that location, these elements became usable by early organisms for fulfilling their biological needs, such as home building or metabolism. Water there acts as a transport mechanism, a mixing agent, and ultimately a removal tool for maintaining a delicate ionic concentration range within the ocean itself. Even more important, however, is the fact that evaporating seawater provides two major features: Its falling, as rain, breaks up rocks and forms soils, with nutrients available for land-based plant life, and it provides the fresh water so necessary to nonocean-dwelling organisms. Without the initial interplay of water on the earth, the globe, instead of being the home of countless billions of creatures, would undoubtedly be a desolate ball, revolving forever around the sun as an improbable abode of life.

Bibliography

Brancazio, Peter J., ed. *The Origin and Evolution of Atmospheres and Oceans*. New York: John Wiley & Sons, 1964. This work is a collection of papers dealing with the chemical problems relevant to the early formation of the fluid parts of the earth. Tracing all the basic arguments, the criteria for water formation is clearly explained and its relationship to minerals and rocks elucidated. Some heavy reading, charts, extra references.

Chamberlain, Joseph W. *Theory of Planetary Atmospheres: An Introduction to*

Their Physics and Chemistry. New York: Academic Press, 1978. A detailed analysis of the characteristics of diverse atmospheres in the solar system, including water contents. By comparisons of chemical compositions and meteorological observations, criteria are established for examining the possible origins for atmospheric gases and oceans. Some mathematics, heavy reading, numerous charts, comprehensive references.

Frakes, L. A. *Climates Throughout Geologic Time*. New York: Elsevier, 1980. A well-written explanation of how the interaction of the earth's atmosphere and oceans has caused the climate of the earth to change over the history of the planet. Beginning with the possible origin of ocean and atmosphere, changes are traced as revealed through the geological and paleontological records. Numerous graphs and charts and extensive references.

Henderson-Sellers, A. *The Origin and Evolution of Planetary Atmospheres*. Bristol, England: Adam Hilger, 1983. This work details the theories of where the volatiles for the earth came from and how the oceans and other planetary atmospheres came into existence from the creation of the solar system. Water as a direct result of outgassing of planetary interiors is considered, as are the effects from lack of water molecules. Harder reading, but an advanced layperson should find it comprehensible. Includes an extensive bibliography.

Holland, Heinrich D. *The Chemistry of the Atmosphere and Oceans*. New York: John Wiley & Sons, 1978. A very detailed reference on the basic chemical elements present in the two media and the wide variety of reactions occurring in each area. The interactions of the two areas are stressed, as are their common origin from materials outgassed from within the earth. The action of their chemicals on the terrestrial areas is described in detail. Contains references and numerous charts of data but is difficult reading.

McElhinny, M. W., ed. *The Earth: Its Origin, Structure, and Evolution*. New York: Academic Press, 1979. A more readable work dealing with all the basic elements of earth science. Starting with the theory of planetary formation, the work covers the origin of oceans, atmosphere, land, and life forms. Excellent description of the changes occurring on the planet throughout geologic time. Well written, it has good pictures and extra references.

Ponnamperuma, C., ed. *Cosmochemistry and the Origins of Life*. Dordrecht, the Netherlands: Reidel, 1982. A collection of works dealing with the distribution of elements in the universe, particularly those necessary for life. Provides information on the formation of the planetary system, showing how the chemicals combined at various temperatures to make the planets as different as they are. Discusses origins of oceans, atmospheres, and life; detailed reading with many charts and an extensive bibliography.

Seibold, E., and W. Berger. *The Sea Floor*. New York: Springer-Verlag, 1982. A delightful book covering the chemistry, geology, and biology of the bottom of the earth's oceans. That the oceans are a result of outgassing is emphasized. Well written, with a very interesting section on the white and black smokers and their relation to the origin of waters and life. Contains excellent illustrations, along with additional references.

Arthur L. Alt

Cross-References

The Atmosphere's Structure and Composition, 128; Elemental Distribution in Earth, 391; The Evolution of Earth's Composition, 496; Fluid Inclusions, 726; The Geochemical Cycle, 818; The Hydrologic Cycle, 1102; Water in Magmas, 1433; Ocean-Atmosphere Interactions, 1779; The Structure of the Oceans, 1871; The Origin of Life, 1961; Precipitation, 2108; Sea Level, 2267; Seawater Composition, 2282; Elemental Distribution in the Solar System, 2434; The Origin of the Solar System, 2442.

THE STRUCTURE OF THE OCEANS

Type of earth science: Oceanography

The ocean has a complex structure, both at its surface and in the vertical dimension descending to the ocean floor. This internal structure results in layering with respect to temperature, salinity, density, and the way in which the ocean responds to the passage of light and sound waves.

Principal terms

CONVECTIVE OVERTURN: the renewal of the bottom waters caused by the sinking of surface waters which have become denser, usually because of decreased temperature

DOLDRUMS: the equatorial zone, where winds are light and variable and there is heavy thunderstorm rainfall

HALOCLINE: a layer within a water body characterized by a rapid rate of change in salinity

HORSE LATITUDES: the belts of latitude approximately 30° north and 30° south of the equator, where the winds are very light and the weather is hot and dry

HYPOTHERMIA: a fall in body temperature below the usual level, which under extreme conditions may result in death

PYCNOCLINE: a layer within a water body characterized by a rapid rate of change in density

SALINITY: the quantity of dissolved solid material in seawater, usually expressed as parts per thousand

SALTWATER WEDGE: a wedge-shaped intrusion of seawater from the ocean into the bottom of a river; the thin end points upstream

THERMOCLINE: a layer within a water body characterized by a rapid change in temperature

Summary of the Phenomenon

One highly significant aspect of ocean structure is a layering based on temperature differences. In order to understand the reasons for the temperature layering of the ocean, one must bear in mind that the primary source of heating for the ocean is sunlight. About 60 percent of this entering radiation is absorbed within the first meter of seawater, and about 80 percent is absorbed within the first 10 meters. As a result, the warmest waters in the ocean are found at its surface.

That does not mean, however, that surface temperatures in the ocean are the same everywhere. Since more heat is received at the equator than at the poles, ocean surface temperatures are closely related to latitude. As a result, they are distributed in bands of equal temperature extending east and west, parallel to the equator. Temperatures are highest along the equator because of the near-vertical angles at which the sun's rays are received here. Toward the poles, ocean temperatures gradually cool as a result of the decreasing angle of the incoming solar radiation.

Measurements of ocean surface temperature range from a high of 33 degrees Celsius in the Persian Gulf, a partly landlocked, shallow sea in a desert climate, to a low of −2 degrees Celsius in close proximity to ice in polar regions. There, the presence of salt in the water lowers the water's freezing point below the normal zero-degree level. Ocean surface temperatures may also vary with time of year, with warmer waters moving northward into the Northern Hemisphere in the summertime and southward into the Southern Hemisphere in the wintertime. These differences are most noticeable in midlatitude waters. In equatorial regions, water and air temperatures change little seasonally, and in polar regions, water tends to be cold all year long because of the presence of ice.

Vertically downward from the equator, toward the ocean floor, water temperatures become colder. That results from the facts that solar heating affects the surface waters only and that cold water is denser than warm water, since its molecules are more closely packed. When waters at the surface of the ocean in polar regions are chilled by extremely low winter temperatures, they become denser than the underlying waters and sink to the bottom. They then move slowly toward the equator along the sea floor, lowering the temperature of the entire ocean. As a result, deep ocean waters have much lower temperatures than might be expected by examination of the surface waters alone. Although the average ocean surface temperature is 17.5 degrees Celsius, the average temperature of the entire ocean is a frigid 3.5 degrees.

Oceanographers recognize the following layers within the ocean, based on its temperature stratification: First, there is an upper, wind-mixed layer, consisting of warm surface water up to 500 meters thick; this layer may be lacking in polar regions. Next is an intermediate layer, below the surface layer, where the temperature decreases rapidly with depth; this transitional layer can be 500-1,000 meters thick and is known as the main thermocline. Finally, there is a deep layer extending to the ocean floor; in polar regions, this layer may reach the surface, and its water is relatively homogeneous, the temperature slowly decreasing with depth.

Because the upper surface layer is influenced by atmospheric conditions, such as weather and climate, it may contain weak thermoclines as a result of the daily cycle of heating and cooling or because of seasonal variations. These are temporary, however, and may be destroyed by severe storm activity. Nevertheless, the vast bulk of ocean water lies below the main thermocline and is uniformly cold, the only exception being hot springs on the ocean floor that introduce water at temperatures of 300 degrees Celsius or higher. Plumes of warm water emanating from these hot springs have been detected within the ocean.

A second phenomenon responsible for layering within the ocean is variation in the water's salinity. For the ocean as a whole, the salinity is 35 parts per thousand, or 35 parts of dissolved solids in every 1,000 parts of water. Considerable variation in the salinity of the surface waters from place to place results from processes that either add or subtract salt or water. For example, salinities of 40 parts per thousand or higher are found in nearly landlocked seas located in desert climates, such as the

Red Sea or the Persian Gulf, because high rates of evaporation remove the water but leave the salt behind. High salinity values are also found at the surface of the open ocean at the same latitudes where there are deserts on land (the so-called horse latitudes). There, salinities of 36 to 37 parts per thousand are common.

At the equator, however, much lower salinity values are encountered, despite the high temperatures and nearly vertical rays of the sun. The reason is that the equatorial zone lies in the so-called doldrums, a region of heavy rainfall. The ocean's surface waters are therefore diluted, which keeps the salinity low. Low salinities are also found in coastal areas, where rivers bring in large quantities of fresh water, and in higher latitudes, where rainfall is abundant because of numerous storms.

Despite the variation in salinity in the ocean's surface water, the deep waters are well mixed, with nearly uniform salinities ranging from 34.6 to 34.9 parts per thousand. Consequently, in some parts of the ocean, surface layers of low-salinity water overlie the uniformly saline deep waters, and in other parts of the ocean, surface layers of high-salinity water overlie the uniformly saline deep layer. Between these layers are zones of rapidly changing salinity known as haloclines. An important exception to this picture is a few deep pools of dense brine—such as are found at the bottom of the Red Sea, for example—where salinities of 270 parts per thousand have been recorded.

Haloclines are very common in coastal areas. Off the mouth of the Amazon River, for example, a plume of low-salinity river water extends out to sea as far as 320 kilometers, separated from the normally saline water below by a prominent halocline. In many tidal rivers and estuaries, a layer of heavier seawater will extend many kilometers inland beneath the freshwater discharge as a conspicuous saltwater wedge.

A prominent density stratification within the ocean results from the variation in ocean temperatures and salinity just described. As has been noted, two things make water heavier: increased salinity, which adds more and more dissolved mineral matter, and lowering of temperature, which results in the water molecules being more closely packed together. Therefore, the least-dense surface waters are found in the equatorial and tropical regions, where ocean temperatures are at their highest. Toward the higher latitudes, the density of these surface ocean waters increases because of the falling temperatures. In these areas, low-density surface water is found only where large quantities of fresh water are introduced, by river runoff, by high amounts of precipitation, or by the melting of ice.

Vertical density changes are even more pronounced. As water temperatures decrease with depth, water densities increase accordingly. This increase in density, however, is not uniform throughout the ocean. At the poles, the surface waters are almost as cold as the coldest bottom waters, so there is only a slight increase in density as the ocean floor is approached. By contrast, the warm surface waters in the equatorial and tropical regions are underlain by markedly colder water. As a result, a warm upper layer of low-density water is underlain by an intermediate layer in which the density increases rapidly with depth. (This middle layer is known as the pycnocline.) Below it is a deep zone of nearly uniform high-density water.

Convective overturning takes place when this normal density stratification is upset. In a stable density-stratified system, the less dense surface water floats on top of the heavier, deeper water. Occasionally, however, unstable conditions will arise in which heavier water forms above lighter water. Then, convective overturning takes place as the mass of heavier water sinks to its appropriate place in the density-stratified water column. This overturning may occur gradually or quite abruptly. In lakes and ponds, it occurs annually in regions where winter temperatures are cold enough. In the ocean, convective overturning is primarily associated with the polar regions, where extremely low winter temperatures result in the sinking of vast quantities of cold water. In addition, convective overturning has been observed in the Mediterranean during the wintertime, when the chilled surface waters sink to replenish the deeper water.

Oceanographers also recognize stratification in the ocean based on the depths to which light penetrates, and they divide the ocean into two zones. The upper zone, which is known as the photic zone, consists of the near-surface waters that have sufficient sunlight for photosynthetic growth. Below this zone is the aphotic zone, where there is insufficient light for photosynthetic growth. The lower limit of the photic zone is generally taken as the depth at which only 1 percent of the surface intensity still penetrates. In the extremely clear waters of the open ocean, this depth may be 200 meters or more.

Stratification in the ocean based on the behavior of sound waves has also been observed. Because sound waves travel nearly five times faster under water than in the air, their transmission in the ocean has been extensively studied, beginning with the development of the echo sounder. So-called scattering layers have been recognized; they are regions that reflect sound, usually because of the presence of living organisms that migrate vertically, as layers within the water column, depending on light intensity. The sofar (sound fixing and ranging) channels are density layers within the ocean where sound waves can become trapped and can travel for thousands of kilometers with extremely small energy losses. These channels have the potential to be used for long-distance communications. Shadow zones are also caused by density layers within the ocean. These layers trap the sound waves and prevent them from reaching the surface. One advantage of shadow zones is that submarines can travel in them undetected.

Methods of Study

The measurement of water temperatures at the ocean's surface is quite simple. A thermometer placed in a bucket of water that has been scooped out of the ocean at the bow of a boat will suffice, provided the necessary precautions have been taken to prevent temperature changes caused by conduction and evaporation. For ocean-wide or global studies, satellites provide near-simultaneous readings of ocean surface temperatures within an accuracy of 1 degree Celsius. These satellites utilize infrared and other sensors, which are capable of measuring the amount of heat radiation emitted by the ocean's surface to within 0.2 degree.

Measuring the temperature of the deeper subsurface waters has always posed a problem, however, because a standard thermometer lowered over the side of a ship will "forget" a deep reading on its way back to the surface. As a result, the so-called reversing thermometer was developed in 1874. This thermometer has an S-bend in its glass tube. When the thermometer is inverted at the desired depth, the mercury column breaks at the S-bend, thus recording the temperature at that depth. Subsequently, electronic instruments which record subsurface water temperatures continuously were introduced. These devices can be either dropped from a plane or ship or moored to the ocean floor.

The measurement of the salinity of seawater is not as easy as one might think. An obvious way to determine water salinity would be to determine the amount of dried salts remaining after a weighed sample of seawater has been evaporated, but in actual practice, that is a messy and time-consuming procedure, hardly suitable for use on a rolling ship. A variety of other techniques have been used over the years, based on such water characteristics as buoyancy, density, or chloride content. By far the most popular relies on seawater's electrical conductivity. In this method, an electrical current is passed through the seawater sample; the higher the salt content of the water, the faster this current is observed to pass. Using this method, oceanographers have been able to determine the salinity of seawater samples to the nearest 0.003 part per thousand—an important advantage, in view of the fact that the salinity differences between deep seawater masses are very minute.

Measurement of the densities of surface water samples can easily be accomplished by determining the water sample's buoyancy or weight, but the real difficulty comes with attempts to determine a subsurface water sample's density. If this water sample is brought to the surface, its temperature, and therefore its density, will change. Although sophisticated techniques are available for the determination of density at depth, in actual practice the density is not measured at all; instead, it is computed from the sample's known temperature, salinity, and depth. It turns out that water's density is almost wholly dependent on these three factors.

Various methods are available for measuring the depth of light penetration in seawater. A crude estimate can be made using the Secchi disk, which was first introduced in 1865. This circular, white disk is slowly lowered into the water, and the depth at which the disk disappears from sight is noted visually. More sophisticated measurements can be made using photoelectric meters. Another good indicator of the maximum depth of light penetration in the sea is the lowest level at which photosynthetic growth can take place. For sound studies within the ocean, various methods are used to create the initial sound, including the use of explosives in seismic profiling. The returning echo is detected by means of a receiver known as a hydrophone.

Context

The only temperature layer in the ocean that most people will experience is the surface zone. Although this layer is warm in equatorial and subtropical regions, in middle latitudes and polar regions it can be quite cold. Cold water can lower the human body's temperature, a condition technically known as hypothermia. In extreme cases, hypothermia can lead to death. For this reason, surfers, snorklers, and scuba divers wear rubber wet-suits to insulate themselves against the effects of cold water. Even warm ocean waters, however, have disadvantages for humans. It is these warm waters that spawn hurricanes.

In many respects, the salinity of seawater is an undesirable characteristic. Persons living near the ocean are familiar with the corrosive effects of salt spray, and countless shipwreck victims have died of thirst while surrounded by water that they could not drink because of its salt content. Nevertheless, it is possible to extract valuable substances, such as magnesium and table salt, from the sea, and some of the dissolved minerals responsible for salinity are the raw materials from which organisms living in the ocean make pearls, seashells, and coral.

The surface layer of the ocean is dense enough to buoy humans and to keep huge ships afloat. At the same time, however, the density of seawater gives waves a massive impact when they strike. Density also causes convective overturning; chilled surface waters sink down to the ocean floor, carrying life-giving oxygen with them. These waters are then spread throughout the oceans by slow-moving currents. The oxygen supports life and burns waste material, thereby keeping the global ocean from becoming stagnant.

Because light waves are highly absorbed by seawater, the ocean is totally dark in the aphotic zone; this lack of light hinders the exploration of the ocean floor. By contrast, sound waves are transmitted faster under water than in air, so underwater sound waves have many important uses. In sonar (sound navigation ranging), sound waves are bounced off the sea floor or other objects in order to determine their depth. In addition, sound channels beneath the sea may someday be used for long-distance communications between humans.

Bibliography

Fairbridge, Rhodes W., ed. *The Encyclopedia of Oceanography*. New York: Reinhold, 1966. An outstanding oceanography source book for the student or the professional. It has sections on the temperature structure of the ocean, salinity, density, underwater light properties, and underwater sound channels. The text is suitable for college-level readers who have some technical background. A well-illustrated and carefully cross-referenced volume.

Gross, M. Grant. *Oceanography: A View of the Earth*. 4th ed. Englewood Cliffs, N.J.: Prentice-Hall, 1987. A well-written and well-illustrated oceanography text. Chapter 7, "Ocean Structure," provides a thorough treatment of the topic. There are many useful diagrams and charts, including color plates showing temperature distribution in the ocean based on satellite imagery. Suitable for college-level readers or the interested layperson.

Ingmanson, Dale E., and William J. Wallace. *Oceanography: An Introduction*. 4th ed. Belmont, Calif.: Wadsworth, 1989. Chapter 7 has useful information on ocean-surface salinities and gives typical salinity profiles for the ocean. Chapter 8 gives similar information regarding temperature, density, light, and sound. The text is well illustrated throughout and is suitable for college-level readers.

McLellan, H. J. *Elements of Physical Oceanography.* Elmsford, N.Y.: Pergamon Press, 1965. A thorough treatment of temperature, salinity, and density distribution within the ocean and the methods used for their measurement. Data are given for selected locations, with helpful tables and charts. There are photographs that help to explain the workings of the reversing thermometer and the bathythermograph.

Pickard, G. L., and W. J. Emery. *Descriptive Physical Oceanography: An Introduction.* 4th ed. Oxford, England: Pergamon Press, 1982. A text designed to introduce oceanography majors to the field of physical oceanography. Chapter 3 has useful sections on the temperature, salinity, density, light, and sound structure of the ocean. Chapter 6 has a discussion of the various instruments and methods used for measuring the above properties.

Sverdrup, H. W., M. W. Johnson, and R. H. Fleming. *The Oceans: Their Physics, Chemistry, and General Biology.* Englewood Cliffs, N.J.: Prentice-Hall, 1942. This text is one of the classics in oceanography. It provides much valuable, detailed information relating to the distribution of temperature, salinity, and density in the oceans. The charts showing the worldwide distribution of temperature and salinity in the ocean have been reproduced in many other oceanography texts. Suitable for college students and the interested nonspecialist.

Von Arx, W. S. *An Introduction to Physical Oceanography.* Reading, Mass.: Addison-Wesley, 1962. Written for readers lacking a strong background in physics and applied mathematics, this book has helpful sections on temperature, salinity, and density distributions in the sea. Also contains an important section on stratification that discusses the concepts of the thermocline, halocline, and pycnocline. For college-level readers.

Donald W. Lovejoy

Cross-References

Coastal Processes and Beaches, 240; Groundwater Pollution, 1028; Groundwater Pollution Remediation, 1035; Groundwater: Saltwater Intrusion, 1042; Ocean-Atmosphere Interactions, 1779; Deep Ocean Currents, 1792; Surface Ocean Currents, 1798; The Origin of the Oceans, 1863; Remote Sensing and the Electromagnetic Spectrum, 2166; Sea Level, 2267; Seawater Composition, 2282; Surface Water, 2504; Water Wells, 2708.

OIL AND GAS EXPLORATION

Type of earth science: Geology
Field of study: Petroleum geology and engineering

Exploration for oil and gas is an important geological activity. By understanding the geologic features with which oil and gas are associated, exploration for these minerals can be made less risky and more economically feasible.

Principal terms

DRY HOLE: a well drilled for oil or gas that had no production
LEASE: a permit to explore for oil and gas on specified land
PERMEABILITY: a property of rocks where porosity is interconnected, permitting fluid flow through the rocks
POROSITY: a property of rocks where empty or void spaces are contained within the rock between grains or crystals or within fractures
PROSPECT: a limited geographic area identified as having all the characteristics of an oil or gas field but without a history of production
REGIONAL GEOLOGY: a study of the geologic characteristics of a geographic area
RESERVOIR: a specific rock unit or bed that has porosity and permeability
SEAL: a rock unit or bed that is impermeable and inhibits upward movement of oil or gas from the reservoir
SOURCE ROCK: a rock unit or bed that contains sufficient organic carbon and has the proper thermal history to generate oil or gas
TRAP: a structure in the rocks that will allow petroleum or gas to accumulate rather than flow through the area

Summary of the Methodology

Exploration for oil and gas involves an application of many geologic principles toward a single goal: the discovery of new reserves of petroleum and natural gas. The exploration geologist may be a specialist in one of the many fields of geology but will also have a strong foundation in other subdisciplines as well as a good background in support sciences such as physics, chemistry, and mathematics. The methodology involved in the search for oil and gas is dependent on human input. Unlike many other procedures in geology, the actual approach used in the exploration for oil and gas will vary with the individual conducting the search. This results in a diversity of opinions as to the best method of oil and gas exploration, dependent upon the diverse geologic characteristics of the region. As no two regions are exactly alike geologically, it would also be expected that no two oil or gas fields are exactly alike. Given this, a diversity of interpretations of a certain area can actually enhance the exploration of this area rather than hinder it. If two geologists look at the same data on a region, they may both develop different theories about potential oil and gas accumulations within the area. Both cannot be correct, but one may be. If only one viewpoint prevailed, it could very easily be the wrong one. The exploration of oil and gas is an optimistic methodology. If a region does not have production, it is considered poorly understood rather than unproductive. This results in a constant reevaluation of regions as ideas in geology change.

Despite the diversity of opinions, ideas generated about the occurrence of oil and gas within a particular region are not merely random thoughts. All theories concerning the potential occurrence of oil and gas within an area must conform to the regional geology, an understanding of the stratigraphy, structure, and depositional and tectonic history of an area. Raw geologic data can be interpreted in many ways. The valid interpretation is one that will fit within the regional understanding of the geology.

As the search for oil and gas begins, the exploration geologist identifies very specific areas within a geologic region, called prospects. A prospect is a potential oil or gas field. A prospect is not merely the extension of an existing field, as such work is classified as development geology. Rather, a prospect would be a potential new field some distance away from preexisting production. In order to locate prospects, a model of what such potential fields will look like needs to be developed. This model will be based on already discovered fields with well-known characteristics, although it is recognized that there will be differences between the two, and this knowledge will serve as a starting point for exploration. Despite differences between prospects and models, all prospects have certain criteria that must be met to demonstrate that a prospect is viable or, in other words, drillable. If one of the criteria cannot be met, the prospect may be regarded as too risky to drill.

The first criterion that an exploration geologist must satisfy is proving the existence of a trap. Proving that a trap is present involves the use of several tools. First, the exploration geologist must refer to the model. The trap type in the model will be the same type of trap in the prospect. Once the geologist knows what type of trap to look for, the specific tool is selected. The tool used to locate a trap is a map constructed on the basis of subsurface data. The type of map constructed will depend on the type of trap present in the model. If the trap is a structural trap, a subsurface structure map showing folds and faults will be constructed, similar to a topographic map. The contours on this map connect points of equal elevation relative to sea level, except that they are in the subsurface rather than on the surface. When studied in the subsurface, hills on a structural contour map represent anticlines or domes, valleys represent synclines or depressions, and sharp cliffs usually indicate faults. If the trap in the model is of a stratigraphic type, then a stratigraphic map showing thickness of a rock unit or bed, differing rock types (facies), or ancient depositional environments is developed. The data to construct such maps are generally derived from subsurface information about the rock units in question derived from previously drilled wells in the vicinity. In addition to well information, data derived through the use of geophysical techniques such as seismic and gravity or magnetic surveys will also add support to a prospect. Surface geologic data are considered but may not accurately reflect the geologic conditions of the subsurface.

Once all the subsurface data have been analyzed and a potential trap located, a detailed examination of the rocks present in the prospect area is needed. Specifically, it must be demonstrated that a rock unit or bed within the trap can function as a reservoir for the oil or gas. The qualities that enable a rock to be a reservoir are porosity, pore spaces between grains or crystals or open fractures, and permeability, the interconnection of pore spaces or fractures that will allow fluid flow (in this case, oil or gas). Demonstrating that these properties exist is usually done through a detailed study of the rocks by using special cylinder-shaped rock samples collected from previously drilled wells called cores. This core analysis is a very important aspect of petroleum geology and is the best way to describe and define reservoirs. Geophysical logs that measure certain physical properties of the rocks are also very valuable in defining a reservoir.

The next thing to be demonstrated is that a source bed for oil or gas exists in the prospect area. This feature is perhaps the most critical, as oil and gas are generated only under very specific chemical and physical conditions. A rock unit or bed must be located in the rocks of the prospect that have the proper chemical consistency and have been subjected to the proper temperatures needed to generate oil or gas. There must also be a pathway or mechanism to allow the oil or gas to migrate from the source bed to the reservoir, as the two will only rarely be the same unit. What is generally needed is a total organic carbon content of a bed to be greater than 1 percent and a temperature history to allow the organic matter to mature into hydrocarbons such as oil or natural gas. The rock type generally involved will be a shale, but some fine-grained limestones and dolomites as well as some cherts will function as source beds. A pathway of migration for the generated oil and gas must be available. This is not a critical problem if the source bed occurs beneath the reservoir bed because of the tendency of upward migration of oil and gas resulting from the lighter density of those fluids compared to the groundwater. If the source bed occurs above the reservoir, it can still function for the prospect if it is dropped down by a fault below the reservoir unit. Direct downward migration of oil and gas is known to occur, but this process would have to be demonstrated as functioning in the prospect area in order to use it to explain the source for a prospect.

If the above criteria for a prospect are met, the next factor to be considered is the presence of a seal. As the tendency is for oil and gas to migrate upward, an impermeable rock unit or bed must be present above the reservoir bed to prevent the oil and gas from flowing through the reservoir unit rather than accumulating in the trap. If oil and gas cannot migrate upward, they will migrate laterally to the highest point (trap) in the last permeable bed (reservoir) they can enter. Seals can be of any impermeable rock type, but common ones are evaporites (rock salt and gypsum) and shales. Fine-grained limestones and dolomites as well as some igneous and metamorphic rocks can also function as seals.

The reservoir, source, and seal are generally determined on a regional basis and do not need to be redemonstrated for each individual prospect in the area, provided that the prospect is consistent with the regional geologic model.

If any dry holes (previously drilled wells without production) are near a prospect, the reason for their lack of production must be explained. Generally this will be done by showing that the wells were drilled away from the prospect in question or that technical or economic problems were encountered. Geologists do not want a prospect with a dry hole in the middle of it unless that well was dry for a reason that the present model can explain.

If all the above criteria have been met, the geologist may have a prospect, provided that a lease can be obtained. An oil and gas lease gives the holder the right to explore and produce oil and gas on the land in question. These are the only rights granted to the lease holder. This lease is usually for a specified term (five or ten years) and pays the landowner an annual rental fee plus a royalty interest in any production. If production is achieved on the lease, the term will not expire until production stops. Production cannot be halted to wait for better economic conditions such as higher prices, as this would endanger the lease. The availability of acreage is a nongeologic factor in the exploration for oil and gas, but it is a critical one. A prospect without at least the potential of acquiring a lease is of little use, as it cannot be drilled and developed.

The final criterion that must be satisfied is the time of oil and gas generation and migration and its relationship to the time of trap formation. In order to determine when these events occurred, a detailed understanding of the geologic history must be attained. In general, the trap must have been formed before the generation and migration of oil and gas in the region. If this is not the case, the trap in question will not likely contain oil and gas. Many excellent traps exist that have been drilled and do not produce because of the timing difference.

Applications of the Method

The outlined method of oil and gas exploration does not represent a rigid methodology. Rather, it represents a guide to exploration that permits many diverse and sometimes unique approaches to a challenge. That challenge is to find oil and gas accumulations large enough to permit economical development.

In order to illustrate how oil and gas exploration activity proceeds, three prospects will be examined. All three resulted in wells being drilled, and all three had different results. The first prospect to be examined was proposed by a geologist working on deep gas potential in the Permian Basin region of West Texas. A regional structural map was made on the top of the major deep reservoir bed in the region. A potential trap in the form of an anticline or dome with an associated fault was located using data from adjacent wells. Because of this, several seismic lines were run over the prospect. The results of this geophysical survey verified the existence of the trap. The trap had the general characteristics of two nearby gas fields and so these fields became the models. The reservoir bed, a chert, was present. Porosity and permeability in the chert were considered to be related to fractures in the rock, and the presence of a nearby fault indicated to the geologist that the reservoir rock should be adequately fractured to permit it to function as an oil or gas reservoir. Studies of the chemistry of the rocks in the region showed that one shale unit could act as a source rock for oil or gas. A problem in the case of this particular prospect was that the source bed was above the reservoir bed. In this region, however, that was a common situation and, in fact, was the source situation in the two model fields. All that had to be demonstrated was that a fault adjacent to the trap had moved the source bed below the reservoir bed. The seismic data indicated that this was the case, and thus the problem could be handled by referring back to the model fields. An impermeable shale unit was present directly above the reservoir bed throughout the region, and, consequently, there was no problem relating to a seal. Only one dry hole was present in the immediate prospect area. Using seismic data, it could be shown that this nonproductive well was, in fact, on the flanks of the prospect and not actually on top of it. As oil and gas tend to flow to the highest possible point within a reservoir, the presence of this dry hole did not eliminate the possibility of production higher in the structure. The timing of the formation of the trap and the generation and migration of the oil and gas was ideal. The trap was formed during the Devonian period (approximately 370 million years ago), and the oil and gas were generated during the Permian period (approximately 280 million years ago). The final criterion to be investigated was the likelihood of attaining a lease. The acreage situation on this prospect was very positive. The geologist's company held two-thirds of the acreage within the prospect. The remaining one-third was held by another oil company. A partnership agreement was established, whereby costs and profits were to be shared. Any well drilled as an exploration well rather than a development well within an existing field is called a wildcat well. The reservoir was expected to be approximately 14,000 feet below the surface. The depth and the model fields indicated that gas was to be the expected product of this well. The well was successful and was the discovery well for a new gas field in West Texas. Approximate cost for this first well to be drilled, including all phases of exploration and lease acquisition, was $3 million. The time from the first presentation of the prospect to the start of drilling operations was twenty-five months, and the well was drilled and completed in six months.

The second example comes from the Gulf Coast region of Texas. In this example, the model was based on fields that were ancient reefs. That is, the traps were small fossil reefs buried in the subsurface. The traps were characterized by thick regions within the reservoir unit, thus the exploration tool in this case was a stratigraphic map showing the thickness of the reservoir bed. Reefs tend to form along the trend of the edge of a shelf, so the potential trap is likely to occur along a line parallel to the shelf edge and along trend with other fields. Several fields were previously discovered near the prospect, and therefore models were in existence. Seismic data were used to verify the position of the shelf edge, but the prospect itself was too small to appear on the seismic data. Based on the stratigraphic map and the existence of nearby production, the potential trap was accepted. The reservoir rock in this case was the reef rock itself, a rock composed of the skeletal remains of large clams that had grown together to form small reefs. The porosity in the model fields was related to these fossils, and adequate permeability was expected in the prospect based on the model fields. The source for the oil was considered to be a shale bed below the reservoir. Studies of the rock chemistry of the region verified this. An impermeable shale unit was directly above the reservoir unit, thus forming an adequate seal. The timing of trap formation and oil and gas generation and migration was consistent with this prospect being a potential oil accumulation. The acreage situation was favorable, and leases were negotiated and a wildcat well drilled. After the well was drilled, the porosity was found to have been closed by the crystallization of calcite. This was only a local phenomenon and not one that could be known before the well was drilled. The results of this drilling demonstrate the potential risk of oil exploration despite solid research and data.

The third example is again from the Permian Basin region of Texas. A prospect had been defined by structural mapping as being a faulted anticline. This work was evaluated and verified by seismic work. Because of its large size, this prospect had the potential of being a truely giant field. The reservoir, source, seal, and timing criteria were the same as for the first example, and no problems were envisioned for this prospect. Problems did develop, however, as a result of the acreage situation. After a careful search of the lease records, it was discovered that the leases were held by a major competitor of the geologist's company. Attempts to develop a partnership were unsuccessful, and thus the prospect was not considered valid. In the search for oil and gas, business and economic factors are as important as geologic ones. Consequently, this last prospect was never drilled. Whatever reason the company in question had for holding this acreage, it must have differed from the model illustrated here, again illustrating the power of differing points of view in oil and gas exploration.

Context

The exploration for oil and gas is an important part of the service aspect of the science of geology. All industrial societies depend on oil and gas as a source of inexpensive energy, and many less developed countries depend on oil and gas exports to fund their economies. Despite the importance of these materials to humanity, world reserves are dwindling and new fields are being discovered at a slow rate.

The process of oil and gas exploration is a difficult one because of the large degree of uncertainty involved. Advances such as high resolution seismic profiling, computer analysis and management of well data, and the use of satellite photographs of the land surface have all improved the way geologists explore oil and gas deposits. Despite the benefits of improved technology, the exploration for oil and gas remains a process of ideas rather than equipment. This does not mean that old, established ideas will dominate the search for oil and gas. In fact, quite the opposite is true. Ideas can and do develop at a much faster rate than technology. Because of this, the potential for change in an approach is always present. Thus, a region that might be considered to have no oil and gas potential may appear differently to geologists who have a different or new idea about the geology of the area. Some new ideas affect all regions of the earth and tend to form a revolution of approaches in the oil and gas industry. Ideas over the last three decades have tended to view geology from a global perspective, and this has changed the exploration for oil and gas. The most important idea of this type is the theory of plate tectonics. This proposed mechanism resulted in a widespread reevaluation of the petroleum potentials of regions, resulting in increased discoveries of new fields.

The effect that the exploration of oil and gas has on society is a very clear one. Oil and gas are needed by almost everyone as sources of relatively inexpensive, clean, and efficient energy. The present structure of the oil industry, including oil exploration and production, is sometimes criticized as being wasteful and inefficient. In some nations, oil and gas exploration has been nationalized and is handled by a team of geologists in order to promote efficiency by eliminating competition for the same prospective new fields. This has been suggested as a model for the oil industry in the United States as a way to increase the known petroleum reserves.

Because the competitive system, in which many geologists develop varying working models of an area, is eliminated by a nationalized approach, only one model is present, and the chances of ever finding oil are greatly reduced. While many nationalized companies are very successful, often their success stories are in areas that simply had not been explored before, and the oil accumulations were very obvious. As these regions mature and oil and gas become harder to find, multiple ideas are needed to locate new fields. A competitive system ensures that as long as a profit can be made, exploration for oil and gas will continue.

Bibliography

American Petroleum Institute. *Primer of Oil and Gas Production.* 3d ed. Washington, D.C.: American Petroleum Institute, 1978. This is a basic introduction to the procedures and techniques of oil and gas production. Chapters on the origin and accumulation of oil and gas and on the properties of reservoirs are included. This book is written as a beginner's text in nontechnical language and contains helpful illustrations.

Baker, Ron. *A Primer of Oil Well Drilling.* 4th ed. Austin: The University of Texas at Austin, 1979. This book is an introduction to the procedures involved in oil and gas well drilling. It includes chapters on exploration and on oil and gas accumulations. The text is well illustrated with many on-site photographs. Suitable for high school or college students.

LeRoy, L. W., and D. O. LeRoy, eds. *Subsurface Geology.* 4th ed. Golden: Colorado School of Mines, 1977. This book is an important reference for all who are interested in the geology of the subsurface. There are many chapters on petroleum geology, but exploration for oil and gas is not the only focus of this book.

The chapters on oil and gas are written by experts in the field and are very complete and well illustrated. Although this book is intended as a reference for college-level students and professionals, it is regularly used as a basic reference for the geology of oil and gas by nongeologists involved in the oil business.

Levorsen, A. I. *Geology of Petroleum.* 2d ed. San Francisco, Calif.: W. H. Freeman, 1967. A full textbook on petroleum geology designed for the college student who has taken some basic geology courses. Serves as a reference for people with an interest in some of the more detailed aspects of petroleum exploration. This book was the training textbook for many present-day exploration geologists. It contains a complete bibliography on each chapter.

Owen, E. W. *Trek of the Oil Finders: A History of Exploration for Petroleum.* Tulsa, Okla.: American Association of Petroleum Geologists, 1975. A detailed history of the development of the petroleum industry throughout the world. It is written from a historical perspective, and the language is technical only when necessary. The text is very well indexed by subject, geographic location, and proper names and is organized into chapters by region.

Selley, R. C. *Elements of Petroleum Geology.* New York: W. H. Freeman, 1985. A well-organized text covering the specifics of oil and gas and their relationship to geology. It is written as a college-level text but does not require extensive knowledge of geology. The book contains subject and proper name indexes, useful illustrations, and appendixes that include a well classification table, a glossary of oil terms and abbreviations, and a table of conversion factors.

West Texas Geological Society. *Geological Examples in West Texas and Southeastern New Mexico (the Permian Basin) Basic to the Proposed National Energy Act.* Midland: West Texas Geological Society, 1979. This short publication was designed to inform state and federal government members about the procedures and costs of exploration for oil and gas. This paper is based on case histories and maps; diagrams and actual costs are included. Although not intended as a basic text on petroleum geology, it is a valuable reference, written in clear, nontechnical language.

Richard H. Fluegeman, Jr.

Cross-References

Diagenesis, 354; Normal Faults, 676; Thrust Faults, 683; Folds, 739; Gravity Anomalies, 997; Oil and Gas: Offshore Wells, 1886; Oil and Gas: Onshore Wells, 1893; The Origin of Oil and Gas, 1901; Oil and Gas: Petroleum Reservoirs, 1909; Oil and Gas: Well Logging, 1915; The Worldwide Distribution of Oil and Gas, 1923; Oil Chemistry, 1931; Oil Shale and Tar Sands, 1939; Seismic Reflection Profiling, 2333.

OIL AND GAS: OFFSHORE WELLS

Type of earth science: Geology
Field of study: Petroleum geology and engineering

Offshore wells are drilled in favorable oil and gas areas that are inundated with either oceanic (salt) or inland lake (fresh) waters. Most of the world's future hydrocarbon reserves may be discovered in offshore provinces.

Principal terms

CONTINENTAL MARGIN: the offshore area immediately adjacent to the continent, extending from the shoreline to depths of approximately 4,000 meters

DIRECTIONAL DRILLING: the controlled drilling of a borehole at an angle to the vertical and at an established azimuth

DRILLING FLUIDS: a carefully formulated system of fluids and solids that is used to lubricate, clean, and protect the borehole

GEOPHYSICS: the quantitative evaluation of rocks by electrical, gravitational, magnetic, radioactive, seismological, and other techniques

HYDROCARBONS: naturally occurring organic compounds that in the gaseous state are termed natural gas and in the liquid state are termed crude oil or petroleum

ROTARY DRILLING: a fluid-circulating, rotating process that is the chief method of drilling oil and gas wells

SEDIMENTARY ROCK: rock formed by the deposition and compaction of loose sediment created by the erosion of preexisting rock

SEISMOLOGY: the application of the physics of elastic wave transmission and reflection to subsurface rock geometry

Summary of the Methodology

Offshore drilling is an extension of on-land oil and gas drilling techniques into waters that either cover or lie adjacent to landmasses of the earth, such as the Great Lakes of North America and the continental margins that surround each continent. The continental margins are the principal arena in which offshore drilling is conducted; they constitute approximately 21 percent of the surface area of the oceans and may contain a majority of the world's future reserves of oil and gas. The offshore continental margin comprises three sections, which are identified by water depths and physical characteristics. The continental shelf is a relatively flat extension of the continent from the shoreline to that depth, an average of 1,350 meters, at which a marked increase in slope is found. Continental slopes, with an average inclination of 4 degrees, extend to depths where the deep-sea floor flattens, between 1,400 and 3,000 meters. Continental rises extend the continental margins into the very deep portions of the oceans, which begin at about 4,000 meters. Because of engineering and economic constraints, the great majority of offshore wells are located on the continental shelf, which ranges from a minimum width of several tens of meters to a known maximum of more than 1,300 kilometers. The broadest shelves, and therefore potentially the most prolific offshore-well regions, occur along the north coasts of the Soviet Union and North America, in the Arctic Ocean, and in the western Pacific Ocean from Australia to the Aleutian Islands.

As of the last decade of the twentieth century, oil and gas production had been established off the coasts of more than forty countries in the continents of Africa, Australia, South America, North America, Asia, and Europe, and offshore drilling had been completed in the waters of more than half the nations on earth. Drilling platforms capable of operating in water deeper than 1,800 meters probe the hydrocarbon potential of the outer continental margin. Even farther offshore, self-propelled drill ships capable of drilling more than 2,000 meters into the sea floor within waters as deep as 6,000 meters have been analyzing the deeper portions of the oceans since the early 1960's.

Offshore drilling for oil and gas, even with the very high costs dictated by its architectural, meteorological, engineering, and safety requirements, is an international priority; it is driven by need, economic return, and national security. Except for difficult-to-explore and environmentally sensitive regions, such as the Arctic, the South American interior, and central Africa, many onshore regions of the world have entered a mature stage of hydrocarbon exploration: Most of the accessible large-volume oil and gas fields have already been discovered. The United States is an excellent example, for it imports almost 50 percent of its daily petroleum requirements, leaving it vulnerable to foreign military and political disturbances. Studies have consistently shown that the best opportunities for increasing the reserves of American oil and gas lie in the continued exploration of the continental margins. Although not all offshore areas contain oil and gas, analyses conducted by the U.S. Geological Survey indicate that within the continental margin of the United States, as much as 40 billion barrels (a barrel equals 42 U.S. gallons, or about 159 liters) of oil and more than 5.7 trillion cubic meters of natural gas are yet to be discovered.

There are many difficulties associated with the drilling of onshore wells. These same difficulties are encountered when drilling is conducted offshore, with additional difficulties being caused by water and wind currents, water depths, and considerations of safety, communications, supply, and maintenance.

Initially, the specific offshore drilling location must be established. Onshore, that is the responsibility of the geologist, who, by studying the various rock exposures and their structures, decides on the best surface site for the drilling equipment. Offshore, such exposures are submerged, and geophysical methods of determining the geology of the sea floor must be used. Offshore geophysics is an indirect technique of studying the rocks composing the sea floor by measuring their physical properties. A magnetometer towed behind an aircraft flying low over the water can be used to measure the magnetic properties of underlying rocks. With a gravimeter mounted in a slow-moving boat, the gravity field associated with the sea floor can be analyzed. A combination of these methods will help the geologist locate a site that is underlain by rocks that may contain hydrocarbons. By far, the most common offshore geophysical tool is the seismic reflection survey. Seismology depends on the artificial generation of an elastic sound wave and its transmission through the layered, sedimentary rocks underlying the sea floor within the continental margin zone. These waves reflect off sedimentary rocks and are transmitted back to the surface of the water, where a vessel will record the time difference between transmission and reflection. Millions of such combined reflection arrival times are interpreted as a cross-sectional view of the underlying sea floor. A series of intersecting seismic sectional views presents a simple three-dimensional portrayal of the best site for offshore drilling equipment.

The type of platform that will be used to contain the drilling equipment is critical, considering the inhospitable weather periodically encountered offshore. There are four types of platforms: the submersible, semisubmersible, and jack-up platforms and the drill ship. A submersible platform is stabilized by flooding the hollow legs and platoons of the platform and establishing seabed moorings. Since these platforms are in contact with the sea floor, they cannot be used in excessively deep waters. In such deep waters, a semisubmersible design is employed; the hollow pontoons are only partially flooded, permitting the platform to settle below the surface of the water but not to rest on the bottom. Inherent in this design is buoyancy that, along with anchor moorings, is sufficient to maintain the platform safely over the drilling site. The ratio of semisubmersible to submersible units in use is approximately 4:1.

By far, the most popular offshore unit is the jack-up platform. These movable structures are towed to the drill location and stationed by lowering massive steel legs to the seabed. In essence, the platform is "jacked-up" on the legs to a level sufficient to protect the unit from storm waves. The fourth design is the drill ship, a free-floating, usually self-propelled vessel that contains amidship an open-water drilling unit. The drill ship is kept on location by computer-activated propellers that maintain the horizontal and vertical motion of the standing ship within safe limits. Regardless of the basic design, all offshore platforms contain a drilling derrick, storage and machinery housing, living and eating quarters, recreation and basic health facilities, and sometimes a helicopter landing pad. The entire structure must be of a size sufficient to house and maintain a normal working crew of forty to sixty individuals.

The equipment employed to drill the offshore borehole into the sea floor does not differ in its fundamental design from similar onshore equipment. The sole method used for drilling offshore wells is the rotary method. Rotary motion is supplied by diesel engines to a length of interconnected drill pipe (the drill string), to the bottom of which is attached the drill bit. Drilling bits come in a variety of styles designed to drill through differing types of sedimentary rock. Each type of drill bit contains an arrangement of high-strength alloy teeth that tear through the rock when rotated under pressure. As the hole deepens, new sections of drill pipe are added. Periodically, the inside of the borehole is lined with cemented casing, which prevents the hole from caving in. During drilling, drilling fluid is circulated through the pipe and hole. This circulating fluid, a mixture of water, special clays, and other minerals and chemicals, is necessary to maintain a safe temperature and pressure in the borehole and to clean the hole of newly created rock chips. All drilling activities take place within the derrick, an open steel structure that often is 60 meters tall. The derrick holds the draw works, whereby the drill string can be drawn out of the borehole and disassembled, one length at a time.

Should a drilling operation discover new reserves of oil or gas, production platforms must be constructed on-site after the movable drilling platform is deployed elsewhere. From these fixed production platforms, as many as fifty or more additional wells are drilled to determine the new hydrocarbon field's size and volume. Each of these boreholes is drilled from the same general location on the production platform; however, at a predetermined depth below the sea floor, individual boreholes veer away from one another, allowing different sectors of the field to be economically developed from one production platform. This process of deviation is termed directional drilling; it requires the assistance of a specialist, as the bottom positions of the boreholes must be very carefully controlled for effective hydrocarbon production. After the final directional hole has been drilled and the limits of the field fully defined, the production derrick is replaced with equipment used to gather the oil and gas from the many active wells flowing into the platform. An offshore pipeline is laid, connecting the producing platform to onshore pipeline and refining systems, and the new field begins its production history.

Applications of the Method

The methods used in drilling offshore wells are similiar to those employed onshore; only the setting is different. Drilling in water up to several thousands of meters in depth requires special procedures that ensure safety to the environment and to those individuals working on the drilling platform.

Because of the expense associated with the siting of an offshore drilling platform, more than one borehole is commonly drilled from the same surface location. More than sixty-five boreholes have been drilled from a single platform. Most are drilled into the seabed at a predetermined angle to vertical, allowing many wells to "bottom" in an oil or gas reservoir rock over a distance as much as 3 kilometers laterally from the platform site. In this manner, the hydrocarbon reservoir can be economically produced with a minimum risk to the aquatic environment.

Such multiple borehole platforms are designed to extend a safe height above sea level. Platforms in use in the Gulf of Mexico, the North Sea, and the Santa Barbara Channel of California are designed to endure the most severe storm that is likely to occur within a one-hundred year cycle, including hurricane force storms, as well as earthquake tremors. Special submersible drilling platforms are designed for operation in polar waters, where ice-free waters exist only for a short time period during summer. These structures, which must be able to withstand strong currents and floating pack ice, are protected below the waterline by a steel or cement caisson. Often the drilling deck is circular, allowing easy passage of floating ice.

Offshore operations are supplied by both boat and helicopter. Conventional supplies, such as drill pipe, drilling mud components, and food are delivered on a regular basis by various-sized crafts. Personnel transfers, priority deliveries, and medical emergencies are conducted by helicopter.

While important in every drilling operation, on a self-contained, isolated offshore platform, the equipment designed to contain a rush of rock formation fluid or gas pressure into the drill hole takes on added significance. When such unexpected pressure is encountered, the drilling crew activate the "blowout preventer stack." Without alert action, a blowout of hydrocarbons can pollute the sea, extensively damage the platform, and cause loss of life.

Floating platforms, semisubmersibles, and drill ships move with wind and water currents. Unless compensated for, these motions affect drilling efficiency. When boreholes are drilled in very deep waters, compliant platforms that yield to weather and water currents are employed.

Offshore drilling is an effort directed toward the discovery of new reserves of hydrocarbons. The first offshore well in the United States was drilled in 1897 off the coast of California from a boardwalk extending 90 meters from the shoreline. In 1947, a steel platform replaced wooden derrick construction in the Gulf of Mexico, and the modern era of offshore exploration was under way. With the need to drill more in distant offshore waters, deep-water technology has greatly advanced.

Offshore operations will continue to occur in all the oceans and seas of the world. Whatever the local environmental and meteorological conditions, evolving offshore technology will continue to meet the challenge of discovering new hydrocarbon reserves.

Context

The drilling of offshore wells for the purpose of discovering economic resources of oil and gas is a natural extension of similar operations that have been conducted onshore since the beginning of the hydrocarbon industry in 1859. Offshore operations continue to expand in response to a global economy increasingly dependent on hydrocarbon-derived energy. Most of the world's future hydrocarbon reserves will be discovered in offshore provinces. The total worldwide volume of onshore sedimentary rocks that are possibly hydrocarbon-bearing has been estimated at about 3 billion cubic meters. In contrast, the volume of continental margin, or offshore, sedimentary rocks that might contain oil or gas totals 7.5-9 billion cubic meters.

The degree and specific locations of offshore exploration and drilling activities depend on political, environmental, and economic factors, all of which affect petroleum products' availability and price. Certain offshore drilling regulations have already been established. In the United States, states' rights generally prevail to approximately 5,500 meters, or 3 nautical miles, offshore. From there out to designated international waters, federal government policies must be followed. The outer limits of American waters and those of other signatory nations is controlled by the ruling of the 1958 United Nations Conference on the Law of the Sea held in Geneva. Because of economic and engineering constraints, these outer limits have not yet been tested with actual drilling. A common cause for the delay in exploration drilling is public concern for the marine environment. An example of a highly publicized and heavily studied American offshore oil spill is a spill that occurred in the Santa Barbara Channel, off California, in 1969; another is the 1989 spill in Prince William Sound, in the Gulf of Alaska. The long-term effects of these spills are unknown. One study, however, has shown that between 1950 and 1980, the commercial fish-catch weight in the Gulf of Mexico increased fourfold, suggesting that offshore compatibility between the fishing and hydrocarbon industries is possible. Yet, as environmentally fragile continental margin areas, such as the shores of Alaska and Canada, continue to be evaluated, intensified concerns for the environment may delay exploration agendas. Finally, the costs of finding and producing oil and gas offshore will continue to climb as deeper waters are probed.

Depending on local conditions, the time gap between the initial geophysical evaluation of an offshore sector and production of oil and gas from that sector normally ranges from ten to fifteen years. As the world continues to rely on hydrocarbons as its principal industrial and domestic fuel, the difficulties attendant on continued offshore exploration and production must be addressed in an orderly and coordinated fashion.

Bibliography

Baker, Ron. *A Primer of Offshore Operations*. 2d ed. Austin: University of Texas Press, 1985. This basic text addresses international offshore operations and is written for the general public. Text covers the chemistry and geology of oil and gas as well as the exploration, drilling, production, and transportation aspects of the business. Illustrated with color photographs and easy-to-understand diagrams.

Duxbury, A. C., and A. B. Duxbury. *An Introduction to the World's Oceans*. 2d ed. Dubuque, Iowa: Wm. C. Brown, 1989. A freshman-level review of the marine environment. Sections are devoted to the physical, chemical, biological, and meteorological structure of the continental margins. Color plates review satellite and research submarine technology.

Ellers, F. S. "Advanced Offshore Oil Platforms." *Scientific American* 246 (April, 1982): 39-49. The methods of construction and emplacement of four different offshore oil platforms, all taller than the World Trade Center and designed to withstand 35-meter waves in water 200 meters deep, are presented in language familiar to readers of this popular monthly magazine.

Engel, Leonard. *The Sea*. Boston: Time-Life Books, 1967. A very easy-to-read introduction to the general physical and chemical composition of the typical ocean. Well illustrated.

Hall, R. Stewart, ed. *Drilling and Producing Offshore*. Tulsa, Okla.: PennWell

Books, 1983. A semitechnical text that introduces the reader to every aspect of the offshore drilling business. Covers drilling, platforms, production, and maintenance, including diving and underwater construction. Up to date.

Maclachlan, Malcolm. *An Introduction to Marine Drilling*. Tulsa, Okla.: PennWell Books, 1986. The purpose of this book is to introduce the new offshore worker to the principal operations of the business. Provides insight into a way of life directly witnessed by only a very small percentage of the general population. Contains a glossary of marine drilling terms.

Myers, A., D. Edmonds, and K. Donegani. *Offshore Information Guide*. Tulsa, Okla.: PennWell Books, 1988. This comprehensive guide may be considered the bible, telephone directory, and database for offshore operations. One section provides some sixteen hundred references to offshore journals, directories, maps, legislation, and conference proceedings.

Albert B. Dickas

Cross-References

Oil and Gas Exploration, 1878; Oil and Gas: Onshore Wells, 1893; The Origin of Oil and Gas, 1901; Oil and Gas: Petroleum Reservoirs, 1909; The Worldwide Distribution of Oil and Gas, 1923; Oil Chemistry, 1931; Oil Shale and Tar Sands, 1939.

OIL AND GAS: ONSHORE WELLS

Type of earth science: Geology
Field of study: Petroleum geology and engineering

Several million wells have been drilled in the exploration for oil and gas within every environment of the earth. Testing, completion, and evaluation technologies of a completed well are similar whether the borehole is dug by the cable-tool or by the rotary method. Downhole, wire-line analyses have evolved from the simple electric log of the 1920's to a modern array of evaluative services.

Principal terms

CABLE-TOOL DRILLING: a repetitive, percussion process of secondary use in the boring of relatively shallow oil and gas wells

COMPLETION PROCEDURES: all methods and activities necessary in the preparation of a well for oil and gas production

DRILL STRING: the length of steel drill pipe and accessory equipment connecting the drill rig with the bottom of the borehole

DRILLING FLUIDS: a carefully formulated system of fluids used to lubricate, clean, and protect the borehole during the rotary drilling process

DRILLING RIG: the collective assembly of equipment, including a derrick, power supply, and draw-works, necessary in cable-tool and rotary drilling

HYDROCARBONS: naturally occurring organic compounds that in the gaseous state are termed natural gas and in the liquid state are termed crude oil or petroleum

ROTARY DRILLING: the principal method of boring a well into the earth using a fluid-circulating, generally diesel-electric generated, rotating process

WELL LOGGING: a graphic record of the physical and chemical characteristics of the rock units encountered in a drilled borehole

Summary of the Methodology

The location of the first drilling operation is lost to history, although it is known that the Chinese drilled for brine and water two thousand years ago using crude cable-tool methods. Similar methods of drilling were still being employed in the 1850's. By this process, a well is created by raising and lowering into the borehole a heavy metal bit suspended from a cable or rope. Gradually, the bit will pound its way through the rocks. With the addition of a jar, a mechanical device that imparts a sharp vertical stress to the bit, the process is greatly improved. Surface equipment, contained within a wooden derrick, or rig, was commonly steam driven and repeatedly withdrew the bit from the hole, allowing it to be again dropped to the bottom of the well. As the bottom of the hole fills with rock chips, a bailer is periodically used to remove this debris.

Cable drilling is a slow process: Its greatest advantage is easy identification of oil- and gas-producing rock units. Because minimal drilling fluids are used, uncontrolled surface flows of encountered hydrocarbons (occurrences known as blowouts) are frequent. For this reason, cable drilling is most applicable within depths of 1,000 meters. As late as 1920, cable-tool rigs drilled as many as 85 percent of all wells completed in the United States.

Introduced to the industry at Corsicana, Texas, in 1895, the rotary method was used to drill 90 percent of American wells in the 1950's. In rotary drilling, the drill bit is attached to connected sections of steel pipe, or drill string, and lowered into the borehole. Pressure is placed on the bit and the drill pipe is rotated, causing the bit to grind against the bottom of the borehole. In contrast to the cable method, new borehole depths are created by the rock being torn, rather than pounded. When the drill bit becomes dull, the drill string is removed from the borehole, disassembled, and stacked within the tall mast, or derrick. A new bit is attached, and the drill string is reassembled.

The application of a drilling fluid system is a key element of the rotary method. Originally ordinary mud, drilling fluids have become a carefully formulated solution of water, clays, and chemical additives. These fluids are circulated under pressure down the center of the drill string, extruded through the drill bit, and pumped back to the surface through the space between the drill string and the borehole. These fluids serve several important functions: to lubricate and cool the drill bit, to remove rock chips from the borehole, and to protect the borehole from dangerous blowouts. Because of its mechanical advantages, the rotary method is approximately ten times faster than is the cable method in drilling a borehole.

After the borehole is completed, and assuming commercial deposits of oil or gas are discovered, completion procedures are initiated. Because surface instruments cannot detect the presence of subsurface hydrocarbons, the rock units exposed in the wall of a borehole must be evaluated for the presence and quality of contained oil and gas. A preliminary analysis is conducted on the rock chips continuously brought to the surface by the drilling fluid system. Later, instruments lowered into the borehole determine the physical and chemical characteristics of the penetrated rocks and their contained fluids and gases. Should the presence of hydrocarbons be indicated, further testing is conducted to determine the economic value of the discovery. Finally, if economic payout is indicated, the borehole undergoes final completion procedures. Special production tubing systems are installed, and the oil or gas is pumped, or flows under its own pressure, from the rocks up the borehole and into a pipeline or surface storage system.

Rotary drilling procedures vary little with geographic location or climate. In urban areas, the derrick is covered with soundproof material and sometimes even disguised for aesthetic purposes. In sensitive areas, such as Arctic regions and offshore operations, safety and environmental preservation precautions are mandated by state and federal law.

Drilling processes other than the cable and rotary have occasionally been used. With the turbodrill method, the drill string remains stationary while the drill bit rotates under the influence of circulating drilling fluid. While this process drills very straight boreholes with minimum mechanical problems, it has not won wide appeal. The hammer drill, a combination of slow rotary motion coupled with percussion impact, produces a faster rate of rock penetration, but again this method has not been accepted in practice. Experiments with vibration and sonic drills have proved unsuccessful or uneconomic. Throughout the world, the rotary drilling method remains standard.

After the location for a borehole is determined, rotary drilling equipment is taken to the chosen site, an area of one or two acres. When the drill rig is assembled, sections of drill pipe, or drill string, are connected within the derrick. The drilling fluid hose is connected to the upper end of the drill string, while a drill bit is attached to the bottom. The rig is now ready to "make hole." The history of a borehole begins with its "spud-in" time, that moment when the ground is broken by the rotating bit.

The rotary table, located in the center of the rig floor and connected to powerful engines, rotates the drill string and attached bit. As the bit rotates, drilling fluid (termed mud) is pumped down the inside of the drill string and through openings in the bit. The density of this mud is carefully controlled so that as it exits the bit, it is capable of lifting rock fragments, or cuttings, from the bottom of the borehole, allowing the bit to rotate against a fresh rock surface. The drilling mud, with its contained cuttings, is circulated up the annulus (passage) created between the wall of the borehole and the outside of the drill string. At the surface, cuttings are separated by flowing the drilling mud through a vibrating sieve. Periodically, a sample of cuttings is collected for geologic analysis. Finally, the cleansed mud circulates through the "mud pit," where, after cooling to surface temperature, it is pumped through the drilling fluid hose back into the drill string. While the borehole is being drilled, this mud system is in continuous circulation. Approximately every 9 meters, as the borehole becomes deeper, a new section of drill pipe is added to the drill string, increasing the depth capability of the rig.

At shallow depths, where the bit is penetrating loose soils and poorly consolidated rock formation, the drilling speed is measured in tens to hundreds of meters per day. With increased depths, penetration rates will diminish to as little as a meter per day, depending on rotation pressure and velocity and rock characteristics. At the surface, "conductor pipe" is driven 6-10 meters into the ground to protect the borehole against collapse. At depths below the conductor pipe, rock units containing fresh water are protected from drilling fluid contamination by cementing "surface casing" through the conductor pipe and into the borehole. At greater depths, progressively smaller radius "intermediate casing" may be cemented into the borehole, keeping the newly drilled hole open while sealing off unusually high or unusually low pressure rock strata. Because each new series of casing must fit into prior cemented casing, the borehole diameter becomes smaller with increased depth. When the borehole reaches programmed total depth (TD), the drilling process is complete. The next phase of activity involves testing for the presence and quantity of oil and gas.

Drill cuttings are periodically collected from the drilling fluid and analyzed in the field in converted mobile-home vehicles. These field tests determine rock type, contained minerals, density, pore space percentage, and association with either natural gas or crude oil (petroleum). Since drilling is an expensive operation, commonly costing millions of dollars, the majority of boreholes are subjected to additional analyses, termed well logging. Conducted by contracted specialists, well-logging operations involve lowering an elongated instrument called a sonde to the total depth of the borehole. As the sonde is slowly pulled up the hole, it records various characteristics of the rocks exposed within the wall of the borehole and their contained fluids and gases. These characteristics, which include electrical resistivity, conductivity, radioactivity, acoustic properties, and temperature, are transmitted to the surface, where they are recorded and filed for future use. It is common for four or five different logs to be recorded, while on a very important borehole, more than twice this number may be taken.

In the office, individuals trained in geology and engineering study the cuttings analyses and logging data and determine the presence and economic extent of oil or gas by calculating rock porosity, permeability, density, thickness, lateral extent, inclination, and pressure at various depths in the borehole. Should these analyses be pessimistic, the borehole is declared "dry and abandoned" and permanently sealed at several depths by cement plugs. Such is the fate of approximately six out of seven boreholes drilled in frontier (new) geographic regions or to unproven depths; such boreholes are termed wildcat wells. For the one in seven wildcat wells in which logging analyses indicate a chance of success, verification analyses in the form of drill-stem testing (DST) will be conducted.

Drill-stem testing equipment is attached to the base of the drill string and lowered to the rock depth to be tested. After this depth is physically isolated from the rest of the borehole, assuring a valid test, the DST tool is activated, allowing fluids or gases contained within the isolated rocks to flow into the drill string and to the surface. From DST, rock pressures and flow capacities are calculated. When DST verifies positive economic results determined by logging analyses, the commercial quantities of either oil or gas, or both, are declared and the well is prepared for its final completion phase.

The borehole is protected by cementing "production casing" through the depth of the production zone. Perforating guns, multibarrel firearms designed to fit into the borehole, are lowered to the target production depth and fired electrically. High-velocity bullets penetrate the casing cement and embed in the rock strata, creating pathways through the strata to the wall of the borehole. Oil or gas emitting from the rock through these pathways flows into installed production tubing and to the surface, where the hydrocarbons are either temporarily stored or directed to a nearby pipeline. At this point the well is completed and "on line."

Applications of the Method

While the basic techniques of drilling onshore oil and gas wells may remain the same worldwide, specialized drilling procedures are used when required by geology or subsurface rock characteristics. The most common of these procedures involves the choice of drilling bit, choice of drilling fluid system, recovery of equipment lost down the borehole (a process known as fishing), and rock coring.

Several types of drilling bits may be used in drilling a borehole to total programmed depth, with the type chosen governed by the rock being drilled. Rock formations are classified by drilling crews as either soft or hard, depending on crushing strength. Soft formations include unconsolidated rocks, shale, siltstone, and sandstones. Dense limestones, chert, quartzite, granite, and lava sequences are examples of hard formations. Drilling bits differ in the quality of steel used in their manufacture, the degree of case-hardening employed, and the design and spacing of the drill bit teeth. In the drilling of hard formations, a high-quality steel, case-hardened bit with short, closely spaced teeth is chosen.

The majority of drilling fluid systems are suspensions of clays and other solids in water called water-base muds. The addition of colloidal clay material to drilling mud creates the viscosity necessary to remove cuttings from the bottom of the borehole. When shale is being drilled, clay particles from this rock disperse in the mud, thus naturally creating viscosity. Inert solids are added to the mud system to increase the mud weight and to prevent the loss of mud circulation. Increased mud system weight decreases the chance of a blowout. On the other hand, too great a mud system weight may cause lost circulation, which is the loss of volumes of drilling mud into cracks or crevices in the rocks exposed in the wall of the borehole. Inert lost circulation material includes wood fibers, ground walnut shells, cellophane flakes, and minerals that expand in the presence of water. The overall chemical and physical characteristics of any mud system is periodically checked and altered with changes in drill depth and geologic conditions.

In the drilling of any borehole, the probability exists of a mechanical failure whereby some of the drilling equipment becomes unattached from the drill string in the borehole. Lost equipment must be removed as soon as possible, as the chances of recovery decrease with time. If removal is not possible, the borehole must be directionally drilled around the zone of lost equipment, or the borehole must be redrilled; both are expensive operations. Because a majority of the equipment used in the drill string is hollow, most fishing tools are designed to attach to the inside of the object, or "fish." Outside fishing tools attach themselves to the fish by passing over the exterior of the fish. Specialized recovery equipment includes the milling tool, used to grind the fish into pieces small enough to be circulated from the borehole by the drilling fluid, and the junk basket, designed to recover articles small enough to be lifted but not circulated from the borehole, by circulating drilling fluid.

In the process of coring, a large specimen of the rock being drilled, in contrast to the small average size of drill cuttings, is cut from its natural depth and removed to the surface of the borehole for examination. Analysis of cored rock material yields the most reliable information on the physical, fluid, and gas-bearing characteristics of a rock potentially capable of containing oil or gas. Physical analyses consist of the measurement of rock pore space, permeability, and water and hydrocarbon saturation. Conventional coring requires a core bit and core barrel, both attached to the bottom of the drill string. Core bits can be either metal teeth or diamond-faced: diamond core drilling increases both the percentage of core recovery and the drill penetration rate. In a coring operation, only the outer rim of the rock formation is cut, leaving a portion—the core—of the formation intact. With continued coring, the lengthening core is retained in the core barrel. After the desired length of core is cut, the drill string is removed from the borehole and the core extracted from the core barrel. A variation involves side-wall coring from the wall of the borehole. Such cores are collected after the drilling of the borehole, in contrast to conventional cores, which are collected while the borehole is being drilled. In side-wall operations, a short length of tube is fired into the borehole wall at the depth of desired core collection. The tube remains attached to the core tube device, or gun, by steel cable. The core is extracted from the borehole wall by pulling the core gun a short distance up the borehole. As many as thirty cores, up to 6 centimeters in length, can be collected in this manner in one trip down the borehole. Because cored rock is the preferred material for geologic and engineering studies of a borehole, all cores are carefully described, identified, and stored in a "core shed" for future evaluation.

Context

The age of hydrocarbons began in the sixth decade of the nineteenth century and will end when safely and economically superseded by a period of history dependent upon a more advanced form of energy. Twentieth century society is principally warmed, transported, fueled, and otherwise dependent upon oil and gas. The best means of extracting these substances from the earth is through the process of drilling. After the Organization of Petroleum Exporting Countries (OPEC) crisis of the early 1970's, drilling activity in the United States increased on an annual basis until 1982, when 88,106 wells were drilled. The borehole depths of these wells totaled in excess of 120 million meters for an average depth of 1,390 meters per well. Of all the wells, those classified as wildcat wells were the most important, as they offer the greatest potential for the discovery of new reserves of hydrocarbons. Of 7,914 wildcat wells drilled in the peak drilling year of 1982, 1,402 were commercially completed, for a success rate of almost 18 percent. In spite of this record activity, production and utilization of domestic hydrocarbons exceeded newly discovered oil and gas reserves. By the mid-1980's, worldwide economic and political factors resulted in a precipitous 85 percent decline in the number of working rotary drilling rigs in the United States: from a 1982 high of 4,530 to a 1986 low of 663. This unprecedented reversal in activity within the oil and gas drilling industry triggered an increase in American dependence on foreign crude oil imports from a low in 1983 of 28 percent to a level approaching 45 percent in 1987, dangerously close to the record high 46 percent in 1977 that resulted from the OPEC era of international influence.

The fortunes of the American oil and gas drilling industry are closely tied to the market value of a barrel (42 U.S. gallons, or about 159 liters) of crude oil. As that value increases, so generally does the number of drilling rigs under contract. Adding confusion to this economy-to-rig-use relationship are considerations such as governmental policies, environmental concern, and marketplace competition for high-risk investment dollars. After thirteen decades of drilling wells in the search for new reserves of oil and gas, terrestrial portions of the United States are considered a mature exploration province. The chances of discovering large new reserves of hydrocarbons on land are very small. The future lies in drilling within the offshore provinces (deep water of the Gulf of Mexico and the Atlantic eastern seaboard) and environmentally protected regions (northern Alaska and national parks and forestlands). In order to maintain a hydrocarbon-based energy economy while reducing dependence upon foreign hydrocarbons, oil and gas well-drilling and production programs may have to take place in these frontier exploration regions. Such programs must be governed by consensus regulatory, environmental, and economic policies until either solar, nuclear, or some unforeseen resource assumes the dominant energy position and oil and gas wells no longer need be drilled into the earth.

Bibliography

Allaud, Louis A., and Maurice H. Martin. *Schlumberger: The History of a Technique*. New York: John Wiley & Sons, 1977. An interesting historical account of the mineral-prospecting methodology invented in 1912 by Conrad Schlumberger and used in modified form in the evaluation of the majority of oil and gas wells drilled throughout the world.

Gray, Forest. *Petroleum Production for the Nontechnical Person*. Tulsa, Okla.: PennWell Books, 1986. After thirty years in the industry, the author wrote this oil and gas story for an audience that also works daily in the industry but has yet to master the technology and its terminology. Each chapter is accompanied with a series of exercises. A detailed glossary is included.

Kennedy, John L. *Fundamentals of Drilling*. Tulsa, Okla.: PennWell Books, 1982. An easy-to-understand basic presentation on oil and gas well drilling. Details the tools and methods used and includes sections on economics, future trends, and an introduction to the industry.

Langenkamp, Robert D. *Oil Business Fundamentals*. Tulsa, Okla.: PennWell Books, 1982. A book for individuals interested in learning business perspectives of oil and gas well drilling. In addition to technology, this nontechnical presentation includes chapters on ownership rules, drilling, financing, and the marketing of hydrocarbons.

Welker, Anthony J. *The Oil and Gas Book*. Tulsa, Okla.: PennWell Books, 1985.

Written to bridge the communication gap between the oil and gas industry and members of the general public, such as bankers, investors, and newspersons. Especially valuable because of special-interest topics covering partnerships, joint ventures, promotions, and working interests.

Albert B. Dickas

Cross-References

Oil and Gas Exploration, 1878; Oil and Gas: Offshore Wells, 1886; The Origin of Oil and Gas, 1901; Oil and Gas: Petroleum Reservoirs, 1909; The Worldwide Distribution of Oil and Gas, 1923; Oil Chemistry, 1931; Oil Shale and Tar Sands, 1939.

THE ORIGIN OF OIL AND GAS

Type of earth science: Geology
Field of study: Petroleum geology and engineering

Oil and gas are two of the most important fossil fuels. The formation of oil and gas is dependent on the preservation of organic matter and its subsequent chemical transformation into kerogen and other organic molecules deep within the earth at high temperatures over long periods of time. As oil and gas are generated from these organic materials, they migrate upward, where they may accumulate in hydrocarbon traps.

Principal terms

FOSSIL FUEL: a general term used to refer to petroleum, natural gas, and coal

HYDROCARBONS: solid, liquid, or gaseous chemical compounds containing only carbon and hydrogen; oil and natural gas are complex mixtures of hydrocarbons

KEROGEN: fossilized organic material in sedimentary rocks that is insoluble and that generates oil and gas when heated; as a form of organic carbon, it is one thousand times more abundant than coal and petroleum in reservoirs, combined

METHANE: a colorless, odorless gaseous hydrocarbon with the formula CH_4; also called marsh gas

NATURAL GAS: a mixture of several gases used for fuel purposes and consisting primarily of methane, with additional light hydrocarbon gases such as butane, propane, and ethane, with associated carbon dioxide, hydrogen sulfide, and nitrogen

PETROLEUM: crude oil; a naturally occurring complex liquid hydrocarbon, which after distillation yields a range of combustible fuels, petrochemicals, and lubricants

RESERVOIR: a porous and permeable unit of rock below the surface of the earth that contains oil and gas; common reservoir rocks are sandstones and some carbonate rocks

Summary of the Phenomenon

The origin of oil and gas begins with the production of organic matter by plants and plantlike organisms, through a process called photosynthesis. Photosynthesis converts light energy from the sun into chemical energy and produces organic matter (or carbohydrates, which include sugars, starches, and cellulose) and oxygen. Carbohydrates burn easily and release considerable amounts of energy in the process. It is this property that makes them ideal fuels.

To become a fossil fuel, the organic matter in an organism must be preserved after the organism dies. The preservation of organic matter is a rare event because most of the carbon in organic matter is oxidized and recycled to the atmosphere through the action of aerobic bacteria. (Oxidation is a process through which organic matter combines with oxygen to produce carbon dioxide gas and water.) Less than 1 percent of the organic matter that is produced by photosynthesis escapes from this cycle and is preserved. To be preserved, the organic matter must be protected from oxidation, which can occur in one of two ways: The organic matter in the dead organism is rapidly buried by sediment, shielding it from oxygen in the environment, or the dead organism is transported into an aquatic environment in which there is no oxygen (that is, an anoxic or anaerobic environment). Most aquatic environments have oxygen in the water, because it diffuses into the water from the atmosphere and is produced by photosynthetic organisms, such as plants and algae. Oxygen is removed from the water by the respiration of aerobic organisms and through the oxidation of decaying organic matter. Oxygen consumption is so high in some aquatic environments that anoxic water is present below the near-surface oxygenated zone. Environments that lack oxygen include such places as deep, isolated bodies of stagnant water (such as the bottom waters of some lakes), some swamps, and the oxygen-mimimum zone in the ocean (below the maximum depth to which light penetrates, where no photosynthesis can occur). Large quantities of organic matter may be preserved in these environments.

Some bacteria, called anaerobic bacteria, can survive in water without oxygen and in sediments with anoxic pore water. These bacteria partially decompose organic matter through processes such as fermentation, sulfate-reduction, nitrate-reduction, and methanogenesis (or methane production). Methane is formed as sediment is buried to relatively shallow depths (centimeters to meters), because of the activity of methanogenic bacteria living in this sediment. Bubbles of methane can be seen rising from stagnant water overlying sediment and are often referred to as "marsh gas."

The major types of organic matter preserved in sediments include plant fragments, algae, and microbial tissue formed by bacteria. Animals (and single-celled animal-like organisms) contribute relatively little organic matter to sediments. The amount of organic matter contained in a sediment or in sedimentary rock is referred to as its total organic content (TOC), and it is typically expressed as a percentage of the weight of the rock. To be able to produce oil, a sediment typically must have a TOC of at least 1 percent by weight. Sediments that are capable of producing oil and gas are referred to as "hydrocarbon source rocks." In general, fine-grained rocks such as shales (which have clay-sized grains) tend to have higher TOC than do coarser-grained rocks.

The organic matter trapped in sediment must undergo a series of changes to form oil and gas. These changes take place as the sediment is buried to great depths as a result of the deposition of more and more sediment in the environment over long periods of time. Temperature and pressure increase as depth of burial increases, and the organic materials are altered by these high temperatures and pressures.

As sediment is gradually buried to depths reaching hundreds of meters, it undergoes a series of physical and chemical changes, called diagenesis. Diagenesis transforms sediment into sedimentary rock by compaction, cementation, and removal of water. Methane gas commonly forms during the early stages of diagenesis as a result of the activity of methanogenic bacteria. At depths of a few meters to tens of meters, organic compounds such as proteins and carbohydrates are partially or completely broken down, and the individual component parts are converted into carbon dioxide and water or are used to construct geopolymers, or large, complex organic molecules of irregular structure (such as fulvic acid and humic acid and larger geopolymers called humins). During diagenesis, the geopolymers become larger and more complex, and nitrogen and oxygen content decreases. With increasing depth of burial over long periods of time (burial to tens or hundreds of meters over a million or several million years), continued enlargement of the organic molecules alters the humin into kerogen, an insoluble form of organic matter, that yields oil and gas when heated.

As sediment is buried to depths of several kilometers, it undergoes a process called catagenesis. At these depths, the temperature may range from 50 to 150 degrees Celsius, and the pressure may range from 300 to 1,500 bars. The organic matter in the sediment, while in a process called maturation, becomes stable under these conditions. During maturation, a number of small organic molecules are broken off the large kerogen molecules, a phenomenon known as thermal cracking. These small molecules are more mobile than are the kerogen molecules. Sometimes called bitumen, they are the direct precursors of oil and gas. As maturation proceeds and oil and gas generation continues, the kerogen residue remaining in the source rock gradually becomes depleted in hydrogen and oxygen. In a later stage, wet gas and condensate are formed. ("Condensate" is a term given to hydrocarbons that exist as gas under the high pressures existing deep beneath the surface of the earth but condense to liquid at the earth's surface.) Oil is typically generated at temperatures between 60 and 120 degrees Celsius, and gas is generated at somewhat higher temperatures, between about 120 and 220 degrees Celsius. Large quantities of methane are formed during catagenesis and during the subsequent phase, which is called metagenesis.

When sediment is buried to depths of tens of kilometers, it undergoes the processes of metagenesis and metamorphism. Temperatures and pressures are extremely high. Under these conditions, all organic matter and oil are destroyed, being transformed into methane and a carbon residue, or graphite. Temperatures and pressures are so intense at these great depths that some of the minerals in the sedimentary rocks are altered and recrystallized, and metamorphic rocks are formed.

Accumulations of oil and gas are typically found in relatively coarse-grained, porous, permeable rocks, such as sandstones and some carbonate rocks. These oil- and gas-bearing rocks are called reservoirs. Reservoir rocks, however, generally lack the kerogen from which the oil and gas are generated. Instead, kerogen is typically found in abundance only in fine-grained sedimentary rocks such as shales. From these observations, it can be concluded that the place where oil and gas originate is not usually the same as the place where oil and gas are found. Oil and gas migrate or move from the source rocks (their place of origin) into the reservoir rocks, where they accumulate.

Oil and gas that form in organic-rich rocks tend to migrate upward from their place of origin, toward the surface of the earth. This upward movement of oil occurs because pore spaces in the rocks are filled with water, and oil floats on water because of its lower density. Gas is even less dense than oil and also migrates upward through pore spaces in the rocks. The first phase of the migration process, called primary migration, involves expulsion of hydrocarbons from fine-grained source rocks into adjacent, more porous and permeable layers of sediment. Secondary migration is the movement of oil and gas within the more permeable rocks. Oil and gas may eventually reach the surface of the earth and be lost to the atmosphere through a seep. Under some circumstances, however, the rising oil and gas may become trapped in the subsurface by an impermeable barrier, called a cap rock. These hydrocarbon traps are extremely important because they provide a place for subsurface concentration and accumulation of oil and gas, which can be tapped for energy sources.

There are a variety of settings in which oil and gas may become trapped in the subsurface. Generally, each of these traps involves an upward projection of porous, permeable reservoir rock in combination with an overlying impermeable cap rock that encloses the reservoir to form a sort of inverted container. Examples of hydrocarbon traps include anticline traps, salt dome traps, fault traps, and stratigraphic traps (see figure). There are many types of stratigraphic traps, including porous reef rocks enclosed by dense limestones and shales, sandstone-filled channels, sand bars, or lenses surrounded by shale, or porous, permeable rocks beneath an unconformity. The goal of the exploration geologist is to locate these subsurface hydrocarbon traps. Enormous amounts of geologic information must be obtained, and often many wells must be drilled before accumulations of oil and gas can be located.

Methods of Study

The origin of oil and gas can be determined using physical and chemical analyses. Petroleum contains compounds that serve as biological markers to demonstrate the origin of petroleum from organic matter. Oil can be analyzed chemically to determine its composition, which can be compared to that of hydrocarbons extracted from source rocks in the lab. Generally, oil is associated with natural gas, most of which probably originated from the alteration of organic material during diagenesis, catagenesis, or metagenesis. In some cases, gas may be of abiogenic (nonorganic) origin. Samples of natural gas can be analyzed using gas chromatography or mass spectrometry and isotope measurements.

Commonly, rocks are analyzed to determine their potential for producing hydrocarbons. It is important to distinguish between various types of kerogen in the rocks because different types of organic matter have different potentials for producing hydrocarbons. In addition, it is important to determine the thermal maturity or evolutionary state of the kerogen to determine whether the rock has the capacity to generate hydrocarbons or hydrocarbons have already been generated.

The quantity of organic matter in a rock, referred to as its TOC, can be measured with a combustion apparatus, such as a Leco carbon analyzer. To analyze for TOC, a rock must be crushed and ground to a powder and its carbonate minerals removed by dissolution in acid. During combustion, the organic carbon is converted into carbon dioxide by heating to high temperatures in the presence of oxygen. The amount of carbon dioxide produced is proportional to the TOC of the rock. The minimum amount of TOC considered adequate for hydrocarbon production is generally considered to be between 0.5 and 1 percent TOC by weight.

The type of organic matter in a rock can be determined indirectly through study of the physical and chemical characteristics of the kerogen or directly by using pyrolysis (heating) techniques. The indirect methods of analysis include examination of kerogen with a microscope and chemical analysis of kerogen. Microscopic examination can identify different types of kerogen, such as spores, pollen, leaf cuticles, resin globules, and single-celled algae. Kerogen that has been highly altered and is amorphous can be examined using fluorescence techniques to determine whether it is oil-prone (fluorescent) or inert or gas-prone (nonfluorescent). Chemical analysis of kerogen provides data on the proportions of chemical elements, such as carbon, hydrogen, sulfur, oxygen, and nitrogen. A graph of the ratios of hydrogen/carbon (H/C) versus oxygen/carbon (O/C) is used to classify kerogen by origin and is called a van Krevelen diagram. There are three curves on a

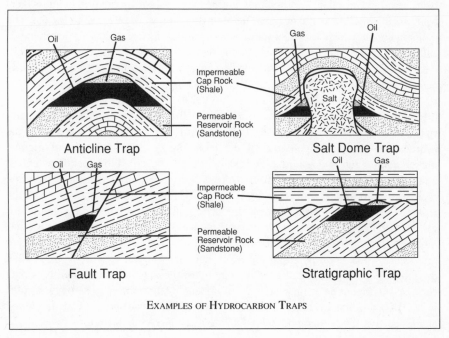

EXAMPLES OF HYDROCARBON TRAPS

van Krevelen diagram, labeled I, II, and III, corresponding to three basic types of kerogen. Type I is rich in hydrogen, with high H/C and low O/C ratios, as in some algal deposits; this type of kerogen generally yields the most oil. Type II has relatively high H/C and low O/C ratios and is usually related to marine sediments containing a mixture of phytoplankton, zooplankton, and bacteria; this type of kerogen yields less oil than Type I, but it is the source material for a great number of commercial oil and gas fields. Type III is rich in oxygen, with low H/C and high O/C ratios (aromatic hydrocarbons), as in terrestrial or land plants; this type of kerogen is comparatively less favorable for oil generation but tends to generate large amounts of gas when buried to great depths. As burial depth and temperature increase, the amount of oxygen and hydrogen in the kerogen decreases, and the kerogen approaches 100 percent carbon. Hence, a van Krevelen diagram can be used to determine both the origin of the organic matter and its relative thermal maturity.

The potential that a rock has for producing hydrocarbons can be evaluated through a pyrolysis, or heating, technique, commonly called Rock-Eval. Rock-Eval yields information on the quantity, type, and thermal maturity of organic matter in the rock. The procedure involves the gradual heating (to about 550 degrees Celsius) of a crushed rock sample in an inert atmosphere (nitrogen, helium) in the absence of oxygen. At temperatures approaching 300 degrees Celsius, heating releases free hydrocarbons already present in the rock; the quantity of free hydrocarbons is referred to as S_1. At higher temperatures (300-550 degrees Celsius), additional hydrocarbons and related compounds are generated from thermal cracking of kerogen in the rock; the quantity of these hydrocarbons is referred to as S_2. The temperature at which the maximum amount of S_2 hydrocarbons is generated is called T_{max} and can be used to evaluate the thermal maturity of the organic matter in the rock. In addition, carbon dioxide is generated as the kerogen in the rock is heated; the quantity of CO_2 generated as the rock is heated to 390 degrees Celsius is referred to as S_3. (The temperature is limited to 390 degrees Celsius because at higher temperatures, CO_2 is also formed from the breakdown of inorganic materials, such as carbonate minerals.) These data can be used to determine the hydrocarbon-generating potential of the rock, the quantity and type of organic matter, and the thermal maturity. For example, $S_1 + S_2$, called the genetic potential, is a measure of the total amount of hydrocarbons that can be generated from the rock, expressed in kilograms per ton. If $S_1 + S_2$ is less than 2 kilograms per ton, the rock has little or no potential for oil production, although it has some potential for gas production. If $S_1 + S_2$ is between 2 and 6 kilograms per ton, the rock has moderate potential for oil production. If $S_1 + S_2$ is greater than 6 kilograms per ton, the rock has good potential for oil production. The ratio, $S_1/(S_1 + S_2)$, called the production index, indicates the maturation of the organic matter. Pyrolysis data can also be used to determine the type of organic matter present. The oxygen index is S_3/TOC, and the hydrogen index is S_2/TOC. These two indices can be plotted against each other on a graph, comparable to a van Krevelen diagram.

Context
Oil and gas are derived from the alteration of kerogen, an insoluble organic material, under conditions of high temperatures (50-150 degrees Celsius) and pressures (300-1,500 bars). After oil and gas are generated, they migrate upward out of organic-rich source rocks and come to be trapped and accumulate in specific types of geologic settings. The search for oil and gas deposits trapped in the subsurface can be expensive and time-consuming, and it requires trained exploration geologists. Once a promising geologic setting has been located, the only way to determine whether oil and gas deposits are actually present in the subsurface is to drill a well. Oil and gas are two of the earth's most important fossil fuels. It is important to understand that a finite amount of these hydrocarbons is present within the earth. They cannot be manufactured when known reserves are depleted.

Bibliography

Durand, Bernard, ed. *Kerogen: Insoluble Organic Matter from Sedimentary Rocks*. Paris: Éditions Technip, 1980. This book consists of a series of papers on various ˙aspects of kerogen, ranging from its origin and appearance under the microscope to its chemical composition and structure as determined by a variety of analytical means. The articles are written by specialists; most of them are in English, but a few are in French. Technical but does contain a number of beautiful color plates illustrating the appearance of kerogen-rich rocks and organic microfossils (pollen, spores, acritarchs, dinoflagellates) as seen through the microscope.

North, F. K. *Petroleum Geology*. Boston: Allen & Unwin, 1985. A long book (607 pages) that covers a wide variety of topics related to petroleum geology, it includes five main parts: introduction; the nature and origin of petroleum; where and how oil and gas accumulate; exploration, exploitation, and forecasting; and distribution of oil and gas. Designed as a college textbook to introduce students to many topics with practical application to exploration and drilling in addition to the basics on the origin of oil and gas. Well illustrated with maps and geologic cross sections representing many oil-producing areas around the world. Suitable for geologists and college students.

Peters, K. E. "Guidelines for Evaluating Petroleum Source Rock Using Programmed Pyrolysis." *The American Association of Petroleum Geologists Bulletin* 70 (March, 1986): 318-329. Although rather technical in nature, this article provides information on Rock-Eval pyrolysis, one of the major analytical techniques for analyzing rocks to determine their hydrocarbon potential. Provides a brief summary of the technique and goes into detail using numerous examples, discussing some of the problems encountered in interpreting samples. Suitable for geologists and advanced college students.

Selley, Richard C. *Elements of Petroleum Geology*. New York: W. H. Freeman, 1985. This book is designed as a college textbook for students near the end of their coursework in geology or for geologists beginning careers in the petroleum industry. Fairly technical, it requires basic understanding of geological concepts.

Tissot, Bernard P., Bernard Durand, J. Espitalié, and A. Combaz. "Influence of Nature and Diagenesis of Organic Matter in Formation of Petroleum." *The American Association of Petroleum Geologists Bulletin* 58 (March, 1974): 499-506. This article discusses the generation of hydrocarbons and changes in kerogen that occur during burial. Somewhat technical but well illustrated with graphs. Provides a concise summary of the types of kerogen and depths at which oil and gas are generated.

Tissot, Bernard P., and D. H. Welte. *Petroleum Formation and Occurrence*. 2d ed. New York: Springer-Verlag, 1984. This book is one of the most comprehensive guides to the origin of petroleum and natural gas and should be considered one of the leading references in the field. The book is divided into five parts: the production and accumulation of geologic matter (a geological perspective); the fate of organic matter in sedimentary basins (generation of oil and gas); the migration and accumulation of oil and gas; the composition and classification of crude oils and the influence of geological factors; and oil and gas exploration (application of the principles of petroleum generation and migration). Each part is divided into chapters, which are well written and well illustrated with line drawings and graphs. Easy to read; up-to-date coverage of the field is provided. An indispensable reference for geologists that is suitable for college-level students.

Waples, Douglas W. *Geochemistry in Petroleum Exploration*. Boston: International Human Resources Development Corporation, 1985. This book provides an overview of the origin of oil and gas and should be considered a leading reference in the field. Concise and well illustrated with line drawings and graphs. Easy to read. A good reference for geologists, it is also suitable for college-level students.

Pamela J. W. Gore

Cross-References

Diagenesis, 354; Oil and Gas Exploration, 1878; Oil and Gas: Offshore Wells, 1886; Oil and Gas: Onshore Wells, 1893; Oil and Gas: Petroleum Reservoirs, 1909; Oil and Gas: Well Logging, 1915; The Worldwide Distribution of Oil and Gas, 1923; Oil Chemistry, 1931; Oil Shale and Tar Sands, 1939; Earth Resources, 2175; Unconformities, 2563.

OIL AND GAS: PETROLEUM RESERVOIRS

Type of earth science: Geology
Field of study: Petroleum geology and engineering

A petroleum reservoir is a body of rock that contains crude oil, natural gas, or both, that can be extracted by a well. Two conditions must be met. First, to contain and permit extraction of its fluids, the reservoir rock must be porous and permeable. Second, there must be a reservoir trap, a set of conditions that concentrates the petroleum and prevents its migration to the earth's surface.

Principal terms

FIELD: one or more pools; where multiple, the pools are united by some common factor
NATURAL GAS: a flammable vapor found in sedimentary rocks, commonly, but not always, associated with crude oil; it is also known simply as gas or methane
PERMEABILITY: a measure of the rate of flow of fluids through a porous medium
PETROLEUM: a dark green to black, flammable, organic liquid commonly found in sedimentary rocks; it looks like used crankcase oil and is also called crude oil or liquid hydrocarbon
POOL: a continuous body of petroleum-saturated rock within a petroleum reservoir; a pool may be coextensive with a reservoir
POROSITY: the percentage of pore, or void, space in a reservoir
RESERVOIR: a body of porous and permeable rock; petroleum reservoirs contain pools of oil or gas
TRAP: a seal to fluid migration caused by a permeability barrier; traps may be either stratigraphic or structural
WELL LOG: a stripchart with depth along a well borehole plotted on the long axis and a variety of responses plotted along the short axis; there are many varieties, including borehole log, geophysical log, electric log, and wireline log; information may be obtained about lithology, formation fluids, sedimentary structures, and geologic structures

Summary of the Phenomenon

Petroleum (from the Latin) literally means "rock oil." Petroleum reservoirs are volumes of rock that contain or have the potential to contain hydrocarbons (crude oil and natural gas) that can be extracted by wells. A reservoir may contain one or more pools, that is, continuous bodies of oil or gas. One or more related pools form a field. The definition of a pool depends on economic as well as geologic considerations—as the price of oil goes up, the size of a pool goes down. There are four components to a petroleum reservoir: the rock, the pores, the trap, and the fluid.

In the vast majority of cases (99 percent-plus), the reservoir rock is a sedimentary rock. Sedimentary rocks form when unconsolidated sediment, deposited on the earth's surface by water or wind, becomes a solid rock. Two types of sedimentary rocks contain 95 percent of the world's petroleum: sandstones and carbonates. Sandstone reservoirs contain approximately half the United States' petroleum. A freshly deposited sand is made up of mineral grains, mostly quartz, deposited from water in rivers, along shorelines, and in the ocean in the shallow water adjacent to the continent; less often, it is deposited by wind in sand dunes. Sand-sized grains range from 0.06 to 2.00 millimeters, or smaller than a small pea.

Carbonate rocks include limestones and dolostones. Limestones are made of the mineral calcite (calcium carbonate, $CaCO_3$). Sand-sized grains of calcite form when organisms, such as clams and corals, extract calcite (and aragonite, a related calcium carbonate mineral) from water to build their skeletons. When the animal dies, the skeletons are broken into fragments, which are then sorted by waves and currents and deposited along beaches or on the sea floor. Very fine-grained, mud-sized calcite and aragonite may be deposited with the sand-sized grains. This fine carbonate comes from calcareous algae (marine plants). In some cases, corals and algae may combine their activity to construct a wave-resistant mass, a coral reef. Reefs form the best potential reservoir rock. Dolostones, although they form a relatively small portion of the world's total carbonate mass, contain almost 80 percent of the petroleum in carbonate reservoirs in the United States. Dolostones are dominated by the mineral dolomite. Dolomite forms by the reaction of preexisting calcium carbonate minerals with magnesium-rich solutions. How this replacement takes place is not well understood.

A petroleum reservoir has the same general attributes as a water aquifer; it is a porous and permeable body of rock that yields fluids when penetrated by a borehole. Porosity is a measure of the pore space in a reservoir, the space available for storage of petroleum. It is usually expressed as a percentage. A freshly deposited unconsolidated sand contains about 25 percent intergranular pore space, normally occupied by water. As the sand is buried deeper and deeper, the grains interpenetrate, and the pores are reduced in size and percentage. At the same time, cements will precipitate in the pores. Thus, the pore space decreases, and the sand becomes a solid—a sandstone. To be a petroleum reservoir, a rock needs 10 percent or more porosity. A good reservoir will have 15-20 percent porosity. Sandstone reservoirs seldom exceed 25 percent porosity, but carbonate reservoirs can have up to 50 percent porosity. This greater porosity is a result of very high porosity in the open structure of reef rocks and cave systems of some limestones.

Porosity can be divided into primary and secondary types. Primary porosity is the porosity present at the time the rock was deposited. It depends on several factors, including the roundness and size range of the grains (sorting). Secondary porosity forms after the rock is solidified, when grains and cements are dissolved. Secondary porosity is most common in limestones but is also important in sandstones.

Permeability is a measure of the rate of flow of fluids through a porous medium. In general, the more porous the rock, the more permeable it is likely to be; however, the relation is not simple. For example, Styrofoam (a type of polystyrene plastic) has very high porosity but almost no permeability. Permeability of petroleum reservoirs is seldom less than 1 millidarcy, and a good reservoir needs 10-100 millidarcies.

A petroleum trap is a geometric situation in which an impermeable layer of rock (a caprock) seals a permeable, petroleum-bearing reservoir rock from contact with the earth's surface. A common type of caprock is shale, or consolidated, lithified mud. There are two common types of traps, structural and stratigraphic. Structural traps form where the originally horizontal sedimentary rock layers are disrupted by warping (folding) and breaking (faulting). A much sought-after type of fold trap is an anticline. Anticlinal folds have a cross section that is concave down (like the letter *A*). Because oil and gas are lighter than water, they migrate to the high point on the anticline and are prevented from reaching the surface by an impermeable caprock. Fault traps occur where a break in a rock layer brings a reservoir rock into contact with an impermeable rock. Salt-dome traps form where bodies of salt flow upward and pierce overlying rock layers. Salt domes form both anticlinal and fault traps on their crest and margins. They are common on the Gulf Coast of the United States. Stratigraphic traps form where the permeability barrier is a result of lateral or vertical changes in the rock, changes as a result of the conditions under which the original sediment was deposited. Stratigraphic traps include buried river channels, beaches, and coral reefs. Geologic methods dominate the search for stratigraphic traps.

Reservoir fluids consist of water, crude oil, and natural gas. When sediments are deposited, they are (or soon become) saturated with water, usually salt water. The oil forms from the alteration (called maturation) of organic material buried in sedimentary rocks. This process takes place in the absence of oxygen at temperatures of 60-150 degrees Celsius when the sediments are buried. Natural gas forms by further thermal alterations of the hydrocarbons (thermogenic gas) or by low temperature alteration of near-surface organic material (biogenic gas, the gas that can be seen bubbling up from the bottom in swamps). After formation, the oil and gas must be expelled from its source rock and migrate into a reservoir rock. As oil is lighter than water, it migrates up the water column to the highest location in the trap. If there is no trap, the oil will seep onto the earth's surface. Although oil seeps are common, in most cases the oil will be prevented from reaching the surface by a trap. The trapped reservoir fluids will then stratify themselves on the basis of density, lightest at the top (natural gas) and densest on the bottom (water).

Petroleum reservoirs are not uniformly distributed in time or space; certain areas of the world and certain intervals of geologic time have a disproportionate amount of the world's petroleum reserves. One unifying characteristic of these major areas of concentration is the presence of a basin. A basin is an area where rocks thicken from the margin to basin center, rather like a mud-filled saucer. The geologic conditions in basins favor the formation of oil and gas in the basin center and its migration into traps along the basin margin.

Globally, most of the world's oil is in the Middle East: Saudi Arabia (170 billion barrels), Kuwait (67 billion barrels), Iraq (43 billion barrels), and Iran (51 billion barrels). Venezuela (25 billion barrels) and Mexico (48 billion barrels) have the major Latin American reserves. Nigeria (18 billion barrels) and Libya (21 billion barrels) in Africa and the Soviet Union (63 billion barrels) in Europe round out the picture. The United States has 27 billion barrels in reserves, of which 85 percent is in four states: Alaska (largely in North Slope fields around Prudhoe Bay), Texas (both along the Gulf Coast salt domes and in the Permian Basin of West Texas), California (southwest), and Louisiana (Gulf Coast salt domes). While the world's major producing areas are widely separated, they were much closer together 100 million years ago (in the Cretaceous period), and many of them shared a common setting, what geologists call the Tethys Sea.

In terms of time, very little oil is found in rocks older than 500 million years. Rocks of Jurassic and Cretaceous age (about 65-200 million years old) contain 54 percent of the world's oil and those about 35-55 million years old, the Eocene epoch, contain 32 percent of the world's oil. It is not clear whether this young age (geologically speaking) is related to the origin of oil or results from the fact that deep wells cost more money so that older rocks are less thoroughly drilled.

Methods of Study

The exploration for petroleum reservoirs has two intimately related aspects, one geophysical and the other geological. In geophysical exploration, the scientist, called an exploration geophysicist, uses the physics of the earth to locate petroleum reservoirs in structural traps. The principal technique is seismic reflection profiling. In this approach, the geophysicist sets off deliberate explosions and uses the energy reflected from subsurface rock layers to interpret the folds, faults, and salt domes that may be present. Variation in the gravity, magnetic, and heat-flow characteristics of the earth may also point to the location of oil and gas pockets in the subsurface.

Geological exploration dominates in the search for stratigraphic traps. Petroleum geologists use facies models to predict the location and extent of petroleum reservoirs. Facies models are based on information about the size, internal characteristics, and large-scale association of modern sediment accumulations. Data based on well logs obtained from previously drilled wells are used to prepare structure maps, which show the "topography" of the reservoir surface, and thickness variation (isopachous) maps. Data from well logs, well cuttings, and cores are used to prepare lithofacies maps, which show the lateral variation in the rocks. These variations influence porosity and permeability trends in the reservoir. Such maps can then be compared to the facies models to make predictions about the size, location, and the location of the edges of stratigraphic traps in the subsurface. Commonly applied facies models for sandstones include those for rivers, beaches, deltas, and sand dunes. Those for carbonate rocks include beaches, reefs, and dolostones.

A technique that combines geology and geophysics is seismic stratigraphy. In this approach, the data from artificial explosions are interpreted in terms of the depositional system of the rocks; for example, a delta system has a seismic signature that is distinct from that of sediments deposited in the shallow waters of the continental shelf. On the whole, the most favorable "prospect" is the portion of a trap closest to the earth's surface. Since oil and gas rise to the top of a trap, this location is the most likely volume to contain petroleum.

Context

Petroleum supplies a major portion of the world's fossil energy and, consequently, is an important element in the complex international play of economic forces. In other words, what decides whether a body of rock is a petroleum reservoir is not simply geology but also the reservoir's economic and political setting. The basic problem centers on the fact that petroleum is a nonrenewable resource, is present in finite amounts, and is not randomly distributed in the earth's subsurface. Millions of oil and gas wells have been drilled in the continental United States, making it the most mature country in the world from the point of view of petroleum exploration. The "easy" oil has been found, and it is becoming harder to find the fewer and fewer undiscovered economically exploitable petroleum pools. On a more positive note, however, as drilling density has increased, so has knowledge. Better information, better understanding of how and when petroleum enters a reservoir, and better techniques for finding traps have improved the success ratio of oil drilling.

Bibliography

Haun, John D., and L. W. LeRoy, eds. *Subsurface Geology in Petroleum Exploration*. Golden: Colorado School of Mines, 1958. This book contains forty-one short articles covering myriad specific techniques of use to petroleum geologists. Chapters cover the analysis of well cuttings, cores, and fluids, well-logging methods and interpretation, subsurface stratigraphic and structural interpretation, geochemical and geophysical methods, well drilling, formation testing, and well evaluation. Most of the articles assume very little prior knowledge on the part of the reader.

Hunt, John M. *Petroleum Geochemistry and Geology*. San Francisco: W. H. Freeman, 1979. Petroleum is a complex organic substance, and its geochemistry is not clearly understood. This book covers many topics, including composition, origin, migration, accumulation, and analysis of petroleum and the application of petroleum geochemistry in petroleum exploration; seep and subsurface prospects; crude oil correlation; and prospect evaluation. While parts of this book are descriptive and explanatory, much of it requires a chemistry background and algebra.

King, Robert E., ed. *Stratigraphic Oil and Gas Fields*. Tulsa, Okla.: American Association of Petroleum Geologists, 1972. Thirteen chapters discuss various exploration techniques and thirty-five chapters discuss case histories of specific reservoirs, pools, and fields. These case histories include information on discovery, development, and trap mechanisms. While written to provide the professional geologist with models upon which to base exploration predictions, some chapters can provide the interested nonspecialist with insights into what a field, pool, and reservoir are.

Levorsen, A. I. *Geology of Petroleum*. 2d ed. San Francisco: W. H. Freeman, 1967. This classic textbook, which was very popular from the mid-1950's to the late 1970's, strongly influenced and unified the way petroleum geologists classify traps and view their discipline. While intended for advanced undergraduate and graduate geology majors in college, it is so well written that its organization, introductory and summary statements on various topics, and specific examples can still serve as a source of general information for the interested nonspecialist. There have been many developments since its publication, however, and its production statistics are out of date.

Moore, Calvin A. *Handbook of Subsurface Geology*. New York: Harper & Row, 1963. Aimed at undergraduate geology students who intend to go into the oil industry, this book has a very pragmatic approach. There is no math or chemistry in it; instead, it stresses the preparation of diagrams of value to the exploration geologist (structure maps, thickness variation maps, lithofacies maps, and cross sections) as well as interpretation of well logs and how to evaluate a formation test.

Selley, Richard C. *Elements of Petroleum Geology*. New York: W. H. Freeman, 1985. This textbook is intended for undergraduate college geology majors. It is more technical than Levorsen's book. Topics covered include the properties of oil and gas, exploration methods, generation and migration of petroleum, reservoir and trap characteristics, and basin classification. Elementary geology, algebra, and chemistry are needed for most of the chapters.

David N. Lumsden

Cross-References

Alluvial Systems, 31; Continental Structures, 290; Thrust Faults, 683; Folds, 739; Gravity Anomalies, 997; Groundwater: Saltwater Intrusion, 1042; Oil and Gas: Well Logging, 1915; Earth Resources, 2175; Strategic Resources, 2188; Sediment Transport and Deposition, 2290; Seismic Reflection Profiling, 2333; Stratigraphic Correlation, 2485; Transgression and Regression, 2534.

OIL AND GAS: WELL LOGGING

Type of earth science: Geophysics
Field of study: Exploration geophysics

Reservoir rock data obtained by well logging are of vital importance to the petroleum industry. With these data, the production potential of a well can be determined and many problems involving the structure, environment of deposition, and correlation of rock strata can be solved.

Principal terms

CONDUCTIVITY: the opposite of resistivity, or the ease with which an electric current passes through a rock formation

CORRELATION: the tracing and matching of rock units from one locality to another, usually on the basis of lithologic characteristics

CUTTINGS: small rock chips that are the pulverized remains of the rocks that have been penetrated by the drill bit

GAMMA RADIATION: electromagnetic wave energy originating in the nucleus of an atom and given off during the spontaneous radioactive decay of the nucleus

HYDROCARBONS: organic compounds consisting predominantly of the elements hydrogen and carbon; mixtures of such compounds form petroleum

LITHOLOGY: the mineralogical composition of a rock unit

NEUTRON: an uncharged, or electrically neutral, particle found in the nucleus of an atom; it is slightly more massive than a proton

PERMEABILITY: measured in millidarcies, the capacity of a rock unit to allow the passage of a fluid; rocks are described as permeable or impermeable

PETROLEUM: a natural mixture of hydrocarbon compounds existing in three states: solid (asphalt), liquid (crude oil), and gas (natural gas)

POROSITY: the volume of pore, or open, space present in a rock

RESERVES: the measured amount of petroleum present in a reservoir rock that can be profitably produced

RESERVOIR: any subsurface rock unit that is capable of holding and transmitting oil or natural gas

RESISTIVITY: a measure of the resistance offered by a cubic meter of a rock formation to the passage of an electric current

SONDE: the basic tool used in well logging; a long, slender instrument that is lowered into the borehole on an electrified cable and slowly withdrawn as it measures certain designated rock characteristics

Summary of the Methodology

A well log is a continuous record of any rock characteristic that is measured in a well borehole. The log itself is a long, folded paper strip that contains one or more curves, each of which is the record of some rock property. Since the first "electric log" was run in a well in France for the Pechelbronn Oil Company in 1927, well logs have been the standard method by which well data have been displayed and stored. Well logs and the information they record can be classified in two ways: by purpose (lithology, porosity, or fluid saturation determination) and by type (electrical, radioactive, or sonic).

After a well has been drilled, it is standard procedure to log it. Logging has been compared to taking a picture of the rock formations penetrated by the borehole. The technique consists of lowering the logging tool, or "sonde," to the bottom of the borehole on the end of an electrified cable that is attached to a truck-mounted winch at the surface. The truck also contains the instruments for recording the logged data. The sonde, which is 4.5-6 meters long and has a diameter of 7.5-13 centimeters, is then pulled up the borehole at a constant rate, measuring and recording the data of interest. Measurements are recorded coming "uphole," rather than going "downhole," because it is easier to maintain a constant sonde velocity by pulling it up. On the downward course, the sonde has a tendency to "hang up" on numerous irregular surfaces in the borehole. It is essential to run logs to evaluate petroleum potential before the borehole is lined with steel pipe, because the well completion process is expensive and will be done only if economically justified. Data obtained from the well by logging are used to determine such rock parameters as lithology, porosity, and fluid saturation.

Of the logging curves that can be run for lithology identification and correlation, the most useful are the gamma-ray, spontaneous potential, and caliper. The gamma-ray log records the intensity of natural gamma radiation emitted by minerals in the rock formations during radioactive decay. An advance in gamma-ray technology has been the development of the gamma-ray spectrometry tool, a device that measures the wavelengths of the gamma rays and makes possible the identification of individual minerals. The spontaneous potential, or SP, log measures small natural potentials (voltages) caused by the movement of fluids within the formations. These currents largely arise as a result of salinity differences between the pore waters of the formations and the mud in the borehole. Although the borehole is drilled with a bit of a particular size, its diameter is never constant from top to bottom. The caliper log provides a continuous measurement of borehole diameter by means of spring-activated arms on the sonde that are pressed against the wall of the borehole.

Porosity is determined by using singly or in combination the sonic, neutron, and density logs. The standard sonic tool has an arrangement of two transmitters, each with its own signal receiver. The transmitters send out sound waves, which are detected back at the receivers after passing through the rock. The neutron log tool bombards the formation with fast neutrons. These neutrons are slowed by collisions with ions in minerals and fluids. Because a hydrogen ion has approximately the same mass as does a neutron, collisions with hydrogen ions are most effective in slowing the neutron for the same reason that a billiard ball is slowed more by a collision with another billiard ball than it is by a collision with the rail of the table. The slowed neutrons are deflected back to the tool to be counted and recorded. Like the neutron log, the density log is a nuclear log. The density sonde bombards the formations with medium-energy gamma rays. The gamma rays collide with electrons in the formation, causing the gamma-ray beam to be scattered and its intensity reduced before it returns to the detector on the sonde.

Most logs used to determine water and oil saturations in the formations employ some method of measuring the passage of an electric current through the rock. The electric logs can be subdivided into induction logs and electrode logs. The induction log measures the conductivity of the formation and is the most commonly used device. The induction-logging sonde generates a magnetic field that induces a current deep in the formation. The passage of this current is measured by the logging tool. In the electrode-log system, electrodes on the sonde put current directly into the borehole fluid or the formation. The resistance to the flow of the electric current through the formation is measured as the formation resistivity. The short normal log, microlog, and microlaterolog measure resistivity immediately adjacent to the borehole, while the laterolog and guard log measure resistivity deep in the formation. Deep readings are made by narrowly focusing the electric current beam and directing it straight into the formation rather than letting it diffuse through the mud and into the adjacent formations. The laterolog and microlaterolog are most commonly used when the borehole mud has a saltwater, rather than a freshwater, base.

The temperature log, a nonelectric log, continuously records borehole temperature and can also be used for fluid identification. The dipmeter log is a resistivity device run with three or four electrodes arranged around the perimeter of the sonde. If the rock layers are inclined at any angle to the horizontal, this inclination, or dip, can be detected, because the electrodes will encounter bed boundaries at slightly different times on different sides of the borehole. An on-line computer converts these differences to angle of dip. The cement-bond log is a sonic device that measures the degree to which cement has filled the space between the steel pipe, or casing, that lines the inside of the borehole and the formations behind it (complete filling is desired).

Applications of the Method

Lithology refers to the mineralogical composition of the rock unit, or formation. Oil and natural gas occur almost exclusively in the sedimentary rocks sandstone, limestone, and dolomite; the latter two are known as carbonate rocks. Shale, the most abundant of all sedimentary rocks, is never a reservoir rock for hydrocarbons, because it is impermeable. An important purpose of well logs is to determine the lithology of the rock formations and, thus, to identify those that possess suitable permeability to serve as reservoir rocks. The principal radioisotopes (thorium, uranium, and potassium), from which most natural gamma radiation emanates, are usually found in minerals in clays and shales. Therefore, the gamma-ray log is used to differentiate shales from sandstones and limestones and to calculate the amount of clay that might be present in some sandstones. Since most fluid movement is in or out of porous and permeable formations, the SP curve may be used to identify such rocks. These rocks are usually sandstones—hence, the identification of lithology. While permeable zones can be located, it is not possible to calculate actual permeability values. Next to permeable formations, the diameter of the borehole is reduced by the buildup of mud cake on the borehole wall. Borehole diameter also changes dramatically through shales, because shale is weak and crumbles, or "caves," thus enlarging the borehole. The caliper log can therefore be used as a lithology log to identify permeable sandstones and "caving" shale.

Porosity is a measure of the total open space in a rock unit that is available for the storage of hydrocarbons. Such space is normally expressed as a percentage of the total rock volume. Knowledge of formation porosity is necessary to determine the total petroleum reserves in the formation or oil field. The sonic log has historically been the most widely used porosity tool. The time, in microseconds, required for a sound wave to travel through one meter of the rock is continuously plotted on the log. This travel time is the reciprocal of velocity, so a wave that has a high velocity has a short travel time. The use of a dual transmitter-receiver system for modern sonic logs eliminates the effects of changing borehole diameter and deviations of the borehole from the vertical. Formation travel times are functions of lithology and porosity. If the formation lithology is known, the porosity can be calculated. Because a sonic wave travels faster through a solid than through a liquid or gas, increasing porosity causes greater travel times. The presence of shale in the rock formations will also cause unusually high travel times and erroneously high porosity calculations. The neutron tool principally senses the hydrogen ions present in the formation fluids, which, in turn, are found in the pore spaces. This log is affected by lithology, because clays in shales have water within their crystal structure, and the tool senses this water as if it were pore water. The density log measures electron density, which is directly related to the overall, or bulk, formation density. The greater the bulk density, the lower the porosity, because mineral matter is denser than fluid-filled pore space. A related log is the variable-density log, which is used to locate rock zones that are highly fractured and, thus, potential reservoir rocks. The fractures in the rock have the effect of lowering the bulk density.

Because accurate interpretation of the data gathered by the three porosity tools is dependent on a knowledge of lithology, it is common practice in the petroleum industry to run porosity tools in combination, particularly the neutron and density logs. Cross-plotting the readings from the two logs provides both lithology and porosity information. In addition, neutron and density logs respond oppositely to the presence of natural gas in a formation. Density porosity readings increase, whereas neutron porosity readings decrease. Therefore, this log combination will detect the presence of gas-bearing zones by the separation of the two curves.

Fluid saturations, water and oil, are the most important quantities to be determined from well-log analysis. Because the water and oil saturations together must equal 100 percent, knowing one necessarily determines the other. The significance of these values is clear: If the rock unit of interest is not oil-bearing or if it contains hydrocarbons in quantities that are not economically feasible to produce, the well will be abandoned rather than completed. To understand the quantitative assessment of formation-fluid saturation, one must first understand what occurs within the borehole and in the formations that are penetrated by the well. Because high temperatures are generated by friction as the drill bit grinds its way through solid rock, specially formulated "drilling mud" is continuously circulated down the borehole to cool the bit. In addition, the mud clears the borehole by bringing to the surface the pulverized rock material, or cuttings. The drilling mud is usually a water-based fluid with various mineral additives. Within the borehole, there is a tendency for the fluid portion of the mud to separate from the mineral fraction. The fluid, or mud filtrate, seeps into the permeable rock formations, completely flushing out and replacing the natural formation fluids adjacent to the borehole. This area is the "flushed zone." Some of the filtrate moves deeper into the formation, where it continues to displace the natural fluids, creating a partially flushed area, or "invaded zone." The solid portion of the mud that has separated from the filtrate forms a "mud cake," lining the inside of the borehole on the surfaces of the permeable formations.

Within a reservoir, the rock matrix, fresh water, and hydrocarbons act as electrical insulators. Any electric current that passes through the rock is carried by dissolved ions in salt water in the pore spaces of the formation. Therefore, where current flows readily, the pore fluid is salt water. Where electrical resistance is encountered, it is likely that hydrocarbons occupy the pore spaces. The principal advantage of the arrangement of the induction log is that the current largely bypasses the invaded zone and gives a better picture of the true formation resistivity (the inverse of the conductivity) deep in the formation. Even so, the flushed zone and the invaded zone are still sampled to some extent, and corrections must be made to obtain the true resistivity of the uncontaminated formation. This can be accomplished by running logs that sample the formations only immediately adjacent to the borehole and, therefore, read either the flushed zone or the invaded zone resistivity. In some instances, the short normal log (a curve that is run with most electric log surveys) can be used. In other circumstances, it is preferable to use the microlog or, when saline drilling mud has been used, the microlaterolog. These last two logs are specifically designed to measure the mud cake and flushed zone resistivities.

In addition to corrections for flushed zone and invaded zone resistivities, other corrections must be applied to the log readings to allow for the effects of changing borehole diameter and bed thickness. With a computed true resistivity value and a knowledge of the formation porosity, one can calculate the percentages of water and oil in the formation and make a quantitative determination of the total volume of hydrocarbons. Such formations that contain natural gas rather than oil can be readily identified with the temperature log. As gas moves out of the formation and into the borehole, it is under less pressure and expands. As it expands, it cools, and the borehole temperature opposite the gas-bearing formation is significantly lowered.

Other special-purpose logs are available to the petroleum industry. One of these, the dipmeter log, provides information on the angle of dip of the formations encountered. This information can be used to determine environments of deposition, because rock layers in channel deposits, reefs, offshore bars, and other sedimentary features will have some unique pattern of dip. Increasingly, geologists have been using other well-log curves to refine their environmental interpretations. This is done by examining the curve patterns within the sedimentary rock units and noting whether the log parameters increase or decrease downward, for example, or change gradually or abruptly. The log, in effect, is measuring rock properties, such as particle size, that are controlled by the physical conditions within the site of deposition.

In addition to assessing rock units for their petroleum content and environmental information, well logs are used extensively for correlation—that is, the matching and tracing of rock units from one locality to another. Since it is lithology, rather than porosity and fluid saturation, that is geologically the most significant factor in rock identification, the lithology logging curves are most commonly used for this purpose. Correlation may be accomplished either by matching log curves "by eye" or by statistical and computer analysis.

Context

Well logging is a little-known but necessary part of the petroleum industry. It is the method whereby geologists and petroleum engineers obtain the information on petroleum reservoir rock characteristics that allow them to make decisions about the economic potential of an oil well—that is, whether it can be completed as a "producer" or must be plugged and abandoned as a "dry hole." Such decisions involve millions of dollars and cannot be made without an examination of all the available relevant data. They must usually be correct, or the oil company will not survive financially.

As the well-logging sonde is drawn up the borehole, it continuously records data on those formation parameters for which it was specifically designed. Information may be provided on the travel times or velocities of sound waves pulsing through the formation; the density of the rock; small, naturally occurring electric currents present in the rocks and adjacent borehole; the ease with which the formation will pass electric currents induced in or directed into it; borehole size; borehole temperature; and natural formation radioactivity resulting from the decay of unstable isotopes in the minerals of the rock formations. With this information, geologists and petroleum engineers can determine the mineralogical composition of the rock formations (lithology), the rock pore space volume (porosity), the presence and amount of crude oil in the pore spaces of the rock (oil saturation), and the location of natural gas-bearing zones within the well.

With the aid of computers in the logging trucks that are tied into the logging instruments, the data can be analyzed and important decisions made at the well site immediately upon completion of the logging run. These decisions concern not only whether the well should be completed but also whether to continue drilling to deeper rock units and which rock zones should be tested for their fluid content and producibility. As in many business endeavors, time saved in the decision-making process can be turned into money earned.

Bibliography

Asquith, George B., with Charles Gibson. *Basic Well Log Analysis for Geologists*. Tulsa, Okla.: American Association of Petroleum Geologists, 1982. An excellent discussion of the theory of well logging and of the application of each of the major types of log. Each section is complete with description, examples, and problems. Several comprehensive case studies are included at the end. Well illustrated, with a comprehensive bibliography. Intended for the working geologist but would be understood by persons with minimal geologic training.

Berg, Robert R. *Reservoir Sandstones*. Englewood Cliffs, N.J.: Prentice-Hall, 1986. This college-level text includes a good summary of well logs and logging procedures. The various types of log are discussed, with particular emphasis on how they are used in specific formation evaluation and sedimentological problems. While the text as a whole would not be suitable for the novice, the basic discussion of well logging would be.

Brock, Jim. *Analyzing Your Logs*. Vol. 1, *Fundamentals of Open Hole Log Interpretation*. 2d ed. Tyler, Tex.: Petro-Media, 1984. A good, fundamental discussion of the basic characteristics of petroleum reservoir rocks is followed by a description of the theory and use of each of the major types of well log. Fairly easy to understand, with good diagrams but no bibliography. Designed for a short course in well log evaluation. Questions and problems accompany each section. The necessary graphs and correction charts for use with each type of log are included.

Pirson, Sylvain J. *Geologic Well Log Analysis*. Houston: Gulf Publishing, 1970. The emphasis in this book is on the use of well logs for sedimentary environment interpretation, structural analysis, facies analysis, and hydrogeology rather than on the evaluation of hydrocarbonate-bearing rock units. Somewhat dated, but the most complete and detailed work of its kind.

Schlumberger, Inc. *Log Interpretations Principles/Applications*. 2d ed. Houston: Schlumberger Educational Services, 1987. An excellent updated summary put out by the largest well service company in the world. Designed for the use of Schlumberger's clients (geologists and petroleum engineers), the publication is available from the company and is an excellent reference for the nonprofessional. Well illustrated, with a comprehensive bibliography.

Selley, Richard C. *Elements of Petroleum Geology*. New York: W. H. Freeman, 1985. An excellent undergraduate text that contains a well-written section on the theory and application of well logging, with a discussion of each of the major types of log. Easily understood by the beginner. Excellent diagrams and an extensive bibliography are included.

Donald J. Thompson

Cross-References

Alluvial Systems, 31; Clays, 210; Diagenesis, 354; Oil and Gas Exploration, 1878; Oil and Gas: Offshore Wells, 1886; Oil and Gas: Onshore Wells, 1893; The Origin of Oil and Gas, 1901; Oil and Gas: Petroleum Reservoirs, 1909; Oil Chemistry, 1931; River Bed Forms, 2196; Physical Properties of Rocks, 2225; Sediment Transport and Deposition, 2290; Sedimentary Rock Classification, 2304.

THE WORLDWIDE DISTRIBUTION OF OIL AND GAS

Type of earth science: Geology
Field of study: Petroleum geology and engineering

Oil and gas have been discovered on every principal landmass on earth. Their potential in any particular series of rocks is determined by analyses of the original environment of deposition and its subsequent geologic history and not by present-day climate or location.

Principal terms

BASIN: a depressed area of the crust of the earth in which sedimentary rocks have accumulated

FRONTIER: a region of potential hydrocarbon production; little is known of its rock character or geologic history

GEOPHYSICS: the quantitative evaluation of rocks by electrical, gravitational, magnetic, radioactive, and elastic wave transmission and heat-flow techniques

HYDROCARBONS: naturally occurring organic compounds that in the gaseous state are termed natural gas and in the liquid state are termed crude oil or petroleum

PERMEABILITY: the measure of the ability of a porous rock to transmit liquids and gases

POROSITY: the presence of pore space in a sedimentary rock in which hydrocarbons collect

SEDIMENTARY ROCK: rock formed by the deposition and compaction of loose sediment created by the erosion of preexisting rock

STRUCTURE: a physical rearrangement of sedimentary rocks into geometric forms that favor the accumulation and entrapment of hydrocarbons

Summary of the Phenomenon

Deposits of petroleum and natural gas are found in sedimentary rocks on every principal continent and within the shallow portions of the ocean basins. Sedimentary rocks cover 75 percent of continental land area and extend into the subsurface to maximum depths of 15,000 meters. The occurrence of hydrocarbons varies greatly among differing continents, countries, and individual sedimentary rock basins. Hydrocarbon quantities vary from oil-stained rock and insignificant surface seeps to subsurface reservoirs containing billions of barrels (1 barrel equals 42 U.S. gallons, or about 159 liters) of petroleum or trillions of cubic meters of natural gas. While hydrocarbons have been discovered in rocks ranging in age from 1 million to 1 billion years, generally the younger the sedimentary rock, the greater the chance of commercial hydrocarbon quantities. Approximately 85 percent of crude oil found occurs within the Gulf-Caribbean and the Persian Gulf regions and is contained in rock deposited less than 250 million years of age.

Edwin L. Drake is credited with drilling, in 1859, the first oil well in the United States, near Titusville, Pennsylvania. Wells were first drilled in the search for oil or gas in Europe (France) in 1813, South America (Peru) in 1863, the Far East (Burma) in 1889, Africa (Egypt) in 1908, and the Middle East (Iran) in 1908. By the late 1980's, hydrocarbons had been discovered in eighty-six countries, and oil was being produced from more than 900,000 wells in eighty-two of these countries. Estimated worldwide proven reserves of petroleum exceed 905 billion barrels; gas reserves approximate 100 trillion cubic meters. Indeed, practically every country, including members of the Third World, has become dependent on oil and gas as primary sources of energy.

The presence of hydrocarbons is related to the environment prevailing at the time localized columns of sedimentary rock were deposited and to the geologic history to which those rocks have been subjected after being deposited. Hydrocarbons are formed by the chemical alteration of the remains of marine life that collect in the pore space (porosity) of sedimentary rocks, most commonly siltstone, sandstone, and porous varieties of limestone and dolostone. An undeterminable amount of oil and gas created and trapped over millions of years of geologic history has been lost to forces of heat and pressure. Such forces, created through the processes of mountain building and volcanic activity, either destroy hydrocarbons or chemically reduce them to an uneconomic solid state. Large regions of the earth's land area that have been subjected in the geologic past to extended periods of mountain building and volcanism are not considered target areas for hydrocarbon exploration. These "shield" regions, composed of rock generally in excess of 600 million years of age, constitute the geologic nucleus of every continent. An excellent example is the Canadian Shield, centering on the Hudson Bay region of North America.

Regions surrounding the centrally positioned shields are commonly composed of downwarpings, or depressions, in the crust of the earth. Within these "sedimentary basins" are accumulations of sedimentary rocks thousands of meters thick. In such basins, of which approximately 750 have been identified throughout the world, oil and gas are found in quantities depending on conditions of hydrocarbon source rock, geologic structure, and geologic history. Assuming that rocks infilling any basin contain source units, plus porous and permeable rocks, hydrocarbons will generate in the course of geologic time in the central and deeper portions of the basin. With increasing overburden pressure and temperature, oil and gas will slowly migrate outward and upward toward the basin periphery, where either entrapment will take place within a structure or surface seeps will occur.

Each basin must be individually evaluated as to its potential for containing economic deposits of oil or gas. Basins that have been infilled with sedimentary rock deposited under marine (saltwater) conditions offer the best potential, while those infilled under terrestrial environments offer the least. Should the sedimentary rock column be thin, overburden pressure would be insufficient to generate crude oil; if the column is excessively thick, the resultant high temperatures will alter the oil to natural gas or even burn off the gas. Hydrocarbons are destroyed when a basin is subjected to mountain-building forces and escape to the surface to form un-economic tar sand deposits.

In North America, the principal hydrocarbon-producing regions include the east coast of Mexico, the plains of Alberta and Saskatchewan, and the coastal areas of Alaska. In the lower forty-eight states, the most important producing areas are the coastal states of Alabama, Louisiana, and Texas, the Great Plains and the lower Great Lakes regions, and California. Approximately 10 percent of world oil reserves and 9 percent of world gas reserves are found in North America. Important frontier regions on this continent include the Arctic waters of Alaska and Canada and the Atlantic coastal waters of the United States. The development of both these regions will, however, be constrained by economic and environmental conditions.

Venezuela alone accounts for 84 percent of the oil and 63 percent of the natural gas reserves of South America. The Lake Maracaibo oil fields have historically accounted for a majority of this production. The only other important hydrocarbon-producing country on this continent is Argentina. With large sections of the middle latitudes of South America composed of the Guyana and the Brazilian shields, most of the oil discovered in South America is found in rock less than 250 million years in age and in structures associated with the creation of the Andean mountain ranges. Recent major discoveries in water depths of 900 meters in the Campos basin, offshore Brazil, indicates that significant reserves are yet to be discovered along the Atlantic seaboard of South America.

Africa contains 6 percent of the oil and 16 percent of the gas reserves of the world. North of the Sahara desert, those countries with the greatest hydrocarbon reserves are Libya, Algeria, and Egypt; all border on the prolific Mediterranean basin. In southern Africa, Nigeria controls the majority of production and reserves, while Angola, Congo, and Gabon possess reserves of secondary value. Many sections of this continent have been minimally evaluated for hydrocarbon potential and are considered frontier status. As the African Shield covers much of the 30-million-square-kilometer area of this continent, the best prospects for new oil and gas discoveries are confined to peripheral sedimentary basins, some of which extend into the offshore Atlantic area. These peripheral basins are characterized by thick sedimentary sequences and the common presence of salt deposits; the latter is a positive indicator of hydrocarbon potential.

In the Middle East and Asia, the Soviet Union and the Saudi Arabia peninsula dominate the distribution pattern of oil and gas. Of the proven world reserves of oil, 63 percent are controlled by the countries of Abu Dhabi, Iran, Iraq, Kuwait, and Saudi Arabia. Saudi Arabia alone possesses 170 billion barrels of proven reserves: 19 percent of the world total. With an additional estimated 70 billion probable reserves, Saudi Arabia has the largest total reserves of any country. These reservoirs are being depleted by only 700 producing wells, with the average well flowing approximately 13,000 barrels of oil per day. In contrast, in the United States, more than 500,000 wells produce 9 million barrels of oil, for an average production rate of 18 barrels per day. All hydrocarbons in Saudi Arabia occur within calcium carbonate sedimentary rocks approximately 155 million years in age. The majority of accumulations are contained within anticline structures, convex upward rock folds formed by compressional forces. These flexures, or folds, are located mainly in eastern Arabia, and the longest (including Ghawar, the largest oil field in the world) extends for more than 400 kilometers.

The Soviet Union contains 6 percent of world reserves of oil and 38 percent of world reserves of natural gas. These reserves are principally concentrated in the West Siberian basin, which accounts for two-thirds of Soviet oil production and more than half of its gas production. The West Siberian basin has a cumulative oil production of more than 25 billion barrels. The old hydrocarbon regions of the Soviet Union, the Volga-Ural and North Caucasus regions west of the Ural Mountains and Caspian Sea, contain hydrocarbon reserves of secondary importance. As many sectors of these regions have reached a mature state of exploration, drilling and exploration efforts are being concentrated in the Siberian sector and basins in the Turkmen and Uzbek republics, bordering on Iran and Afghanistan.

West European hydrocarbon reserves are concentrated in the offshore, North Sea extensions of Norway, Denmark, and the United Kingdom. Western Europe contains only 2 percent of world reserves of oil and an insignificant amount of world reserves of natural gas. The increases in European production over the past several decades have been derived mainly from basins located offshore; onshore basins, historically, have never been important producers. Australasia, extending from New Zealand to Malaysia, contains approximately 1 percent of world hydrocarbon reserves. Historically, the principal producing areas have been Sumatra, Java, and Borneo, but exploration programs are assessing the offshore waters of this vast region.

In addition to thickness of sedimentary rock column, type of sedimentary rock, and geologic structure, the geologic age of hydrocarbon source and reservoir rock is significant in evaluating worldwide distribution of oil or gas. The economic presence of hydrocarbons is the result of deposition of an organic shale that undergoes maturation, thus producing the oil or gas (the "source"), followed by migration into a porous and permeable reservoir rock structure. Because source rock maturation occurs within a short period of geologic time, usually measured in millions of years, hydrocarbon distribution is dependent on basin age. In general, the younger the basin and its contained sediments, the greater the volume of hydrocarbons. Approximately 85 percent of known hydrocarbons are contained within rocks younger than 250 million years. These reserves are principally located in California, the Rocky Mountains, the Gulf Coast of Louisiana, Venezuela, the southern Soviet Union, Mexico, Saudi Arabia, Iraq, and Iran. Fourteen percent of world reserves are associated with rocks 250-600 million years in age. These reserves are mainly located in Canada, North Africa, the Soviet Union, and the states of Texas, Oklahoma, Kansas, Illinois, Michigan, Ohio, and Pennsylvania. Small volumes of oil and gas have been found in rocks older than 600 million years, in the Soviet Union, China, Australia, and the United States.

Methods of Study

In the evaluation of the oil and gas potential of a sedimentary basin, whether it be a frontier region or the deeper zones of a mature production area, a routine of analyses has been established. As the geographic distribution of oil and gas accumulations is controlled by regional as well as local factors, such factors must be initially evaluated. The most important of regional factors are those of depositional environment and deformational history.

As a result of the commonly accepted belief that hydrocarbons are derived from oceanic organic matter deposited within sedimentary rocks, basins that have been developed under conditions of marine deposition are given favorable initial evaluation. Minority opinion suggests that hydrocarbons are inorganically (or "abiogenically") derived and, thus, may be found in any type of rock that possesses porosity and permeability. In addition to sedimentary types, such rock might include fractured lava and other igneous rock derived from crystallization of magma (molten rock). This inorganic theory has been tested by the drilling of a deep well in the Scandinavian Shield region of Sweden; an area dominated by heavily fractured granite. As geologic reviews indicated only traces of natural gas and little porosity, the organic theory of hydrocarbon origin appears to be vindicated.

If a world geologic map is superimposed on a hydrocarbon distribution map, relationships dependent on deformational history become apparent. Regionally, oil and gas fields are concentrated in areas of the earth's crust that are downwarped, such as continental margins, coastal plains, and inland plateaus that are low in elevation in comparison to surrounding areas. Such areas generally contain adequate thicknesses of sedimentary rock possessing the organic material, porosity, and permeability necessary to function as source and reservoir rocks.

After a frontier region is evaluated from the above considerations and found to possess potential for oil or gas accumulation, geophysical technology is used to further localize possible hydrocarbon-bearing structures. The most commonly used geophysical techniques are those that employ seismology (the analysis of basin structure by artificially generated elastic wave reflections), gravitational technology (the association of density distributions with rock types), and magnetic technology (the measurement of the earth's magnetic field at different locations). Geophysics technology is used to define fundamental basin architecture and geologic history.

As the surface area of a typical basin is on the order of many thousands of square kilometers, each basin must be studied from the viewpoint of preferred habitats of known oil and gas accumulations. Studies of oil accumulations indicate that more than half (54 percent) of world reserves occur along a basin hinge belt, that zone separating intense downwarping of a basin center from the modest downwarping of the basin periphery. Within the deep basin, only 11 percent of the oil is found, while the peripheral shelf contains the remaining 35 percent.

In the final evaluation of oil and gas distribution patterns, it must be emphasized that the majority of known hydrocarbon deposits are concentrated in three intercontinental depressions in the crust of the earth. In the Western Hemisphere, between North and South America, lies the depression forming the Caribbean Sea and the Gulf of Mexico. Here are found the great oil and gas deposits of Venezuela, Colombia, Mexico, and the Gulf Coast. The second of these depressions contains the hydrocarbon reserves bordering the Red, Mediterranean, Caspian, and Black seas and the Persian Gulf and is formed within the corners of Africa, Europe, and Asia. The last depression is found in the southwest Pacific, between the continents of Asia and Australia, and includes the great fields found in Borneo, Sumatra, and Java. A fourth intercontinental depression, in the early stages of evaluation, occupies the northern limits of North America, Europe, and Asia, surrounding the North Pole. While this region offers great promise and is the site of the largest oil field discovered to date in the United States—the Prudhoe Bay field of Alaska— expanded exploration will be constrained by environmental considerations.

Even with the wide array of available geological and geophysical research procedures, worldwide drilling for new oil and gas reserves is a high-risk endeavor. In spite of continued introduction of new exploration methodologies, approximately 30 percent of all wells drilled since 1859 have been declared dry, and more than 70 percent of the wells drilled annually in frontier areas are unsuccessful.

Context

The worldwide hydrocarbon industry was created in the middle of the nineteenth century to fuel the Industrial Revolution. The recognition of oil and gas as a cheap and efficient energy resource marked the end of wood as an important source of fuel and ultimately reduced "King Coal" to secondary status. By the final decade of the twentieth century, however, the burning of oil and gas was being associated with atmospheric pollution and the greenhouse effect, among other environmental problems. Yet, the promises of solar power have not been realized, and nuclear energy, while economically viable, has been generally considered unsafe.

Oil and gas continue to function in the role that they rapidly assumed after the completion of Edwin Drake's well in 1859; they are the wonder fuels, lubricants, and chemical sources of the modern scientific world. It was popular in the 1960's to predict that the end of the hydrocarbon age would be closely associated with the year 2000, but such predictions have proved premature. The continued exploration for new reserves of oil and gas is partially controlled by economics. Actions taken by the Organization of Petroleum Exporting Countries (OPEC) in the early 1970's caused the value of a barrel of petroleum in the United States to increase from $3 to $35 by 1981. Spurred by this incentive, the American hydrocarbon industry in 1974 created the first annual increase in proven oil reserves in the United States since 1960. In that same year, the world consumption of petroleum products approximated 7 billion barrels annually. Thirty years later, the United States alone was consuming 6 billion barrels of crude oil every year, with some 45 percent of this supply being imported. Worldwide, the demand for oil and gas, in terms of crude oil equivalent energy, is close to 90 million barrels per day.

Oil and gas will probably continue for decades to be the world's primary energy source, and new reserves will continue to be sought worldwide. The distribution of oil and gas in the future will be determined by the same factors governing its distribution today. Geologic factors will continue to dictate the best locations for exploration, with local political stability and economic considerations entering into the decision when and whether to explore.

Bibliography

Baker, Ron. *Oil and Gas: The Production Story*. Austin: University of Texas Petroleum Extension Service, 1983. The first four sections of this primer are easy-to-read introductions to the origin and accumulation of hydrocarbons, exploration and testing technologies, and production stimulation procedures. Each section contains full-color diagrams.

Ball, Max W. *This Fascinating Oil Business*. New York: Bobbs-Merrill, 1940. Although an older reference, this 444-page book contains a wealth of information found in no other review of the business. It is especially valuable for its history of early global exploration in remote regions ranging from Afghanistan to Manchukuo. Written for general readers.

Nawwab, Ismail I., Peter C. Speers, and Paulk F. Hoye, eds. *Aramco and Its World: Arabia and the Middle East*. Washington, D.C.: Arabian American Oil, 1980. A beautifully illustrated volume that explores the history of the discovery and development of oil in a region that possesses 63 percent of the world's petroleum reserves.

Pratt, Wallace E., and Dorothy Good, eds. *World Geography of Petroleum*. Princeton, N.J.: Princeton University Press, 1950. A classic comparative study of the petroleum-producing regions of the world. Coedited by an internationally recognized geologist. A college-level text.

Schackne, Stewart, and N. D'Arcy Drake. *Oil for the World*. 2d ed. New York: Harper & Brothers, 1960. A brief introduction to all aspects of an integrated oil and gas company, from discovery through drilling operations, refining, and marketing.

Tiratsoo, Eric N. *Natural Gas*. 3d ed. Houston: Gulf, 1980. A college-level review of natural gas drilling, production reserves, and economics. Eight chapters discuss principal geographic regions in detail. Includes a valuable compilation of natural gas statistics for the Soviet Union and Eastern Europe.

_____. *Oilfields of the World*. 3d ed. Houston: Gulf, 1985. This easy-to-read companion reference to the above entry describes oilfields in approximately seventy countries. The geology of each field is presented at a college freshman level.

Albert B. Dickas

Cross-References

Oil and Gas Exploration, 1878; Oil and Gas: Offshore Wells, 1886; Oil and Gas: Onshore Wells, 1893; The Origin of Oil and Gas, 1901; Oil and Gas: Petroleum Reservoirs, 1909; Oil Chemistry, 1931; Oil Shale and Tar Sands, 1939.

OIL CHEMISTRY

Type of earth science: Geology
Field of study: Petroleum geology and engineering

Crude oil is fossil organic tissue that has been transformed by geologic processes into a complex mixture of many different chemical compounds called hydrocarbons. Although the composition of oils varies widely, the most abundant hydrocarbons in most oils are the paraffins, naphthenes, aromatics, and compounds with nitrogen, sulfur, and oxygen attached (NSOs). Less abundant compounds, called biomarkers, are true "geochemical fossils" that retain the original molecular structure of the organisms from which the oil is derived.

Principal terms

AROMATIC HYDROCARBONS: ring-shaped molecules composed of six carbon atoms per ring; the carbon atoms are bonded to one another with alternating single and double bonds

BIOMARKERS: chemicals found in oil with a chemical structure that definitely links their origin with specific organisms; also called geochemical fossils

HYDROCARBONS: natural chemical compounds composed of carbon and hydrogen, usually of organic origin; they make up the bulk of both petroleum and the tissues of organisms (plants and animals)

KEROGEN: organic matter that has been buried with sediments and gently heated until it is physically condensed and chemically transformed into a dark, waxy substance; the primary chemical precursor to oil

MOLECULAR WEIGHT: a measure of the mass of the molecule of a chemical compound, as determined by both the total number and the size of atoms in the molecule

NAPHTHENE HYDROCARBONS: hydrocarbon molecules with a ring-shaped structure, in which any number of carbon atoms are all bonded to one another with single bonds

OXIDATION: a very common chemical reaction in which elements are combined with oxygen—for example, the burning of petroleum, wood, and coal, the rusting of metallic iron, and the metabolic respiration of organisms

PARAFFIN HYDROCARBONS: hydrocarbon compounds composed of carbon atoms connected with single bonds into straight chains; also knows as n-alkanes

SATURATED HYDROCARBONS: hydrocarbon compounds whose molecules are chemically stable, with carbon atoms fully bonded to other atoms

Summary of the Phenomenon

Oil is a product of both geologic and biologic processes; it is what remains of animal and plant tissues that have been changed over time into a liquid of bewildering complexity, containing an enormous number of individual chemical compounds. In unraveling the details of this chemistry, geologists have discovered a fundamental connection between oil, organisms, geologic processes, and the primary energy source of most life on earth, the sun.

Almost all organisms rely on sunlight, either directly or indirectly, for their existence. Green plants use the process of photosynthesis to combine water (H_2O) and carbon dioxide (CO_2) into their body tissues and into energy for living. Almost all animals survive either by eating plants or eating other organisms that do. All plants and animals are composed largely of chemical compounds of carbon and hydrogen called hydrocarbons. These "organic" chemical compounds sometimes include small amounts of nitrogen, sulfur, oxygen, and phosphorus. Oil, being a biological product, is made up almost completely of hydrocarbons, some of which are the original chemicals of the organic tissues from which the oil was derived.

When oil is burned in an automobile, steam boiler, or home furnace, the hydrocarbon molecules are rapidly combined with oxygen in a process known as oxidation, which converts the hydrogen and carbon in oil hydrocarbons back into water and carbon dioxide. Oxidation converts other organic fuels, such as coal, wood, and natural gas, in a similar way. A very common geochemical process, oxidation at lower temperatures converts metallic iron into rust. When plants and animals consume organic matter (hydrocarbons) as food and convert them into energy for growth, metabolism, and reproduction, they are combining these organic compounds with oxygen in the oxidation reaction called respiration. Respiration is the slow, controlled oxidation of organic hydrocarbons that takes place within cells. The natural decay of organic matter as it decomposes is another slow oxidation process. An oil fire in an automobile motor can also be thought of as geologically delayed respiration. Consequently, organic matter, a product of photosynthesis, is eventually returned to the carbon dioxide and water from which it was made by a variety of processes (respiration during life, slow decay or burning after death) in a never-ending cycle of biogeologic change. Oil, formed from the tissues of organisms living many millions of years ago, is often called a fossil fuel because as people burn it, they are using solar energy that was stored by organisms long ago in the geologic past.

Petroleum hydrocarbons are formed when organic tissue is buried to great depth within a thick pile of sediments. During burial, the increase in temperature and pressure brings about a complex physical and chemical transformation of the organic matter. The molecules of organic matter first condense and combine to form larger molecules of a substance called kerogen. Kerogen, which resembles soft plastic or wax, is the primary precursor to oil. Kerogen forms most easily and abundantly when the majority of buried organic matter is mostly of animal origin and high in fat or is rich in plant wax, the protective coating on the outer surfaces of terrestrial plants that helps keep them from drying out from evaporation. The burial of plant tissue from species low in wax results in molecular condensation into peat and lignite, both precursors of coal. The formation of kerogen and lignite is always accompanied by the production of methane gas (CH_4), a natural hydrocarbon, as a by-product. If kerogen is compressed or buried somewhat further (under at least 900 meters of sediment) and heated within the range of 50-150 degrees Celsius, the process of catagenesis takes place, during which the kerogen condenses further to form liquid petroleum. Under higher temperature and pressure conditions, the oil will be transformed into natural gas. At higher temperatures, oil and gas form more quickly than at low temperatures, but even if low temperatures are maintained for long enough periods of time, the same volume of petroleum will eventually form.

The various hydrocarbon compounds found in petroleum differ from one another in two fundamental ways: the number of carbon and hydrogen atoms in the hydrocarbon molecule and the shape of the molecule. Hydrocarbon molecules are classified according to the number of carbon atoms they contain. A simple numbering system is used where C_2, for example, refers to a molecule with 2 carbon atoms, and C_3 is a molecule with 3 carbons. In most oils, compounds of very low molecular weight (less than C_5) are dissolved in the oil as natural gas. When the crude oil is pumped out of the ground, these molecules evaporate from the liquid petroleum and are either burned off or collected to be used as fuel.

Carbon atoms can be bonded to one another in straight chains, rings, or combinations of these basic forms. In many hydrocarbon molecules, small molecular fragments, called side chains, are attached like branches of a tree to the main chain or ring of the molecule. The simplest and most abundant petroleum hydrocarbons in crude oils are straight carbon chain molecules, referred to as the paraffin series. The smallest and simplest paraffin hydrocarbon molecule is methane, the most common component of natural gas. The methane molecule is composed of a central carbon atom bonded to four hydrogen atoms in a three-sided pyramid arrangement, or tetrahedron. The structure of paraffin molecules of higher molecular weight (C_2 to C_{30}) is made when additional carbon atoms are attached to the basic methane tetrahedron, making a carbon chain. As these carbon atoms are successively added, a chainlike arrangement of carbon atoms develops, with hydrogen atoms bonded to all the carbon atoms. This series of chainlike molecules is called the n-alkane series, with "n" denoting the number of carbon atoms in the chain. For example, the compound pentane, an abundant component of natural gas, is a five-carbon alkane chain (C_5H_{12}). Octane, the hydrocarbon compound by which gasolines are graded, is an eight-carbon alkane (C_8H_{18}). The highest molecular weight n-alkane found as a liquid in oil is heptadecane ($C_{17}H_{36}$), a hydrocarbon with a boiling point of 303 degrees Celsius.

All carbon atoms have four positions, called bonding sites, at which other atoms can attach themselves to form a molecule. In petroleum hydrocarbons, the carbon atoms are usually bonded to either hydrogen atoms or other carbon atoms. In order for the molecule to be stable so that it does not spontaneously react chemically with other molecules in the oil, all four bonding sites of each carbon atom must be occupied; these stable molecules with filled bonding sites are called saturated hydrocarbons. For any saturated n-alkane in the paraffin series, the number of hydrogen atoms in the molecule ($\#H$) can be predicted from the number of carbon atoms (n) in the chain by the simple equation $\#H = 2n + 2$. Note that for all n-alkane hydrocarbons the carbon-to-hydrogen ratio is always less than 1:2.

If the ends of a paraffin hydrocarbon chain are linked together to form a ring, the result is the shape of the other abundant group of hydrocarbon compounds in crude oils, the naphthene series. Naphthene molecules are composed of carbon atoms bonded together in rings; molecules with this molecular geometry are usually referred to as cyclic hydrocarbons or ring compounds. The simplest naphthene hydrocarbon is cyclopropane (C_3H_6), a three-carbon ring molecule that is a gas dissolved in crude oil. Cyclopropane, like other hydrocarbons of low molecular weight, bubbles out of the oil solution when it reaches the low-pressure conditions of the earth's surface in the same way that carbon dioxide gas bubbles out of a soft drink when the bottle is opened. In this way, it becomes part of the natural gas that is associated with crude oil production. The liquid naphthene with the lowest molecular weight is cyclopentane (C_5H_{10}); this compound and cyclohexane (C_6H_{12}) are the dominant cyclic hydrocarbons in most oils. Saturated naphthene hydrocarbon molecules have hydrogen atoms bonded to all the carbon atom bonding sites in a manner similar to that of n-alkanes. In this case, two hydrogen atoms are bonded to each carbon, and the ratio of carbon to hydrogen for these compounds is 1:2.

Less abundant in oils than the paraffins and naphthenes are the aromatic hydrocarbons. This group of petroleum hydrocarbons, which constitute from 1 to 10 percent of most crude oils, is so named because many of the compounds have pleasant, sometimes fruity, odors. The aromatics also have a carbon ring structure, but this structure has a different geometry from that of the naphthenes. Aromatic hydrocarbon molecules are formed of one or more six-carbon rings in which the carbon atoms are bonded to one another with alternating single and bouble bonds. For this reason, the aromatic hydrocarbons have a carbon-to-hydrogen ratio of 1:1. The petroleum aromatic with the lowest molecular weight is benzene (C_6H_6), a chemical commonly used as an industrial solvent.

Many of the aromatic hydrocarbons are cancer-causing (carcinogenic) substances; most potent are the high molecular weight, multiringed aromatic molecules referred to as PAH (poly-aromatic hydrocarbons). The first carcinogen ever discovered is benzopyrene, an aromatic molecule composed of five carbon rings. In the late 1800's, Sir Percival Pott linked this substance with cancer of the scrotum in London chimneysweeps. Their daily exposure to the aromatic hydrocarbons in coal tar and soot, coupled with their poor personal hygiene, was responsible for epidemic proportions of this disease.

A small percentage of the hydrocarbons found in oils have distinctive molecular fragments bonded onto basic hydrocarbon structures. These nonhydrocarbon fragments most commonly contain nitrogen, sulfur, and oxygen; hydrocarbon compounds with these attached fragments are called NSOs for this reason. NSO molecules tend to have much higher molecular weights than do the hydrocarbon molecules described earlier. One of the most interesting of the NSO molecular fragments is the amino group; it contains nitrogen and has the formula NH_2. The amino group is the essential component of the amino acids, the building blocks for the many different proteins of which animal organs, muscles, and other tissues are composed. Amino acids are simple molecules that can form by organic or inorganic processes, but their presence in oil is best explained by inheritance from the organic matter source of the oil.

The minor, or trace, hydrocarbon components in crude oil generally make up much less than 1 percent of the total oil; they are probably the most interesting of all petroleum compounds. Many of these chemicals have a chemical composition and molecular structure that definitely links their origin to specific organisms; they are termed geochemical fossils or biological markers (biomarkers) for this reason. Biomarker chemicals were synthesized by the organisms from which the oil originated and have been preserved through the long and complex history of sediment deposition and burial, oil formation (catagenesis), and migration of the oil from its source to the reservoir rock. Biomarkers are generally large molecules, with much higher molecular weights than those of the more abundant oil hydrocarbons, that have a carbon-to-hydrogen ratio greater than 1:2.

Some of the long chain paraffin hydrocarbons are among the best-known biomarkers. One relatively abundant group, the isoprenoid hydrocarbons, have chain-type molecules based on the isoprene group (C_5H_8); isoprene is the primary source of synthetic rubber. Isoprenoids are common in the waxes and chlorophyll of terrestrial green plants and are present in many crude oils and ancient sediments, which indicates that the petroleum isoprenoids are derivatives of chlorophyll and that kerogen from terrestrial plants is a significant source of oils. The most interesting of the plant-derived isoprenoids found in petroleum is pristane, a C_{15} carbon chain with four CH_3 molecular fragments, called methyl groups, attached to the main paraffin chain as side chains. Phytane is an isoprenoid similar to pristane but is composed of a C_{16} carbon chain with four methyl group side chains. The ratio of pristane to phytane is useful to geologists trying to determine the type of organic matter from which the oil was derived. Oil derived mostly from terrestrial plant tissue, for example, has a high pristane-to-phytane ratio (greater than 4:1), while oils from marine animal tissue have much lower ratios.

Methods of Study

To determine the chemical composition of an oil, petroleum geochemists employ many different techniques, most of which are modifications of standard techniques of organic chemistry. Crude oils are composed of a vast number of individual chemical compounds that differ from one another in their molecular weight and shape and in the distribution of electric charges on the outer portions of the molecules. These individual compounds are separated from one another by a technique called chromatography. Portions of the oil are slowly passed through a long glass or metal column packed with a chemical substance (usually an organic chemical) that attracts hydrocarbon molecules having certain size or charge characteristics. The attractive chemical inside this "chromatographic column" has a greater affinity for the heaviest or most highly charged molecules, so hydrocarbon molecules of different sizes and charges move through the column at different rates and emerge from the end of the column at different times. For example, the n-paraffins are separated from one another by their molecular weight, so the lightest of these molecules emerges first from the column, and the others come out in the order of their carbon number. It should be noted that no column exists that separates all petroleum hydrocarbons, and several different chromatic columns are needed to separate an oil into its constituent chemicals. At the end of the column, a detector that is sensitive to molecular weight, charge, or other characteristics measures the amounts of each hydrocarbon compound as it emerges from the column and graphs the results. As with chromatographic columns, no one detector is able to separate all petroleum hydrocarbon compounds, and several different types are used. One of the most valuable and interesting of these detectors is the mass spectrometer. This detector breaks a hydrocarbon molecule into fragments as it leaves the chromatographic column and measures the molecular weight of these fragments. Laboratory studies have confirmed the way in which various known hydrocarbon compounds are fragmented in a mass spectrometer; this information is stored in the memory of a computer connected to the detector. During the analysis of an unknown hydrocarbon compound in an oil sample, its fragments are recognized and "reassembled" by the computer to determine the composition of the original hydrocarbon.

Context

Oil is a basic raw material from which many thousands of products are made; it is also a natural substance with a chemical composition that varies greatly from place to place. The refining and petrochemical industry separates crude oil from the well into its many different constituent chemical compounds and breaks up some of the larger hydrocarbon molecules to render oil into thousands of useful commodities, such as liquid and gaseous fuels, plastics, industrial chemicals, and a wide variety of synthetic substances. The types and quantity of petroleum products that can be obtained by refining crude oil are determined by its bulk chemical composition. For example, paraffin-rich oils with low aromatic content usually yield the highest quantity of hydrocarbon fuels, while highly aromatic oils refine into the best lubricating oils. Oils containing a large percentage of n-alkanes of low molecular weight (C_5-C_{13}) yield high quantities of gasoline, kerosene, jet fuel, and expensive hydrocarbon solvents used in many manufacturing processes; oils rich in n-alkanes of higher molecular weight (C_{14}-C_{40}) yield high quantities of diesel fuel and lubricating oils. Oils dominated by hydrocarbons of high molecular weight (heavy oils) yield asphalt and the hydrocarbons used to make plastics and synthetics.

Oils from different areas of the world can be divided into various types based on their bulk chemistry. Oils composed primarily of paraffins, termed paraffin-based crudes, are the most sought-after of all oil types by the refining industry but represent only a small percentage of the oil being produced worldwide. Most paraffin-based crude oils in North America are of Paleozoic age (about 600-250 million years ago) and are produced from oil fields in the midcontinent region. One of these is the famous Pennsylvania crude, which has historically been the standard against which all oils are compared. Similar oils on other continents are usually much younger. Paraffin-based oils of Mesozoic age (about 250-65 million years ago) are produced in Chile, Brazil, and the Caucasus region of the southern Soviet Union. Paraffin-based oils of Cenozoic age (the last 65 million years) are found in Africa, Borneo, and China.

Crude oils dominated by naphthene hydrocarbons, sometimes called asphalt-based oils, are relatively rare. These oils are usually thermally immature, meaning that catagenesis has not gone to completion during formation of these oils because of relatively low temperatures or insufficient time of burial. Significant production of naphthenic oils occurs in the Los Angeles-Ventura area of southern California and some oil provinces of the United States' Gulf Coast, the North Sea, South America, and the Soviet Union. Highly aromatic oils are generally the heaviest and most viscous of all oil types; some are actually solids at surface temperatures. Many of these oils are also relatively rich in NSO compounds and are particularly high in sulfur. These oils are most often the result of the degradation of a more paraffin- and naphthene-rich oil because of evaporation, water washing in the subsurface, and certain hydrocarbon-consuming bacteria living in subsurface sediment. Important deposits of this unusual oil type include the famous black oils of Venezuela, the very large Athabasca tar sand deposits of western Canada, and certain oils from West Africa. Oils of intermediate composition, called mixed-base oils, make up the bulk of worldwide petroleum production.

The study of the biomarker composition of oils has given geologists valuable insight into the origin of petroleum and is used as a valuable tool in oil exploration as well. Every oil has a unique biomarker composition that it inherits from the kerogens that generated the oil and the conditions of catagenesis. Certain biomarker compounds, even when present in exceedingly minute quantities, can be detected with the mass spectrometer. This "geochemical fingerprint" allows petroleum geologists to recognize distinctive chemical similarities between oils and their source sediments. The geochemical fingerprinting technique is routinely used to distinguish different oils from one another, to correlate similar oils from different areas, and to demonstrate a similarity between kerogen-bearing source sediments and the oil that was generated from them. It is also used to increase oil-exploration efficiency by serving as a critical clue to the presence of undiscovered petroleum. The technique has also been used at the sites of oil spills and polluted groundwater and in other instances of oil pollution to identify the source pollutant; it has been successfully used as evidence in courts of law to determine the guilty party and to calculate damages for episodes of oil pollution.

Bibliography

Barker, Colin. *Organic Geochemistry in Petroleum Exploration*. Tulsa, Okla.: American Association of Petroleum Geologists, 1979. Published for professional geologists as a short course in petroleum chemistry. The first half of this manual is so well organized and well written that most readers should be able to use it. Not as well illustrated as some of the texts below but an excellent resource on the subject.

Chapman, R. E. *Petroleum Geology*. New York: Elsevier, 1983. Written to emphasize petroleum production and minimize the geological aspects. This book is the best of all listed here for gaining an understanding of petroleum production and aspects of refining oil. Has a good section on basic chemistry.

Hobson, G. D., and E. N. Tiratsoo. *Introduction to Petroleum Geology*. Houston: Gulf Publishing, 1981. An excellent text for the basics of petroleum geology. Accessible to most readers.

Link, Peter K. *Basic Petroleum Geology*. Tulsa, Okla.: Oil and Gas Consultants International, 1987. A concise treatment of those aspects of petroleum chemistry most important to the science and business of oil exploration.

North, F. K. *Petroleum Geology*. Boston: Allen & Unwin, 1985. One of the best general texts on all aspects of petroleum geology. Sections on petroleum chemistry are not as detailed as in some texts but explain basic information very well. Well illustrated.

Selley, Richard C. *Elements of Petroleum Geology*. New York: W. H. Freeman, 1985. Best among the books in this list for explaining advances and discoveries in the petroleum field.

Tissot, B. P., and D. H. Welte. *Petroleum Formation and Occurrence*. New York: Springer-Verlag, 1978. A standard textbook for college-level courses in petroleum geology. A comprehensive text, with a well-written and complete section on petroleum biomarkers. Most readers will find this text informative, but a few of the sections on oil chemistry do require a basic organic chemistry background.

James L. Sadd

Cross-References

The Geochemical Cycle, 818; Geothermometry and Geobarometry, 922; Mass Spectrometry, 1521; Oil and Gas Exploration, 1878; Oil and Gas: Offshore Wells, 1886; Oil and Gas: Onshore Wells, 1893; The Origin of Oil and Gas, 1901; The Origin of Life, 1961; Sedimentary Rocks: Biogenic, 2312.

OIL SHALE AND TAR SANDS

Type of earth science: Geology
Field of study: Petroleum geology and engineering

Although oil shales and tar sands are not generally thought of as potential sources of petroleum products, these resources have been developed slowly as the possible replacement for today's dwindling oil fields. Tremendous reserves exist worldwide, but the current costs and technology preclude the use of oil shales and tar sands on a full scale.

Principal terms

BARREL: the standard unit of measure for oil and petroleum products, equal to 42 U.S. gallons or approximately 159 liters
BITUMEN: a generic term for a very thick, natural semisolid; asphalt and tar are classified as bitumens
HYDROCARBON: an organic compound consisting of hydrogen and carbon atoms linked together
KEROGEN: a waxy, insoluble organic hydrocarbon that has a very large molecular structure
OIL SHALE: a sedimentary rock containing sufficient amounts of hydrocarbons that can be extracted by slow distillation to yield oil
RESERVOIR ROCK or SAND: the storage unit for various hydrocarbons; usually of sedimentary origin
RETORT: a vessel used for the distillation or decomposition of substances using heat
TAR SAND: a natural deposit that contains significant amounts of bitumen; also called oil sand

Summary of the Phenomenon

Oil shales, or "rocks that burn," are typically fine-grained, stratified sedimentary rock. The term "oil shale" is actually a misnomer because the reservoir rock does not have to be a shale, nor does it contain oil as it is generally known. Organic matter is present in the pores of these rocks in the form of kerogen. Kerogen is the most abundant type of organic material on earth, having an average abundance of about 0.3 weight percent in sedimentary rocks. Using this figure, there is almost 600 times as much kerogen present in the earth's crust as there is coal. In an average oil shale, kerogen can be 10-12 weight percent of the sample. Bitumen, a major component in tar sands, is also present in oil shale but usually represents less than about 3 weight percent of the sample.

The organic material in kerogen was originally resins, algae, waxes, and wind-blown plant spores and pollens. If hydrocarbons are subjected to sufficient heat and pressure as the reservoir rocks are buried, petroleum in the form of oil or natural gas is formed. Insufficient burial, however, will result in kerogen being formed. Kerogen is slowly produced in a reducing (oxygen-depleted) environment over a long time as the original organic-rich sediments are transformed into complex hydrocarbons. Unlike oil and natural gas, which move relatively easily in the subsurface, hydrocarbons in oil shale migrate at an almost imperceptible rate or not at all, because the sedimentary parent rock often has a very low porosity and permeability. The highly viscous nature of kerogen limits its movement through any small pore spaces that might exist in the shales or in the more porous sandstone and limestones in which it is also found.

The physical properties of oil shale depend on the amount of organic material in the rock. Oil shale, having a lower organic content, has a higher density, because the density of the mineral matter is at least twice that of the organic matter. John W. Smith and Howard B. Jensen provide a range of density values based on the presence of varying amounts of organic components (see Bibliography). They also offer an equation for determining rock density given certain criteria with respect to the amount of organics present.

The U.S. Geological Survey has estimated worldwide reserves of 3,000 billion barrels of oil incorporated in shales, which could yield 38 liters (0.24 barrel) of oil per ton of shale. By comparison, the richest known oil shales produce between 320 and 475 liters (2-3 barrels) of oil per ton of processed rock. Based on current technology, though, less than 7 percent of these reserves are recoverable.

When examined on a global basis, the United States has large oil shale reserves. Oil shales are located under more than 20 percent of the land area of the United States. Roughly 50 percent of the worldwide reserves are found in the Green River formation, a shale and sandstone unit that formed during the Eocene epoch about 50 million years ago. This formation, the only one in the western United States that has been extensively studied for oil shale potential, covers approximately 42,000 square kilometers of southwest and south-central Wyoming, northeast Utah, and northwest Colorado. The thickest portions of the Green River formation are located in large structural basins that allowed large, shallow lakes to form in the topographically depressed areas. Subsequent deposition of rich organic sediments and later burial and thermal alteration led to the present deposits. Up to 540 billion barrels of oil exist in the rock units having a thickness greater than 10 meters, a thickness that is sufficient to produce enough hydrocarbons to be cost-effective using present-day recovery methods. Estimates of the total oil shale reserves for the Green River formation range as high as 2,000 billion barrels of oil. Unfortunately, wide-scale development of these resources will probably not happen, because the extraction process requires large amounts of water, a commodity in small supply in the arid western United States. Approximately 3 liters of water are required to extract 1 liter of oil, so each barrel of oil would require that almost 480 liters of water be used to remove the oil from the reservoir rock. Major projects have been initiated in the Green River formation in western Colorado to set up entire cities to handle the processing of the reservoir rock and its eventual products. Almost all these projects, however, have been terminated or put on indefinite hold because of changes in the worldwide petroleum market.

Although the richest oil shale deposits are in the western United States, another 15-20 percent of worldwide reserves are found in Devonian and Ordovician rocks located from New York to Illinois and into southwestern Missouri. These deposits, however, are not economically usable, because the cost to extract the small amount of oil present far exceeds the value of the oil produced. Several nations attempted using oil shale as a source for petroleum products during World War II, but postwar economic variations shut most of them down within a few years.

Tar sands constitute another major potential source of unconventional oil reserves. These highly viscous deposits—sometimes referred to as tar, asphalt, and bitumen—probably formed as residues from petroleum reservoirs after the lighter, more hydrogen-rich crude oils migrated toward the surface. These porous sands contain asphaltic hydrocarbons, which are extremely viscous. Thus, the hydrocarbons are not bound up as tightly in the reservoir as they are in oil shales. G. Ronald Gray defines these heavy substances as one of the following: bitumen, an oil sand hydrocarbon that cannot be produced using conventional processes; extra-heavy oils; and heavy oils (see Bibliography). These three types are usually lumped together when discussing worldwide reserve estimates, which are set at about 5,000 billion barrels.

The seven largest tar sand fields have roughly the same amount of oil as do the three hundred largest conventional oil fields in the world. The three largest tar sand deposits are, in descending order, in northern Alberta, Canada; northeastern Siberia, Soviet Union; and along the northern bank of the Orinoco River, Venezuela. The amount of heavy oil in place in the tar sands in the Athabasca deposit of Alberta is essentially equal to all the petroleum reserves found in the Middle East. Tar sand deposits are found in twenty-two states in the United States, the largest deposits being situated in Utah. Given the massive reserves of tar sands throughout the world, they could potentially supply modern society with as much oil as that obtained from conventional flowing wells. The major problem in the future is developing the technology to recover the usable hydrocarbon products in a cost-effective manner.

Methods of Study

Oil shales are found in deposits associated with shallow-water marine, freshwater lake, or deltaic swamp environments. A vast number of shales formed in large lakes tend to be associated with carbonate-rich rocks, which have been shown to be major sources of kerogen. Shallow-water marine deposits are formed in silica-rich sedimentary rocks, which usually produce smaller amounts of oil shale. In the latter instance, perhaps less organic material is transported to the oceanic setting than reaches the closed lakes situated on the continents.

Geochemical analyses of the organic components in oil shale are quite variable, because the environments present during formation and following have not been constant. The reducing conditions have severely altered the organic matter. Some rocks that contain relatively high percentages of organic material, such as the Green River formation, take on the physical properties of the organic matter. These rocks tend to deform as a plastic in that they bend rather than break, a property that makes them difficult to crush when the rock is processed for extraction of the hydrocarbons.

In 1978, Richard V. Hughes reported that an average analysis of a sample of oil shale from the Green River formation consists of about 86 percent inorganic and 14 percent organic matter. The inorganic portion includes about 55 weight percent carbonates, 19 percent feldspars, 15 percent clay, 10 percent analcite (a feldspar mineral), and 1 percent pyrite. The bulk composition of the organic matter is approximately 80 percent carbon and 10 percent hydrogen; the remaining 10 percent consists of varying amounts of nitrogen, sulfur, and oxygen. Kerogen serves as the cementing agent that binds the inorganic grains together. An average of several analyses of oil shales from the Green River formation shows that about 11 weight percent of each sample is kerogen, and 2.75 weight percent is bitumen. The latter is soluble in most organic solvents and, thus, can be easily removed from the oil shale.

Once the hydrocarbons are detected in the reservoir rock, they must be extracted. One of two primary mining techniques is used to recover the oil. After the upper soil and rock layers overlying the oil shale are stripped away, the reservoir rock is removed, crushed, and transported to a large retort, where it is heated. This process involves raising the temperature of the rock and hydrocarbons to about 480 degrees Celsius, the temperature at which kerogen vaporizes into volatile hydrocarbons and leaves a carbonaceous residue. When oil shale is heated, the amount of organic matter that is converted to oil increases as the amount of hydrogen in the deposit increases. This vapor is then condensed to form a very viscous oil. After the introduction of hydrogen, the mixture can be refined in a manner similar to that used to refine crude oil, which is drawn from the ground using conventional methods of drilling and pumping for extracting petroleum sources. One obvious problem with this method is that a considerable amount of heat (energy) must be expended in order to yield products that themselves are potential energy sources.

The second technique used to recover oil from oil shales involves in-situ heating of the reservoir rock after it has been fractured with explosives or water under pressure. Researchers at the Sandia National Laboratories in New Mexico may have discovered a method to enhance the extraction of kerogen from the reservoir rocks. Underground fracturing of the rock by controlled explosions increases the number and size of passageways for air to pass through. Air is a necessary component to complete the chemically driven thermal reactions that release the hydrocarbons from kerogen. Heating the rock by pumping superheated water into it loosens the viscous hydrocarbons from the pores and cracks. Hydrocarbons are driven off by the heat, collected, and then pumped to the surface for further distillation and refining.

A key factor in the removal of hydrocarbon compounds from the ground is the carbon-to-hydrogen ratio. Carbon is twelve times heavier than hydrogen, so carbon-rich heavy crude oils are more dense than conventional oil, which contains a higher percentage of hydrogen. Carbon-rich crude oil yields smaller amounts of the more desirable lighter fuels, such as kerosene and gasoline. Heavy crudes, such as those derived from oil shale and tar sands, can be chemically upgraded by removing carbon or adding hydrogen in the refining process. These procedures, however, are rather complex and certainly add to the already high cost of extraction and refining.

Progress has been made in the recovery rate of hydrocarbons from reservoir rock. Extraction technology has increased the amount recovered from about 12 percent in 1960 to more than 50 percent in some instances by the late 1980's. The recovery rate is dependent on the percentage of complex hydrocarbons present, which varies from formation to formation. One main problem impeding the all-out effort to continue full-scale production is the economics of oil shale mining. When the price of oil, especially that which is imported, is low and the amounts abundant, it is not feasible to consider oil shale as a source.

Several major environmental problems exist with oil shale production. The refining process actually generates more waste than the original amount of rock that is processed. The processed rock increases in volume by about 30 percent, because the hot water and steam used to extract the kerogen from the oil shale enter into the clay molecules present in the rock and cause them to expand. The problem then is what to do with the increased volume of material, as it will overfill the void produced by mining the rock. This expanded material also weathers very rapidly so that it will not remain in place and form a stable terrane. In-situ retorting precludes the need to mine the shale and, thus, circumvents this disposal problem.

Another environmental concern is that of the air quality in the vicinity of the processing plant. Large amounts of dust being thrown into the atmosphere have an adverse effect on the air in the immediate area surrounding the plant. On a large scale, the overall air quality on a global basis can be affected with a marked increase in oil shale production through increases in carbon dioxide. Research has shown that high-temperature retorting methods (those using temperatures exceeding 600 degrees Celsius) may produce more carbon dioxide from the carbonate rocks containing the oil than does the actual burning of the oil produced by the process. This process adds to the amount of carbon dioxide, thus increasing the worldwide greenhouse effect. Additional carbon dioxide is generated through the combustion of free carbon, which is present in the kerogen.

Tar sands are formed in environments different from those in which oil shales are produced. While oil shales appear to form in lake environments, especially those characterized by sandstone and limestone deposits, tar sands are often found in conjunction with deltaic or nonmarine settings. Most of the major deposits of tar sands are in rocks which are of Cretaceous age or younger, whereas oil shales are often associated with older sedimentary formations. The lack of a cement to hold the sand grains together results in high porosities and permeabilities, thus affording the viscous tars an opportunity to flow. Another geologic setting that enhances the formation of large tar deposits includes areas that have an impermeable layer overlying the deposits. The impermeable layer acts as a barrier to prevent the upward movement of the hydrocarbons.

The mining of tar sands must usually be done at or near the deposits, as large amounts of the sands are handled. The actual production of oil from tar sands in the Athabasca field involves large amounts of material being processed. For each 50,000 barrels of oil, almost 33,000 cubic meters of overburden must be removed and about 100,000 tons of tar sand mined and then discarded. Extraction of bitumen and heavy oils from tar sands is relatively difficult because of high levels of viscosity of the hydrocarbons. Bitumen at room temperature is heavier than water and does not flow. The viscosity of these substances can be changed dramatically by applying heat. If tar sands are heated to about 175 degrees Celsius, the bitumens present flow readily and are capable of floating on water. In some cases, the injection of steam into the reservoir sands increases the flow, thus allowing the material to be pumped out of the ground. Hot water can also be used, but this method requires vast volumes of water, something not available in many regions of the west where these sands are presently found. Underground combustion techniques utilize burning the tar sands underground, allowing the resulting heat to warm the bitumens to the point at which they flow and can be pumped to the surface.

Context

The existence of oil shales and tar sands has been known for several centuries. Deposits were used as a source of oil for lamps in Europe and colonial America. Native Americans used them to patch their canoes. Once commercial production of petroleum expanded in the latter half of the nineteenth century, interest in developing and using oil shales and tar sands as a source of oil decreased. Interest increased, however, during World War II and also in the mid-1970's as a result of shortages in petroleum imports. Once the short-term oil crisis was over, though, both the federal government and private industry in the United States dropped most of their research and development associated with extracting oil from oil shale. The Canadian government has moved ahead with its development of extensive tar sand deposits. Undoubtedly, interest in developing oil shale reserves in the United States will increase as the national reserves of petroleum diminish and imports become scarcer and more expensive. It must be recognized that even the worldwide reserves of oil shale and tar sand are finite and that other energy sources must be developed in the twenty-first century.

Bibliography

Carrigy, M. A. "New Production Techniques for Alberta Oil Sands." *Science* 234 (December, 1986): 1515-1518. A succinct, fact-filled discussion of tar sand production in Canada. The article is clearly written, so it is suitable for high school readers.

De Nevers, Noel. "Tar Sands and Oil Shales." *Scientific American* 214 (February, 1966): 21-29. A good review of the status of the development of these deposits in the earlier days of production. The author makes some comparisons of the Green River formation oil shale fields and the tar sand sources in the Athabasca tar sand area of Alberta.

Duncan, Donald C., and Vernon E. Swanson. *Organic-Rich Shale of the United States and World Land Area*. U.S. Geological Survey Circular 523. Washington, D.C.: Government Printing Office, 1965. A classic work that serves as the basis for much of the present-day knowledge of worldwide deposits of oil shale, in terms of both locations and reserves. A very readable presentation, it is highly recommended as a key reference. Data presented have since been updated in other works.

Gray, G. Ronald. "Oil Sand." In *McGraw-Hill Encyclopedia of the Geological Sciences*, edited by S. P. Parker. 2d ed. New York: McGraw-Hill, 1988. This article discusses several geological factors that control the environments of formation of tar sands, along with providing specific information on worldwide reserves. Good source of data for those desiring to make comparisons of various areas.

Hughes, Richard V. "Oil Shale." In *The Encyclopedia of Sedimentology*, edited by R. W. Fairbridge and J. Bourgeois. Stroudsburg, Pa.: Dowden, Hutchinson and Ross, 1978. A brief discussion of the environments and characteristics of selected oil shale deposits. More than a dozen technical references are provided for those readers looking for the scientific basis and interpretation of oil shales.

Smith, John W. "Synfuels: Oil Shale and Tar Sands." In *Perspectives on Energy, Issues, Ideas, and Environmental Dilemmas*, edited by L. C. Ruedisili and M. W. Firebaugh. 3d ed. New York: Oxford University Press, 1982. A superb article that discusses the definitions, characteristics, resources, and production of oil shales and tar sands in a well-outlined presentation. Its very complete reference list provides more sources to readers desiring either general or technical details. This article would serve as an excellent starting point for someone researching the topic. Suitable for high school students.

Smith, John W., and Howard B. Jensen. "Oil Shale." In *McGraw-Hill Encyclopedia of the Geological Sciences*, edited by S. P. Parker. 2d ed. New York: McGraw-Hill, 1988. An excellent summary article, with several figures showing oil shale deposits in the United States. Explains the technical aspects of oil shale properties. An extensive bibliography lists more than a dozen technical references. Suitable for high school readers and beyond.

Yen, T. F., and G. V. Chilingarian, eds. *Oil Shale*. New York: Elsevier, 1976. A compilation of twelve chapters authored by experts in the various facets of oil shale studies. Some articles are suitable for high school and college students; others are very specific and are suitable for researchers. Numerous references provided with each chapter.

David M. Best

Cross-References

Surface Mining Techniques, 1703; Underground Mining Techniques, 1710; Mining Wastes and Reclamation, 1718; Oil and Gas Exploration, 1878; The Origin of Oil and Gas, 1901; The Worldwide Distribution of Oil and Gas, 1923; Oil Chemistry, 1931; Sedimentary Rocks: Biogenic, 2312.

OIL SPILLS

Field of study: Urban geology and geologic hazards

Growing demand for petroleum has set the stage for colossal oil spills along coastlines. Major sources are supertanker groundings and offshore drilling. Nature's resilience has been the main protection from catastrophic impacts.

Principal terms

DETERGENTS: a numerous class of water-soluble preparations able to emulsify oil and thus clean surfaces and disperse the oil; in oil spills, commonly referred to as emulsifiers or dispersants

EMULSION: a colloidal system consisting of a liquid dispersed in a liquid, as oil in water or water in oil, composed of very tiny droplets

GROUNDING: the entrapment of ships on rocks or soil, from which they normally cannot escape without the help of tugs, offloading of cargo, or both

OIL: a common term for petroleum, a diverse mixture of mostly liquid hydrocarbons (combinations of hydrogen and carbon) obtained from oil wells

SUPERTANKERS: gigantic oil tankers of more than 100,000 tons deadweight, which, because of their sheer size, cause catastrophic spills when breached

Summary of the Phenomenon

Oil spills are all too common events in this technological age. Humankind depends heavily upon energy resources for industry, commerce, and personal comfort. Prior to the 1973 Organization of Petroleum Exporting Countries (OPEC) oil embargo, demand for petroleum products had been doubling every decade. This demand exhausted local resources and led major consuming nations to rely more and more on oil imported from distant sources, such as the Persian Gulf and the Arctic region of Alaska, and to pursue vigorously offshore exploration. Wars in the Middle East, however, especially the 1956 Arab-Israeli conflict, demonstrated the vulnerability of the Suez Canal. At the same time, new ship-building techniques made it feasible to construct vastly larger tankers that could carry oil as cheaply around Africa, in spite of the much longer journey. By the 1960's, the term "supertanker" was being applied to vessels of 100,000 tons and larger. Supertankers of 500,000 tons have become possible, and design studies have been made for ships up to 1 million tons. The upward spiral of reliance on these behemoths has been halted only by the stabilization of demand during the 1970's and the 1980's, largely through price-induced conservation.

Oceanic oil spills are far more difficult to handle than are those on land. Because oil floats on water and rapidly thins, it can cover vast surfaces and pollute many miles of coastline. The 1989 grounding of the Exxon *Valdez* near Valdez, Alaska, spilled only 20 percent of its cargo, yet it blackened 1,300 kilometers of rocky, often inaccessible shoreline about the same length as the United States' Atlantic coastline. During the winter of 1983, a combination of storm and war damage to producing wells resulted in an oil slick that covered most of the Persian Gulf. In the years since the first catastrophic oil spill from the *Torrey Canyon* off the southwest coast of England, little progress has been made. Nevertheless, much has been learned about how to handle the oil, its impact on aquatic life, and how natural processes degrade it (break it down to harmless elements).

The most publicized oil spills involve tanker accidents, which actually account for only 10-15 percent of the annual input into the oceans, and blowouts at offshore drilling rigs. Media reports and books often cite a bewildering array of statistics, making comparisons difficult. Part of the problem lies in the difference between measurements by volume—in barrels and gallons—versus weight—in tons and metric tons. Volume measurements use the industry standard of barrels, a relic from the days when whale oil was stored in barrels holding 42 gallons. There is no set conversion possible between volume and weight measurements, since oil from different reservoirs and regions varies in density and composition; however, 1 metric ton (1,000 kilograms, or about 2,200 pounds) is approximately equal to 7 barrels.

Evidence suggests that ecosystems are well able to handle modest amounts of oil pollution in dilute proportions. It is the "catastrophic" spills that are so damaging; the five largest have been *Torrey Canyon*, Santa Barbara, Amoco *Cadiz*, Ixtoc I, and Exxon *Valdez*. Vastly different quantities are involved in even these spills. The significance of a given event has much more to do with its timing and location than with quantity. The Santa Barbara spill, though far smaller than Ixtoc I, had a vastly greater impact on public opinion and legislation. The Exxon *Valdez* spill is notable for occurring in Prince William Sound, an environmentally sensitive and especially picturesque, Subarctic region comparable to the Alps. One common thread in tanker accidents is the combination of chance events required to cause them, a montage of errors and factors. Vigilance and redundant safety systems seem to be the only safeguards.

In 1967, the *Torrey Canyon* grounded on protruding granitic rocks called the Seven Stones, located between the Scilly Isles and Lands End at the extreme southwestern corner of England. Off-course and needing to meet a critical high tide, the captain chose to sail east of the Scilly Isles through an unfamiliar channel, rather than the normal unrestricted passage to the west. Confused by fishing boats in his path and the questionable positions determined by his deck officer as well as beset with a temporarily nonresponsive steering wheel, the captain just missed clearing the rocks upon which his ship foundered. For Lloyds of London (the insurers), the cause was clearly the pressure on the captain to make port at a specific time; as an example, there is a notable increase in collisions and accidents just before Christmas.

Torrey Canyon was the first major accident involving a supertanker, with no precedents. Existing maritime law was unclear, especially as to the rights of the British government when the only apparent solution was to bomb the ship in an effort to burn up the remaining oil. Lines of authority for cleanup operations had to be evolved on the spot, a similar problem in France when oil hit the Brittany coast a few weeks later. The English shoreline at that point is a major vacation spot, so the government decided to focus efforts on clean beaches, depending mainly on detergents to do the job. They paid for their clean beaches with a heavy loss of aquatic life in the intertidal zone (area between high and low tide), especially grazers that had heretofore kept the slimy green algae under control. By contrast, the French, with some time to judge the British effort, opted to clean up the oil that came ashore as best they could, using straw and other absorbent materials. Heroic efforts included the massive, though mostly futile, attempts by the English to save oiled seabirds, and the successful protection of a hundred-year-old research section at Roscoff, France. The latter involved making a long boom out of burlap stuffed with straw and wood cuttings, an operation dubbed "Operation Big Sausage." Because they had not recognized the need to anchor this boom, students physically held it in place while the tide rolled in, with new troops relieving those who could no longer endure the cold water.

The Santa Barbara spill occurred in January, 1969, when a new well being drilled 10 kilometers offshore blew out through weak and fractured geologic structures. Permission had been granted by the U.S. Department of the Interior to place initial casing down to a depth of only 72.5 meters instead of the 268 meters required by regulations. This exception was not uncommon; when a competent formation was lacking, it was thought best to drill the well as rapidly as possible and then cement the entire borehole. This accident was the first to occur in the area, even though ample evidence, in the form of natural seepages, strongly indicated its potential. After twelve days, the blowout was brought under initial control through the high pressure injection of heavy drilling mud and by cementing the upper part of the borehole. Oil continued to seep, however, until the pressure was relieved by new wells installed to drain the reservoir. In the shoreline cleanup efforts, straw was again the most effective weapon. Probably the most important impact of the Santa Barbara blowout was political. Television images of blue water and white sand smeared with black oil—and birds and people similarly smeared—had a powerful public impact that would lead to the formation of the Environmental Protection Agency. For the United States, Santa Barbara introduced "the environmental decade" of the 1970's.

The Amoco *Cadiz* spill (March, 1978), nearly twice that of *Torrey Canyon*, and the blowout of Ixtoc I (June, 1979) have been by far the largest, yet they received relatively light coverage. The Amoco *Cadiz* lost its steering, foundered on rocks, and broke up during a period of extremely stormy weather and rough seas a few kilometers off the western edge of Brittany, the same general region of France blackened by *Torrey Canyon* oil. Fortunately, the high wave energy there provided optimal conditions for high rates of biodegradation.

Ixtoc I was being drilled by Petroleos Mexicanos in the Bay of Campeche, 77 kilometers off Ciudad del Carmen in 45-meter-deep water. Shutoff valving failed to work, and strenuous efforts to plug the well were unsuccessful. The flow rate exceeded 3.75 million liters per day for a number of months and was controlled only when relief wells reduced the reservoir pressure. Fortunately, much damage that might have occurred did not. Aromatics are the most toxic fractions of the oil; because they have the lowest boiling point, they largely evaporate within a day. The fact that this spill was located well offshore and within the large surface area of the Gulf of Mexico certainly contributed to the relatively low impact. Also, much of the oil that came ashore landed along several hundred kilometers of sparsely populated coast between Yucatan and the United States border. After three months, with help from the U.S. Coast Guard, half the daily leakage was being recovered through the use of booms and skimmer craft. This spill raised international issues between Mexico and the United States, especially through political pressure from Texas over losses in tourist trade. The two governments did cooperate in efforts to save the endangered Atlantic ridley turtle, however, airlifting fifteen thousand hatchlings from their Mexican beach near the spill site to the open sea.

The Exxon *Valdez* accident in March, 1989, though causing the loss of only 20 percent of its cargo, was still the largest oil spill in American history. The accident apparently occurred when the allegedly intoxicated captain set the ship on a course heading straight for Bligh Reef and then left the bridge, placing the responsibility for navigation in the hands of the third mate. Local Alyeska Pipeline crews were unprepared for a spill of this magnitude. Furthermore, their response took ten to twelve hours, rather than the five hours required by law. The ten years of trouble-free operation, where eight hundred tankers a year load up with oil for West Coast refineries, had apparently lulled all involved into complacency. The gross human error involved is implied by the fact that the grounding occurred in good weather and clear visibility, within range of Coast Guard radars, good radio contact, and light traffic. A major impact was on the credibility of the oil industry, at a time when it was seeking permission to develop Alaska's Arctic National Wildlife Refuge—the nation's most promising source of new oil. Exxon took out full-page ads in many local newspapers to express regrets and promise cleanup action, estimated to cost $100 million.

Methods of Study

Oil spills stimulate a tremendous quantity and diversity of research, which can generally be classified as legal, ecological, or hydrological. Legal studies focus on causes and liabilities, effectiveness of abatement procedures and contingency plans, and needed legislation, including international agreements. The Santa Barbara spill especially produced a notable shift among scientists and engineers, from detached onlookers to active participants in the setting of standards and policies.

Unfortunately, while much progress has been made in assigning financial responsibilities and developing contingency plans, the sheer magnitude and infrequency of catastrophic spills tend to overwhelm abatement efforts. Containment and recovery efforts become trivial in the face of high seas and the rapid spread of massive oil slicks over vast areas. Hard lessons are still being learned about the need for quick action while the oil is still concentrated. Furthermore, within a day, untreated oil exposed to heavy wave agitation begins to form a water-in-oil emulsion, commonly described as "chocolate mousse," which is far more difficult to clean up.

After decades of research, detergent-based emulsifiers and dispersants remain the only effective abatement tool. Most of them are toxic, however, especially to larvae on the surface (where most live) and to animal life within the intertidal zone. Fortunately, the worst problems are confined to the short-lived aromatic solvents (chemically similar to those described for Ixtoc I) used to disperse the heavier oils in the spill. The goal in using these dispersants is to create an oil-in-water emulsion (the opposite of naturally formed "mousse"). These tiny droplets then spread throughout the upper surfaces, where they are more readily biodegraded by zooplankton and bacteria. Unfortunately, this course of action also allows easier penetration of oil and other pollutants into gills and other vital organs of fish. When used offshore, the ecological impact of detergents is greatly reduced. Remembering the hard lesson associated with the *Torrey Canyon*, however, workers still rely on straw as one of the most effective cleanup materials, as it retains ten to thirty times its own weight in oil.

Another tragic lesson from the *Torrey Canyon* and Santa Barbara incidents involved the plight of seabirds, especially those that dive for food or rely primarily on swimming for locomotion. The oil soaked their plumage and destroyed its waterproofing and insulating properties so that the birds became chilled and often died from exposure and exhaustion. In spite of heroic efforts to save them, most cleaned birds perished, and few of the survivors were psychologically fit to return to the wild. Some scientists recommend a policy of concentrating resources on the survival of unaffected colonies of endangered species hit by the spill, a form of ecological triage (or prioritized treatment). In the Exxon *Valdez* spill, sea otters, dependent for insulation on fur, suffered a similar fate. By contrast, animals that depend on subcutaneous fat are much less affected, as their skin easily sheds the oil. Also, the higher developed mammals seem able to sense danger and take evasive action, as evidenced by migratory whales in the Santa Barbara Channel.

Research has discovered an amazing ability of aquatic organisms to survive in oil once the toxic aromatic compounds have evaporated. Long-term ecological effects are disputed, however, with some scientists voicing concern about the residual effects of oil in the water column and stored in the fecal pellets of zooplankton in ocean-bottom sediments. Hydrologic research has sought to determine where the oil goes and how it is degraded by physical, chemical, and biological processes. The greatest concern is for the polar environments, where the pace of chemical and biological activity is much slower.

Many similarities are seen among oil spills. Consequently, the extensive research from the *Torrey Canyon*-Santa Barbara period is still highly relevant. There is no "right" method, however, as the immense variability of local conditions dictates local plans of action, materials, and equipment. Fortunately, with each massive spill, commitment grows to handle these catastrophes better.

Context

The impact of major spills on the oil industry has been overwhelmingly negative, while conversely, those groups seeking environmental action and support have been clearly strengthened. To repair the public relations damage, oil companies are accepting full responsibility for cleanup operations.

Catastrophic spills have been a powerful force in stimulating political action. The Santa Barbara incident directly influenced the establishment of the Environmental Protection Agency and helped launch "the environmental decade" of the 1970's. The *Torrey Canyon* demonstrated the international nature of oil movements: an American-owned ship under the Liberian flag, with Italian sailors, charted to British Petroleum, grounded in international waters, and severely polluting both English and French coasts. The Exxon *Valdez* spill halted efforts to develop Alaska's Arctic National Wildlife Refuge, and *Time* magazine printed a cover story, "The Two Alaskas," describing the conflict over wilderness preservation versus development. Heavy pressure has been placed on petroleum geologists and engineers to take far more care in reservoir development and extraction.

Fortunately, nature is highly resilient. Oil spill impacts are mostly short-term, damaging amenities such as beaches and rocky coastlines and causing economic losses to tourist and seafood industries. Nevertheless, scenes of dying, oil-caked seabirds leave indelible imprints on the mind. Ecosystems and coastlines do recover, but the trauma of these spills is a powerful stimulus to future prevention, and prevention is still by far the option of choice. The magnitude of these catastrophes is so great that only nature's ravages are comparable. One cannot help but wonder about the necessity for controls similar to those governing commercial air traffic. When accidents do occur, a quick and massive response is needed. Ultimately, people living in modern industrial nations need to recognize a corporate responsibility. Calls for conservation seek to reduce the risks associated with the present high energy age.

Bibliography

Cowan, Edward. *Oil and Water: The Torrey Canyon Disaster*. Philadelphia: J. B. Lippincott, 1968. Similar to Petrow's British-oriented book but a more detailed, less readable treatment from an American perspective. Includes striking photographs and an index.

Easton, Robert. *Black Tide: The Santa Barbara Oil Spill and Its Consequences*. New York: Delacorte Press, 1972. This account focuses on the people and politics that radicalized Santa Barbara and led to milestone national environmental legislation. A must for anyone interested in the history of the environmental movement. Includes photographs, an extensive list of sources, and an index.

Gundlach, Erich R., et al. "The Fate of Amoco *Cadiz* Oil." *Science* 221 (July 8,

1983): 122-129. This work is one of the few major scientific articles on this large tanker spill. Focuses on the physical-chemical degradation of the oil and includes forty-nine references and notes.

Hill, Gladwin. "Ixtoc's Oil Has a Silver Lining." *Audubon* 81 (November, 1979): 150-159. This article is a succinct, contemporary account of the events surrounding and the issues raised by this oil spill. Describes an effective Coast Guard control plan and the international relations issues between Mexico and the United States from the blowout.

Jackson, J. B. C., et al. "Ecological Effects of a Major Oil Spill on Panamanian Coastal Marine Communities." *Science* 243 (January 6, 1989): 37-44. Important because of its data on before-and-after conditions from a 1986 spill of about 4,500 barrels, this study cites much higher mortality rates than are commonly reported, especially among plant communities. Detailed figures and fifty-nine references and notes.

Lemonick, Michael D., and Eugene Linden. "The Two Alaskas." *Time* 133 (April 17, 1989): 56-62. A cover story contrasting wilderness and industry, this article presents the raging debate set off by the Exxon *Valdez* grounding. Also considers the question of the need for development versus conservation.

Nelson-Smith, Anthony. *Oil Pollution and Marine Ecology.* New York: Plenum Press, 1973. This detailed survey of the literature by a top British marine ecologist contains an extensive bibliography and index but limited illustrations. Only the introductory chapters are appropriate for the general reader, but the whole is a vital source for the serious researcher.

Petrow, Richard. *In the Wake of Torrey Canyon.* New York: David McKay, 1968. A very readable discussion of the causes, consequences, and lessons from this disaster, including a few photographs and an index. Provides detailed coverage of the navigational aspects and the inadequacies of existing maritime law.

Roberts, Leslie. "Long, Slow Recovery Predicted for Alaska." *Science* 244 (April 7, 1989): 22-24. This short, but highly informative, contemporary account in a prestigious journal summarizes the problem of oil spills as well as current knowledge, including the 1985 National Research Council report entitled "Oil in the Sea."

Wardley-Smith, J., ed. *The Control of Oil Pollution on the Sea and Inland Waters.* London: Graham & Trotman, 1976. A surprisingly readable primer, with consistent articles by diverse experts. Well organized, thorough, heavily illustrated, and indexed. Includes an appendix on the recommended treatment of oiled seabirds.

Nathan H. Meleen

Cross-References

Coastal Processes and Beaches, 240; Ocean-Floor Drilling Programs, 1805; Ocean Tides, 1832; Oil and Gas Exploration, 1878; Oil and Gas: Offshore Wells, 1886; Oil and Gas: Petroleum Reservoirs, 1909; Oil Chemistry, 1931.

OPHIOLITES

Type of earth science: Geology
Field of study: Tectonics

Ophiolites are a unique assemblage of rocks found in many mountain belts throughout the world. They were formed in the oceans and subsequently transported to land during mountain-building processes. Ophiolites are useful to geologists as indicators of the location of ancient oceans. They are important to society because they are major sources of asbestos, nickel, and copper minerals.

Principal terms

IGNEOUS ROCK: a rock formed when magma (molten rock) cools and forms minerals; it can form on the surface of the earth when volcanoes erupt, or it can form at depth, without reaching the earth's surface

LITHOSPHERE: the upper, rigid 100 kilometers of the earth that forms the moving plates; beneath oceans it is called oceanic lithosphere, and beneath continents it is continental lithosphere

MAFIC: a rock rich in iron and magnesium minerals; ultramafic rocks are very rich in these minerals

OLIVINE: a mineral consisting of magnesium, iron, silicon, and oxygen

PERIDOTITE: an igneous rock consisting of minerals rich in magnesium; serpentinized peridotite has been heated such that the mineral olvine is partially converted into serpentine

PILLOW LAVA: the lava that is formed when molten rock erupts into water and cools in the shape of a pillow

PLATE TECTONICS: the theory that the upper part of the earth consists of a number of "plates," or rigid parts, that can move across the interior of the earth and also move relative to one another on the surface

SERPENTINE: a mineral consisting of magnesium, iron, silicon, oxygen, and water

Summary of the Phenomenon

Ophiolites are a unique assemblage of rocks that have fascinated geologists for centuries. The word "ophiolite" is derived from the Greek *ophis,* meaning snake or serpent. The term first appeared in the geological literature in the 1820's, when Alexandre Brongniart of France used it to describe rocks called serpentinite, which are made entirely of the mineral serpentine. The term "ophiolite" is appropriate because serpentinite, like some snakes, has a mottled green appearance. The usage of the term "ophiolite" changed early in the twentieth century when the close association of serpentinite or serpentinized peridotite with deep-water sediments and with pillow lavas was noted. This assemblage of three rock types became known as the Steinmann Trinity. In the late 1960's, with the advent of plate tectonics as a unifying theory in geology, the definition of "ophiolite" again changed and was used to describe the Steinmann Trinity plus other rocks arranged in a particular sequence. At the same time, the interpretation that ophiolites formed in the oceans became the cornerstone for reconstructing the history of mountains. As defined for modern usage by a Geological Society of America conference in 1972, ophiolite refers to a distinctive assemblage of mafic and ultramafic rocks. A completely developed ophiolite is 10-12 kilometers thick and covers an area of hundreds of square kilometers.

Rocks in ophiolites occur in layers in the following order (starting from the bottom and working up): peridotite, gabbro, sheeted dike complex, pillow lavas, and chert. Peridotite is an ultramafic igneous rock formed below the earth's surface, dark in color, consisting of large grains (greater than 5 millimeters) of the minerals olivine (an olive-green mineral rich in magnesium, iron, silicon, and oxygen) and pyroxene (a black mineral rich in iron, magnesium, silicon, and oxygen). In many ophiolites, peridotite has been subjected to heat and hot water since its formation, resulting in some of the olivine minerals changing to serpentine, some of which is asbestos. Gabbro is a mafic igneous rock formed below the earth's surface that has a salt-and-pepper appearance. It consists of large grains (greater than 3 millimeters) of the minerals pyroxene and feldspar (a white mineral rich in calcium, sodium, aluminum, and oxygen). Sheeted dike complex is made up of mafic igneous rocks formed just below the earth's surface, similar to gabbro but with smaller mineral grains (less than 3 millimeters). Pillow lavas are mafic igneous rocks formed on the earth's surface as lava erupts into water, similar to gabbro but with much smaller grains (less than 1 millimeter). Chert is a sedimentary rock formed in deep water, consisting of very small grains (some too small to be seen with a microscope) of various minerals and organic remains. Not all ophiolites exhibit the complete sequence of rocks; some were formed with certain layers missing, and others were dismembered subsequent to their formation. A very important observation is that beneath all ophiolites there is a fault (fracture in the earth) separating them from underlying rocks. Furthermore, there is evidence that ophiolites have probably moved hundreds of kilometers along those faults.

Ophiolites can form in two different plate tectonic environments, both of which are in oceans. In one environment, such as in the middle of the Atlantic Ocean, two plates are moving away from each other. As they do so, magma from the interior of the earth moves up to the bottom of the oceans and cools to form long mountain chains called oceanic ridges (for example, the Mid-Atlantic Ridge). The solidified rock becomes part of an outer layer of the earth called the oceanic lithosphere. The newly formed oceanic lithosphere then moves away from the ridge at which it formed, resulting in widening of the ocean. (For example, the Atlantic Ocean is growing wider as North America moves westward, away from Europe.) Ophiolites are believed to be remnants of the top part of oceanic lithosphere that was created at ancient oceanic ridges. All the igneous rocks in ophiolites formed by the cooling of magma produced deep in the earth and spewed forth at an oceanic ridge. Pillow lavas form when the magma erupts into seawater; sheeted dikes, gabbros, and peridotites form when that magma cools at various depths below the surface. Chert forms when fine particles, including mineral grains, animal parts, and plants, fall to the bottom of the newly created ocean floor to form sedimentary deposits. A second environment where ophiolites may form is the region where two plates are moving toward each other. In this environment, oceanic lithosphere that formed at oceanic ridges disappears down into the interior of the earth, resulting in melting at depth, the production of highly explosive volcanoes, and the generation of dangerous earthquakes. This general area is known as a subduction zone. When oceanic lithosphere has just begun to subduct (descend into the earth's interior) beneath another oceanic lithospheric plate, ophiolites may form in the region above the subducting plate. The processes involved in formation of these ophiolites are the same as at an oceanic ridge, though the environments are different.

Another important part of the geological history of ophiolites is how they are moved from their place of formation in the oceans to their current location on continents. The key lies in understanding how mountains are built. Ophiolites have been described from all the world's major mountain belts: the Appalachian Mountains of eastern North America, the Rockies in western North America, the Alps in Europe, the Himalaya in Asia, the Urals in the Soviet Union, the Andes in South America, and the mountains of Papua New Guinea. They range in age from about 600 million years old to as young as 15 milion years old. The movement of ophiolites from the ocean floor to mountains is related to plate tectonics. Subduction zones, where plates are moving toward each other, provide the mechanism for emplacement of ophiolites.

To get a better idea of how ophiolites may have been put into place in the past, scientists consider what might happen to the Pacific Ocean in the future. The Pacific plate (that is, the oceanic lithosphere beneath the Pacific Ocean) is moving westward toward, and subducting beneath, the Asian plate along the Japanese islands, resulting in volcanoes and earthquakes along the zone. The Pacific plate is also subducting eastward beneath western North America. Therefore, the Pacific Ocean will become smaller, the North American continent will move closer to the Asian continent, and they will eventually collide (maybe in a hundred million years). During this span of time, probably 99.99 percent of the Pacific oceanic lithosphere (potential ophiolites) will be lost to the interior of the earth at the subduction zones. At the time of collision of North America and Asia, however, a small portion (less that 0.01 percent) of the oceanic lithosphere may not slip back into the interior but instead may be pushed up onto the continents, because when the two continents collide, mountains are being built, and some of the Pacific oceanic lithosphere, sandwiched in the zone of collision, may be pushed up with the mountains. These portions of the Pacific oceanic lithosphere will then be called ophiolites. In a similar fashion, the ophiolites that are now visible in mountain belts are tiny remnants of ancient oceanic lithosphere pushed onto continents during ancient mountain building.

The occurrence of ophiolites in mountains has helped geologists to understand how mountains are built. Ophiolites lie in narrow bands that continue for thousands of kilometers along a mountain belt. This narrow band represents the zone where two continents have come together to build the mountains. Thus, by locating ophiolites, geologists can identify and then characterize the two (or more) continents that existed separately before the mountains were built. For example, in the Appalachian Mountains of eastern North America, a narrow band of ophiolites extends from western Newfoundland, Canada, through Quebec, Canada, into Vermont and as far south as Alabama in the United States. This zone may represent the boundary between the ancient North American continent to the west and the ancient African continent to the east; the two ancient continents were plastered together during the building of the Appalachians over a span of time between 500 million and 350 million years ago.

Methods of Study

Geologists have used a variety of techniques to study ophiolites, including field mapping, seismic studies, electron microprobe techniques, and X-ray techniques. Field mapping of ophiolites involves identifying rock types, noting their locations on maps, and ascertaining the relationship of the ophiolites with neighboring rocks; it is the basic tool used by the geologist to analyze the origin of ophiolites, and it precedes any laboratory techniques.

Seismic studies have been employed to compare ophiolites to the modern oceanic lithosphere. Seismic (shock) waves travel through the earth after earthquakes; they can also be created by man-made explosions or by hitting the ground hard with a sledgehammer. Seismic waves travel at different speeds through different rock types. Thus, if scientists can identify the velocities of seismic waves as they travel through different types of rock, the type of rock can be identified even though it cannot be seen. In the oceans, seismic velocity measurements through rocks beneath the ocean floor have shown that the modern oceanic lithosphere is made up of layers that correspond exactly in rock type and in thickness to what is observed in ophiolites, which is very good evidence to support the interpretation that ophiolites formed as portions of oceanic lithosphere.

X-ray techniques have been used to determine the chemical composition of rocks in ophiolites. In a technique called X-ray fluorescence, X rays bombard a powdered rock sample and interact with electrons of the chemical elements to produce secondary X rays. The secondary X rays generated by specific elements can be isolated and counted to determine the amounts or percentages of specific elements present in the rock. Results of such studies on ophiolites have shown that pillow lava and sheeted dike rocks are similar to lavas erupted in modern oceans. In particular, low percentages of potassium oxide and of light rare earth elements are common to both ophiolitic rocks and modern oceanic rocks.

The electron microprobe is also used extensively to help interpret the origin of ophiolites. In the electron microprobe, electrons hit a rock sample at high speed and interact with electrons in chemical elements in the rock to produce X rays. In the same way as in X-ray techniques, amounts of the chemical elements can be determined. In electron microprobe work, however, the rock sample, rather than being a crushed or powdered specimen, is a thin section (0.03 millimeter thick) of an intact rock that can be viewed through a microscope. Thus, minerals in the rock can be seen, selected, and analyzed for their chemical constituents. Chemical analyses of minerals are most useful in the peridotite and gabbro layers of ophiolites. For example, chemical analyses of olivine, pyroxene, and feldspar from gabbro layers and upper parts of peridotite layers have shown that these layers precipitated from a magma of the same composition as the pillow lavas and sheeted dikes. Therefore, nearly all the igneous rocks in ophiolites can be related to one magma, part of which cooled at shallow depths (about 5 kilometers below the surface) to produce gabbro and peridotite and some of which was injected into higher levels in the earth to produce the sheeted dikes and pillow lavas. The lower parts of the peridotite layer, however, must have originated in a different way. The amounts of aluminum in the mineral pyroxene reveal that the lower peridotite layer formed under high pressure at considerable depth, as much as 30 kilometers below the surface of the earth—good evidence for the suggestion that ophiolites that now exist on the surface of the earth must have been moved since the time of their formation.

Context

Ophiolites contain important mineral deposits, such as asbestos, nickel, chromium, platinum, and copper. Most of the world's asbestos has been mined from ophiolites, principally in the province of Quebec, Canada. Asbestos is a fibrous form of the mineral serpentine commonly found in the peridotite layer of ophiolites. Serpentine forms long after ophiolites become solid rock. Hot water—between 300 and 400 degrees Celsius—penetrates into fractures in ophiolites, comes in contact with olivine in the peridotite layer, and changes (metamorphoses) the olivine into serpentine. Olivine is readily changed into serpentine because the alteration merely involves adding water to olivine and adjusting the proportions of magnesium, iron, and silicon. It is not clear which chemical and physical conditions favor the formation of the fibrous asbestos over other varieties of serpentine. Asbestos has been used mainly in insulating and fire-proof materials, although its use has delined markedly because of associated health hazards.

Nickel, chromium, and platinum occur together in the peridotite layer of some ophiolites. Unlike asbestos, which forms after the ophiolite formed, nickel, chromium, and platinum precipitate from magmas and thus are incorporated into ophiolites at the time of formation. Nickel is mined chiefly from ophiolites in tropical latitudes, where intense weathering of peridotite concentrates the nickel so that it can be mined profitably. Nickel is preeminently an alloy metal used in nickel steels and in nickel cast irons, to which it adds toughness, strength, lightness, and anticorrosive, electrical, and thermal qualities. Chromium, like nickel, is used primarily as an alloy in steel. Platinum, because of its scarcity, is very valuable. The chief uses for platinum are in the electrical, chemical, and petroleum industries. It is used as a setting for diamonds because of its white color and hardness, and it is used in resistors and contacts in delicate instruments such as telephones, televisions, and radios. The chemical industry uses platinum for containers, wire, electrodes, coils, X-ray equipment, and acid making.

Copper deposits are found in pillow-lava layers of most ophiolites. Copper is present in small amounts in the lava when it cools to form solid rock. It is concentrated into small, minable bodies by hot water passing through the solid lava. Pillow lavas in ophiolites form on the ocean floor and fracture as they cool. Seawater penetrates into these fractures to depths of about 5 kilometers. The seawater is heated as it descends beneath the ocean floor, and it also becomes more acidic. Many elements, including copper, are dissolved from the lavas and are concentrated in the water during this process. Once the water reaches a certain depth, it becomes too hot and starts to rise back to the ocean floor. When the hot water from depth reaches the cold ocean water on the sea floor, the dissolved copper precipitates to form copper deposits. Modern oceans are rich in these deposits. Similar ancient ocean deposits are preserved in ophiolites that are emplaced onto land. Although copper from ophiolites is not the primary source of the world's copper, it is an important source. Copper is one of the minerals essential to modern industry. Most wires and electrical equipment are made of pure copper, and copper is used also as an alloy to manufacture brass and bronze.

Bibliography

Coleman, R. C. "The Diversity of Ophiolites." *Geologie en Mijnbow* 63 (1984): 141. A very good review of the state of knowledge on the origin of ophiolites. Suitable for more advanced students of geology.

_____. *Ophiolites: Ancient Oceanic Lithosphere?* New York: Springer-Verlag, 1977. the most detailed treatment of ophiolites available. Includes sections on field descriptions, chemistry of the rocks, and models to explain the origin of ophiolites. Also includes detailed descriptions of four major ophiolites in the world. Suitable for those with previous exposure to geology.

Duxbury, A. C., and A. B. Duxbury. *An Introduction to the World's Oceans.* 2d ed. Dubuque, Iowa: Wm. C. Brown, 1989. A general textbook on the oceans with particularly good chapters (2 and 3) on the sea floor and the not-so-rigid earth. Suitable for any reader.

Francheteau, Jean. "The Oceanic Crust." *Scientific American* 249 (September, 1983): 130. Summarizes information on how modern oceanic crust is formed. Relevant to ophiolites because they are thought to have formed as ancient oceanic crust. Suitable for advanced high school and college students.

Gass, Ian G. "Ophiolites." *Scientific American* 247 (August, 1982): 122. A comprehensive treatment of the evolution of ideas on the origin of ophiolites. Well illustrated with colored diagrams and photographs. Suitable for advanced high school students, college students, and interested adults.

Hamblin, W. K. *The Earth's Dynamic Systems.* 4th ed. New York: Macmillan, 1985. A very good general text to introduce readers to the field of geology. Chapters 17 through 20 are particularly informative on plate tectonics, ocean-floor processes, and mountain building. Suitable for anyone interested in geology.

McKenzie, Dan P. "Tectonics and Sea-Floor Spreading." *American Scientist*, July, 1972: 425. Describes plate tectonics and processes that occur at oceanic ridges. Suitable for anyone with an interest in earth science.

Strahler, Arthur. *Physical Geology.* New York: Harper & Row, 1981. An introductory text in geology. Chapters 4, 10, and 13 deal with igneous rocks and with tectonics in ocean basins. Suitable for general readers.

Raymond A. Coish

Cross-References

Hydrothermal Mineralization, 1108; Igneous Rock Classification, 1138; Igneous Rocks: Ultramafic, 1207; Lithospheric Plates, 1387; Sub-Sea-Floor Metamorphism, 1614; Mountain Belts, 1725; The Oceanic Crust, 1846; Plate Margins, 2063; Plate Motions, 2071; Plate Tectonics, 2079; Sedimentary Rock Classification, 2304; Subduction and Orogeny, 2497; Volcanism at Spreading Centers, 2607.

THE ORIGIN OF LIFE

Type of earth science: Paleontology and earth history

At some time after the formation of the earth some 4.5 billion years ago and before the earliest known microfossils some 3.5 billion years old, life evolved from widely available organic compounds into unicellular creatures similar to modern blue-green algae. Plausible schemes for their evolution from abiotically produced organic matter remain elusive. Much research into the origin of life is based on the idea that the environment of early life was as important as its nature and is comparing the relative merits of the ocean, submarine volcanic vents, and soil as possible places where life began.

Principal terms

AMINO ACID: an organic acid consisting largely of carbon, oxygen, and hydrogen but with an amino group and sometimes also sulfur, phosphorus, and iron

CHERT: a hard rock of minutely crystalline, and often partly hydrous, silica

CHONDRITE: a kind of meteorite that has conspicuous globular grains (chondrules) of high-temperature minerals such as pyroxene and olivine

CLAY: a hydrous aluminosilicate mineral with sheetlike crystal structure

CYANOBACTERIA: commonly known as blue-green algae, a group of microscopic unicellular organisms that lack a membrane dividing their polynucleotides (DNA) from the rest of the cell (thus prokaryotic) and that have a photosynthetic metabolism

ENANTIOMER: a particular version of the same kind of asymmetric chemical compound, such as sugars and amino acids, that may be left- or right-handed and so polarize light in a clockwise (D enantiomer) or counterclockwise (L enantiomer) direction, respectively

FERMENTATION: a metabolic process found in microbes such as yeast, whereby complex organic molecules are partially broken down to alcohol and carbon dioxide, thus releasing energy for work

PHOTOSYNTHESIS: a metabolic process found in plants and microbes whereby the energy of the sun and the catalytic properties of a pigment (bacteriophyll or chlorophyll) are used to reduce carbon dioxide to organic matter

POLYNUCLEOTIDE: a high-molecular-weight compound formed from many units of a sugar joined to an organic base and to a phosphate group; includes ribonucleic acid (RNA) and deoxyribonucleic acid (DNA), both of which carry genetic information in all living cells

PROTEIN: a high-molecular-weight compound that is a long chain or aggregate of amino acids joined by hydrogen bonds

RESPIRATION: a metabolic process found in animals and microbes whereby complex organic molecules ("food") are oxidized to carbon dioxide, thus releasing energy for work

Summary of the Phenomenon

Life on earth is probably no older than the solar system, which accreted, or built up, some 4.5 billion years ago. Early stages in this accretionary process are revealed by meteorites, most of which have been radiometrically dated to about this age. A particular kind of meteorite called a carbonaceous chondrite is characterized by the high-temperature globular mineral grains called chondrules, mixed with low-temperature iron-rich clays and organic compounds. Most of the organic compounds are dispersed among the clays, but some of them form organic lumps and globules. These latter have been mistakenly identified as microfossils, but the organic compounds of carbonaceous chondrites have some diagnostic features of organic matter formed abiotically in solution from mixtures of gases including carbon dioxide. Many organic molecules, such as sugars, are asymmetric. When synthesized in the laboratory, there are about equal amounts of left-handed and right-handed versions (each is known as an enantiomer) that polarize light in a clockwise or counterclockwise direction, respectively. Organic matter behaves similarly in carbonaceous chondrites, whereas organisms are highly selective for a particular enantiomer of a compound, including, for example, only D enantiomers of sugars. Organic compounds that also are presumed to have formed abiotically have been detected from the characteristics of light spectra reflected from asteroids, comets, and interstellar dust. Thus, simple organic compounds used by living creatures are widely available in the universe and have been for at least 4.5 billion years.

It is an enormous step from a tarry mixture of simple organic compounds to a fully functioning organism, with its long polynucleotide instructions and messengers and its complex molecular assembly line and controlling compounds of protein all bound up within a system of membranes and cell wall. This degree of complexity, seen in some of the simplest living forms of unicellular life, was attained by about 3.5 billion years ago. Microscopic fossils of unicellular cyanobacteria have been found permineralized in black cherts of this age in the Pilbara region of Western Australia. These are among the oldest little-deformed sedimentary rocks in which such fossils are likely to be found. Highly deformed and metamorphosed sedimentary rocks as old as 3.8 billion years crop out around Isua in southwestern Greenland. These rocks have not yet yielded convincing microfossils, but the isotopic composition of carbon in these rocks appears to be a metamorphosed version of compositions found in younger rocks with this isotopic signature of photosynthetic life. Older fossil evidence of life on earth is unlikely. There is, however, a younger fossil record from cherts and shales of increasingly complex microfossils in rocks ranging from 3.5 billion years ago to the present. By 700 million years ago, there were also complex multicellular creatures. Fossil plants and animals become increasingly familiar in rocks of younger geological age.

The vast gulf between primordial organic compounds and functioning cells revealed in the rock and meteorite record also is apparent from experimental studies in organic chemistry designed to investigate how life originated. It has been shown many times that organic compounds including amino acids are produced readily within water in sealed flasks containing reducing gases such as carbon dioxide energized by electrical discharges, ultraviolet light, or even shock waves. The exact gas mixture or energy source is not critical to organic matter production, although yields are limited in gas mixtures including oxygen or with weak energy sources. Clay, siderite, and other minerals added to these reaction flasks have been shown to promote both the production of simple organic compounds and their assembly into larger compounds. How they accomplish it is not certain: They may act as a template to hold molecules in a favored orientation for combination, either as a catalyst participating in reversible reactions that tend to promote a particular combination or as a chemostat in buffering solutions from extreme acidity. Thus the origin of organic compounds such as those in carbonaceous chondrites can to some extent be duplicated in a chemistry laboratory.

Chemical experiments fall far short of creating such complex organic molecules as ribonucleic acid (RNA) and deoxyribonucleic acid (DNA). There have been cases where some parts of nucleotides have been synthesized and where nucleotides have been aggregated into polynucleotides. It remains a problem how there could arise a nucleotide-rich environment of the correct chemical nature under abiotic conditions. Nevertheless, it is clear from much experimental work in molecular biology that polynucleotides such as RNA and DNA are the basis for a system of information storage and transfer in all known life forms on earth.

The odds of tarry abiotic organic matter becoming organized into a functioning cell by pure chance are astronomically unfavorable. It has been argued that, given the long period of time available, even the rarest of chances becomes a certainty. This argument now has little appeal, because geological and meteoritic evidence constrains the origin of life to within the first billion years of earth's history and because studies in molecular biology have revealed astounding complexity in even the simplest of organisms. One escape from this dilemma is to postulate seeding of the earth with some form of extraterrestrial life, either by long-distance transport of spores across space or by the technological enterprise of an extraterrestrial civilization. These views have not proven very productive, because they are difficult to test and, in addition, do not solve the problem. Even the simplest life forms are well suited to earth and are made of materials commonly available here. Thus, if life is extraterrestrial, it originated under broadly earthlike conditions elsewhere in the universe. It remains a useful exercise to speculate on how life might have arisen from natural causes here on earth.

The most widely held hypothesis for the origin of life until recently has been that life arose in the primordial soup of the world ocean. The early atmosphere of the earth probably included little or no free oxygen, like that of most planets. Under these conditions, organic matter would have been produced in the sea by lightning strikes, ultraviolet light from the sun, and shock waves from earthquakes or meteorite impacts. This vast organic nutrient solution is viewed as the source of ever more complex molecules, some of which attained the critical innovation of self-replication. These early versions of RNA and DNA then evolved increasingly complex mechanisms for self-preservation, such as cell organelles, cells, and bodies. By this view, the primitive molecular ecosystem fed on abiotically produced organic compounds, and the earliest organisms may have been fermenters. It was only when primordial organic compounds of the ocean were depleted that there arose more sophisticated cellular machinery for the biological production of organic matter by photosynthesis. The most serious problem of this hypothesis is the gap between abiotic organic matter and organized self-replicating molecules. The ocean is, and probably was, too dilute a solution, too low in dissolved phosphorus and too uniform in its alkalinity and oxidation state for synthesis and maintenance of complex organic molecules. The laboratory synthesis of DNA requires many different reactions under very different chemical conditions: acidic and alkaline, oxidizing and reducing, wet and dry. Such fluctuating conditions can be imagined during the intermittent evaporation of seawater ponded on ice floes or in tidal flats, but low temperatures and the formation of salts would retard production of complex organic molecules.

The discovery of deep-sea volcanic vents prompted a second group of hypotheses about the origin of life. These "black smokers" are openings along mid-ocean ridges where internal water of the earth as well as seawater percolating through seafloor basalt has been heated by contact with hot volcanic rocks and is vigorously expelled into the sea at temperatures of up to 380 degrees Celsius. The water gushing from the vents is also strongly acidic and depleted in oxygen. The "black smoke" billowing forth, as well as the vent chimneys, consists of dark sulfide minerals. The idea that ocean vents are flow reactors capable of stripping oxygen from carbon dioxide to produce organic matter is one of the arguments that they may prove pertinent to the origin of life. In addition, the complex system of fractures and vesicles in volcanic rocks around vents would have encouraged a variety of simultaneous and very different chemical reactions, in contrast to the tendency for chemical uniformity in the open ocean. Furthermore, experimental studies have shown that proteins aggregate into spheres and sheets at high temperatures, and such structures can be imagined as crude membranes and cell walls. If life did evolve in oceanic vents, then it would initially have lived by fermentation or respiration of abiotically produced organic compounds, and photosynthesis would have arisen with more complex organic systems of those few vents exposed to sunlight on land or in shallow water. Despite some appealing features of this hypothesis, it remains to be demonstrated whether the minute amounts of organic matter detected in submarine volcanic vents were produced abiotically or are remains of the distinctive fauna of tube worms, clams, and crustaceans that now colonize the sea floor around vents. The high temperatures and strongly acidic nature of vent water are incompatible with the production and preservation of complex proteins and nucleotides. These problems are reduced considerably even a short distance away from the vent, but then there remain the problems already mentioned for an oceanic origin of life.

A third set of hypotheses, that life evolved in soil, can be taken to include ideas involving clay minerals. Soils are, and probably were, the principal sites where clay is formed on earth. Soil hypotheses for the origin of life combine many of the desirable features of ocean and vent hypotheses. Soil water could have been enriched in organic matter like the early ocean, and soils are in a sense flow reactors driven by the energy of the sun at the surface. Soil water is compartmentalized and evaporates into a complex array of films around mineral grains and other particles. Soils enjoy moderate temperature and mild chemical conditions. The most critical advantage of the soil hypothesis is that the production of clay by weathering or of organic matter by abiotic synthesis would have been encouraged because clayey and organic soils are less easily eroded than are sandy, inorganic soils. This matter of advantage can be imagined as a crude form of "natural selection" in which the most clayey and organic soils survived erosion for the longest periods of time. Thus, even the least efficient mechanisms of abiotic weathering and organic synthesis could result in soils as organic and clayey as carbonaceous chondrites. Increasingly complex compounds such as sugars and proteins would be preserved preferentially to the extent that they could bind the soil and maintain it within the zone of materials and energy transfer at the surface. In this view, the primary production of organic matter would initially have been fueled by light from the sun at the surface, and photosynthetic organisms may well have preceded fermenting and respiring creatures. The idea that life arose in soils reduces some of the difficulties of forming functioning cells from tarry organic matter, but it cannot be claimed to eliminate them.

Methods of Study

There was a time when it was thought that the origin of life might be detected from the study of Precambrian microfossils. Although their fossil record is known back to the base of the useful sedimentary record, an appreciation of the nature of the most ancient microfossils still provides constraints on the origin of life. Most of the microfossils have been found in silicified limestones of a distinctive domed and banded kind called stromatolites. Black, organic-rich cherts are collected, because these have proven most fossiliferous. The cherts are cut and polished as thin, petrographic sections for observation under the microscope. Such studies also can be supported by isotopic and chemical research on the organic matter preserved in the chert.

Other constraints on the investigation of the origin of life come from the study of meteorites, particularly carbonaceous chondrites. There are not many of these in meteorite collections because they are rapidly destroyed by weathering after they land on earth, unlike iron meteorites. Deliberate search for meteorites by following the course of "shooting stars" estimated from at least three observation points is beginning to yield more carbonaceous chondrites. They can be studied in thin sections and by an array of methods for mineralogical and chemical characterization of their constituents: X-ray diffraction of their clays, transmission electron microscopy of their minerals and organic structures, electron microprobe chemical analysis of their minerals, and mass spectrometric separation and identification of their organic compounds.

Much useful information on the origin of life also has come from laboratory experiments on the synthesis of organic matter, on the biochemistry of living organisms, and on the nature of clays and other minerals. Organic synthesis experiments involve placing water and mixtures of gases in a sealed flask and applying an energy source, such as an electrical spark. The resulting tarry organic matter can be analyzed by a variety of methods, including spectrometric separation and identification of organic compounds.

A major enterprise of molecular biology is working out the structure of the various complex organic molecules found in living creatures, using such methods as X-ray diffraction, nuclear magnetic resonance, and mass spectrometry. Molecular biologists also strive to understand how the molecules may work from experiments with simple organisms such as bacteria and viruses.

Context

Few topics in science are as inaccessible to direct observation or as fraught with philosophical and religious implications as the origin of life. Scientific techniques are not designed to answer such questions as why humankind exists, but evidence from astronomical, geological, chemical, and biological sciences is revealing some possibilities of how life may have originated. It is doubtful that any of the hypotheses concerning the origin of life will ever become so firmly established as are the laws of physics. The long-accepted concept of molecular evolution in the primordial soup of the world oceans is challenged by alternative views of life's origin in submarine vents and in soils. This work is based on the idea that the way in which life interacts with its environment is as important in defining it as are its physical nature and the way in which it reproduces. Scientists may never satisfactorily reveal how life came about, but they are discovering many fundamental features of the earth, of life, and of their interrelationship.

Bibliography

Bernal, J. D. *The Origin of Life.* New York: World Books, 1967. This comprehensive introduction to the topic, written at a level accessible to the informed layperson, emphasizes the origin of life in the sea. An appendix includes a translation of the original Russian article on this idea, first published by I. A. Oparin in 1924.

Cairns-Smith, A. G. *Genetic Takeover.* Cambridge, England: Cambridge University

Press, 1982. This masterpiece of logic develops the startling theory that clay not only encouraged the origin of organic-based life but also can be considered as part of a quasi-living system itself. This book assumes a university-level background in science, but care is taken to explain technical lines of evidence in various scientific specialties. Also offered is a comprehensive bibliography.

Crick, Francis. *Life Itself: Its Origin and Nature.* New York: Simon & Schuster, 1981. In this slim volume, a Nobel laureate in biochemistry explains, in terms easily understood by the layperson, why life is too complex a phenomenon to have developed on earth within the limited geological time available. In arguing that the earth was deliberately seeded with microbial life by alien civilizations, he also reviews a variety of other hypotheses for the extraterrestrial origin of life.

Fox, S. W., and K. Dose. *Molecular Evolution and the Origin of Life.* San Francisco: W. H. Freeman, 1972. Pitched at the level of university students and professional scientists, this general treatment of the origin of life includes an overview of experiments with the natural aggregation of proteins by the authors.

Hartman, H., P. Morrison, and J. G. Lawless, eds. *Search for the Universal Ancestors: The Origins of Life.* Palo Alto: Blackwell Scientific, 1987. This short book for a popular audience outlines the scientific quest to understand the origin of life and introduces the current ferment of ideas on how life may have evolved.

Miller, S. L., and L. E. Orgel. *The Origins of Life on Earth.* Englewood Cliffs, N.J.: Prentice-Hall, 1974. In this well-referenced and carefully worded account aimed at university students and professional scientists, emphasis has been placed on experimental studies on the abiotic synthesis of organic compounds.

Monod, Jacques. *Chance and Necessity.* Translated by Austryn Wainhouse. New York: Alfred A. Knopf, 1971. In an extended essay aimed at a general audience, this distinguished French molecular biologist develops a critical theme for evaluating theories about the origin of life: Given the complexity of living creatures, it is hardly likely that they originated by chance; some kind of "natural selection" is needed to convert these long odds to a necessity.

Nisbet, Evan G. *The Young Earth: An Introduction to Archaean Geology.* Winchester, Mass.: Unwin Hyman, 1987. This colorful account of the basic data and controversies of geologists researching the oldest rocks on earth is aimed at an audience with at least high school training in science. It is an excellent guide for the primary geological literature on these rocks and especially for the idea that life originated in and around submarine volcanic vents.

Schopf, J. W., ed. *Earth's Earliest Biosphere.* Princeton, N.J.: Princeton University Press, 1983. The text of this long and well-referenced monograph is aimed at university students and professional scientists. It is encyclopedic in scope, with both reviews and original scientific reports of chemical and paleontological studies on early life on earth. Of more general interest are summary tables of data, an extensive glossary of technical terms, and many photographs of stromatolites and microfossils.

Gregory J. Retallack

Cross-References

ORTHOSILICATES

Type of earth science: Geology
Field of study: Mineralogy and crystallography

The orthosilicates are a large and diverse group of rock-forming minerals. The group contains a number of minerals of geologic importance, among them olivine, which may be the most abundant mineral of the inner solar system. Orthosilicates have a few special but limited industrial uses and include a number of important gemstones.

Principal terms

ANION: an atom that has gained electrons to become a negatively charged ion

CATION: an atom that has lost electrons to become a positively charged ion

CRYSTAL STRUCTURE: the regular arrangement of atoms in a crystalline solid

IGNEOUS ROCK: a rock formed by the solidification of molten, or partially molten, rock

METAMORPHIC ROCK: a rock formed when another rock undergoes changes in mineralogy, chemistry, or structure owing to changes in temperature, pressure, or chemical environment at depth within a planet

MINERAL: a naturally occurring, solid, inorganic compound with a definite composition and an orderly internal arrangement of atoms

SILICATES: minerals containing both silicon and oxygen usually in combination with one or more other elements

SOLID SOLUTION: a solid that shows a continuous variation in composition in which two or more elements substitute for each other on the same position in the crystal structure

TETRAHEDRON: a four-sided pyramid made out of equilateral triangles

Summary of the Phenomenon

The orthosilicates are one of the major groups of silicate minerals. Oxygen and silicon are the two most common elements in the rocky outer layers of the earth-like inner planets. Thus, it is not surprising that the silicates are the most abundant, rock-forming minerals on these planets. They are not only very abundant, but also very diverse: It has been estimated that almost one-third of the roughly 3,000 known minerals are silicates. In all but a few of these minerals, each silicon atom is surrounded by a cluster of four oxygen atoms distributed around the silicon in the same way that the corners of a tetrahedron are distributed around its center. Silicate tetrahedra can join together by sharing one oxygen at a corner. By this means, two or more silicate tetrahedra can link together to form pairs, rings, chains, sheets, and three-dimensional frameworks. This linking provides the basis of the classification of silicate structures: Sorosilicates contain pairs of tetrahedra; cyclosilicates contain rings; inosilicates contain chains; phyllosilicates contain sheets; and tectosilicates contain three-dimensional frameworks. In the orthosilicates, however, silicate tetrahedra do not link to each other. Each silicate tetrahedra is isolated from the others as if it were an island, and hence these minerals are sometimes known as island silicates. In the structure of some minerals, isolated silicate tetrahedra are mixed with silicate pairs formed when two tetrahedra share an oxygen at a common corner. Many scientists classify these structures as orthosilicates and use the term nesosilicates to refer to a subdivision of the orthosilicates containing minerals in which all the silicon occurs in isolated tetrahedra.

The electrostatic attraction between negatively charged ions (anions) and positively charged ions (cations) is the basis of the ionic chemical bond. The chemical bonding in orthosilicates is predominantly ionic. Under normal geological conditions, silicon loses four electrons to become a cation with a charge of $+4$, while oxygen gains two electrons to become an anion with a charge of -2. The ionic bond between oxygen and silicon is usually the strongest bond in orthosilicate structures. For a mineral to be stable it must be electrically neutral; in other words, the total number of negative charges on the anions must be equal to the total number of positive charges on the cations. It would take two oxygen anions to balance the charge on one silicon cation. In the silicate tetrahedra, however, the silicon cation is surrounded by four oxygen anions, so in the group as a whole there are four excess negative charges. In the orthosilicate structures this excess negative charge is balanced by the presence of cations outside the silicate tetrahedra. It is the bond between the oxygen in the tetrahedra and these other cations that holds the tetrahedra together to form a coherent, three-dimensional structure. The most common cations to play this role are aluminum with a charge of $+3$, iron with a charge of $+3$ or $+2$, calcium with a charge of $+2$, and magnesium with a charge of $+2$. Aluminum, iron, and calcium are, respectively, the third, fourth, and fifth most abundant elements in the earth's crust, while magnesium is the seventh most abundant. Conspicuously absent from the common orthosilicate structures are the two alkali cations sodium and potassium, which are the sixth and eighth most abundant elements in the earth's crust.

Of all the different kinds of silicates, orthosilicates have the lowest ratio of silicon to oxygen. Thus, they often form in environments relatively low in silicon. The atoms in orthosilicates tend to be packed closer together than the atoms in many other silicates, causing them to be somewhat denser. Greater densities are favored at higher pressure, hence a number of the more important minerals stable at high pressure are orthosilicates. Orthosilicates also tend to be harder (resistant to being scratched) than the average silicate. This property helps give many orthosilicates high durability (resistance to wear), which contributes to their use as gemstones.

The orthosilicates are a large and diverse group, and a description of more than the most common of them is well beyond the scope of this article.

The mineral olivine is the most common and widespread of the orthosilicates: Indeed, it is probably the most abundant mineral in the inner solar system. Olivine contains magnesium (Mg) and iron (Fe) in addition to silicon (Si) and oxygen (O). The chemical formula of olivine is generally written as $(Mg,Fe)_2SiO_4$. The parentheses in this formula indicate that olivine is a solid solution; in other words, magnesium and iron can substitute for each other in the olivine structure. Pure magnesium olivines (Mg_2SiO_4) are known as forsterite, and pure iron olivines (Fe_2SiO_4) are known as fayalite. Most olivines have both magnesium and iron and hence have compositions that lie between these two extremes. Each iron and magnesium atom is surrounded by six oxygen atoms, while each oxygen atom is bonded to three iron or magnesium atoms and one silicon atom, thereby creating an extended three-dimensional structure. Olivine is usually a green mineral with a glassy luster and a granular shape. Rocks made up mostly of olivine are known as peridotites. Although peridotites are relatively rare in the earth's crust (that layer which begins at the surface and extends to depths of between 5 and 80 kilometers), it is the rock that makes up most of the earth's uppermost mantle. This olivine-rich layer begins at depths ranging from between 5 and 80 kilometers and extends downward to depths of roughly 400 kilometers. Evidence indicates that the Moon and the other inner planets (Mercury, Venus, and Mars) also have similar olivine-rich layers. Olivine can also be an important mineral in basalts and gabbros, which are the most abundant igneous rocks in the crusts of the inner planets. In addition, it is an abundant mineral in many different kinds of meteorites and some kinds of metamorphic rocks.

The garnets are a group of closely related orthosilicate minerals, each of which is a solid solution. The chemistry of the common garnets can be fairly well represented by the somewhat idealized general formula $A_3B_2Si_3O_{12}$ where the A stands for either magnesium, iron (with a charge of $+2$), manganese (Mn), or calcium (Ca), and the B stands for either aluminum (Al), iron (with a charge of $+3$), or chromium (Cr). In the crystal structures of these minerals, the cations in the A site are surrounded by eight oxygen anions, while the cations in the B site are surrounded by six oxygens. Most garnets can be described as a mixture of two or more of the following molecules: pyrope $(Mg_3Al_2Si_3O_{12})$, almandine $(Fe_3Al_2Si_3O_{12})$, spessartine $(Mn_3Al_2Si_3O_{12})$, grossular $(Ca_3Al_2Si_3O_{12})$, andradite $(Ca_3Fe_2Si_3O_{12})$, and uvarovite $(Ca_3Cr_2Si_3O_{12})$. The most abundant and widespread garnets are almandine-rich garnets, which form during the metamorphism of some igneous rocks and of sediments rich in clay minerals. Grossular-rich and andradite-rich garnets are found in marbles formed through the metamorphism of limestone. The formation of spessartine-rich or uvarovite-rich garnets occurs during the metamorphism of rocks with high concentrations of manganese or chrome. Rocks with these compositions are relatively unusual, and hence these garnets are fairly rare. Pyrope-rich garnets are widespread in the earth's mantle, although they typically do not occur in abundance (more than 5 or 10 percent of the rock). Garnets that have weathered out of other rocks are sometimes found in sands and sandstones. Garnets may also occur in small amounts in some igneous rocks.

Two or more minerals are called polymorphs if they are made up of the same kinds of atoms in the same proportions but in different arrangements. Polymorphs are minerals with the same compositions but different crystal structures. The aluminosilicates are a group of orthosilicate minerals containing three polymorphs: kyanite, sillimanite, and andalusite. Each of these minerals has the chemical formula Al_2SiO_5. The differences in the structures of these minerals are best illustrated by considering the aluminum atoms; in kyanite, all the aluminum atoms are surrounded by six oxygen atoms; in sillimanite, one-half of the aluminum atoms are surrounded by six oxygens, while the other half are surrounded by four oxygens; in andalusite, half the aluminum atoms are surrounded by four oxygens, and half are surrounded by five oxygens. Kyanite usually forms elongated rectangular crystals with a blue color. Sillimanite typically occurs as white, thin, often fibrous crystals. Andalusite is most commonly found in elongated crystals with a square cross section and a red to brown color. The aluminosilicates typically form during the metamorphism of clay-rich sediments; such rocks have the relatively high ratios of aluminum to silicon necessary for the formation of these minerals. The identity of the aluminosilicate formed depends upon the temperature and pressure of metamorphism; kyanite forms at relatively high pressures, sillimanite forms at relatively high temperatures, and andalusite forms at low to moderate temperatures and pressures.

Topaz is another aluminum-rich orthosilicate; although this mineral also contains fluorine (F) and/or the hydroxyl molecule (OH). The chemical formula of topaz is $Al_2SiO_4(F,OH)_2$. As the parentheses indicate, this mineral is a solid solution in which fluorine and hydroxyl can substitute for each other. Topaz is formed during the late stages in the solidification of a granite liquid.

The mineral zircon contains the relatively rare element zirconium (Zr). Zircon has the chemical formula $ZrSiO_4$; it generally also contains small amounts of uranium and thorium. The decay of these radioactive elements can be used to obtain the age of a rock, making zircon particularly important to geologists. It is most commonly found as brown rectangular crystals with a pyramid on either end. It is a widespread mineral in igneous rocks, although it generally occurs in relatively minor amounts.

Titanite ($CaTiSiO_5$), sometimes known as sphene, is one of the most common minerals bearing titanium (Ti). It is a fairly widespread mineral, occurring in many different kinds of igneous and metamorphic rocks, but is rarely present in abundance.

Epidote ($Ca_2(Al,Fe)Al_2Si_3O_{12}(OH)$) contains both isolated silicate tetrahedra and tetrahedral pairs: Hence, it would be classified as an orthosilicate but not a nesosilicate. Epidote is a fairly common mineral most typically formed during low-temperature metamorphism in the presence of water. It most often occurs as masses of fine-grained, pistachio-green crystals.

Methods of Study

To characterize a mineral requires both its chemical composition and crystal structure. There are many different analytical techniques that will give chemical compositions; probably the most popular to use on orthosilicates is electron microprobe analysis. In this technique, part of the mineral is bombarded by a high-energy beam of electrons, which causes it to give off X rays. Different elements in the mineral give off X rays of different wavelengths, and the intensities of these different X rays depend on the abundance of these elements. By measuring the wavelengths and intensities of the X rays, the composition of the mineral can be obtained. This technique has the advantages of being nondestructive (the mineral is still available and undamaged after the analysis) and being applicable to very small spots on a mineral: The typical electron microprobe analysis gives the composition of a volume of mineral only a few tens to hundreds of cubic microns (millionths of a meter) in size.

The crystal structures of orthosilicates are generally obtained using the technique of X-ray diffraction. In this technique an X-ray beam is passed through the mineral. As the beam interacts with the atoms in the mineral, it breaks up into many smaller, diffracted beams traveling in different directions. The intensities and directions of these diffracted beams depend on the positions of atoms in the mineral. By analyzing the diffraction pattern, a scientist can discover the crystal structure of a mineral.

Context

Orthosilicates are one of the important building blocks of the planets of the inner solar system, and this reason alone provides an important scientific rationale for studying them. Despite their importance in nature, these minerals have had only a limited technological use. The relatively high hardness of garnet makes it suitable as an abrasive, and it is used in some sandpapers and abrasive-coated cloths. The aluminosilicates are used in the manufacture of a variety of porcelain that is noted for its high melting point, resistance to shock, and low electrical conductivity. This material is used in spark plugs and brick for high-temperature furnaces and kilns. Zircon is mined in order to obtain zirconium oxide and zirconium metal. Zirconium oxide has one of the highest known melting points and is used in the manufacture of items that have to withstand exceptionally high temperatures. Zirconium metal is used extensively in the construction of nuclear reactors. Titanite is mined as a source of titanium oxide. Titanium oxide has a number of uses but is most familiar as a white pigment in paint.

Probably the most widespread uses of the orthosilicates are as gemstones. Especially fine, transparent crystals of olivine make a beautiful green gem generally known as peridot, although the names chrysolite and evening emerald are sometimes used instead. Relatively transparent garnets also make very beautiful gems. The most common garnets are a deep red, and this is the color usually associated with the stone. Yet gem-quality garnets can also be yellow, yellow-brown, orange-brown, orange-yellow, rose, purple, or green. Garnet is a relatively common mineral and therefore is typically among the least valuable of gemstones. The major exception is the green variety of andradite garnet: Known in the gem trade as demantoid, this relatively rare material is one of the more valuable gems. When properly cut, zircon has a brilliancy (ability to reflect light) and fire (the ability to break white light up into different colors) second only to diamond and is a popular gemstone. Topaz is also widely used as a gem. The most valuable topaz is orange-yellow to orange-brown in color; unfortunately, all yellow gems are sometimes incorrectly referred to as topaz: When this practice is followed, true topaz is generally known as precious topaz or oriental topaz. Gem-quality topaz may also be colorless, faintly green, pink, red, blue, and brown.

Bibliography

Deer, W. A., R. A. Howie, and J. Zussman. *Rock-Forming Minerals*. Vol. 1A, *Orthosilicates*. 2d ed. New York: Longman, 1982. This is one of the most complete treatments of the orthosilicates in English. A very well-written book, it is an excellent place to go for detailed information on individual minerals. Most suitable for college-level audiences.

Gait, R. I. *Exploring Minerals and Crystals*. Toronto: McGraw-Hill Ryerson, 1972. This is a lower-level introduction to the science of mineralogy. Well written and illustrated, it is more scientific than the typical rock-hound manual but less detailed than the introductory textbook. Suitable for high school students.

Hurlbut, Cornelius S., Jr., and G. S. Switzer. *Gemology*. New York: John Wiley & Sons, 1979. Written in the style of an introductory textbook, it is a very good starting point for someone whose primary interest in mineralogy is gems. It includes an introduction to the chemistry, physics, and mineralogy needed for the study of gems, a discussion of the general technical aspects of gemology, and a description of individual gemstones. Suitable for upper-level high school students.

Klein, Cornelis, and Cornelius S. Hurlbut, Jr. *Manual of Mineralogy*. 20th ed. New York: John Wiley & Sons, 1985. A popular textbook for a first course in mineralogy, this is an excellent book for someone interested in an introduction to the scientific study of minerals. Contains a very good sixteen-page section on the nesosilicates. Suitable for upper-level high school students.

Ribbe, P. H., ed. *Orthosilicates: Reviews in Mineralogy*. Vol. 5. Washington, D.C.: Mineralogical Society of America, 1980. This book consists of eleven articles, all but one of which specialize in a specific mineral or mineral group. The articles tend to be fairly technical, and some previous exposure to mineralogy or chemistry would be very helpful to the reader. Suitable for college-level students.

Sinkankas, J. *Mineralogy for Amateurs*. New York: Van Nostrand Reinhold, 1964. Not quite as rigorous as an introductory text, this book still contains much more scientific detail than the average book on minerals written for amateurs. Suitable for high school students.

Edward C. Hansen

Cross-References

Igneous Rocks: Basaltic, 1158; Igneous Rocks: Kimberlites, 1186; Igneous Rocks: Ultramafic, 1207; Ionic Substitution in Minerals, 1245; Metamorphic Rocks: Pelitic Schists, 1570; Contact Metamorphism, 1594; Regional Metamorphism, 1606; Meteorites: Achondrites, 1630; Meteorites: Carbonaceous Chondrites, 1638; Meteorites: Chondrites, 1645; Meteorites: Stony Irons, 1659; Physical Properties of Minerals, 1681; The Structure of Minerals, 1693.

OXIDES

Type of earth science: Geology
Field of study: Mineralogy and crystallography

The oxides represent one of the most important classes of minerals. They are the source of several key metals upon which the world is dependent; these metals include iron, aluminum, titanium, manganese, uranium, and chromium. Products manufactured from these metals touch virtually every aspect of modern living.

Principal terms

CRUST: the outer layer of the earth; it extends to depths of from 5 kilometers to at least 70 kilometers and is the only layer of the earth directly accessible to scientists

IGNEOUS ROCK: a major group of rocks formed from the cooling of molten material on or beneath the earth's surface

METAL: an element with a metallic luster and high electrical and thermal conductivity; it is ductile, malleable, and of high density

METAMORPHIC ROCK: a major group of rocks that are formed from the modification of sedimentary or igneous rocks by elevated temperatures and/or pressures beneath the earth's surface

MINERAL: a naturally occurring, solid chemical compound with a definite composition and an orderly internal atomic arrangement

ORE: a mineral or minerals with a valuable constituent present in large enough amounts in a given deposit to be minable for the metal(s) at a profit

QUARTZ: a very common silicate mineral

ROCK: an aggregate of one or more minerals

SEDIMENTARY ROCK: a major group of rocks formed from the breakdown of preexisting rock material or from the precipitation of minerals by organic or inorganic processes

Summary of the Phenomenon

At first glance, the earth appears to be composed of a chaotic arrangement of soils, rocks, and minerals, but a more careful evaluation reveals far less complexity. Compositionally, the earth contains eighty-eight elements, but only eight of these comprise more than 99 percent (by weight) of the crust. These eight elements combine to form some two dozen minerals that make up more than 90 percent of the crust.

The elements in these minerals are substances that cannot be broken down by ordinary physical and chemical methods. The smallest division of the element is the atom. Atoms have two basic parts—the nucleus, which is composed of protons (heavy particles, each with a positive charge), and neutrons (heavy particles with no charge)—surrounded by clouds or orbitals of highly energized, lightweight, negatively charged electrons. Elements are characteristically identified by the number of protons in the nucleus, which is referred to as the atomic number. Oxygen, for example, has an atomic number of 16. Although the number of protons in an element must by definition be fixed, the number of neutrons may vary slightly. The number of neutrons and protons in an atom is called the mass number. Because oxygen typically contains 8 neutrons, its most common mass number is 16. These values are characteristically written in the abbreviated form, $_8O^{16}$, where the subscript eight indicates the atomic number and the superscript sixteen is the mass number. The most common forms of iron and aluminum are expressed as $_{26}Fe^{56}$ and $_{13}Al^{27}$, respectively.

Within the rocks and minerals of the crust, oxygen accounts for almost 94 percent of the total volume. On the atomic scale, that implies that most minerals are virtually all atoms of oxygen, with the other elements filling in the intervening spaces in orderly arrangements. Most minerals form because ions (atoms that have gained or lost one or more electrons) become mutually attractive. More precisely, ions with positive charges (cations), which have lost electrons, become attracted to ions with negative charges (anions), and if the charges are balanced and several rules of crystal chemistry are satisfied, a mineral will form. A simple example is the combination of the sodium cation (Na^{+1}) and the chlorine anion (Cl^{-1}) to form the mineral halite ($NaCl$).

Ionic combinations include complex anions (radicals) that are strongly bound cation and anion groupings. These radicals take on a negative charge and will attract more weakly bound cations. Silica and carbonate are examples of these complex anions. These anion radicals and the simple anions form the basis for one of the most widely used classification systems of minerals, with the following classes of minerals recognized: the native elements; sulfides and sulfosalts; oxides and hydroxides; carbonates; halides; nitrates; borates; phosphates, arsenates, and vanadates; sulfates and chromates; tungstates and molybdates; and silicates.

Although this classification is based entirely on chemical composition, subdivisions within these classes are based on both structural and additional chemical criteria. Of these eleven classes, the silicates dominate the crust, forming approximately 97 percent of this layer. Although all the other classes represent only 3 percent of the crust, these classes include the majority of the minerals that society has come to depend upon. In economic value alone, the oxides undoubtedly rank at or near the top of all the classes of minerals, including the silicates.

The oxides are those minerals that have oxygen combined with one or more metals. Generally, the oxides are subdivided according to the ratio of the number of metals to the number of oxygens in the formula. Many of the oxides have relatively simple metal (A) to oxygen (O) ratios, so the following categories are recognized: AO, A_2O, AO_2, and A_2O_3. Some oxides have atomic structures in which different metals occupy different atomic (structural) sites. These minerals are commonly referred to as complex or multiple oxides, and most have the general formula

AB_2O_4, where A and B are separate atomic sites.

In both the AO and A_2O oxides, there are no minerals that are considered common. In the AO_2 oxides, however, several minerals are important, with two subdivisions recognized: the rutile group and the individual mineral uraninite. The three important minerals that occur in the rutile group are rutile (TiO_2), cassiterite (SnO_2), and pyrolusite (MnO_2). Rutile is a common minor mineral in a wide variety of quartz-rich igneous and metamorphic rocks. It is also found in black sands along with several other oxides. Pyrolusite is a very widespread mineral found in manganese-rich nodules on the floors of the oceans, seas, lakes, and bogs. Cassiterite is a common minor constituent in quartz-rich igneous rocks. Uraninite (UO_2) is a separate AO_2 oxide that, like cassiterite and rutile, is characteristically associated with quartz-rich igneous rocks. In several places it also occurs with gold in stream deposits modified by metamorphism.

Even more common than the AO_2 oxides are the A_2O_3 oxides, which include the common minerals hematite (Fe_2O_3), corundum (Al_2O_3), and ilmenite ($FeTiO_3$). Hematite, the most widespread iron oxide mineral in the crust, occurs in a wide variety of conditions, such as metamorphic deposits, quartz-rich igneous rocks, and sedimentary rocks. Corundum is a widespread minor constituent in metamorphic rocks low in silicon and relatively rich in aluminum. It is also found in igneous rocks that have low silicon contents. Ilmenite is another mineral that typically occurs in small amounts in many types of igneous rocks and in black sands with several other oxides.

In the more complex oxides (AB_2O_4), the most common minerals occur in the spinel group, but the individual mineral columbite-tantalite ($(Fe,Mn)(Nb,Ta)_2O_4$) is also commonly given consideration. The spinel group contains many minerals that have complex interrelationships. Several, however, are more abundant than others. Spinel ($MgAl_2O_4$) is common in some metamorphic rocks formed at high temperatures and in igneous rocks rich in calcium, iron, and magnesium. Magnetite (Fe_3O_4) is a common minor mineral in many igneous rocks. Relatively resistant to weathering, it also occurs in black sands and in very large sedimentary banded iron deposits. Chromite ($FeCr_2O_4$), another important mineral in the spinel group, is found only in calcium-poor and iron- and magnesium-rich igneous rocks. Unlike members of the spinel group, columbite-tantalite is a separate subdivision of the AB_2O_4 oxides. Like so many of the other oxides, it is characteristically associated with quartz-rich igneous rocks.

The hydroxides are a group of minerals that includes a hydroxyl group $(OH)^{-1}$ or the water (H_2O) molecule in their formulas. These minerals tend to have very weak bonding and, as a consequence, are relatively soft. Five hydroxides are briefly considered here: brucite ($Mg(OH)_2$), manganite ($MnO(OH)$), and three minerals in the goethite group (diaspore, $AlO(OH)$; goethite, $FeO(OH)$; and bauxite, a combination of several hydrous aluminum-rich oxides including diaspore). Brucite occurs as a product of the chemical modification of magnesium-rich igneous rocks and is associated with limestones. Manganite tends to occur in association with the oxide pyrolusite. Of the minerals in the goethite group, diaspore commonly is associated with corundum and occurs in aluminum-rich tropical soils. Goethite, an extremely common mineral, occurs in highly weathered tropical soils, in bogs, and in by-product of the chemical weathering (breakdown) of other iron oxide minerals. Bauxite is also found in highly weathered tropical soils.

Methods of Study

There are several general approaches to the study and identification of the oxide minerals. They include the study of hand specimens, optical properties, the internal atomic arrangements and their external manifestations (crystal faces), chemical compositions, and the synthesis of minerals. In the study of hand specimens, minerals possess a variety of properties that are easily determined or measured. These properties both aid in identification and may make the minerals commercially useful. Several properties are important for the oxides and hydroxides. Luster describes the way the surface of the mineral reflects light. Many minerals have the appearance of bright smooth metals, and this sheen is referred to as a metallic luster. Some minerals, like hematite and goethite, do not readily transmit light but may exhibit this type of luster. Other minerals that are able to transmit light have nonmetallic lusters, regardless of how shiny the outer surface of the mineral may be. Some common nonmetallic lusters include glassy, vitreous, and resinous. Minerals that have metallic lusters also characteristically produce powders that have diagnostic colors. The color of the powdered mineral is called the streak. Hematite, for example, may be silvery gray in color, but its powder is red. The shapes of minerals can also be important. Corundum, for example, is typically hexagonal in outline; magnetite forms octahedrons; and hematite has thin plates that grow together in rosettes. Specific gravity, the ratio of the weight of a substance to the weight of an equal volume of water, is also an important property of many of these minerals. Oxides tend to have much higher than average specific gravities. Heavy liquids, the Jolly balance, the pyncometer, and the Berman balance are all means by which specific gravity may be determined. Hardness is another property that is used for identification purposes and makes some of the oxides useful. Hardness is simply the measure of a substance's resistance to abrasion. Some minerals like corundum have particularly high hardnesses and therefore can be used commercially as abrasives.

The study of the optical properties of the oxides is conducted either in polarized light transmitted with a petrographic microscope or in reflected light. One important optical property of minerals in transmitted light is refractive index, which is a measure of the velocity of light passing through them. Minerals have up to three unique refractive indices, because light may travel at different velocities in different directions. Minerals that are nontransparent, such as many of the oxides, are studied in reflected light with an ore microscope. Such properties as reflectivity, color, hardness, and reactivity to different chemicals are all considered.

The study of the orderly internal atomic arrangements within minerals and the associated external morphologies is called crystallography. The primary methods used to study these internal geometries are a variety of X-ray techniques that look at single crystals or powered samples of minerals. The most commonly used procedure is the X-ray diffraction powder method. This technique takes advantage of the principle that the internal atomic arrangement in every mineral is different from all others. X rays striking the powdered sample are reflected or diffracted at only specific angles (dictated by internal geometries). Thus, the measurement of the specific angles of diffraction provides enough information to identify the substance. Single crystals, however, are normally used in the more detailed studies with X rays. With respect to the study of crystal faces on mineral specimens, a reflecting goniometer allows for the precise measurement of the angular relationships between these faces.

Until the latter part of the twentieth century, most chemical analyses of minerals were conducted by methods generally referred to as wet-chemical analyses. In these analyses, the mineral is first dissolved in solution. The amounts of the individual elements in the solution are then determined either by separation and weighing of precipitates or by measurement via spectroscopic methods of elemental concentrations in solution. Over the years, the accuracy and speed of completing these analyses have been improved, but several problems have never been completely solved. The invention of the electron microprobe in the 1950's has revolutionized mineral analyses and has largely eliminated many of the problems and greatly decreased the time necessary to conduct most analyses. The beam of electrons that is used can be precisely focused on samples or areas of samples as small as 1 micron (10^{-3} millimeter) in diameter. Thus, not only small samples may be analyzed, but also individual crystals may be evaluated in several places to check for compositional variations.

Another important method used to study and understand the oxides and other minerals in the laboratory involves the synthesis of minerals. The primary purpose of these studies is to determine the temperature and pressure conditions at which individual minerals form. In addition, the roles of fluids and interactions with other minerals are also evaluated. High-temperature studies are typically conducted in furnaces containing platinum or tungsten heating elements. High-pressure studies are produced in large hydraulic apparatus or presses.

Context

The oxides are one of the most important mineral groups because they have provided civilization with some very important metals. Iron, titanium, chromium, manganese, aluminum, and uranium are several of these key metals extracted from the ores of the oxides. Iron is the second most common metal in the crust. Along with aluminum, manganese, magnesium, and titanium, iron is considered an abundant metal because it exceeds 0.1 percent of the average composition of the crust. The steelmaking industry uses virtually all the iron mined. Steel, an alloy in which iron is the main ingredient, also includes one or more of several other metals (manganese, chromium, cobalt, nickel, silicon, tungsten, and vanadium) that impart special properties to steel. Hematite, magnetite, and goethite are three of the most important ore minerals of iron.

Aluminum is the most common metal in the crust, but by comparison, it accounts for only 2 percent of production levels for iron. Although many of the common silicates contain large amounts of aluminum, most of the aluminum is extracted from the complex hydroxide bauxite. Unlike iron, which has been utilized for more than three thousand years, aluminum is a metal that has gained prominence only in the twentieth century. Since aluminum is light in weight and exhibits great strength, it is widely used in the automobile, aircraft, and shipbuilding industries. It is also utilized in cookware and food and beverage containers. In many situations, aluminum is replacing copper in the manufacture of electrical wiring.

A third abundant metal that is primarily extracted from oxide and hydroxide minerals is manganese. Pyrolusite (MnO_2) is the main ore mineral; 90 percent of the manganese is consumed in the production of steel. The other abundant metal in the crust that is produced from oxides is titanium. Ilmenite ($FeTiO_3$), the major source of this metal, is used predominantly in the production of TiO_2, which forms as a pigment in paints. Titanium is also important as a metal and an alloy because of its great strength and light weight. It is a principal metal in the engines and essential structural components of modern aircraft and space vehicles.

Several scarce metals, representing less than 0.1 percent of the average composition of the crust, that occur as oxides and have important uses include chromium, uranium, tin, tantalum, and niobium. Of these metals, chromium and uranium are the most prominent. Chromite is the only ore mineral of chromium. The bulk of the chromium produced is utilized in the steel industry, where chromium is a principal component in stainless steel. In addition, because of its high melting temperature, chromium is used in bricks for metallurgical furnaces. Uranium is an important metal becaue it spontaneously undergoes nuclear fission and gives off large amounts of energy. Uranium is utilized in nuclear reactors to generate electricity and to produce the materials for nuclear weapons. Tin is another scarce metal that for tens of centuries was utilized as an alloy in bronze. It has lost many of its older uses, but remains a prominent metal as new applications are developed. Whereas tin is a metal discovered in antiquity, tantalum and niobium, derived from columbite-tantalite, are products of the twentieth century. Tantalum is highly resistant to acids, so it is used in equipment in the chemical industry, in surgical inserts and sutures, and in specialized steels and electronic equipment. Niobium is used in the production of stainless steels and refractory alloys (alloys resistant to high temperatures) used in gas turbine blades in aircraft engines.

Emery, a combination primarily of black corundum, magnetite, and hematite, is used as an abrasive. Several oxides also form gemstones. Rubies are the red gem variety of corundum, and sapphire is also a gemstone of corundum that can have any other color. Spinel, if transparent, is a gem of lesser importance. If red, the gem is called a ruby spinel.

Bibliography

Berry, L. G., Brian Mason, and R. V. Dietrich. *Mineralogy*. 2d ed. San Francisco: W. H. Freeman, 1983. A college-level introduction to the study of minerals that focuses on the traditional themes necessary to understand minerals: how they are formed and what makes each chemically, crystallographically, and physically distinct from others. Descriptions and determinative tables include almost two hundred minerals (with twenty-eight oxides and hydroxides).

Dietrich, R. V., and B. J. Skinner. *Rocks and Rock Minerals*. New York: John Wiley & Sons, 1979. This short, readable college-level text provides a relatively brief but excellent treatment of crystallography and the properties of minerals. Although the descriptions of minerals focus on the silicates, several important oxides are considered. Very well illustrated and includes a subject index and modest bibliography.

Hurlbut, C. S., Jr., and G. S. Switzer. *Gemology*. New York: John Wiley & Sons, 1979. A well-illustrated introductory textbook for the reader with little scientific background. Coverage includes the physical and chemical properties of gems, their origins, and the instruments used to study them. Later chapters treat methods of synthesis, cutting and polishing, and descriptions of gemstones.

Klein, Cornelis, and C. S. Hurlbut, Jr. *Manual of Mineralogy*. 20th ed. New York: John Wiley & Sons, 1985. An excellent second-year college-level text that is an introduction to the study of minerals. Topics discussed include external and internal crystallography, crystal chemistry, properties of minerals, X-ray crystallography, and optical properties. Also systematically describes twenty-two oxide minerals.

Ransom, Jay E. *Gems and Minerals of America*. New York: Harper & Row, 1974. A readily available book intended for the nonscientist who is interested in rock and mineral collecting. Introductory chapters introduce basic mineral characteristics and their environments of formation. Later chapters focus on the locations and collection of gems and minerals throughout the United States. A number of oxides are considered.

Skinner, Brian J. *Earth Resources*. 3d ed. Englewood Cliffs, N.J.: Prentice-Hall, 1986. A compact, well-illustrated introductory text that discusses the distribution of and rates of use of a variety of mineral and energy resources. Chapters 5 and 6 cover a number of important metals that are derived from oxides and hydroxides. Indexed and includes a modest bibliography.

Tennissen, A. C. *Nature of Earth Materials*. 2d ed. Englewood Cliffs, N.J.: Prentice-Hall, 1983. A text written for the nonscience student that treats minerals from the perspective of both the internal relationships (atomic structure, size, and bonding) and external crystallography. Includes an excellent overview of the physical properties of minerals and the classification and description of 110 important minerals.

Ronald D. Tyler

Cross-References

Carbonates, 190; Gem Minerals, 802; Ionic Substitution in Minerals, 1245; Physical Properties of Minerals, 1681; The Structure of Minerals, 1693; Non-Silicates Other Than Oxides and Carbonates, 1741; Radioactive Minerals, 2143.

PALEOBIOGEOGRAPHY

Type of earth science: Paleontology and earth history

Paleobiogeography concerns the study of the geographic distribution of past life forms. Paleobiogeographic studies, coupled with reconstructions of ancient plate configurations, serve as tools for reconstructing a detailed history of the earth's changing geography and environments through time and the concurrent evolution of the organisms living in these environments.

Principal terms

BARRIER: any sort of physical, chemical, or biological obstacle that prevents the migration of a species into or out of a given geographic area

BIOGEOGRAPHIC PROVINCE: a geographic region distinguished by a unique set of endemic organisms that live in the region

CONVERGENT ORGANISMS: evolutionarily unrelated organisms that come to resemble one another through adaptation to the same life habit

COSMOPOLITAN: having a broad, essentially worldwide distribution

DIVERSITY: the variety of life, usually described in terms of the number of species present

ENDEMIC: restricted to a specific, limited geographic region

EPICONTINENTAL SEAS: shallow seas that periodically covered large portions of the continents in the geologic past

LIMITING FACTORS: the physical, chemical, and biological factors that govern the distribution of a given organism

PALEOBIOGEOGRAPHY: the study of the geographic distribution of past life forms

PLATE TECTONIC THEORY: the concept that the earth's exterior is divided into an interlocking mosaic of moving plates

Summary of the Phenomenon

Life is distributed on the earth's surface in complex patterns, governed by local environmental conditions and distributed in specific geographic regions. Very few living species of plants or animals are cosmopolitan in their distribution. *Homo sapiens* (modern humans) is one of the few cosmopolitan species. Most organisms evolve, exist, and eventually become extinct all in the same limited geographic region; these organisms are said to be endemic in their distribution. Endemic species may be restricted to a continent (the African elephant in sub-Saharan Africa), a portion of a continent (the snow leopard in the Himalaya), an island (the orangutan in Borneo), or even smaller geographic areas (the giant sequoia redwood in northern California).

Most organisms are adapted to a specific set of narrowly defined environmental requirements that must be met if the organism is to exist in a given area. If only one of these environmental requirements or limiting factors is not present in the right proportion, the species will be unable to exist in a particular environment. These limiting factors include all the physical, chemical, and biological properties that define a given environment. For all organisms, an adequate food supply or source of nutrients is basic for continued existence. Factors controlling the distribution of organisms in terrestrial (land) environments include the availability of water, the temperature, and the altitude above sea level; humidity, precipitation, soil type, and sunlight intensity are limiting factors for plants, and types of vegetation are limiting factors for animals. For aquatic organisms, factors such as water depth, salinity, temperature, dissolved oxygen content, current flow, clarity, and bottom conditions become important. These various environmental factors in a particular geographic area are critical to determining the kinds of animal and plant life that can exist there.

Each environment within a given geographic region supports flora and fauna that are adapted to the specific conditions of that environment and are known collectively as biota. These geographically restricted biotas can be used to define biogeographic provinces, specific geographic regions distinguished by their endemic floras and faunas. The boundaries between biogeographic provinces are marked by the development of barriers to the free movement of species from one area to another. These barriers might be physical, chemical, or biological in nature. For example, land areas would be barriers to the dispersal of marine organisms, open oceans would be barriers to the dispersal of terrestrial organisms, and deep oceanic waters might be barriers to the dispersal of shallow-water, nearshore organisms. Many barriers differentiating biogeographic provinces today are climatic in nature, marking zones of changing atmospheric or water temperature.

At the present, the major continental land areas can be divided into seven major biogeographic provinces, based primarily on the occurrence of distinctive groups of large mammals (figure 1). These provinces are delineated by climate and vegetation, which, in turn, control the distribution of these animals. These land areas and the terrestrial organisms they support are isolated by large oceans. The greater the isolation of these provinces (that is, the more effective the barriers between provinces), the more distinctive the flora and fauna characteristic of each province. Similarities between faunas in North America and Eurasia result from similar climatic conditions in these land areas and the development of a "corridor," the Bering Land Bridge, within the past two million years; this corridor allowed the unobstructed interchange of land animals between the two continents. Australia, on the other hand, until the nineteenth and twentieth centuries, maintained its geographic isolation and, thus, its distinctive marsupial mammalian fauna. The fossil record shows that a similar marsupial fauna existed in South America until the Pliocene epoch (about 5 million years ago), when the Central American isthmus was uplifted, allowing for the invasion of South America by more advanced placental North American mammalian forms. This endemic South American fauna is now largely extinct; survivors include the opossum and armadillo.

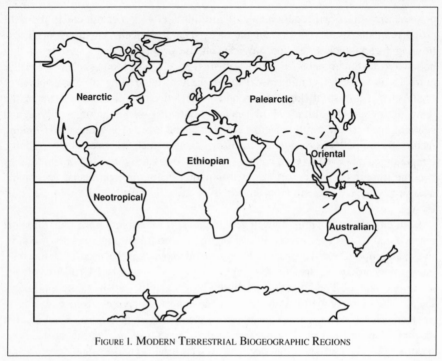

FIGURE 1. MODERN TERRESTRIAL BIOGEOGRAPHIC REGIONS

The great diversity of animal and plant life in the world at present is largely the result of the present-day configuration of the continents. As seen in figure 1, the continents are spread all over the globe, in rough north-south alignments that cross the entire spectrum of latitudinal climatic belts, from the Arctic Circle to the equator and from the equator to Antarctica. These climatic belts, as noted above, delineate many of the presently defined biogeographic provinces. The north-south arrangement of continents separated by large ocean basins allows cold-water polar currents to flow nearly unimpeded toward the equator, generating cooler climatic conditions on a global scale. In addition, large, deep oceanic basins separate the continents, forming formidable barriers to the dispersal not only of land animals and plants but also of shallow-water marine life. The development of these bio-geographic barriers is an important evolutionary mechanism, promoting increases in species diversity through the creation of new species by geographic isolation. The more effective these barriers are in preventing the interchange of species between provinces, the more genetically isolated faunas and floras in these provinces be-come, promoting greater differences between organisms living in these areas. As a result, similar environments in different geographic regions will support totally separate but often convergent faunas and floras. If these barriers did not exist, the same organisms would occupy the same environments in all geographic regions.

At present, nearly all the large continents are emergent, or above sea level. Their emergence resulted from a draw-down of worldwide sea level caused by relatively recent continental glaciation in the Northern Hemisphere (Pleistocene epoch, about two million to twelve thousand years ago). The formation of this enormous mass of ice tied up much of the available surface water, which would otherwise have flowed into the ocean basins. Thus, sea level was depressed, and shallow seas were drained off most of the continents. Shallow epicontinental seas had previously covered portions of the continents and had had a climatically ameliorating effect, for bodies of water tend to hold heat longer than exposed land areas. Their disappearance contributed to the development of extreme climatic conditions. The development of emergent continents and intervening deep-water ocean basins also isolated shallow-marine faunas living in the narrow continental shelf regions ringing the continents. In this way, numerous marine biogeographic provinces have developed in these coastal areas, and the diversity of endemic shallow-marine faunas in these areas has increased.

The lateral motions of the continents because of plate tectonic activity have been a powerful force in reshaping the distribution of biogeographic boundaries in time and space. According to the plate tectonic theory, the earth's exterior is divided into an interlocking mosaic of moving plates composed of low-density crustal rocks and underlying, denser mantle rocks. These plates are created at spreading centers, where dense volcanic rocks well up from below and flow away laterally. Continental crust at these spreading centers is rifted apart, allowing for the formation of a new ocean basin dividing what was once a continuous continent. Such is the case in the Near East, with the formation of the Red Sea between the rifting African continent and the Arabian plate. Plates can also move together, colliding with each other. At the point of impact, the crust shortens, thickens, and is deformed, leading to the formation of a new mountain belt that welds the colliding continents together into one larger continent. An example of this continent-to-continent collision is the collision between India and Eurasia, upthrusting the Himalaya. Plates also slide past each other along enormous linear cracks in the crust, termed strike-slip or transform faults. The San Andreas fault in California is such a fault, with California west of the fault moving north relative to the rest of North America. Such fault systems serve to displace continental crust horizontally along plate boundaries. All these plate tectonic activities cause the continents to change their shape and geographic position with time as well as result in the rise and fall of topographic features on the earth's surface.

Plate tectonic reconstructions for the major continents indicate major geographic realignments of these continents over the past 600 million years. These reconstructions show a pattern of cyclic periods of plate divergence (plates moving away from each other) followed by plate convergence (plates converging and eventually colliding). Plate divergence causes the formation of large ocean basins separating the continents. Convergent cycles culminate in the development of supercontinental masses composed of multiple, sutured continental plates. These "supercontinents" exist for several tens of millions of years, only to rift apart with the initiation of the next divergent cycle, which would fractionate the continents and disperse them over the globe. Detailed studies of the fossil organisms preserved in the sedimentary rocks on these continents indicate that the large-scale evolution of life over the past 600 million years parallels these plate tectonic events, with the changing geographic patterns having a profound effect on the evolution and extinction of organisms.

An example of this relationship is the Early Paleozoic interval of geologic time (Cambrian and Ordovician periods, about 600-450 million years ago). This was a time of plate divergence, with the continents aligned into rough east-west belts. The various continents that now make up the Northern Hemisphere were situated as isolated masses along the equator, in tropical latitudes. The present-day Southern Hemisphere continents were sutured into one large supercontinent, which scientists call Gondwanaland, located at higher, cool-temperate latitudes south of the equator (figure 2). The continents were eroded down to flattened platforms and were flooded (over perhaps 95 percent of their surface area) by shallow, epicontinental seas. Sea level was comparatively high because of the absence of continental collisions (which would elevate the continents through mountain building) and a lack of glaciation through much of the period. World climate was uniformly mild. The continents were separated by deep ocean basins and, as a result of the flooding of the continents by these epicontinental seas, shallow-marine environments were abundant.

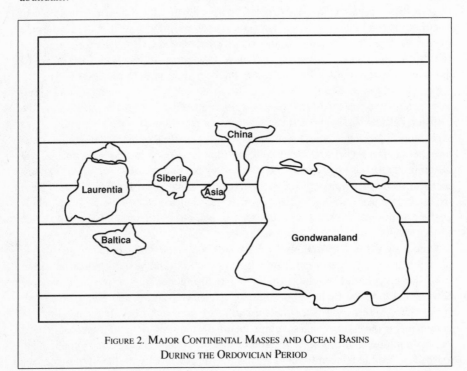

FIGURE 2. MAJOR CONTINENTAL MASSES AND OCEAN BASINS
DURING THE ORDOVICIAN PERIOD

This Cambro-Ordovician plate tectonic scenario coincides with a seemingly explosive evolution of shallow-marine animal life, especially the major groups of shell-secreting invertebrates (corals, brachiopods, snails, clams, nautiloids, trilobites, and echinoderms). These shallow marine faunas were highly provincial for much of this time interval because of the divergent nature of the major continental masses, with the intervening deep-water oceanic basins forming formidable barriers to the dispersal of these shallow-water marine animals. The highly endemic nature of these faunas and the mild climatic conditions promoted high levels of diversity. Terrestrial floras and faunas are unknown for this time interval, with the earliest land plants and animals being known from the succeeding Silurian period (about 425 million years ago).

Methods of Study

Reconstructing the biogeography of ancient life forms is a complex process that requires the research of geologists, paleontologists, geophysicists, oceanographers, meteorologists, and biologists. The basic information that must be assembled includes detailed local, regional, and worldwide studies of fossils in order to determine the total lateral (geographic) and vertical (time) range of these fossil organisms. The fossils and rocks that contain them must be dated as precisely as possible—through relative dating, as determined by the presence or absence of time-specific fossil species, and through radiometric dating of the rocks, or analyzing their enclosed radioactive minerals. The plate tectonic arrangement of the continents must be reconstructed to determine the geography that existed at the time when the fossil organisms were living. The continental configuration is indicated by remnant paleomagnetism preserved in the rocks and by the presence of key geologic features that are associated with various plate-to-plate interactions (faults, fold belts, regional metamorphic belts, and volcanic and other igneous rocks). Detailed paleoenvironmental reconstructions for each geographic region during each interval of time are made through analysis of sedimentary rock types present and sedimentary structures (ripple marks, mud cracks, cross-bedding, and the like). The fossils themselves are compared with the various types of organisms associated with the array of environments on the earth's surface today. (This use of the present to infer the past is an example of the principle of uniformitarianism, a basic concept in the geological sciences.) Using the present as a living laboratory, scientists seek to understand the factors that control the present distribution of organisms and to apply this knowledge to the apparent paleobiogeographic distributions preserved in ancient rocks.

Clearly, paleobiogeographic studies require the collaborative efforts of many scientists with various areas of expertise. The synthesis of all this information into a coherent paleobiogeographic model for a particular period of geologic history is a complex affair. The detailed geology is worked out for a specific local area, including determining the sequence of rocks present, their lithology, and sedimentary structures present. Fossil species present are collected, studied, and identified.

Analysis of these data permits scientists to infer the physical environment represented by this sequence of rock layers. The sequence of rocks is assigned a relative geologic age, based on the presence or absence of time-specific fossil forms, and radiometric dating may also be done. These rocks and their fossils are then compared (correlated) with rocks of the same age exposed elsewhere in the same general region. From these data, a paleoenvironmental map of the region for the time interval under study is constructed. A paleogeographic map of the continent for that time period brings together an array of such regional maps. Worldwide paleogeographic maps result from the assembling of continental maps for the period. The positions of the various continents for each geologic period are determined through paleomagnetic studies of crustal rocks; this information is integrated with data on the occurrence and distribution of the various plate tectonic geologic features and paleoenvironmental data refined from the rocks and fossils. With the positions of the various continent-bearing plates established for each time interval, fossil faunas and floras are analyzed in terms of their geographic distribution and the type of environment with which they are associated. Finally, from analogy with the present and knowledge of the effects of geography and environment on the dispersal, evolution, and extinction of organisms, paleobiogeographic provinces are determined for each geologic period.

These paleobiogeographic reconstructions will change as the body of knowledge increases, that is, with refined plate tectonic reconstructions, more accurate age determinations for rocks and fossils, more complete information on the distribution of the fossil organisms, and a better understanding of the relationship between geography and the distribution and evolution of life on earth.

Context

Paleobiogeographic studies are intrinsically important, for they make possible a graphic record of how the present-day diversity and structure of life came about. History can also aid in projecting the future. Paleobiogeographic studies shed some light on how geography and environment affect evolution and extinction. The continued existence of the present diversity of organisms is dependent upon humans' gaining an understanding of these factors. Such an understanding is especially critical in the light of the rapid and widespread destruction of natural ecosystems by humankind. Extinction that rivals the mass extinction events identified from the fossil record is already occurring.

Misuse of environments and resources has resulted in the development of a global increase in carbon dioxide and predictions of the onset of the "greenhouse effect," altering world climatic patterns and having implications for a host of critical human activities. The burning of fossil fuels releases carbon dioxide into the atmosphere. Another critical factor fueling the increase in carbon dioxide, however, is the wholesale destruction of tropical rainforests at an unprecedented rate in the 1980's. At the same time, coastal and open-ocean surface waters have been polluted by oil spills and the flushing of toxic chemicals and wastes into the sea. This pollution can seriously harm marine phytoplankton—tiny, photosynthetic microorganisms that float in surface waters. Both rainforests and marine phytoplankton absorb tremendous amounts of carbon dioxide in the process of photosynthesis and generate oxygen as a by-product.

Human beings often consider themselves separate from other life forms on the planet and think that their continued existence is independent of that of plants and animals. It is easy to believe that technology insulates the human species from the natural world so that the limiting factors that constrain all other species do not apply. It has become apparent, however, that while technology can break down certain limitations and allow humans to exist in marginal environments, it can manufacture environmental problems of its own that threaten not only the stability and viability of natural ecosystems but the very existence of human beings as well.

Bibliography

Bambach, Richard K., C. R. Scotese, and A. F. Ziegler. "Before Pangea: The Geographies of the Paleozoic World." *American Scientist* 68 (January/February, 1980): 26-38. An important article for its reconstructions of the arrangement of the plates and the distribution of land and sea areas during the Paleozoic era. Suitable for advanced high school and college-level readers.

Hallam, A., ed. *Atlas of Palaeobiogeography*. New York: Elsevier, 1973. One of the first volumes to be devoted exclusively to paleobiogeography and to incorporate plate tectonic information. Includes chapters by individual experts detailing the paleobiogeography of individual groups of fossil organisms for specific geologic periods. An important source of paleobiogeographic information. Most articles are well written and illustrated. Suitable for the informed layperson and college-level students with a basic knowledge of paleontology.

Kurten, Björn. "Continental Drift and Evolution." *Scientific American* 220 (March, 1969): 54-64. An early paper relating paleobiogeography and evolution to plate motions. The article shows how the diversity of mammalian faunas is related to the divergent arrangement of the continent-bearing plates. Well written and illustrated. Suitable for the informed general reader.

Moody, R. *Prehistoric World*. Secaucus, N.J.: Chartwell Books, 1980. A "picture book" illustrating the evolution of animals and plants through time. The text is informative, relating the evolution of various plants and animals to the development of biological communities characteristic of specific environments. Contains paleogeographic maps for each geologic period. Some references are made to the paleobiogeographic distribution of organisms, especially in later chapters.

Robison, Richard, and Curt Teichert, eds. *The Treatise of Invertebrate Paleontology*. Lawrence: Geological Society of America and University of Kansas Press, 1976. "Biogeography and Biostratigraphy," in part A, gives a synopsis of the faunas and floras and their occurrence in time (biostratigraphy) and space (biogeography). Each section is written by an expert on the fossil organisms of a particular period. The text is suitable for college-level students with a good knowledge of paleontology. Some readers, however, may struggle with the technical language.

Smith, Alan G., and J. C. Briden. *Mesozoic and Cenozoic Paleocontinental Maps*. New York: Cambridge University Press, 1977. A companion piece to Bambach, Scotese, and Ziegler (see above), documenting the arrangement of the plates and land and sea areas in the Mesozoic and Cenozoic eras of geologic time. Appropriate for college-level readers.

Stanley, Steven N. *Earth and Life Through Time*. San Francisco: W. H. Freeman, 1986. A college-level historical geology textbook, this volume contains information on many aspects of plate tectonics, paleogeography, and evolution. Plate arrangements and the distribution of fossil organisms and environments are well illustrated for each geologic period.

Tarling, D. H. *Continental Drift and Biological Evolution*. Burlington, N.C.: Carolina Biological Supply, 1986. Part of the Carolina Biology Readers series. Describes some of the evidence for continental drift and provides examples of how the arrangement of the continents has affected the biogeography of groups of organisms in the geologic past. In particular, there is a good section on how barriers or migration routes might be developed as the result of plate tectonic activity. Suitable for advanced high school and college-level readers.

Robert C. Frey

Cross-References

Biostratigraphy, 173; Cambrian Diversification of Life, 183; Colonization of the Land, 246; Dinosaurs, 370; The Evolution of Life, 655; Gondwanaland and Pangaea, 982; Ice Ages, 1115; Mammals, 1453; Mass Extinctions, 1514; Paleoclimatology, 1993.

PALEOCLIMATOLOGY

Type of earth science: Paleontology and earth history

Climate is the average of weather elements over long periods of time and over large areas. The study of ancient climates, termed paleoclimatology, utilizes sedimentologic, paleontologic, and geochemical data to reconstruct ancient temperature, wind patterns, precipitation, and evaporation.

Principal terms

ATMOSPHERIC CIRCULATION: the movement of air as a result of regional pressure differentials; general global atmospheric circulation greatly influences the creation of regional climates

CLIMATE: the accumulative effects of weather; its basic elements include radiation, temperature, atmospheric moisture and precipitation, evaporation, and wind

INSOLATION: incoming solar radiation; differences in global insolation at various places on the earth's surface create weather and climate patterns

PALEOCLIMATOLOGY: the study of ancient climates; primary sciences utilized in this study include paleontology, sedimentology, and geochemistry

WEATHER: the condition of the atmosphere at a given moment and at a given place

Summary of the Phenomenon

The basic elements of climate include radiation, temperature, atmospheric moisture and precipitation, evaporation, and wind. The features of ancient climates that have been most studied are temperature, wind patterns, amount of precipitation, and evaporation. In order to understand ancient climates, it is necessary to understand the fundamentals of modern climatic processes.

Solar radiation is the electromagnetic radiation emitted by the sun's surface; this radiation is primarily within the infrared, visible, and ultraviolet ranges. The incoming solar radiation is termed global insolation. The amount of energy received by the earth at any one time is essentially constant, although paleoclimatic evidence indicates that it has not always been so. The amount of global insolation received depends on the output energy of the sun, the distance between the earth and the sun, the angle at which the sun's rays strike the earth's surface, the duration of daylight, and atmospheric composition. Therefore, global insolation depends primarily on the latitude and the seasons: Regions within the higher latitudes receive the least amount of insolation, primarily because of the angle at which the sun's rays strike the earth, and they have the greatest seasonal variation. The result is an energy deficit poleward of 40 degrees north and 40 degrees south latitude, respectively; the equator has the least variation, so that between these degrees of latitude there is an energy surplus. Therefore, a continuous horizontal exchange of energy between these regions occurs, which is the cause of atmospheric circulation and weather patterns.

The unequal heating of the earth's surface creates pressure differences. Since gases move from areas of high pressure to areas of low pressure, this differential heating and pressure variation causes the wind to blow. If the earth were not rotating, its general circulation pattern would be one of ascending air at the equator and descending air at the poles, with continuous horizontal flow between. The Coriolis effect, however, changes this ideal pattern, and free-moving objects are deflected from a straight-line path in response to the earth's rotation: In the Northern Hemisphere, the deflection is to the right, and in the Southern Hemisphere, it is to the left. Ocean surface circulation patterns are therefore typically clockwise in the Northern Hemisphere and counterclockwise in the Southern, yet atmospheric patterns are in fact more complex because air parcels are ascending and descending as well as moving horizontally. General atmospheric circulation patterns from the equator poleward include the doldrums, the trade winds, the horse latitudes, the westerlies, and the easterlies. In the geologic record, general atmospheric circulation patterns are difficult to determine as a result of the scarcity of data points necessary for accurate calculation of such large-scale phenomena. Wind patterns, however, may be calculated for some areas on the basis of sedimentary structures, and general atmospheric circulation patterns may be inferred from models based on modern atmospheric circulation and the distribution of the earth's land and water areas through time.

In order for precipitation to occur, there must be atmospheric instability. An air parcel will rise until it reaches an altitude where the surrounding air is of equal temperature; this process may be enhanced where intense solar heating creates lower pressures, where the air mass is heated by a warm surface below it, where sloping terrain such as mountains forces air to ascend, or where cool air acts as a barrier over which warmer, lighter air rises. As the unstable air parcel moves vertically, it cools as a result of the expansion of gases (the adiabatic process). Condensation will occur when the dew point temperature is reached, which varies according to the initial relative humidity of the air parcel. Provided that there is sufficient moisture and that nuclei are present around which the moisture may accumulate, precipitation may occur. The major types of precipitation include rain, freezing rain, sleet, snow, and hail. The type of precipitation that occurred in ancient times is difficult to determine, although occasional examples of raindrop prints are found as casts in sediments, and ancient glacial deposits indicate the accumulation of frozen precipitation. In some situations, the amount of precipitation may be inferred, typically through the utilization of fossil plants. In other cases, the amount of precipitation versus evaporation may be indicated, primarily through the utilization of sedimentary mineral types such as evaporites.

The result of the interaction of these climatic processes is the formation of regional climates. On the modern earth, a wet equatorial belt lies within about 20 degrees of the equator. The adiabatic cooling of very moist and warm air results in heavy precipitation within these regions, yielding a wet tropical climate. These air parcels then begin descending, adiabatically heat up through compression, and the now-dry air encounters the earth's surface. The result is the formation of tropical deserts, centered at approximately 25-30 degrees north and south latitude. At the middle latitudes (approximately 35-65 degrees), the interaction of air masses between the polar and tropical regions and the variation in global insolation throughout the year result in large variations in temperature and seasonality. Polar regions are characterized by cold and dry conditions, because the sun's rays are typically at low angles and cold air parcels in those regions are unable to accumulate large amounts of moisture.

One phenomenon that seems to affect climate, at least for relatively short cycles of earth history, is sunspot activity. Although the data are incomplete, the increase and decrease in these solar disturbances seems to suggest that they create variations in global insolation and subsequent warming and cooling trends. The cooling of the earth's climate during the early-to-middle portion of the second millennium has been linked to variations in sunspot activity. Another explanation of causes of earth-climate cyclicity was put forth in the twentieth century by Milutin Milankovitch. Milankovitch suggested that the earth's orbit around the sun may vary from more elliptical (with more pronounced differences in global insolation during the summer versus the winter) to more circular (with less seasonality). Such a cycle would take about 100,000 years to complete. Other Milankovitch cycles proposed include changes in the tilt of the earth's axis in relationship to the sun (a 40,000-year cycle) and the wobble of the earth upon its axis (a cycle of 21,000 years). Studies on ocean-floor sediments for the Pleistocene (within the past 2 million years of earth history) and in lake basin sediments of the Triassic and Jurassic (approximately 200-180 million years before the present) of the east coast of the United States indicate that such cycles may indeed exist.

Another possible cause of short-term changes in climate may be asteroid impacts. Scientists have theorized that such impacts would increase the particulate levels in the atmosphere to such an extent that a phenomenon similar to "nuclear winter" would occur. Overall global insolation would decrease dramatically and temperatures plummet. Suggestions have been made that this phenomenon could account for the periodic extinctions that take place on the earth.

Another possible cause of changes in the earth's atmosphere involves changes in carbon dioxide levels: a heating trend caused by increasing levels (the greenhouse effect) or a cooling trend caused by decreasing levels. Such changes may be caused by changes in the overall metabolism of organisms or by decreases and increases in volcanic activity. Increases in volcanic activity could also cause cooling trends because of a decrease in global insolation as a result of volcanic particles suspended in the atmosphere. Ocean current patterns tremendously influence weather patterns and regional climates, and it has been suggested that the atmosphere and oceans can be viewed as a single, interacting unit. Changes in oceanic circulation would certainly modify climates, although the geologic evidence of a definite link between the two is equivocal. Stronger evidence for causes of variation may be related to plate tectonics. The movement of continental plates over polar areas may certainly account for the buildup of ice during certain periods of earth history, such as occurred on the southern continents during the Permian period (about 290-240 million years before the present). In part, such shifting of plates may also account for the last ice ages in Europe and North America, although the presence of several periods of glaciation and interglacial episodes indicates that each episode of glaciation during the Pleistocene cannot be explained this way.

Methods of Study

The study of ancient climates utilizes many techniques over a broad range of earth science disciplines. Especially utilized are studies of paleontology, sedimentology, and geochemistry. Plants, especially the flowering plants or angiosperms, have provided a considerable amount of evidence of climatic change during a portion of the Cretaceous period and the subsequent Cenozoic era (covering approximately the last 100 million years of earth history). One of the most important tools for determining ancient climate zones concerns the utilization of leaf characteristics. In cold climates, leaf margins are typically nonentire (that is, they are lobed, indented, or toothed) and leaf venation is typically palmate (radiating). Entire, or smooth-margined, leaves are more typical of the tropics. Other leaf features that are diagnostic of plants that grow in tropical climates are large and thick leaves, leaves with pinnate (featherlike) venation, and compound leaves (in which the leaves grow in clusters). Leaf margin features have been utilized in studies of climatic changes throughout the Cenozoic era. Other studies have utilized the growth rings of plants. In areas marked by seasonality, either warm-cool or dry-wet, the woody annular rings of trees vary in diameter. Studies have been made on these structures to detect seasonal changes in climate for the Paleozoic, Mesozoic, and Cenozoic eras. Results are mixed, because the cause of growth rings is difficult to interpret and because annular ring development has varied on plants in the past. Other interpretations have been based on the types of plants that grew in particular areas within a given period of earth history. Cycads are limited currently to tropical and subtropical areas and probably grew under similar conditions throughout their history. During the Mesozoic era (approximately 240-63 million years before the present), these plants were especially common. Another study that has been important in interpretation of ancient climates is palynology, or the study of pollen and spores. These tiny organic remains are especially important as fossils because they are easily preserved, very abundant, and widely distributed in many continental-derived sediments. They have been most widely utilized for the interpretation of climates over the past 2 million years. For example, palynological studies document in detail the shift in colder temperatures southward during the last ice age. Other palynological studies as well as studies of large plant fossils have been utilized to reconstruct the earth's ancient biomes, or animal and plant provinces.

Several other biologic criteria may also indicate regional climates. Tropical climates contain more diverse plant and animal communities, with the number of species and genera increasing from high latitudes toward the tropics. Although preservational problems often limit the utilization of this technique to the rock record, studies on the diversity of one-celled foraminifers have been used to differentiate glacial and interglacial episodes as reflected in marine environments during the Pleistocene. Like plants, animal species have been used to indicate regional climates. Stenothermal organisms are those that can withstand only minor temperature fluctuations; eurythermal types can withstand much greater temperature variation. The former group may be very useful in determining paleotemperatures, provided that accurate determination of their temperature tolerances has been properly determined. Planktonic (floating) animals that secrete silica shells, such as diatoms and radiolarians, are more abundant in cooler waters than in warmer areas, as there is more dissolved silica for shell formation in cooler waters. The presence of musk-ox and reindeer indicates cooler climates (or at least cooler summers) for portions of the southern United States during the last ice age, and the presence of tapirs and other South American tropical animals suggests that warmer temperatures (at least warmer winters) were also characteristic for portions of the Pleistocene. Hermatypic corals, which form the bulk of our modern reef systems, are limited to areas where water temperature seldom falls below 18 degrees Celsius. Although ancient reefs were composed of a wide variety of plant and animal types, studies indicate that most grew under tropical or subtropical conditions similar to those under which modern corals grow.

The form of ancient animals has also been used to indicate ancient climate conditions. Growth rings, indicating alternation of cool and warm conditions, are found in bivalve mollusk shells and have been used as indications of nontropical climates. Marine snails tend to have thicker, more ornamented shells in tropical regions as opposed to cooler areas. As tropical waters are less viscous than cooler oceanic waters, many planktonic species increase their surface areas in order to suspend themselves better within the water column. One-celled, shell-secreting animals, such as the foraminifers and radiolarians, may evolve long spines or other structures in tropical areas in order that any minor increase in water activity will keep them suspended. Marine planktonic plants, such as the acritarchs and dinoflagellates, have also developed more intricate ornamentation in tropical and subtropical waters to aid in keeping them afloat, both now and in the geological past. Application of habitat preferences and regional climate controls on modern plant and animal distribution to interpret the climates of more ancient periods of earth history must be approached with caution, as the preferences of extinct animals may have little in common with their modern counterparts.

Analysis of ancient sedimentary sequences may give an indication as to climatic conditions during their formation, as indicated by sedimentary textures and structures. Soil types are especially related to climatic influences that determine the amount of moisture and vegetation essential to their development. Soils in hot areas often have calcium carbonate or silica precipitated within their upper layers as a result of capillary action during evaporation. Under wetter conditions, the dissolved solutes are flushed to lower horizons, where they precipitate as hardpans. In tropical areas, accumulation of iron and aluminum in the upper soil horizons creates brick-red lateritic soils. Formation of large desert areas depends primarily on global atmospheric circulation patterns. Ancient desert environments may be indicated by rocks formed from the deposits of ancient alluvial fans, sand dunes, ephemeral streams, or temporary (playa) lakes. Rocks and sedimentary particles may be faceted and pitted by desert winds or coated with precipitates. Certain types of sand dune may be utilized to indicate ancient wind direction, as sediment layers created on the front (slipface) of sand dunes are tilted away from the ancient wind direction. The formation of salt and gypsum minerals in playa lakes—and for continental and marine evaporite minerals in general—is directly influenced by global atmospheric circulation patterns creating desert conditions where evaporation exceeds precipitation. Carbonate rocks, such as limestone and dolomite, form primarily under tropical or subtropical conditions. Rainfall amounts and periodicity are indicated by the types of rivers formed, with braided types indicating a more "flashy" precipitation pattern and meandering indicating a more stable input of water. The effects of colder climates may be indicated by the presence of glacial sediments. Glacial tills may be formed through bulldozing by glacial ice; light- and dark-colored ringular sedimentary couplets, termed varves, may be deposited in glacier-bordering lakes; and thick deposits of silt, termed loess, may accumulate near the margins of large glacial masses. Underlying rocks may be scratched and scraped by the movement of glacial ice over them, and even smaller sedimentary particles may have glacial striations upon them. It should be noted, however, that many of the above sedimentary features may be formed in environments other than their typical settings. Also, the effects of age and later environmental factors may conceal the true relationships of sedimentary textures, structures, and climate.

The isotopes oxygen 16 and oxygen 18 have been widely utilized for determining paleotemperatures. Warm seawater is typically more enriched in the heavier isotope, oxygen 18, because the lighter isotope, oxygen 16, is usually lost during evaporation. Subsequent precipitation may store oxygen 16 in large ice sheets during glacial episodes or under cold conditions at higher latitudes. Therefore, the accumulation of large amounts of the oxygen 16 isotope within these ice sheets may cause ratios of oxygen 18 to oxygen 16 to increase within surrounding ocean basins; if these ice sheets are melted, the meltwaters that return to the sea will enrich the marine waters near the glacial areas in oxygen 16. Oxygen isotope ratios have been obtained by analysis of the chemistry of shells from a number of fossil groups, although the one-celled foraminiferans seem to be best suited for such studies. Isotope studies have been utilized in paleotemperature analyses in rocks from Permian through Quaternary age, although the most successful utilization has been on rocks deposited during the past 2 million years.

Context

The origin of fossil fuels is directly related to paleoclimate. Ancient swampy, humid tropical environments are the only places where large amounts of coal were deposited. Marine organisms, whose death and decomposition eventually form oil and gas deposits, seem to be found especially in rock layers that indicate ancient tropical or subtropical conditions. The formation of evaporite minerals, such as gypsum and the many varieties of salt, occurred primarily under hot and dry conditions. Without knowledge of paleoclimatology, the exploration and exploitation of these materials would be severely curtailed.

Ancient climatological data indicate that there are climate cycles that repeat through geologic time. As climate controls the most essential elements of daily human life, including where and how people live and eat, it is important to try to unlock the secrets of this climatic cyclicity. Studies of paleontology, sedimentology, and geochemistry may help scientists to predict future climate cycles.

At certain times in earth history, great periods of extinction have eradicated many of the earth's plants and animals. There is some indication that these catastrophes result from periodic asteroid impacts upon the earth. The particulate matter thrown into the air upon impact may have caused overall global insolation to decrease, so that severe cooling trends followed. This paleoclimate model is very similar to that proposed for the effects of nuclear war; therefore, analysis of paleoclimatological data may assist in determining the consequences that nuclear war would have upon climate and the earth's ecosystem.

Bibliography

Boggs, Sam, Jr. *Principles of Sedimentology and Stratigraphy.* Westerville, Ohio: Charles E. Merrill, 1987. As many of the paleoclimatological methodologies rely on sedimentological features, any detailed study of paleoclimates will require some knowledge of sedimentology. This text is one of the best books on the subject in terms of readability and accuracy. The chapters on sedimentary textures, sedimentary structures, and sedimentary environments are especially useful for understanding the sedimentological results of paleoclimatological processes. Designed for junior- or senior-level geology students.

Cox, C. B., and P. D. Moore. *Biogeography: An Ecological and Evolutionary Approach.* 4th ed. Palo Alto, Calif.: Blackwell Scientific Publications, 1985. This book contains a wealth of information on many aspects of biogeography, but certain sections may be too detailed for the general college-level reader. Discussions of climate and other atmospheric limits on biogeography and coverage of ecology and plate tectonics serve as a useful overview for analysis of paleoclimate conditions and influences through time.

Dodd, Robert J., and Robert J. Stanton, Jr. *Paleoecology: Concepts and Applications.* New York: John Wiley & Sons, 1981. A comprehensive treatment of many aspects of paleoecology. Provides detailed coverage of various plant and animal groups as concerns their utilization in analysis of ancient ecologies and climates as well as detailed analysis of the use of isotope studies in paleoecology and paleoclimatology. Also included are discussions of ecosystems and communities in paleoecology and paleobiogeography. Written at the introductory college level.

Lapedes, D. N., ed. *McGraw-Hill Encyclopedia of the Geological Sciences.* New York: McGraw-Hill, 1978. This encyclopedia gives a comprehensive overview of geology. In general, the articles are well written, and they provide the reader with the essentials of each subject. Many articles would be understandable to high school students, including the article on paleoclimatology; approximately half of this article is devoted to an overview of paleoclimate changes upon the earth through geologic time.

Raup, David M., and Steven M. Stanley. *Principles of Paleontology.* San Francisco: W. H. Freeman, 1978. Rather than treating each group of fossil animals in detail, this text discusses the utilization of fossils in unraveling the history of the earth. The section on biogeography is especially informative, as the authors include material on modern and ancient climates, distributions of plants and animals, plate tectonic theory, and extinctions. Written for lower-level college students in biology or geology.

Stanley, Steven M. *Earth and Life Through Time.* 2d ed. San Francisco: W. H. Freeman, 1985. A well-written and accurate introductory text on historical geology; high school students with some training in earth science would be able to use it. Three chapters are devoted to ancient environments and principles of paleoecology and paleoclimatology. Approximately half of the text is devoted to a review of earth history, in which many examples of the interpretation of paleoclimates and the evolution of earth climate are documented.

Ziegler, B. *Introducton to Palaeobiology: General Palaeontology.* Translated by R. Muir. New York: Halsted Press, 1983. Like Raup and Stanley's text, this book stresses the utilization of fossils in understanding earth history rather than detailing particular fossil plant and animal groups. The last two chapters are devoted to ecology and biogeography, including discussions of light, temperature, rainfall, and oxygen. Designed for upper-level college students of geology and paleontology.

Phillip A. Murry

Cross-References

The Atmosphere's Global Circulation, 121; The Atmosphere's Structure and Composition, 128; Climate, 217; Evaporites, 631; Fossil Plants, 753; The Fossil Record, 760; Glacial Deposits, 937; The Greenhouse Effect, 1004; Micropaleontology: Microfossils, 1674; Paleobiogeography, 1984; Paleosols, 2011; Sediment Transport and Deposition, 2290; Sedimentary Rocks: Biogenic, 2312; Sedimentary Rocks: Chemical Precipitates, 2318.

PALEONTOLOGY: SYSTEMATICS AND CLASSIFICATION

Type of earth science: Paleontology and earth history

The modern classification of both fossil and living organisms attempts both to organize life forms in a logical and uniform manner, based primarily on structural similarities between organisms, and to illustrate the evolutionary relationships between different groups of animal and plant life. Only 250,000 fossil species have been described, while it has been estimated that some 500 million species have come and gone over the past 3.4 billion years of geologic time. Thus, there are enormous numbers of fossil species still awaiting discovery and classification.

Principal terms

BINOMIAL SYSTEM: the current system of classifying organisms, which gives each organism a dual name, consisting of the genus and the species

GENUS: a group of closely related species that share a common ancestry and similar morphological characteristics

KINGDOM: one of the five large subdivisions of life, differentiated on the basis of gross body plan (single-celled versus multicellular) and method of obtaining food or nutrients (produces own food or obtains it from other organisms)

NOMENCLATURE: the names and terms used in a classification system

PHYLOGENY: the study of the evolutionary relationships between organisms

PHYLUM: a major grouping of organisms, distinguished on the basis of basic body plan, grade of anatomical complexity, and pattern of growth or development

SPECIES: a group of actually or potentially interbreeding organisms; the basic taxonomic unit

SYSTEMATICS: the identification and classification of fossil organisms into structurally and evolutionarily related groups; the study of taxonomy

TAXON: one of several systematic groups or categories into which a particular organism may be placed

TYPE SPECIMENS: the original fossil specimens upon which a species was first erected

Summary of the Phenomenon

Historically, there has been a tendency for people to organize and arrange into groups large numbers of items in order to understand the complex world in which they live. To accomplish this, systems of classification are developed. Most types of classification scheme attempt to group things of a similar kind together in the same category. This is true of the system utilized by biologists and paleontologists to classify both living and fossil organisms. This system of classification is based on the premise that a similarity in morphology or structure provides evidence of a biological kinship between organisms. Indeed, the biological classification employed by biologists and paleontologists not only expresses the similarities and differences between groups, but also summarizes or conveys a vast amount of information concerning these groups, especially the general phylogenetic or evolutionary relationships between groups.

"Systematics" is the term applied to the study of taxonomy which is concerned with the identification and classification of fossil organisms into morphologically and evolutionarily related groups. These groups or taxonomic categories are referred to as taxa. The system of classification in use the world over is the Binomial System, a system of nomenclature proposed by the Swedish naturalist Carolus Linnaeus in the 1700's. The fundamental unit, or taxon, in this classification is the species. A species can be defined as a group of morphologically similar individuals whose ecological demands and physiologic functions are the same and whose members interbreed to produce fertile offspring. Groups of closely related species that share a common ancestry and possess a set of similar morphological characteristics are termed "genera" (singular, genus). Under the Binomial System, each plant or animal is given two names, the genus name first, the species second. The human species, for example, is referred to as *Homo* (genus) *sapiens* (species). The names of both the genus and the species are printed in italics. Species names are given in Latin, as originally this was the universal language of science in the Western world and naturalists were looking for a standardized nomenclature recognizable to scientists from all countries. The Latinized names of species have remained universal names, equally recognizable to biologists and paleontologists in areas as diverse as South America, England, China, and the Soviet Union.

There are also taxonomic categories above the genus level. Similar genera are grouped into a single family; groups of related families are placed into an order; similar orders into a class; and closely related classes form a phylum. The more than thirty-five phyla are placed into one of five large groups termed kingdoms. These include the Monera (single-celled organisms with no cell nucleus), the Protista (single-celled organisms with a cell nucleus), the multicellular Plantae (organisms that produce their own food via photosynthesis), the multicellular Animalia (organisms that gain nutrients from the ingestion of other organisms), and the Fungi (multicellular organisms that absorb nutrients from their environment). Whereas the species represents a real, natural taxonomic unit, all taxonomic categories above the species level are to a large extent artificial and subjective. The classification of the fearsome carnivorous dinosaur *Tyrannosaurus rex* would be as follows: kingdom, Animalia; phylum, Chordata; class, Reptilia; order, Saurischia; family, Tyrannosauridae; genus, *Tyrannosaurus*; species, *Tyrannosaurus rex*. The basic categories of higher taxa are sometimes supplemented by additional categories with the use of a sub-prefix or super-prefix.

This type of classification is referred to as a hierarchical system. In such a system, each fossil specimen belongs to one and only one "lower" taxonomic category or species and only one of each of the "higher" or superspecific categories. From the highest rank (kingdom) to the lowest rank (species), these categories become progressively narrower in scope. For example, 1.5 million or more species comprise the kingdom Animalia, but one and only one species constitutes the species *Homo sapiens*. The criteria used to diffferentiate different taxonomic groups also becomes narrower and more trivial as one goes from higher to lower taxa.

As indicated above, the Binomial System attempts not only to divide organisms into structurally differentiated groups but also to illustrate the phylogenetic, or evolutionary, relationships between these groups. This classification scheme serves as a phylogenetic outline for the evolution of life on earth and as an indicator of the diversity of basic body plans available to organisms through time. This is often diagrammatically depicted in the rough form of a branching tree (see figure), with the more primitive, structurally simpler organisms at the base and the more advanced, structurally more complex forms in the crown. In the figure, one can see how animals evolved from simple, single-celled protozoans through increasingly more complex multicellular organisms with successively more sophisticated grades of development. These evolutionary pathways are determined from studies of the comparative anatomy of living organisms and by information provided by the fossil record (especially in regard to the timing and order of evolutionary events).

The identification of fossils and the integration of fossil organisms into the system of biological classification allows for reconstructing the history of life on earth. The present records just one instant in the long history of life on this planet—a "snapshot" of life as it exists today. The fossil record, however, extending back some 3.4 billion years, provides the whole epic motion picture. To be sure, there are some frames missing or blurred by the effects of time, but the fossils

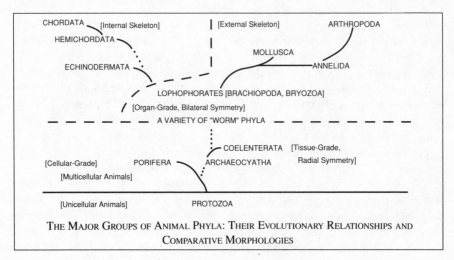

THE MAJOR GROUPS OF ANIMAL PHYLA: THEIR EVOLUTIONARY RELATIONSHIPS AND
COMPARATIVE MORPHOLOGIES

provide the only record of life on earth. It is this fossil record that is the sole source for the factual documentation of the evolution and extinction of organisms through time. The systematic study of fossil organisms provides four types of evolutionary information: It allows scientists to reconstruct the phylogenetic relationships that exist between various taxonomic groups; it reveals the times of major evolutionary events, that is, the times of major evolutionary radiations and the timing of so-called mass extinction events; it gives some idea as to the rates of evolutionary change; and it reveals patterns of evolutionary change.

Methods of Study

It has often been said that to identify a fossil correctly is the first step, if not the key, to finding out further information about the fossil. Determining the identity of a particular fossil provides an outline of its biological affinities, evolutionary pedigree, anatomical complexity, and some idea of how the organism lived in its environment. With its identification and classification, a fossil becomes more than a curiously shaped stone; it becomes the remains of a once-living organism that, in itself, is a time capsule for information about that interval of geologic time during which the organism lived and eventually died.

The basic tools of the systematic paleontologist traditionally have been the various implements and equipment used to remove the fossils from the rock matrix and prepare them for description, calipers to measure morphological dimensions, and an adequate reference library to aid in determining the identity and relationships of the fossils under study and compare them with those already described. Today, computers can store and compare the dimensions of large suites of specimens and statistically analyze large sets of data in order to determine the possible relationships between fossil taxa. Studies of shell microstructure and geochemistry have also provided new approaches to fossil identification and classification, beyond the study of the external features of a fossil specimen.

The basic approach to fossil identification, however, remains essentially the same as it has been for the past two centuries. A fossil is discovered and collected, with the details of its occurrence—that is, the rock layer or stratum and geographic locality where it was found—being determined and recorded with the fossil. Ideally, associated fossil species should also be noted, as well as the orientation of the fossil specimens in the rock and the nature of their preservation. This may help the paleontologist to infer something as to the life habits and habitats of the fossils under study. Today, a single specimen of a particular fossil taxon is not enough; the larger the number of specimens of the fossil available for collection from the site, the better for the purposes of statistical analysis of the species.

The fossil specimens are removed from the enclosing rock matrix, and rock matrix adhering to the specimens is removed using preparatory equipment ranging from hammers and chisels to air-abrasive equipment and vibra-tools. This preparation is necessary to expose the main morphological features of the shell or bone, features critical in determining the fossil's identity. Following mechanical removal of rock matrix, occasionally paleontologists have to resort to sonic cleaners, weak acids, or strong detergents to remove more stubborn matrix adhering to the fossils. Fortunately, many fossils weather cleanly from soft sedimentary rocks like shales, marls, and poorly cemented sandstones and require very little cleaning and preparation.

Following preparation and cleaning of the fossil specimen, a detailed description of the specimen is formulated, including the dimensions of the specimen (measurements of length, width, height, thickness, and so on), the general arrangement of the parts that compose the fossil, and a description of the external and internal morphological features that distinguish the specimen. For certain fossil groups, especially corals, bryozoans, and nautiloid cephalopods, it is necessary to section or cut open specimens with rock saws, both longitudinally and tangentially to expose critical internal structures and the microstructure of the shell if it is preserved. If more than one specimen was collected of the fossil type under study, each specimen is described and then compared with its associates in order to determine any morphological variation that is present within the fossil population or to determine whether one or more than one distinct species are present in the collection.

To classify the fossil specimen(s), the fossil at hand is compared to fossil forms already described in the scientific literature. The usual process for identifying a fossil specimen is to determine its phylum first and then proceed from the general to the specific. Information to aid in the identification of fossils can be found in a number of reference books, textbooks, and popular field guides on fossils. Invertebrate fossils (remains on animals that lack backbones) constitute the majority of fossils found. Fortunately, these primarily marine animals are also the easiest to identify. This is largely a consequence of the possession of hard parts consisting of mineralized external or internal shells that usually are composed of a minimal number of parts that are preserved intact. Good general systematic reference books for the invertebrates include any of a number of college-level paleontology textbooks, such as E. N. K. Clarkson's *Invertebrate Paleontology and Evolution* (1986) or that edited by R. S. Boardman, A. H. Cheetham, and A. J. Rowell, *Fossil Invertebrates* (1987). These books provide good descriptions of the major invertebrate phyla and the classes and orders within these phyla. More specific identification at the genus and species levels requires texts such as those by H. W. Shimer and R. R. Schrock, *Index Fossils of North America* (1944), R. C. Moore, C. G. Lalicker, and A. F. Fischer, *Invertebrate Fossils* (1952), and the various volumes of the Geological Society of America's *Treatise on Invertebrate Paleontology*, edited by Moore. Determination of the species of a particular fossil may require further research utilizing more obscure paleontological monographs that describe select genera or groups of related species.

The fossil remains of vertebrate animals and plants are much less common and more difficult to identify and classify. This is attributable, in part, to the fact that these organisms are most common in terrestrial environments where the rapid and complete burial necessary for preservation as a fossil is not a common process. The internal skeletons of vertebrates consist of a multitude of individual bones held together by tendons, cartilage, and fleshy tissue. Upon the death of the organism, these soft parts will decay and the skeleton readily disaggregates into a pile of loose bones that, upon transport by stream action or scavengers, are spread over a broad area and are difficult to reassemble into the original skeleton. Plant remains lack mineralized hard parts and consist of multiple parts (roots, stems, leaves, seeds, and the like) that also are easily separated from one another in the process of burial. These problems in preservation and the complexity of the component parts make identification of these fossil remains difficult and best left to professional paleontologists and paleobotanists. General references for identification and classification of the major vertebrate groups include A. S. Romer's *Vertebrate Paleontology* (1971), E. H. Colbert's *Evolution of the Vertebrates* (1983), and L. Radinsky's *The Evolution of Vertebrate Design* (1987).

After comparing the fossil specimens with species that have already been described, one of two conclusions can be made. Either the fossil specimens can be identified as those of an existing species or they constitute a species new to science. If the specimens are identified as a preexisting species, they should be closely compared with the type specimens of the known species to ascertain if any variation exists between the two suites of specimens. The "type specimens" are the original specimens for which the fossil species was first erected. They are usually preserved for posterity in collections held at major natural history museums. The occurrence, both the age of the rock unit and the geographic locality of the collecting site, should be compared to that of the existing species to determine whether these new specimens extend the range of the species in time and/or space. If it is determined that the fossil specimens are sufficiently distinct from existing species, then a new species is created for these specimens.

The description of a new species has to follow a specific format that has been established by biologists and paleontologists and which is specified in the Code of Zoological Nomenclature established by the International Commission on Zoological Nomenclature. This format was established in the early 1900's to bring a measure of uniformity to animal taxonomy. A comparable set of procedures has been established for plants. This code specifies the choice of the species name, publication of the name, description of the new species, and the designation of one or more type specimens.

The name given to a new species must be binomial, consisting of the genus name and the species name. A specific name by itself is meaningless. The new species name cannot be already in use, or "occupied." This means the name used for the species cannot already be in use with the genus name with which it is to be associated. The names of the species and the genus must be Latin words or words that have been Latinized. Species names can be Latinized place-names, the names of people, or descriptive words. A species cannot be named anonymously and the author's name is part of the official species name. For example, the official name for the living species of the chambered nautilus from the southwest Pacific would be

Nautilus pompilius Linnaeus, Carolus Linnaeus being the original author of the species.

For a new species to be officially recognized, the name and a description of the distinctive features that identify the new species must be published in an approved medium; that is, it must be in print, published in quantity, and circulated to libraries to ensure that the announcement of the new name is readily available to scientists around the world. The description of a new species should include a diagnosis listing the characteristics distinguishing the new species from other, similar species as well as a fuller description of the various morphological aspects of the species, along with its geographic locality, geologic occurrence, and a reference to the museum where the designated type specimens for the species are stored. Currently, it is also strongly recommended that an illustration of the new species be included in this description.

The International Code also specifies that each new species description must be accompanied by the designation of a type specimen or set of type specimens. These are the actual original fossil specimens upon which the species is based. The code requires that type specimens be clearly labeled as such and that measures be taken to ensure their preservation and accessibility to interested scientists. This usually means that specimens are deposited in a major natural history museum, where such facilities are available. If the new species is based on a single specimen, this specimen is designated the type specimen, or "holotype." If several specimens serve this purpose, they are designated the "syntypes" for the species.

The naming of new species is best left to a professional paleontologist who is familiar with the rules of zoological nomenclature and the accepted format for publication. Nevertheless, amateur fossil collectors, who typically find the bulk of new species in the field, are often recognized for their contributions by being named a coauthor of the new species or having the new species named for them.

Reconstruction of the phylogenies, or evolutionary family trees, of fossil organisms operates in a manner opposite that of fossil identification and classification. A paleontologist starts at the species level, reconstructing evolutionary relationships between species, and then works up the taxonomic hierarchy, from the narrow to the broad. Species phylogenies are reconstructed on the bases of morphologic similarity and the stratigraphic occurrence of fossil species. If a biological classification system is to reflect the evolutionary relationships between taxa, the amount of genetic difference between species must be determined. One cannot observe this directly in the fossils, so the paleontologist must use morphological difference as a rough measure of genetic difference. The two species in a group that have the largest number of morphological features in common are most likely to be descended from a common ancestor and hence are more closely related. A large number of species, defined using a multitude of taxonomic features, make determination of the phylogenetic relationships between fossil species difficult. Often, only a few morphological features are singled out as being of greater evolutionary importance than the rest, and determining relationships between species is based on these characters. The stratigraphic occurrence of these fossil taxa allows one to determine the order of appearance of fossil species, providing a check of the ancestor-descendant relationships based on morphology alone.

Similar phylogenies can be reconstructed for groups of related genera, families, orders, and so on up the taxonomic hierarchy. The characters utilized become less trivial as the taxonomic rank under study becomes higher. Through detailed studies, or "monographs," of groups of related species and genera, the phylogenies of most of the major animal groups have been mapped out. These reconstructions, however, are constantly undergoing change, primarily as the result of the description of newly discovered fossil taxa and the restudy of older, established species.

Context

The biological classification of both living and fossil forms allows for a better understanding of the enormous variety of life on the earth as well as the planet's evolutionary history. This classification serves as a biological outline that summarizes the various anatomical and morphological combinations available to life on earth and demonstrates the evolutionary pathways that lead from one group to another. It also provides a standardized nomenclature that serves as a universal language, allowing biologists and paleontologists from many different countries and cultures to communicate effectively with one another.

The identification and classification of fossils also allow them to be used to reconstruct the evolutionary history of life on earth. From detailed studies of fossil species, phylogenies can be reconstructed, illustrating the evolutionary relationships between groups of species and higher taxa as well. These fossil phylogenies provide models of how the processes of evolution and extinction operate over long periods of time—time intervals far beyond that of human experience. From the information provided by studies of evolution based on these tabulations of fossil species and higher taxa, computer-generated models have been developed to identify patterns and trends in the evolutionary history of life and to explain their causes and their effects on subsequent evolutionary events. These fossil examples reveal information that allows scientists to interpret the long-term consequences of the evolutionary changes occurring on the earth today and how these will affect the subsequent evolution of life in the future.

The models developed for these various evolutionary processes are only as good as the data on which they are based. The taxonomic information used by paleontologists today is derived from systematic studies that are decades old or older. Only some 250,000 fossil species have been described—5 percent of the total number of species that have been described as living on the planet's surface today. It has been estimated that some 500 million species of organisms have come and gone over the past 3.4 billion years of geologic time, which suggests that there are enormous numbers of fossil species, residing in crustal rocks or in museum drawers, awaiting discovery and classification. These new sources of information are critical to improving the reality of these evolutionary models.

Bibliography

Andrews, H. N. *Studies in Paleobotany.* New York: John Wiley & Sons, 1960. Somewhat dated but standard paleobotany textbook, with the major emphasis on Paleozoic and Mesozoic vascular plants. Suitable for college-level readers.

Beerbower, J. R. *Search for the Past.* Englewood Cliffs, N.J.: Prentice-Hall, 1968. An introductory paleontology textbook with discussions of classification and evolution plus descriptions of the major groups of both vertebrate and invertebrate fossils. Suitable for college-level readers.

Boardman, R. S., A. H. Cheetham, and A. J. Rowell, eds. *Fossil Invertebrates.* Oxford: Blackwell Scientific, 1987. Up-to-date college-level text on invertebrate paleontology, with individual sections that each describe a major phylum and its component classes and orders. Very good illustrations of the major invertebrate groups and their characteristic morphological features.

Clarkson, E. N. K. *Invertebrate Paleontology and Evolution.* London: Allen & Unwin, 1986. A college invertebrate textbook up-to-date with good description of the major invertebrate phyla, classes, and orders. Good illustrations of the major morphological features that distinguish each group. A brief general description of taxonomy and fossil systematics.

Colbert, E. H. *Evolution of the Vertebrates.* New York: John Wiley & Sons, 1983. An introduction to the major groups of vertebrate animals, with general descriptions of the major taxonomic groups. More elementary than Romer (below), with less emphasis on morphology and classification. For college-level readers.

Moore, R. C., ed. *Treatise on Invertebrate Paleontology.* 27 vols. Lawrence: University of Kansas Press, 1953-1975. This series of volumes (with some volumes currently being revised) includes descriptions and illustrations of all fossil invertebrate groups, down to the genus level. Each volume concentrates on a particular phylum or class and includes general chapters on evolution, ecology, and classification. The standard reference for the identification and classification of fossil invertebrates. Some basic knowledge of biology or paleontology required.

Moore, R. C., C. G. Lalicker, and A. F. Fischer. *Invertebrate Fossils.* New York: McGraw-Hill, 1952. A "classic" textbook on invertebrate fossils, outdated but profusely illustrated with line drawings of the more important genera and species representative of the major invertebrate groups. Still a useful reference for identification of fossil invertebrates. Suitable for college-level readers.

Radinsky, Leonard B. *The Evolution of Vertebrate Design.* Chicago: University of Chicago Press, 1987. A very good introductory text to the vertebrates. Well written and illustrated, with a unique approach to vertebrate classification, relating important morphological features in each group to their function. Highly readable and understandable to the college-level reader.

Raup, D. M., and S. M. Stanley. *Principles of Paleontology.* San Francisco: W. H. Freeman, 1978. An excellent college-level text emphasizing paleontological concepts, including thorough sections on fossil classification, the description of new species, and reconstruction of fossil phylogenies. Suitable for college-level readers with some background in biology or paleontology.

Romer, A. S. *Vertebrate Paleontology.* Chicago: University of Chicago Press, 1971. The authoritative text on vertebrate paleontology, stressing morphology and classification. An important reference but requiring a considerable knowledge of vertebrate anatomy for effective comprehension.

Shimer, H. W., and R. R. Schrock. *Index Fossils of North America.* Cambridge, Mass.: MIT Press, 1944. A compendium of many of the more commonly found fossils in North America, providing short descriptions and illustrations of these taxa. Emphasis on marine invertebrates. Some generic names are now out-of-date. Still a good reference for fossil identification at the species level. Suitable for high school and college readers.

Tidwell, W. D. *Common Fossil Plants of Western North America.* Provo: Brigham Young University Press, 1975. A good handbook for the identification of fossil plants. Well illustrated and useful for any region, although the emphasis is on the fossil floras of the western United States.

Robert C. Frey

Cross-References

Biostratigraphy, 173; Dinosaurs, 370; Human Evolution, 641; The Evolution of Life, 655; Fossil Plants, 753; The Fossil Record, 760; Fossilization and Taphonomy, 768; Ediacarian Fossils, 776; Mammals, 1453.

PALEOSOLS

Field of study: Soil science

Paleosols are ancient soils that have been buried. Although natural acids (largely dissolved carbon dioxide) are almost entirely supplied by the atmosphere during modern soil formation, that does not seem to have been the case with all paleosols, particularly the most ancient paleosols and those that are associated with ore deposits. Paleosols that were produced by ancient atmospheric gases may record the environmental conditions of the ancient earth.

Principal terms

CALICHE: a type of soil or paleosol that contains a high proportion of calcium carbonate, calcium sulfate, or both

CLAY MINERAL: a type of mineral that is the most common product of soil formation; it is composed of silicon, oxygen, hydrogen, usually aluminum, and possibly other elements

PARTIAL PRESSURE: the proportion of a gas mixture (for example, the atmosphere) that a particular type of molecule (for example, carbon dioxide) comprises

SOIL: all material which has been substantially altered at the earth's surface by interaction with the atmosphere, living things, or both, and which has not been laterally displaced subsequent to that alteration

SOIL HORIZON: a distinct layer in a soil

Summary of the Phenomenon

Soil is one of the best-known yet least precisely defined geologic entities. Many definitions would not exclude beds of graded sediment; other definitions would not exclude sediment that has experienced only mild physical and chemical alteration. Additionally, many soil science textbooks restrict "soil" to that lying within the depth of plant roots, but such a definition is inappropriate for Precambrian and Early Paleozoic soils, which formed before the evolution of rooted plants.

The rock record of the earth covers the past 3.9 billion years (out of a total earth history of 4.6 billion years). Throughout the known rock record, soil formation (weathering) has involved more energy than other geologic processes, such as mountain building. Mountain building is driven by the internal energy of the earth (for example, by natural radioactivity), whereas soil formation is driven by solar energy and by chemical reactions between acidic atmospheric gases and exposed rock. Solar energy fuels photosynthetic plants, which concentrate the most abundant atmospheric acid (carbon dioxide), and subsequent decay of these plants releases concentrated carbon dioxide into soil waters, which thereby become acidic and dissolve minerals. The downward solar flux of energy, which enhances weathering, currently is about 7,500 times greater than the upward flux of internal energy. The internal energy of the earth has progressively decreased with time as radioactive elements decay; solar radiation has progressively increased. In addition, the input of solar energy has exceeded the output of internal energy by at least a factor of 1,000 since the beginning of the rock record.

The collective volume of soils produced throughout earth history may have been comparable to the present volume of the continental crust, but only an insignificant volume of these soils has become preserved by burial within the crust. Paleosols now constitute a smaller proportion of continental crust than most other well-known rock types. The proportion of paleosols appears to be particularly small in the oldest rocks. In these rocks, the preserved portion is so small and the conditions for preservation of paleosols appear to have been so peculiar that it is dangerous to make sweeping interpretations of ancient earth environments based on paleosols.

Virtually all old soils have been eroded to become sediment rather than buried to become paleosols. Intense weathering causes a high proportion of rock to dissolve, and the remnant soil becomes rich in insoluble elements such as aluminum. Erosion of this soil produces aluminum-rich sediment, which usually accumulates in the shallow ocean as a clay-rich rock (mudrock), such as shale. Sedimentary rocks therefore may be environmental indicators, and the vastly greater volume of sedimentary rock has resulted in most interpretations of ancient environments coming from study of sedimentary rock rather than from study of paleosols. Environmental study of paleosols is less constrained, however, than that of sedimentary rock because the unweathered parent of the weathered material (soil) is observable beneath a paleosol, whereas the parent for a weathered sediment generally cannot be deduced with certainty; the parent rock for any given sediment may lie thousands of miles from where the sediment accumulates—for example, the Andean Mountain parent for much of the Amazon deltaic sediment.

Paleosols are known from all major divisions of earth history, from the Archean eon to the present epoch. The proportion of paleosols to other rock types roughly increases with time, consistent with the theory of continental growth through earth history; an increase in the area of exposed continents would lead to an increase in the volume of soil. Although the area of exposed continents probably was smallest in the Archean, well-preserved Archean paleosols are known from Canada and from South Africa, where Archean continental crust never has been so deeply buried that regional metamorphism could destroy evidence of the weathering processes which produced the paleosols. The area of exposed continents apparently increased dramatically from the Archean to the Proterozoic, so Proterozoic paleosols are correspondingly more abundant.

The role that plant life may have played in the weathering of these Proterozoic soils is unclear. Plants currently concentrate so much carbon in the upper portion of a typical soil that oxidation of this carbon provides more carbon dioxide to the underlying soil than does diffusion of carbon dioxide directly from the atmosphere. Much of this carbon dioxide comes from roots, but roots did not evolve until after the Proterozoic. Plant life in Precambrian (Archean plus Proterozoic) soils was limited to bacteria. Mats of photosynthesizing cyanobacteria (also called blue-green algae) lay at the surface, and other bacteria occurred deeper in the soil. Modern soil contains abundant bacteria below the surface, but the soil surface generally is occupied by complex photosynthesizing plants—for example, trees—instead of by cyanobacteria. A partial image of Precambrian soils may be obtained by studying cyanobacterial mats that grow in environments too harsh for more complex plants—for example, on salt flats and around geysers. These environments are not only harsh but also highly variable. The chemical composition of water on a modern salt flat may vary from hypersaline to nonsaline following a thunderstorm. The water temperature around a geyser may vary by several tens of degrees within a few minutes. The ability of cyanobacteria to withstand such variations may indicate that the environmental conditions of Precambrian soils either were consistently harsh or were more variable than those of more recent soils.

Ancient paleosols generally are too scarce for study of the geographic variation of soil types. Geographic variations in rainfall and temperature are the two prime variables that control the distribution of modern soils, because the atmosphere mixes so rapidly that any local variation in the partial pressure of oxygen or carbon dioxide rapidly becomes globally homogenized. Molecular oxygen and carbon dioxide also would have been evenly distributed in ancient atmospheres, but their proportions of the atmosphere may have varied throughout earth history. The oldest paleosols therefore are studied to examine variation in the earth's atmosphere through earth history, whereas the youngest paleosols are studied to learn about geographic variation in climate. Paleosols and other indicators record dramatic variation in climates on earth during the past 2 million years, related to the growth and melting of enormous continental glaciers.

Tropical climates produce distinct soils and thus distinct paleosols. Both wet and dry tropical climates characteristically produce yellow-to-red soils because of oxidation and retention of iron in the soil. Wet tropical conditions can produce soils which are so rich in aluminum that these soils may be mined profitably. In such soils, the more soluble elements have been leached away by groundwater draining lush vegetation. Decay of the vegetation produces acids that attack even quartz, leaving only aluminum-rich minerals. Aluminum-rich paleosols are among the oldest (Archean) paleosols on earth, so wet tropical conditions appear to have existed long ago, despite the fact that solar radiation should have been much smaller during the Archean eon.

Warm dry climates may produce little soil of any kind. For example, more characteristic of the Sahara than the "sand seas" that are commonly illustrated in documentaries are vast stretches of bare rock. Caliche is a characteristic soil and paleosol produced in such a climate. Caliche generally forms by precipitation of calcium carbonate from upwardly moving groundwater as the groundwater approaches the earth's surface. The upward decrease in pressure may allow carbon dioxide to be released, just as carbon dioxide is released upon opening a bottle of soda pop. Release of carbon dioxide favors precipitation of calcium carbonate; this precipitation may be aided by evaporation of the groundwater—which points to a dry climate for the formation of an ancient caliche. A caliche paleosol generally may be interpreted to record an ancient dry climate, even if the precipitation of calcium carbonate was not related to evaporation within soil but was simply the result of release of carbon dioxide. The original excess of carbon dioxide could have been provided by the escape of gases to the earth's surface during metamorphism of carbon-bearing sedimentary rocks at great depth. The abundant infiltration of rain-water in a wet climate would dissolve calcium carbonate from soil, whatever its origin, so the preservation of calcium carbonate in a caliche paleosol generally records a dry climate, even if the precipitation of calcium carbonate were induced by deep crustal processes independent of climate.

Interpretation of the elemental composition and mineralogy of a paleosol generally is controversial, especially for paleosols older than 570 million years (Precambrian paleosols), because paleosols potentially have experienced substantial modification (diagenesis) after burial. One of the most consistent chemical peculiarities of Precambrian paleosols is that they contain extreme ratios of potassium to sodium, unlike modern clayey soils. No known weathering process could fractionate sodium from potassium so severely. Precambrian paleosols commonly contain more than ten times as much potassium as sodium, whereas these two elements generally behave similarly under modern weathering conditions. This potassium in Precambrian paleosols mostly occurs in fine-grained, aluminum-rich mica. The potassium either is a record of pervasive diagenetic alteration of Precambrian paleosols or indicates that, unlike modern soils, they did not form as a result of atmospheric acid-forming gases. The majority of Precambrian paleosols could represent alterations on the ancient land resulting from exhalation of acid-containing mud from deep in the earth. Although paleosols which are older than 570 million years generally have the greatest ratios of potassium to sodium, paleosols which are 250-570 million years old (Paleozoic paleosols) also are more potassium-rich than are modern soils. In these Paleozoic paleosols, the potassium-bearing mineral typically is a clay mineral called illite. In illite-bearing paleosols, some investigators attribute the high potassium content to peculiar weathering conditions, whereas others attribute it to precipitation of potassium from through-flowing groundwater long after burial of the soil.

Methods of Study

Paleosols are studied in many of the ways that modern soils are studied. Like a modern soil, a paleosol exhibits a profile, that is, a progressive downward variation in chemical composition and mineralogy. Detailed sampling is conducted on a paleosol in the field so that subsequent analysis of the samples in a laboratory may reveal gradations within the profile. Modern soil profiles generally are more obvious than are paleosol profiles, given greater contrast in color and grain size among modern soil horizons; paleosol profiles therefore may require more systematic sampling than would sampling of a modern soil—for example, sampling every 5 centimeters.

Paleosol samples typically are analyzed for elemental abundances, both major and minor elements. A wide variety of analytical techniques have been used to measure elemental abundances in paleosols, including X-ray fluorescence, atomic-absorption spectrophotometry, and neutron activation analysis. The mineralogy of a paleosol generally is determined by X-ray diffractometry. Thin slices of paleosol rock (thin sections) may be cut and polished for study under a petrographic microscope. Microscopic identification of the minerals should corroborate the mineral identification by X-ray diffraction and should reveal the presence of additional minerals, given that X-ray diffraction generally cannot detect minerals which constitute less than about 10 percent of a rock. Many of the minerals in paleosols differ from those in the original soil, as the original minerals have been transformed after burial.

Observation of textures and sedimentary structures in and above paleosols is essential for a clear demonstration that a given rock is indeed a paleosol. The occurrence of plant roots in growth position has long been the favored indicator of the soil environment, but rooted plants have existed on earth for only the past 10 percent of earth history. Other diagnostic criteria are thus needed for older paleosols and for the many young paleosols which lack plant roots. Such indicators include ripped-up clasts and differential compaction.

Most paleosols are overlain by sedimentary rock. It is common to find that pieces of the former soil were eroded during deposition of the overlying sediment and that those pieces (ripped-up clasts) have become concentrated near the base of the overlying sedimentary bed. Ripped-up clasts are a useful genetic indicator for paleosols, especially if there is sufficient exposure of the paleosol surface to show that the clasts had become concentrated in pockets on the original surface of the eroding soil.

Some ancient soils have included a saprolite horizon like that which characterizes most modern soils found in tropical to subtropical areas. Saprolite is sufficiently weathered to be porous but retains the original volume and much of the original structure which characterized the rock prior to weathering. Upon weathering to saprolite, quartz veins in the original rock remain unchanged but become surrounded by porous weathered material. Upon burial, the porous saprolite compacts, and these quartz veins become broken and compressed. Recognition of such differential compaction helps in the identification of paleosols.

Context

Air-breathing animals—including human beings—living on land are highly susceptible to changes in atmospheric composition. It is important, therefore, to learn whether the atmosphere remains constant in composition or there are occasional digressions. If paleosols were to provide clear evidence of potentially rapid variation in atmospheric composition, industrialized societies could construct emergency shelters with artificial atmospheres. Evidence of recent atmospheric change has not yet emerged from paleosol studies, but some type of global atmospheric event has been shown to coincide with the extinction of the dinosaurs about 65 million years ago. Nevertheless, if the odds of a recurrence of such an event were in fact one in one million (assuming a human life span of sixty-five years), it is questionable that even the richest societies would invest in precautionary shelters.

Paleosols have economic importance for iron, aluminum, and nickel ore deposits but have little agricultural importance. An exception involves some farms in Kansas, where the soil is a paleosol that thoroughly weathered tens of thousands of years ago, froze about 20,000 years ago during the most recent ice age, and then thawed during the past 10,000 years to become fertile soil again.

The richest iron ore deposits are paleosols that developed on voluminous iron formations. The iron formations originally contained substantial silicon but lost it to through-flowing groundwater during alteration that extended downward from a land surface (paleosol alteration). There is general agreement that the paleosol alteration involved vast quantities of dissolved acid-forming gases, but there remains substantial controversy whether those acid-forming gases descended from the atmosphere or rose from deep in the earth. A similar controversy involves aluminum deposits. Most extensive aluminum deposits are at least partly paleosols because they contain portions which are chemical alterations of aluminum-bearing rocks that lay at or near the earth's surface during the alteration. A better understanding of the relationship between ordinary paleosols and ore-bearing paleosols would help in the search for richer ore deposits and thereby lower the cost of mining. Lower mining costs would subsequently lower the cost of domestic products that contain iron, aluminum, or nickel and thus benefit consumers.

Bibliography

Holland, Heinrich D. "Oxygen in the Precambrian Atmosphere: Evidence from Terrestrial Environments." In *The Chemical Evolution of the Atmosphere and Oceans*. Princeton, N.J.: Princeton University Press, 1984. Archean and Proterozoic paleosols are described and interpreted to deduce the composition of the ambient atmosphere before the dawn of animal life.

Kimberley, M. M., and D. E. Grandstaff. "Profiles of Elemental Concentrations in Precambrian Paleosols on Basaltic and Granitic Parent Materials." *Precambrian Research* 32 (1986): 133-154. All papers in this issue are devoted to Precambrian paleosols. This particular paper compares Precambrian paleosols that developed on basalt with those that developed on granitic rocks.

Reinhardt, J., and W. R. Sigleo. *Paleosols and Weathering Through Geologic Time: Principals and Applications*. Special Paper 216. Boulder, Colo.: Geological Society of America, 1988. Several paleosols in the United States (from Pennsylvania, Kentucky, Georgia, Alabama, Colorado, and California) are described in this volume, along with field methods and theoretical models for the development of ancient paleosols.

Retallack, G. *Laboratory Exercises in Paleopedology.* Eugene: University of Oregon Press, 1985. Practical exercises are outlined for the study of paleosols. Examples of paleosols are described from several localities around the world.

Samama, J. C. *Ore Fields and Continental Weathering.* New York: Van Nostrand Reinhold, 1986. Some paleosols are ore deposits for aluminum or nickel; part of this book reviews the characteristics and metal-concentrating processes which produce such paleosols. Another part reviews a different class of paleosol-related ore in which subsurface holes in limestone coincidentally or subsequently become filled with metal-precipitating solutions. Research subsequent to this book has shown that the dissolution of ore-bearing limestone probably shortly preceded precipitation of the lead-zinc minerals and that both the limestone-dissolving and metal-precipitating fluids rose from deep in the earth.

Wright, V. P., and Alfred Fischer, eds. *Paleosols: Their Recognition and Interpretation.* Princeton, N.J.: Princeton University Press, 1986. This volume emphasizes paleosols that occur outside the United States, particularly those in the British Isles, Spain, and New Zealand. Chapter 6 reviews selected paleosols in the western United States.

Michael M. Kimberley

Cross-References

THE PALEOZOIC ERA

Type of earth science: Geology
Field of study: Stratigraphy

Paleozoic stratigraphy concerns the study of rock sequences that date from 570 to 245 million years before the present. The primary method by which the stratigraphic relationships of the Paleozoic are established is stratigraphic analysis of distinctive types of fossils.

Principal terms

BIOSTRATIGRAPHY: defining rock layers on the basis of their fossil content

CORRELATION: matching rock units of equivalent age

INDEX (GUIDE) FOSSIL: the remains of an ancient organism that are useful in establishing the age of rocks; index fossils are abundant and have a wide geographic distribution, a narrow stratigraphic range, and a distinctive form

PALEOZOIC: a geologic era dating from 570 to 245 million years before the present

SERIES: a time-rock unit representing rock deposition during a geologic epoch

STAGE: a time-rock unit representing rock deposition during a geologic age

STRATIGRAPHY: the study of rock layers (strata)

SYSTEM: a time-rock unit representing rock deposition within a geologic period

Summary of the Phenomenon

The Paleozoic is the oldest era of the Phanerozoic eon, ranging from approximately 570 to 245 million years before the present. In North America, it is divided into seven periods. Beginning with the oldest, these are the Cambrian, Ordovician, Silurian, Devonian, Mississippian, Pennsylvanian, and Permian. Outside North America, the Mississippian and Pennsylvanian are combined to form the Carboniferous period. In stratigraphy, strata laid down during a particular period are referred to as a system. Systems are subdivided into series (the time-rock unit equivalents of epochs), which may be further subdivided into stages (the time-rock unit equivalents of ages). These subdivisions are very important in subdividing time-rock units of the Paleozoic and other eras of earth history.

The Cambrian is the oldest system in the Paleozoic, ranging from approximately 570 to 505 million years before the present. It was named by Adam Sedgwick in 1835 on the basis of rock exposures in northern Wales. The Cambrian system is subdivided globally into a Lower (Early), Middle, and Upper (Late) series. The earliest rocks of the Phanerozoic eon are stratigraphically difficult to interpret. One reason is that although most rocks of the Paleozoic are subdivided primarily on the basis of their included fossils, the record of Precambrian and Early Cambrian life is poorly known. By Middle Cambrian times, the composition of the fossil communities had changed greatly; this proliferation of forms preserved in the rock record has enabled paleontologists to establish fairly well the stratigraphy of the Middle and Upper Cambrian series. The primary tool used in the establishment of Middle and Upper Cambrian stages is the stratigraphic distribution of trilobites, marine arthropods that somewhat resembled modern pill bugs. Acritarchs, tiny planktonic algae that form a resistant, fossilizable covering, were another group that have become useful index fossils for the Proterozoic (Upper Precambrian) through Devonian. Another common Cambrian fossil group is the brachiopods. These two-valved suspension feeders were of relatively simple form during the Cambrian, a fact that lessens their utility as stratigraphic indicators. During the Late Cambrian, a series of events caused many types of trilobites to become extinct. These events of extinction and evolutionary radiation are especially useful in precise definition of Cambrian stratigraphy. The last of these extinction episodes, which occurred at the very end of the Cambrian, eliminated numerous trilobite species. After this event, the trilobites never rebounded; in post-Cambrian strata they cannot be widely used as index fossils.

The second Paleozoic system is the Ordovician. It ranges from approximately 505 to 438 million years before the present. The Ordovician was named in 1879 by Charles Lapworth, who combined portions of the Cambrian and Silurian systems as first defined in Wales, thus ending a debate that had developed concerning those sequences of strata. The Ordovician may also be subdivided into Early, Middle, and Late series, and for these the stages are much better established than in the Cambrian. Strata of Ordovician age are often characterized by an abundance of carbonate (limestone and dolomite) rocks, which were deposited upon shallow seaways extending over many of the continents. Although trilobites declined in number throughout the Ordovician, many other animal groups became abundant or appeared for the first time. Especially important for biostratigraphy are graptolites, primitive hemichordate animals that lived in colonies; often they are preserved as black marks that resemble tiny hacksaw blades on rocks. Also of biostratigraphic importance are the acritarchs and the nautiloids. The latter group were predatory mollusks that at this time typically had straight shells, with tentacles emanating from one end. The chitinozoans are another group used in biostratigraphy for rocks of Ordovician through Devonian age. Although they are often classified as algae, the precise relationships of these microscopic, typically vase-shaped organisms are unknown. Finally, the evolution of more complex, hinged-shell groups of brachiopods with distinctive form enables stratigraphers to utilize this group in biostratigraphy from Late Ordovician through Early Pennsylvanian series rocks. The end of the Ordovician is marked by another mass extinction event, in which approximately one hundred families of marine animals were wiped out.

The Silurian system was named by Roderick Murchison in 1835 on the basis of rock exposures in southern Wales. The age of the Silurian ranges from 438 to 408 million years before the present. Worldwide, an Early and a Late series are recognized. In the best-known exposures of Silurian rocks, however, various series designations are used. Silurian rocks are common on all continents and were deposited in continental or marine environments. The most common rocks of the Silurian are limestones and dolomites, although many dark, clay-rich marine rocks containing graptolites are present. As in the Ordovician, this group is a useful index fossil for the Silurian. Brachiopods, acritarchs, and chitinozoans are other important fossils used in determining the age of Silurian strata.

The fourth system of the Paleozoic is the Devonian, ranging from 408 to 360 million years before the present. The Devonian system was named by Murchison and Sedgwick in 1839 for rock exposures in Devon and Cornwall, in southwest England. Globally, the Devonian is subdivided into Early, Middle, and Late series. Devonian rocks are very common; they are present on all continents, where they formed in a great variety of environments. Thick sequences of Devonian-age sediments accumulated along the edges of ancient continents and record a time of changing climate and environments. On land, red bed sequences, colored by oxidation of iron-bearing minerals, are widely distributed for the first time. Of these units, the Old Red Sandstone of the British Isles is best known. As in the Ordovician and Silurian, graptolites, brachiopods, and chitinozoans are important marine index fossils for the Devonian. The proliferation of different groups of organisms also adds to the list of fossils used in stratigraphic correlation. Here, for the first time, pollen and spores can be used to define strata; they are especially important in correlating Devonian continental rocks. Also of biostratigraphic utility are the strange, tiny, toothlike conodont fossils (from animals of unknown affinity) and ostracods (minuscule, two-valved crustaceans). In addition, for the first time, ammonoids (cephalopods with typically coiled shells) are of widespread use in biostratigraphy. Goniatite ammonoids are of major importance in defining rocks of the Devonian through Permian age.

The term "Carboniferous" was first applied to rocks within the area of north-central England by William Conybeare and William Phillips in 1822. Yet, no type section (the area in which rock units are first described) was ever designated. The Carboniferous lasted from approximately 360 to 286 million years before the present. Although the system is named for coal-bearing strata, only its upper portion contains large amounts of coal; the lower portion typically consists of carbonates. In North America, a different classification is employed, based largely on these rock differences. In 1870, Alexander Winchell proposed the name "Mississippian" for Lower Carboniferous exposures in the Mississippi River valley between southeastern Iowa and southern Illinois. Rocks of the Mississippian range from 360 to 320 million years before the present. In 1891, Henry Williams named Upper Carboniferous exposures the Pennsylvanian, after the widespread coal-bearing strata in that state. The Pennsylvanian ranges from 320 to 286 million years before the present. The widespread application of these names to Carboniferous-age rocks in North America led to the formal recognition of the Mississippian and Pennsylvanian as systems by the U.S. Geological Survey in 1953.

The Mississippian system (Lower Carboniferous series) is characterized by the widespread distribution of limestone and dolomite, formed by marine incursions over many continents. Cyclic successions are developed in many places within Mississippian-age strata, especially within the upper portion of the system, in which sequences of limestones, sandstones, and shale were repetitively deposited one upon the other. Goniatites, brachiopods, spores, and pollen are all utilized in the Mississippian-age strata for correlation purposes.

Within North America, there is a widespread unconformity (a gap in the rock record) between the Mississippian and Pennsylvanian (Upper Carboniferous). The Pennsylvanian was a time of extensive coal deposition within low-lying swamps within North America, Europe, and many portions of Asia. Coal deposits are often found capping cyclical sequences consisting of limestone, shale, sandstone, and more shale (with the associated coal). Within the marine sequences, goniatite ammonoids are utilized for determining age and, at the base of the system, brachiopods are used for correlation. In addition, fusulinid foraminifers (small fossils—resembling grains of rice—but giants of this one-celled group) become important for Upper Pennsylvanian correlation. With the abundance of coal-producing plants, fossil spores and pollen serve as valuable index fossils for continental sediments of the Upper Carboniferous.

The Permian system was named for the region of Perm, in the western Ural Mountains of Russia. The system, first proposed by Murchison in 1841, roughly corresponds to a period of earth history between 286 and 245 million years before the present. The Permian may be subdivided into a Lower and Upper series. Permian deposits are thick and widespread in many parts of the world and indicate a time of climatic complexity. Permian stratigraphic sequences are quite varied. Coal was still present but was no longer being extensively formed in North America or central Europe. Continental deposits of the Permian are primarily known for extensive red bed sequences, created through the oxidation of iron-rich sediments. Extensive evaporites are also present, especially in Upper Permian-age strata, with thick layers of gypsum and salt. Large reefs are found and, on the Gondwana continents, tillite deposits give evidence for extensive Permian glaciation. Major index fossils for the Permian include goniatite ammonoids and fusulinids for the marine sequences and spores and pollen for continental deposits. The end of the Permian is marked by an extinction event of major significance. Fusulinids, tabulate and rugose corals, and trilobites became extinct; brachiopods, bryozoans, and echinoderms sustained huge losses, and substantial numbers of bivalve and gastropod mollusks also became extinct. On land, many groups of the larger coal-swamp trees became extinct, and several major groups of vertebrates also died out. These huge losses in plant and animal types mark the stratigraphic boundary between the Paleozoic era ("the era of ancient life") and the subsequent Mesozoic era.

Methods of Study

Studies of Paleozoic stratigraphy primarily utilize analyses of rock units, paleontological studies, and radiometric dating techniques. Lithostratigraphy defines strata (rock layers) on the basis of rock, or lithologic, characteristics. Distinctive rock layers are very useful in determining the position and relative age of local outcroppings of Paleozoic strata. Most Paleozoic systems tend to be dominated by specific rock types. For example, carbonate rocks (limestones and dolomites) are characteristic of many Ordovician, Silurian, and Mississippian sequences. Clastic rocks, including sandstones and mudrocks with their included coals, are diagnostic of Pennsylvanian-age deposits. Red bed deposits, consisting of oxidized iron-rich sediments, are often associated with clastic sequences in Devonian- and Permian-age strata. Unconformities—gaps in the rock record representing periods of erosion or nondeposition—often separate the Paleozoic systems and form natural boundaries for their separation. A major unconformity also typically separates Precambrian rocks from those of the earliest Paleozoic.

Biostratigraphy defines rocks on the basis of their fossil content. The basic unit of biostratigraphic classification is the biozone, in which strata are characterized by the occurrence of a certain fossil or fossils. These index or guide fossils are abundant, distinctive forms with a wide geographic distribution but narrow stratigraphic range and are therefore useful in correlation and in determining the age of strata. The fossils most often used are planktonic (floating) or nektonic (swimming) forms. Of special importance for the study of Paleozoic stratigraphy are trilobites, brachiopods, and graptolites. For certain portions of the Paleozoic, acritarchs, conodonts, chitinozoans, fusulinids, pollen, and spores, as well as nautiloid and ammonoid cephalopods, are widely utilized in biostratigraphic studies.

Lithostratigraphic and biostratigraphic studies can establish only the relative ages of strata. Determination of the absolute age of Paleozoic rocks is done primarily through radiometric dating techniques. These studies utilize the known decay rates of radioactive isotopes to establish the age of rocks in terms of years. Isotopes used for studies of Paleozoic rocks are uranium 235, uranium 238, and thorium 232, all of which decay to lead. Also used are potassium 40, which decays to argon 40, and rubidium 87, whose daughter isotope (product of decay) is strontium 87. Igneous and metamorphic rocks are generally utilized in radiometric dating techniques.

Context

Probably the most important application of Paleozoic stratigraphy is in the search for natural resources. Without knowing the age of the rocks being evaluated or the economic products potentially included within them, the exploration geologist's job would be impossible. Of particular significance is the widespread presence of coal in rocks of Pennsylvanian and Permian age. Most of the coal produced in North America and central Europe has been mined from Pennsylvanian-age rocks. As these coal beds often occur within the same portion of a cyclical sequence of sediments, the search for them is made easier through knowledge of Paleozoic stratigraphy. Permian-age coal sequences are found in Australia, China, the Soviet Union, India, and South Africa. There are also great quantities of oil and natural gas within rocks of Paleozoic age. Significant finds of hydrocarbons have been made in Devonian- and Carboniferous-age rocks, and discoveries of huge oil and gas fields in the Permian Basin of west Texas were a result of exploration of Upper Paleozoic marine strata. Arid conditions, especially common during the Permian, resulted in huge deposits of sodium and potassium salts as well as gypsum and anhydrite. Mountain-building events during the Paleozoic also created tremendous deposits of both precious metals and metals that are imporant for industry. Without an understanding of the stratigraphic occurrence of these valuable resources, the recovery of these materials would be impossible.

Bibliography

Bruton, David L., ed. *Aspects of the Ordovician System*. New York: Oxford University Press, 1984. A symposium volume from the Fourth International Symposium on the Ordovician system, held in Norway in 1982. The introductory paper and a few of the papers on the stratigraphic framework and sea-level changes of the Ordovician would be understandable to a college-level student with some training in geology. The sections on Ordovician environments and their included faunas are written by and for specialists in those areas.

Dineley, D. L. *Aspects of a Stratigraphic System: The Devonian*. New York: John Wiley & Sons, 1984. A well-written and well-illustrated book covering many aspects of Devonian stratigraphy, sedimentology, and fossils. Because it is a single-authored text, it possesses much more continuity than do most symposium volumes. The text would be understandable and very readable for a college student with some training in geology.

Hallam, A. *Atlas of Palaeobiogeography*. New York: Elsevier, 1972. This volume gives an overview of changing animal and plant compositions through time and is especially useful in reviewing fossil groups commonly used in biostratigraphy. Not extremely technical. The various chapters can typically be understood by a college student with some training in paleontology or systematic biology.

House, M. R., C. T. Scrutton, and M. G. Bassett, eds. *The Devonian System: A Palaeontological Association International Symposium*. London: Palaeontological Association of London, 1979. A series of papers devoted to various studies of the Devonian system. Although several of the papers give a general overview, most are technical accounts of Devonian tectonics, fossils, and stratigraphy, written for the specialist.

Levin, Harold L. *The Earth Through Time*. 3d ed. Philadelphia: Saunders College Publishing, 1987. An introductory college-level text that covers aspects of historical geology. A large section is devoted to Paleozoic-age rocks. Well written and profusely illustrated.

Stanley, Steven M. *Earth and Life Through Time*. 2d ed. New York: W. H. Freeman, 1988. This introductory college-level text is well written and well illustrated and contains very few technical errors. Would be accessible to high school students with some training in geology.

Whittington, H. B. *The Burgess Shale*. New Haven, Conn.: Yale University Press, 1985. Whittington reviews the beautifully preserved animals from the Middle Cambrian of the Rocky Mountains in Canada and gives a detailed look at the often strange animals from that famous locale. A review of the stratigraphy and sedimentology of the locality is given, along with comments on the evolutionary significance of the Early Paleozoic animals. The work is written for general audiences.

Phillip A. Murry

Cross-References

Biostratigraphy, 173; Cambrian Diversification of Life, 183; Colonization of the Land, 246; Fossil Plants, 753; The Fossil Record, 760; Fossils of the Earliest Life Forms, 782; The Geologic Time Scale, 874; Gondwanaland and Pangaea, 982; Micropaleontology: Microfossils, 1674; Paleobiogeography, 1984; Stratigraphic Correlation, 2485; Unconformities, 2563; Uniformitarianism, 2571.

PEGMATITES

Type of earth science: Economic geology

Pegmatites are veinlike bodies of coarse-grained granitic rock that host the world's major supply of the rare metals lithium, beryllium, rubidium, cesium, niobium, and tantalum. They are also major sources of tin, uranium, thorium, boron, rare earth elements, and certain types of gems. Pegmatite-forming fluids evolve by efficient crystal-liquid fractionation and extreme concentration of water, boron, phosphorus, and fluorine in the residual melt.

Principal terms

APLITE: a light-colored, sugary-textured granitic rock generally found as small, late-stage veins in granites of normal texture; in pegmatites, aplites usually form thin marginal selvages against the country rock but may also occur as major lenses in the pegmatite interior

CRYSTAL-LIQUID FRACTIONATION: physical separation of crystals, precipitated from cooling magma, from the coexisting melt, enriching the melt in elements excluded from the crystals; this separation, or fractionation, leads to extreme concentration of incompatible elements in the case of pegmatite magma

FLUID INCLUSIONS: microscopic drops of parental fluid trapped in a crystal during growth; inclusions persist indefinitely unless the host crystal is disturbed by deformation or recrystallization

INCOMPATIBLE ELEMENTS: chemical elements characterized by odd ionic properties (size, charge, electronegativity) that tend to exclude them from the structures of common minerals during magmatic crystallization

SOLIDUS/LIQUIDUS TEMPERATURE: the liquidus temperature marks the beginning of crystallization in magmas, and the solidus temperature marks the end; crystals and melt coexist only within the liquidus-solidus temperature interval

VISCOSITY: a property of fluids that measures their internal resistance to flowage; the inverse of fluidity or mobility

Summary of the Phenomenon

Pegmatites are relatively small rock bodies of igneous appearance that are easily distinguished from all other rock types by their enormous range of grain size and textural variations. Typically, fine-grained margins of aplite are abruptly succeeded by discontinuous interior layers of coarse, inward-projecting crystals, which, in turn, give way to zones of graphically intergrown quartz and alkali feldspar. Most pegmatites contain numerous isolated pockets, rafts, and radial clusters of abnormally large, even giant, crystals and are cut by fractures filled with late-stage products. The spatial inhomogeneity of mineral distribution, rock texture, and chemical elements exhibited in pegmatites is unequaled in any other igneous product.

The majority of pegmatites are narrow lens-shaped, tabular, or podiform masses measuring from a few meters to several tens of meters in length. Even large, commercially exploited pegmatites rarely exceed 1 kilometer in length and 50 meters in width. Nearly all pegmatites have a bulk composition approximating that of granite. They are composed predominantly of quartz, alkali feldspar, and muscovite, with minor quantities of tourmaline and garnet. Those containing only these minerals are termed simple pegmatites, the word "simple" referring to their mineralogy, chemistry, and internal structural features collectively. Complex pegmatites are composed of the same major mineral assemblage but, in addition, contain a great variety of exotic accessory minerals which host rare metals such as lithium, rubidium, cesium, beryllium, niobium, tantalum, and tin. These pegmatites are also called rare-element or rare-mineral pegmatites, and they are of major economic and strategic importance. In contrast to simple types, they are complex in terms of mineralogy, chemistry, and internal structure. Beyond their economic value, rare-element pegmatites are of interest because they crystallize from the most evolved, or fractionated, granitic magmas in nature. They are the extreme product of extended crystal fractionation and therefore occupy a unique position between normal igneous rocks and hydrothermal vein deposits. The remainder of this article deals exclusively with this important class of pegmatites.

Major rare-mineral pegmatites may exhibit systematic internal variations in mineralogy and texture that are termed zoning. The usual zonal pattern begins with a thin selvage of aplite, a few centimeters thick at most, which typically grades into the country rock. The aplite selvage is abruptly succeeded by a coarse-grained muscovite-rich zone which, by decrease in muscovite abundance, passes into a zone dominated by quartz and feldspar that may also carry abundant spodumene. The innermost zone is composed mainly or exclusively of quartz. Ideally, the zones are crudely parallel structures symmetrically disposed with respect to the center line of the host pegmatite. In a real pegmatite, however, it is usually found that individual zones vary in terms of width, continuity, and position with respect to the center line of the body. The zonal pattern records the inward growth of a pegmatite from the enclosing walls of country rock. The bulk chemical composition of each individual zone is an approximate indication of the composition of the parental magma at the time the zone formed. It follows that the inward zone sequence is an approximate record of compositional changes that occurred in the evolving parent magma as the pegmatite formed. The existence of a common zonal pattern must mean that most pegmatite magmas evolve in a broadly similar fashion.

In most zoned pegmatites, the zone structure is disrupted by crosscutting units of replacement minerals that extend outward from the core. The replacement bodies postdate the zones they cross and are formed by fluids derived from the parent magma at an advanced stage of fractionation. Late-appearing fluids migrate upward along fractures in the solidified pegmatite walls, making space for replacement minerals by dissolving susceptible zone minerals in their path. In spite of the general similarity in zone pattern shown by rare-mineral pegmatites as a class, no two bodies are ever exactly alike in terms of the size, shape, and spatial distribution of their zones. The mineral assemblages and textures that comprise individual zones are, however, surprisingly consistent. Excluding the selvage, most zoned pegmatites are composed of five distinct mineral assemblages: coarse microcline with or without pollucite; quartz with subordinate lithium aluminosilicate minerals and with amblygonite-montebrasite; massive quartz (virtually monomineralic bodies); albite (sodium feldspar) or fluorine-rich mica bodies that contain abundant tourmaline, apatite, beryl, iron- and manganese-bearing phosphates, rare earth element phosphates, zircon, and niobium-tantalum-tin oxides; and mixed zones of sequential deposition (composed of very coarse-grained microcline and spodumene or petalite within a finer-grained matrix of albite).

Gross chemical inhomogeneity and remarkable concentrations of exotic minerals have earned zoned rare-mineral pegmatites a reputation for complex chemistry. In fact, the overall bulk composition of most such rock bodies is a rather simple one, dominated by the common elements oxygen, silicon, aluminum, sodium, and potassium, which comprise the major pegmatite mineral phases of quartz, albite, microcline, and muscovite. Water and lithium oxide are next in importance, water forming generally 0.5-1.0 weight percent, and lithium oxide being present in amounts up to roughly 1.5 weight percent. Oxides of phosphorus and iron usually comprise several tenths of a percent each. The elements calcium, magnesium, and manganese are present in trace amounts only. The total concentration of rare elements (beryllium, boron, cesium, rubidium, tantalum, niobium, tin, tungsten, uranium, thorium, fluorine, and rare earths), for which pegmatites are famous, is somewhat less than 1 percent by weight in almost every case. This composition, except for the high lithium component, is essentially that of normal alkali granite. The lithium concentration in normal granites, however, is only approximately one-seventieth of that in typical lithium-bearing pegmatites. The reason for the extreme concentration of lithium in the final stage of pegmatite formation is not yet understood but is presumed to involve an extremely efficient fractionation process. The bulk composition of a pegmatite body is often assumed to be approximately equivalent to its parent magma. That does not apply to the water content, because most pegmatite magmas exsolve water during crystallization, which then diffuses outward into the surrounding country rock. This loss of water raises the important issue of the loss of additional elements that may be present in the exsolved aqueous solution. Most major pegmatites that have been studied in detail are, in fact, surrounded by intense metasomatic aureoles enriched in pegmatite-derived potassium, sodium, fluorine, and boron. Therefore, in any given pegmatite, the assumed equivalence between pegmatite parent magma and bulk rock composition should be viewed with caution until the degree of host rock metasomatism is known.

Granitic magmas, irrespective of their origin, always contain small initial quantities of dissolved water and incompatible elements such as boron, phosphorus, and fluorine. These components do not participate in the formation of the large amounts of feldspar and quartz that ultimately crystallize from such a magma. Instead, they are concentrated in the remaining melt (also called residual melt or rest liquid), which systematically diminishes in volume as a result of crystallization. Magma normally begins to solidify along its contacts with the surrounding, cooler country rocks, and as a result, the walls and roof of a crystallizing pluton grow inward and confine the residual melt to a central position beneath the pluton roof. Generally, the residual melt either is consumed by crystallization or escapes along roof/wall fractures to form granitic or aplitic dikes before it becomes water saturated. If the initial water content of a magma is abnormally high or the crystallization of anhydrous phases is particularly efficient, however, water saturation may occur in the residual magma while a significant volume of it yet remains. Continued crystallization will produce a separate aqueous fluid, which increases in volume as the residual melt solidifies. The appearance of a distinct aqueous fluid, coexisting with a residual water-saturated silicate melt, is called the "first boiling" of the magma. Because cooling and crystallization proceed inward from the enclosing rock, it seems reasonable to assume that saturation occurs first near the margins of the magma body. The condition of saturation in the marginal silicate melt tends to make it impermeable to water movement (either into or out of the residual melt). Consequently, additional crystallization causes boiling within this "closed system," and the resulting aqueous fluid exerts increasing pressure on the surrounding shell of solidified magma. If the roof rocks rupture during this stage, the accumulated aqueous fluid will rapidly move up through the fractures and into the cooler country rock. This process is referred to as the "second boiling" of a magma.

Experiments have firmly established that water, as a dissolved constituent in magma, lowers both the liquidus and solidus temperatures significantly. Water also lowers the viscosity of the residual melt, which is a major factor in promoting the growth of the large crystals that distinguish pegmatites from normal igneous rocks. Traditionally, pegmatites have been considered to be "post-boiling" phenomena produced by complex but unspecified interactions between water-saturated silicate melt of low viscosity, a separate coexisting aqueous fluid, and the enclosing rocks. Several important experiments, however, have shown that water vapor in equilibrium with coexisting granite melt has relatively low solvent power with respect to certain major and trace elements concentrated in rare-mineral pegmatites. Further, fluid inclusion data from pegmatite minerals, a field studied intensively by Soviet geologists, indicate that the trapped fluids are relatively dense and thus intermediate in character between silicate melt and simple aqueous solutions. These data are important because they imply that pegmatite minerals crystallize from highly evolved silicate magma rather than from any aqueous solution that may be present. If that is true, it is likely that one or several incompatible elements in the magma are responsible for the extreme concentration of rare metals in pegmatite magma.

A number of lines of evidence suggest that boron, phosphorus, and fluorine play key roles in this regard. On account of their incompatible nature, these elements will be highly concentrated, along with water, in a residual melt prior to "first boiling." Theoretical considerations suggest that high levels of these elements will have two major effects in silicate magmas. First, they will delay water saturation, or "boiling," by increasing the solubility of water in the residual melt, and, second, they will promote concentration of Group I elements (lithium, sodium, potassium, rubidium, cesium) in that melt. Thus, the result will be a water-rich, sodium-aluminosilicate-rich, late-stage melt from which albite, tourmaline, phosphate minerals, fluorine-rich micas, beryl, zircon, and niobium-tantalum-tin oxides can crystallize prior to boiling. Such a melt would possess the required low viscosity and low solidus temperature (below 500 degrees Celsius) required to enable pegmatite magma to migrate significant distances from the parent pluton prior to crystallization. High concentrations of boron, phosphorus, and fluorine in the late-stage melt can produce the additional important effect known as immiscibility. At some critical concentration, the single parent melt can split into two mutually insoluble "partner melts" with drastically contrasting chemical compositions. One partner melt will be very rich in silica and could form massive quartz zones enriched in lithium minerals. The remaining partner melt would be a strongly alkaline silicate melt capable of producing albite-dominated zones. The eventual boiling of the boron-phosphorus-fluorine-enriched late-stage melt is not excluded in this theoretical sequence of events, but it does not play the pivotal role in forming pegmatite that has long been attributed to it. The appearance of a mobile aqueous fluid, capable of transporting excess potassium, sodium, fluorine, and boron into the surrounding host rocks, is required for those pegmatites enclosed by intense metasomatic aureoles. At the present stage of knowledge, however, aqueous solutions do not appear to be chemically capable of concentrating major quantities of lithium, rubidium, cesium, beryllium, zirconium, niobium, and other metals that must, therefore, remain in the silicate melt. The fine-grained aplite border selvage displayed by most pegmatites suggests that the initial injection of pegmatite magma occurred while it was still in a water-unsaturated state. The abrupt inward textural transition to coarse-grained interior zones may be an indication that water saturation occurs during (not before) the emplacement process. The crystallization of tourmaline has been shown to be a very effective means of concentrating water in the residual melt and has been suggested to be a "triggering process" to produce rapid water saturation.

Methods of Study

In the past, studies of pegmatites have mainly concerned either the evaluation of their economic potential or their exotic mineralogy. Surprisingly few efforts have focused on pegmatites in a coherent and systematic fashion, and as a result, satisfying theories for their origin are poorly developed relative to other areas of igneous petrology. A comprehensive study of pegmatites in a particular region would include not only the pegmatites but also the country rocks that enclose them and any bodies of exposed granitic rock. Study begins with preparation of a geologic map showing the distribution of pegmatite bodies, by type, throughout the area of interest. The map is compiled from firsthand, detailed observations of rock out-croppings obtained by numerous foot-traverses across the area. Additional useful information may be obtained from earlier geologic maps, aerial photographs, satel-lite imagery, and mine records. In most cases, the geologic map will show numer-ous, small, discontinuous pegmatite veins cutting older, high-grade metamorphic country rocks. These are known as external pegmatites. If any granite plutons are present in the area, they must be examined closely, as they are potential parent bodies of the pegmatites. Such granites may themselves host so-called internal pegmatites. External and internal pegmatites, even if derived from the same peg-matite magma (cogenetic pegmatites), generally will differ in mineralogy and zon-ing traits. It is a considerable achievement if a study can demonstrate that groups of external and internal pegmatites derive from the same parent body of granite. In such a case, the geologist has the rare opportunity to study the chemical and temporal relationships between parent rock, host rock, and an evolving, mobile pegmatite magma. This happy state of affairs is seldom realized, because of the all-important "level of erosion." Since external pegmatites form by migration of peg-matite magma upward and away from the parent body along fracture pathways, they will normally be destroyed by erosion before their deeper parent and internal "relatives" are exposed.

By examining a large pegmatite-bearing area, rather than a single pegmatite body (as is often done), it is possible to determine if systematic differences exist in the exposed pegmatites relative to host-rock type, local or regional fracture patterns in the host rock, or distance from igneous plutons. Individual pegmatites can also be compared in terms of shape, size, orientation, mineralogy, and zone characteristics. Systematic variations of these parameters on the scale of a geological map con-stitute "regional zoning." Increased recognition of such effects is needed to provide greater insight to the operation of the pegmatite-forming process.

After regional geologic relationships are determined, individual pegmatites are mapped in the greatest detail possible (often at scales as large as 1 inch per 10 feet). The objective is to determine the size, shape, and zone sequence of each pegmatite body, which, in turn, will provide a basis for sampling and determining the com-position of the pegmatite as a whole. Every effort is made to establish the correct sequence of zone crystallization, because the bulk compositions and fluid inclusion data from each member of the zone sequence can then be used to trace chemical changes in the pegmatite magma during the emplacement process.

Once the bulk composition of a pegmatite body is known, it is then compared with the theoretical "minimum" composition of granite. The minimum composi-tion is that of the last drop of granite melt to crystallize; it shifts systematically with temperature and pressure. If a pegmatite bulk composition approximates that of the minimum, the pegmatite probably is of strictly igneous derivation, and its crystalli-zation temperature and pressure are approximately given by that of the minimum.

On the other hand, if the bulk composition differs significantly from the minimum, a more complex history, probably involving metasomatism, is indicated. Even in cases where metasomatism is not indicated by pegmatite bulk compositions, it is a good idea to determine the average composition of the country rock that hosts the pegmatite. Samples for this purpose must be collected well away from the pegmatite and any other potential sources of contamination. The host rock is then sampled at varying distances from the pegmatite contact. If these samples vary among themselves in chemical composition, and especially if they show systematic variation from the average host rock composition, metasomatism is indicated (meaning that chemical exchange has occurred between the host rock and the pegmatite magma and that the pegmatite did not evolve as a pure igneous system). This important aspect of pegmatite study has been so neglected that, at present, it is impossible to specify how important a role metasomatism plays in pegmatite formation.

Context

Pegmatites are relatively small, veinlike, igneous bodies noted for their textural and chemical inhomogeneity. Most are simple coarse-grained equivalents of granite, consisting mainly of quartz, microcline, albite, and muscovite. In the past, large and favorably located simple pegmatites were often worked for mica, quartz, and feldspar by the glass and ceramic industries, but production of this type has all but ceased. The post-World War II electronics revolution and other technological advances, such as the new lithium batteries, have fueled ever-increasing demands for the rare elements found in complex pegmatites.

Rare-element pegmatites with commercial grades and reserves that are sufficiently close to the surface for low-cost open-pit mining are distinctly uncommon. The few that do exist are the only sources for the elements lithium, beryllium, cesium, rubidium, tantalum, and niobium; they are important sources for boron, tin, tungsten, uranium, thorium, fluorine, and rare earth elements (lanthanides) as well. Because many of the pegmatites in current commercial production are located in Third World countries, some industrialized countries (the United States among them) stockpile rare-element commodities of strategic importance in case of national emergencies or supply disruptions.

As an example of how important a single Third World pegmatite can be, consider the Bikita pegmatite located some 250 kilometers southeast of the capital city of Zimbabwe, Africa. This pegmatite is a low-dipping, sheetlike, zoned body, 2.36-2.65 billion years old, which cuts even older country rocks of Archean greenstone. With an exposed length of 2 kilometers and a true width of 45-60 meters, the Bikita pegmatite is a fraction of the size of most producing mines. Yet, it is the largest, most productive pegmatite in the world, and its reserves of lithium, beryllium, and cesium are the largest on the planet. Bikita was formerly known for the production of tin, tantalum, and niobium from high-grade "pockets" of cassiterite, tantalite, and microlite in the quartz-rich zone, but these are now largely depleted. Current production of lithium, beryllium, and cesium is sustained by vast quantities of the ore minerals petalite, lepidolite, spodumene, pollucite, beryl, eucryptite, and amblygonite.

Complex pegmatites are valued for reasons other than commercial production of rare elements. From ancient times, they have been mined for precious and semiprecious gems. The intermediate zones of certain pegmatites are the major source of gem-quality topaz, tourmaline, and beryl (including morganite, aquamarine, and emerald). Each year, hundreds of small, commercially subeconomic rare-element pegmatites are prospected by amateur and professional collectors of rare minerals and fine crystals. These pegmatites are, in fact, supporting a small but vigorously growing industry. Many, perhaps even most, of the spectacular crystal specimens displayed in museums were obtained from subeconomic pegmatites by amateur collectors.

Bibliography

Best, Myron G. *Igneous and Metamorphic Petrology*. New York: W. H. Freeman, 1982. A popular university text for undergraduate majors in geology. A well-illustrated and fairly detailed treatment of the origin, distribution, and characteristics of igneous and metamorphic rocks. Chapter 4 treats pegmatites briefly; chapter 8 discusses late-stage magmatic processes pertinent to pegmatite formation.

Cameron, Evan N., R. H. Jahns, A. H. McNair, and L. R. Page. *Internal Structure of Granitic Pegmatites*. Urbana, Ill.: Economic Geology Publishing, 1949. This classic study of North American pegmatites during wartime illustrates the strategic nature of pegmatite deposits. The detailed maps and descriptions of American pegmatites are the basis for most textbook treatments of pegmatites. Valuable descriptions are given of bodies subsequently removed by mining. Aimed at professionals but can be understood by college-level readers with some background in geology. Will be found in any university library.

Desautels, Paul E. *The Mineral Kingdom*. New York: Grosset & Dunlap, 1972. One of many superbly illustrated books devoted to minerals and gems for hobbyists and serious collectors. A skillful blend of art, science, and history of minerals, with a useful index. Very suitable for high school readers and those interested in the aesthetic aspects of gems and crystals.

Guilbert, John M., and Charles F. Park, Jr. *The Geology of Ore Deposits*. 4th ed. New York: W. H. Freeman, 1985. A splendid new edition of a traditional college text for undergraduate geology majors. Pegmatites are treated on pages 487-507. The influence of the early work by Cameron (1949) is striking. Excellent photographs of pegmatite textures and outcrops and a comprehensive review of traditional American perspectives on pegmatites.

Hutchison, Charles S. *Economic Deposits and Their Tectonic Setting*. New York: John Wiley & Sons, 1983. An economic geology text for undergraduate majors in geology. The strength of this book is its modern international perspectives (in contrast to the Guilbert and Park text) on various classes of ore bodies, including pegmatites (pages 125-129). Figure 6-10 presents the Varlamoff spatial classification of pegmatites, which is widely known outside the United States, as well as an excellent cross section of the famed Bikita pegmatite.

Klein, Cornelis, and Cornelius S. Hurlbut, Jr. *Manual of Mineralogy.* 20th ed. New York: John Wiley & Sons, 1985. This twentieth edition of a standard mineralogy text for college students with some geology background provides an excellent index of mineral names and tabulates chemical formulas, crystal systems, and physical properties of all the common mineral species and many of the rare ones encountered in pegmatites. This basic mineralogy text is essential for anyone embarking on a study of rare-mineral pegmatites. A brief pegmatite summary is given on pages 485-486.

Norton, James J. "Sequence of Minerals Assemblages in Differentiated Granitic Pegmatites." *Economic Geology* 78 (August, 1983): 854-874. This article updates the classic zone sequence of Cameron (1949) by constructing one that takes into account the Bikita and Tanco pegmatites (the world's largest). The account is technical but understandable by college-level readers with some background in geology. The data tables and bibliography will be useful to anyone with a serious interest in pegmatites.

Gary R. Lowell

Cross-References

Hydrothermal Mineralization, 1108; Igneous and Contact Metamorphic Mineral Deposits, 1124; Crystallization of Magmas, 1420; Water in Magmas, 1433; Earth Resources, 2175; Strategic Resources, 2188.

PETROGRAPHIC MICROSCOPES

Type of earth science: Geochemistry
Field of study: Analytical techniques

The petrographic microscope is an essential tool for studying the mineral content and texture of fine-grained rocks. It also provides a rapid and accurate means for identifying minerals through their optical properties.

Principal terms

ANISOTROPIC CRYSTAL: a crystal with an index of refraction that varies according to direction with respect to crystal axes

BIREFRINGENCE: the difference between the maximum and minimum indices of refraction of a crystal

CRYSTAL AXES: directions in a crystal structure with respect to which its molecular units are organized

INDEX OF REFRACTION: the ratio of the speed of light in vacuum to its speed in a particular transparent medium

INTERFERENCE: the combining of waves or vibrations from different sources so that they are in step and reinforce each other or are out of step and oppose each other

INTERFERENCE COLOR: a color in a crystal image viewed under crossed polars, caused by subtraction of other colors from white light by interference

INTERFERENCE FIGURE: a shadow shape caused by the blocking of polarized light from certain areas of a crystal image

POLARIZATION: filtration of light so that only rays vibrating in a specific plane are passed

PRINCIPAL VIBRATION DIRECTIONS: directions in a crystal structure in which light vibrates with maximum or minimum indices of refraction

RETARDATION: the progressive falling behind of part of a ray vibrating in a slower direction compared to a part vibrating in a faster direction

Summary of the Methodology

The crystals of many rocks and deposits are too small to be distinguished—much less identified—by the naked eye. Individual crystals can be distinguished under an ordinary microscope, but identification in this manner is still difficult. A powerful improvement was discovered in 1828 by William Nicol when he applied to the microscope his newly invented polarizing prisms cut from calcite crystals and found that different minerals have very distinctive appearances in polarized light. The modern petrographic microscope is a refinement of Nicol's discovery.

The petrographic microscope is similar to a standard biological microscope but has adaptations for use with polarized light. A polarizer (or "polar") beneath the condenser lenses polarizes the light before it passes through the specimen. A circular, rotatable stage allows the slide and specimen to be turned with respect to the polarized light. A second, removable polarizer called the analyzer, oriented crosswise to the lower polar, can be inserted into the light path in the tube, providing "crossed polars." There are other accessories used for special purposes. Under the polarizing microscope, crystals show bright, distinctive colors called interference colors. As the stage is turned, these colors move and change or become dark ("extinct") in ways that can be used to identify the minerals. It is the interaction of light with the crystal structure that causes the distinctive behavior.

Light is an electromagnetic wave. As a ray of light travels along, its electric field strength oscillates back and forth transverse to the path of the ray, somewhat like the vibration that travels along a horizontal rope when it is shaken up and down at one end. The vibration direction and the travel path are perpendicular. The distance traveled by the ray between one maximum of the transverse field and the next is the wavelength of the light. Each color of visible light has its own particular wavelength, ranging from roughly 700 nanometers for red to 400 nanometers for violet (a nanometer is one-billionth of a meter). White light is a mixture of all colors.

All light travels at the same speed in vacuum, but in a transparent medium, it is slowed by interaction with matter. The speed is characteristic of a given medium and is indicated by its index of refraction; the greater its index, the slower light moves through it. The speed in air (index 1.000) is essentially the same as in vacuum; but in quartz (index 1.54), it is only 65 percent of that, and in diamond (index 2.42), it is only 40 percent.

The atoms or molecules in crystals are arranged in a strict order, repeated over and over to make the crystal structure (or "lattice"). The structure is responsible for many characteristic features of minerals, such as the natural shapes and faces of crystals and the likelihood of breaking along flat surfaces called cleavages. The pattern of any given mineral is very distinctive, so the ways in which light interacts with the different structures can be used to identify the various minerals.

Minerals are classified as isotropic or anisotropic. In isotropic crystals, light can travel any direction at the same speed, and the index of refraction has the same value for all orientations. Isotropic minerals all have a molecular structure and spacing that are identical along each of three perpendicular crystal axes. Some common examples are halite (rocksalt) and garnet. Glass substances, which are equally disordered in all directions, are also isotropic. In anisotropic minerals, the molecular structure and spacing are different along one or more crystal axes. In such crystals, the interaction of light vibrations with matter—and, therefore, the speed of light and the index of refraction—depend on the direction of travel. The analyst, in order to identify the minerals, must know the detailed differences among the crystal structure systems and how light interacts with them. For the present purposes, however, a single fact is important: The speed of light traveling along most paths through anisotropic crystals depends on the direction of vibration. Even along the same path, light vibrating in one direction may be faster or slower than light vibrating in another (with both vibration directions being perpendicular to the travel path).

The polarizer under the stage allows the analyst to select the vibration direction. Without it, the rays of light rising vertically through the specimen vibrate parallel to the stage but with random orientation. The polarizer absorbs all these rays except those vibrating in one specific direction, which is usually fixed back-to-front or sideways in the field of view. The analyst turns the specimen on the stage to change the orientation of the crystals to the polarized light.

An anisotropic crystal viewed down the microscope tube, in general, has one direction with maximum index of refraction and another perpendicular to it with minimum index. A ray vibrating parallel to the first would be the slowest, while the other would be the fastest. A ray oriented in any other direction actually separates into two parts, each part vibrating in one of the two directions but following the same vertical path. The part vibrating in the higher index direction is slower than is the other and falls progressively farther behind; it is said to be retarded. The amount of retardation depends on how far the parts travel (the thickness of the crystal) and on the difference in their speeds (and, thus, on the difference of their indices of refraction, called the birefringence). Because each color has its own particular wavelength, the amount of retardation affects whether the vibrations of the two parts of a given color are in step with each other (in phase) as they exit the crystal or determines how much they are out of step.

The analyzer (the upper polarizer) blocks all light vibrating parallel to the lower polarizer because it is oriented at right angles. Thus, the glass of the slide and any isotropic crystals appear black, as they do not alter the polarization. Similarly, the two separated parts of a ray from an anisotropic crystal, if they happen to emerge in step, recombine in the original polarization, and this light is blocked also. Although if one part is retarded out of step with the other (so that, recombined, they have a rotating "elliptical polarization"), the analyzer in effect deals with each part individually. It resolves each part once more and allows only those portions parallel to the analyzer vibration direction to pass. The passed portions of each part now vibrate in the same plane but are out of step with each other. Depending on how much they are out of step, the vibrations may reinforce each other and strengthen the color or oppose each other and weaken the color. Colors that are weakened or canceled are subtracted from the original white light, and what remains to be viewed is the complementary color. A sheet of mica placed between crossed Polaroids shows this effect well even without a microscope.

The interference colors that result from this process are one of the most striking features of crystals viewed under crossed polars. Because they result from the subtraction of specific colors from white light, some more and some less, they fall in a sequence that is distinctly different from an ordinary spectrum. Beginning with black when there is no retardation (the passed rays are in step), as retardation increases, the colors go through gray and white to orange and red for the first "order," then through several cycles from red through blue for higher orders, eventually merging to pinks and greens, and finally to more or less white for very high orders. The sequence is displayed on a Michel-Levy chart (which shows the sequence of colors as a function of birefringence). The colors that actually appear in a given crystal give important information about the mineral.

Applications of the Method

Samples for microscopic examination are usually prepared either as a powder or as a thin section. The powder is made by crushing a mineral grain and screening it very fine; a small amount of the powder is then placed on a microscope slide with a drop of oil. The thin section is made by sawing a slice off of the sample, gluing it to a slide, then further sawing and grinding the slice until it is only 0.03 millimeter thick. In such thin samples, most minerals are transparent or translucent, although metals and many sulfide minerals are still opaque. Special reflection techniques can be used to examine opaque minerals.

With either preparation, the first goal is to identify the minerals present by observing their visible properties. Features of shape, such as a characteristic crystal form, habit, cleavage, or fracture (keeping in mind that only a cross section is visible), give the first clues to identity. For example, garnets often exhibit a polygon-like cross section of their characteristic crystal form, and mica usually shows its perfect one-directional cleavage. Typical colors may be present (with polars un-crossed), although they are much fainter than in a hand sample. Some minerals, like tourmaline or biotite mica, change color as they are turned in the polarized light; these minerals are called pleochroic.

The relief of a crystal indicates the contrast between its index of refraction and that of its surroundings. Minerals with high relief appear to stand out from their background and have very distinct boundaries, while those with low relief are hard to distinguish from their background. If neighboring minerals or a medium (mounting or immersion) of known index are present, the analyst can estimate the index of refraction of an unknown mineral from its relief. The analyst can measure the index of minerals in powdered form exactly by comparison with standard index oils (called the immersion method). If the index of the mineral matches the oil closely, the grain boundary almost disappears. Anisotropic crystals require a different oil for each vibration direction. Having measured the indices, the analyst can then consult a table to identify the mineral.

If the indices cannot be measured directly, as in a thin section, the birefringence (the difference between maximum and minimum indices) gives useful information for identification. The interference colors in a crystal depend on its birefringence and its thickness (usually approximately 0.03 millimeter in a thin section). The analyst compares the highest interference colors found in a crystal to a Michel-Levy chart, determines the corresponding birefringence, and consults a table to identify the mineral.

The relationships between the vibration directions and visible features such as crystal faces and lines of cleavage give another clue to identity. At every quarter-turn as an anisotropic crystal is turned on the stage, there is a point at which the crystal becomes completely dark, or extinct. Extinction occurs whenever the crystal's vibration directions are parallel to the polarizer or analyzer. The angle between an extinction direction and a crystal face or cleavage can distinguish between many otherwise similar minerals, such as the pyroxenes and amphiboles. Isotropic minerals like garnet are extinct at all positions of the stage.

Interference figures provide another powerful means of identifying crystals. They are shadows with distinctive shapes that appear with crossed polars and diverging light because polarized light is blocked from certain areas of the crystal image. Special lenses are used to cause the light to diverge and to change the focus of the eyepiece. The shadow figures, which depend on the nature and orientation of the crystal, take the shapes of Maltese crosses or sweeping curves that move in distinctive ways as the stage is turned. The analyst can use them to determine many details about the crystal structure, the relationships of the vibration directions, and other features useful for identification.

Microscopic analysis of crushed mineral grains (powder) is the most efficient way to identify any mineral (and some nonmineral substances) whose crystals are large enough to distinguish with a microscope. Thin sections are less efficient, but they have other advantages because they preserve the structure of the original sample; they are essential for the study of fine-grained rocks. By calculating the relative abundance of each kind of mineral, examining the shapes of grains and the ways they contact each other, and studying the distribution of grains and larger structures like bedding, the analyst can identify the rock type, estimate its properties, and interpret clues to its history. For example, a thin section of sandstone under the microscope would show the shape of the sand grains, fine details of its bedding, the amount of cement between grains, the amount of empty space, or porosity, and the presence and distribution of any mineral grains besides the quartz sand. This information could be used to estimate its mechanical strength for engineering purposes, its ability to hold water or oil, or its potential as a quarry stone, raw material for glassmaking, or an ore of uranium.

A polarizing microscope adapted to view reflected rather than transmitted light is commonly used by metallurgists to study the identity, size, and texture of metal crystals produced in industrial processes. Economic geologists use the reflection microscope to identify opaque, metal-bearing minerals and to determine their abundance in samples from an ore body.

Context

The petrographic microscope is an important tool for identifying many kinds of minerals and other substances that cannot easily be distinguished by ordinary physical and chemical tests. It has been used, for example, to determine the nature of corrosion products on metal surfaces; the corrosion products indicate which chemical reactions might be responsible for the damage and, therefore, how the surfaces might be protected. In another application, the microscope has been used to study the different materials traded commercially or displayed in museums as "jade." Officially, the name "jade" is applied to rocks composed of either an amphibole called nephrite or a pyroxene called jadeite, but the microscope revealed that much of what has been called jade is really composed of other minerals similar in appearance. The study showed historically significant patterns in the use of different kinds of jade in various cultures.

The petrographic microscope has many applications to areas in which geology touches on the economy or on public safety. Rock that has been sheared and fractured, as by faulting, shows distinctive texture and structure in thin section. Knowledge of these features in the rock of a given region can be important in the prediction of earthquake potential or in the evaluation of stability for engineering projects. Thin sections also show the amount of empty space, or porosity, between the grains in a rock, which is essential for estimating the potential of the rock for bearing oil, for carrying groundwater, or for allowing the passage of pollutants and radioactive waste. In the mining industry, thin sections are used to identify and evaluate the abundance of ore minerals and also to determine their grain size and how they are locked into the rock structure; all these factors determine whether the minerals can be recovered at a profit.

There are many anisotropic substances besides minerals. Whenever there is a distinct alignment of long molecules in a substance, polarized light may interact with it and reveal interference colors. Some biological tissues, structures in cells, plastics, and glasses have such anisotropic structures, and polarized light is useful for studying them. In one application, polarized light is used to study the distribution of stress in engineering structures such as machine parts and architectural members. The structure is modeled with a plastic such as Lucite and viewed through crossed polars. When the model is placed under load, the plastic develops interference colors that are concentrated at points of maximum stress.

Fiber-optic systems for transmission lines and optical switching devices developed for telephone and computer communications depend on the differences of the indices of refraction of their various parts. The polarizing microscope, which shows the differences by interference colors, is a key instrument for designing and testing such systems. New kinds of microscope systems using other kinds of radiation are becoming widely employed, but the polarizing light microscope will continue to hold a central importance both in the field of geology and outside it.

Bibliography

Craig, James R., and D. J. Vaughan. *Ore Microscopy.* New York: John Wiley & Sons, 1981. The first three chapters (on the reflection microscope, preparation of polished specimens, and qualitative properties of minerals) give a compact overview of how the technique of reflection microscopy is used. Knowledge of basic mineralogy is assumed. Most of this college-level text is beyond the interests of the casual reader. The index is thorough, but the tables and references are technical.

Hecht, E., and A. Zajac. *Optics*. Reading, Mass.: Addison-Wesley, 1974. A college-level text with considerable advanced mathematics, so well written and illustrated that a courageous nonmathematical reader can ignore the equations and still gain insight on many topics, especially polarization. Interesting examples and home experiments. Technical bibliography. An excellent index including many historical references.

Kerr, Paul E. *Optical Mineralogy*. 4th ed. New York: McGraw-Hill, 1977. A college-level textbook emphasizing the identification of minerals in and interpretation of thin sections. The chapters on theory presume a knowledge of basic optics and mineralogy but provide a good summary of applications to the microscope. An ample bibliography, a selective index, excellent tables, and individual mineral descriptions make this a solid reference work for identifying common minerals.

Klein, Cornelis, and Cornelius S. Hurlbut, Jr. *Manual of Mineralogy*. 20th ed. New York: John Wiley & Sons, 1985. A college-level introduction to mineralogy. Contains a thorough discussion of crystal systems and concise descriptions of all common minerals, including essential optical data. Chapter 6 contains a summary of the construction and use of the petrographic microscope. Well illustrated and indexed, with key references after each chapter.

MacKenzie, W. S., and C. Guilford. *Atlas of Rock-forming Minerals in Thin Section*. New York: Halsted Press, 1980. The bulk of this short atlas consists of excellent color photographs of thin sections designed to show how common minerals appear with crossed and uncrossed polars. The minimal text identifies the minerals and key points of interpretation. Illustrates typical features but also shows the beauty of rocks in thin section.

Rochow, T. G., and E. G. Rochow. *An Introduction to Microscopy by Means of Light, Electrons, X Rays, or Ultrasound*. New York: Plenum Press, 1979. Thorough coverage of basic principles and the construction of various types of microscope. Very readable (high school level), with little scientific background presumed. The reader willing to cross-reference in this well-indexed volume will find technical terms carefully defined. Abundant useful illustrations, including views of thin sections. Michel-Levy chart included. Broad bibliography.

Sinkankas, John. *Mineralogy*. New York: Van Nostrand Reinhold, 1975. A wide-ranging and effective introduction to the nature and properties of crystals, written for the amateur. Very helpful illustrations. Chapter 8 contains an easy approach to many concepts needed to understand the petrographic microscope but applied instead to the simpler polariscope. Roughly one-half of the 585 pages are devoted to individual minerals. Useful tables and selected bibliography, with index.

Stoiber, Richard E., and S. A. Morse. *Microscopic Identification of Crystals*. Reprint. Malabar, Fla.: Robert E. Krieger, 1981. A compact, college-level text emphasizing the use of immersion oils for identification. The explanation of polarization and interference is clear and detailed, with many helpful illustrations, using a mostly geometrical approach.

James A. Burbank, Jr.

Cross-References

Earthquake Engineering, 430; Fluid Inclusions, 726; Foliation and Lineation, 747; Geochronology: Fission Track Dating, 826; Igneous and Contact Metamorphic Mineral Deposits, 1124; Igneous Rock Classification, 1138; Lunar Rocks, 1414; Metamorphic Rock Classification, 1553; Metamorphic Textures, 1578; Micropaleontology: Microfossils, 1674; Physical Properties of Minerals, 1681; The Structure of Minerals, 1693; Physical Properties of Rocks, 2225; Sedimentary Mineral Deposits, 2296; Sedimentary Rock Classification, 2304.

PHASE CHANGES

Type of earth science: Geochemistry

Phase changes among liquids, solids, or gases are important in many geologic processes. The formation of ice from water, of minerals from magma, of gases bubbling out of magma, and of halite (sodium chloride) precipitating out of a lake are examples of phase changes in nature. Many of these phase changes aid in the understanding of deposits that are of economic importance.

Principal terms

GAS: a substance that can spontaneously fill its own container

IGNEOUS ROCK: a rock formed from molten rock material (magma or lava)

LIQUID: a substance that flows

MAGMA: a liquid, usually composed of silicate material and suspended mineral crystals, that occurs below the earth's surface

METAMORPHIC ROCK: a rock in which the minerals have formed in the solid state as a result of changing temperature or pressure

PHASE: that part of nature that has a more or less definite composition and thus homogeneous physical properties, with a definite boundary that separates it from other phases

PRECIPITATE: the process in which minerals form from water or magma and settle out of the liquid

SEDIMENTARY ROCK: a rock that has formed from the accumulation of sediment from water or air; the sediment might be fragments of rocks, minerals, organisms, or products of chemical reactions

SOLID: a substance that does not flow and has a definite shape

Summary of the Phenomenon

A phase has a more or less constant chemical composition and physical properties, with a boundary that separates it from other phases. Phases can include many different kinds of solids and liquids, but there can be only one gas phase.

Three different minerals in a rock—for example, quartz, plagioclase, and alkali feldspar—constitute three separate phases. The number of separate mineral grains is not the same, however, as the number of phases. There might be 231 grains of quartz, 257 grains of alkali feldspar, and 199 grains of plagioclase in a given rock, but the rock does not contain this many different phases. Instead, there are only three phases in the rock, corresponding to the three different minerals with the same composition and physical properties. Some minerals have the same composition but different arrangements of the atoms, so they may be considered separate phases. The calcium carbonate minerals calcite and aragonite are examples. Ice is another example of a solid phase.

There are also many liquid phases. Water is a liquid with the same composition as ice. Ice cubes and the water in which they float may be considered as two separate phases, since the ice and water have different physical properties (ice is lighter or less dense than the water, for example) and are separated by boundaries. Melted rocks form liquid rock material called magma. The magma may be considered one phase, while any minerals suspended in it are considered separate phases.

Two or more liquids may coexist as separate phases if they do not mix. Oil and water form separate layers with a boundary between them, so they are separate phases. Being less dense than the water, the oil floats on top of the water. Similarly, carbonate-rich magmas may not mix with many silicate-rich magmas, and they may form separate liquid phases. Water and ethyl alcohol, on the other hand, mix in all proportions and thus form only one homogeneous phase with no boundary surfaces. In a similar fashion, two silicate magmas of somewhat different composition may mix and form a homogeneous magma of an intermediate composition.

Though it may seem difficult to visualize, some solids of different composition may be able to mix partially or completely in all proportions. The silicate mineral olivine, for example, can accommodate any ratio of magnesium to iron into its composition; the magnesium end member is said to have a complete solid solution with the iron end member. Gases, in contrast to solids and liquids, mix in all proportions. The earth's atmosphere, for example, is a fairly homogeneous mixture of nitrogen (the predominant gas) and oxygen. There are also small amounts of other gases, such as water vapor and carbon dioxide.

Phase changes abound in nature. Ice changes to water at 0 degree Celsius, and at one atmosphere pressure and 100 degrees Celsius, water changes to steam. Such phase changes may differ with changes in atmospheric pressure. At about 200 times atmospheric pressure, the boiling point of water is more than 300 degrees Celsius, and the freezing point is less than 0. At a pressure of less than 0.006 atmosphere, liquid water is not stable; rather, ice changes directly to water vapor at less than 0 degree Celsius without any intervening water phase. There is even one temperature (0.1 degree Celsius) and pressure (0.006 atmosphere), called the triple point, in which ice, water, and steam coexist.

The phase relations of water have direct application to understanding the formation of certain features on Mars. Some features appear to have been formed by a running fluid such as water. The atmospheric pressure of Mars is currently too low for the planet to have any running water. Billions of years ago, however, Mars's atmospheric pressure might have been high enough to permit stabilized water to exist there. Thus, water could have been an erosional agent on Mars early in that planet's history.

Important phase changes also occur among solids in metamorphic rocks. Metamorphic rocks were formed from other rocks by chemical reactions in the solid state because of differing temperature and pressure. The minerals kyanite, andalusite, and sillimanite are different aluminum silicate minerals with the same composition occurring in metamorphic rocks. Phase changes among these three solids depend on temperature and pressure, as in the ice-water-steam system; no liquid or gas, however, is involved in the aluminum silicate minerals. The triple point of the aluminum silicate minerals is at about 600 degrees Celsius and nearly 6,000 times atmospheric pressure (6 kilobars), so changes among these minerals take place only deep within the earth. Sillimanite is stable from about 600 degrees Celsius and 5-6 kilobars up to more than 800 degrees and 1-11 kilobars. In contrast, andalusite is stable at pressures up to only 6 kilobars over a wide range of temperature (200 to 800 degrees). Kyanite is also stable over a wide temperature range but at a higher pressure for a given temperature than is the case for either andalusite or sillimanite. For a geologist, then, knowing which of these aluminum silicate minerals is present in a rock helps to show the range of temperature and pressure at which the rock formed. There are also solid-to-liquid phase changes in sedimentary systems. A variety of minerals may crystallize or precipitate from water to form sediments.

In igneous rocks, too, there are many phase changes among solids and liquids. Igneous rocks form from the crystallization of minerals from magma or melted rock, usually of silicate composition. As magma slowly cools within the earth, it forms minerals that gradually either sink or float in the magma, depending on their density (weight in relation to volume). The minerals that are heavier or denser than the magma gradually sink, and the lighter or less-dense minerals gradually float upward. The magma composition gradually changes as the minerals are extracted, because the minerals' composition is different from that of the magma. Magma forms by the melting of solid rock in the lower crust or upper mantle of the earth. The magma's composition will depend on the composition of the rock melted, the pressure, and the degree of melting. Also, the magma composition will be different from that of the solid. The melting of a typical rock in the upper mantle, for example, will produce a basaltic magma. A basaltic magma will produce a dark, fine-grained rock of low silica content, called basalt, when extruded at the surface of the earth. The melting of a silica-rich rock in the continental crust is more likely to produce magma with a high silica content. These high-silica magmas will crystal-lize to light-colored rocks called dacite or rhyolite when extruded at the surface.

The maximum amount of a mineral that may be dissolved in water is called its saturation point. Different minerals have different saturation points in water. Con-siderably less calcite (calcium carbonate mineral) may dissolve in water than gyp-sum (calcium sulfate mineral). Even more halite (sodium chloride) may dissolve in water than gypsum. If the saturation points for these minerals are exceeded, the minerals will begin to crystallize or precipitate and sink to the bottom of the water. Saturation points of minerals may be exceeded when water evaporates or when the temperature changes. If seawater is present in a bay in which evaporation exceeds the influx of new seawater, calcite, gypsum, and halite may precipitate, in that order, as the water gradually evaporates. Vast amounts of salt deposits of halite and gypsum are believed to have formed in this fashion during the geologic period called the Permian (about 250 million years ago) in Kansas and Oklahoma. Such salt deposits are not nearly as common as are limestones. Limestones are sedimentary rocks composed of mostly calcite. The calcium carbonate is believed to have precipitated in warm, shallow seas either by inorganic precipitation or by organisms forming calcite or aragonite. The precipitation of calcite or aragonite is aided by the evaporation of seawater in shallow seas and by warming of the water.

Methods of Study

A variety of techniques are used to study phase changes. The technique selected to study phase changes depends on the pressure, temperature, and types of phases. The easiest phase changes to study are those involving precipitation of minerals from water solutions at atmospheric pressure and temperature. One of the intriguing problems in the study of sedimentary rocks, for example, is why among ancient rocks so much limestone that is composed of calcite and dolostone is composed of dolomite (a calcium/magnesium carbonate mineral), as modern sediments seem to be forming mostly aragonite and calcite. Little dolomite is apparently forming today. Experiments in the laboratory have helped geologists to explain such observations. The precipitation of calcite and aragonite in the laboratory is temperature-dependent. A temperature of about 35 degrees Celsius, for example, favors precipitation of needlelike crystals of aragonite. In contrast, a lower temperature of 20 degrees favors precipitation of mostly stubbier crystals of calcite.

To identify the minerals, scientists observe them under a microscope or by X-ray diffraction. X-ray wavelengths and the distances between atoms in the minerals are about the same, so the X rays will be reflected off planes of atoms in the mineral. The angle of reflection depends on the distance between the atoms and the wavelength of the X rays. Since every mineral has different spacings between atoms, the reflections of different minerals have different angles and serve as a "fingerprint" for the mineral. Thus, calcite and aragonite can easily be distinguished; it is difficult, however, to produce dolomite under any conditions in the laboratory. Such laboratory observations are consistent with the observed abundance of aragonite needles in warm, shallow seas and with the greater abundance of calcite forming from cooler waters. They are also consistent with the lack of observed dolomite formation.

Other experiments in furnaces at high pressure tell geologists that aragonite is in reality stable only at a pressure much higher than atmospheric pressure. Aragonite is unstable at atmospheric pressure, so any aragonite forming presently should slowly revert to the more stable calcite with time. This fact explains why there is no aragonite in ancient rocks.

The only dolomite that can form in the laboratory is produced by the conversion of calcite to dolomite in contact with concentrated waters with a high magnesium-to-calcium ratio. Thus, only under special geologic conditions below the land surface will calcite convert—slowly—into dolomite. Waters high in magnesium moving through calcite-rich rocks below the surface will convert the calcite into dolomite over long periods of time. This process may be occurring in certain places presently, though it simply cannot be observed.

Experiments involving phase changes at higher pressure and temperature are more difficult to carry out because of the problem of controlling and measuring the temperature and pressure. In some experiments, a cylindrical container or hydrothermal vessel composed of a special steel alloy is hollowed out in the center so that a sample container may be placed inside of it. The sample container is composed of pure gold or platinum and is sealed at one end. The sample and some water are placed in the container, and the other end is sealed. The container is placed inside the hydrothermal vessel, and water is pumped into the container and heated to the desired temperature. As the temperature gradually rises, the water vapor must periodically be released so that the pressure does not rise too high and rupture the hydrothermal vessel. The gold or platinum container distorts easily and transmits the pressure to the sample inside the container. After the experiment has continued for the desired length of time, the container is suddenly cooled so that the sample is frozen in the state it had reached at the higher temperature and pressure. Suppose the experimenter is studying the melting of rocks. After the sudden cooling, he may find that some of the sample is glass with embedded crystals of one or more minerals. Presumably the glass represents liquid that was quickly "frozen." The minerals may be identified by observing them under a microscope or by using X-ray diffraction. The exact mineral and glass composition may be determined through the use of an electron microprobe. In this technique, a narrow electron beam is focused on a part of the material to be analyzed, causing electrons of various elements to be removed from the atoms. Other electrons take the places of the removed electrons. X rays of certain specific energies are then emitted; because these are characteristic of a given element, that element may now be identified. The number of gamma rays or their intensity depends on the amount of the element in the sample; thus, the concentration of the element may be determined.

The mineral and glass composition at a series of temperatures and pressures may be determined during the gradual solidification of a silicate liquid, for example, to understand how the crystallization of the minerals may change the composition of the liquid. These liquid changes in the experiment may then be related to the changing composition of a series of natural lavas to see whether they might have formed by a similar process.

Context

Phase changes occur in familiar processes every day. The phase changes from ice to water to water vapor are familiar to most people. Ice is less dense than water, so the ice takes up more space than does the original water. A drink placed in a freezer may explode as a result of this phase change. This effect is avoided in automobile cooling systems when ethylene glycol is mixed with the water; the freezing point of this mixture is much lower than that of water. Ice floats in water because of its lower density. What if ice were more dense than water? Then ice would surely sink to the bottom of lakes and oceans, and it might remain there the year round. Profoundly different oceanic, lake, and atmospheric circulation and very different climates and ecosystems would be the result.

People cook with boiling water. It is generally known that the boiling point of water decreases with increased elevation as the pressure is reduced. Cooking time must thus be increased to compensate for this lowered boiling temperature at higher elevations. Alternately, salt could be added to the water to raise the boiling point.

Water vapor in the atmosphere can increase only up to a certain maximum point, called the saturation point. This saturation point varies with temperature. More water vapor may be contained in warmer air. Rainfall results when warm, saturated air rises and cools. The cooler air cannot hold as much moisture as can warmer air, so rain falls.

An understanding of phase changes is essential for an understanding of geological processes. The concentration of elements in geologic systems involves one or more phase changes. The so-called fractional crystallization process, for example, involves the precipitation of minerals from a slowly cooling magma. The minerals either sink or rise in the magma, depending on whether they are heavier or lighter than the same volume of the magma. Some elements are more concentrated in the minerals than in the magma; others are more concentrated in the magma than in the minerals. Some elements may boil out of magma with water vapor and become concentrated in hydrothermal deposits. Common table salt (sodium chloride) forms vast deposits where large, saline bodies of water evaporated slowly over long periods of geologic time, much as the Great Salt Lake in Utah is doing today. Animal matter may slowly change to petroleum or natural gas when buried gradually below the surface of the earth. As large swamps are gradually buried, they may be transformed into coal. Buried deep, some of this material may change to graphite (all carbon). The mineral diamond (also all carbon) may have existed as graphite before it was transformed to diamond at even greater pressure within the earth.

Bibliography

Brownlow, Arthur H. *Geochemistry*. Englewood Cliffs, N.J.: Prentice-Hall, 1979. A variety of phase changes are discussed in this introductory text in geochemistry. Suitable for a college student who has taken introductory courses in geology and chemistry. Many illustrations.

Ehlers, Ernest G. *The Interpretation of Geological Phase Diagrams*. San Francisco: W. H. Freeman, 1972. An excellent and very detailed discussion of the principles used to interpret geological phase diagrams in geology. Suitable for college-level students with basic knowledge of mineralogy and chemistry.

Ernst, W. G. *Earth Materials*. Englewood Cliffs, N.J.: Prentice-Hall, 1969. This book is part of a series which supplements introductory textbooks in geology. Discusses mineralogy, igneous rocks, sedimentary rocks, and metamorphic rocks in more detail than do most introductory textbooks. Features good treatments of phase changes and phase diagrams in all the rock types. Accessible to the college-level student who has studied general geology.

_____. *Petrologic Phase Equilibria*. San Francisco: W. H. Freeman, 1976.

A detailed treatment of phase diagrams in geologic processes. Appropriate for college students with background in chemistry and mineralogy. Illustrated.

Krauskopf, Konrad B. *Introduction to Geochemistry.* New York: McGraw-Hill Book Company, 1979. In this well-written introductory geochemistry text a variety of phase changes are discussed in detail. College students who have taken geology and chemistry courses will find it helpful. Contains many figures.

Mason, Brian. *Principles of Geochemistry.* New York: John Wiley & Sons, 1968. An introductory college-level text in geochemistry. Includes some discussion of phase changes. Illustrated with many figures.

Robert L. Cullers

Cross-References

PHASE EQUILIBRIA

Type of earth science: Geochemistry

The mineral assemblages in most igneous and metamorphic rocks preserve a record of the chemical equilibrium related to the initial rock-forming process. Phase equilibria studies attempt to determine quantitatively the pressure/temperature conditions of rock formation from these mineral assemblages.

Principal terms

DEGREE OF FREEDOM: the variance of a system; the least number of variables that must be fixed to define the state of a system in equilibrium, generally symbolized by F in the phase rule $(P + F = C + 2)$

EQUILIBRIUM: the condition of a system at its lowest energy state compatible with the composition (X), temperature (T), and pressure (P) of the system; the smallest change in T, P, or X induces a state of disequilibrium that the system attempts to rectify

ISOCHEMICAL PROCESSES: processes that leave rock compositions unchanged; in thermodynamic terms, a system in which X remains constant even if T and P change

MOLE: the amount of pure substance that contains as many elementary units as there are atoms in 12 grams of the isotope carbon 12

PHASE: any part of a system—solid, liquid, or gaseous—that is physically distinct and mechanically separable from other parts of the system; a boundary surface separates adjacent phases

PHASE DIAGRAMS: graphical devices that show the stability limits of rocks or minerals in terms of the variable T, P, X; the simplest and most widely used are P-T diagrams $(X = \text{constant})$ and T-X diagrams $(P = \text{constant})$

SYSTEM: any part of the universe (for example, a crystal, a given volume of rock, or an entire lithospheric plate) that is set aside for thermodynamic analysis; open systems permit energy and mass to enter and leave, while closed systems do not

THERMODYNAMICS: the science that treats transformations of heat into mechanical work and the flow of energy and mass from one system to another, based on the assumption that energy can neither be created nor destroyed (the first law of thermodynamics)

Summary of the Phenomenon

The traditional methods of studying rock bodies are descriptive in nature and involve mapping large-scale outcrop features in the field and detailed microscopic observations of rock textures and mineralogy in the laboratory. These methods, successful by themselves, are supplemented by a second, more theoretical, approach wherein rocks are treated as chemical systems and the principles of phase equilibria are applied to determine the conditions of their origin. A full and complete description of a rock body is still required, but that is no longer the main goal of petrologic study. The principles of phase equilibria are simply the laws that govern attainment of equilibrium of chemical reactions such as $A + B = C + D$, where A and B are known as reactants, and C and D are known as products. Before exploring how these principles cast light on rock-forming processes, the concept of chemical equilibrium must first be developed. By analogy with gravitational potential, there must exist a similar tendency in chemical systems to lower their energy state through chemical reactions. Reasoning along these lines, J. Willard Gibbs introduced the term "chemical potential" to describe the flow of chemical components from one site (of high potential) to another (of lower potential) during reactions that lead a chemical system toward its lowest energy state. The total energy available to drive a chemical reaction must therefore be the sum of the chemical potentials of each component in the system multiplied by the number of moles of each component. The usual definition of chemical potential of a phase (or pure substance) is "the molar free energy" (or free energy per mole). This simple statement leads to a workable, three-part definition of chemical equilibrium, which is central to the understanding of phase equilibria: First, if the chemical potential of a component is the same on either side of a reaction equation, the component can have no tendency to participate in the reaction; second, in a multicomponent system consisting of several phases under uniform temperature (T) and pressure (P), equilibrium must prevail when the chemical potential of each component is the same in all phases in which the component is present; third, the condition of equilibrium is one of maximum chemical stability. The second part of the definition is equivalent to saying that, for a given chemical reaction, the free energy of the reactants must equal the free energy of the products if a condition of chemical equilibrium prevails under fixed conditions of T and P. If either T or P changes, the system is no longer in equilibrium, but it will immediately adjust itself in such a way as to "moderate" the effect of the disturbing factors. The last statement is known as the moderation theorem, or Le Chatelier's principle. If the free energy on the product side of an equation is less than the free energy on the reactant side, the reaction will be spontaneous. If the opposite is true, no reaction is possible. Scientists are thus able to predict the result of any chemical reaction if the free energy of the reactants and products under the reaction conditions (T, P) is known.

The major rock-forming processes—magmatism, metamorphism, and sedimentation—all involve large-scale flow of energy and movement of matter that produce an uneven distribution of chemical potential. Inevitably, the result must be chemical reactions tending to restore these natural systems to a state of equilibrium. The equilibrium state of a system is governed by its bulk composition (X), temperature (T), and pressure (P). For most geological processes, T and P change slowly relative to the rates of most chemical reactions, which means that most rock-forming reactions may be considered to take place under constant T and P and, if X also remains constant, most such reactions should easily attain chemical equilibrium. In geology, the major concern then is not so much with achievement of equilibrium but rather with preservation of equilibrium mineral assemblages through hundreds of millions of years, which must follow before deep-seated rocks are finally exposed at the surface. Rocks formed at depth must clearly undergo significant reductions in T and P prior to exposure at the surface, and there are several mechanisms that may induce changes in X during this lengthy period. Geologists are acutely aware of the implications of the moderation theorem: Retrograde metamorphism, mineralogical inversions and exsolutions, hydrothermal alteration, and weathering are but a few of the processes that could trigger reequilibration in rock bodies before they are exposed for study. Fortunately, microscopic studies coupled with Gibbs's pioneering work in phase equilibria provide the means to discern whether a given mineralogical assemblage preserves a former equilibrium.

The "phase rule," now generally called the Gibbs phase rule, was initially derived by Gibbs in 1878 from the mathematical formalities of thermodynamics. The phase rule, which is fully applicable to all chemical systems, expresses the relationship between the governing variables T, P, X and the number of phases that may coexist in a state of equilibrium. Usually the phase rule is expressed in equation form as $P + F = C + 2$, where P = number of phases, C = number of chemical components, and F = degrees of freedom possessed by the system (normally T, P, X). Phases are chemically pure, physically separable subparts of the system and may be gases, liquids, or solids. In the formal sense C is the minimum number of chemical entities needed to define completely the composition of each reactant and product phase in a given reaction.

Although the objective of phase rule applications is to determine F for major rock-forming reactions, a far simpler situation that could be experimentally verified in any high school laboratory or even in an ordinary kitchen may be considered. Pure water (H_2O) boils at T = 100 degrees Celsius at sea level (P = 1 bar; atmospheric pressure). The effect of dissolving common salt (NaCl) in water is to raise the boiling temperature approximately 0.8 degree Celsius for each mole percent NaCl in the liquid phase. The steam given off by boiling is pure H_2O and, therefore, the salt concentration in the remaining liquid must progressively increase with temperature during boiling. To apply the phase rule to this simple system, one first must tally up the participating phases: there is steam and there is liquid salt solution, and one must conclude that P = 2. Both pure water and salt are required to form these coexisting phases and, therefore, C = 2. The phase rule for this process (boiling), under conditions of fixed pressure (P = 1 bar), tells one that

$$
\begin{aligned}
F &= C - P + 2 \\
&= 2 - 2 + 2 \\
&= 2
\end{aligned}
$$

Therefore, the system has two degrees of freedom and is said to be "divariant," which means that, because one degree of freedom is utilized by fixing P = 1 bar, only one additional variable need be known to specify completely the state of the system. That may be either T (boiling temperature) or X (composition of boiling solution); in other words, T and X are dependent variables at constant P. This T-X compositional dependence is easily determined for P = 1 bar by direct experiment. If the resulting T-X data were graphically plotted, the diagram would indicate, for example, that the boiling temperature for an 8 mole percent solution is close to 106 degrees Celsius. Conversely, if it were known only that the boiling temperature of a salt solution were 106 degrees Celsius, that would necessitate a solution concentration of 8 mole percent at P = 1 bar.

To apply the phase rule to a reaction that has some geological significance, consider the appearance of diopside in siliceous dolomite during contact metamorphism by the reaction

$$CaMg(CO_3)_2 + 2\ SiO_2 = CaMgSi_2O_6 + 2\ CO_2$$
$$\text{(dolomite)} \quad \text{(quartz)} \quad \text{(diopside)} \quad \text{(gas)}$$

The reaction involves three mineral phases and a fugitive gas phase, which is necessarily lost from the rock if diopside appears; P = 4. Note that the Ca:Mg (calcium-to-magnesium) ratio is the same in the reactant phase (dolomite) and the product phase (diopside); consequently, the minimum number of components needed to define the compositions of the four phases in the reaction is three. Therefore, C = 3. Substituting these values into the phrase rule, one obtains

$$F = C - P + 2$$
$$= 3 - 4 + 2$$
$$= 1$$

and the reaction above has one degree of freedom and is said to be univariant. For any given reaction pressure, the phases appearing in that reaction can coexist in equilibrium at one, and only one, temperature. Univariant reactions are of great interest to petrologists because it is frequently possible to estimate the depth of a rock-forming reaction and, hence, P, from field relationships. It is then a simple matter to estimate the reaction temperature from the P-T diagram for the univariant reaction involved. For example, suppose that field relationships lead to the conclusion that diopside-bearing contact metamorphic rocks formed by the reaction above at an estimated depth of 4 kilometers. The pressure equivalent of this depth is about 1,000 bars; the experimentally derived P-T diagram indicates a reaction temperature of about 450 degrees Celsius.

The principles of phase equilibria were first applied to rocks in 1911 by V. M. Goldschmidt in his classic account of contact metamorphism in the Oslo area in Norway. Countless similar attempts have followed, with most authors concluding, as did Goldschmidt, that rocks, in general, record a state of chemical equilibrium governed by the temperature and pressure prevailing at their time of origin. The major generalization emerging from eighty years of such studies is that rocks with a large number of mineral phases tend to have a low number of degrees of freedom. Goldschmidt recognized that, at Oslo, metamorphism must be controlled mainly by T and P and that divariant equilibrium (F = 2) is the general case for isochemical rock-forming reactions. For F = 2, the phase rule reduces to P = C. Dubbed "the mineralogical phase rule," this equation cannot be mathematically derived from thermodynamic principles. It simply reflects the common case in nature where rock-forming processes are approximately isochemical and their phase equilibria are controlled by both T and P operating as independent variables. It follows that rocks recording univariant equilibria are more restricted in occurrence than those recording divariant equilibria. Similarly, the rarity of rocks recording invariant equilibria (F = 0) can be understood, as the phase rule requires that both a unique T and a unique P be maintained during their formation. Rocks of complex mineralogy are occasionally encountered in which the number of phases, P, exceeds C + 2 and, consequently, the value of F is negative. Phase rule departures, indicated by negative F values, are a sure sign of disequilibrium and serve as a reminder that not all mineral assemblages can be treated by the methods of phase equilibria.

Methods of Study

The temperature and pressure range in which any mineral may exist is limited, and it is the task of experimental petrology to ascertain these limits for rock-forming minerals. The data resulting from this experimental work are utilized to construct "phase diagrams." Such diagrams show the effects of changing P, T, X values on mineral stability fields and are, therefore, simply graphical expressions of the phase rule. In metamorphic petrology, the major use of phase equilibria data has been for construction of "petrogenetic grids." A petrogenetic grid, initially conceived by N. L. Bowen in 1940, is a P-T diagram on which experimentally derived univariant reaction curves are plotted for a particular metamorphic rock type (for example, blueschists, marbles, calcsilicates, or pelites). The value of such "grids" lies in the fact that each natural equilibrium assemblage recognized in the field will fall within a definite P-T pigeonhole and thereby inform the field geologist immediately of the P-T conditions of the metamorphic terrane under study. This goal, so simple in concept, has proven elusive even after half a century of vigorous experimental, theoretical, and field effort. The problem lies in the lack of truly univariant reactions. For nearly seventy years, field geologists mapped isograds recording the "first appearance" of notable zone minerals such as biotite, garnet, staurolite, kyanite, and sillimanite under the impression that they represented the intersection of the ground surface with a plane of univariant equilibrium. Virtually all such "isograds" have proven to be the result of divariant equilibria and thus plot as a "band"—which may be rather wide—on a P-T diagram. This undesirable result has the effect of "smearing" grid boundaries and rendering them less useful as metamorphic indicators.

The general absence of univariant reactions in metamorphic rocks was eventually recognized because of theoretical and experimental advances in phase equilibria studies. The problem stems from the fact that most mineral phases participating in metamorphic reactions are solid solutions of variable composition and the commonest reactions lead to the release of a fluid, the composition of which may vary with time. Each of these effects introduces an additional degree of freedom in phase rule terms, and, as a result, virtually all important reactions are divariant. In spite of these difficulties, petrogenetic grids, based on divariant and quasi-univariant equilibria, have gradually evolved for all major metamorphic rock types. These are not the simple, quantitative grids envisioned by Bowen, but they do provide quick, reliable, and fairly narrow estimates of P-T conditions for common metamorphic mineral assemblages. Modern grids, continually subject to refinement, are phase equilibria's greatest contribution to metamorphic petrology.

In the area of igneous petrology, phase equilibria methods and data have become indispensable. Natural rocks, spanning the compositional spectrum, are melted under strictly controlled laboratory conditions to determine solidus and liquidus temperatures at pressures ranging from 1 to 35,000 bars. The results of such experiments place tight constraints on depths and temperatures of magma generation. They also permit the experimentalist to explore P-T effects on partial melting (anatexis) in terms of melt composition and refractory solid phases. The resulting phase diagrams, like metamorphic grids, permit petrologists to "see" deep into the crust and upper mantle and to test hypotheses dealing with the origin of magma.

For nearly a century, igneous petrologists have studied crystal-melt equilibria of simplified, synthetic melts as models for complex, natural magmas. The objective is to reduce the number of equilibrium phases by elimination of minor components of real magmas. Studies of this type were introduced by Bowen at the Geophysical Laboratory of the Carnegie Institution in Washington, D.C. Through its many subsequent researchers, this laboratory published hundreds of phase diagrams and earned a reputation for meticulous and exhaustive experimental work.

Phase equilibrium studies have provided a rather complete understanding of two fundamentally different modes of magma crystallization. Equilibrium crystallization occurs when P-T-X conditions change so slowly that chemical reactions within the melt are able to maintain the state of chemical equilibrium. On the other hand, fractional crystallization results when changes in P-T-X conditions outpace the compensating reactions. This disequilibrium process greatly influences the behavior of natural magmas and extends the range of melt compositions that can be derived from a given parent magma. This latter type of behavior, recognized through the early phase equilibria studies of the Geophysical Laboratory, is the major factor in explaining the compositional diversity of igneous rocks.

The relatively simple phase diagrams of synthetic systems unraveled the complexities of sequential crystallization, cast light on the mechanics of crystal nucleation, and exposed the crucial role that water plays in magmatic processes. Collectively, these diagrams are the foundation of modern igneous petrology.

Context

Geologists look at rocks in three fundamentally different ways: as large mappable bodies in the field, as mineral mosaics under the microscope, and as "fossilized" products of chemical reactions from the distant past. The study of phase equilibria encompasses the latter point of view—and its goal is understanding the chemical nature of rock-forming processes. Each of the three approaches to rock study plays an important role in modern geology, but phase equilibria studies, alone, have the potential for quantitative determination of the pressure/temperature conditions of rock formation.

The origin of the phase equilibria approach is rooted in the mathematical formalisms of classical thermodynamics, which treats the flow of mass and energy from a general viewpoint. The basic relations that apply to chemically complex systems like rock bodies were derived by J. Willard Gibbs in a memoir entitled "On the Equilibrium of Heterogeneous Substances" (1876-1878). From his fundamental equation relating energy, entropy, and the masses of chemical constituents, Gibbs derived the conditions necessary for a state of chemical equilibrium. These conditions are now formalized in the powerful Gibbs phase rule, which lies at the center of phase equilibria study.

The refined symbolic notation and elegant mathematical derivations of thermodynamics are likely to remain unappreciated by the majority of laypersons and geologists alike. It is precisely these formalisms, however, that place phase equilibria on a quantitative footing and permit calculation of mineral stability fields from compositional data. Future development in the area of phase equilibria will follow this theoretical line.

The qualitative form of phase equilibria is expressed in phase diagrams rather than equations. Such diagrams have been a major part of petrology since the 1950's. Historically, emphasis in phase equilibria studies has been on high-temperature igneous and metamorphic rocks, which are most likely to preserve former equilibrium mineral assemblages. This preservation is the fundamental prerequisite for any application of phase equilibria methods. For this reason, the phase equilibria approach has generally not been applied to sedimentary rocks, except saline deposits formed by intense evaporation of seawater and record chemical equilibrium.

The phase diagrams and sophisticated calculations utilized in phase equilibria studies are often imposing, but that merely reflects the compositional complexity of natural rocks and minerals. What must be appreciated is that the goal of such studies is both simple and practical: to determine how rocks form. All processes taking place on or within the earth (as well as all other solar system bodies) involve the flow of energy and mass. If scientists wish to advance beyond simply describing these processes—that is, to understand the chemical nature of the world—the phase equilibria approach must be employed.

Bibliography

Angrist, Stanley W., and Loren G. Hepler. *Order and Chaos: Laws of Energy and*

Entropy. New York: Basic Books, 1967. An elementary treatment of basic thermodynamic concepts that lie behind phase equilibria studies. One of very few books that present this topic in nonmathematical terms. Aimed at high school readers.

Best, Myron G. *Igneous and Metamorphic Petrology.* New York: W. H. Freeman, 1982. A widely used text for undergraduate geology majors. The treatment skillfully balances the traditional and phase equilibria approaches to petrology. Chapter 1 introduces basic thermodynamic concepts from the geological perspective. Chapters 8 and 14 summarize phase equilibria applications to igneous and metamorphic processes, respectively. For college-level readers with some background in geology and chemistry.

Bowen, Norman L. *The Evolution of the Igneous Rocks.* Mineola, N.Y.: Dover, 1956. A reprint of the 1928 classic that first brought the phase equilibria approach to American geologists. Still valuable as an introduction to igneous processes, though some parts are dated. Suitable for college-level readers who have had a course in physical geology.

Ehlers, Ernest G. *The Interpretation of Geological Phase Diagrams.* San Francisco: W. H. Freeman, 1972. Aptly titled, this book is a "must" for those interested in the practical side of phase equilibria. A well-indexed guide to most chemical systems relevant to igneous petrology. Theoretical aspects of the subject are omitted, except for a terse presentation of the phase rule in chapter 1. For college-level readers with a knowledge of mineralogy.

Fermi, Enrico. *Thermodynamics.* Mineola, N.Y.: Dover, 1956. A reprint of the 1937 work by one of the most prominent physicists of the twentieth century. Concepts are presented simply and without regard to applications. For college-level readers with some background in calculus; others may still find the text valuable as the emphasis on mathematical derivation is minimal compared with modern books on the subject.

Fyfe, W. S., F. J. Turner, and J. Verhoogan. *Metamorphic Reactions and Metamorphic Facies.* New York: Geological Society of America, 1958. This monumental book established the thermodynamic approach in metamorphic petrology, and its influence is seen in all subsequent texts on the subject. A major reference for any serious student of metamorphism. Will be found in all university libraries.

Powell, Roger. *Equilibrium Thermodynamics in Petrology: An Introduction.* New York: Harper & Row, 1978. This text, as well as many others of recent vintage, treats phase equilibria as a problem-solving methodology rather than as a body of knowledge derived through field and laboratory work. Written for advanced students of geology, but chapters 1 and 2 are suitable for general readers seeking an introduction to equilibrium concepts and phase diagrams.

Gary R. Lowell

Cross-References

PHOBOS AND DEIMOS

Type of earth science: Planetology
Field of study: Large solar system bodies

The two moons of Mars, Phobos and Deimos, almost certainly originated as asteroids and will provide the first close look at these small components of the solar system. The two moons will also probably act as future bridgeheads to the exploration of Mars; as orbital way stations, they may provide future explorers of Mars with an orbital base and perhaps even with essential resources.

Principal terms

CARBONACEOUS ASTEROID: an asteroid made up principally of carbon and carbon-based materials

ELECTROLYSIS: a process whereby molecular water is broken down into oxygen and hydrogen

EQUATORIAL ORBIT: an orbit that directly overlies a planet's equator

OPPOSITION: when one planet or other astronomical body moves close to another in their respective orbits

REFLECTIVITY: a technique used to examine the amount of light reflected from a body

ROCHE LIMIT: the inner orbital limit of a natural satellite (moon) where the gravitational-tidal forces of the planet will break the moon into pieces

Summary of the Phenomenon

In early August of 1877, astronomer Asaph Hall began his search for the moons of Mars at the U.S. Naval Observatory in Washington, D.C. His search was initiated for two primary reasons. First, he found that many astronomy texts and ephemerides of the day contained serious errors and misstatements, one of which contended that Mars had no moons. Second, Hall knew from consulting Frederick Kaiser's summary of Martian observations in the Annals of the Leiden Observatory (1872) that few before had even looked. So, while Mars made its close approach to the earth in 1877 (an event called opposition), Hall used the Naval Observatory's 26-inch Clark refractor telescope to search for Martian moons.

Even as he began his search, Hall knew the chance of finding a Martian moon was slim. Any object even a fraction of the size of the earth's own moon would have been discovered long before. Any smaller object could not even exist at any great distance from Mars, as the sun's gravitational influence would snatch it away. Hall therefore began his search looking for a very small moon, probably orbiting very close to the planet, and therefore obscured in its glare, very close to the visible disk of the planet as seen through the telescopic lens. In view of these discouraging considerations, Hall said, "I might have abandoned the search had it not been for the encouragement of my wife." (This statement would become indelibly etched on the discovery.) On August 12, 1877, Hall first glimpsed one of Mars' two moons, which he confirmed on August 16. The next evening, he discovered a second moon. The announcement was made several days later by Navy admiral John Rodgers, the observatory's superintendent. The moons were named Deimos (meaning "flight" or "panic") and Phobos (fear) from Homer's *Iliad*: "He [Mars] spake, and summoned Fear and Flight to yoke his steed, and put his glorious armor on."

The first clear images of the moons were made from the U.S. Spacecraft Mariner 9 in 1972, and five years later, even more dramatic and detailed photographs were obtained by the U.S. Viking orbiter probes. The photographs revealed that the two moons are among the darkest bodies in the solar system; their surface is a flat black. Because of their density, size, and curious orbital characteristics, they are widely thought to be asteroids captured by the gravitational field of Mars. They are not circular in shape; some have even described their appearance as potato-shaped. Their tiny size allows for the weakest of gravitational fields, which will not permit the body to collapse into a spherical shape like that of planets and larger moons. Phobos, the larger of the Martian moons, has a diameter of 28 by 23 by 20 kilometers. Deimos' diameter measures 16 by 12 by 10 kilometers.

Phobos' orbit is exceptionally low—directly above the equator only 9,378 kilometers over the planet's surface—so low that it cannot be observed from the surface at latitudes greater than 70 degrees north or south. The orbit of Phobos is just above the Roche limit (where the planet's tidal forces would tear it apart). In fact, it probably will be torn apart and crash into the surface of Mars in the next 38 million years. Its orbital period is very fast; it circles the planet in only 7 hours and 39 minutes, making the moon appear to rise in the west and set in the east. Deimos' orbit is considerably higher, some 23,459 kilometers above the equator, with a period of 30 hours and 18 minutes. Deimos' orbit is high enough that it will eventually escape Mars' gravitational field and fly off into an independent orbit around the sun.

The first observations of the two moons showed them to be heavily cratered. Such cratering suggests their surfaces to be very old, nearly as old as the solar system itself, some 3-4 billion years. There are two very large craters (relative to the body's size) on Phobos. The largest crater, dominating Phobos' northern hemisphere, has been named Stickney, for discoverer Hall's wife. The astronomer himself has been remembered by a lesser surface marking: Crater Hall is a 6-kilometer depression on the moon's southern pole. Crater Roche lies near Phobos' north pole, a reminder of the moon's eventual fate as a result of Mars' dominant gravitational influence. As the Viking probe flew to within 88 kilometers of Phobos' surface, it photographed what appeared to be cracks, as wide as several hundred meters and up to 10 kilometers in length, emanating from Crater Stickney. These appear to be cracks in the moon's surface caused by the impacting body that formed the crater itself.

The surface of Deimos is not as spectacular as that of the larger moon. The

Viking probe flew to within 23 kilometers and resolved a relatively quiescent sur-face, with smaller craters (the largest discovered is only 2.3 kilometers across), no visible cracks, and a lack of a single spectacular formation.

The theory of asteroid origins was bolstered by the visual images. The extraor-dinarily dark surface and a density only twice that of water (half that of Mars) lent credibility to the theory that the moons were made of carbon and carbon com-pounds such as are conjectured for type C asteroids, which populate the outermost regions of the asteroid belt. The bodies may contain up to 20 percent water by weight. Why their orbits should be so nearly perfectly circular and equatorial has no easy explanation. In terms of capture probability, captured asteroids would not necessarily fit into such neat orbits (they would most likely be inclined and noncir-cular). Hence, for confirmation, such theories will have to await both the physical exploration of their surfaces and a firsthand look at carbonaceous asteroids them-selves.

The Soviet Union's probes to the Martian moon's surface were collectively called the Phobos mission. Two craft, Phobos 1 and Phobos 2, were launched from earth in the summer of 1988; their mission was to land on Phobos to analyze its surface. Communication with Phobos 1 was lost before it reached Mars' orbit. Phobos 2 successfully attained orbit around Mars in 1989 and began returning photographs of Phobos and Mars. On March 27, 1989, merely days before the probe's planned close encounter with Phobos and release of its landers, the spacecraft spun irretrievably out of control, and the mission was lost.

The intense interest in the tiny moons of Mars has been generated for several reasons. They provide a natural "space station" for future Mars explorers. Their tiny gravitational fields require very little energy to overcome, but they offer a stable platform for the staging of landing and observation parties. They may also contain substantial quantities of water that may one day be mined to provide (through electrolysis) hydrogen fuel and oxygen for space travelers, thus reducing the neces-sary burden of transporting it from earth or even from the surface of Mars. Finally, it will require less energy to fuel a mission to the moons of Mars than to and from the surface of the earth's own moon (because of the weak gravitational fields of Phobos and Deimos). Such a mission, which would require a minimal travel time of two to three years, is being seriously discussed by both the Soviet government and certain interests in the United States.

Methods of Study

The data obtained from the United States' space probes of Phobos and Deimos are photographic studies from the spacecraft cameras and mass studies based upon flyby navigation studies. The most detailed photographic studies were conducted with the Viking orbiter cameras. Viking Orbiter 1 flew by Phobos on February 12, 1977. Viking Orbiter 2 flew by Deimos on September 25, 1977. The photographic system on the orbiters was called the Viking Imaging System, which returned a total of 51,539 images of Mars and its moons to earth during the mission. The mass of

Phobos and Deimos was estimated by determining how much the spacecraft were deflected in their orbits around Mars by the mass of the moons and the resulting gravitational field produced by the mass of the bodies. Until the probe flybys, the moons' masses were unknown.

Photographic studies alone produced a wealth of information. A technique known as reflectivity—measuring the amount of light reflected from the surface of the moons—enabled planetary scientists to speculate that the moons may have been captured asteroids, as it has long been speculated that a class of asteroids made of carbon and carbon compounds would be exceedingly dark, as Phobos and Deimos proved to be.

The surfaces of the moons were saturated with craters, which indicated that their surfaces were very old, perhaps as old as the solar system itself. This finding enabled dating of the asteroids. In addition, the peculiar 10-kilometer crater on Phobos named Stickney displayed very large cracks down the surface of the moon, which hinted to some planetary geologists that the composition of the body may contain substantial amounts of water ice. The cracks also indicated other subsurface structural features as well as the depth of the regolith, or top layer of soil overlying the bedrock.

Context

The moons of Mars—Phobos and Deimos—will soon become two of the most important way stations in the solar system. As the earth's focus of exploration turns to Mars as the next most logical frontier of exploration and colonization after this planet's moon, Phobos and Deimos will serve as stepping-off points to the surface of Mars. They will provide a base for operations to and from the planet. They will also provide a communications base for ground to space and earth information exchanges. The two tiny moons may also be able to supply resource water for fuel and oxygen to equip future space explorers.

Plans are currently under way to consider sending a manned mission to Phobos as a dress rehearsal for a later mission to the surface of Mars. This mission would test the critical life-support and medical issues that are the current limiting factors to a Mars mission, at a fraction of the energy that would be required to land on the surface of the planet itself.

Bibliography

Beatty, J. Kelly, et al. *The New Solar System*. Cambridge, Mass.: Sky Publishing, 1982. This beautifully illustrated and well-crafted book was intended to bring the most recent planetary discoveries to light in a single source. Details the Martian moons. Written for the general reader; extensively illustrated.

Ezell, Edward, and Linda Ezell. *On Mars: Exploration of the Red Planet, 1958-1978*. NASA SP-4212. Washington, D.C.: Government Printing Office, 1984. This book is an official National Aeronautics and Space Administration (NASA) history of the Viking program, from the original ideas in 1958 to the culmination of the project some twenty years later. A detailed assessment of the political and technical history that also discusses details of the Martian moons. Written for all readers, it is generally nontechnical.

Flinn, E., ed. *Scientific Results of the Viking Project*. Washington, D.C.: American Geophysical Union, 1977. A compendium of articles about the Viking project as originally published in the *Journal of Geophysical Research*. Detailed, technical articles about the assessments of data from the Viking landers on the surface of Mars. Suitable for college-level readers.

Hartmann, William K., et al. *Out of the Cradle: Exploring the Frontiers Beyond Earth*. New York: Workman Publishing, 1984. This combination picture book and narrative of future human exploration discusses Mars as a logical next step for human exploration and settlement after the moon. It depicts the struggle of future colonists on Mars and includes a discussion of the Martian moons. The book is written for the general reader and is illustrated with an artist's conception of future planetary bases and explorers.

Joels, Kerry Mark. *The Mars One Crew Manual*. New York: Ballantine Books, 1985. This facsimile of what a future explorer's crew manual might look like is an excellent reference for what the future colonist may find on arrival at Mars. Written for all backgrounds; illustrated.

Miles, Frank, and Nicholas Booth. *Race to Mars: The Harper & Row Mars Flight Atlas*. New York: Harper & Row, 1988. A futuristic crew manual that relates the process of a flight to Mars and what the expedition members will encounter while there. Exquisitely photographed and illustrated. Provides a very detailed discussion of Phobos and Deimos and the Soviet Phobos mission. Written for all readers.

Mutch, Thomas A., et al. *The Geology of Mars*. Princeton, N.J.: Princeton University Press, 1976. This technical book is written in textbook style and is accessible to those with a college-level science background. A complete analysis of the recovered Viking data in a geological narrative. Illustrated, with photographs and tables.

Dennis Chamberland

Cross-References

Asteroids, 98; Lunar History, 1400; Mars' Craters, 1480; Mars' Polar Caps, 1487; Meteorites: Carbonaceous Chondrites, 1638; The Origin of the Solar System, 2442.

PLATE MARGINS

Type of earth science: Geology
Field of study: Tectonics

The outer 70-200 kilometers of the earth comprise a number of rigid plates that move about independently of one another. Each plate interacts with the adjacent plate along one of three types of plate margin: convergent, divergent, or conservative. The interactions of the moving plates along these margins cause most earthquakes as well as much of the volcanic activity on the surface of the earth.

Principal terms

ACCRETIONARY PRISM: a complex structure composed of fault-bounded sequences of deep-sea sediments mechanically transferred from subducting oceanic lithosphere to the overriding plate; it forms the wall on the landward side of a trench

ASTHENOSPHERE: the soft, partially molten, layer below the lithosphere

CONVECTION CELL: a single circular path of rising warm material and sinking cold material

LITHOSPHERE: the outer, rigid shell of the earth that contains the oceanic and continental crust and the upper part of the mantle

RIFTING: the process whereby lithospheric plates break apart by tensional forces

SEA-FLOOR SPREADING: the concept that new ocean floor is created at the ocean ridges and moves toward the volcanic island arcs, where it descends into the mantle

SUBDUCTION ZONE: a region where a plate, generally oceanic lithosphere, sinks beneath another plate into the mantle

TRANSFORM FAULT: a fault connecting offset segments of an ocean ridge along which two plates slide past each other

VOLCANIC ISLAND ARC: a curving or linear group of volcanic islands associated with a subduction zone

WADATI-BENIOFF ZONE: the inclined band of earthquake focus points interpreted to delineate the subducting oceanic lithosphere; better known as the Benioff zone

Summary of the Phenomenon

The surface of the earth is a mosaic of several large and more numerous smaller plates that move about laterally. The boundaries, or margins, of these plates are the sites of most of the volcanic and earthquake activity on the earth. The geological concept of the plate and plate margins ultimately has its origins in the theory of continental drift. The first comprehensive theories of continental drift were independently proposed around 1910 by the American geologists F. B. Taylor and H. H.

Baker and the German meteorologist Alfred Wegener. Wegener's work was particularly thorough, and he is generally considered to be the person who first made the theory of continental drift an important scientific issue. Wegener devoted much time and effort to matching geological features and fossil types on both sides of the Atlantic Ocean. He argued, based on this work, that approximately 230 million years ago, all the continents were joined as one supercontinent that he named Pangaea. Furthermore, Wegener suggested that Pangaea broke apart approximately 170 million years ago. Since then, the various parts of the supercontinent—the modern continents—have moved to their present positions. Wegener also postulated that as the continents move through the oceans, their leading edges become crumpled and often collide with other continents, thereby forming the mountain belts.

In the period after World War II, several important discoveries made by oceanographers studying the ocean basins lent support to Wegener's scoffed-at theory. This postwar research ultimately led to the formulation of the theory of sea-floor spreading proposed by Harry Hammond Hess of Princeton University. According to Hess's theory, new ocean floor is continuously forming at the ocean ridges, or the large subsea mountain ranges that traverse the earth, in a conveyor belt fashion. As this process continues, the newly formed sea floor moves laterally away from the ocean ridge on both sides of the ridge. The opening in the earth's surface created by the spreading of the sea floor at the ridge is filled with magma, or molten rock, from the mantle, which cools to form new sea floor. Hess and other scientists suggested that if the sea floor is continuously moving, the continents must also be moving with it. Thus, the concepts of continental drift and sea-floor spreading were combined into the more comprehensive theory of plate tectonics. This revolutionary theory in the earth sciences describes the movement of rock in the earth's 70- to 200-kilometer-thick outer brittle shell, the lithosphere, as it moves over the deeper, more ductile, partially molten asthenosphere. The lithosphere, which includes continental and oceanic crust and the upper part of the mantle, comprises a number of large and small, rigid lithospheric plates that move independently of one another. As these plates move, they interact along one of three types of plate margin: divergent or accreting margins, convergent or destructive margins, and conservative or neutral margins.

Divergent or accreting plate margins are tensional plate boundaries that correspond to the ocean ridges. According to plate tectonic theory, ocean ridges, also referred to as spreading centers, are sites on the earth's surface where new oceanic lithosphere is formed by the process of rifting, or the tensional separation of plates. Rifting can occur in the oceans as well as on the continents, as in the case of the East African rift zone. If rifting begins on a continent and continues for an extended period of time, a new ocean basin will ultimately form—as is now occurring in the Middle East, where the Red Sea rift is creating a new ocean between Saudi Arabia and northeastern Africa.

The crests of ocean ridges are characterized by deep valleys believed to have been caused by tensional faulting in response to oppositely directed lateral movement of the plates bound by the ocean ridge. This valley is referred to as the rift valley and is marked by a high degree of earthquake activity. The rift valley is also the site of voluminous outpourings of basaltic magma, or molten rock enriched in iron and magnesium.

Some of the most dramatic evidence of the processes occurring at divergent plate margins has come from a series of observations made from submersibles on the Galápagos spreading ridge near the equator, just west of South America and that part of the East Pacific Rise south of the Gulf of California. Researchers observed undersea hot springs and mounds of iron-rich clay minerals and manganese dioxide precipitated from the hot ore-carrying springs. Similar submersible dives to the Mid-Atlantic Ridge southwest of the Azores permitted observation of submarine volcanism and yielded abundant evidence of tensional faulting within the narrow rift valley.

Convergent or destructive plate margins are those areas of the earth's surface where the lithospheric plates grind together head-on and are then recycled back into the asthenosphere. Thus, these margins are characterized by compressive tectonic forces. Submarine features typical of convergent plate margins are long, narrow troughs on the sea floor referred to as trenches. Hess postulated that the trenches mark the positions where ocean lithosphere created at ocean ridges is drawn down or sinks into the mantle. The trenches, which are the deepest points of the oceans, are closely associated with volcanic island arcs, or linear or arcuate groups of volcanic islands such as Japan or the Aleutian Islands.

Convergent margins are characterized by a high incidence of earthquakes, many of which originate at depths greater than 600 kilometers within the earth. Scientists have demonstrated that the focus points of these earthquakes (those points within the earth from where the seismic energy is first generated) are generally found within a band inclined from the trench toward the volcanic island arc or continent called the Wadati-Benioff zone (better known as the Benioff zone). Realization of this distribution of earthquakes at convergent margins led scientists to speculate that the Wadati-Benioff zone delineates a slab of dense lithosphere formed at an ocean ridge that, according to plate tectonic theory, is sinking at the trench into the mantle. This process of lithospheric sinking at convergent margins is referred to as subduction. In general, the most powerful earthquakes at convergent margins are the shallow focus earthquakes generated close to the trenches. These earthquakes occur when a sinking lithospheric plate moves beneath an island arc or a continent and drags the overriding plate down a bit. Eventually, this process reaches a critical point, and sudden slip occurs along the boundary of the sinking plate and the plate beneath which it is moving, thereby creating the earthquake.

The volcanic island arcs, like the distribution of earthquake focus points, can be considered in terms of the process of subduction. The basic question concerns how the magma that spewed from the volcanic islands forms beneath the island arcs. It is generally agreed that island arc volcanism is caused by melting of the subducting plate as it descends into the hot mantle. Generation of magma may also be assisted by frictional melting along the upper surface of the subducting plate as it moves beneath the island arc.

A final point regarding convergent margin processes concerns the fate of marine sediments on subducting oceanic lithosphere. Initially, it was postulated that all the marine sediments on descending oceanic lithosphere should be piled up and folded on the bottom of the trench. Studies of modern trenches, however, indicate that trenches generally contain only minor amounts of sediment. A more complete understanding of this problem was gained when more sophisticated geophysical techniques were applied to the study of convergent margins. Results of these investigations suggest that marine sediments carried on a subducting plate are stripped off the plate at the trench. These sediments are attached to the leading edge of the overriding plate to form a complexly deformed sequence of sedimentary rocks called an accretionary prism that builds the landward wall of the trench.

In summary, convergent plate margins display a series of features that have been interpreted in terms of subduction, the dominant plate tectonic process occurring at these margins. Trenches mark the locations on the earth where oceanic lithosphere, formed at a divergent plate margin, sinks into the mantle. At least a portion of the deep marine sediment carried atop this plate is mechanically transferred to the leading edge of the overriding plate to form an accretionary prism. As the plate moves deeper into the mantle, it fractures and generates earthquakes along its length. Additionally, it begins to melt, thereby producing magma that rises to the surface of the earth to form a volcanic island arc. If the oceanic plate is attached to a continent, that continent eventually reaches the trench. Because, however, continental lithosphere is less dense and therefore more buoyant than oceanic lithosphere, the continent cannot be subducted, and instead it collides with the volcanic island arc or the overriding continent. This collision results in the formation of a mountain belt, as in the case of the collision of the Indian subcontinent and the Tibetan plateau to the north, which is still forming the Himalaya belt.

The third type of plate margin is the conservative, or neutral, margin. These margins, along which lithosphere is neither created nor destroyed, are characterized by oppositely directed horizontal movement of adjacent plates. The actual boundaries of the moving plates are marked by transform faults, or faults along which plates slide horizontally past one another. The San Andreas fault of California, perhaps the best-known example of a transform fault, marks the boundary between the northwest-moving Pacific plate and the North American plate. This plate boundary is characterized by contrasting geology on both sides of the fault, by little if any volcanic activity, and by powerful shallow focus earthquakes such as the kind that devastated San Francisco in 1906.

Transform faults separate offset segments of ocean ridges. Although ocean ridges extend continuously for thousands of kilometers, they are actually broken into much smaller segments separated by transform faults that are oriented at nearly right angles to the ridge segments. The relative movement of the two plates along a transform fault is caused by creation of new sea floor at the two offset ridge segments. As ocean lithosphere forms at and moves away from one ridge segment, it slides in the opposite direction past lithosphere forming at the other ridge segment. The transform fault, therefore, marks the contact of the oppositely moving plates and is situated between the ridge segments.

Plate tectonic theory requires that there be single points, called triple junctions, at which three lithospheric plates meet. In the Middle East, for example, three divergent plate margins—the Gulf of Aden, the East African rift, and the Red Sea rift—meet at what is referred to as a ridge-ridge-ridge triple junction. Almost any combination of the three plate margins—ridge, trench, and transform fault—can form triple junctions. Some types of triple junctions move with the plates, and they may even be subducted.

Methods of Study

Much of what is known about plate margins, particularly convergent and divergent margins, has come about through detailed study of the surface and interior structure of the ocean floor. One of the most important techniques developed in this regard is echo sounding. In echo sounding, a sound pulse generator-receiver system mounted on the hull of a ship emits sound pulses at regular intervals. Each pulse travels to the ocean floor at a known velocity and echoes back to the ship, where its return is detected by the pressure-sensitive receiver. The recording apparatus, a precision depth recorder, indicates the travel time of the sound pulse to and from the ocean bottom on an advancing paper chart. As the ship moves across the ocean, travel time marks for a succession of pulses detected by the receiver are displayed on the chart profile. The depth to the sea bottom is then calculated by multiplying the velocity of the sound pulse by one-half its travel time. This method was most instrumental in defining the ocean ridges and trenches on the ocean floor.

A somewhat more sophisticated approach using seismic waves allows scientists to study the internal structure of the upper part of oceanic lithosphere. In this approach, referred to as seismic reflection profiling, a ship emits sound waves powerful enough to penetrate the bottom of the ocean and then to reflect back to the ship. More specifically, these sound waves, which may be generated either by undersea explosions or by compressed air, reflect from the surface of the ocean floor and from internal sediment layers and faults back to the ship, where they are picked up by a receiver, or hydrophone, towed behind the ship. The travel times of the waves reflected off and from within the sea floor are recorded on charts by a sparker-profiler. Seismic reflection profiling has helped scientists to understand better the interior structure of the ocean bottom. For example, the faults bounding the slivers of marine sediments in accretionary prisms at convergent margins were recognized through the use of this technique.

Measurement of terrestrial heat flow (the amount of heat that escapes from the earth's interior through the sea floor) yielded particularly valuable information regarding the nature of plate margins. Results of heat flow studies indicated that the ocean ridges, once thought to be dormant submarine mountain ranges, are actually sites where large amounts of heat from the interior of the earth reach the earth's surface. This finding fit in well with Hess's convection-cell interpretation of ocean ridges. In addition, heat-flow studies demonstrated extremely low heat-flow values in the trenches, an observation consistent with Hess's proposal that convection cells sink into the mantle at convergent margins.

The Deep Sea Drilling Project (DSDP), a multinational research program initiated in 1968, attempted to understand better the evolution and geologic history of the modern oceans by drilling through the deep-sea sediments into the underlying igneous floor of the ocean. A specially designed ship, the *Glomar Challenger*, was used in the drilling. Among other things, results of the DSDP indicated that the age of the igneous ocean floor increases away from ocean ridges, thereby substantiating the major tenet of sea-floor spreading: that oceanic lithosphere is produced at, and moves away from, the ridges. The Deep Sea Drilling Project was superseded by a new program of research with many of the same goals, the Ocean Drilling Program (ODP).

Many details of plate margins, particularly divergent ocean ridges, have been revealed through direct observation of the sea floor. The French-American Mid-Ocean Undersea Study (project FAMOUS) of 1973 and 1974, for example, concentrated on a small area of the Mid-Atlantic Ridge southwest of the Azores. Several deep-sea submersible submarines were used to dive to the ridge to map the shape of the rift valley and to collect samples of the ocean floor. This project permitted observation of the tensional faults that formed the rift valley and extrusion of basaltic magma. In several submersible dives to transform faults, scientists recovered igneous rock samples that showed evidence of the shearing associated with horizontal plate movement along the transform faults. A number of submersible dives to the East Pacific rise in the eastern Pacific Ocean have allowed marine geologists to observe submarine hot springs associated with lava extrusion at a divergent margin.

Finally, studies of modern plate margins have been supplemented by investigations of rock sequences exposed on land and interpreted to have formed at ancient plate margins. This approach is particularly useful to the study of convergent plate margins. For example, highly deformed or chaotic rock units, referred to as mélanges and exposed in the Appalachian belt, along coastal California, and elsewhere, have been interpreted as marine sediments that were incorporated into ancient accretionary prisms. By studying these exposed sedimentary rocks, geologists can understand better the processes occurring at modern convergent plate margins.

Context

Plate margins are generally not a major concern of most people unless they happen to live or work near one. Nevertheless, one has only to pick up a newspaper to see the effects of plate margins and their attendant processes on human life. Convergent margins, for example, are characterized by frequent earthquakes and are generally prone to volcanic activity, some of which may be violent. The powerful earthquakes and deadly volcanoes of the Aleutian Islands, Central and South America, Japan, and Indonesia attest the potentially dangerous conditions of convergent plate margins. Conservative plate margins, like the San Andreas fault, are susceptible to powerful earthquakes, although volcanic activity is not likely. The instability of plate margins must be kept in mind by community planners so that proper building codes can be created and followed to reduce the potential for catastrophe in these areas.

Despite the obvious dangers of living close to or along plate margins, there can be some benefits. In Iceland, for example, the heat emanating from the Mid-Atlantic Ridge is used as geothermal energy. Indeed, Reykjavík, the capital of Iceland, is heated entirely by geothermal energy.

Understanding the relation of plate tectonics and metal deposits is of paramount importance given the growing global need for various metals. At ocean ridges, for example, marine geologists and oceanographers have observed the formation of metallic sulfide ores. These deposits, which form in association with the basalt magma extruded at the ridge, precipitate out of the hot water that circulates through the newly erupted basalt. Convergent plate margins are characterized by various types of metal deposits formed in association with magma generated during subduction. In the Andes belt of South America, iron, copper, and gold ores accumulated in response to subduction of the Pacific ocean floor beneath the western coast of South America.

Bibliography

Bonatti, E., and K. Crane. "Ocean Fracture Zones." *Scientific American* 250 (May, 1984): 40. Excellent discussion of transform faults and associated oceanic fractures. Suitable for the college-level reader.

Dewey, J. F. "Plate Tectonics." *Scientific American* 226 (May, 1972): 56. A good overview of the theory of plate tectonics and plate margins. Can be read by the high school or college student.

Heirtzler, J. R. "Sea-floor Spreading." *Scientific American* 219 (December, 1968): 60. This article provides an excellent discussion of the theory of sea-floor spreading. Suitable for high school students.

Heirtzler, J. R., and W. B. Bryan. "The Floor and the Mid-Atlantic Rift." *Scientific American* 233 (August, 1975): 78. Excellent discussion of divergent plate margins, with the Mid-Atlantic Ridge as the example. Can be read by high school and college students.

Marsh, B D. "Island-Arc Volcanism." *American Scientist* 67 (March/April, 1979): 161. A detailed discussion of volcanic activity at convergent margins. Suitable for college students.

Tokosoz, M. N. "The Subduction of the Lithosphere." *Scientific American* 233 (November, 1975): 88. This article describes the process of subduction at convergent margins and can be read by high school and college students.

Uyeda, Seiya. *The New View of the Earth: Moving Continents and Moving Oceans.*

San Francisco: W. H. Freeman, 1971. An excellent presentation of the evolution of the theory of plate tectonics from continental drift. Convergent and divergent plate margins are particularly well discussed, with numerous examples from the Pacific Ocean. Probably most suitable for college-level readers.

Gary G. Lash

Cross-References

Continental Rift Zones, 275; Geosynclines, 898; Island Arcs, 1261; Lithospheric Plates, 1387; Mountain Belts, 1725; Ocean Basins, 1785; The Ocean Ridge System, 1826; The Oceanic Crust, 1846; Plate Motions, 2071; Plate Tectonics, 2079; Subduction and Orogeny, 2497.

PLATE MOTIONS

Type of earth science: Geology
Field of study: Tectonics

In order to trace the geological history of the earth, it is necessary to know how the tectonic plates have moved around upon its surface. Using geological evidence, scientists can determine their relative locations at various times in the past. Such information can help in understanding the distribution of geological provinces and also in locating economically important formations.

Principal terms

DECLINATION: the angle in the horizontal plane between true north and the direction that the magnetization of a rock points

EULER POLE: the point on the surface of the earth where an axis, about which a rotation occurs, penetrates that surface

FRAME OF REFERENCE: a part of the planet, with respect to which all velocities are quoted

HOT SPOT: a point on the earth's surface, unrelated to plate boundaries, where volcanic activity occurs

INCLINATION: the angle in the vertical plane between horizontal and the direction of magnetization of a rock

PANGAEA: a supercontinent consisting of all the present continental fragments; it existed approximately 200 million years ago

RELATIVE VELOITY: the velocity of one object measured relative to another

TRIPLE JUNCTION: a point where three plate boundaries meet

VECTOR: a quantity that is defined by both magnitude and direction

VELOCITY: speed and direction of motion

Summary of the Phenomenon

A central tenet of the plate tectonic theory is that the plates are moving across the surface of the earth. Though all motion is relative in the context of plate tectonics, motion must be defined with respect to a given frame of reference. There is also the difficulty of treating an enormous period of time over which the plate motion has taken place. Some of the geological methods available to earth scientists can be utilized to find the position of a plate millions of years ago, while other methods can yield its present velocity. It may be difficult, however, to resolve these two pieces of information into a consistent pattern describing the history of the plate's motion.

In order to measure a plate's motion, the first step is to find its velocity with respect to an adjoining plate; that is termed a relative velocity. Such a relative velocity is actually a linear velocity and, like any velocity, is a vector, which means that it is described not only by the speed of the plate (the magnitude of the vector) but also by the direction in which the plate moves. Some of the methods that geologists employ to find plate velocities give both magnitude and direction; others provide only one of these quantities.

Yet, plates do not move in straight lines, as they are constrained to be on the surface of a globe. In fact, the plates are moving along curved paths, so their velocities should be described as angular velocities, strictly speaking. If one is considering only a very small area on the earth's surface, then linear velocities are an acceptable approximation. While linear velocities are quoted in units of millimeters per year, angular velocities are quoted as degrees per year, or radians per year. Furthermore, angular velocities are described as a change in angle per unit time around a pivot point (or axis). An everyday analogy might be a door: When a door opens, it pivots at the hinge, and the entire door moves at a particular angular velocity around this pivot. Note that the linear velocity of various parts of the door varies. Near the hinge, the distance moved in the time taken to open the door is small, so the linear velocity here is small too. The door handle moves a much greater distance in the same time, so its linear velocity is greater. Note also that as the door opens the linear velocity of any point on the door changes continually, as any point on the door is constantly changing direction. Considering the door handle, at every instant during the opening its direction of motion is changing (even though the speed may be constant); hence, the velocity is also changing. Now consider a plate on the surface of the earth: The linear velocity of the plate has a small magnitude near the pivot point around which it moves. This pivot point is called an Euler pole (for a Swiss mathematician, Leonhard Euler, who developed these concepts). Farther away from the Euler pole, the magnitude of the linear velocity increases. Suppose that two plates are spreading apart and that the pivot point is the north geographic pole. The mid-ocean ridge between the plates would lie on a line of longitude. The linear velocity of one plate wth respect to the other (at any instant) would be zero at the Euler pole and increase to a maximum at the equator. On the other side of the equator, the linear velocity would decrease until it reached zero again at the south pole, where another Euler pole would be located. In fact, the two Euler poles are just the points where the axis around which the rotation is taking place penetrates the earth's surface.

Knowledge of relative velocities and Euler poles enabled the reconstruction of the position of the continental landmasses in the past. Approximately 200 million years ago, the continents were grouped in a single supercontinent called Pangaea. Pangaea then split into a northern fragment (Laurasia) and a southern part (Gondwanaland) separated by the Tethys Sea. Since then, the fragmentation has continued, and the plates have shifted such that the continents have drifted to the positions they occupy today. Some of the continental fragments have drifted quite rapidly, such as the Indian subcontinent, which broke from Africa and Antarctica and drifted north until colliding with Asia to form the Himalayan mountains.

Using the known present relative velocities, how the plates will move in the future can be predicted. For example, the Atlantic Ocean will continue to open, mostly at the expense of the shrinking Pacific Ocean. Australia and Africa will continue to move north, as will Baja California and parts of southern California as the San Andreas fault lengthens. In roughly 10 million years, Los Angeles and San Francisco will become neighbors.

Although relative velocities are clearly very useful, the absolute motions of plates can be defined from a frame of reference that is geologically determinable. What is needed is a frame of reference fixed with respect to the interior of the planet, beneath the lithosphere; this region of the interior is termed the mesosphere. It appears that there are locations on the earth's surface that are in some way tied to the mesosphere: hot spots. Hot spots are places where there is volcanic activity that is apparently unrelated to plate boundary activity. These regions are often typified by lavas that are geochemically dissimilar to those formed at either mid-ocean ridges or island arcs, and the suggestion is that the dissimilarity results from the fact that their magma source is much deeper.

Perhaps the best example of a hot spot trace is the Hawaii-Emperor chain of seamounts, which is basically a chain of extinct volcanoes except for the island of Hawaii itself. As one moves away from Hawaii along this seamount and island chain, the ages of the lava flows become progressively older. In the hot spot hypothesis, this is explained by the postulation that each island (or seamount) formed over the hot spot, but that the motion of the Pacific plate over the hot spot continually moved the islands away from the magma source—rather like a conveyer belt moving over a static Bunsen burner, leaving a progressively lengthening scorch mark. Interestingly, the Hawaii-Emperor chain has a bend in it, at about the location of Midway Island, which is interpreted as meaning that the Pacific plate motion changed direction at the time that that island formed (some 37 million years ago). Because it is possible to date the lava flows on these islands, the velocity of the Pacific plate relative to this particular hot spot can be calculated (its direction being obtained from the bearing of the seamount chain). The same can be done for other hot spots, too, and thus geologists can ultimately find the velocities of the hot spots relative to one another. The result of this procedure is the discovery that the hot spots move with respect to one another but at rates much slower than do the plates. Assuming that these relative motions are insignificant and that the hot spots are in reality fixed with respect to their proposed source, the mesosphere, then the mean hot spot frame of reference can be defined and all plate motions calculated with respect to that. In fact, this method essentially determines the velocities of the plates with respect to a mantle velocity that best simulates all the known hot spot traces. Absolute plate velocities determined by this method are commonly given in contemporary global plate motion analyses.

The analysis of absolute plate motions has a bearing on theories concerning why the plates move. One group of plates is apparently moving quite slowly, with velocities of between 5 and 25 millimeters per year. This group includes the Eurasian plate, the North and South American plates, and the African and Antarctic plates. In contrast, the Indian, Philippine, Nazca, and Pacific plates move much more rapidly, and the Cocos plate has a velocity of roughly 85 millimeters per year. This observation has led to the realization that it is the plates with actively subducting margins that move the fastest. None of the slower group has a significant percentage of its margin being subducted, whereas all in the faster group do; the implication may be that the subduction process itself plays an important role in driving plate motions. This idea is in contradiction to the earlier hypothesis that the lithospheric plates rode on the back of giant convection cells within the mantle. If this latter view were correct, one might expect the larger plates to move faster (although that is debatable, depending on the geometry of the convecting cells). At the least, a passive plate theory such as that would not produce the correlation noted above. It seems that the plates are not passive players in the plate tectonic cycle but are an active part of convection.

Methods of Study

Geologists have a variety of ways to determine how plates have moved in the past and how they may move in the future. Crucial to this endeavor is determining the location of Euler poles, but finding the location of an Euler pole for the relative motion between two plates can be difficult. As indicated in the previous section, however, if one follows a line of longitude along which a ridge lies, one must eventually arrive at the Euler pole. Unfortunately, ridges do not always lie on the geographic longitude lines of the earth. The ridge system separating two plates describes its own set of longitude lines, which may not correspond with geographic longitude lines. To distinguish them, these longitude lines can be referred to as great circles. (In fact, any circle that is drawn around the earth is a great circle. All great circles would be identical in length on a perfectly spherical earth. Latitude lines, on the other hand, are not great circles, with the exception of the equator, and vary considerably in length. They are referred to as small circles.) Fortunately, mid-ocean ridge segments are offset by transform faults; therefore, a set of great circles can be drawn through the various segments of the ridge system and hence reveal the Euler pole. The transform faults can also be used; small circles drawn through these also define the position of the Euler pole. This latter case has the added advantage that the fracture zones on either side of the transform fault effectively extend their length and make the geometric construction easier, as it is advantageous to have as long a feature as is possible to which to fit the circle in order to cut down on the errors inevitably involved with any line-fitting method.

When a plate does not have a mid-oceanic ridge system separating it from a neighboring plate, other methods must be employed. Such is the case with the Philippine plate, which is surrounded entirely with subduction zones. In this instance, finding its velocity with respect to its neighboring plates and the Euler pole around which the rotation occurs is much more difficult. The motion of the Philippine plate is usually found by adding the velocities of all the other plates on the earth's surface and finding the resultant. The velocity that exactly cancels this resultant is taken to be the velocity of the Philippine plate. Locations where three plates meet at a single point (triple junctions) can be analyzed by vector addition also, and if the velocities of two of the plates are known, then the velocity of the third can be determined. Significantly, the relative velocity of the triple junction itself can be determined; from that number it can be determined if any of the plate boundaries is lengthening or shortening. In this fashion geologists were able to determine that the San Andreas fault is lengthening. At its southern end, the triple junction (a convergence of all three types of plate boundaries) migrates south, and at its northern end, the triple junction (two transform faults meet a subduction zone) moves north. This deduction led to the realization that part of the ancient Pacific sea floor, the Farallon plate and part of the East Pacific Rise, had been subducted down a trench that used to lie offshore of western North America. The two remnants of this older plate are the Cocos plate to the south and the Gorda (or Juan de Fuca) plate to the north.

The relative motions of two plates can also be measured by more direct approaches. One technique is to try to measure directly the changes in positions occurring over a few years, which, from a geological point of view, is instantaneous. These are referred to as instantaneous velocities. One example of how that may be done is using geodetic measurements, essentially surveying the region across a plate boundary at regular intervals and, therefore, observing the motion. This technique does not lend itself to the examination of mid-ocean ridges but has been extensively used in studying the San Andreas fault in California. The results of these measurements give the magnitude of the relative linear velocity between the Pacific plate and the North American plate to be between 50 and 75 millimeters per year, the direction of this relative velocity being known from the bearing of the fault line. These numbers agree quite well with other estimates based upon geological evidence, such as the separation of once-continuous geological features that has taken place over much longer time periods. Another example is the use of satellite laser ranging (SLR); this technique employs a laser beam bounced off a satellite, which affords a method to calculate the distance between two points on the surface of the earth with great accuracy. The distance between two points on separate plates is regularly found, and hence the velocity between the points is calculated. By this method, the relative velocity between North America and Europe has been found to have a magnitude of approximately 15 ± 5 millimeters per year. Once again, that is in agreement with geological data for much longer time periods. In some cases, however, the agreement between the results of SLR and geological evidence is not as good. In the Zagros mountains of Iran, the two methods do not agree, implying that the instantaneous velocity indicates a change in the relative motion of the two plates on either side of this plate boundary.

The velocities calculated by geological means over much longer time spans are referred to as finite velocities. One major technique used to determine finite velocities depends upon the Vine and Matthews theory of sea-floor spreading. The geomagnetic polarity record is now well established and the dates of the geomagnetic reversals known (although it is still undergoing refinement and short polarity episodes are sometimes added to the known record). This time scale can be used to identify marine magnetic anomalies caused by the magnetization of the sea floor and affords a method by which to date a point on the sea floor. If one measures the distance between two locations of the same age, located on either side of a mid-ocean ridge, then it is quite simple to calculate the relative velocity between the two plates (the direction of the motion being, in most cases, perpendicular to the ridge or parallel to the transform faults). If the separation of two points on the ocean floor, on the same plate but of different ages, is measured, then geologists can still find the "half spreading rate" of the ridge (the amount of new crustal material added per year at the ridge), but this is not a relative velocity.

Because the oceanic crust is quite young, the oldest approximately 160 million years old (as compared to 4.5 billion years of earth history), the techniques described above are not applicable to the majority of the history of the earth. In order to work out plate motions for older periods, other methods must be employed. The most prevalent of these methods is the use of the remanent magnetization of rocks. Remanent magnetization is acquired when rocks form, and it is oriented parallel to the geomagnetic field at the time and place at which they are forming. This magnetization is retained in much the same way that a bar magnet retains its magnetization. If the rock is subsequently moved, by being carried along with a moving plate, the rock may end up at a location where the direction of the geomagnetic field is substantially different from that of its magnetization. It is this difference between the field and magnetization directions that was critical in proving that continents do indeed drift across the earth's surface and that was a contributing factor in the acceptance of this theory by geologists. The angle that the geomagnetic field makes with the horizontal varies considerably, from vertically up at the south magnetic pole to horizontal at the equator to vertically down at the north magnetic pole. This angle is referred to as the inclination. By calculating the inclination of the magnetization of the rock, the latitude at which the rock formed, called the paleolatitude, can be ascertained. If a series shows paleolatitudes for successively older rocks, the latitudinal motion of the plate over time can be traced. Unfortunately, the same cannot be done for longitude, for the simple reason that while latitude is an inherent property of a spinning planet, longitude is not.

Plates not only shift in latitude but also rotate as they move with respect to one another. The angle between true north and a rock's magnetization is referred to as the declination, and it is this angle that allows such rotations to be determined. It is interesting that in recent years geologists have been able to delineate rotations of small blocks near the edges of the major plates, which means that a considerably more complex story unravels concerning the interactions at plate boundaries. In both southern California and Southeast Asia, there are numerous microplates that may have rotated between larger plates.

Context

The understanding of plate motions may not initially appear particularly relevant to the general public; however, some economic decisions that may be made, in part based upon that understanding, are. Economic deposits, such as oil or coal, may have originally formed before the breakup of Pangaea. Therefore, if the location of one such deposit is known, then, by reconstructing the ancient landmasses, it may be possible to determine the full paleogeographic extent of the environment that gave rise to the deposit in the past. By using this method, geologists can predict where further economic sites may lie, even if these sites are currently thousands of miles from the known deposit on a separate continent.

Although plate motions are very slow, the consequences of those motions can often be very abrupt and dramatic. Study of plate tectonics has led to an understanding of why certain regions of the earth are prone to such hazards as earthquakes and volcanic eruptions. It would be to everyone's benefit to be able to predict when these events will take place, and some of the methods that are used to determine plate motions can give direct information concerning these phenomena. In a region such as southern California, measurements of relative velocities along the San Andreas fault can be applied to the forecasting of earthquakes, and are, therefore, of direct interest to the local population.

Bibliography

Cox, Allan, and R. B. Hart. *Plate Tectonics: How It Works*. Palo Alto, Calif.: Blackwell Scientific, 1986. A well-illustrated and detailed account of the methodology of plate tectonics. Includes information on many different aspects of plate tectonic theory and supplies explanations of the mathematical techniques utilized in solving plate tectonic problems. Suitable for those with a good mathematical background.

Dewey, J. F. "Plate Tectonics." In *Continents Adrift and Continents Aground*. San Francisco: W. H. Freeman, 1976. This article appears in a book of articles reprinted from *Scientific American*. The first part of the article gives a succinct explanation of plate rotations and includes several excellent diagrams. While not giving a full mathematical treatment, the article does approach some complex ideas in an understandable fashion. Suitable for high school readers who have some prior knowledge of the subject.

Press, Frank, and Raymond Siever. *Earth*. 4th ed. New York: W. H. Freeman, 1986. A general geology text. The chapter on global plate tectonics is quite thorough and contains "boxes" that explain the motions of the plates. Hot spots are explained elsewhere in the text and not related to plate motions. The diagrams, although only two-tone, are quite detailed. The text is appropriate for advanced high school readers.

Uyeda, Seiya. *The New View of the Earth*. San Francisco: W. H. Freeman, 1978. A very readable account of the development of plate tectonics up to the early 1970's. Does not go into mathematical detail concerning plate motions but does give many examples. Suitable for high school readers.

Wyllie, Peter J. *The Way the Earth Works*. New York: John Wiley & Sons, 1976. A good introductory geology text written from the point of view of plate tectonics. The author does not go into detail concerning the mathematics involved with determining plate motions. Well illustrated and easy to read. Information concerning plate motions is disseminated throughout the text. Suitable for high school readers.

Ian Williams

Cross-References

Continental Rift Zones, 275; Gondwanaland and Pangaea, 982; Hot Spots and Volcanic Island Chains, 1079; Ocean Basins, 1785; Plate Margins, 2063; Plate Tectonics, 2079; Subduction and Orogeny, 2497.

PLATE TECTONICS

Type of earth science: Geology
Field of study: Tectonics

Plate tectonics is the theory that the earth's surface is composed of major and minor plates that are being created at one edge by the formation of new igneous rocks and consumed at another edge as one plate is thrust, or subducted, below another. This elegant theory accounts for the formation of earthquakes, volcanoes, and mountain belts, the growth and fracturing of continents, and many types of ore deposits.

Principal terms

ANDESITE: a volcanic rock that occurs in abundance only along subduction zones

BASALT: a dark-colored, fine-grained igneous rock

CONTINENTAL RIFT: a divergent plate boundary at which continental masses are being pulled apart

CONVERGENT PLATE BOUNDARY: a compressional plate boundary at which an oceanic plate is subducted or two continental plates collide

DIVERGENT PLATE BOUNDARY: a tensional plate boundary where volcanic rocks are being formed

EARTHQUAKE FOCUS: the area below the surface of the earth where active movement occurs to produce an earthquake

OCEANIC RISE: a type of divergent plate boundary that forms long, sinuous mountain chains in the oceans

SUBDUCTION ZONE: a convergent plate boundary where an oceanic plate is being thrust below another plate

TRANSFORM FAULT: a large fracture transverse to a plate boundary that results in displacement of oceanic rises or subduction zones

Summary of the Phenomenon

Plate tectonics is the theory that the earth's crust is composed of six major rigid plates and numerous minor plates with three types of boundaries. The divergent plate boundary is a tensional boundary in which basaltic magma (molten rock material that will crystallize to become calcium-rich plagioclase, pyroxene, and olivine-rich rock) is formed so that the plate grows larger along this boundary. The rigid plate, or lithosphere, moves in conveyer-belt fashion in both directions away from a divergent boundary across the ocean floor at rates of 0-18 centimeters per year. The lithosphere consists of the crust and part of the upper mantle and averages about 100 kilometers thick; it is thicker over continental than over oceanic crust. The lithosphere seems to slide over an underlying plastic layer of rock and magma called the asthenosphere. Eventually, the lithosphere meets a second type of plate boundary, called a convergent plate margin. If lithosphere-containing oceanic crust collides with another lithospheric plate containing either oceanic or continental crust, then the oceanic lithospheric plate is thrust or subducted below the second plate. If both intersecting lithospheric plates contain continental crust, they crumple and form large mountain ranges, such as the Himalaya or the Alps. Much magma is also produced along convergent boundaries. A third type of boundary, called a transform fault, may develop along divergent or compressional plate margins. Transform faults develop as fractures transverse to the sinuous margins of plates, in which they move horizontally so that the plate margins may be displaced many tens or even hundreds of kilometers.

Divergent plate margins in ocean basins occur as long, sinuous mountain chains called oceanic rises that are many thousands of kilometers long. The rises are often discontinuous, as they are displaced long distances by transform faults. The two longest oceanic rises are the East Pacific Rise, running from the Gulf of California south and west into the Antarctic, and the Mid-Atlantic Ridge, running more or less north-south across the middle of the Atlantic Ocean. The oceanic rises are deep-sea mountain ranges, and there is a rift valley that runs down the middle of the highest part of the mountain chain. The rift valley apparently forms along the ocean rises as the plates move outward from the rises in both directions and pull apart the lithosphere. The oceanic floor descends from a maximum elevation at the oceanic rises to a minimum in the deepest trenches along subduction zones. Thus, the lithosphere moves downhill from the oceanic rises to the convergent plate margins. It is thought that the lithosphere gradually cools and contracts as it moves from the oceanic rises to the convergent margins.

The oceanic rises are composed of piles of basalts forming gentle extrusions. There is high heat flow out of oceanic rises because of the large volume of magma carried up toward the surface. The magnetic minerals in the lavas are frozen into alignment with the earth's magnetic field. Half the magnetized lavas move out from the oceanic rises in one direction, and the other half move out in the opposite direction. The magnetic field of the earth appears to reverse itself periodically over geologic time. The last magnetic reversal occurred about 730,000 years ago. This last reversal can now be observed at the same distance in both directions away from the oceanic rises. A series of such magnetic reversals can be traced back across the Pacific ocean floor for a period of about 165 million years. Many shallow-focus earthquakes occur at depths of up to 100 kilometers below the surface, along the rises and transform faults. Presumably they result from periodic movement that releases tension in the lithosphere.

A second type of divergent plate margin, called a continental rift zone, occurs in continents. Examples are the Rio Grande Rift, occurring as a sinuous north-south belt in central New Mexico and southern Colorado, and the East African Rift, occurring as a sinuous north-south belt across eastern Africa. These rift zones occur as down-dropped blocks forming narrow, elongate valleys that fill with sediment. The rift valleys often contain rivers or elongate lakes. They are characterized by abundant basalts with high potassium contents and, often, smaller amounts of more silica-rich rocks called rhyolites. Rhyolites are light-colored volcanic rocks containing the minerals alkali feldspar (potassium, sodium, and aluminum silicate), quartz (silica), sodium-rich plagioclase, and often minor dark-colored minerals. Shallow-focus earthquakes result in these areas from the tension produced as the continental crust is stretched apart, much as taffy is pulled.

Many rift valleys never become very large. Others grow and may actually rip apart the continents to expose the underlying oceanic crust and rise, as is occurring in the Red Sea. There the oceanic crust is near enough to the continents that it is covered with sediment. Eventually, the continents on both sides of the Red Sea may be pulled apart so far that the underlying oceanic floor will be exposed, with no sediment cover. About 240 million years ago, the continents of North and South America, Europe, and Africa were joined in an ancient landmass called Pangaea. They slowly broke apart along the north-south Mid-Atlantic Ridge from about 240 to 70 million years ago. At first, only a rift valley similar to the East African Rift was formed. Later it opened, much like the area of the Red Sea today. Finally, the continents drifted far enough apart during the last 70 million years to form a full-fledged ocean basin, the Atlantic Ocean.

As the lithosphere moves slowly across the ocean floor, minor volcanic activity is generated over hot spots on the ocean floor. The Hawaiian Islands are situated over one of these hot spots. The basalts produced there are much richer in potassium than are those formed over oceanic rises. The Hawaiian Islands are part of a linear, northwest-trending chain of islands, about 2,000 kilometers long, that extends to the island of Midway. The volcanic rocks become progressively older from the Hawaiian Islands to Midway Island. Presumably, Midway Island formed first as the plate slid over the hot spot. As the plate moved to the northwest, the source of magma was removed from Midway, and newer volcanoes began progressively to form over the same hot spot.

Eventually, the lithospheric plate with oceanic crust reaches a compressional plate boundary and may be subducted below other oceanic crust; one result is the island arcs in the western Pacific Ocean, such as Japan. Or they may be pulled below continental crust, often at angles of 20-60 degrees to the horizontal (the Andes in western South America are the result of such movement). The intersection of the two colliding plates is marked by a sinuous, deep trench forming the deepest portions of the ocean floors. Sediment collects along the slopes of the trench, carried down from the topographic highs of the upper plate. Mountain belts are built up on the nonsubducted plate, as a result of the tremendous amounts of igneous rock that form and of the compressional forces of the plate collision, which throw much sediment and metamorphic rock in the nonsubducted plate to higher elevations.

The subducted plate can be traced to depths as great as 700 kilometers. Some of the sediments collecting along the trench are carried rapidly to great depths, where they undergo a very high-pressure and low-temperature metamorphism. (Metamorphism is the transformation of minerals in response to high temperatures and pressures deep within the earth.) Some rocks are carried more slowly to great depths and have a more normal, higher-temperature metamorphism. During metamorphism, many minerals containing water along the subducted plate gradually break down and give off water vapor, which moves up into the overlying plate. The water vapor is believed to lower the melting point of these rocks within the subducted and overlying plates so that widespread melting takes place, producing the abundant basalts and andesites that build up island arcs or continental masses above the subducted plate. In addition, much rhyolitic magma is formed in the continental crust, presumably through the melting of some of the higher-silica rocks in the continents.

Sometimes a continent is carried by an oceanic plate into another continent at a subduction zone, which happened when India collided with the Asian continent. Such a collision crumples the continents into very high mountains; the Himalaya were formed in this way. This process produces an earthquake zone that is more diffuse (with foci to depths up to 300 kilometers) than are those along subducted plates. No volcanic rocks are produced in these continental-continental plate collisions. Instead, abundant granites crystallize below the surface. Granites contain the same minerals as do rhyolites. Rhyolites form small crystals by quick cooling when they crystallize rapidly in volcanic rocks; granites form larger crystals from magma of the same composition by slow cooling below the earth's surface.

Methods of Study

Plate tectonics is a major, unifying theory that clarifies many large-scale processes on the earth. The major concepts to support the theory were put together only in the late 1950's and the 1960's. Yet, many of the keys to developing the theory had been known for many years. Beginning in the seventeenth century, a number of people noticed the remarkable "fit" in the shape of the continents on opposing sides of the Atlantic Ocean and suggested that the continents could have been joined at one time. It was not until the early twentieth century that Alfred Wegener put many pieces of this puzzle together. Wegener noticed the remarkable similarity of geological structures, rocks, and especially fossils that were currently located on opposite sides of the Atlantic Ocean. Most notably, land plants and animals that predated the hypothesized time of the breakup of the continents, at about 200 million years before the present, were remarkably similar on all continents. Subsequently, their evolution in North and South America was quite different from their development in Europe and Africa. Climates could also be matched across the continents. For example, when the maps of the continents were reassembled into their predrift positions, the glacial deposits in southern Africa, southern South America, Antarctica, and Australia could be explained as having originated as one large continental glacier in the southern polar region.

One of the biggest problems with the concept of continental drift at that time was the lack of understanding of a driving force to explain how the continents could have drifted away from one another. Then, in 1928, Arthur Holmes proposed a mechanism that foreshadowed the explanation geologists later adopted. He suggested that the mantle material upwelled under the continents and pulled them apart as it spread out laterally and produced tension. The basaltic oceanic crust would then carry the continents out away from one another much like rafts. When the mantle material cooled, Holmes believed, it descended back into the mantle and produced belts along these areas. From the 1920's to the early 1960's, however, continental drift theories had no currency, for there was no real evidence for driving forces that might move the continents. It was not until the ocean floors began to be mapped that evidence was found to support a plate tectonic model. The topography of the ocean floor was surveyed, and large mountain ranges, such as the Mid-Atlantic Ridge with its rift valleys, and the deep ocean trenches were discovered. Harry Hess suggested in the early 1960's that the oceanic ridges were areas where mantle material upwelled, melted, and spread laterally. Evidence for this sea-floor spreading hypothesis came from the mirror-image pattern of the periodically reversed magnetic bands found in basalts on either side of the ridges. The symmetrical magnetic bands could be explained only by the theory that they were originally produced at the ridges, as the earth's magnetic field periodically reversed, and then were spread laterally in both directions at the same rate.

Supporting evidence for plate tectonics began to accumulate during the 1960's. Further magnetic pattern surveys on ocean floors confirmed that the symmetrical pattern of matching magnetic bands could be found everywhere around ridges. Also, earthquake, volcanic rock, and heat-flow patterns were discovered to be consistent with the concept of magma upwelling along rises and sea-floor material being subducted along oceanic trenches. Oceanic and lithospheric plates could then be defined, and the details of the interaction of the plate boundaries could be understood. With this overwhelming evidence, most geologists became convinced that the plate tectonic model was valid.

Context

The plate tectonic theory is highly significant in that it accounts for a wide variety of phenomena: the formation of volcanoes, earthquakes, mountain belts, and many types of ore deposits, as well as the growth, drift, and fracturing of continents. For scientists, it is a rich and fascinating theory with many implications.

Plate tectonics is important economically because of the theory's usefulness in predicting and explaining the occurrence of ore deposits. Plate boundaries such as the mid-oceanic rises are areas of high temperature in which hot waters are driven up toward the surface. These hot waters are enriched in copper, iron, zinc, and sulfur, so sulfide minerals such as pyrite (iron sulfide), chalcopyrite (copper and iron sulfide), and sphalerite (zinc sulfide) form along oceanic rises. One such deposit in Cyprus has been mined for many centuries. Tensional zones sometimes formed in basins behind subduction zones may form deposits similar to those at oceanic rises. In addition, ferromanganese nodules form in abundance in some places by chemical precipitation from seawater. These nodules are enriched in cobalt and nickel, as well as in iron and manganese as complex oxides and hydroxides. They could potentially be mined from ocean floors.

Deposits enriched in chromium occur in folded and faulted rocks on the nonsubducted plate next to the oceanic trench in subduction zones. This deposit is found in some peridotites (olivine, pyroxene, and garnet rocks) or dunites (olivine rock) that have been ripped out of the upper mantle and thrust up into these areas. The ore mineral chromite (magnesium and chromium oxide) is found in pods and lenses that range in size from quite small to massive. Many intrusions of silica-rich magma above subduction zones contain water-rich fluids that have moved through the granite after it solidified. The water-rich fluids deposit elements such as copper, gold, silver, tin, mercury, molybdenum, tungsten, and bismuth throughout a large volume of the granite in low concentrations. Hundreds of these deposits have been found around subduction zones in the Pacific Ocean.

Bibliography

Motz, Lloyd M., ed. *The Rediscovery of the Earth*. New York: Van Nostrand Reinhold, 1979. An unusual book, as it is written by many of the experts who developed the plate tectonic model. Begins at an elementary level so that someone without much background in plate tectonics should be able to understand the discussion; the discussion progresses, however, to an advanced level. Beautifully illustrated with photographs and diagrams.

Press, Frank, and Raymond Siever. *Earth*. 4th ed. New York: W. H. Freeman, 1986. A well-written introductory textbook on geology. Chapters 19 and 20 deal with plate tectonics. Well illustrated; contains a glossary. Appropriate for general readers.

Seyfert, Carl K., and L. A. Sirkin. *Earth History and Plate Tectonics*. New York: Harper & Row, 1973. This book integrates the plate tectonic concept with the evolution of plants and animals through geologic time. Some understanding of plate tectonics, rocks, and minerals would be helpful before using this source. Written as an introductory text in historical geology, so important concepts are reviewed. Good illustrations.

Skinner, Brian J., et al. *Resources of the Earth*. Englewood Cliffs, N.J.: Prentice-Hall, 1988. A good book for the layperson who is interested in the history, use, production, environmental impact, and geological occurrence of ore deposits. Technical terms are kept to a minimum. Well illustrated; contains a glossary. Suitable for someone who is taking a course in geology.

Windley, Brian F. *The Evolving Continents*. 2d ed. New York: John Wiley & Sons, 1984. A more advanced source than the others listed. Summarizes how the continents have evolved through geologic time. The reader should understand plate tectonic processes well before attempting to read this book.

Robert L. Cullers

Cross-References

PLATINUM GROUP METALS

Type of earth science: Economic geology

Although platinum group metals are among the rarest elements known, their chemical inertness, high melting points, and extraordinary catalytic properties make them an indispensable resource for modern industrial society.

Principal terms

CATALYST: a substance that facilitates a chemical reaction but is not consumed in that reaction

IMMISCIBLE LIQUIDS: liquids not capable of being mixed or mingled

LAYERED IGNEOUS COMPLEX: a large and diverse body of igneous rock formed by intrusion of magma into the crust; it consists of layers of different mineral compositions

MAFIC/ULTRAMAFIC: compositional terms referring to igneous rocks rich (mafic) and very rich (ultramafic) in magnesium- and iron-bearing minerals

MAGMA: molten rock material that solidifies to produce igneous rocks

PLACER: a mineral deposit formed by the concentration of heavy mineral grains such as gold or platinum during stream transport

REEF: a provincial ore deposit term referring to a metalliferous mineral deposit, commonly of gold or platinum, which is usually in the form of a layer

SPECIFIC GRAVITY: the ratio of the weight of any volume of a substance to the weight of an equal volume of water

TROY OUNCE: unit of weight equal to 31.1 grams used in the United States for precious metals and gems

Summary of the Phenomenon

Platinum is a beautiful silver-white metal that, when pure, can be hammered into shape. Its specific gravity of 21.45 is extremely high. It has a high melting point of 1,769 degrees Celsius, does not oxidize at room temperature, and is extremely resistant to chemical attack. In addition, platinum has the unusual property of being able to absorb large volumes of hydrogen at ordinary temperatures and release it at high temperatures. Technological society has taken advantage of platinum's distinctive properties and is becoming increasingly dependent on the metal.

Platinum, like gold, can be found as a pure metal in stream placer deposits, where its density and resistance to corrosion have resulted in concentration of the metal during stream transport. Platinum appears to have been recovered from placer deposits since earliest times. A hieroglyphic character forged from a grain of platinum has been dated from the seventh century B.C., and ancient South American metalsmiths used platinum as an alloy to improve the hardness of gold as early as the first millennium B.C.

The name "platinum" is derived from the Spanish word for silver, to which it was originally considered to be inferior. Spanish conquistadors called the metal *platina del Pinto* (little silver of the Pinto) after its discovery in placer gold deposits of the Rio Pinto. Although the metal looked like silver, it proved to be more difficult to shape. Also, with a density similar to that of gold, platinum in small quantities mixed with gold was difficult to detect. Fear of its being used to degrade gold and silver led to a temporary ban against the importation of platinum to Europe. The metal was eventually brought to Europe and was described by Sir William Watson in 1750.

The platinum group metals consist of six elements so named because they occur with and have similar properties to platinum. In addition to platinum, they include osmium, iridium, rhodium, palladium, and ruthenium. These five metals were discovered in the first half of the nineteenth century by scientists who examined the residue left when crude platinum was dissolved in aqua regia, a mixture of hydrochloric and nitric acids. Because of their resistance to corrosion, all six platinum group metals and gold are referred to by chemists as the noble metals. Economic geologists classify these metals together with silver as the precious metals. The weight of precious metals, like that of gems, is given in troy ounces.

Four of the platinum group metals were discovered by British scientists in 1803. Smithson Tennant discovered osmium and iridium. The name "osmium" was taken from the Greek word *osme* (meaning "smell"), because the metal exudes a distinctive odor, actually toxic osmium tetroxide, when it is powdered. Osmium is bluish white and extremely hard. Its melting point of about 3,045 degrees Celsius is the highest of the platinum group. The specific gravity of osmium has been measured at 22.57, making it the heaviest known element.

Iridium was named by Tennant for the Latin word *iris*, a rainbow, because of the variety of colors produced when iridium is dissolved in hydrochloric acid. Iridium is white with a slight yellowish cast. Like osmium, it is very hard, brittle, and dense. It has a melting point of 2,410 degrees Celsius and is the most corrosion-resistant metal known.

Rhodium and palladium were first discovered by William Hyde Wollaston, who named rhodium for the Greek word *rhodon* (a rose) because of the rose color produced by dilute solutions of rhodium salts. The metal is actually silvery white, has a melting point of about 1,966 degrees Celsius, exhibits a low electrical resistance, and is highly resistant to corrosion. Wollaston named palladium for Pallas, a recently discovered asteroid named for the Greek goddess of wisdom. Palladium is steel-white, does not tarnish in air, and has the lowest specific gravity (12.02) and melting point (1,554 degrees Celsius) of the platinum group metals. Like platinum, it has the unusual property of absorbing enormous volumes of hydrogen.

The existence of ruthenium was proposed in 1828 but not established until 1844 by Russian chemist Karl Karlovich Klaus. He retained the previously suggested name ruthenium in honor of Ruthenia, the Latinized name for his adopted country of Russia. Ruthenium is a hard, white, nonreactive metal with a specific gravity slightly greater than that of palladium (12.41) and a melting point of 2,310 degrees Celsius.

The average crustal abundance of the platinum group metals is not known exactly but is comparable to that of gold. Estimates are that iridium, osmium, rhodium, and ruthenium have rock concentrations of only 1 part in 1 billion, while platinum is five and palladium ten times that amount. The platinum group metals are found as native metals, as natural alloys, and as compounds with sulfur and arsenic. They occur most abundantly in igneous rocks of mafic and ultramafic composition. Economic concentrations of the metals are found in primary igneous deposits and secondary sedimentary placer deposits. The metals are also recovered as a by-product of the refining of nickel, copper, and gold ores. Important deposits of platinum group metals are found in the Bushveld complex, Republic of South Africa; in the Stillwater complex, Montana; at Sudbury, Ontario; and in Norilsk and the Ural Mountains in the Soviet Union.

The Bushveld complex holds a special place as history's greatest source of platinum, and it still contains the world's largest reserves of platinum group elements. Bushveld is a large layered igneous complex. It is located north of the town of Pretoria in the northeast corner of South Africa, and it covers an area roughly the size of the state of Maine. It formed 1.95 billion years ago when an enormous intrusion of mafic magma, the largest known mafic igneous intrusion, was injected and slowly cooled in the earth's crust. As cooling and solidification occurred, the denser, mafic minerals became concentrated downward in the magma chamber, and the igneous rock became stratified with ultramafic layers at greater depth and layers of increasingly less mafic rocks upward.

Placer platinum was discovered in South Africa in 1924 and was subsequently traced by Hans Merensky to its source, a distinctive igneous layer which became known as the Merensky Reef. The reef is located in the lower part of the Bushveld complex, about one-third of the distance from the base to the top. Although commonly less than 1 meter in thickness, it has been traced for 250 kilometers around the circumference of the complex, and nearly one-half of the world's historic production of platinum group metals has come from this remarkable layer.

The average metal content in the layer is about one-third of a troy ounce per ton of rock, or about 1 part platinum group metals in 100,000 parts rock. Platinum is the most abundant metal extracted from the reef. Other platinum group minerals in order of abundance are palladium (27 percent), ruthenium (5 percent), rhodium (2.7 percent), iridium (0.7 percent), and osmium (0.6 percent). Also produced are significant quantities of gold, nickel, and copper. Mining of such a narrow layer is so labor-intensive that each South African miner produces only about 30 ounces of platinum group metals per year.

The Stillwater complex, Montana, is a large-layered, mafic to ultramafic igneous complex remarkably similar to Bushveld. It is exposed for about 45 kilometers along the north side of the Beartooth Mountains in southwest Montana. The Stillwater area has long been famous for its large but low-grade chromium-rich layers, and platinum was discovered there in the 1920's. Serious exploration for economic concentrations of platinum, however, was initiated in 1967 by the Johns-Manville Corporation. This led, in the 1970's, to identification of the J-M Reef, a palladium-land platinum-rich horizon between 1 and 3 meters thick, which, like the Merensky Reef, can be traced through most of the complex.

The Stillwater complex formed 2.7 billion years ago. Like Bushveld, the complex is layered from ultramafic igneous rocks at the base to mafic rocks upward. The J-M Reef lies slightly above the ultramafic zone. It has an average ore grade of 0.8 ounce of platinum group metals per ton of rock with a 3:1 ratio of palladium to platinum. Mining of the J-M Reef commenced in 1987. The ore is concentrated at the mine site and then shipped to Antwerp, Belgium, for refining. The J-M Reef is the only significant source of platinum in the United States, and the Stillwater mine is projected to be in production until about 2020.

The Sudbury complex, just north of Lake Huron in southeast Ontario, Canada, is similar in many ways to Bushveld and Stillwater, but it is not conspicuously layered. Also, nickel and copper are the main products with platinum group metals being produced as a by-product. Nickel was discovered in the Sudbury area in 1856. At that time, the region was largely wilderness, and government survey parties were engaged in running base, meridian, and range lines in preparation for a general survey and subdivision of northeast Ontario. Considerable local magnetic attraction and the presence of iron were noted during the survey. An analysis of the rock showed that it contained copper and nickel as well. The Sudbury magma was intruded 1.85 billion years ago and now appears as an elliptical ring of mafic igneous rock 60 kilometers long by 27 kilometers wide. At depth, the intrusive is believed to have the shape of a funnel, and some fifty ore deposits are found along and just outside its outer edge. The origin of the ore and of the complex itself continues to be the subject of spirited debate.

A large deposit similar to that at Sudbury exists at Norilsk in Siberia. The Soviet Union has other deposits as well, including placer platinum from the Ural Mountains. Platinum, commonly accompanied by gold, is by far the most common platinum group metal in placer deposits, as the other platinum group metals are preferentially dissolved and lost during placer formation.

Methods of Study

Although platinum has long been important as a precious metal, recent industry demands for the metal have stimulated research into the origin of platinum group metal deposits. Much of this research has been directed toward understanding the world's great mafic igneous complexes. Other avenues of investigation include laboratory studies and identification of future sources of platinum group metals.

It has long been recognized that the origin of the Merensky and J-M reefs is tied to the formation of the layering within these mafic igneous complexes. Geologists have firmly established that the mafic magmas originate in the earth's mantle and that they derive trace amounts of the platinum group metals from their mantle source rocks. It is also well known that as these magmas crystallize, the various minerals are precipitated from the magma in a fairly well-established sequence. Geologists have long believed that the layered mafic igneous complexes represent the settling of precipitated mineral grains into layers according to their densities. Repetitions and modifications in the layering are considered to be the result of currents churning within the hot magma. As crystallization proceeds, volatile elements such as water, carbon dioxide, and sulfur gradually become concentrated in the remaining magma. Sulfur has the ability to scavenge many metals, including iron, copper, nickel, and platinum group metals. Laboratory studies have shown that if the sulfur concentration is high enough, metallic sulfide droplets can form a separate, immiscible liquid. Like water in oil, the denser sulfide magma droplets sink and accumulate toward the base of the intrusion. Many geologists believe the layers and masses of metallic sulfide ore found in the large mafic igneous complexes formed in this manner.

Detailed studies of the chemical composition of the Stillwater complex, however, suggest that the crystallization sequence was interrupted at about the level of the J-M Reef by an influx of new, somewhat different magma. The evidence suggests that the magma was sulfur-saturated, and its influx is believed to have triggered the precipitation of the platinum minerals. Research on the Bushveld complex has also suggested multiple episodes of magma injection, with the Merensky Reef forming at the base of one of the magma pulses. It should be emphasized, however, that even after a century of investigation, the origin of the ore at the Bushveld, Stillwater, and Sudbury complexes is still a subject of considerable debate.

The hypotheses for ore formation at Sudbury include the separation of droplets of immiscible sulfide liquid from a mafic magma, but a lively debate exists as to the mechanism by which the mafic magma was produced. It has long been noted that a distinctive zone of broken and shattered rock many kilometers wide underlies and surrounds the Sudbury igneous complex. Overlying the complex is a thick sequence of fragmentary rocks, originally interpreted as being volcanic in origin. In 1964, Robert Dietz suggested that Sudbury was the site of a tremendous meteorite impact that formed a large crater and shattered the surrounding rock. It was later proposed that the impact caused the melting that produced the mafic igneous rock and that the supposed volcanic rock was actually material that had been ejected during the meteorite impact and had fallen back into the crater. This theory continues to cause controversy. The evidence for a meteorite impact is strong, but some geologists consider any impact to be unrelated to the Sudbury deposit. Others not only believe the impact theory but also suggest that the Bushveld magma was triggered by a meteorite impact. The debate continues, and its outcome has implications for the presence or absence of metallic ore deposits beneath the large lunar craters.

While field and laboratory work on the great platinum deposits of the world continue, so too does experimental work aimed at understanding the conditions under which these ore deposits formed. Laboratory scientists are duplicating conditions found in nature in order to increase their understanding of the behavior of platinum group elements during crystallization from magmas, their behavior during formation of immiscible liquids, and their mobility at submagmatic temperatures in water-rich solutions.

Research also continues to search for new sources of platinum group metals. A potential source may be in the incrustations of iron and manganese found on the submerged slopes of islands and seamounts throughout the world's oceans. These metallic crusts and nodules are believed to have formed by extremely slow precipitation from seawater. Although they are composed mostly of iron and manganese, they contain many metals, including those of the platinum group, and the volume of these deposits is staggering. While commercial development is unlikely before the early part of the twenty-first century, these ferromanganese crusts are considered to be an attractive, long-term resource.

Context

The platinum group metals are used extensively in modern industrial society because of their chemical inertness, high melting points, and extraordinary catalytic properties. Platinum group metals are important parts of the automotive, chemical, petroleum, glass, and electrical industries. Other important uses are found in dentistry, medicine, pollution control, and jewelry. The automotive industry is the single largest consumer of platinum group metals. Since 1974, platinum-palladium catalysts have been used in the United States to reduce emission of pollutants from automobiles and light-duty trucks. A typical catalytic converter contains 0.057 ounce of platinum, 0.015 ounce of palladium, and 0.006 ounce of rhodium. In the European Economic Community, all cars with engines larger than 2 liters produced after October, 1988, must have converters.

The electrical industry is the second largest consumer of platinum group metals. Palladium is used in low-voltage electrical contacts, and platinum electrical contacts protect ships' hulls from the corrosive activity of seawater. The dental and medical professions utilize nearly as much platinum group metals as the electrical industry. Palladium is alloyed with silver, gold, and copper to produce hard, tarnish-resistant dental crowns and bridges. Other medical uses include treatment for arthritis and some forms of cancer. Platinum group metals are also used internally in cardiac pacemakers and in a variety of pin, plate, and hinge devices used for securing human bones.

The chemical industry uses platinum and palladium as catalysts for a variety of reactions involving hydrogen and oxygen. Molecules of either of these gases are readily adsorbed onto the surface of the metals, where they dissociate into a layer of reactive atoms. Oxygen atoms on platinum, for example, increase the rate at which sulfur dioxide, a common industrial pollutant, is converted into sulfur trioxide, a component of sulfuric acid, the most widely used industrial chemical. Other pollution-control devices include the control of ozone levels in the cabins of commercial jet airplanes and oxidation of noxious organic fumes from factories and sewage treatment plants. Platinum group catalysts are also used in the production of insecticides, some plastics, paint, adhesives, polyester and nylon fibers, pharmaceuticals, fertilizers, and explosives. In the petroleum industry, platinum group metals are used by refineries both to increase the gasoline yield from crude oil and to upgrade its octane level. Because material used as a catalyst is not consumed in the chemical reactions (although small amounts are lost), the many important chemical uses actually consume only a small amount of the platinum group metals.

Platinum group metals' ability to withstand high temperatures and corrosive environments has led to its use in the ceramics and glass industry. Thin strands of glass are extruded through platinum sieves to make glass fibers for insulation, textiles, and fiber-reinforced plastics. High-quality optical glass for television picture tubes and eyeglasses is also melted in pots lined with nonreactive platinum alloys. Crystals for computer memory devices and solid-state lasers are grown in platinum and iridium crucibles. As ingots and bars, platinum group metals are sold to investors, and platinum and palladium alloys are commonly used for jewelry. Brilliant rhodium is electroplated on silver or white gold to increase whiteness, wear, and resistance to tarnishing.

The world's reserves of platinum group metals are large, but distribution is concentrated in a relatively few locations. South Africa is the largest producer of platinum, but the Soviet Union is the world's principal supplier of palladium and the second largest platinum producer. Japan is the largest consumer nation and the United States is second.

Historically, U.S. production has been extremely small and has consisted almost entirely of platinum and palladium extracted during the refining of copper. Stillwater's J-M Reef is a significant discovery, but it is expected to supply only about 7 percent of the nation's projected needs. As a result, the U.S. State Department has added the platinum group metals to a list of strategic materials that are considered to be essential for the economy and for the defense of the United States and that are unavailable in adequate quantities from reliable and secure suppliers.

Bibliography

Guilbert, John M., and Charles F. Park, Jr. *The Geology of Ore Deposits*. New York: W. H. Freeman, 1985. The best of the available college-level texts on ore deposits. The geology of the Sudbury and Bushveld complexes is covered in the chapter on deposits related to mafic igneous rocks. The book is widely available in university and large public libraries.

Loebenstein, Roger J. "Platinum-Group Metals." In *Mineral Facts and Problems*. Washington, D.C.: Department of the Interior, 1985. *Mineral Facts and Problems* is published at five-year intervals by the U.S. Department of the Interior as one of its public service functions. The book provides information on the status of all significant mineral and fuel commodities. It is available from the Bureau of Mines in Washington, D.C., and is found with other government documents at all university and large metropolitan libraries.

_____. "Platinum-Group Metals." In *Minerals Yearbook*. Washington,

D.C.: Department of the Interior, 1988. *Minerals Yearbook* is published annually in three volumes by the United States Department of the Interior. Volume 1 contains general information on nonmetallic resources and all metals, including platinum. Volume 2 has information on U.S. resources by state, and volume 3 has comparable information for other countries of the world. These volumes are widely available in university and large public libraries.

Mertic, J. B., Jr. *Economic Geology of the Platinum Metals*. U.S. Geological Survey Professional Paper 630. Washington, D.C.: Government Printing Office, 1969. A comprehensive survey and extensive bibliography of all platinum deposits, widely available in university and public libraries.

St. John, Jeffrey. *Noble Metals*. Alexandria, Va.: Time-Life Books, 1984. This book is part of Time-Life's Planet Earth series. It is an available source of good information on platinum and is written for a general audience.

Weast, Robert C., ed. *CRC Handbook of Chemistry and Physics*. Boca Raton, Fla.: CRC Press, 1988. Ths widely available reference book is the result of the collaboration of a large number of professional chemists and physicists. It contains in condensed form an immense amount of information from the fields of chemistry and physics. Section B contains an alphabetized description of all the known elements and is written in a manner understandable to those with little scientific background. New editions are published at frequent intervals, ensuring that the information is up-to-date.

Young, Gordon. "The Miracle Metal: Platinum." *National Geographic* 164 (November, 1983): 686-706. This article has excellent pictures and covers many of the uses of platinum.

Eric R. Swanson

Cross-References

The Abyssal Sea Floor, 1; Air Pollution, 24; The Archean Eon, 92; Astroblemes, 106; Igneous and Contact Metamorphic Mineral Deposits, 1124; Igneous Rock Bodies, 1131; Igneous Rocks: Ultramafic, 1207; Crystallization of Magmas, 1420; Meteorite and Comet Impacts, 1623; Future Resources, 2182; Sediment Transport and Deposition, 2290; Sedimentary Mineral Deposits, 2296.

PLUTO AND CHARON

Type of earth science: Planetology
Field of study: Large solar system bodies

Pluto and Charon constitute a double planet located far from the sun. These objects are different in composition from any of the other large planets of the solar system. In size and composition, Pluto and Charon resemble the asteroids more closely than they resemble the planets.

Principal terms

ALBEDO: the fraction of light reflected by a planet or satellite

DENSITY: the mass of a unit volume of a material

ECLIPSE: an event where all or part of the light emitted, or reflected, by an astronomical object is obscured by another astronomical object

OCCULTATION: an eclipse of any astronomical object other than the sun or the Moon caused by the Moon or any planet, satellite, or asteroid

RESOLVE: to produce separate images of objects that are close together

SPECTROSCOPY: the study of spectra to determine the properties of the source of the light

SPECTRUM: light from an object separated into its component colors

TRANSIT: the passage of a small object across the face of a larger object

Summary of the Phenomenon

Pluto was discovered by U.S. astronomer Clyde Tombaugh in 1930; its moon Charon was discovered in 1978 by James W. Christy of the U.S. Naval Observatory. (The reader should note that in the United States, the accepted pronunciation of "Charon" when referring to the moon of Pluto is *shar'on*; this pronunciation is used because it is reminiscent of Charlene, the wife of the discoverer. In the rest of the world, the pronunciation *kar'on* is usually preferred.) Less is known about Pluto than any of the other planets; it is the only planet that has not been visited by a satellite from the Earth. Earth-based telescopes cannot provide much information about Pluto and Charon, as they are too far away for surface details to appear even in the largest telescopes. In fact, Pluto and Charon are so far away that Earth-based telescopes cannot even separate them, and they appear as a single unresolved image. The discovery of Charon has rendered all that was written prior to its discovery unreliable.

Pluto is the smallest planet in the solar system, smaller even than the Moon; it is usually the outermost planet. Pluto takes 247.7 Earth years to orbit the sun and rotates on its axis once every 6.39 Earth days. The orbits of all the planets are ellipses; the orbit of Pluto is more eccentric than that of any other planet; that is, the deviation from a circle is greatest in the case of Pluto. The eccentricity of Pluto's orbit is so large that it is sometimes closer to the sun than is the planet Neptune: That is the situation between January 21, 1979, and March 14, 1999. After this date,

Pluto will be beyond the orbit of Neptune until 2226.

The distances between objects in the solar system are usually measured in astronomical units. The astronomical unit is the average distance between the Earth and the sun. Pluto can be as close to the Sun as 29.64 astronomical units and as far away as 49.24 astronomical units. At Pluto's distance from the sun, the sun appears as a starlike point, but a point more than one hundred times brighter than a full moon. The amount of solar energy received by Pluto varies greatly because of the large variation in distance between the sun and Pluto. This variation in solar energy is expected to cause the thickness of Pluto's atmosphere to vary markedly in different parts of its orbit.

Charon is similar in size to Pluto. The diameter of Pluto is approximately 2,284 kilometers, and the diameter of Charon is approximately 1,192 kilometers. The average distance between Pluto and Charon is 19,700 kilometers. Because of this proximity, along with their similar sizes, Pluto and Charon are referred to as a double planet. The orbital period of Charon about Pluto is 6.39 days; that is, the orbital period of Charon is the same as the rotation period of Pluto. That results in the same face of Pluto always pointing toward Charon. In fact, an observer on the surface of Pluto would always see Charon in the same position relative to the horizon.

The orbit of Charon is not in the plane of Pluto's orbit about the sun. Instead, the plane swept out by Charon's orbit is almost perpendicular to the plane swept out by Pluto's orbit. From the perspective of the Earth, depending on where Pluto is in its orbit, the orbit of Charon can appear as a circle, an ellipse, or a line. When the plane of Charon's orbit presents its edge to the Earth, it appears as a line, and a series of occultations and transits between Pluto and Charon occur. This series of transits and occultations results in a series of mutual eclipses being observed from the Earth. These mutual eclipses can be observed at two positions in Pluto's orbit, and so they occur every 124 years. The mutual eclipses last for about six years. The series of mutual eclipses that began in 1985 enabled the measurement of the sizes of Pluto and Charon reported above.

The surface temperature of Pluto is uncertain because the fraction of sunlight that it reflects (known as the albedo) is uncertain. It has been determined that the surface temperature is no colder than 45 Kelvins (that is, -228 degrees Celsius), above which it is unlikely to increase more than 15 degrees. The uncertainty arises because the surface composition of Pluto and the extent of its atmosphere are uncertain. The surface temperature of Charon is estimated to be 8-10 degrees warmer than Pluto's.

The density of the Pluto and Charon system has been determined to be of the order of 1,800 kilograms per cubic meter (separate density measurements have not been made). This density, almost twice that of water, indicates that Pluto and Charon are composed of a variety of ices and that as much as half of their mass could be made up of rocky material. The surface of Pluto has, in fact, been determined to contain methane ice. It is thought that, rather than the methane being uniformly distributed over the surface, there are two large polar ice caps made of methane and a thin, warmer equatorial region, where the methane has become depleted, leaving water ice.

Pluto is too small to trap a permanent atmosphere, but in the late 1980's, a thin atmosphere of methane was detected. Scientists believe that the atmosphere of Pluto was at its thickest during this period because Pluto was near its perihelion passage. At perihelion, its closest approach to the sun, Pluto receives more energy from the sun than it does during other parts of its orbit; in other words, it is heated more strongly. Methane under the conditions prevailing on Pluto acts much as frozen carbon dioxide (dry ice) does on the Earth: When it is heated sufficiently, it will form a gas directly from the solid without first forming a liquid (the process is called sublimation). It has been theorized that the atmosphere detected on Pluto may result from the sublimation of the methane from the equatorial region of its surface to form an atmosphere. Pluto will have to be observed through its entire orbit before it is known if it has an atmosphere throughout that orbit, and if it does, how the atmosphere's thickness varies. It has been suggested that when Pluto is close to aphelion (when it is most distant from the sun), only the side of Pluto facing the sun would be warm enough to maintain a methane atmosphere, and that the atmosphere on the far side of Pluto would precipitate on its surface as frost.

The surface of Charon has been determined to be covered with water ice; no frozen methane has been detected. It is expected that the interior of Charon contains methane. The composition of Charon is similar to that of some of the satellites of the Jovian planets. In fact, the surface of Charon appears to be almost identical in composition to Miranda, one of the moons of Uranus. Charon is not expected to trap an atmosphere, even temporarily. It is difficult to make an exact determination because of the great distance of Charon from the sun, but an upper limit of no more than one-twentieth of the thickness of Pluto's atmosphere has been determined. The equatorial region of Pluto that is depleted in methane is thought to have the same composition as its similarly methane-depleted moon, Charon.

Methods of Study

All the information that scientists possess about Pluto and Charon has been gained by observing from a distance. Most of the information has come through an analysis of data gathered by Earth-based telescopes. Spacecraft can travel to the outer planets in a reasonable amount of time only if they are accelerated by the gravitational fields of other planets. These gravitational boosts require a fortuitous alignment of the planets, and such an alignment will not occur for a mission to Pluto in the next hundred years.

Most of the information currently available about the dual planet has been derived from the electronic recording of telescopic images of Pluto and the computer processing of the images. The rotation period of Pluto was measured by noting that the brightness of Pluto varies periodically (the period over which the brightness varies is the rotation period of the planet). The brightness varies because the surface distribution of methane ice and water ice is not uniform, and different ices reflect different amounts of ice. Charon was discovered when James Christy was examining some electronic images of Pluto. He noticed that there was a bump on the edge of Pluto that appeared to move; this "bump" was Charon. No Earth-based telescope has been able to resolve Pluto and Charon into separate images because the presence of the Earth's atmosphere limits the maximum magnification power that can be used with the largest telescopes to about five hundred times.

The atmospheres of Pluto and Charon have been studied by two different methods: observation of occultations and spectroscopy. An occultation occurs when the light from an astronomical object is extinguished by another astronomical object, such as when Pluto passes in front of a star. The observation of occultations is the standard technique used to determine whether a planet has an atmosphere or rings. If the planet has no atmosphere, it is possible to observe the star with undiminished brightness until the disc of the planet crosses it. It then disappears completely and reappears with its usual brightness. If a planet has an atmosphere, the light from the star dims gradually as the starlight passes through the atmosphere of the planet, and when it reappears, it is faint and brightens as the planet moves farther away from the star. The atmosphere of Pluto was first detected in this manner.

Spectroscopy involves the analysis of the light reflected by Pluto. Different colors are reflected by different amounts, and some colors are completely absent from the reflected light. The spectrum of reflected light can be used to identify the chemical elements and compounds present on the surface of a planet and in its atmosphere. This procedure works because each element or compound produces a unique spectrum that can be measured in the laboratory. The infrared spectrum of Pluto has also been probed to add to the information. The main problem encountered in the Pluto-Charon system is that normally the spectra of Pluto and Charon are obtained simultaneously. The mutual eclipse events described above have enabled spectrum of Pluto alone to be obtained when Charon is behind Pluto. This Pluto spectrum can then be subtracted from the usual combined spectra to obtain the spectrum of Charon. Using this method, scientists have been able to determine the different surface compositions of Pluto and Charon.

Occultations could also be used to measure the sizes of Pluto and Charon, but instead scientists have used the series of mutual eclipses. The rotation period of Charon about Pluto is known, so if the durations of the eclipses of Charon by Pluto and of Pluto by Charon are timed, these eclipse times can then be used to estimate the diameter of Pluto and Charon. The masses of the outer planets are usually measured by their effects on the orbits of planets closer to the sun. This method, however, has not worked in the case of Pluto and Charon, because their combined mass is too small to have an observable effect on Neptune. Fortunately, the discovery of Charon has enabled the determination of the mass of Pluto from the orbital period of Charon. Kepler's third law of planetary motion states that the square of a planet's orbital period divided by the cube of its orbital radius is equal to a constant. The constant depends on the mass of the object orbited; hence, scientists have found that the mass of Pluto is about one five-hundredth Earth's mass. The mass of Charon is determined from its size by assuming it has the same density as Pluto.

Context

Pluto is the outermost planet and the most difficult to investigate. What has been learned about it indicates that it is different from all the other planets. The other four planets of the outer solar system (Jupiter, Saturn, Uranus, Neptune) have low densities and are composed primarily of gases. The density of Pluto is greater, indicating the presence of rocky material. Nevertheless, the density is lower than the densities of the rocky planets of the inner solar system (Mercury, Venus, Earth, Mars). Pluto has features in common with the Galilean moons of Jupiter and some of the moons of Saturn, Uranus, and Neptune, but none has exactly the same makeup. Charon is in many ways similar to an asteroid. In fact, models developed for asteroids covered with water ice are applicable to Charon, and they have been used profitably in an attempt to gain a deeper understanding of Charon.

This pair of small worlds may seem insignificant in comparison with the other, larger planets of the outer solar system, but if scientists are ever to develop a complete understanding of the origins and evolution of the solar system, they will need a detailed knowledge of all its members. Pluto is usually the farthest planet away from the sun, but in many ways, it has more in common with the debris of the solar system—the comets, meteoroids, and asteroids—than it does with the other major planets. Pluto could well be one of a large number of similar objects in the outer solar system. Although there are no large objects in the solar system even ten times farther away from the sun than is Pluto, there is a spherical swarm of debris far from the sun, called the Oort Cloud, that is the source of comets. In developing an understanding of Pluto and Charon, scientists may be laying the groundwork for a better understanding of the Oort Cloud.

Study of the Pluto-Charon system may also answer some questions about Neptune and its moons. One of the theories for the origin of Pluto is that it was once a moon of Neptune. That appears less likely since scientists have learned that Pluto has a moon, but an exact determination of its orbit would provide a definitive answer. The mysteries of the solar system include the eccentric orbit of Neptune's satellite Nereid and the clockwise direction (as viewed from the North Pole) of the orbit of another satellite, Triton, when all the other large moons of the solar system orbit their planets in a counterclockwise direction. Both of these oddities could be explained by a collision in which Pluto broke free.

Bibliography

Burns, Joseph A., and Mildred Shapley Matthews, eds. *Satellites*. Tucson: University of Arizona Press, 1986. A review of the properties of all the satellites of the solar system that had been discovered prior to its publication. Despite the title of the book, Pluto and Charon are both discussed in articles that are suitable for general readers.

Greeley, Ronald, and Michael H. Carr, eds. *A Geological Basis for the Exploration of the Planets*. Washington, D.C.: National Aeronautics and Space Administration, 1976. This publication defines the geological goals of planetary geology. Primarily concerned with the strategy of planetary exploration, the work describes the development of different methods, using the knowledge gained from the earliest planetary explorations. The different roles played by Earth-based observations and satellite exploration are discussed. Provides strong justification for continued planetary exploration. Easily accessible to high school and general readers.

Larson, Harold P. "Infrared Spectroscopic Observation of the Outer Planets, Their Satellites, and the Asteroids." *Annual Review of Astronomy and Astrophysics* 18 (1980): 43-75. This publication is written to present current knowledge of the state of astronomy to a wide audience; although the series is not specifically intended for the lay reader, the majority of articles are usually accessible. This particular article describes how the basic composition of the outer planets was measured. Confined to methods and omitting the mathematical background, it is more suited to the lay reader than to a technical audience.

Morrison, David, and Tobias Owen. *The Planetary System*. Reading, Mass.: Addison-Wesley, 1988. An introduction to the properties of all the major objects of the solar system. At the level of a college descriptive astronomy text. A good source of data about the solar system, it provides a detailed comparative planetology.

Pasachoff, Jay M. *Contemporary Astronomy*. 4th ed. Philadelphia: Saunders College Publishing, 1989. A textbook for use in college descriptive astronomy courses that devotes more space to Pluto than most; there are, however, still only five pages. The limited coverage is wide-ranging and presents an account of methods as well as summarizes information. Recommended to any reader seeking a broad knowledge of the current state of astronomy.

Pollack, James B. "Origin and History of the Outer Planets." *Annual Review of Astronomy and Astrophysics* 22 (1984): 389-424. This article provides general information about the evolution of the planets and satellites of the outer solar system. Uses some technical terminology but should present no undue difficulties to the lay reader with an interest in astronomy.

Tombaugh, Clyde W., and Patrick Moore. *Out of the Darkness: The Planet Pluto*. New York: New American Library, 1981. A book about the discovery of Pluto, written by the discoverer and a well-known popularizer of astronomy. Tombaugh describes his career and his discovery of Pluto. Moore describes the discovery of Neptune and Uranus. Of interest primarily from a historical perspective, as much of the material on the physical properties of Pluto and Charon is outdated.

Stephen R. Addison

Cross-References

Asteroids, 98; Comets, 253; Infrared Spectra, 1232; The Jovian Planets, 1283; The Jovian Planets' Satellites, 1303; Meteors and Meteor Showers, 1666; Phase Changes, 2042; Phase Equilibria, 2049; Elemental Distribution in the Solar System, 2434; The Origin of the Solar System, 2442.

POLAR WANDER

Type of earth science: Geophysics
Field of study: Geomagnetism and paleomagnetism

Evidence from several of the earth sciences clearly demonstrates that the earth's magnetic and geographic poles have been located at widely separated places relative to its surface during the planet's geological history.

Principal terms

ASTHENOSPHERE: a hypothetical zone of the earth that lies beneath the lithosphere and within which material is believed to yield readily to persistent stresses

ICE AGES: periods in the earth's past when large areas of the present continents were glaciated

LITHOSPHERE: the outer layer of the earth

NORTH GEOGRAPHIC POLE: the northernmost region of the earth, located at the northern point of the planet's axis of rotation

NORTH MAGNETIC POLE: a small, nonstationary area in the Arctic Circle toward which a compass needle points from any location on the earth

PALEOMAGNETISM: the intensity and direction of residual magnetization in ancient rocks

PLATE TECTONICS: the study of the motions of the earth's crust

Summary of the Phenomenon

Shortly before World War II, geophysicists discovered a method of determining the location of rocks on the earth's surface at the time they were formed, relative to the north magnetic pole. Thus began the study of paleomagnetism. Paleomagnetic studies quickly yielded very puzzling and often contradictory results. The new science produced evidence that the north magnetic pole has changed its location by thousands and even tens of thousands of miles hundreds of times during the earth's geologic history. Since earth scientists are generally agreed that the north magnetic pole has always corresponded closely with the north geographic pole, this evidence seemed to indicate that the earth's axis of rotation must have changed, a highly unlikely occurrence.

As the paleomagnetic evidence for different locations of the poles in the past accumulated through measurements of rock formations from around the world, more and more earth scientists began to accept the theory of continental drift. This theory offered an explanation of the paleomagnetic evidence without the necessity of postulating that the earth's axis of rotation had changed in the past. Alfred Wegener, early in the twentieth century, had drawn attention to the theory that the continents moved in relation to one another. Most geologists initially greeted his theories with derision, but many others agreed with him, causing an often bitter controversy in the earth sciences that lasted almost half a century. The ever-growing body of paleomagnetic evidence could be explained by postulation that the surface areas of the earth move in relationship to the planet's axis of rotation. This explanation proved to be more acceptable to geologists than the idea that the axis of rotation changed.

With the growing acceptance of the theory of continental drift in the 1940's, geologists began trying to explain the mechanism that caused it. They postulated that the earth has a stable and very dense core overlain by an area called the asthenosphere, which is made up of rock rendered plastic by heat and pressure. Floating on the asthenosphere is the earth's outer crust, or lithosphere. Dislocation within the earth caused by the action of heat and pressure result in the movement of the lithosphere relative to the core and to the axis of rotation. The initial attempts to explain continental drift have been considerably revised and refined into the modern theories of plate tectonics and ocean-bed spreading, but the basic premise remains the same: The surface areas of the earth move in relationship to its core and to its axis of rotation. The result of the movement of the earth's lithosphere is that the surface area located at the axis of rotation does not remain the same over long periods of time. This shifting accounts for the apparent "wandering" of the poles as well as for several other puzzling aspects of earth's geologic history.

Striking evidence that the surface areas of the earth have moved enormous distances during geologic history relative to its axis of rotation comes from the study of glaciers. Observations from around the globe show that almost all the land areas of the earth have been glaciated at some time in the past, including parts of Africa, India, and South America presently located on or near the equator. Without postulating either a substantial shifting of the earth's surface relative to its axis of rotation or a change in the axis, equatorial glaciation is inexplicable. If global temperatures dropped to levels sufficient to glaciate even the equator at some time in the past, all life on earth would have been destroyed. If, however, the areas of Africa, India, and South America which are presently located in tropical locales once shifted to the polar regions and shifted from there to their present locations, their ancient glaciation is not at all mysterious.

Shifting of the earth's surface relative to its axis of rotation is almost certainly a major cause of the so-called ice ages, the origins of which have puzzled glaciologists since the beginnings of that science. Previous explanations of the ice ages— including global drops in temperature, the passage of the earth through exceptionally cold regions in space or through areas containing "spacedust" that blocked out a significant amount of the sun's radiation, and unexplained fluctuations in the amount of radiation generated by the sun—are all unsatisfactory. It seems much more likely that areas of the earth that were glaciated in the past, such as northern Europe and North America as far south as present-day New Jersey, were located much closer to one or the other of the poles at the time they were covered with ice.

The study of paleoclimatology has also produced evidence supporting the proposition of the shifting of the earth's crust relative to its axis of rotation. Paleoclimatologists study the climates of past ages on the various parts of earth's surface. They have found that Antarctica once supported rich varieties of plant and animal life, many of which could only have lived in temperate and even subtropical climates. Explorations in the far northern regions of Canada, Alaska, and Siberia have revealed that those areas also supported multitudes of animals and luxurious forests in the past, as did many of the islands presently located within the Arctic Circle. Obviously, those regions must have had much warmer climates at the times when the plant and animal life flourished there, which can be explained in only one of two ways: Either the climate of the entire world was much warmer in the past, or those areas now located near the poles were once located in much more temperate latitudes. If the entire world had warmed to the point that the polar areas had temperate climates, the tropical and subtropical areas of the earth would have been much too hot to support life, which is demonstrably untrue according to the fossil record. Thus, the areas now near the poles must have been located in temperate climatic latitudes in the past.

Earth scientists, using the evidence discussed above and paleomagnetism, have established an approximate chronology showing which areas of the earth's surface were located at its north rotational axis during past ages. At the beginning of the Cambrian period (roughly 600 million years ago), the area of the Pacific Ocean now occupied by the Hawaiian Islands was at or near the earth's north rotational axis. By the Ordovician period 100 million years later, the surface of the earth had shifted in such a manner that the area approximately 1,000 miles north and east of modern Japan was on or near the North Pole. Fifty-five million years later, during the Silurian period, modern Sakhalin Island north of Japan was within the Arctic Circle. During the next 20 million years, the area of modern Kamchatka in eastern Siberia shifted to a position very near the pole. Earth scientists have identified ninety-nine separate locations that occupied the polar regions at one time or another during the ensuing 395 million years from the Silurian to the Pleistocene. During the past million years, forty-three different areas of the earth's surface have been on or near the north geographic poles, averaging over 1,500 miles distance from each other.

Although contemporary earth scientists have reached a consensus that the surface of the earth has shifted relative to the planet's axis of rotation many times in the past, several problems remain. One area on which there is no unanimity of opinion is the mechanism responsible for crustal shift. The answer most likely lies in high-pressure physics and the nature of the asthenosphere. Another, more controversial, problem concerns the speed of crustal shifts. During most of the twentieth century, almost all the geologists who were daring enough to accept the theory of continental drift assumed that the movement of surface features of the earth relative to the axis of rotation and relative to one another was very slow, on the order of a few inches per year at most. Then an increasing number of earth scientists began arguing for short periods of relatively rapid movement of the earth's crust and long periods of stability.

These problems notwithstanding, there can no longer be any doubt that the surface of the earth has shifted many times relative to its rotational axis. The phenomenon has led to the mistaken assumption that the rotational axis has moved relative to the earth's surface—thus the term "polar wander." The rotational axis of the earth has remained constant throughout its history; apparent polar wander is caused by the shifting of the earth's crust.

Methods of Study

The study of paleomagnetism during the twentieth century has yielded irrefutable evidence that many different areas of the earth's surface have occupied polar positions during the history of the planet. Scientists studying paleomagnetism measure the weak magnetization of rocks. Virtually all rocks contain iron compositions that can become magnetized. In the study of paleomagnetism, the most important of these compositions are magnetite and hematite, which are commonly found in the basaltic rocks and sandstones. Paleomagnetism may also be measured in less common rocks that contain iron sulfide. In igneous rocks, magnetization takes place when the iron compositions within the rocks align themselves with the earth's magnetic field as the rocks cool. In sedimentary rocks, small magnetic particles align with the magnetic field as they settle through the water and maintain that alignment as the sediments into which they sink solidify.

Magnetized rocks not only indicate the direction of the north magnetic pole at the time they were formed but also show how far from the pole they were at formation by the angle of their dip. Scientists call their horizontal angle the variation and their dip the inclination. Variation reveals the approximate longitude of the rock sample at the time of its formation, relative to the north magnetic pole, and inclination gives its approximate latitude. By ascertaining the date at which the rock sample being examined was formed, using well-known dating methods, scientists are able to establish the area of the earth's surface relative to the north magnetic pole that was occupied by the rock at the time of its formation.

There are, however, many pitfalls for the unwary scientist investigating paleomagnetism. A rock whose magnetism is being studied may have moved considerable distances from its place of formation by glacial action or by crustal movement along a major fracture in the earth's surface, such as the San Andreas fault on North America's west coast. High temperatures, pressure, and chemical action can distort or destroy the magnetization of a rock. Folding and the movement of the continents relative to one another may also alter the original orientation of the rocks whose magnetism is being studied. All these pitfalls may be avoided through the expedient of basing estimates of the relative position of the north magnetic pole on a great number of rock samples of the same age, gathered from many different locations on all the continents.

Another problem in paleomagnetic studies involves the constant movement of the north magnetic pole relative to the north geographic pole. Recent studies show that the north magnetic pole moved from 70 degrees to 76 degrees north latitude (approximately 345 miles, or 576 kilometers) during the period 1831-1975. This phenomenon might accurately be called true polar wander, though it does not involve any alteration either of the earth's axis of rotation or of the surface of the planet relative to its axis of rotation. Most geophysicists studying this movement have concluded that over a period of several thousand years, the average position of the north magnetic pole coincides closely with that of the north geographic pole. Thus, when scientists learn that the north magnetic pole was located near Hawaii 600 million years ago, it is a virtual certainty that modern Hawaii was at that time located near the north geographic pole.

Context

The most immediate and pressing question facing all residents of planet Earth concerning apparent polar wander is the speed with which the phenomenon may occur. A historian of science, Charles H. Hapgood, compiled a huge amount of compelling evidence in the 1950's that massive shifts of the earth's crust relative to its axis of rotation occur in geologically brief periods of time. Hapgood made a very strong case for the surface area of the Canadian Yukon, which is now located at approximately 62 degrees north latitude and longitude 137 degrees west, having occupied the north geographic pole prior to 80,000 years ago. Then, in a massive movement which took less than 5,000 years, the earth's surface shifted in such a way that an area of the Greenland Sea now located at approximately 72 degrees north latitude and longitude 10 degrees east occupied the north polar region. This shift involves a distance of almost 5,000 miles.

Hapgood offers further evidence that the earth's surface remained stable relative to its axis of rotation for approximately twenty thousand years, then began another massive shift resulting in the area of Hudson's Bay that now occupies the surface region located at about 60 degrees north latitude and longitude 83 degrees west, moving to the earth's north rotational axis. This movement of approximately 3,500 miles took less than 5,000 years. Again the earth's surface became stable, according to Hapgood, this time for more than 30,000 years, until about 17,000 years ago. At that time, the earth's surface began another movement lasting nearly 5,000 years and resulting in the present surface-pole relationship.

If Hapgood is right about the surface of the planet shifting enormous distances in relatively short periods of time, the period during which the shift actually occurs must be a traumatic era for the earth's flora and fauna, including humankind. Such rapid movement would certainly produce earthquakes and volcanic action of almost unimaginable proportions throughout the globe. Weather and tidal patterns would be greatly and unpredictably altered, which could have fatal consequences for many plant and animal species. This last result offers yet another piece of powerful evidence for the rapid-shift hypothesis.

The earth's fossil record offers examples of the mass extinction and extermination of many species of flora and fauna during the geological history of the planet. The most recent such event occurred at the end of the Pleistocene epoch, about 12,000 years ago. Literally tens of millions of animals in North America alone died in a relatively short period of time, leaving their sometimes remarkably well-preserved remains lumped together in huge "boneyards," stretching geographically from Alaska to Florida. This mass extermination of fauna must have been caused by the events accompanying crustal displacement: Volcanic action on a gigantic scale not only would throw huge amounts of ash into the air, causing a lowering of global temperatures and an increase in rainfall producing widespread flooding, but also would produce enormous quantities of poisonous gases lethal to animals and humans in the vicinity; rapid and pronounced weather changes would destroy food supplies which may have been the ultimate cause of extinctions of many species; widespread earthquakes could also take a large toll on animal life.

If, as more and more geophysicists are coming to believe, the shifting of the earth's surface does take place rapidly at infrequent intervals and for reasons not currently well understood, the phenomenon is of the utmost importance. Modern civilization could not survive the enormous climatic dislocations that must accompany such a shift. It is therefore imperative that the phenomenon known as polar wander be studied to the point that it can be, if not prevented, at least predicted and prepared for.

Bibliography

Brooks, C. E. P. *Climate Through the Ages*. New York: McGraw-Hill, 1949. This work synthesizes data from many earth sciences to demonstrate clearly that every surface area of the earth has at different times in the planet's history been subjected to every extreme of climate, from arctic to equatorial and everything in between.

Daly, R. A. *Our Mobile Earth*. New York: Scribner's, 1926. Daly was one of the first earth scientists to propose that the earth's surface has shifted over long distances relative to its axis of rotation and over relatively brief periods of time; this book explains Daly's views and his theory on the mechanism that causes the shifts. Suitable for anyone with a high school education.

Doell, Richard R., and Allan Cox. *Paleomagnetism*. Vol. 8, *Advances in Geophysics*. New York: Academic Press, 1961. Despite its extensive use of technical terms, this book can prove informative to the layperson interested in the scientific underpinnings of paleomagnetism and associated problems.

Hapgood, Charles H. *Earth's Shifting Crust*. Philadelphia: Chilton, 1958. Revised and reissued by Chilton in 1970 as *The Path of the Poles*. Hapgood's pioneering work presents a sound and clear argument that the earth's surface has shifted rapidly many times relative to its axis of rotation. Includes a foreword by Albert Einstein. Readily understandable to the layperson.

Hibben, Frank C. *The Lost Americans*. New York: Thomas Y. Crowell, 1946. Hibben provides a wealth of information concerning the great animal extermination at the end of the Pleistocene. His evidence shows clearly that the extermination was the result of one or more natural catastrophes of enormous proportions.

Material is presented in nontechnical language accessible to any reader with a high school education.

Hooker, Dolph Earl. *Those Astonishing Ice Ages*. New York: Exposition Press, 1958. Hooker's book is designed to make information concerning past ice ages accessible to a general audience. Includes evidence that areas now on or near the equator were once glaciated.

Irving, E. "Pole Positions and Continental Drift Since the Devonian." In *The Earth: Its Origins, Structure, and Evolution*, edited by M. W. McElhinny. New York: Academic Press, 1980. Irving uses the results of half a century of magnetic measurements to establish which areas at the earth's surface were located at its magnetic pole during the various geological periods. A layperson can follow the gist of his arguments.

King, Lester C. *Wandering Continents and Spreading Sea Floors on an Expanding Earth*. New York: John Wiley & Sons, 1983. Most of this book is written in language much too technical for the general public. It does contain, however, a chapter on paleomagnetism with a good explanation of the techniques and pitfalls of that science and a chapter of plate tectonics with considerable evidence that shiftings of the earth's crust have occurred rapidly and at irregular intervals over geological history.

Munyan, Arthur C., ed. *Polar Wandering and Continental Drift*. Tulsa, Okla.: Society of Economic Paleontologists and Mineralogists, 1963. The articles contained in this publication range in topic from ancient climates through the study of paleomagnetism. Although a background in geology is necessary to understand all the nuances in the articles, most of them can be followed by the general reader.

Whitley, D. Gath. "The Ivory Islands of the Arctic Ocean." *Journal of the Philosophical Society of Great Britain* 12 (1910). Whitley describes in detail the myriad bones of large land mammals which lived during the Pleistocene, stacked to heights of more than 100 feet on many of the islands within the present Arctic Circle. That these animals could not have lived in those areas given present climatic conditions is axiomatic.

Paul Madden

Cross-References

Earth's Crust, 518; Earth's Rotation, 576; The Fossil Record, 760; Continental Glaciers, 967; Ice Ages, 1115; Mass Extinctions, 1514; Paleoclimatology, 1993; Plate Tectonics, 2079; Rock Magnetism, 2217.

PRECIPITATION

Type of earth science: Hydrology

Precipitation consists of particles of liquid or frozen water that fall from clouds to the earth's surface. Thus, precipitation links the atmosphere with the other reservoirs of the global hydrologic cycle, replenishing oceanic and terrestrial reservoirs (rivers, lakes, groundwater). In addition, precipitation is the ultimate source of fresh water for irrigation, industrial consumption, and supplies of drinking water.

Principal terms

ACID PRECIPITATION: rain or snow that is more acidic than normal, usually because of the presence of sulfuric and nitric acid

BERGERON PROCESS: precipitation formation in cold clouds whereby ice crystals grow at the expense of supercooled water droplets

COLD CLOUD: a visible suspension of tiny ice crystals, supercooled water droplets, or both at sub-freezing temperatures

COLLISION-COALESCENCE PROCESS: precipitation formation in warm clouds whereby larger droplets grow by merging with smaller droplets

RAIN GAUGE: an instrument for measuring rainfall, usually consisting of a cylindrical container open to the sky

SUPERCOOLED WATER DROPLETS: liquid droplets at subfreezing temperatures

WARM CLOUD: a visible suspension of tiny water droplets at temperatures above freezing

Summary of the Phenomenon

Precipitation consists of liquid or frozen particles of water that fall from clouds and reach the earth's surface. Probably the most familiar types of precipitation are raindrops and snowflakes. Perhaps surprisingly, most clouds, even those associated with large storm systems, do not produce precipitation. A special set of circumstances is required for the extremely small water droplets and/or ice crystals that compose a cloud to grow into raindrops or snowflakes. A typical cloud particle is about one-millionth the size of a raindrop.

Cloud particle diameters are typically in the range of 2-50 micrometers (a micrometer is one-millionth of a meter). They are so small that they remain suspended within the atmosphere unless they vaporize or somehow undergo considerable growth. Upward-directed air currents (updrafts) are usually strong enough to prevent cloud particles from leaving the base of a cloud. Even if cloud droplets or ice crystals descend from a cloud, their fall rates are so slow that they quickly vaporize in the relatively dry air under the cloud. In order to precipitate, therefore, cloud particles must grow sufficiently massive that they counter updrafts and survive thousands of meters of descent to the earth's surface. Cloud physicists have identified two processes whereby cloud particles grow large enough to precipitate: the Bergeron process and the collision-coalescence process.

Most precipitation originates via the Bergeron process, named for the Scandinavian meteorologist Tor Bergeron, who, about 1930, first described the process. It occurs within cold clouds, that is, clouds at a temperature below freezing (0 degrees Celsius). Cold clouds are composed of ice crystals or supercooled water droplets or a mixture of the two. Supercooled water droplets are tiny drops that remain liquid even at subfreezing temperatures. Bergeron discovered that precipitation is most likely to fall from cold clouds composed of a mixture in which supercooled water droplets at least initially greatly outnumber ice crystals. In such a circumstance, ice crystals grow rapidly while supercooled water droplets vaporize. As ice crystals grow, their fall rates within the cloud increase. They collide and merge with smaller ice crystals and supercooled water droplets in their paths and thereby grow still larger. Eventually, ice crystals become so heavy that they fall out of the cloud base. If air temperature is subfreezing during at least most of the descent, crystals reach the earth's surface as snowflakes. If, however, the air below the cloud is above freezing, the snowflakes melt and fall as raindrops.

Growth of ice crystals at the expense of supercooled water droplets in the Bergeron process is linked to the difference in the rate of escape of water molecules from an ice crystal versus a water droplet. Water molecules are considerably more active in the liquid phase than in the solid phase; hence, water molecules escape water droplets more readily than they do ice crystals. Within a cold cloud, air that is saturated for water droplets is actually supersaturated for ice crystals. Consequently, water molecules diffuse from the water droplets and deposit on the ice crystals; that is, water droplets vaporize and ice crystals grow.

The collision-coalescence process occurs in warm clouds (clouds at temperatures above 0 degrees Celsius). Such clouds are composed entirely of liquid water droplets. Precipitation may develop if the range of cloud droplet sizes is broad. Larger cloud droplets have greater fall velocities than do smaller droplets; as a result, larger droplets collide and coalesce with smaller droplets in their paths. Collision and coalescence are repeated a multitude of times until the droplets become so large and heavy that they fall from the base of the cloud as raindrops.

Once a raindrop or snowflake leaves a cloud, it enters drier air—a hostile environment in which some of the precipitation vaporizes. In general, the longer the journey to the earth's surface and the drier the air beneath the cloud, the greater the amount of rain or snow that returns to the atmosphere as vapor. It is understandable, then, why highlands receive more precipitation than do lowlands, which are farther from the base of clouds.

Precipitation occurs in a variety of liquid and frozen forms. Besides the familiar rain and snow, precipitation also occurs as drizzle, freezing rain, ice pellets, and hail. Drizzle consists of small water drops less than 0.5 millimeter in diameter that drift very slowly to the earth's surface. The relatively small size of drizzle drops stems from their origin in low stratus clouds or fog. Such clouds are so shallow that droplets originating within them have a limited opportunity to grow by coalescence.

Rain falls mostly from thick nimbostratus and cumulonimbus (thunderstorm) clouds. The bulk of rain originates as snowflakes or hailstones, which melt on the way down as they enter air that is warmer than 0 degrees Celsius. Because rain originates in thicker clouds, raindrops travel farther than does drizzle, and they undergo more growth by coalescence. Most commonly, raindrop diameters range from 0.5 to 5 millimeters; beyond this range, drops are unstable and break up into many smaller drops. Freezing rain (or freezing drizzle) develops when rain falls from a relatively mild air layer into a shallow layer of subfreezing air at ground level. Drops become supercooled, then freeze immediately on contact with subfreezing surfaces. Freezing rain forms a layer of ice that sometimes grows thick and heavy enough to bring down tree limbs, snap power lines, disrupt traffic, and make walking hazardous.

Snow is an assemblage of ice crystals in the form of flakes. Although it is said that no two snowflakes are identical, all snowflakes have hexagonal (six-sided) symmetry. Snowflake form varies with air temperature and water vapor concentration and may consist of flat plates, stars, columns, or needles. Snowflake size also depends in part on the availability of water vapor during the crystal growth process. At very low temperatures, the water vapor concentration is low so that snowflakes are relatively small. Snowflake size also depends on collision efficiency as the flakes drift toward the ground. At temperatures near freezing, snowflakes are wet and readily stick together after colliding, so flake diameters may eventually exceed 5 centimeters. Snow grains and snow pellets are closely related to snowflakes. Snow grains originate in much the same way as drizzle, except that they are frozen; diameters are generally less than 1 millimeter. Snow pellets are soft conical or spherical white particles of ice with diameters of 1-5 millimeters. They are formed when supercooled cloud droplets collide and freeze together, and they may accompany a fall of snow.

Ice pellets, often called sleet, are frozen raindrops. They develop in much the same way as does freezing rain except that the surface layer of subfreezing air is so deep that raindrops freeze before striking the ground. Sleet can be distinguished readily from freezing rain, because sleet bounces when striking a hard surface, whereas freezing rain does not.

Hail consists of rounded or irregular masses of ice, often characterized by concentric layering, resembling the interior of an onion. Hail develops within severe thunderstorms as vigorous updrafts transport ice pellets upward into the upper reaches of the cloud. (Often, severe thunderstorms reach altitudes of more than 10 kilometers.) Along the way, ice pellets grow via coalescence with supercooled water droplets and eventually become too heavy to be supported by updrafts. Ice pellets then descend through the cloud, exit the cloud base, and enter air that is typically above freezing. As ice pellets begin to melt, those that are large enough may survive the journey to the ground as hailstones. Most hail consists of harmless granules of ice less than 1 centimeter in diameter, but violent thunderstorms may spawn destructive hailstones the size of golf balls or larger. Hail is usually a spring and summer phenomenon that is particularly devastating to crops.

Over the past few decades, considerable concern has been directed at the environmental impact of changes in the chemistry of precipitation. The global hydrologic cycle purifies water through distillation, but as raindrops and snowflakes fall from clouds to the ground, they wash pollutants from the air. In this way, the chemistry of precipitation is altered. Rain is normally slightly acidic, because it dissolves atmospheric carbon dioxide, producing weak carbonic acid. Where air is polluted with oxides of sulfur and oxides of nitrogen, these gases interact with moisture in the atmosphere to produce droplets of sulfuric acid and nitric acid. These acid droplets dissolve in precipitation and increase its acidity. Precipitation that falls through such polluted air may become two hundred times more acidic than normal.

Field studies have confirmed a trend toward increasingly acidic rains and snows over the eastern third of the United States. Much of this upswing in acidity can be attributed to acid rain precursors emitted during fuel combustion. Coal-burning for electric power generation is the principal source of sulfur oxides, while high-temperature industrial processes and motor vehicle engines produce nitrogen oxides. Where acid rains fall on soils or bedrock that cannot neutralize the acidity, lakes and streams become more acidic. Excessively acidic lake or stream water disrupts the reproductive cycles of fish. Acid rains leach metals (such as aluminum) from the soil, washing them into lakes and streams, where they may harm fish and aquatic plants.

Methods of Study

Precipitation is collected and measured with essentially the same device that has been used since the fifteenth century: a container open to the sky. The standard U.S. National Weather Service rain gauge consists of a cone-shaped funnel that directs rainwater into a long, narrow cylinder that sits inside a larger cylinder. The narrow cylinder magnifies the scale of accumulating rainwater so that rainfall can be resolved into increments of 0.01 inch. (Rainfall of less than 0.005 inch is recorded as a "trace.") Rainwater that accumulates in the inner cylinder is measured by a stick, which is graduated in centimeters or inches. Rainfall is measured at some fixed time once every twenty-four hours, and the gauge is then emptied.

With regard to snow, scientists are interested in measuring snowfall during each twenty-four-hour period between observations, the meltwater equivalent of that snowfall, and the depth of snow on the ground at each observation time. New snowfall is usually collected on a simple board that is placed on top of the old snow cover. When new snow falls, the depth is measured to the board; the board is then swept clean and moved to a new location. The meltwater equivalent of new snowfall can be determined by melting the snow collected in a rain gauge (from which the funnel has been removed). Snow depth is usually measured with a special yardstick or meterstick. In mountainous terrain where snowfall is substantial, it may be necessary to use a coring device to determine snow depth (and meltwater equivalent). Snow depth is determined at several representative locations and then averaged.

The average density of fresh-fallen snow is 0.1 gram per cubic centimeter. As a general rule, 10 centimeters of fresh snow melts down to 1 centimeter of rainwater. This ratio varies considerably depending on the temperature at which the snow falls. "Wet" snow falling at surface air temperatures at or above 0 degrees Celsius has a much greater water content than does "dry" snow falling at surface air temperatures well below freezing. The ratio of snowfall to meltwater may vary from 3:1 for very wet snow to 30:1 for dry, fluffy snow.

Monitoring the timing and rate of rainfall is often desirable, especially in areas prone to flooding. Hence, some rain gauges provide a cumulative record of rainfall. In a weighing-bucket rain gauge, the weight of accumulating rainwater (determined by a spring balance) is calibrated as water depth. Cumulative rainfall is recorded continuously by a device that either marks a chart on a clock-driven drum or sends an electrical pulse to a computer or magnetic tape. During subfreezing weather, antifreeze in the collection bucket melts snow as it falls into the gauge so that a cumulative meltwater record is produced.

Both rainfall and snowfall are notoriously variable from one place to another, especially when produced by showers or thunderstorms. The siting of a precipitation gauge is particularly important in order to ensure accurate and representative readings. A level site must be selected that is sheltered from strong winds and is well away from buildings and vegetation that might shield the instrument. In general, obstacles should be no closer than about four times their height.

Context

Without precipitation, the earth would have no fresh water and thus no life. When water vaporizes from oceans, lakes, and other reservoirs on the earth's surface, all dissolved and suspended substances are left behind. Hence, water is purified (distilled) as it cycles into the atmosphere and eventually returns to the earth's surface as freshwater precipitation. In this way, the global hydrologic cycle supplies the planet with a fixed quantity of fresh water.

As human population continues its rapid growth, however, demands on the globe's fixed supply of fresh water are also increasing. In some areas, such as the semiarid American Southwest, water demand for agriculture and municipalities has spurred attempts to enhance precipitation locally through cloud seeding. Usually, cold clouds that contain too few ice crystals are seeded by aircraft with either silver iodide crystals (a substance with properties similar to ice) or dry-ice pellets (solid carbon dioxide at a temperature of about -80 degrees Celsius) in an effort to stimulate the Bergeron precipitation process.

Cloud seeding, although founded on an understanding of how precipitation forms, is not always successful and at best may enhance precipitation by perhaps 20 percent. The question remains as to whether the rain or snow that follows cloud seeding would have fallen anyway. Even if successful, cloud seeding may merely bring about a geographical redistribution of precipitation so that an increase in precipitation in one area is accompanied by a compensating reduction in a neighboring area. Cloud seeding that benefits agriculture in eastern Colorado, for example, might also deprive farmers of rain in the downwind states of Kansas and Nebraska. The uncertainties of cloud seeding underscore the need for conservation of the planet's freshwater resource. Conservation should entail not only strategies directed at wise use of fresh water but also measures to manage water quality. Abatement of water pollution not only reduces hazards to human health and aquatic systems but also increases the supply of fresh water.

Bibliography

Colbeck, Samuel C. "What Becomes of a Winter Snowflake?" *Weatherwise* 38 (1985): 312-315. This article describes the processes taking place within a snowbank. Well illustrated.

Leopold, Luna B. *Water: A Primer.* New York: W. H. Freeman, 1974. A concise and well-illustrated treatment of the global hydrologic cycle. Provides the context within which precipitation processes take place.

Moran, Joseph M., and Michael D. Morgan. *Meteorology: The Atmosphere and the Science of Weather.* 2d ed. New York: Macmillan, 1989. A well-illustrated survey of atmospheric science. Includes chapters on the hydrologic cycle, cloud development, and precipitation processes.

Oliver, John E., and Rhodes W. Fairbridge, eds. *The Encyclopedia of Climatology.* New York: Van Nostrand Reinhold, 1987. A comprehensive treatise on the basics of climatology. Includes a detailed discussion of the global and seasonal distribution of precipitation.

Oliver, John E., and John J. Hidore. *Climatology: An Introduction.* Westerville, Ohio: Charles E. Merrill, 1984. A well-written survey of the principles of climate and the climates of the globe. Provides a background on the factors that control the spatial and temporal distribution of precipitation.

Schaefer, Vincent J., and John A. Day. *A Field Guide to the Atmosphere.* Boston: Houghton Mifflin, 1981. An exceptionally well illustrated survey of cloud and precipitation processes. Includes suggested simple experiments and demonstrations.

Schindler, D. W. "Effects of Acid Rain on Freshwater Ecosystems." *Science* 239 (1988): 149-156. An excellent summary of what is currently understood about the impact of acidic precipitation.

Snow, J. T., and S. B. Harley. "Basic Meteorological Observations for Schools: Rainfall." *Bulletin of the American Meteorological Society* 69 (1988): 497-507. This article discusses rainfall measurement and evaluates inexpensive rain gauges suitable for classroom use.

Joseph M. Moran

Cross-References

Acid Rain, 9; Climate, 217; Clouds, 224; Drainage Basins, 384; Freshwater Chemistry, 795; The Hydrologic Cycle, 1102; Storms, 2477; Weathering and Erosion, 2723.

PROKARYOTES

Type of earth science: Paleontology and earth history

Prokaryotes are primitive, one-celled organisms that have left an extensive fossil record in the form of sedimentary structures produced by physiological activity of cell communities. For 80 percent of earth history, communities of prokaryotes made up the biosphere of the earth. They are a well-defined group of organisms and occupy a highly diverse variety of habitats.

Principal terms

AEROBES: prokaryotes (usually bacteria) that live in the presence of elemental oxygen

ANAEROBES: prokaryotes that can live only in an atmosphere that is free of elemental oxygen

DEOXYRIBONUCLEIC ACID (DNA): a molecule made up of two strands of nucleotides arranged in a double helix; the molecular basis of heredity

GRAZING and CROPPING EUKARYOTES: single-celled (protists) or multicelled (metazoans) eukaryotes (cells with a definite nucleus), which appear in the fossil record during the close of the Precambrian eon, about 1 billion years ago

NUCLEOTIDE: a molecule made up of a series of amino acids that, when linked together, are capable of carrying genetic information

PRECAMBRIAN EON: the first 3.5 billion years of the geologic record; it is followed by the Paleozoic era of the Phanerozoic eon

RIBONUCLEIC ACID (RNA): a complex compound made up of nucleotide bases that acts as a template, or "messenger," in the replication of DNA

RIBOSOME: a large multienzyme found associated with cell nuclear materials, composed of RNA and protein molecules

Summary of the Phenomenon

From about 3.5 to 1 billion years ago, life on earth, as determined from the fossil record, consisted entirely of one-celled organisms that have a cell morphology and a metabolism different from those of all other life forms. These organisms, the prokaryotes, are characterized by their lack of a cell nucleus, their lack of sexual reproduction (meiosis), the small size of the prokaryotic cell, and their distinctive biochemistry. Prokaryotes are neither plants nor animals, although the aerobic photosynthetic forms, often called blue-green algae, have in the past been placed with the plants. Eukaryotes, organisms with a cell nucleus and a larger, more complex cell, make up the animals, plants, fungi, and protists. Prokaryotes are thus quite separate from all other life forms in terms of their cell biology. Prokaryotes and eukaryotes are the two most basic categories of living things. These two fundamental life forms have basic differences in their biologic processes that are greater than those that exist between animals or plants or between any of the other kingdoms.

Prokaryotes are mainly single-celled organisms, usually found living together in "colonies" consisting of immense numbers of cells. Their deoxyribonucleic acid (DNA) is distributed throughout the cell, not, as in the case with the eukaryotes, localized in a cell nucleus surrounded by a nuclear membrane. The prokaryote cell is smaller by a factor of ten than the average eukaryote cell. It lacks chloroplasts and mitochondria and consequently is considered primitive when compared with the eukaryote cell.

Prokaryotes constitute the kingdom Monera, one of five kingdoms in modern taxonomy. (The other kingdoms are the protists, fungi, animals, and plants, all of which have more complex eukaryotic-type cells.) Phyla, or categories, within the kingdom Monera include the bacteria, the cyanobacteria (or blue-green algae), the archaebacteria, and the prochlorophytes. The bacteria, as well as the other moneran phyla, are further subdivided into a number of classes. Bacterial classes of the Monera include the eubacteria, photosynthetic bacteria, myxobacteria (slime bacteria), actinomycetes (moldlike bacteria), and other groups, each characterized by its own distinctive metabolism and biochemistry. The bacteria consist of obligate or strict anaerobes and facultative anaerobes; the former include the photosynthetic bacteria, which differ from the cyanobacteria not only in their ability to function, if required, under anaerobic conditions and low light levels but also in their different photosynthetic pigment.

The archaebacteria are considered by some to be the most primitive and ancient of the monerans. Archaebacteria have a number of biochemical and metabolic characteristics that allow them to live under very adverse conditions—conditions such as those that appear to have existed during the early history of the earth. The archaebacteria are defined from their ribosomal ribonucleic acid (RNA), which in sequencing is quite different from that of all other monerans. The archaebacteria differ fundamentally from the other bacteria classes in structural and biochemical aspects as well.

Fossil prokaryote cells of great antiquity have become widely known from the fossil record. They were first reported in the 1910's by C. D. Walcott from 1.5-billion-year-old strata of western Montana (Belt series); however, the authenticity of these fossils was doubted until the discovery, in 1954, of one of the oldest known paleontological "windows" on life of the past, the two-billion-year-old Gunflint biota. Since then, many occurrences of prokaryote cell fossils have been reported, most from very fine-textured flinty cherts associated with stromatolites of the Proterozoic (latter part of the Precambrian) eon.

The geologic significance of the prokaryotes is great: Not only do they (at present as well as in the geologic past) play an important part in the recycling of many chemical elements, but they also have a role in basic geologic processes such as weathering and other alteration of rocks. For example, prokaryotes are involved in the formation of stromatolites. Stromatolites are layered organosedimentary structures, frequently found fossilized in rock strata of many different geologic ages. Stromatolites come in a considerable variety of shapes and sizes; the different types have often been given Linnaean biological names because, when originally discovered, they were thought to be fossil organisms like corals or sponges. (Linnaean names are not italicized as are "official" biological names.) Most stromatolites are dome-shaped, finger-shaped, or laminar structures that have a characteristic "signature"; they can form significant parts of rock strata, particularly in limestone and dolomites. Stromatolites are found in rock strata as ancient as the Archean (former part of the Precambrian) eon and are particularly diverse and abundant in strata of the Proterozoic; locally, they can be quite common in early Paleozoic marine strata as well.

The origin of stromatolites was debated for many years; as late as the 1950's, many paleontologists seriously doubted their biogenic origin. This doubt stemmed, at least in part, from the fact that stromatolites occur so much further in the geologic past than do any other fossils. Through thousands and thousands of meters of Precambrian strata, they are the only fossils that can be found. Early workers on stromatolites, such as Walcott, suggested a cyanobacterial origin for them. The discovery of the well-preserved cells of prokaryotic type in digitate (fingerlike) stromatolites of the Gunflint chert of Ontario in the 1950's led to a gradual acceptance by most geologists and paleontologists of the organic origin of the majority of stromatolites. It became clear that, under the right conditions, small, fragile cells could be preserved in very ancient strata. During the 1970's and 1980's, studies on Precambrian stromatolites and the prokaryotic organisms responsible for them became widespread. Stromatolite occurrences going as far back as 3.5 billion years have been documented. These ancient stromatolites yield not only morphological information but also carbon isotope ratios indicative of a biogenic origin. They sometimes supply biochemical information in the form of hydrocarbons, amino acids, and porphyrins (the latter is apparently a degradation product of original photosynthetic pigment).

The morphology of a prokaryotic organism is simple. Unlike fossils of eukaryotic organisms, fossils of most prokaryotes provide little specific information about the actual living organism. Prokaryotic cells can be single coccoid (spherical) forms, or they can be elongate chains of cells, as with the filaments, or trichomes, of the cyanobacteria.

Methods of Study

A standard petrographic thin section mounted on a glass slide is the common mount for observing cells preserved in a stromatolite. Oil immersion is usually required if fossil prokaryote cells are to be observed. Thin slivers of a stromatolite can also be examined under oil immersion; however, the best results are generally with well-made thin sections. Often considerable trial and error is involved in finding stromatolites that preserve cells and then in actually locating those cells; different parts of a particular stromatolite specimen usually have varying degrees of cell preservation. Very fine-grained sediments, such as those that occur with stromatolites preserved by black cherts or finely crystalline limestones, generally give the best results.

In thin section under high optical magnification, a stromatolite may exhibit fossil cyanobacterial cells as either filaments or rod-shaped forms. If preservation of these small prokaryote cells is excellent, as in the stromatolites of the Gunflint formation, the biogenic origin of the cells will be clear, and distinct cell types can be observed. When most stromatolites are examined in thin section under high magnification, however, the biogenicity of the small objects seen is usually not so certain. Often, small black globules of carbon, suggestive of macerated cells, are evident, but their origin usually cannot be proved. Contaminants such as spores, pollen grains, bacteria cells, and fungi fragments can be a problem, particularly in examination of suspected fossiliferous rocks when thin sections are not used. Even with most thin sections, the unequivocal verification of a biogenic origin for fossil cells is rare. In the case of the Gunflint prokaryotes, the detail preserved in these fossil cells is highly remarkable; some of them show internal cell structure and cells in the process of division.

The earliest stromatolites that yield these fossil cells are generally either broad domes or laminar forms. Associated cells either are single-cell coccoid forms or consist of probable chains of photosynthetic bacteria. Chains of cells of filamentous cyanobacteria generally first appeared about 2.3 billion years ago, and this appearance of filaments agrees fairly well with the first appearance of branched or digitate stromatolites, for which filamentous cyanobacteria seem to be responsible.

Often more significant than single-cell morphology or the megascopic morphology of a stromatolite is the chemical signature left by a group of prokaryotes as a consequence of their metabolic activity. Prokaryotes are classified according to their type of metabolism; some prokaryotes have a metabolism that enables them to occupy a wider variety of ecological niches than do eukaryotic organisms. Anaerobic and aerobic forms are the two fundamental forms of prokaryotic metabolism. In these two categories are the autotrophs and the heterotrophs; heterotrophic prokaryotes require previously formed organic material on which to live, while autotrophs do not. The autotrophs obtain their energy from their environment either in the form of sunlight (photoautotrophs) or through chemical reactions such as oxidation, as in the sulfur-oxidizing bacteria; such bacteria are called chemoautotrophs. This type of metabolism is unique in the organic world, for all other life forms obtain their energy from photosynthesis or through utilization of the chemical energy contained in previously formed organic compounds. The cyanobacteria are photoautotrophs and are responsible for the formation of the various types of stromatolites. The process of photosynthesis changes the microenvironment around the photosynthesizing prokaryote; the mineral precipitation that results is responsible for the formation of stromatolite layers.

Some stromatolites contain oxidized manganese, cobalt, or other "transitional" elements, possibly incorporated into these fossil communities by oxidative metabolism of bacteria. Chemoautotrophic prokaryotes, which are various types of bacteria, may leave a chemical signature in the form of these oxides and precipitate their production of a layered stromatolite-like structure containing these oxidized metals. A number of bacteria oxidize manganese to higher oxidation states so that it is precipitated; deep-sea manganese nodules presently being formed are believed to have such an origin. Sectioning of these nodules shows a finely layered, stromatolite-like structure. Some of the heavy-metal-bearing stromatolites of the early Precambrian may reflect a similar chemoautotrophic metabolism. Analysis of organic residues present in many stromatolites in small quantities can sometimes shed light upon the specific organisms responsible for forming them. This technique, however, has met with only limited success, although degradation products of the photosynthetic pigment present in cyanobacteria have been identified, supporting the cyanobacterial origin of many ancient stromatolites.

The earliest stromatolites, those of Archean age (about 3.5 billion years old), exhibit certain distinctive morphological and chemical aspects. Some of these early stromatolites may be products of anaerobic assemblages of photosynthetic bacteria rather than of cyanobacteria communities. Geochemical evidence suggests that the atmosphere in the Archean may have been anoxygenic (oxygen-free) and that the photosynthetic bacteria, not being obligate aerobes, would have been favored by such an environment.

Context

Prokaryotes, primitive one-celled life forms without a cell nucleus, make up the kingdom Monera. Monerans represent one of the earliest life forms on earth and are represented by the various forms of bacteria, archaebacteria, and cyanobacteria (blue-green algae). As fossils, they occur both as actually preserved cells and (more commonly) as megascopic structures, called stromatolites, produced as a consequence of the life activities of these organisms. A typical stromatolite is usually a multicomponent, complex community of strict aerobes at the surface, with an "understratum" of anaerobic photoautotrophs (usually photosynthetic bacteria). Below this layer, in turn, can exist various strict anaerobes, archaebacteria, and other non-light-requiring monerans that decompose and metabolize the organic matter formed before the stromatolite grew upward. The peak of stromatolite diversity, and possibly of prokaryotic diversity as well, appears to have been during the mid-Proterozoic (about 1.5 billion years ago). During the late Proterozoic (after about 0.8 billion years ago), stromatolite diversity and abundance diminished sharply, a phenomenon that appears to correlate with the rise of eukaryotic autotrophs (green algae and seaweeds) and grazing and cropping eukaryotic metazoans (multicelled animals). Stromatolite abundance and diversity increased again in the Cambrian and Early Ordovician periods of the Paleozoic era, but not to the same extent as before; stromatolites then declined and became as they are presently, restricted to those places that are generally inhospitable to eukaryotic life forms, such as hypersaline water.

The very early appearance of prokaryotes in the rock record, more than 3.5 billion years ago, implies that life has existed for most of the earth's history. Prokaryotic life forms were the only organisms on earth for some 80 percent of this history; the more complex eukaryotic cell appeared around 1 billion years ago.

Bibliography

Broadhead, T. W., ed. *Fossil Prokaryotes and Protists: Notes for a Short Course*. Knoxville: University of Tennessee, 1987. Information on a broad range of fossil prokaryotes and protist microfossils is presented. This work is the text of one of a series of "short courses" sponsored by the Paleontological Society, but it can be useful to anyone interested in the various fossil groups covered.

Margulis, Lynn, and Karlene V. Schwartz. *Five Kingdoms*. 2d ed. New York: W. H. Freeman, 1987. A concise, useful, and readable examination of five kingdoms: the prokaryotes, protists, fungi, plants, and animals. The prokaryotes are presented within a framework that easily permits one to compare their taxonomic diversity and evolutionary radiation with those of the other kingdoms.

Nisbet, Evan G. *The Young Earth: An Introduction to Archean Geology*. Boston: Unwin Hyman, 1987. A highly comprehensive coverage of geologic phenomena of the earth's earliest geologic time span, the Archean eon. Included in this work is information on both crustal evolution and biosphere. The book's sections vary considerably in technical coverage and terminology, some parts being readily comprehensible to the lay reader while others are quite technical and require considerable background in trace element geochemistry, isotope geochemistry, and petrology.

Schopf, J. William, ed. *Earth's Earliest Biosphere: Its Origin and Evolution*. Princeton, N.J.: Princeton University Press, 1983. This book deals with the record of life in the Archean eon. A product of the Precambrian Paleobiology Research Group, a group of specialists assembled to examine geologic records of earth's earliest biosphere, it covers a diversity of subject matter related to these early geologic records. This 15-chapter, 543-page book addresses theory as well as hard data on the early biosphere.

Walter, M. R., ed. *Stromatolites*. New York: Elsevier, 1976. A symposium-type compilation of papers dealing with multiple aspects of stromatolites and their formation. Topics include classification and systematics of stromatolites, abiogenic stromatolite-like structures, recent stromatolites, and biology of stromatolites (including prokaryotes responsible for producing them and the environments in which they formed). A wide-ranging coverage, presenting a variety of basic information on these ubiquitous organosedimentary structures.

Bruce L. Stinchcomb

Cross-References

Archaebacteria, 78; The Archean Eon, 92; The Atmosphere's Evolution, 114; Eukaryotes, 623; Fossils of the Earliest Life Forms, 782; Micropaleontology: Microfossils, 1674; The Origin of Life, 1961; Paleontology: Systematics and Classification, 2001; The Proterozoic Eon, 2122; Sedimentary Rocks: Biogenic, 2312.

THE PROTEROZOIC EON

Type of earth science: Geology
Field of study: Stratigraphy

The Proterozoic eon is the interval between 2.5 billion and 570 million years ago. During this period in the geologic record, processes presently active on earth first appeared, notably the first clear evidence for plate tectonics. Rocks of the Proterozoic eon also document changes in conditions on the earth, particularly an apparent increase in atmospheric oxygen.

Principal terms

ARCHEAN EON: the period of geologic time from about 4 billion to 2.5 billion years ago

OROGENIC BELT: a belt of crust that has been severely compressed, deformed, and heated, probably by convergence of crustal plates

PALEOMAGNETISM: the study of magnetism preserved in rocks, which provides evidence of the history of earth's magnetic field and the movements of continents

PHANEROZOIC EON: the period of geologic time with an abundant fossil record, extending from about 570 million years ago to the present

PLATE TECTONICS: the theory that the outer surface of the earth consists of large moving plates that interact to produce seismic, volcanic, and orogenic activity

PRECAMBRIAN: the collective term for all geologic time before the Phanerozoic, that is, before about 570 million years ago

RADIOMETRIC DATING: the use of radioactive elements that decay at a known rate to determine the ages of the rocks in which they occur

TERRANE: a structurally distinct block of crust added to a continent by plate tectonic processes

Summary of the Phenomenon

The largest subdivision of geologic time is the eon. Three eons comprise the known history of earth: Phanerozoic, Proterozoic, and Archean. The Phanerozoic, whose abundant fossil record permits fine subdivisions of geologic time and intercontinental correlation of strata, is the interval about which the most is known. The Proterozoic, by contrast, is generally characterized by a sparse fossil record of simple life forms that do not permit the sort of stratigraphic subdivision possible in the Phanerozoic. Ages of rocks in the Proterozoic can be established only by radiometric dating. For rocks as old as the Proterozoic, the inherent uncertainty in even the best dating is on the order of 10-20 million years, comparable in length to some Phanerozoic periods.

The Proterozoic has been subdivided only into intervals comparable to eras (several hundred million years), and these subdivisions are not global but are defined in terms of major geologic events in separate regions. The principal Proterozoic subdivisions are the following (all figures represent time in billions of years ago): for the United States, Precambrian X (2.5 to 1.6), Precambrian Y (1.6 to 0.9), and Precambrian Z (0.9 to 0.57); for Canada, Aphebian (2.5 to 1.8), Helikian (1.8 to 1.0), and Hadrynian (1.0 to 0.57); for Europe, Svecofennian (2.5 to 2.0), Gothian or Karelian (2.0 to 1.6), and Riphean (1.6 to 0.57); and for Australia, Nullaginian (2.5 to 1.9), Carpentarian (1.9 to 1.4), and Adelaidean (1.4 to 0.57). In addition to these regional terms, the term "Eocambrian" or "Ediacarian" (sometimes "Ediacaran") is often used for the latest Proterozoic, from about 800 to 570 million years ago.

Much of the significance of the Proterozoic derives from the first appearance of processes that are still operating on earth. The Archean, in contrast, may have experienced a quite different set of processes. It is therefore impossible to discuss the Proterozoic without also discussing the Archean to some extent. There are many unanswered questions about major earth processes in the Archean. In particular, the Archean lacks structures that closely resemble Phanerozoic orogenic belts. Whether plate tectonics operated in its present form during the Archean is still unresolved. Dynamic processes within the earth may have undergone a significant change about 2.5 billion years ago.

The contrast between Archean and Proterozoic geology is striking if still imperfectly understood. The Archean is dominated by two principal types of regional structure: greenstone belts and gneiss-migmatite terrains. Greenstone belts are troughs of volcanic rocks and deep-water sedimentary rocks intruded by elliptical granite bodies. Gneiss-migmatite terrains are bands of very highly metamorphosed and deformed rocks. Structures similar to both the greenstone belts and the gneiss-migmatite terrains have formed throughout the history of the earth and can form through conventional plate tectonic processes, but the almost complete lack of other types of structure in Archean time is perplexing. It is widely (though not universally) believed that the Archean crust was more mobile than at later times and that large masses of continental crust did not exist then. The first extensive shallow-water rocks deposited in a continental-shelf or stable continent setting occur in the latest Archean rocks of South Africa and are abundant throughout the Proterozoic and Phanerozoic. The appearance of such rocks may mark the first appearance of stable continental crust.

During the Proterozoic, there is the first widespread evidence for plate tectonics and orogeny (mountain building) comparable to that of the Phanerozoic. There seem to have been two major periods of plate collision during which large continents were assembled out of small continental plates. North America was assembled between about 1.9 and 1.6 billion years ago by the collision of several smaller Archean blocks plus the accretion of many smaller terranes. This episode is known as the Trans-Hudson Event. The overall process was very similar to the accretion that is known to have added large areas to western North America during the Phanerozoic. Between about 900 and 600 million years ago, South America and Africa also appear to have been assembled in much the same way to form part of the early Phanerozoic supercontinent of Gondwanaland. The sequence of events that assembled South America and Africa is called the Pan-African Event.

Some Proterozoic crustal events are still poorly understood. In particular, there was a widespread heating event that resulted in the intrusion and eruption of silica-rich igneous rocks (granite and rhyolite) between about 1.5 and 1.3 billion years ago across much of North America. This interval also resulted in the intrusion of large bodies of anorthosite, an igneous rock made mostly of feldspar minerals, on many continents. Anorthosite is otherwise uncommon, and the reason it was formed so extensively in the Proterozoic is not known.

A number of significant developments took place on the surface of the Proterozoic earth. There is evidence for increasing oxygen content of the atmosphere, as indicated by the appearance of the first "red beds," red sandstone and conglomerate colored by iron oxide. Also, there were a number of major ice ages during the Proterozoic. One occurred about 2.3 billion years ago, and there is widespread evidence for a series of ice ages between about 900 and 600 million years ago.

The early earth probably lacked free oxygen, except in minor amounts. Free oxygen is not a component of the raw materials that formed the planets, and oxygen is a highly reactive gas that would rapidly have combined with other substances. Oxygen originally was given off as a waste product by early organisms (and is actually toxic to some organisms even today). How and when the present oxygen level of the atmosphere was attained is controversial. Many scientists consider that increasing oxygen was related to the abrupt expansion of life at the start of the Phanerozoic. There is also evidence that a significant threshold in oxygen level was crossed about 2.0-1.8 billion years ago.

Several types of sedimentary deposit, all closely related to the availability of free oxygen, either ceased or began to be deposited about 1.8 billion years ago. Detrital uranium deposits and banded iron formations, both believed to indicate low oxygen levels, become very uncommon in the geologic record after that time, while red beds appear at roughly the same time. Detrital uranium deposits are sandstone deposits in which dense minerals were concentrated by current action. This process is common today, but the Proterozoic deposits include uranium minerals, which are highly susceptible to weathering, and even pyrite (iron sulfide), which oxidizes extremely quickly and which is almost never found in recent sedimentary deposits.

A detrital uranium deposit at Okolo, in the African nation of Gabon, is remarkable for another reason. The uranium ore from the deposit was found to be greatly depleted in uranium 235, the isotope used in nuclear reactors. Further investigation showed that the ore deposit had been a natural nuclear reactor. Present-day uranium is too poor in uranium 235 to sustain a nuclear chain reaction except under very controlled conditions. Yet, 2.2 billion years ago, when the Okolo deposit formed, uranium 235 was far more abundant, abundant enough for a sustained chain reaction to begin when sedimentary processes collected enough uranium minerals in one place. So far the remarkable deposit at Okolo is unique; other detrital uranium deposits were studied for effects of natural chain reactions, and no other examples were found.

Another type of ore deposit common in early Proterozoic rocks is banded iron formation. Banded iron formations consist of layers of iron oxides and silicates interbedded with fine-grained silica, or chert. The significance of these ore deposits, apart from their great importance as sources of iron, lies in the degree of oxidation of the iron. Iron in nature has two oxidation states. Ferrous iron, the less oxidized state, consists of iron atoms that have lost two electrons and thus have a positive electric charge of $+2$. Ferric iron atoms have lost three electrons and have a $+3$ charge. Common rust is mostly ferric iron oxide, as would be expected in the earth's presently oxygen-rich atmosphere. The iron in banded iron formations, however, is mostly ferrous, even though it was deposited on the surface of the earth. The ferrous iron in banded iron formations presents one of the strongest arguments for an oxygen-poor atmosphere on the early earth. The iron was originally dissolved in seawater and was probably precipitated by microorganisms. Indeed, some of the best-preserved Proterozoic fossils are those of microorganisms preserved in the chert of banded iron formations. Ferrous iron is far more soluble in water than is ferric iron, so the Proterozoic seas may have been richer in dissolved iron than are the present oceans. Iron deposits precipitated by microorganisms have also formed in the Phanerozoic, but the iron is mostly ferric.

Both detrital uranium deposits and banded iron formations become rare in the geologic record after 1.8 billion years ago. At about the same time, red sandstones appear in abundance. Red sandstones owe their color to ferric (highly oxidized) iron, and are most commonly deposited on land or in shallow water. One of the earliest extensive red bed deposits is in northwestern Canada. These rocks were deposited shortly after the crust of the region had experienced a major orogeny about 1.8 billion years ago and represent debris eroded from the newly formed mountain range. A deposit of this sort is termed molasse. These red beds furnish not only evidence for the oxygen level of the atmosphere but also some of the first evidence for topographically high mountains.

The Proterozoic experienced a number of major glacial events about 2.3 billion years ago and again from 900 to 600 million years ago. The intervening period appears to have been largely ice-free. The glaciation 2.3 billion years ago is best documented in the Gowganda formation of Ontario, where virtually every type of glacial deposit occurs. Other deposits in Wyoming and Quebec have been interpreted as glacial deposits of the same age, but the Gowganda formation remains the clearest evidence for a 2.3-billion-year-old glaciation.

The glacial deposits 900-600 million years old are far more problematical. Many of these rocks are diamictites, fine-grained sedimentary rocks with scattered large pebbles. Diamictites cannot have been simply deposited by running water; slow-moving water could not have transported the pebbles, while sediment deposited by fast-moving water would have a much higher proportion of coarse material than do diamictites. Only a few plausible ways of forming diamictites exist. One way is for floating glacial icebergs to melt and drop trapped rocks into otherwise fine-grained sediment. When the sediments are finely layered, the occurrence of so-called dropstones is generally taken as clear evidence of glaciation. Diamictites can also form from nonglacial processes. For example, submarine landslides can mix a small amount of coarse debris into a large amount of fine sand and silt. The glacial origin of many diamictites has been controversial, and some of the late Proterozoic diamictites may not be glacial.

An additional problem with the late Proterozoic glaciation is the geographic distribution of the deposits. Glacial deposits by themselves indicate cold climates, but in many cases there are nearby carbonate rocks (dolomite and limestone) of similar age that typically form in warm climates. Also, paleomagnetic studies indicate that some areas with glacial deposits, notably Australia, were at low latitudes during the late Proterozoic. A number of possible explanations, none entirely satisfactory, have been proposed. A few geologists find a flaw in the evidence: in the climatic indicators or the paleomagnetic evidence. Others propose that the late Proterozoic earth was abnormally cold, still others that the temperature decrease with altitude was much greater than at present, allowing warm climates at sea level but glaciers at even moderate elevations.

Throughout most of the Proterozoic, simple life forms dominated on earth. The first life forms, already established in the Archean, were prokaryotes, organisms without a cell nucleus, such as bacteria and blue-green algae. About 2 billion years ago, eukaryotes, or organisms with a cell nucleus, appeared. The only common Proterozoic fossils of large size are stromatolites, domelike masses of calcium carbonate or silica deposited by colonies of algae in shallow water. The first widespread evidence for large multicelled organisms appears in rocks about 800 million years old. These organisms are rare as fossils because they lacked hard body parts but seem to have resembled jellyfish and marine worms. Many are unrelated to present-day organisms and seem to represent extinct evolutionary lines.

Methods of Study

On a local scale, the methods used in studying Proterozoic rocks are the standard methods of geology, such as geologic mapping and microscopic examination of thin sections of rock. The Precambrian, however, presents particular problems in broader interpretation for many reasons: lack of a fossil record, great depth of erosion, concealment by younger rocks, and the possibility that fundamental processes may have operated differently on the early earth.

The lack of a detailed fossil record in the Proterozoic greatly hampers scientists' ability to discuss Proterozoic events on more than a local scale. Radiometric dating is used to establish the absolute age of rocks for both the Phanerozoic and the Precambrian, but fossils in the Phanerozoic make it possible to distinguish intervals of time shorter than those distinguishable by radiometric dating and to correlate events on a regional or even global scale. Finally, many kinds of rock simply cannot be dated radiometrically because they lack the required radioactive elements or because they have been chemically altered. The same rocks may contain fossils that make it easy to establish their place in the geologic sequence relative to other rocks.

Without fossils that can be correlated worldwide, the Precambrian geologist must rely on radiometric dating to establish the ages of the rocks. A very good radiometric age might be accurate to within 1 percent or, for a rock 2 billion years old, 20 million years. Twenty million years is almost the length of the Silurian period. Thus, it is not possible to correlate widely separated events in the Precambrian more closely than a few tens of millions of years. The picture of Proterozoic events is therefore very coarse.

Where rocks lack suitable compositions for radiometric dating, it may be possible only to bracket the ages of the rocks. For example, the Huronian supergroup, a sequence of sedimentary rocks in Ontario that includes the Gowganda formation, is between 2.5 and 2.15 billion years old. The rocks contain igneous intrusions 2.15 billion years old and rest on Archean rocks 2.5 billion years old. (For comparison, the interval between 2.5 and 2.15 billion years is 350 million years, equal to the time since the Devonian period.)

In many cases, processes in Precambrian rocks have been recognized only after comparable processes were recognized in Phanerozoic rocks. For example, geologists were able to recognize that western North America had been assembled out of small crustal blocks, or terranes, because, in many cases, adjacent terranes had markedly different fossils, often from very different climatic zones. It seems certain that a similar process occurred during the Trans-Hudson and Pan-African events in the Proterozoic, but lack of suitable fossils prevented easy recognition of the different terranes.

One concept widely applied to Precambrian terranes is the "province" concept. A province is a region with a common geologic history, usually involving major orogeny. Different provinces are often easily visible on regional geologic maps because they are often sharply bounded by faults or have belts of rock units with sharply different orientations. Radiometric dating usually reveals that adjacent provinces consist of rocks of sharply different ages. In many cases, provinces represent crustal plates or zones where terranes have been accreted to a larger plate.

Proterozoic rocks in many regions, like much of the United States, are covered by younger rocks. What scientists know of these rocks is derived from widely scattered outcrops, samples from deep wells, and geophysical evidence (such as study of the magnetic and gravitational effects of the buried rocks). The history of buried Proterozoic rocks is known in broad outline, but not in fine detail.

A major problem in interpreting very ancient rocks is that they have been eroded to great depths, exposing levels of the crust rarely seen in younger rocks. Students of the Precambrian, and especially the Archean, must always bear in mind that supposedly inexplicable structures may actually be the very deep levels of familiar crustal features. Thus, geologists are very cautious about drawing generalizations about global processes in the Precambrian. They can neither assume that processes were the same as at present nor be too quick to assume that processes were different.

Context

The Proterozoic eon is economically important as the time when many major ore deposits formed. Many of the world's largest iron ore deposits are of Proterozoic age, including the Mesabi Range and other iron ore districts in the Great Lakes region of the United States, as well as other great deposits in Labrador and Australia. Some of the largest uranium deposits in the world are also of Proterozoic age. The conditions that allowed these ore deposits to form appear to have been unique to the Proterozoic because similar deposits do not occur in younger rocks.

The Proterozoic is of interest because it provides insights into the evolution of the earth. The Proterozoic lasted nearly 2 billion years. Scientists do not understand the Proterozoic with the detail that they understand more recent geologic time, but, on the other hand, it is possible to see broad patterns in the Phanerozoic that are obscured by the welter of detail in younger rocks. There appear to be periods when different geologic processes dominate. For example, there were major ice ages 2.3 billion years ago and from 900 to 600 million years ago, but the intervening period was apparently ice-free. There is some evidence that the entire earth was unusually cold during the later ice age. A major episode of continent formation by the collision of small plates took place about 1.9-1.6 billion years ago, a crustal-heating event occurred 1.5-1.3 billion years ago, and another episode of continent formation happened 900-600 million years ago. There also appear to be long-term changes in the earth. Continents apparently did not exist as large stable blocks of crust until just before the Proterozoic, and the earth's atmosphere has become richer in oxygen over geologic time; both of these changes are recorded in Proterozoic rocks.

Bibliography

Cowan, George A. "A Natural Fission Reactor." *Scientific American* 235 (July, 1976): 36-47. An account of the remarkable Okolo uranium deposit, which functioned as a nuclear reactor some 2 billion years ago. *Scientific American* is written for nonspecialists at a college reading level and is probably the best generally available source of detailed, recent scientific information for nonspecialists.

Groves, David I., J. S. R. Dunlop, and R. Buick. "An Early Habitat of Life." *Scientific American* 245 (October, 1981): 64-73. A description of Archean stromatolites in Australia, but the descriptions apply to Proterozoic life as well. Stromatolites were abundant in the Precambrian but diminished after grazing organisms evolved that feed on them.

Hoffman, Paul F. "United Plates of America, the Birth of a Craton: Early Proterozoic Assembly and Growth of Laurentia." *Annual Review of Earth and Planetary Sciences* 16 (1988): 543-603. Probably the most comprehensive general account of the Trans-Hudson Event that assembled North America between 1.9

and 1.6 billlion years ago. Uses fairly technical language. Suitable for advanced college students.

Kasting, James B., O. B. Toon, and J. B. Pollack. "How Climate Evolved on the Terrestrial Planets." *Scientific American* 258 (February, 1988): 90-97. This article compares the evolution of Earth, Venus, and Mars. Its relevance to the Proterozoic is that the early sun was fainter than is the present sun, and the earth's atmosphere must have been different to have trapped enough heat to allow liquid water to exist on the early earth.

McMenamin, Mark A. S. "The Emergence of Animals." *Scientific American* 256 (April, 1987): 94-102. This article describes the transition from the latest Proterozoic animals to Phanerozoic animal life forms. The most common Proterozoic animal fossils are tracks and burrows, rather than actual remains. Lack of hard body parts and the evolution of scavengers make Proterozoic animal fossils rare.

Medaris, L.G., C. W. Byers, D. M. Michelson, and W. C. Shanks, eds. *Proterozoic Geology: Selected Papers from an International Proterozoic Symposium.* Memoir 161. Boulder, Colo.: Geological Society of America, 1983. One of the most general available overviews of the Proterozoic, with papers on tectonics, glaciation, and the geology of selected regions. Papers vary in reading level from relatively simple to advanced.

Meyer, Charles. "Ore Deposits as Guides to Geologic History of the Earth." *Annual Review of Earth and Planetary Sciences* 16 (1988): 147. A synthesis of a lifetime of experience as a mining geologist. Meyer documents the changing patterns of ore deposits through geologic time, with strong emphasis on the Precambrian. Uses fairly technical language. Suitable for college students.

Stanley, Steven M. *Earth and Life Through Time.* San Francisco: W. H. Freeman, 1985. A college textbook on historical geology for freshman and sophomore students. Covers the entire history of the earth, with an extensive (73-page) section on the Precambrian in part 4. Includes a brief summary of Precambrian rocks on each continent and a description of Precambrian fossils. One of the very few references on the Precambrian at a nontechncial level.

Van Schmus, W. R., and W. J. Hinze. "The Midcontinent Rift System." *Annual Review of Earth and Planetary Sciences* 13 (1985): 345-383. A comprehensive description of a major rifting event in central North America about 1.1 billion years ago. Uses fairly technical language. Suitable for advanced college students.

Vidal, Gonzales. "The Oldest Eukaryotic Cells." *Scientific American* 250 (February, 1984): 48-57. About 1.4 billion years ago, cells with nuclei first appeared. These organisms include plankton with geometric shells and filamentous algae. Many good photographs illustrate the various fossil forms.

Steven I. Dutch

Cross-References

Archaebacteria, 78; The Archean Eon, 92; Eukaryotes, 623; Ediacarian Fossils, 776; The Geologic Time Scale, 874; Ice Ages, 1115; Iron Deposits, 1254; Paleoclimatology, 1993; Plate Tectonics, 2079; Prokaryotes, 2115; Sedimentary Mineral Deposits, 2296; Uranium Deposits, 2580.

PYROCLASTIC ROCKS

Type of earth science: Geology
Field of study: Volcanology

Pyroclastic rocks form from the accumulation of fragmental debris ejected during explosive volcanic eruptions. Pyroclastic debris may accumulate either on land or under water. Volcanic eruptions that generate pyroclastic debris are extremely high-energy events and are potentially dangerous if they occur near populated areas.

Principal terms

ASH: fine-grained pyroclastic material less than 2 millimeters in diameter

IGNIMBRITE: pyroclastic rock formed from the consolidation of pyroclastic-flow deposits

LAPILLI: pyroclastic fragments between 2 and 64 millimeters in diameter

PUMICE: a vesicular glassy rock commonly having the composition of rhyolite; a common constituent of silica-rich explosive volcanic eruptions

PYROCLASTIC FALL: the settling of debris under the influence of gravity from an explosively produced plume of material

PYROCLASTIC FLOW: a highly heated mixture of volcanic gases and ash that travels down the flanks of a volcano; the relative concentration of particles is high

PYROCLASTIC SURGE: a turbulent, low-particle-concentration mixture of volcanic gases and ash that travels down the flanks of a volcano

STRATOVOLCANO: a volcanic cone consisting of both lava and pyroclastic rocks

TEPHRA: fragmentary volcanic rock materials ejected into the air during an eruption; also called pyroclasts

TUFF: a general term for all consolidated pyroclastic rocks

VOLATILES: fluid components, either liquid or gas, dissolved in a magma that, upon rapid expansion, may contribute to explosive fragmentation

Summary of the Phenomenon

Pyroclastic rocks form as a result of violent volcanic eruptions such as that of Mount St. Helens in 1980 or Mount Vesuvius in A.D. 79. Molten rock, or magma, within the earth sometimes makes its way to the surface in the form of volcanic eruptions. These eruptions may produce lava or, if the eruption is highly explosive, fragmental debris called tephra or pyroclasts. The term "pyroclastic" is from the Greek roots *pyros* (fire) and *klastos* (broken). Dissolved water and gases (volatiles) are the source of energy for these explosive eruptions. All molten rock contains dissolved fluids such as water and carbon dioxide. When the molten rock is still deep within the earth, the confining pressure of the overlying rock keeps these volatiles from being released. When the magma rises to the surface during an eruption, the pressure is lowered, and the gases and water may be violently released, causing fragmentation of the molten rock and some of the rock surrounding the magma. This type of explosive eruption is more common in rocks rich in silica, which are more viscous (flow more thickly) than those that are silica-poor. External sources of water, such as a lake or groundwater reservoir, may also provide the necessary volatiles for an explosive eruption.

Pyroclastic debris can be produced from any of three different types of volcanic eruptions: magmatic explosions; phreatic, or steam, explosions; and phreatomagmatic explosions. Magmatic explosions occur when magma rich in dissolved volatiles undergoes a decrease in pressure such that the volatiles are rapidly released or exsolved. The solubility of volatiles in magma is partially controlled by confining pressure, which is a function of depth. Solubility decreases as the magma rises toward the surface. At a certain depth, carbon dioxide and water begin exsolving and become separate fluid phases. At this point, the magma may undergo explosive fragmentation either through an open vent or by destroying the overlying rock in a major eruptive event.

As a magma rises toward the surface, it may encounter a groundwater reservoir or, in a subaqueous vent, interact with surface water. In both cases, the superheating and boiling of water followed by its explosive expansion to gas may fragment the magma and the surrounding country rock. The ratio between the mass of water and the mass of magma controls the type of eruption. If there is little water in relation to magma, the explosive activity may be confined to the eruption of steam and is called a phreatic explosion. If the magma contains significant quantities of dissolved volatiles and encounters a large amount of water, the resulting explosion is termed phreatomagmatic.

Pyroclastic deposits are composed of tephra, or pyroclasts. These fragments can have a wide range of sizes. Particles less than 2 millimeters in diameter are termed ash, those between 2 and 64 millimeters are called lapilli, and those greater than 64 millimeters are called blocks, or bombs. There are three principal components that make up pyroclastic debris: lithic fragments, crystals, and vitric, or juvenile, fragments. Lithic fragments can be subdivided into pieces of the surrounding rock explosively fragmented during an eruption (accessory lithics), pieces of already solidified magma (cognate lithics), and particles picked up during transport of eruptive clouds down the flanks of a volcano (accidental lithics). Crystal fragments are whole or fragmented crystals that had solidified in the magma before eruption. Vitric or juvenile fragments represent samples of the erupting, still molten, magma. They may be either partly crystallized or uncrystallized (glass). Pumice is a type of juvenile fragment that contains many vesicles, or holes, as a result of the rapid exsolution of gases during eruption. Small, very angular glass fragments are called shards.

Three types of pyroclastic deposit can be distinguished based on the type of process that forms the deposit: pyroclastic-fall deposits, pyroclastic-flow deposits, and pyroclastic-surge deposits. These types can all be formed by any of the previously described different types of volcanic eruption. Any of these deposits may be termed a tuff if the grain size is predominantly less than 2 millimeters.

Pyroclastic-fall deposits form from the settling, under the influence of gravity, of particles out of a plume of volcanic ash and gases erupted into the atmosphere forming an eruption column. Tuffs formed in this way are coarsest near the eruption center and become progressively finer farther away. Ash falls can also be derived from the tops of more dense pyroclastic flows, as the finer-grained material is turbulently removed from the upper portion of the pyroclastic flow and then settles to the ground.

Two types of pyroclastic deposits result from the formation of dense clouds of ash during an eruption and the subsequent transport of debris in the form of a hot cloud of ash, lapilli, and gases. Pyroclastic flows have a relatively high particle concentration and, in some areas, the western United States for example, form enormous deposits with volumes as large as 3,000 cubic kilometers. Pyroclastic-flow deposits rich in pumice are termed ignimbrites. Pyroclastic surges are expanded, low-particle-concentration density currents that are generally very turbulent. Surge deposits are volumetrically less important than those of pyroclastic flows but can be very destructive. Both flows and surges may have emplacement temperatures of up to 800 degrees Celsius. Pyroclastic surges, however, because of their lower density and turbulent nature, may attain velocities up to 700 kilometers per hour. It is this combination of speed and temperature that makes pyroclastic surges so dangerous.

Most pyroclastic rocks are associated with stratovolcanoes, also called composite volcanoes. These volcanic edifices are built by a combination of extrusive and explosive processes and thus are formed of both pyroclastic debris and lava. Well-known examples of stratovolcanoes include Mount St. Helens, Mount Fuji, and Mount Vesuvius. Volcanoes such as those found on the Hawaiian Islands are of a less energetic variety called shield volcanoes and produce insignificant quantities of pyroclastic material. Stratovolcanoes are located around the world and are associated with the global process of plate tectonics, which explains the movement of the continents, the generation of new "plates," which include oceanic crust, and the destruction of old plates. It is at the zone of plate destruction that rock is melted and makes its way to the surface, sometimes producing pyroclastic eruptions.

Methods of Study

Geologists study pyroclastic rocks using field techniques, laboratory analyses, and theoretical considerations of eruption processes. Observations of deposits in the field remain the cornerstone of much of geologic interpretation. Pyroclastic deposits form essentially as sedimentary material, that is, as fragments or clasts moved in air or water and deposited in layers. As such, many of the techniques used by sedimentologists (geologists interested in the formation and history of sedimentary rocks) are employed in the study of pyroclastic deposits. Careful examination of a variety of different sedimentary features within pyroclastic deposits can aid in the interpretation of the processes of transport and deposition. This information, studied over as wide a geographic area as possible to ascertain systematic changes in the deposits, will assist in understanding the geologic history of the region.

Much can be learned through analysis of the composition of pyroclastic rocks, which is generally done using a variety of laboratory techniques. The use of specialized microscopes allows geologists to examine very thin sections of rock in order to observe textures and to discern mineral composition. Geochemical techniques have become very popular and powerful in the study of all kinds of rocks, including pyroclastic rocks. By looking at the amounts of certain elements that occur in extremely low abundances and also at relative proportions of certain types of isotopes (naturally occurring forms of the same element that differ only in the number of neutrons in the nucleus), scientists can understand more about the processes taking place deep within the earth that lead to the formation of magma and eventually to the eruption of pyroclastic debris. Scanning electron microscopes have been used to study in detail the surface features and textures of fine volcanic ash particles. This information can lead to better understanding of eruptive and transport processes that formed and deposited the pyroclastic particles.

Theoretical studies associated with pyroclastic rocks revolve primarily around considerations of the mechanics of high-temperature, high-velocity eruption clouds and their transport and deposition. This type of reasoning allows a geologist to infer certain conditions of eruption from an analysis of the deposits. The geologic rock record has abundant pyroclastic deposits, and it is through this type of inference that geologists interpret the geologic history of a region. A comprehensive understanding of pyroclastic deposits must include a thorough understanding of the processes by which the deposit forms.

Context

Violent volcanic eruptions that may produce pyroclastic deposits are among the most powerful events occurring on the earth. Historically, many of the most destructive volcanic eruptions have involved pyroclastic surges. The eruption in A.D. 79 of Mount Vesuvius generated pyroclastic debris that buried the towns of Pompeii and Herculaneum, killing most of the inhabitants. In 1902, on the island of Martinique in the Caribbean, the violent eruption of Mount Pelée produced a pyroclastic surge that swept down on the city of St. Pierre, killing all but a handful of a population of about thirty thousand. The eruption of Mount St. Helens in 1980 and of El Chichón in Mexico in 1982 both produced pyroclastic surges. Two thousand people were killed as a result of the El Chichón eruption. Pyroclastic surges and flows generally do not present a hazard beyond about a 20-kilometer radius.

Pyroclastic deposits form a major portion of some volcanic terrains. Some of these deposits are enormously extensive, indicating that the eruptions that produced them were much larger than any witnessed in modern times. It is not clear whether these deposits reflect an overall increase in volcanic activity in the earth's past or whether this type of titanic eruption occurs sporadically throughout geologic time. Titanic eruptions inject so much debris into the upper atmosphere that global weather can be affected. The earth experienced brilliant red sunsets and lowered temperatures because dust blocked the sun for several years following the 1883 eruption of Krakatoa in the strait between Java and Sumatra, which completely destroyed an island and discharged nearly 20 cubic kilometers of debris into the air. The explosion was heard nearly 5,000 kilometers away in Australia, and darkness fell over Jakarta, 150 miles away. Some geologists speculate that enormous volcanic eruptions in the earth's past have even led to extinctions, including that of the dinosaurs, by producing so much ash that the amount of sunlight received on the earth's surface is reduced, and the entire food chain is disrupted.

Bibliography

Blong, R. J. *Volcanic Hazards: A Sourcebook on the Effects of Eruptions*. Sydney: Academic Press, 1984. Discusses the nature of volcanic hazards with case histories. Suitable for college-level students.

Cas, R. A. F., and J. V. Wright. *Volcanic Successions: Modern and Ancient*. Winchester, Mass.: Unwin Hyman, 1987. Eleven of the fifteen chapters in this excellent book deal wholly or in part with pyroclastic rocks. Takes a sedimentological approach to the study and interpretation of pyroclastic deposits. Indispensable for geologists interested in pyroclastic rocks. Suitable for college-level students.

Decker, Robert, and Barbara Decker. *Volcanoes*. San Francisco: W. H. Freeman, 1981. This book provides the reader with a good overview of different types of volcanoes and volcanic processes, including those that produce pyroclastic debris. Suitable for high school students.

Fisher, R. V., and H. U. Schmincke. *Pyroclastic Rocks*. New York: Springer-Verlag, 1984. This book, along with that of Cas and Wright, provides the most comprehensive treatment of pyroclastic deposits and the processes which form them. Suitable for college-level students.

Simkin, Tom, L. Siebert, L. McClelland, D. Bridge, C. Newhall, and J. H. Latter. *Volcanoes of the World: A Regional Directory, Gazeteer, and Chronology of Volcanism During the Last Ten Thousand Years*. Stroudsbourg, Pa.: Hutchinson & Ross, 1981. Suitable for all readers.

Bruce W. Nocita

Cross-References

Continental Rift Zones, 275; Igneous Rock Classification, 1138; Island Arcs, 1261; Plate Tectonics, 2079; Volcanic Hazards, 2601; Volcanoes: Krakatoa, 2645; Volcanoes: Mount Pelée, 2653; Volcanoes: Mount St. Helens, 2659; Volcanoes: Recent Eruptions, 2673; Volcanoes: Stratovolcanoes, 2688; Volcanoes: Types of Eruption, 2695.

RADIOACTIVE DECAY

Type of earth science: Geochemistry
Field of study: Geochronology

Radioactive decay is the release of energy by nuclei through the emission of electromagnetic energy or several types of charged particles. In geology, radioactive decay is important not only as the basis for most of the standard dating techniques and as a tracer for fluid flows and chemical reactions but also for its role in heating the interior of the earth and changing the character of minerals.

Principal terms

ALPHA PARTICLE: the nucleus of a helium atom, which consists of a tightly bound group of two protons and two neutrons

ATOM: the smallest piece of an element that has all the properties of the element

ELECTRON: a negatively charged particle that forms the outer portion of the atom and whose negative charge is equal in magnitude to the positive charge of the proton

GAMMA RADIATION: high-energy electromagnetic radiation emitted when a nucleus emits excess energy

HALF-LIFE: the time during which half the atoms in a sample of radioactive material undergo decay

NEUTRON: the uncharged particle that is one of the two particles of nearly equal mass forming the nucleus

NUCLEUS: the central portion of the atom, which contains all the positive charge and most of the mass of the atom

POSITRON: a positively charged electron, a form of antimatter

PROTON: the positively charged particle that is one of the two particles of nearly equal mass forming the nucleus

Summary of the Phenomenon

Radioactive decay is the release of energy by the nucleus of an atom. Nuclei discharge energy either through the emission of electromagnetic radiation, a form of pure energy that does not alter the chemical nature of the atom, or through the emission of a particle that changes the atom into an atom of a different chemical element. In order to understand radioactive decay, it is necessary to understand the behavior of atomic nuclei.

Atomic nuclei occupy a very tiny central portion of the atom; if the atom were the size of a two-story house, the nucleus would be the size of the head of a pin. In spite of its small size, the atomic nucleus contains nearly all the mass of the atom. Nuclei are composed of two particles with nearly identical masses: the proton, which carries one unit of positive electric charge; and the neutron, which is uncharged. The nucleus is orbited by the electrons. Each electron carries one unit of negative electric charge equal in size to the positive charge of the proton—even though the mass of the electron is only five-hundredths of a percent of that of a proton or neutron. The atom is electrically neutral; thus, the number of electrons orbiting the nucleus under normal conditions equals the number of protons contained in the nucleus. The number of protons or electrons determines the chemical element to which the atom belongs.

The particles in the nucleus are held together by the nuclear force, which is strong enough to overpower the electrical repulsion of the protons at very short distances. Just as the atomic electrons orbit the nucleus in patterns with definite energies, the nuclear particles fill states of definite energy within the nucleus. The energies of the neutron states are a little lower than those of the protons, because the neutrons are not forced apart by electrical repulsion. For elements with few protons in the nucleus, the numbers of protons and neutrons in the nucleus are nearly equal. For elements with larger numbers of protons, the electrical repulsion becomes strong enough so that neutrons in heavier atoms considerably outnumber protons. For most elements, there are several types of nuclei that contain different numbers of neutrons but have the same number of protons. Such atoms with equal numbers of protons but different numbers of neutrons are called isotopes of an element.

If a nucleus has extra energy, it will seek to rid itself of that extra energy by emitting either electromagnetic radiation or a particle. This emission is called radioactive decay. The time at which an excited nucleus (one with extra energy) will decay is not predictable except as a probability, which depends on the time elapsed since the nucleus was formed. This probability is described in terms of the half-life of the decay, which is the time it takes for half the excited nuclei in a sample to decay. For example, if there are originally four hundred excited nuclei in a sample, two hundred of them will undergo radioactive decay during the first half-life, one hundred of them in the second, fifty in the third, and twenty-five in the fourth. After the first half-life, there will be two hundred excited nuclei left in the sample, one hundred left after the second, fifty left after the third, and twenty-five excited nuclei left after the fourth. Nuclei with short half-lives decay rapidly and disappear quickly, but the large number of particles they emit may do much damage to their surroundings. Nuclei with longer half-lives exist much longer. Their radioactive decay will do less immediate damage to their surroundings but will continue to do damage over a considerable period of time.

Three major types of radioactive decays are found in nature. They are called alpha, beta, and gamma decay (named for the first three letters of the Greek alphabet); the particles emitted in the decay are called alpha, beta, and gamma particles or rays. The mechanisms for the decays, their half-lives, and their effect on their surroundings differ widely.

Emission of electromagnetic radiation, called gamma decay, allows the protons and neutrons to settle into lower energy states without changing the number of protons in the nucleus that decayed. Gamma decay particles carry no charge and have no mass. Because they are electromagnetic radiation, they travel long distances through matter and do little damage to atoms through which they pass compared to the damage done by the passage of charged particles. The half-lives of gamma decays are usually very short. Common half-lives are about a billionth of a second; it is rare to find a gamma half-life as long as a second. The energy of the gamma is characteristic of the energy levels of the protons and neutrons in the nucleus that emitted it. The pattern of emitted gammas can be used to identify a particular nuclear species.

Alpha decay occurs mostly in heavy nuclei that emit an alpha particle—the nucleus of a helium atom, consisting of two protons and two neutrons. This massive particle is believed to form a tightly bound unit inside these heavy nuclei. It takes advantage of a unique phenomenon of quantum mechanics to escape far enough from the vicinity of the nucleus that the positive electrical repulsion of the nucleus acts on the alpha's positive charge to drive it out of the atom. Because they are very massive and carry two units of positive charge, alphas heavily damage their surroundings even though they travel very short distances in matter and are easily stopped by a thin sheet of paper. Like gamma decay, each alpha decay is characterized by a unique energy determined by the energy structure of the nucleus from which is has escaped. The remaining nucleus now forms an atom of a different element, with two fewer protons and therefore two fewer electrons in the neutral atom. The half-lives of alpha decays are usually very long. Uranium 238, for example, has a half-life of 4.51 billion years, which is believed to be approximately the age of the earth.

There are two types of beta decay: negative (the emission of an electron and changing of a neutron to a proton in the nucleus) and positive (the emission of a positron—a positively charged electron—and changing of a proton to a neutron in the nucleus). Both types of beta particles lie between alphas and gammas in the damage they do to their environment. They are typically stopped by thin blocks of aluminum and do less damage than alphas. Positrons, a form of antimatter, destroy themselves by uniting with an electron and annihilating themselves with the emission of two gamma rays that damage their surroundings. The half-lives of beta decays range from a few seconds to thousands of years. One of the more important beta decays is the decay of the isotope of carbon with six protons and eight neutrons to the isotope of nitrogen with seven protons and seven neutrons by the emission of an electron. This decay has a half-life of 5,730 years. If a positron is emitted, the remaining nucleus has one proton fewer than it did before. Several varieties of beta decay involve phenomena such as the capture of one of the atomic electrons by a proton to turn itself into a neutron. In this case, there is no emitted positron, but an observer sees an X ray as other electrons fall close to the nucleus to replace the electron that was captured.

When they were first discovered, beta decays puzzled researchers because they did not exhibit the definite energies that characterized alpha and gamma decays. It was finally realized that nuclei undergoing beta decay emit not only an electron or a positron but also a tiny uncharged particle called a neutrino. Neutrinos carry off part of the definite energy of the nuclear charge so that the beta particles from a particular nuclear transition exhibit a statistical energy distribution. Because they are uncharged and interact very little with other atomic particles, neutrinos can pass through the mass of several earths with less than a 50 percent chance of interacting. Consequently, they are very difficult to detect. (An example of a neutrino detector is a hole in a mine the size of a ten-story building, filled with water and surrounded by detectors.) Despite their small chance of interacting, neutrinos are important to scientists' understanding of the structure of the universe, as they are believed to be produced in the nuclear reactions at the core of the sun and other stars. Thus, they may constitute a large portion of the mass of the universe. A debate rages over whether the neutrino is massless or has a very tiny mass that has not yet been measured. The answer to this question may determine whether the universe will expand forever or will eventually stop expanding and collapse back on itself.

Methods of Study

Radioactive decay was discovered by accident when Antoine-Henri Becquerel (1852-1908) accidentally left a piece of uranium-bearing rock on top of a photographic plate in a darkened drawer. The rock left its image on the film. The first studies of radioactive decay used film as a detector for radiation. The next generation of radiation detectors used fluorescent screens which would glow when struck by a decay particle. The screens could not be connected to electronic timers, and the flashes had to be counted through a microscope.

The Geiger-Müller counter is a gas-filled tube with a charged wire running up its center. When a gamma or a beta enters the tube, it knocks electrons off the gas atoms and makes the gas a conductor. The electrons are collected by the center wire and can be counted electronically or used to activate a speaker and make the characteristic click of a counter in the presence of radiation. Geiger-Müller counters often are not sensitive to alpha particles, as the metal used to keep the gas inside the tube also keeps alpha particles from entering the counter. The proportional counter, also a gas-filled tube, works on the same principle as does a Geiger-Müller counter except that it carefully measures the number of electrons that reach the central electrode. Because the number of electrons knocked off gas atoms is directly related to the energy of the particle that knocked them off, the number of electrons reaching the central electrode is directly related to the energy of the particle that produced them.

Scintillation counters utilize transparent materials that emit a flash of light when a particle passes through them. The amount of light is proportional to the kind of particle that passes through and its energy. The light is collected by a special tube, called a photomultiplier tube, that converts the light into a current pulse whose size is proportional to the amount of light emitted. The pulse can be used to drive an electronic counting system.

Many modern studies of gamma decay use solid-state detectors which take advantage of the fact that silicon and germanium crystals can be grown with very small amounts of impurities. If the crystals are carefully prepared, they will become conductors when radiation knocks electrons off the atoms in the regions containing the impurities. Once again, the number of electrons produced depends on the energy of the gamma that originated them. The crystal is placed between electrodes with a large voltage across them, and the electrodes collect the electrons produced by the gamma.

Modern detectors produce a pulse of electrons—an electric current—the strength of which is proportional to the energy of the radioactive decay particle that produced it. This current pulse is amplified and its size determined to study the energy of the decay particle that produced it. Such studies typically involve several stages of amplification during which the researcher must be careful not to alter the shape of the current pulses he or she is studying. The pulses are then fed into a device called a multichannel analyzer, which sorts them according to their strength and which stores each pulse as a count in a series of electronic bins. The bins can be displayed to show the number of counts received at each energy level. Called a spectrum of the decay, it is used to identify the nucleus that emitted the decay product. In modern systems, the multichannel analyzer is replaced by a dedicated computer that automatically identifies the energy of the decay and, in many cases, can tell the researcher what nucleus produced it. Such systems have memories stored with data on energies and half-lives of numerous radioactive decays that have been accumulated since World War II and carefully tabulated.

Radiation detectors and their associated counting systems have become smaller and more rugged. Studies of radioactive decays were once conducted only in laboratories; however, portable systems can now be taken into the field and are found, for example, at petroleum drilling sites. Detection systems are frequently carried into space and have been used in studies of the cosmic radiation and numerous other phenomena. The more sensitive systems used in radioactive dating are still confined to the laboratory, as they must be protected from the radiation in the environment produced by cosmic radiation and by radiation from common minerals.

Context

Since World War II, radioactive decay has ceased to be a laboratory curiosity and has become a widely used tool. The understanding of radioactive decay has led to the development of the means to date geological and archaeological specimens. Radioactive-dating techniques take advantage of the fact that each species of excited nucleus will decay so that half of it disappears after a particular amount of time elapses. If no new excited nuclei have been added to the sample since it was formed, one can compare the number of excited nuclei remaining in the sample to the number of nuclei in the sample formed by the radioactive decay and thus determine how long it has been since the sample was formed. The understanding of geologic time is based largely on radioactive dating.

In addition to its importance as a dating tool, radioactive decay is believed to be a major source of the heating of the earth. This heat flow is important to the overall heat budget of the earth and may be partially responsible for present temperatures on the earth's surface. Radioactive decay may also contribute to driving convection currents in the earth's interior, and it is probably at least partially responsible for the heat extracted as geothermal energy. Radioactive decay is also responsible for changing the nature of certain minerals, as in metamictization.

The presence of a large number of nuclei undergoing radioactive decay makes nuclear wastes hazardous. Although short-lived nuclei decay within a year and disappear, wastes from nuclear reactors are characterized by the presence of nuclei with long half-lives. They must therefore be stored in such a manner that they will not come in contact with the environment for tens of thousands of years. Only very stable geologic formations where wastes cannot be reached by groundwater will permit such storage. The search for suitable areas has covered many states. Radioactive decay has become a concern of many home owners with the discovery that seepage of radioactive radon gas, produced by the decay of minerals in the earth, has raised radiation levels in some homes above levels deemed healthy.

Despite its hazards, radioactive decay has become a useful tool in many types of geological research. For example, small amounts of short-lived radioactivity have been injected into geothermal systems along with cooled water to see how long it takes the reinjected water to reach the production end of the system. Radiation detectors are inserted into boreholes during petroleum exploration to map the presence of radioactive minerals along the walls of the borehole, which assists in the identification of shaley layers within a sandstone formation. In many other cases, radioactive decay has proved to be a useful tool for research and exploration.

Bibliography

Dull, Charles E., A. Clark Metcalfe, and John E. Williams. *Modern Physics.* New York: Holt, Rinehart & Winston, 1963. A widely used high school physics text in the United States, this source is readily available in public libraries. Chapters 6 and 7, which treat atomic structure and nuclear physics, provide a very readable introduction to radioactivity (although there are no applications given to geology). The treatment is elementary.

Durrance, Eric M. *Radioactivity in Geology: Principles and Applications.* New York: John Wiley & Sons, 1987. This monograph presents a very thorough review of the principles of radioactive decay and its many applications in geology. In addition to its thoroughness, this book is written for a nonspecialist in nuclear physics and is fairly readable as well as complete, discussing not only dating methods but also exploration methods, the use of radioactivity in petroleum studies, environmental radioactivity, and the role of radioactivity in heating the earth's interior.

Keller, C. *Radiochemistry.* New York: John Wiley & Sons, 1988. In addition to covering the basic theory of radioactive decay, this volume stresses the applications of radioactive decay in the study of problems of geological interest. Unlike the preceding reference, it emphasizes radioactivity produced by humans for their own purposes and is of less general interest than is Durrance's monograph.

Levinger, Joseph S., and George L. Carr. *Secrets of the Nucleus.* New York: McGraw-Hill, 1967. This slim volume presents a solid introduction to the structure of the nucleus and radioactive decay. Produced under the auspices of the National Science Teachers Association and geared for high school and junior high school students, it presents a very clear picture of the way in which the nucleus works.

Mann, W. B., R. L. Ayres, and S. B. Garfinkel, eds. *Radioactivity and Its Measurement.* 2d ed. Elmsford, N.Y.: Pergamon Press, 1980. This volume is designed to introduce radioactivity to nonphysicists who are interested in nuclear medicine. Although not specifically designed for earth scientists, it presents a solid introduction to the physics and technology used in the study of nuclear radiation.

Rhodes, Richard. *The Making of the Atomic Bomb.* New York: Simon & Schuster, 1986. The early chapters of this excellent history of nuclear physics are devoted to a detailed description of the discovery of nuclear decay and the development of a theory of the nucleus. The historically important experiments and ideas are presented in detail. Because the emphasis is on people and the development of a theory, Rhodes has written a very readable as well as technically accurate description of the theory of radioactive decay.

Serway, Raymond A., and Jerry S. Faughn. *College Physics.* Orlando, Fla.: Saunders College Publishing, 1985. Chapter 31 ("Nuclear Structure") provides a solid introduction to radioactive decay, oriented toward the reader with no background in the subject. In addition, this text provides brief introductions to carbon dating, radioactive decay chains found in nature, and nuclear reactions. Chapter 32 ("Nuclear Physics Applications and Elementary Particles") introduces technology of radiation detection and discusses the interaction of radiation with matter as well as treating fission and fusion power.

Ruth H. Howes

Cross-References

Earth's Age, 490; Geochronology: K-Ar and Ar-Ar Dating, 833; Geochronology: Radiocarbon Dating, 840; Geochronology: Rb-Sr Dating, 848; Geochronology: Sm-Nd Dating, 855; Geochronology: U-Th-Pb Dating, 862; Heat Sources and Heat Flow, 1065; Metamictization, 1545; Neutron Activation Analysis, 1734; Nuclear Power, 1749; Nuclear Waste Disposal, 1758; Nucleosynthesis, 1764; Radioactive Minerals, 2143; Radon Gas, 2150; Uranium Deposits, 2580.

RADIOACTIVE MINERALS

Type of earth science: Geology
Field of study: Mineralogy and crystallography

Radioactive minerals combine uranium, thorium, and radium with other elements. Useful for nuclear technology, these minerals furnish the basic isotopes necessary not only for nuclear reactors but also for advanced medical treatments, metallurgical analysis, and chemicophysical research.

Principal terms

AUTORADIOGRAPHY: a method by which a photograph of radioactive minerals is taken, using the emissions of the minerals themselves

CARNOTITE: an important ore of uranium, formed by reaction of groundwater with minerals already present

HALF-LIFE: the amount of time required for exactly one-half of an element's original material to decay into a daughter product

ISOTOPES: atoms of the same element with identical numbers of protons but different numbers of neutrons in their nuclei

MONAZITE: a rare earth phosphate widely disseminated over the crust; the major ore source for thorium

PEGMATITE: a very coarse-grained granitic rock, often enriched in rare minerals, including uranium and thorium

RADIOACTIVE EMISSIONS: particles and radiation thrown off during the breakdown of a nucleus, including alpha and beta particles and gamma rays

RADIOACTIVITY: the spontaneous breakdown of elements in nature into other elements with differing nuclear properties

URANINITE: the chief ore of uranium and radium, formed of uranium oxide in combination with rare earth elements

Summary of the Phenomenon

Of the more than twenty-five hundred species of minerals known to exist on the earth, only a small fraction are characterized by the presence of radioactive elements, primarily uranium, thorium, and radium. These elements are in a continuous state of radioactive breakdown, over time changing the chemical and structural composition of the minerals in which they occur. Approximately 150 of these compounds have uranium or thorium as an essential element in their crystallographic structure. Many of these minerals are quite rare; others, more important economically, can be characterized as present in small and variable amounts, paired with other elements in a solid solution of variable composition. Many such compounds, whether abundant or sparse, have current or future economic potential as sources for usable uranium and thorium.

Although in the earth's crust uranium possesses an average concentration of only 4 parts per million, its abundance is much higher in several minerals that have become of great economic interest. Uranium itself is a dense, very electropositive, reactive metal that forms many alloys that are usable in nuclear technology. Uranium reacts with almost all nonmetallic elements and their binary compounds. Several hundred uranium-containing minerals have been identified, including such rare ones as tyuyamunite, torbernite, autunite, eudialyte, pyrochlore, and rinkite.

The chief ore of uranium is uraninite, which is basically uranium oxide (UO_2). Numerous other elements are often present, particularly thorium, rare earths (mostly cerium), and lead, the latter element formed as a radioactive decay by-product of the uranium breakdown. A complete solid-solution series covers the range between uranium oxide, thorianite (ThO_2), and cerianite (CeO_2). The material has been found in pegmatites with zircons, in hydrothermal deposits with compounds of arsenic (such as cobalt, bismuth, and silver), and in some sedimentary deposits associated with coal. Because uraninite is the chief ore source of uranium and radium, the basic raw material of nuclear energy, it is extremely important. Its chemical variants include bröggerite and cleveite.

Another important ore of uranium and radium is carnotite, a secondary mineral resulting from the reaction of groundwater with preexisting uranium-bearing minerals. Existing as a hydrous vanadate of potassium and uranium (the water varying from one to three molecules depending on the temperature), the largest deposits are in the Colorado Plateau, in Australia, and in Zaire.

Minerals containing uranium possess the element in two ionic forms: as a quadrivalent ion and as a hexavalent one known as the uranyl ion. Minerals with the positive four-valence ion are often black, do not fluoresce in ultraviolet light, and usually occur as primary deposits. Such minerals include uraninite and coffinite. Most uranium-containing minerals, however, are in the uranyl ion form, characterized by a bright lemon-yellow to green color and fluorescing in ultraviolet as a lemon-yellow color. All these minerals are secondary in origin, deriving from preexisting sediments, and are formed from solutions at relatively low temperature and pressure.

With an average concentration of 12 parts per million, thorium is much more abundant in the crust than is uranium. The major source for thorium is the mineral monazite, a rare earth phosphate containing 3-10 percent thorium as thorium oxide (ThO_2). Thorium substitutes for cerium (Ce) and lanthanum (La), giving a series of monazite minerals that may range all the way to 30 percent thorium oxide. Monazite is very widely disseminated in granites, pegmatites, and gneiss rocks as accessory grains and crystals. The weathering products of such materials, found in the form of beach sands or fluvial deposits, often include large amounts of thorium.

Thorium has a half-life of 1.4×10^{10} years. Its decay series, going through ten successive disintegrations, terminates at lead 208. It is useful as an alloying agent in some structural metals and in magnesium technology; in a nuclear reactor, it can be converted to uranium 233, an atomic fuel.

Radium, with a decay half-life of 75,400 years, is another radioactive element usually found in uranium minerals but only in concentrations of 1 part to 3 million parts uranium. Thirteen radium isotopes are known, all radioactive, but only radium 226 is technologically important. The best mineral source at present is pitchblende. Radium salts tend to ionize the surrounding atmosphere, causing a bluish glow to appear. Radium compounds also cause other compounds in mineral form, such as zinc sulfide, to phosphoresce and fluoresce.

All three elements occur in high concentrations in the continental crust compared to the oceanic material. The reason relates to the large ionic radii of the isotopic elements compared to those of silicon, aluminum, magnesium, and iron, which combine with oxygen to make up the bulk of the earth's oxide minerals. The larger ions do not fit as readily into the crystal lattice formed with oxygen, so that in magmatic and metamorphic events, they are freely mobile and tend to follow magmatic products and volatiles upward into the crust. There, they incorporate themselves more easily into the more open crystal structures found in the lower-pressure environments of the surface crustal material.

Uranium, in one mineral form or another, has been found in every geologic environment of the United States, with the exception of ultramafic igneous rocks. Concentrations of radioactive elements have been located in igneous rocks, veins, clastic sediments, precipitates, evaporites, coals, marine black shales, and limestones. The principal sources of uranium in the United States are in terrestrial sandstones and limestones, principally in areas characterized by simple folded mountains alternating with broad basins, such as the Black Hills of South Dakota. There is no confining age range when the ore-bearing sediments were laid down, for they date from Jurassic, Permian, Devonian, and Mississippian geologic time periods. The ore bodies themselves originate by a number of means, including deposits from molten magma, hot fluids, groundwater, surface solutions, volcanic ash, and seawater.

Three major types of uraniferous veins have been recognized by their mineral associations: nickel-cobalt-native silver veins, silica-iron-lead veins, and iron-titanium veins. The first group is characterized by pitchblende, as is the second (with different associated minerals), while the third type of vein is characterized by uranium titanites, such as davidite, occurring mainly in igneous intrusive rocks, such as at Radium Hill, South Australia. The geologic processes that lead to the formation of mineral deposits include differentiation by fractional crystallization in magmas, the escape of hot liquids and gases from cooling melts into surrounding rocks, concentration by underground waters, concentration by sedimentation (the principal process for the formation of monazite), and fixation by biochemical processes such as plant roots. All these mechanisms have been shown, for one mineral or another, to be active in depositing uranium and thorium in the surface rocks.

Because of the nature of the means by which uranium is produced and concentrated, uranium and thorium can be, as with most metals, shown to cluster within broad, poorly defined areas of the globe. Initial concentration probably occurred during the formation of the earth's crust. Geologic analyses and histories provide detailed information on where to look, what minerals to expect, and the feasibility of extracting the radioactive minerals located in a particular area.

Methods of Study

Because concentrations of the radioactive elements in rocks are usually in trace amounts, measured in parts per million, very precise chemical and geological analysis is required. The isotopic abundance is most often obtained through multi-channel gamma-ray spectrometry, a technique by which gamma-ray emissions from the various elements are separated and counted on the basis of energy. For each elemental decay, gamma radiation has very characteristic energies, which the decay counter can detect. The counts at specific levels of the energy spectrum are indicative of the particular isotopic abundance in the sample.

Concentration studies can also be done using atomic absorption spectrometry. This involves heating the sample to a vapor, then passing a light through the gas to see which wavelengths are absorbed. The elements present and their abundances can be easily determined in this way. Three different methods of physically separating the isotopes are common. Gaseous diffusion involves passing the gases through a porous material; the light elements pass through more swiftly than do the heavier ones. In a mass spectrograph, the particles are forced to follow a curved path in a vacuum chamber under the influence of a magnetic field, the amount of bending of the path depending on the mass of the element. In thermal diffusion, the sample is heated to 500 degrees Celsius and allowed to move in a convection gradient, separating because of the ability of lighter particles to move faster than heavier ones.

Minerals with radioactive elements can be detected by many techniques. Auto-radiography uses the interaction of the radiation emitted by radioactive elements with a photographic plate, causing an ion trail that essentially breaks down the photographic emulsion. The density of the image depends on the concentration of radioactive elements present. In this very direct method, results can be quantified if the tracks are clearly defined, for the numbers of trails can simply be counted. The fission track method, used for uranium and thorium, is similar, in that a polished sample is broken apart by the emitted radiation, leaving tracks which can be seen once the sample is etched. Generally, the material is embedded in plastics that record the tracks upon themselves. Such a technique has been used to detect concentrations of uranium from 4,000 parts per million in zircons to 10^{-3} parts per million in hypersthene and anorthite.

Identification can also be done by four somewhat similar methods. With the polarizing microscope, particular minerals can be identified by their color changes under the action of polarized light. In X-ray diffraction, the mineral is powdered and bombarded with X rays. The radiation will be diffracted by the planes of atoms present, forming a diffractogram, which reveals the crystal structure. In electron microscopy, a small sample, as small as 1 micron, is bombarded with an electron beam, so that X rays with wavelengths characteristic of the particular radioactive element are produced. The intensity of radiation also reveals the concentration of the element in the sample. Finally, with the scanning electron microscope, the sample is coated with a gold-palladium layer and bombarded with electrons, revealing the detailed topography of the mineral. Magnifications of up to 100,000 are possible.

To obtain purified materials, the major technique used with all the minerals is the extraction method, which permits high selectivity and complete separation. For uranium, the best method is extraction of uranyl nitrate with ether from a nitrate acid solution saturated with ammonium nitrate. Tributyl phosphate may replace the ether, while adding salts, such as trivalent aluminum or iron, or divalent zinc, causes a salting-out effect to occur, precipitating even more uranium oxide. Ion exchange is used to extract the other radioactive elements (and works for uranium as well). In this process, complex anions on various exchange media, most commonly sulfuric acid or carbonate solutions, are used for their sorbable qualities. The material is passed through a column of basic anion (negatively charged) exchangers. Under the appropriate conditions, uranium, for example, in a nitrate acid in 80 percent alcohol solution, separates completely from other rare earth metals.

Context

Though radioactive minerals are rare, they have become extremely important scientifically and economically. Uranium, thorium, and radium are useful in many fields: medicine, industrial processes, and physics and chemical theoretical studies. The study of radioisotopes, formed from the radioactive elements separated from the earth's minerals, has led to immense increases in knowledge of how the human body works, how plants employ photosynthesis, and how individual cells manage to maintain homeostatic equilibrium. In chemistry, such isotopes provide a picture of intermediaries in chemical reactions, allowing better understanding of the workings of chemical compounds such as enzymes. In physics, a theoretical understanding of the nuclear structure itself—down to the fundamental level of quarks, the supposed elementary particles of the universe—has been gained through watching the breakdown of radioactive nuclei in nature. In the iron and steel industries, their use has helped to shed light on the thermodynamics and kinetics of metal-slag reactions, the hydrodynamics of molten steel, the movement of charged materials in a blast furnace, and crystallization in metallurgical products.

In the field of geochronology, the only means of setting absolute dates on events in the distant past is to examine the breakdown, at a precise decay rate, of radioactive elements. Not only can geoscientists investigate the origin of the earth and the rest of the solar system in this way, but they can also study the evolution of the earth's surface, oceans, and atmosphere—the collage of geological events, such as mountain building or wandering continents, that have shaped the globe.

More important for the average person, however, is the fact that radioactive elements provided the basic materials necessary for the development of nuclear fission as an energy source. Nuclear technology is dependent on a continuous supply of such minerals to create the energy required to meet the demands of industrialized countries at present; such demands are likely to increase. Unfortunately, the hazards posed by the manufacture of nuclear weapons, radiation fall-out from accidents at energy plants, and nuclear waste disposal loom large. It is to be hoped that as these rare minerals continue to be mined and used, the attendant problems will be addressed and eventually solved.

Bibliography

Ehlers, Ernest, and Harvey Blatt. *Petrology: Igneous, Sedimentary, and Metamorphic*. San Francisco: W. H. Freeman, 1982. A study of the major rock types, tracing the processes by which igneous, sedimentary, and metamorphic materials are formed. Discusses mineral concentration factors and relates minerals, including radioactive ones, to global tectonics. Contains a section on the use of isotopes. Well written but detailed; includes many references to other works.

Faul, Henry, ed. *Nuclear Geology*. New York: John Wiley & Sons, 1954. After a readable introduction into the realm of nuclear physics, which defines terms and describes instruments used, the work details the distribution of uranium and thorium in rocks and the ocean. Discusses types of minerals, how they are found geographically, and how they are used geochemically. Contains extensive references.

Faure, Gunter. *Principles of Isotope Geology*. 2d ed. New York: John Wiley & Sons, 1986. This well-written work explains how isotopic data are used to interpret and solve geologic problems, showing how radioactive isotopes make important contributions to virtually every area of science. Includes discussion of minerals, geochronology, and the uses of natural radioactivity. Features helpful references.

Glasstone, Samuel, et al. *Principles of Nuclear Reactor Engineering*. New York: Van Nostrand Reinhold, 1955. Dealing with the entire scope of reactor engineering, this work has two important chapters on reactor materials and the processing of radioactive minerals. Provides a detailed overview of how reactors work, how energy is produced from radioactive minerals, the types of radiation emitted, and the nature of the reactions. Rather extensive mathematics but very interesting.

Gurinsky, David, and G. J. Dienes. *Nuclear Fuels*. New York: Van Nostrand Reinhold, 1956. A guide to the metallurgy of uranium and thorium, including means of preparation and production for use. Describes the metals' growth and formation in nature and discusses alloys and properties useful for technology. A well-written presentation of radiation effects. Includes numerous references and explanatory diagrams.

Lavrukhina, Augusta K., et al. *Chemical Analysis of Radioactive Materials*. Cleveland: CRC Press, 1967. This work discusses the states and behaviors of radioactive elements and the theoretical bases for methods of analysis. Topics include detecting radioisotopes, concentrating elements, and means of isolating each one. The references are helpful. Features detailed analysis and chemistry.

Mason, Brian, and Carleton B. Moore. *Principles of Geochemistry.* 4th ed. New York: John Wiley & Sons, 1982. A well-written work on elements that are significant in the earth's structures. Covers their physical and chemical evolution within the system. Contains chapters on isotope geochemistry for stable isotopes, radiation emitters, and their usefulness in geochronology. A very competent discussion of the important radioactive minerals. Good references are provided.

Nininger, Robert D. *Minerals for Atomic Energy.* New York: Van Nostrand Reinhold, 1954. A comprehensive work on the analysis of the radioactive minerals. Covers ore deposits and formations and the types of minerals containing uranium, thorium, and radium in association with other elements. Describes where such minerals occur in nature. Informative identification guide to the majority of important minerals, with good illustrations.

_____. *Formation of Uranium Ore Deposits.* Vienna: International Atomic Energy Agency, 1974. This work appraises the world supply of uranium minerals. Mechanisms for the formation and concentration of minerals are examined closely, and the isotope geology and mineralogy of diverse deposits around the world are surveyed. Includes numerous maps and illustrations. Some of the papers are not in English. Well equipped with references.

Arthur L. Alt

Cross-References

Elemental Distribution in the Earth, 391; Earth's Oldest Rocks, 561; Hazardous Wastes, 1059; Metamictization, 1545; Nuclear Power, 1749; Nuclear Waste Disposal, 1758; Radioactive Decay, 2136; Earth Resources, 2175; Future Resources, 2182; Strategic Resources, 2188.

RADON GAS

Field of study: Urban geology and geologic hazards

Radon is a radioactive gas that is naturally occurring, colorless, odorless, and almost chemically inert. Interest in indoor levels of radon was created by the discovery of high levels of radon in homes in the Reading Prong area of Pennsylvania, New Jersey, and New York starting in 1985.

Principal terms

ALPHA PARTICLE: a positively charged atomic particle that is ejected from the nucleus of certain radioactive elements and is composed of two neutrons and two protons

BETA PARTICLE: an electron emitted from the nucleus of a radioactive element

DAUGHTER: a decay product resulting from the radioactive disintegration of a radioactive element

GAMMA RAYS: short-wavelength electromagnetic radiation similar to X rays, which is emitted by many radioactive elements

HALF-LIFE: the time required for one-half of any quantity of identical radioactive atoms to undergo decay

PERMEABILITY: the capacity of a solid to transmit a fluid, which is dependent on the porosity as well as the extent of interconnection among pores

WORKING LEVEL: a measure of decay product concentration, which indicates the extent of alpha particle release from short-lived decay products; also, a measure of the total alpha activity in air caused by the presence of radon daughters

Summary of the Phenomenon

Far down on the list of the earth's ingredients, making up a tiny four parts per million of the crust, is the heavy element uranium 238. Uranium is radioactive, and as the unstable atoms of the element break down into atoms of more stable elements (a process known as decay), they spontaneously give off radiation. The time that it takes uranium, and every other radioactive element, to decay and release its radiation is measured as its half-life. Uranium 238 has a half-life of 4.5 billion years, so it will always be present in the materials found in the earth's crust. About halfway through its decay chain sequence, uranium sheds one identity and becomes radium 226, which possesses a half-life of 1,602 years. At this point, where the radium 226 begins to decay, the long decay chain that started with uranium 238 begins to cause problems. As it decays, radium 226 breaks the chain of solid elements and turns itself into a gas, radon. Radon resembles other so-called inert gases in that it is colorless, odorless, tasteless, and nonflammable. It essentially does not react or combine with other chemicals or elements, nor is it readily absorbed by them. Radon can travel long distances through rock, soil, and water and emerge unchanged.

Wherever uranium is found in rocks and soil, radium will also be found. Where there is radium, radon gas and its daughters are sure to be present. Although uranium can be found in about 150 minerals, some types of rock and soil formed from breakdown contain much more of the radioactive element than do others. Among these types are granite, phosphate, shale, and uranium itself. In terms of the United States' overall radon problem, granite is the worst offender, partly because it contains so much uranium and also because there is so much of it. Deposits of phosphate often contain high levels of uranium. One-third of the world's phosphate comes from north and west-central Florida, but there are also mines in Idaho, Montana, North Carolina, Tennessee, and Wyoming. Shale is nothing more than hardened and compacted clay and mud, so its uranium content depends on what kind of soil it was created from, which varies dramatically from place to place. In the United States, some deposits, among them the Chattanooga Shale in eastern Tennessee, are high in uranium. Large deposits of uranium ore, pure enough to be mined for atomic fuel, are located in parts of western Colorado, eastern Utah, northeastern Arizona, northwestern New Mexico, Wyoming, Texas, and western Canada. Radon levels in the soil near these uranium deposits are high. The ore contains about one thousand times more uranium than does the average soil.

Outdoor concentration of radon emanating from soil is small. The soil gas can build up, however, and occur at high concentrations indoors. There are two other sources of radon in structures: building materials and domestic water supplies. These sources are less important than is soil gas emanation; nonsoil sources account for less than 10 percent of total exposure to radon.

The infiltration of radon from soil into buildings generally occurs through cracks and openings in the foundation and under crawl spaces. Basements appear to be the most susceptible to high rates of radon entry from soil. The radon entry is caused by two effects. One is the movement of radon by molecular diffusion through air pores in the soil. A second, more significant air flow occurs because of the indoor-outdoor pressure differential. This pressure-driven flow is the main component of radon entry into homes and is created by the thermal "stack effect" and wind loading on the building. The stack effect relates to the pressure difference across any wall separating air masses of different temperature. In the cold seasons, this effect causes a net inward flow of soil gas into a heated building. Wind loading produces differential pressure across different walls of a building. It also causes an exchange of air between the building and the soil, but it is less important than the stack effect.

For given conditions, concentration of radon in a building is affected by the natural ventilation rate. Based on limited data, it appears that the ventilation rate in most conventional houses varies from 0.5 to 1.0 air exchanges per hour, averaged over cold and warm seasons, respectively. For new homes with tight, energy-efficient construction, the rate is expected to be substantially lower. As a result, the average level of indoor radon has been increasing in the past few years and is expected to continue to increase in the future.

Another source of indoor radon is domestic water. Because radon is highly soluble, it may accumulate at high concentrations in groundwater after being generated in the earth's crust. Groundwater thus can be a significant source of indoor radon in houses supplied by private wells where the storage time is usually too short to allow for radon to decay. While radon concentrations of 100 picocuries per liter are rare for indoor air, waterborne radon has been found in excess of 100,000 picocuries per liter. Waterborne radon appears to account for less than 5 percent of deaths from exposure to indoor levels of radon.

Methods of Study

When a building is tested for radon, the results will probably be reported in one of two ways: picocuries per liter (pCi/l), which refers to levels of radon gas in the building, or working levels (WL), a measure of exposure to radon's radioactive daughter products. One pCi/l of air equals about two radon atoms per minute decaying in every quart of air in a room. Generally, living in a house that contains 10 pCi/l carries the same lung-cancer risk as smoking one pack of cigarettes a day.

Although pCi/l is easier to determine than is WL, radon gas is not really the problem. It is exposure to the alpha radiation from radon's daughter products that is dangerous, and that is measured in WL. The concept of WL was developed in the 1950's as a way of calculating the amount of radon daughters to which uranium miners were being exposed underground. WLs are measurements of energy released by the radon daughters during their decay. In a typical house, 200 pCi/l of radon gas in the air convert to 1 WL. If the test measurement for a house is determined to be 4 pCi/l, then the occupants are living with 0.02 WL of radon daughters. It is difficult to predict what standard, if any, might eventually be adopted for private homes in the United States. The U.S. Environmental Protection Agency (EPA) has recommended a standard for remedial action of 0.02 WL, or 4 pCi/l in the living area of a house. EPA officials are quick to point out, however, that they do not consider 0.02 WL "safe" or even "acceptable," only a realistic target at which to aim. It is probably financially impractical to reduce radon to much below this level in all houses. According to EPA estimates, the average indoor level of radon in the United States (about 0.006 WL or 1.3 pCi/l) causes four thousand or more deaths per million population.

Predicting the risk from the radon decay chain in air requires a knowledge of the average concentration of each of the radon daughters throughout the period of exposure. Regardless of the method used to estimate the concentration of radon or daughters, there are a few features of radon and daughter measurements common to designing any measurement program. These features are essential in ensuring that the measurements reflect the actual conditions of exposure throughout the period of interest. The most accurate and precise measurements will yield unrealistic risk estimates if the measurements are not performed at times representative of exposures.

One of the first considerations is that the radon concentration, and hence the concentration of the daughters, can vary significantly over the course of the year. These variations arise from changes in the water content of soil and fluctuations in atmospheric pressure, each of which influences the emanation of radon from soil. In addition, infiltration rates in buildings depend on the season, as doors and windows are opened and closed in response to the changes in temperature. Radon concentrations also can vary widely within a given day, usually displaying a distinct pattern of rises and falls throughout the cycle of day and night. Because of the daily and seasonal fluctuations, measurements should be performed throughout the year and at varying times during each day. Regardless of the sampling schedule adopted, the measurement times should accurately reflect the distribution of infiltration conditions. Failure to do so can result in large errors in estimates of the average annual exposure.

The measurement plan also must account for potential differences in concentration throughout a structure. Radon and daughter concentrations can vary at different points within a single building, since rooms may differ in distance from the source (such as soil) and in local infiltration conditions.

With these factors in mind, a method must be chosen to collect measurement data. Conceptually, measurement techniques can be divided into three broad categories: grab sampling, continuous and active sampling, and integrative sampling. The choice of category will depend upon the costs involved, the time over which an instrument can be devoted to measurements at a single location, the kind of information required, and the desired accuracy with which measurements can be related to an estimate of risk.

Grab samples consist of essentially instantaneous measurements of the radon or radon daughter concentration in air over time intervals that are short (on the order of minutes) compared to the time scale of fluctuations in concentration. Continuous sampling involves measurements taken automatically at closely spaced time intervals over a long period of time. The result is a series of measurements that can provide information on the pattern with which the concentration varied throughout the measurement interval. Finally, integrating devices collect information on the total number of radiation events (such as alpha decays) that occur throughout some fairly long period of time, usually several days to months. The result from integrating devices is an estimate of the approximate average concentration through the measurement interval. Unfortunately, information about the temporal pattern of concentration within the measurement is lost in the integration.

The activated-charcoal canister and alpha track methods for measuring radon have become quite popular because of the low cost and small size of the devices. The activated-charcoal device utilizes the fact that radon is partially adsorbed onto the surface of activated charcoal and will remain loosely attached until heating. The method is very simple and requires a minimum of equipment, most of which is available in most radiation counting labs. The activated charcoal can be purchased in bulk and is loaded into small containers using almost any available materials (although the containers must be impervious to radon diffusion once they are sealed). Approximately 50-100 grams of the charcoal are placed into each container, and the container is sealed. It is then opened in the area to be monitored and left exposed for two to seven days to allow equilibrium with the ambient air. After this time, the canister is sealed and returned to the lab for counting.

Another method for measurement of radon involves direct exposure of alpha track material to ambient radon. In a typical system, a small slab of alpha track material is placed at the bottom of a small cup (any material for the cup will suffice so long as the radon daughters cannot diffuse through the walls). Often, a filter is added across the front of the cup to remove the daughters. In this way, the radon alone is free to diffuse into the space of the cup, where it will decay to the daughters. The alpha emissions from the radon and any daughters produced in the cup then irradiate the alpha track material, leaving microscopic "damage" along the track of each alpha particle. After exposure for the desired period of time (extending up to a year), the material is removed from the cup and etched in an acidic or basic solution operated upon by an alternating electric field. This etching extends the region of damage around each track, and the separate tracks become visible as small holes on the surface of the material. These tracks are counted visually using a wide-screen microscope. The number of tracks are proportional to the number of alphas striking the material surface during exposure. The accuracy of the method can be modified partially by varying the fraction of the surface examined for tracks. A wide range of materials is available for use as the alpha track material, and several commercial firms now market services that include rental of the device and counting of the tracks. For periods of time of up to a year, the system provides a true integration measurement of the average exposure conditions (at least within the variability of the method itself).

Context

In the United States, radon concentrations in single-family homes vary by more than four orders of magnitude—from a few becquerels per cubic meter (Bq/m^3) of air to more than ten thousand, with an average level of around 50 Bq/m^3 of air (1 Bq = 1 radioactive decay per second; 37 Bq/m^3 = 1 pCi/l). The average indoor radon level represents a radiation dose approximately three times greater than the dose most people would receive from medical X rays in the course of their lifetimes.

Hundreds of thousands of Americans living in homes that have high radon levels receive as large an exposure of radiation annually as do those persons who resided near the Soviet Union's Chernobyl nuclear power plant in 1986, when one of its reactors exploded and released radioactive material into the environment. To estimate a risk factor for indoor radon levels, results from epidemiological studies of underground miners who were exposed to high concentrations of radon's decay products are extrapolated to the lower exposures characteristic of radon in the typical home. Based on these estimates, the average indoor concentration of radon in the United States corresponds to a chance of contracting lung cancer of about 1 in 250, or 0.4 percent, which would account for about ten thousand lung-cancer deaths per year in the United States. People who have lived for twenty years in homes that have radon concentrations of 1,000 Bq/m^3 of air (37 pCi/l) face an additional 2 or 3 percent chance of contracting lung cancer. (There are tens of thousands of these houses in the United States.) There is probably no way to know which homes should be tested and which need not. The federal government has indicated a one-in-ten chance that any house in the United States is contaminated with unhealthy levels of radon. Other agencies and scientists say the odds are even higher.

Fortunately, most people are not exposed to enough radon to harm them. Unfortunately, for those who have lived or worked for years in an environment heavily contaminated with radon, the risk appears to be great. The National Cancer Institute has singled out radon exposure as the number-one cause of lung cancer among nonsmokers, accounting for as many as 30,000 deaths every year in the United States. Others say the number may be even higher. The damage done by radon is never immediately apparent. Radioactivity from radon does its damage imperceptibly, injuring the body a few cells at a time. Only after twenty to thirty years, or longer, may the disease make itself known.

The decay of radon gas produces a series of short-lived daughters (bismuth, lead, and polonium), which are all radioactive. About 90 percent of the radioactivity emitted by radon and its daughters is in the form of alpha particles, the most dangerous type of radioactive emissions. By far the largest internal radon radiation exposure, and the most dangerous, comes by inhaling radon gas. Inhaling radon gas itself is relatively harmless, as the gas is exhaled before any significant decay takes place. (Radon has a half-life of 3.8 days; the average breath stays in the lungs only about 17 seconds.) What threatens health are the radon daughters that are formed directly in the air from the decay of the radon gas. Once deposited in the lungs, in the stomach, or in other internal organs, radon daughters continue to decay, transmitting radiation to nearby cells. Whether the radon is ingested or inhaled, the damage that alpha particle radiation can inflict on living tissue is virtually the same. Unlike beta and gamma radiation, which can penetrate far into the body and disperse their radiation energy over a wider area, an alpha particle travels a relatively short distance through human tissue and concentrates its radiation energy on a small area of cells.

There is no doubt that radon in sufficient doses can produce lung cancer in humans. When a person inhales radon-contaminated air, as many as one-third of the dust particles with radon daughters attached, and most of the unattached daughters, remain in the lungs. Some travel deeply into the lungs, but most lodge in the moist upper bronchi, the two main branches that lead from the trachea to the lungs. At the surface of these large bronchi is a layer of tissue about 38 microns thick. Of all the parts of the human body, this layer, called the epithelium, is one of the most sensitive to radiation. The epithelium is sensitive to radiation because it is composed of basal cells, which reproduce much more rapidly than do other types of cells. Trapped in this delicate tissue, the short-lived radon daughters—especially polonium 218 and polonium 214, with half-lives of only three minutes and two ten-thousandths of a second, respectively—deliver their load of alpha particles to the sensitive tissue around them. The range of these particles is about 25 microns or less, so nearly the entire release of radioactivity is concentrated in the outermost lung tissue.

Lung cancer is the only documented disease linked directly to radon gas. It seems at least possible, however, that drinking radon in water may be a factor in some cases of stomach cancer, especially among people who ingest large amounts of radon from contaminated well water in certain parts of the United States.

Bibliography

Cothern, C. R., and J. E. Smith, Jr. *Environmental Radon*. New York: Plenum Press, 1987. This volume is intended for the newcomer to the area of environmental radon. It is arranged so that anyone with some basic college-level chemistry and physics can develop a clear understanding of the different aspects involved. The reader will find references for each individual chapter, a good glossary, an excellent appendix, and a table of often-used conversion factors.

Eisenbud, Merril. *Environmental Radioactivity: From Natural, Industrial, and Military Sources*. 3d ed. San Diego, Calif.: Academic Press, 1987. This book was written as a reference source for the scientist, engineer, or administrator with a professional interest in the subject, but it may also be of value to the general reader who wishes to understand the facts behind the public debate. For the interested college student, this work will contribute to a deeper understanding and a better appreciation of what is fundamentally a complex subject. Excellent illustrations, charts, and graphs as well as very extensive references are an integral part of this volume.

Gesell, Thomas, Wayne M. Lowder, and James E. McLaughlin, eds. *Natural Radiation Environment III: Proceedings*. Washington, D.C.: U.S. Department of Energy, 1983. A comprehensive and thorough compilation of papers dealing with the entire spectrum of naturally occurring environmental radioactivity in general, with numerous excellent reports on radon and radon-related problems. Suitable for most college-level students with at least a minimal science background. A well-referenced, up-to-date volume containing material by some of the leading modern authorities in the field.

Lafavore, Mike. *Radon: The Quiet Killer*. Emmaus, Pa.: Rodale Press, 1987. The first "popular" book to deal with the radon threat. Timely and sensible answers to tough questions about the radon problem and its potential threat to public health are provided. A listing of federal and state agencies (with addresses) that one can contact for assistance, a list of commercial testing companies that do household radon tests, and a short glossary of some of the more technical terms are included.

National Water Well Association Staff, eds. *Radon in Ground Water: Hydrogeologic Impact and Application to Indoor Airborne Contamination.* Chelsea, Mich.: Lewis Publishers, 1987. This reference work focuses on the following topics: geologic and hydrogeologic controls influencing radon occurrence; monitoring radon, radium, and other radioactivity from geologic and hydrogeologic sources; mining impacts on the occurrence of radon, radium, and other radioactivity in groundwater; sampling and analysis of radon, radium, and other radioactivity in groundwater; radon and radium in water supply wells; predictive models for the occurrence of radon, radium, and other radioactivity; and remedial action for radon, radium, and other radioactivity. A compilation of papers presented at a conference on radon, radium, and other radioactivity in groundwater. Suitable for advanced high school or college-level students as well as the interested layperson. Well illustrated, with excellent references sited, this volume is a storehouse of pertinent information.

Dan R. Quisenberry

Cross-References

Environmental Health, 615; Groundwater Movement, 1020; Groundwater Pollution, 1028; Radioactive Decay, 2136; Radioactive Minerals, 2143.

REEFS

Type of earth science: Geology
Field of study: Sedimentology

Reefs are among the oldest known communities, existing at least 2 billion years ago. They exert considerable control on the surrounding physical environment, influencing turbulence levels and patterns of sedimentation. Ancient reefs are often important hydrocarbon reservoirs.

Principal terms

CALCAREOUS ALGAE: green algae that secrete needles or plates of aragonite as an internal skeleton; very important contributors to reef sediment

CARBONATE ROCKS: sedimentary rocks such as limestone, which is composed of the minerals calcite or aragonite, or dolostone, which is composed of the mineral dolomite

CORALLINE ALGAE: red algae that secrete crusts or branching skeletons of high-magnesium calcite; important sediment contributors and binders on reefs

REEF: a biogenically (organically) produced carbonate structure including an internal framework that traps sediment and confers resistance to wave action

RUGOSE CORALS: a Paleozoic coral group also known as "tetracorals"; sometimes colonial, but more often solitary and horn-shaped

SCLERACTINIAN CORALS: modern corals or "hexacorals," different from their more ancient counterparts in details of the skeleton and the presence of a symbiosis with unicellular algae in most shallow-water species

STROMATOLITES: layered columnar or flattened structures in sedimentary rocks, produced by the binding of sediment by blue-green algal (cyanobacterial) mats

STROMATOPOROIDS: spongelike organisms that produced layered, mound-shaped, calcareous skeletons and were important reef builders during the Paleozoic era

TABULATE "CORALS": colonial organisms with calcareous skeletons that were important Paleozoic reef builders; considered to be more closely related to sponges than to corals

Summary of the Phenomenon

Reefs or reeflike structures are among the oldest known communities, extending back more than 2 billion years into the earth's history. These earliest reefs were vastly different in their biotic composition and physical structure from modern reefs, which are among the most diverse of biotic communities and display amazingly high rates of biotic productivity (carbon fixation) and calcium carbonate deposition, despite their existence in a virtual nutrient "desert." Reefs are among the few communities to rival the power of humankind as a shaper of the planet. The Great Barrier Reef of Australia, for example, forms a structure some 2,000 kilometers in length and up to 150 kilometers in width.

It is necessary to distinguish between "true," or structural, reefs and reeflike structures or banks. Reefs are carbonate structures that possess an internal framework. The framework traps sediment and provides resistance to wave action; thus, reefs can exist in very shallow water and may grow to the surface of the oceans. Banks are also biogenically produced but lack an internal framework. Thus, banks are often restricted to low-energy, deep-water settings. "Bioherm" refers to moundlike carbonate buildups, either reefs or banks, and "biostrome" to low, lens-shaped buildups.

Modern reefs are classified into several geomorphic types: atoll, barrier, fringing, and patch. Many of these may be further subdivided into reef crest or flat, back-reef or lagoon, and fore-reef zones (see figure). Atoll reefs are circular structures with a central lagoon, thought to form on subsiding volcanic islands. Barrier reefs are elongate structures that parallel coastlines and possess a significant lagoon between the exposed reef crest and shore. These often occur on the edges of shelves that are uplifted by faulting. Fringing reefs are elongate structures paralleling and extending seaward from the coastline that lack a lagoon between shore and exposed reef crest. Patch reefs are typically small, moundlike structures, occurring isolated on shelves or in lagoons. The majority of fossil reefs would be classified as patch reefs, although many examples of extensive, linear, shelf-edge trends are also known from the geologic record.

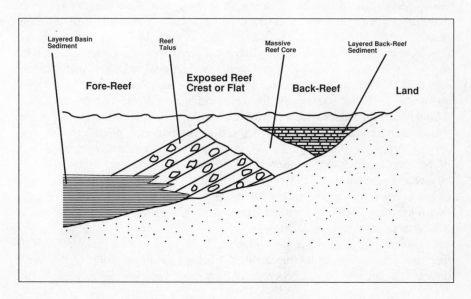

Reefs form one of the most distinctive and easily recognized sedimentary facies (or environments). In addition to possessing a characteristic fauna consisting of corals, various algae, and stromatoporoids, they are distinguished by a massive (nonlayered) core that has abrupt contacts with adjacent facies. Associated facies include flat-lying lagoon and steeply inclined fore-reef talus, the latter often consisting of large angular blocks derived from the core. The reef core is typically a thick unit relative to adjacent deposits. The core also consists of relatively pure calcium carbonate with little contained terrigenous material.

Knowledge of modern reef communities is much greater than that of their ancient counterparts. Information gained from the study of modern reefs will enhance scientists' knowledge of ancient reefs as well. Modern reefs are restricted to certain environments. They occur abundantly only between 23 degrees north and south latitudes and tend to be restricted to the western side of ocean basins, which lack upwelling of cold bottom waters. This restriction is based on temperature, as reefs do not flourish where temperatures frequently reach below 18 degrees Celsius. Reef growth is largely restricted to depths greater than 60 meters, as there is insufficient penetration of sunlight below this depth for symbiont-bearing corals to flourish. Reefs also require clear waters lacking suspended terrigenous materials, as these interfere with the feeding activity of many reef organisms and also reduce the penetration of sunlight. Finally, most reef organisms require salinities that are in the normal oceanic range. It appears that many fossil reefs were similarly limited in their environmental requirements.

Some of the most striking features of modern reefs include their pronounced zonation, great diversity, and high productivity and growth rates. Reefs demonstrate a strong bathymetric (depth-related) zonation. This zonation is largely mediated through depth-related changes in turbulence intensity and in the quantity and spectral characteristics (reds are absorbed first, blues last) of available light. Shallow (1- to 5-meter) fore-reef environments are characterized by strong turbulence and high light intensity and possess low-diversity assemblages of wave-resistant corals, such as the elk-horn coral, *Acropora palmata*, and crustose red algae. With increasing depth (10-20 meters), turbulence levels decrease and coral species diversity increases, with mound and delicate branching colonies occurring. At greater depths (30-60 meters), corals assume a flattened, platelike form in an attempt to maximize surface area for exposure to ambient light. Sponges and many green algae are also very important over this range. Finally, corals possessing zooxanthellae, which live in the coral tissues and provide food for the coral host, are rare or absent below 60 meters because of insufficient light. Surprisingly, green and red calcareous algae extend to much greater depths (100-200 meters), despite the very low light intensity (much less than 1 percent of surface irradiance). Sponges are also important members of these deep reef communities.

Coral reefs are among the most diverse of the earth's communities; however, there is no consensus on the mechanism(s) behind the maintenance of this great diversity. At one time, it was believed that reefs existed in a low-disturbance, highly stable environment, which allowed very fine subdivision of food and habitat resources and thus permitted the coexistence of a great number of different species. Upon closer inspection, however, many reef organisms appear to overlap greatly in food and habitat requirements. Also, it has become increasingly apparent that disturbance, in the form of disease, extreme temperatures, and hurricanes, is no stranger to reef communities.

Coral reefs exhibit very high rates of productivity (carbon fixation), which is a result of extremely tight recycling of existing nutrients. This is necessary, as coral reefs exist in virtual nutrient "deserts." Modern corals exhibit high skeletal growth rates, up to 10 centimeters per year for some branching species. Such high rates of skeletal production are intimately related to the symbiosis existing between the hermatypic or reef-building scleractinian corals (also gorgonians and many sponges) and unicellular algae or zooxanthellae. Corals that, for some reason, have lost their zooxanthellae or that are kept in dark rooms exhibit greatly reduced rates of skeleton production.

In addition to high individual growth rates for component taxa, the carbonate mass of the reefs may grow at a rate of some 2 meters per 1,000 years, a rate that is much higher than that of most other sedimentary deposits. This reflects the high productivity or growth rates of the component organisms and the efficient trapping of derived sediment by the reef frame. Although the framework organisms, most notably corals, are perhaps the most striking components of the reef system, the framework represents only 10-20 percent of most fossil reef masses. The remainder of the reef mass consists of sedimentary fill derived from the reef community through a combination of biosynthesis (secretion) and bioerosion (breaking down) of calcium carbonate. An example of the relative contributions of reef organisms to sediment can be found in Jamaica, where shallow-water, back-reef sediment consists of 41 percent coral, 24 percent green calcareous algae, 13 percent red calcareous algae, 6 percent foraminifera, 4 percent mollusks, and 12 percent other grains. The most important bioeroders are boring sponges, bivalves, and various "worms," which excavate living spaces within reef rock or skeletons, and parrot fish and sea urchins, which remove calcium carbonate as they feed upon surface films of algae.

A diversity of organisms has produced reef and reeflike structures throughout earth history. Several distinct reef community types have been noted, as well as four major "collapses" of reef communities. The oldest reefs or reeflike structures existed more than 2 billion years ago during the Precambrian eon. These consisted of low-diversity communities dominated by soft, blue-green algae, which trapped sediment to produce layered, often columnar structures known as stromatolites. During the Early Cambrian period, blue-green algae were joined by calcareous, conical, spongelike organisms known as archaeocyathids, which persisted until the end of the Middle Cambrian. Following the extinction of the archaeocyathids, reefs again consisted only of blue-green algae until the advent of more modern reef communities in the Middle Ordovician period. These reefs consisted of corals (predominantly tabulate and, to a much lesser extent, rugose corals), red calcareous algae, bryozoans (moss animals), and the spongelike stromatoporoids. This community type persisted through the Devonian period, at which time a global collapse of reef communities occurred. The succeeding Carboniferous period largely lacked reefs, although algal and crinoidal (sealily) mounds are common. Reefs again occurred in the Permian period, consisting mainly of red and green calcareous algae, stromatolites, bryozoans, and chambered calcareous sponges known as sphinctozoans, which resembled strings of beads. These reefs were very different from those of the earlier Paleozoic era; in particular, the tabulates and stromatoporoids no longer played an important role. The famous El Capitan reef complex of West Texas formed during this interval. The Paleozoic era ended with a sweep-ing extinction event that involved not only reef inhabitants but also other marine organisms.

After the Paleozoic extinctions, reefs were largely absent during the early part of the Mesozoic era. The advent of modern-type reefs consisting of scleractinian corals and red and green algae occurred in the Late Triassic period. Stromatoporoids once again occurred abundantly on reefs during this interval; however, the role of the previously ubiquitous blue-green algal stromatolites in reefs declined. Late Cretaceous reefs were often dominated by conical, rudistid bivalves that developed the ability to form frameworks and may have possessed symbiotic relationships with algae, as do many modern corals. Rudists, however, became extinct during the sweeping extinctions that occurred at the end of the Cretaceous period. The reefs that were reestablished in the Cenozoic era lacked stromatoporoids and rudists and consisted of scleractinian corals and red and green calcareous algae. This reef type has persisted, with fluctuations, until the present.

Methods of Study

Modern reefs are typically studied by scuba (self-contained underwater breathing apparatus) diving, which enables observation and sampling to a depth of approximately 50 meters. Deeper environments have been made accessible through the availability of manned submersibles and unmanned, remotely operated vehicles that carry mechanical samplers and still and video cameras. The biological compositions of reef communities are determined by census (counting) methods commonly employed by plant ecologists. Studies of symbioses, such as that between corals and their zooxanthellae, employ radioactive tracers to determine the transfer of products between symbiont and host. Growth rates are measured by staining the calcareous skeletons of living organisms with a dye, such as Alizarin red, and then later collecting and sectioning the specimen and measuring the amount of skeleton added since the time of staining. Another method for determining growth is to X-ray a thin slice of skeleton and then measure and count the yearly growth bands that are revealed on the X-radiograph. Variations in growth banding reflect, among other factors, fluctuations in ocean temperature.

Reef sediments, which will potentially be transformed into reef limestones, are examined through sieving, X-ray diffraction, and epoxy impregnation and thin-sectioning. Sieving enables the determination of sediment texture, the relationships of grain sizes and abundance (which will reflect environmental energy and the production), and erosion of grains through biotic processes. X-ray diffraction produces a pattern that is determined by the internal crystalline structure of the sediment grains. As each mineral possesses a unique structure, the mineralogical identity of the sediment may be determined. Thin sections of embedded sediment or lithified rock are examined with petrographic microscopes, which reveal the characteristic microstructures of the individual grains. Thus, even highly abraded fragments of coral or algae may be identified and their contributions to the reef sediment determined.

Because of their typically massive nature, fossil reefs are usually studied by thin-sectioning of lithified rock samples collected either from surface exposures or well cores. Reef limestones that have not undergone extensive alteration may be dated through carbon 14 dating, if relatively young, or through uranium-series radiometric dating methods.

Context

Modern reefs serve as natural laboratories, enabling the geoscientist to witness and study phenomena, such as carbonate sediment production, bioerosion, and early cementation, that have been responsible for forming major carbonate rock bodies in the past. The study of cores extracted from centuries-old coral colonies shows promise for deciphering past climates and perhaps predicting future trends. This is made possible by the fact that the coral skeleton records variations in growth that are related to ocean temperature fluctuations. The highly diverse modern reefs also serve as ecological laboratories for testing models on the control of community structure. For example, the relative importance of stability versus disturbance and recruitment versus predation in determining community structure is being studied within the reef setting.

Modern reefs are economically significant resources, particularly for many developing nations in the tropics. Reefs and the associated lagoonal seagrass beds serve as important nurseries and habitats for many fish and invertebrates. The standing crop of fish immediately over reefs is much higher than that of adjacent open shelf areas. Reef organisms may one day provide an important source of pharmaceutical compounds, such as prostaglandins, which may be extracted from gorgonians (octocorals). In addition, research has focused upon the antifouling properties exhibited by certain reef encrusters. Reefs also provide recreational opportunities for snorkelers and for scuba divers, a fact that many developing countries are utilizing to promote their tourist industries. Finally, reefs serve to protect shorelines from wave erosion.

Because of the highly restricted environmental tolerances of reef organisms, the occurrence of reefs in ancient strata enables fairly confident estimation of paleolatitude, temperature, depth, salinity, and water clarity. In addition, depth- or turbulence-related variation in growth form (mounds in very shallow water, branches at intermediate depths, and plates at greater depths) enables even more precise estimation of paleobathymetry or turbulence levels. Finally, buried ancient reefs are often important reservoir rocks for hydrocarbons and thus are important economic resources.

Bibliography

Bathurst, Robin G. C. *Carbonate Sediments and Their Diagenesis*. 2d ed. New York: Elsevier, 1975. Provides an excellent general reference on carbonate sediments, from reef and other environments, and their diagenesis.

Darwin, Charles. *The Structure and Distribution of Coral Reefs*. Berkeley: University of California Press, 1962. Darwin's book, originally published in 1851, is replete with observations on coral reefs from around the world. In addition, the theories presented on the formation of reef types such as atolls have withstood the test of time.

Frost, S. H., M. P. Weiss, and J. B. Sanders, eds. *Reefs and Related Carbonates: Ecology and Sedimentology*. Tulsa, Okla.: American Association of Petroleum Geologists, 1977. Includes a broad array of papers covering such aspects of the ecology and geology of modern and ancient reefs as bioerosion, diagenesis, paleoecology of ancient reefs, the role of sponges on reefs, and sedimentology of basins adjacent to modern reefs.

Goreau, Thomas F., et al. "Corals and Coral Reefs." *Scientific American* 241 (August, 1979): 16, 124-136. A good overview of the ecology of modern coral reefs. The discussion of coral physiology and the symbiotic relationship with zooxanthellae is particularly valuable.

Jones, O. A., and R. Endean, eds. *Biology and Geology of Coral Reefs*. 4 vols. New York: Academic Press, 1973-1977. This series of volumes encompasses both biological and geological aspects of coral reefs. Of particular value are review chapters covering, for example, the reefs of the western Atlantic.

Kaplan, Eugene H. *A Field Guide to Coral Reefs of the Caribbean and Florida, Including Bermuda and the Bahamas*. Boston: Houghton Mifflin, 1988. In addition to providing descriptions and illustrations (many in color) of common reef organisms, this book provides an excellent overview of modern reef community structure, zonation, and environments.

Laporte, Leo F., ed. *Reefs in Time and Space: Selected Examples from the Recent and Ancient*. Tulsa, Okla.: Society of Economic Paleontologists and Mineralogists, 1974. Includes papers on reef diagenesis, reef geomorphology, and the distribution of carbonate buildups in the geologic record.

Newell, Norman D. "The Evolution of Reefs." *Scientific American* 226 (June, 1972): 12, 54-65. Provides an overview of the composition of reef communities throughout the earth's history, including the various collapses and rejuvenations.

Smith, F. G. *Atlantic Reef Corals: A Handbook of the Common Reef and Shallow-Water Corals of Bermuda, the Bahamas*. Rev. ed. Baltimore, Md.: University of Miami Press, 1971. Smith provides taxonomic keys, descriptions, illustrations, and zoogeographic distributions for the Atlantic reef corals. In addition, he provides much general information on the distribution of coral reefs and their ecology.

Stoddart, D. R. "Ecology and Morphology of Recent Coral Reefs." *Biological Reviews* 44 (1969): 433-498. This article provides a review of the global distribution of coral reefs with emphasis on their ecology and geomorphology.

W. David Liddell

Cross-References

Carbonates, 190; Continental Structures, 290; Fossil Plants, 753; Fossilization and Taphonomy, 768; Geochronology: Radiocarbon Dating, 840; Earth Resources, 2175.

REMOTE SENSING AND
THE ELECTROMAGNETIC SPECTRUM

Field of study: Remote sensing

Remote sensing is the technique of observing details of an object from a great distance, obtaining reliable information about physical objects and the environment through the process of recording, measuring, and interpreting photographic images and patterns of electromagnetic radiant energy from space.

Principal terms

DIELECTRIC CONSTANT: the measure of how a material reduces an electrical field by producing an opposing field; this constant is used in insulators and determines how much of a radio signal will be reflected or passed

DOPPLER SHIFT: a phenomenon that increases the apparent frequency of radiation emitted by an approaching object, and decreases that of a receding object; by measuring the shift of an emission from its known original frequency, the relative motion of two objects can be measured

ELECTROMAGNETIC RADIATION: a general term encompassing all radiated energy forms, including radio waves, visible light, X rays, and gamma rays ("cosmic rays" comprise atomic and nuclear particles); electromagnetism is one of the four fundamental forces in nature

GEOSTATIONARY ORBIT: an orbit in which a satellite appears to hover over one spot on the planet's equator; this procedure requires that the orbit be high enough that its period matches the planet's rotational period, and have no inclination relative to the equator; for earth, the altitude is 35,903 kilometers

INFRARED RADIATION: electromagnetic radiation extending from just below the sensitivity of the human eye (infra = below) to millimeter-wavelength radio waves; the band is further divided into optical infrared and thermal infrared, and is popularly called heat radiation

LASER: Light Amplification by Stimulated Emission of Radiation, a device that emits radiation at a precise wavelength and with all the waves "in step," or coherent; because the emitted radiation is precisely known it is valuable as a light source for various kinds of measurements

POLARIZATION: the emission or filtering of radiation so that all the waves are vibrating in the same plane; radiation, normally emitted in all planes at once, can be polarized by the strong magnetic fields at the source, or by passage through or reflection from matter

SPECTROSCOPY: the study of the chemical and physical state of matter by splitting a stream of radiation into the spectrum and observing the relative intensity at different wavelengths; this can be applied to radiation from an object (emission spectroscopy) or passing through an object (absorption spectroscopy)

ULTRAVIOLET RADIATION: electromagnetic radiation extending from just above the sensitivity of the human eye (ultra = above) to "soft" X rays; the cut-off is not sharp, and what is called extreme ultraviolet (XUV) in some fields of research is considered to be soft X rays in others

Summary of the Methodology

Remote sensing provides earth scientists with the powerful extension of the third dimension—altitude—in studying the earth. Remote-sensing aircraft and satellites observe weather and climate processes, crop and city growth, and weapon reductions or buildups.

The use of cameras from aircraft in World War I gave birth to aerial combat when its importance to tactical planning was discovered. Aerial mapping has been used extensively ever since, limited only by the altitude that can be achieved by aircraft, which limits the field of view. Images can be joined as a mosaic, but slight mismatches, largely caused by the earth's curvature, distort the result.

Spaceflight extended this third dimension and offered the possibility of mapping the entire planet in a relatively short period of time, then repeating those observations to measure natural or man-made changes. A satellite in earth's orbit operates continually (as long as the craft is functional) and never returns to base. Proper selection of the orbit allows observations to take place in a variety of ways. An orbit crossing from pole to pole at approximately 400 to 500 kilometers in altitude will cross the equator at the same local time each orbit. That means that the sun angles in each set of images will be roughly the same, allowing fair comparisons of images taken days or weeks apart. The orbit can be further tailored so that the pattern is repeated every few days or weeks. From geostationary orbit a satellite can observe almost one-half of the planet. Only a fifth of the earth's surface can be observed effectively, because of the planet's curvature and the longer visual path through the atmosphere at shallow angles, but placing four or five satellites in geostationary orbit provides complete coverage of everything except the poles.

Remote sensing generally encompasses the detection of electromagnetic radiation. Sound and pressure waves may be used in a more limited manner to analyze the interior of the planet (through explosives or earthquakes), but radiation is the method most commonly used in remote sensing. For convenience, the electromagnetic spectrum is divided into segments based on how different wavelengths interact with matter. Progressing from the shortest wavelength (with the highest energy), the three major categories are X rays, light (visible radiation), and radio waves. The boundaries are not absolute. Visible light spans the 400- to 700-nanometer wavelength range (blue to red, respectively). Because matter generally absorbs or scatters shortwave radiation, radiation from X rays down to blue light is of limited use to remote-sensing techniques. Aerosols and dust scatter blue light very efficiently, so images taken in blue tend to be hazy and obscured. Most remote sensing of the surface of the earth is done from the green portion of the visible-light spectrum downward to red, infrared, and radio wavelengths. The range from 700 to 5,500 nanometers covers the reflected infrared spectrum; one encounters emissions by an object's body heat in the thermal infrared region (5,500 to 10,000 nanometers); and the microwave and radio regions, consisting of even longer wavelengths, lie beyond. These portions of the spectrum are not fully usable, since distinct bands are absorbed by the gases or water vapors in the atmosphere.

Remote-sensing techniques generally can be divided into passive and active categories. The former, which is far more common, involves instruments that simply collect natural radiation emitted or reflected by an object. The latter, which requires more complex systems, emits radiation and collects what is reflected by the object. Passive remote sensing also involves analysis of the spectrum of a known light source (usually the sun) as it is filtered by the atmosphere, or of emissions caused by chemical activities in the atmosphere, such as the aurora or dayglow.

Active techniques involve many of the concerns just discussed, but with the major difference that they first emit the radiation that they later detect. These methods are difficult to employ without a controllable source of radiation. Radar was the first remote-sensing technique to be employed: Radio waves are emitted and bounced off an object; the "echo" is analyzed to determine the identity of the object that the waves struck. Radar is used in a variety of methods, including altimetry and simple mapping. The most sophisticated version now used is called synthetic aperture radar (SAR), in which several sets of echoes are combined by computer to generate a single image that otherwise would have to be produced by a much larger aperture. The frequencies used by the radar will vary with the type of data to be collected; in general, shorter frequencies allow smaller objects to be observed. Other factors affecting reflectivity include surface roughness and the dielectric constant, which regulates how an object reacts to radiation (how good an antenna it is). Lasers are the second active remote-sensing method. These measure wind speed by the Doppler shift of the return signal reflected by aerosols and dust.

Remote sensing also can be considered as photographically or electronically sensed. Photography provides the highest-resolution imagery (because of the fine size of the photo emulsion grains compared to relatively coarse electronic sensors) and requires no transmission of data to the ground. It spans only the range of nearultraviolet to infrared light (roughly 280 to 1,500 nanometers), however, and is susceptible to radiation and other elements that can damage the film. Electronic sensors can provide an immediate reading of the intensity of the incident radiation with greater spectral sensitivity and across a broader range of the spectrum. This information can more readily be disseminated and manipulated than photographic images (selected portions of photographs are sometimes digitized to bring out low-contrast details). Typically, though, data obtained by electronic sensors such as television cameras and scanners are presented as color-coded images representing ratios between reflections in different energy bands or exaggerated contrasts to show subtle differences. In this manner the human eye can readily recognize the information contained within the scene.

As a rule, the greater the altitude of the observing platform, the larger the scene observed and the lower the resolution. Weather satellites have a resolution of a few kilometers, while spy satellites are reputed to have resolutions of a few centimeters. The atmosphere through which the reflected radiation must pass is the chief limiting factor on resolution, and turbulence or aerosols will significantly degrade it. Resolution can also be enhanced or degraded by contrast. White lines on a black parking lot will show up clearly even if they are smaller than the instrument's resolution. Conversely, concrete may be difficult to distinguish from desert floor in white light (but viewing in infrared bands may provide sharper contrast).

Applications of the Method

Remote-sensing systems are generally devised and used to address particular problems in gathering environmental data; only in the early years were they used in a "see what you can see" fashion. The operating systems commonly in use are generally oriented toward weather observations, renewable and nonrenewable resource mapping, and climatology.

Passive remote sensing was the first to be employed from air and later from space. Initially it involved the use of simple cameras to produce images of the surface, beginning with the TIROS weather satellites (starting in 1960) and hand-held cameras used by astronauts from the first manned spaceflight (1961). Modern remote sensing uses multispectral systems that produce images in several discrete bands of the spectrum at the same time. This approach was first used with the Landsat satellites starting in 1974.

A common imaging system will focus the scene onto a diffraction grating that scatters light much as a prism would, only more efficiently. Light sensors are located at positions corresponding to different wavelengths (more properly, wavelength bands) and measure the intensity of the scene. Various techniques are used to gather, focus, and spread the light beam to achieve the desired signal. In the "push broom" technique, the sensors are arrayed in a straight line and see only a single point spread into a line with the spectrum spread out. A rotating mirror scans the field of view from side to side while the spacecraft motion moves the scan line forward. The effect is to build an image line by line in a series of colors. More advanced two-dimensional arrays have thousands of detectors, like squares on graph paper. An entire slice of the scene is imaged across the rows, for example, and the color or detected wavelength changes from column to column. Spacecraft motion moves the field of view so a complete image may be made.

Which "color" is to be observed is a highly complex matter that depends closely on the information desired. Early weather satellites were easy to design because meteorologists only wanted to see where the clouds were. A simple camera that showed cloud tops against the dark ocean was a major step forward, one that allowed hurricanes and other major storm systems to be detected well in advance of landfall. Current instrumentation allows meteorologists to measure the temperature at the cloud tops by the amount of infrared radiation they emit. Colder cloud tops mean clouds with greater altitude and, therefore, more powerful circulation to drive them to altitude. Advances in weather and climatology studies show that it is necessary to know the distribution of moisture within the clouds and where it falls. Because light does not penetrate clouds, scientists are now moving deeper into the spectrum with microwave sensors. The earth "glows" with its own heat. Since this microwave radiation is absorbed or scattered most effectively by water, any dimming of the terrestrial background glow means water in the air; the dimmer the glow, the greater the moisture content.

Selection of the correct portion of the spectrum involves observations with ground and airborne instruments and comparative studies, "ground truth data," of the objects themselves. This is necessary because in one or two colors several different objects can appear the same, just as all trees look green to the untrained eye. Grass reflects strongest at approximately 800 nanometers, but deciduous trees are stronger from 700 nanometers onward. Further, the time of day and time of year can change the response of plants to sunlight. Early in the growing season, crops will reflect light differently from the way they reflect light at harvesttime. Crops will also reflect light differently depending on whether they are properly watered, dehydrated, or waterlogged. Often it is necessary to take two or more spectral bands and, by computer, measure the ratios of the plants' reflectivity. The result is compared with a catalog of known responses and turned into assessments of the scene. One field of crops may be seen to be healthy, while another crop may be seen to be ravaged by fungus. Another image may be seen to indicate specific metallic ores on the surface, indicating that larger veins may lie below.

One of the most valuable aspects of remote sensing is simple mapping. Despite centuries of exploration, large portions of the globe are not mapped properly. This may seem odd when one thinks of the fine atlases that are now available, but there are large regions where the mapping has been done at low resolution or with low accuracy, leaving the location of major features uncertain to within a few hundred meters or even kilometers.

Satellite mapping can also be a highly effective tool to monitor land use. An initial set of images can be used to generate highly accurate maps of city streets, crop fields, or shorelines. Subsequent images over time can be compared to determine changes such as city growth or coastal erosion that might not easily be mapped by conventional means.

An interesting but little-discussed application of remote sensing is spy satellites, the use of satellite cameras to observe the buildup and movement of military forces by other nations. Although atmospheric effects limit resolution, advanced image-processing techniques allow resolution to approach a few centimeters. Further, multispectral imaging allows objects to be classified on the basis of differing colors and thermal emissions (just as with plants and minerals).

Many Third World nations are concerned that remote sensing can be used to their disadvantage, that First World governments or countries will use remotely sensed data to determine their economic or resource potential, then make decisions to their disadvantage. The United States has applied just this technique by having Department of Agriculture experts examine spy satellite photographs to project Soviet crop yields and, therefore, the impact on the Soviet economy.

SAR is used commonly aboard aircraft and is coming into use on satellites. Radar has several advantages, including use independent of local illumination and through clouds. Other techniques can be used to determine the composition of the surface. The strength of the signal is related to the dielectric constant of the surface materials. Some wavelengths may penetrate deeper than others and thus allow subsurface features to be imaged. Polarization may be measured in a variety of schemes which measure strength of the transmitted signal along one plane relative to the strength of the return signal along another (such as vertical-versus-horizontal, called V-H, or vertical-versus-vertical, called V-V). Radar is especially useful for mapping surface rocks beneath tropical forest canopies or river flooding beneath storm systems. Images from several passes at different angles may be combined to produce synthetic stereo image pairs or computer animation showing all sides of a scene.

A more limited form of radar remote sensing is altimetry. In this method the round-trip time for a signal from a satellite to the ground can be converted into the distance to the ground. With precise calculations about the location of the satellite in space, this can reveal the variations in the surface from a theoretically spherical shape. An especially dramatic application of this technique was the mapping of the ocean floor by the Seasat 1 satellite in 1979. Seasat's altimeter measured the spacecraft altitude from the ocean surface, which was not at "sea level" (sea level is a local condition) but varied in height by tens of meters depending on whether there were valleys or mountains which exerted slight tidal forces that raised or lowered the average sea height in those areas. These data were translated into a medium-resolution map that inferred the structure of the ocean floor in great detail. Details about the interior structure of the earth can be inferred by measuring slight changes in the velocity and altitude of a satellite over a long series of orbits. Although the spacecraft does not use electromagnetic radiation to observe the earth, the Doppler shifts in signals transmitted to and from the spacecraft are used to measure changes in velocity, which are interpreted as variations in the local gravitational field.

X rays and gamma rays are used in the remote sensing of planets without atmospheres. Gamma radiation reflected or fluoresced by surface rocks, when compared with the galactic background, can reveal the chemical composition of the surface. This technique is of little or no use when there is any appreciable atmosphere. Atmospheres themselves may be studied by ultraviolet backscatter, which measures the amount of the sun's ultraviolet radiation that is reflected back into space. Subtracting that from the solar output will provide a measure of the amount absorbed by the atmosphere.

Atmospheres may also be explored by absorption and emission spectroscopy. In the former, the chemistry of the atmosphere is assayed by measuring sunlight as it passes through the atmosphere at dawn and sunset. The solar continuum will have specific gaps (called spectral lines) where it is absorbed by different chemicals. In the latter, instruments measure light emitted by the atmosphere as a result of different chemical phenomena, such as airglow and auroras.

Lasers are used in another principal form of active remote sensing. These are coming into use for analyzing aerosol and particle distribution and wind speed of the atmosphere, largely in "clear" air, without the need for instruments carried by balloon or rocket. The advantage is that hundreds of measurements can be taken over a wide range of distances in a short period of time. Again, the echo from the emitted radiation is collected and a signal extracted. Simple backscatter will tell the size and distribution of particles in the air, somewhat like watching dust in a sunbeam. Measuring the Doppler shift of the return signal will tell the velocity of the dust or aerosol, but only along the line of sight. A second measurement taken at the same time (or within a few seconds) from a different angle will provide a second component of the wind, which allows the true direction and speed to be calculated. This technique has been demonstrated with a single laser carried aboard an aircraft. The laser scans from fore to aft several times a second as the aircraft moves forward. A series of such measurements over a few minutes produces a grid pattern, each with a specific measurement of wind velocity and direction. An advanced version of this system is being developed for use aboard a satellite so that winds can be measured in clear air on a global scale.

Context

Remote sensing has provided scientists and others with unique views and under-standings of the earth. Some scientists and philosophers believe that the most important image obtained from this field is one from which few usable data could be obtained: It was the earth photographed by the crew of Apollo 8 from the neighborhood of the moon. This image gave substance to the concern being voiced by environmentalists that the earth needed to be treated as a single, irreplaceable system in which all humans are participants, not passive observers or unconcerned consumers. Because the image was on color film and taken from a great distance, it was of little immediate scientific use. Yet it has been used many times in documents justifying additional exploration and exploitation of space.

The most important remote-sensing field has been weather satellites. These have allowed meteorologists to detect and track weather patterns with great precision. Images from geostationary satellites are well known to evening television news viewers, who often are presented computer-enhanced, stop-action images of the weather systems moving across the United States. Because of the early warnings provided by weather satellites, no hurricane has struck the United States without warning since the early 1960's. The prevention of deaths and property damage alone is believed to have repaid the investment in weather satellites. There are major gaps in the satellites' capabilities, however, which are to be addressed by the next generation of satellites.

Although governments decline to acknowledge their existence, spy satellites are believed to have done much to stabilize international politics by providing national leaders with "inside" views of other nations' military activities. In the nuclear arms arena, these satellites are simply referred to as "national technical means of verification." Advances in resolution in recent years have led news organizations to use earth resources satellite photographs, notably during the Chernobyl reactor disaster.

At a global level, the Earth Radiation Budget Experiment, involving several instruments, is measuring the total solar energy striking the earth and the total energy returned to space in order to track the impact on climate. Other satellites have provided vital information on the formation and activity of the ozone holes that are allowing life-threatening shortwave ultraviolet light into the atmosphere.

Radar mapping of the earth has been performed on countless aircraft missions and on three civilian space missions to date (more are planned). The Seasat 1 radar provided advanced maps of the ocean "topography." Seasat observations of sea ice showed that new ice could be distinguished from old ice, and that ice island movements can be tracked over a period of time. Over open water, the Seasat radar was able to detect the boundaries between major current systems in the oceans, ocean fronts, and mid-scale eddy structures. Sea surface roughness was readily detected and could be interpreted as wind-water interactions at the surface, especially in tropical rain cells. Radar mapping has also been used in prospecting for oil and gas by revealing promising geological structures that normally conceal fossil fuels. This technique is even being applied to archaeology in stripping away desert floors or tropical vegetation to discover ancient river features or dwellings.

Passive microwave sensors have been used to show the concentration of sea ice over much of the Arctic Ocean by measuring microwave radiation at two different frequencies. Because brine pockets and inhomogeneities in the ice change the transmission of microwaves by ice, it is possible to distinguish new ice from older "multiyear ice." Other measurements have been made of soil moisture in the ground, snow depth on the ground, and sea surface temperature. This latter measurement is especially important for understanding ocean currents. Knowing where the ice margin is located around the polar seas is essential for navigation and for fishing, since nutrient-rich waters rise from the ocean bottom in these areas. The extent of the polar ice caps is also an important factor for studies of whether the globe is warming. The poles reflect a large amount of sunlight back into space; a reduction in that reflection would increase the rate of warming.

Because the field is relatively new, many applications are still in development. The Earth Observing System planned for the 1990's and other complementary satellites show that the limits have not yet been reached.

Bibliography

Harper, Dorothy. *Eye in the Sky: Introduction to Remote Sensing*. 2d ed. Brookfield, Vt.: Gower Publishing, 1983. An introductory text written for the general reader. Some portions are somewhat technical but are acceptable to most readers.

Holz, Robert K. *The Surveillant Science: Remote Sensing of the Environment*. 2d ed. New York: John Wiley & Sons, 1985. An outstanding collection of essays and articles covering various aspects of the field of remote sensing. Some portions are technical, but several articles give the reader a good foundation in the field.

Lewis, Richard. *Illustrated Encyclopedia of Space Technology*. London: Salamander Press, 1985. Well-illustrated volume surveying all space activities, including chapters on weather satellites and remote sensing. Diagrams give excellent depictions of remote-sensing methods and instruments.

National Aeronautics and Space Administration. *Earth Observing System*. 9 vols. Washington, D.C.: Government Printing Office, 1987. Set of nine reports detailing data needs and proposed instruments for the Earth Observing System. Volumes 1 and 2 cover science and mission requirements and strategy. Volumes 2a through 2h provide details of proposed instruments, including those flown to date. Highly detailed, although the introductory sections are useful to the general reader.

_____. *High Altitude Perspective*. NASA SP-427. Washington, D.C.: Government Printing Office, 1978. Color booklet describing remote-sensing work conducted from the high-altitude U-2 surveillance aircraft. Well illustrated and nontechnical.

National Aeronautics and Space Administration Advisory Council, Earth System Sciences Committee. *Earth System Science: A Closer View*. Washington, D.C.: Government Printing Office, 1988. A detailed and intriguing examination of the earth from core to outer space, with the atmosphere as one of the most important systems comprising the environment.

Dave Dooling

Cross-References

EARTH RESOURCES

Type of earth science: Economic geology

The earth's resources of metals, nonmetals, and energy supplies undergird every modern, technological society.

Principal terms

ALLOY: a substance composed of two or more metals or of a metal and certain nonmetals

BY-PRODUCT: a secondary or incidental product of the refining process

FOSSIL FUEL: an energy source, such as coal, oil, or natural gas, which is formed from the remains of partly decayed organic matter

MINERAL: a naturally occurring, inorganic crystalline substance with a unique chemical composition

NONRENEWABLE RESOURCE: an earth resource that is fixed in quantity and will not be renewed within a human lifetime

ORE DEPOSIT: a natural accumulation of mineral matter from which the owner expects to extract a metal at a profit

RESERVOIR ROCK: the geologic rock layer in which oil and gas often accumulate; often sandstone or limestone

SOURCE ROCK: the geologic rock layer in which oil and gas originate; often the rock type known as shale

Summary of the Phenomenon

All earth resources can be subdivided into two broad categories. The first category contains the renewable resources. The word "renewable" means that these resources are replenished by nature as rapidly as humans use them up, provided good judgment is used. Renewable resources include the energy of the wind, the timber cut in a forest, or the animals used for food. Each of these earth resources is constantly being renewed by the energy reaching the earth's surface from the sun. As long as the sun's rays reach the earth, this pattern of replenishment will continue.

The resources in the second category are known as the nonrenewable resources. These are resources that will not be renewed in a human lifetime. Only limited quantities of these resources are present in the earth's crust, and they are not replenished by natural processes operating within short periods. Examples of non-renewable resources include coal, oil, iron, diamonds, and aluminum. While it is true that certain of these resources, such as coal and oil, are being formed within the earth's crust continuously, the processes by which they are formed are exceedingly slow, being measured in thousands or millions of years.

The earth resources of primary interest to the economic geologist can be divided into the three categories: metals, nonmetals, and energy sources. The metals are a group of chemical elements that have certain features in common, the most noticeable of which is a high metallic luster, or shine. In addition, they can all be melted, they all conduct heat and electricity, and most of them can be pounded in thin sheets or drawn into thin wires.

Metals can be divided into two classes based on their abundance in the earth. The first class, which has been called the abundant metals, consists of those metals that individually constitute 0.1 percent or more of the earth's crust by weight. The metals in this category are iron, aluminum, manganese, magnesium, and titanium. The second class of metals, which are called the scarce metals, consists of those metals that individually constitute less than 0.1 percent of the crust. This class includes such metals as copper, lead, zinc, nickel, mercury, silver, gold, and platinum.

Certain common metals, such as steel, brass, bronze, and solder, are not pure metals but rather alloys, chemical mixtures of two or more metals that have characteristics of strength, durability, or corrosion resistance superior to those of the component metals. Steel, for example, is an alloy in which iron is the main constituent.

Metals are rarely found in the pure state within the earth's crust. Only the metals gold, silver, copper, platinum, and iron are ever found uncombined. All other metals are found chemically combined with additional elements to form minerals. Geologists use the term "ore deposit" to describe a rock containing metals or metal-bearing minerals from which the pure metal can be profitably extracted. Whether a rock is an ore deposit depends on a variety of factors, including how difficult it is to extract the metal from the metal-bearing mineral, how large the ore deposit is and how accessible, whether valuable by-products can be obtained, and what the current price of the metal is on world markets.

The second major category of earth resources is the nonmetals. The term "nonmetal" is widely employed by geologists to describe substances extracted from the earth that are neither sources of metals nor sources of energy. Nonmetals are mined and processed either because of the nonmetallic elements they contain or because they have some highly desirable physical or chemical characteristic. Some of the earth's major nonmetallic resources are fertilizers, chemicals, abrasives, gems, and building materials.

Fertilizers contain the elements nitrogen, potassium, and phosphorus. Most of the nitrogen required for fertilizer production is chemically extracted from the air, so the supply is renewable. The potassium and the phosphorus, however, come from rocks dug out of the ground—potash salt layers and phosphate rocks—and the supply of these is nonrenewable.

Several earth resources provide important raw materials for the chemical industry. They include salt, which is obtained from underground beds of rock salt and from seawater; sulfur, a by-product of oil production; and substances such as borax and soda ash, which are obtained from the beds of dry desert lakes. Abrasives are very hard substances that are used for grinding, polishing, and cleaning. They are obtained from rock and mineral substances dug out of the earth and then pulverized. Gems are earth materials that are attractive to the eye. They can be categorized as precious and semiprecious.

Building materials include the stones obtained from quarries, such as granite, sandstone, limestone, marble, and slate. There is also a high demand for crushed rock, which is used as highway roadbeds and for concrete aggregate. Sand and gravel are also used in making concrete. A number of other useful products are prepared from earth materials, such as cement; plaster, from the mineral gypsum; brick and ceramics, from clay; glass, from very pure sand or sandstone rock; and asbestos, from flame-resistant mineral fibers that can be woven into fireproof cloth or mixed with other substances to make fireproof roofing shingles and floor tiles.

The third major category of earth resources are energy sources. Energy sources are frequently divided into the mineral fuels, which are nonrenewable, and a second, renewable group. The first group contains oil and gas, coal, and uranium.

Crude oil, natural gas, and petroleum provided 66 percent of the United States' energy in 1985. Crude oil is a naturally occurring liquid composed of the elements hydrogen and carbon combined into compounds known as hydrocarbons. Natural gas is a gaseous form of these hydrocarbons. The oil and gas accumulate underground over long periods in source rocks and then migrate into reservoir rocks, where they are trapped. Extraction is accomplished by means of drilling. Two related earth resources are oil shale, a source rock that still contains oil, and tar sands, reservoir rocks exposed at the surface.

Coal is the third most important energy source in the United States; in 1985, it met 24 percent of that nation's energy needs. Coal originates when partly decayed plant material accumulates on the floor of bogs and swamps and is then buried by overlying sediments that compact the plant material into carbon-rich rocks. The various grades of coal are lignite (brown coal), bituminous coal (soft coal), and anthracite (hard coal). Peat is partly decayed plant material that was never buried at all. Coal is mined at the surface in strip mines or is mined underground. Coal, oil, and gas are sometimes referred to as "fossil fuels."

Uranium is a silver-gray metal used in nuclear reactors to produce electricity. In 1985, nuclear reactors met 5.5 percent of American energy needs. Within a reactor, uranium undergoes spontaneous disintegration, producing heat. This heat is used to drive an electrical generator, just as in conventional power plants. Uranium occurs as veins or grains within a variety of rock types and is mined with standard mining methods.

There are many potential energy sources that are renewable and are mostly underutilized. Foremost among these is hydroelectric power, or water power. This power is generated by means of water falling from a dammed reservoir; the force of the falling water turns the turbine of an electric generator. Barring unforeseen climate changes or silting of the reservoir behind the dam, hydroelectric power can be considered a renewable resource. Sunlight, the wind, the tides, and the steam from geysers are also renewable energy sources, as are living things, in the form of firewood and animal power. Newer applications are gasahol- and methane-fired boilers that use gases fermented from seaweed or cow manure. The controlled burning of garbage has tremendous potential for the future, as does the use of hydrogen from the ocean to operate "clean" nuclear reactors—a peaceful use of the same chemical reaction that powers the hydrogen bomb.

Methods of Study

Mineral deposits are quite rare in the earth's crust; either they consist of substances that are uncommon to begin with (gold, for example) or else they are composed of common substances, such as the very pure sand used to make glass, that have been concentrated into workable accumulations. Much study has gone into why such concentrations exist. One valuable tool has been the plate tectonics theory, which proposes that the earth's surface is divided into a few large plates that are slowly moving with respect to one another. Intense geologic activity occurs at plate boundaries, and many mineral deposits are believed to have been formed by this activity.

It becomes more and more difficult to find mineral deposits, as all the easily discoverable ones have already been found. Aerial prospecting was made possible by the airplane, and it has now been replaced by satellite imaging. Most prospecting, however, is based on the search for buried deposits, and utilizes indirect methods for detecting favorable underground geologic conditions. A preferred technique is seismic prospecting, in which sound waves are created underground by means of small explosive charges and are then bounced off underground rock layers in order to determine their structure.

A variety of techniques have been developed for the economical extraction of mineral resources from the earth. Frequently, extraction costs are the controlling factor in whether a mineral deposit can be profitably worked. In general, extraction techniques can be divided into two groups: surface and underground methods. Surface methods are preferred whenever possible, because they are lower in cost. The traditional surface methods are quarrying, open-pit mining, and strip mining. Strip mining involves the removal of large amounts of worthless overburden so that the mineral deposit can be reached. Underground mining methods include the excavation of shafts, tunnels, and rooms; fluids such as petroleum can be removed by means of drilled wells.

Mineral resources extracted from the earth are rarely ready to be sent directly to market. Generally, they will require processing to separate undesirable substances from desirable ones. This processing may involve physical separation, as in the case of separating diamonds from rock pebbles of the same size, or chemical separation, such as is required to remove metals from the sulfur with which they are combined in certain ores. Even after the pure mineral substance is obtained, further treatment may be required, as in the smelting of iron to obtain steel or the refining of petroleum to obtain gasoline.

Further ways in which earth resources are studied include calculations of estimated available reserves in view of anticipated future demands; comparison of the fuel values of various energy sources; analysis of the environmental problems and types of pollution caused by the extraction, refining, and utilization of various mineral resources; and investigations of ways to conserve, recycle, or develop substitutes for mineral resources that are in short supply.

Context

The earth's resources of metals, nonmetals, and energy supplies support all modern technology. Houses and automobiles, televisions and refrigerators, airplanes and roads, jewelry and sandpaper, the electricity that lights a playing field and the gasoline that powers a car—an almost unending list of goods depend on the ability to utilize or harness the resources of the earth.

Despite the importance of the various earth resources, one is seldom mindful of them until forced to do without. Such a deprivation occurred in the 1970's, when an energy crisis struck. In the 1950's, the huge oil fields of the Middle East started coming into production, resulting in a worldwide oil glut. Oil prices dropped as low as $1.30 per barrel, and that translated into gasoline prices of about 20 cents per gallon at the pump. In September, 1959, the oil ministers of several leading oil producing countries banded together to form the Organization of Petroleum Exporting Countries (OPEC) in an effort to bolster oil prices. Despite their best efforts, however, world oil prices were still less than $3.00 per barrel in 1971, because of excess production.

Then came the rapidly escalating political tensions in the Middle East, resulting in voluntary production cutbacks and a refusal to sell oil to the United States and several European countries in retaliation for their support of Israel. Immediately, oil prices on the world market soared, eventually reaching a high of $35.00 per barrel in 1980. Panic gripped the industrial nations of the Western world, because their principal source of energy, which had always been cheap and plentifully available, was suddenly expensive and hard to obtain. Americans spent long hours waiting in line to buy limited amounts of gasoline when any was available at all. It became clear that plentiful supplies of basic earth resources cannot be taken for granted.

A technological society relies on metals. Iron is needed for steel making, aluminum for lightweight aircraft construction, manganese for toughening steel for armor plate, and titanium for making heat-resistant parts in jet engines. Among the scarcer metals, copper is needed for electrical wiring, lead for car batteries and nuclear reactor shielding, zinc for galvanized roofing nails, nickel for stainless steel, and mercury for thermometers and silent electric switches. Silver is used for making photographic film, silverware, jewelry, and coins; gold for coins, jewelry, and dental work; and platinum for jewelry and industrial applications where corrosion resistance is essential.

Among the nonmetallic earth resources, fertilizers are used for agriculture; salt, sulfur, and soda for the chemical industry; and abrasives for sandpaper and grinding wheels. Cut stone, crushed rock, cement, plaster, brick, glass, and asbestos are all needed by the construction industry.

The energy sources obtained from the earth enable humans to perform tasks faster than they could manually. Because most machines run on electricity, the output of the energy source often must first be converted into an electric current. Automobiles, however, convert gasoline directly into power by means of the internal combustion engine. Probably the most direct use of an energy source is the powering of a sailboat by the wind. That is a way of using energy that has not changed in the past five thousand years.

Bibliography

Bartholomew, John C., ed. *The Times Atlas of the World*. New York: Times Books, 1980. A well-written overview entitled "Resources of the World" is followed by large, eight-color maps. The world mineral map shows the world distribution of metals and nonmetals, and world geology. The world energy map shows the distribution of energy sources and comparative consumption by nations. Excellent graphs. Suitable for general audiences.

Bertin, Léon. *The Larousse Encyclopedia of the Earth*. New York: Prometheus Press, 1965. This reference book has lengthy and well-written sections on minerals and mineral ores, mineral fuels, petroleum, hydroelectric power, and energy generated from the wind, tides, rivers, ocean heat, the sun, and the atom. The text is copiously illustrated with excellent black-and-white and color plates. Suitable for high school and college readers.

Bramwell, M., ed. *The Rand McNally Atlas of the Oceans*. Skokie, Ill.: Rand McNally, 1977. A beautifully illustrated atlas. The section entitled "The Great Resource" has outstanding subsections on the various energy sources available in the ocean, the mineral deposits of the continental shelves, manganese nodule deposits on the deep sea floor, and offshore oil. There are excellent color photographs, maps, and line drawings. Suitable for high school readers.

Craig, J. R., D. J. Vaughan, and B. J. Skinner. *Resources of the Earth*. Englewood Cliffs, N.J.: Prentice-Hall, 1988. A well-written and well-illustrated text with numerous black-and-white photographs, color plates, tables, charts, maps, and line drawings. It provides an excellent overview of the metal, nonmetal, and energy resources of the earth. There is a useful chapter on earth resources through history. Suitable for college-level readers or the interested layperson.

Jensen, M. L., and A. M. Bateman. *Economic Mineral Deposits*. 3d ed. New York: John Wiley & Sons, 1979. This economic geology text has detailed information on the different metallic and nonmetallic mineral deposits and their modes of formation. There are excellent sections on the history of mineral use and the exploration and development of mineral properties. Cross sections of individual deposits are provided. For college-level readers.

Judson, S., M. E. Kauffman, and L. D. Leet. *Physical Geology*. 7th ed. Englewood Cliffs, N.J.: Prentice-Hall, 1987. An outstanding physical geology text. Chapter 18, "Energy," and chapter 19, "Useful Materials," provide an excellent overview of the major energy sources and the categories of metallic and nonmetallic earth resources. Chapter 18 includes a section on OPEC. Illustrated with photographs and diagrams. Tables provide important data.

Skinner, B. J. *Earth Resources*. 3d ed. Englewood Cliffs, N.J.: Prentice-Hall, 1986. An overview of all the earth's resources. It is well written and contains helpful line drawings, maps, tables, and charts, although photographs are few. There are excellent suggestions for further reading and a list of principal ore minerals and production figures for 1982.

Tennissen, Anthony C. *The Nature of Earth Materials*. 2d ed. Englewood Cliffs, N.J.: Prentice-Hall, 1983. This reference book contains detailed descriptions of 110 common minerals, with a black-and-white photograph of each. There are helpful sections on the modes of formation and the classification of igneous, sedimentary, and metamorphic rocks. Chapter 7, "Utility of Earth Materials," is an overview of metallic and nonmetallic mineral resources. Suitable for college-level readers.

Donald W. Lovejoy

Cross-References

Aluminum Deposits, 46; Building Stone, 178; Coal, 232; Diamonds, 362; Fertilizers, 706; Gem Minerals, 802; Geothermal Power, 915; Gold and Silver, 975; Hydroelectric Power, 1095; Igneous and Contact Metamorphic Mineral Deposits, 1124; Iron Deposits, 1254; Ocean Power, 1818; The Worldwide Distribution of Oil and Gas, 1923; Future Resources, 2182; Strategic Resources, 2188; Sedimentary Mineral Deposits, 2296; Uranium Deposits, 2580.

FUTURE RESOURCES

Type of earth science: Economic geology

During the twenty-first century, new resources may well be required to build and energize civilization on other planets and in space as well as to enhance accelerated change in a dynamic earth-based society.

Principal terms

CERAMICS: nonmetal compounds, such as silicates and clays, produced by firing the materials at high temperatures

FIBER-REINFORCED COMPOSITES: materials produced by drawing fibers of various types through a material being cast to produce a high weight-to-strength ratio

HYDROLYSIS: the breakdown of water by energy into its constituent elements of water and hydrogen

OFF-PLANET: pertaining to regions off the earth in orbital or planetary space

PERMAFROST: a layer of soil and water ice frozen together

PHOTOVOLTAIC CELL: a device made commonly of layered silicon that produces electrical current in the presence of light; also, a solar cell

REGOLITH: that layer of soil and rock fragments just above the planetary crust

SUPERCONDUCTORS: materials that pass electrical current without exhibiting any electrical resistance

Summary of the Phenomenon

In the largest possible sense, there will be two broad categories of resources during the twenty-first century: earth-based resources and off-planet resources. The reason for the distinction is an economic one, based on where the materials will be used, and is driven by consideration of the gravitational field of the earth. The earth's gravitational field is very strong in comparison with extraterrestrial space, where there is little gravitational influence. It is also strong in relation to the moon and Mars, where the gravitational field is much weaker than the earth's. Hence, materials required in space will be dramatically more economical if mined from small bodies in space (such as asteroids or comets) or the moon. The same resources, if shipped into space from the earth, would cost many times more. This example is provided as an insight into the distinctive ways of looking at future resources in the developing economy of the twenty-first century. In a more systematic approach to categorization, one could fundamentally classify tomorrow's most basic resources in the same broad classes as are used currently: agricultural products, chemicals (including petroleum and derivatives), metals, ceramics, energy, wood (and derivatives), and power.

Though the same broad categories of resources will be required in the future as are required today, many of their individual identities and uses will be much different. Scientists are beginning to foresee new types of materials that will have a vital use. Such an example was afforded in 1989 when two scientists announced that they thought they had discovered a revolutionary power source. One determinant element in their design was a rare earth metal called palladium. Until their announcement, there had been few other uses for the metal; after their announcement, the price of palladium temporarily increased many times as a result of its presumed importance. As new discoveries are made, new uses for existing materials such as metals will cause the demand for the resource to change as dictated by availability.

Scientific discovery and technological development are often the key to the advancement and change of society and the resources that drive it. Examples from the past are abundant: Tungsten presently used for light filaments had few uses before the invention of the incandescent light bulb; silicon (the key element of common beach sand) assumed vital importance with the discovery of microelectronics. Probably no other single resource has had a more far-reaching impact on humankind or planet Earth than petroleum and its derivatives. The science of superconductivity produces materials that conduct electrical current without resistance. Late in 1986, this branch of physics took a revolutionary turn when it was discovered that synthetically produced materials could become superconductive at temperatures much higher than had been thought possible. The synthetic materials were described as "artificial rocks" and were made by mixing together various metal oxides under very specific conditions. As the ultimate goal of room-temperature superconductivity is approached, the materials used in producing the superconductors are likely to become highly sought-after and valuable resources.

The use of ceramic materials increased dramatically in the 1980's. Ceramic materials are nonmetal compounds produced by firing at high temperatures. Ceramics can be lightweight, resilient, and heat-resistant. Materials used in the production of ceramics are clays, silicates, and calcium carbonates. Uses of ceramics include refractories (heat-shielding or heat-absorbing materials, such as those used to construct the space shuttle's heat-shielding tiles) and electrical components. They have also been used in tests as automobile engine blocks. The resources that produce such ceramics are projected to have even broader applications in the future.

Another type of product that has become quite important and is thought will play a vital role in the future is fiber-reinforced composites. Such composites are made by drawing fibers through a material being cast. When the material hardens, the fibers cast inside it make even very light products, such as aircraft wings and space vehicle fuselages, much stronger. The materials from which these composites are made (fiberglass, boron, tungsten, aluminum oxide, and carbon) will assume new importance with any increase of the use of fiber-reinforced composites.

Because the exploitation and possible settlement of space will probably be the most significant development of the twenty-first century, resources that will drive that revolution will become highly valuable in the future. The value of these space materials will be based on their origin. It will always be expensive to ship resources into space from the surface of the earth. A kilogram of aluminum mined and processed on the moon and shipped to earth could one day cost a tenth of the amount of the same aluminum shipped to orbit from the earth because of launch-energy costs. Even under the best of circumstances, in a well-developed launch system, a liter of water launched from the earth into space will always cost thousands of times more than will a liter of water on the surface. One must always keep the gravitational interfaces in mind when considering the economics of space resources. Many studies have been conducted concerning the utilization of off-planet resources, their availability and uses. Such studies have been conducted concerning the construction of moon and Mars bases and colonies as well as the construction of enormous space colonies.

The most valuable resources in space will be the two resources of survival, water and energy; the use of one is dependent on the other. Water and energy yield two other vital resources: oxygen and hydrogen. Water is the most basic of all resources necessary for human survival. Aside from the obvious purposes of direct consumption and hygiene, water will be necessary for cleaning, cooling, and producing food. Raw water can be broken down by a process called hydrolysis into elemental hydrogen and oxygen. The hydrogen may be used for energy production and the oxygen for breathing.

The mass of water is great enough that launching volumes of the substance from the earth that are sufficient to meet the needs of space resources will play a significant role in determining the use of space. Much attention has been paid to the likely sources of water off-planet, especially in the most exploitable deposits. First, the moon may contain deposits of water ice, locked up beneath the regolith, or surface dust and rocks, as glaciers of variable size. The most likely location of potential water ice is at the poles of the moon. Such deposits are presumed by some to have been generated in the primordial epochs of the moon's formation, when large amounts of gases were trapped beneath the surface as the moon cooled. Second, there is considerable evidence that Mars may contain vast amounts of water locked up beneath its regolith as permafrost (water ice mixed with soil). Third, some asteroids may contain water ice, and comets are generally considered to be mostly water ice. It is speculated that these resources may be captured and relocated to an orbit suitable for mining. Finally, pure water is produced as a waste product of fuel cells that react hydrogen and oxygen to produce power. Such cells, if used extensively for power, may become an important source of water off-planet.

Another source of energy is direct conversion, by photovoltaic (solar) cells, of sunlight into electricity. Such cells may be produced off-planet by using lunar materials such as silicon, a significant constituent of lunar soil. Future space colonists may want to locate reserves of radioisotopes for nuclear power. Such reserves, if found, could be exploited with an excellent promise of safety, especially in high earth, lunar, or solar orbit, as the isolation of the radioactive contaminants and power plant itself would be assured. Questions concerning other power sources, such as high-temperature fusion and unconventional fusion techniques, remain unresolved. Such devices, when perfected, would overcome nearly every known deterrent, allowing the fullest exploitation of space.

Aside from the most basic resources of survival off-planet (water, power, hydrogen, and oxygen), space colonists will require massive building-material resources off-planet. Launching millions of tons of raw building materials into space is as infeasible as hauling volumes of water there. A Princeton University physicist, Gerard K. O'Neill, has addressed the question of producing such quantities of building materials for construction of off-planet colonies. O'Neill and his Princeton-based Space Studies Institute have designed a mass driver, a device that could catapult "buckets" of lunar soil into lunar or earth orbit for processing—in automated space factories—into sheets of aluminum, magnesium, titanium, glass, and other materials for use in construction of lunar or orbiting colonies. Lunar soil has been found to be rich enough in the necessary materials to produce such materials in space. Current studies on the moon rocks brought back from the Apollo program indicate that roughly 50,000 metric tons of aluminum sheets per year could be produced from 900,000 metric tons per year of moon ores catapulted into space by the mass drivers.

Methods of Study

Space probes have been utilized to recover information on the location of resources in space and their amounts. The Apollo mission astronauts returned samples from the lunar surface that were analyzed extensively and used in subsequent detailed engineering and economic studies to reveal how the lunar material might be processed into building materials. One such study was performed by Gerald W. Driggers of the Southern Research Institute of Birmingham, Alabama. In Driggers' account, he estimated the cost of building an orbiting metals factory ($20 billion) and its power requirements (300 megawatts). He also estimated the final cost of the aluminum sheeting ($22 per kilogram) and compared it to the cost of the earth-produced material ($2.2 per kilogram); he then compared it to the cost of the earth-based material launched into space ($88 per kilogram). Such economic studies will drive the capital outlays that will be necessary to fund and justify such substantial expenditures.

The resources of Mars were surveyed at two landing sites in 1976 by the United States' Viking landers. The Viking landers were not designed to return samples directly from Mars but were sent with a device called an X-ray fluorescence spectrometer, which would analyze the Martian soil for its inorganic materials. No probe has ever taken a direct observation of an asteroid, although many scientists are convinced that the Martian moons Phobos and Deimos are captured asteroids. Probes will probably land on these bodies for assays prior to the twenty-first century. Flyby studies of these bodies indicate that their densities are low enough that they could be made up of some water ice in their interiors. In 1986, several space-craft flew past Halley's comet as it approached the sun, returning spectacular, close-up photos of the body and taking measurements of its density. These flybys have supported earlier speculation that comets are largely water ices covered over by exceptionally dark, carbonaceous material.

The ability of humans to live and work in space is being confirmed daily by U.S. and Soviet manned missions. The Soviet and American space stations will return detailed information on the requirements for even longer-term missions. These will ultimately translate into the resources necessary to extend missions and ultimately to settle off-planet on a long-term basis.

Context

The survivability and quality of every human's life is directly affected by the resources available to each individual. From water and power to food and building materials, humankind has been in a constant struggle to improve the availability and quality of resources while reducing the magnitude of the struggle to obtain them. The historical propensity of civilization, if not its fundamental purpose, is to ease that struggle and increase the availability of the resource base while constantly improving its superiority and basic usefulness.

The resources of the future will follow this trend, with momentous advances being made in the most elemental domain: power, or energy. Energy production directly affects the acquisition of all other resources. The lives of all humans should benefit by this resource development. Improved ways of generating power will directly influence food production for all people but, most profoundly, those populations in regions fixed on the edge of continual famine. High-temperature super-conductivity would change the basis of electronic devices, resulting in more efficient and cheaper electrical power production, storage, transmission, and use. The exploitation of this science would enable supercomputers that operate at unprecedented speed. Transportation on earth and in space would be revolutionized.

Bibliography

Cadogan, Peter. *The Moon: Our Sister Planet*. New York: Cambridge University Press, 1981. This work discusses the discoveries arising from the exploration of the moon during the decade of the 1960's. Details the resources discovered from the close analysis of the Apollo moon rocks. Also speculates about water on the moon and other possible moon-based resources. Well illustrated, although its index is somewhat limited.

Cooper, Henry S. F., Jr. *The Search for Life on Mars: Evolution of an Idea*. New York: Holt, Rinehart and Winston, 1980. Although this book is a superlative accounting of the search for life on Mars, it relates the instruments used in all the Viking lander science, including a discussion of the device that measured the constituents of Martian soil. An excellent work for understanding how scientists comprehend the details of another planet's resources by automated robotics and how the inferences to planetary resources are thus enabled. Although not illustrated, a well-written scientific narrative.

Hazen, Robert M. *The Breakthrough: The Race for the Superconductor.* New York: Summit Books, 1988. A story that features the discovery of high-temperature superconductors in 1987. Relates what resources were used in the construction of the "artificial rocks" that were made superconductive. Also describes the revolutionary changes that such discoveries would bring.

Heppenheimer, T. A. *Colonies in Space.* Harrisburg, Pa.: Stackpole Books, 1977. This detailed, illustrated book depicts what resources will be required to settle space en masse. It names and enumerates studies that have independently addressed the issue in sufficient particulars that the reader will understand the complexity and degree of effort required to make this next great "leap" of humankind.

Miles, Frank, and Nicholas Booth. *Race to Mars: The Harper & Row Mars Flight Atlas.* New York: Harper & Row, 1988. This book specifies the details for a flight to Mars and its ultimate settlement. Discusses the possibilities of Mars' resources, such as water, availability of building materials, and power sources. An excellent accounting of the difficulties in finding sufficient resources to set up colonies off-planet and the efforts required to establish a foothold on new frontiers.

O'Neill, Gerard K. *2081: A Hopeful View of the Human Future.* New York: Simon & Schuster, 1981. O'Neill discusses the facts as they will be encountered in delivering raw materials not only to the space and planetary colonies but also to the earth from space. He discusses the "capture" of asteroids and the use of moon-based mass drivers to deliver raw materials for use in space. Illustrated; written for all readers.

Dennis Chamberland

Cross-References

Lunar History, 1400; Lunar Rocks, 1414; Mars' Polar Caps, 1487; Mars' Water, 1508; Nuclear Power, 1749; Oil and Gas: Petroleum Reservoirs, 1909; Phobos and Deimos, 2058; Earth Resources, 2175; Solar Power, 2427.

STRATEGIC RESOURCES

Type of earth science: Economic geology

A nation's strategic resources are those resources that are essential for its major industries, military defense, and energy programs. For the United States, these resources include manganese, chromium, cobalt, nickel, platinum, titanium, aluminum, and oil.

Principal terms

ALLOY: a substance composed of two or more metals or of a metal and certain nonmetals

BAUXITE: the principal ore of aluminum; a mixture of aluminum compounds produced by prolonged weathering of bedrock in tropical or subtropical climates

CATALYST: a chemical substance that speeds up a chemical reaction without being permanently affected by that reaction

MANGANESE NODULES: rounded, concentrically laminated masses of iron and manganese oxide found on the deep-sea floor

OIL RIGHTS: the ownership of the oil and natural gas on another party's land, with the right to drill for and remove them

ORE DEPOSIT: a natural accumulation of mineral matter from which the owner expects to extract a metal at a profit

PROVEN RESERVE: a reserve supply of a valuable mineral substance that can be exploited at a future time

SALT DOME: an underground structure in the shape of a circular plug resulting from the upward movement of salt

Summary of the Phenomenon

Reference is frequently made to strategic resources, but unfortunately, there is no general agreement on what makes resources "strategic." Because the word "strategy" has a military connotation, strategic resources are often considered to be those resources that would be of critical importance in wartime. A somewhat broader definition of strategic resources is that they are those resources that a nation considers essential for its major industries, military defense, and energy programs. Similarly, there is no general agreement as to just which of the many earth resources are the strategic ones. Several authors have restricted the definition to metals that are in short supply, with some even limiting the definition to the six metals alloyed with iron in the making of steel. Others, taking a broader view, have included among the strategic resources nonmetals such as fertilizers and energy sources such as petroleum.

In listing those earth resources that are strategically significant, it is important to realize that each nation's list will be different. In other words, a resource that is in critically short supply for one nation may be possessed in abundance by a second. The United States, for example, imports 98 percent of its manganese, a substance that is alloyed with iron in the making of the tough steel needed for armor plate in tanks and warships. The Soviet Union, on the other hand, is the world's largest manganese producer. Not only does the Soviet Union produce enough manganese to meet its own needs, but it has enough left over for export to the United States, as well.

Furthermore, what is considered to be a strategic resource today may not be considered one tomorrow or a hundred years from now. In early times, for example, salt was one of the most sought-after earth resources. Not only was it an essential ingredient in the human diet, but it was also necessary for the preservation of meat before the introduction of refrigeration. Salt was a commodity of exchange, just as gold was later, and because Roman soldiers received part of their pay in salt, there arose the expression "worth his salt." Governments even taxed salt because they found that higher prices did not diminish its use. In time, ample salt was obtained from the evaporation of seawater or the mining of underground salt deposits, so now, salt is cheap and in plentiful supply.

Now consider an example of a substance that was once cheap and plentiful and that suddenly became scarce. Before the 1970's, the opening of the large Middle Eastern oil fields had driven the price of oil down to $1.30 per barrel and the price of gasoline at the pump as low as 20 cents per gallon. Excess production capacity continued until the early 1970's, when increasing political tensions in the Middle East finally resulted in a united front on the part of the members of the Organization of Petroleum Exporting Countries (OPEC). First came voluntary production cutbacks, then the Arab oil embargo of 1973-1974. Eventually, the price of oil reached $35.00 per barrel, and gasoline was selling for more than $1.50 per gallon, when it could be obtained at all. A resource which everyone had taken for granted had suddenly become a strategic resource.

To ensure adequate oil supplies for the United States in future emergencies, the U.S. government authorized the establishment of the Strategic Petroleum Reserve. The purpose of this legislation was to purchase 1 billion barrels of oil and to store them in large caverns hollowed out of underground salt domes in coastal Texas and Louisiana. The creation of the Strategic Petroleum Reserve illustrates an important principle. Nations can protect themselves against a possible interruption in supplies of imported strategic resources by stockpiling them during peacetime. Shortages during World War I, for example, caused the U.S. Congress to pass the Strategic Materials Act of 1939 and to begin stockpiling tin, quartz crystals, and chromite in anticipation of the outbreak of another war.

Another way that a major industrial nation protects itself against possible wartime shortages of stategic materials is by arranging for access to supplies of these materials in the event of war. Frequently, this preparation will involve trade agreements with neutral nations or with nations to which a country is bound by political alliances. In extreme cases, it may be necessary to invade a neighboring nation in order to obtain access to strategic resources. The history of Alsace-Lorraine in Europe exemplifies such a situation. This important iron-mining district is traditionally French, but it shares a border with Germany. In both world wars, Germany occupied Alsace-Lorraine in order to assure access to these iron ore deposits.

A third way that a nation can ensure adequate supplies of strategic resources during wartime is to develop substitutes for scarce materials using cheap materials already available. Certain mineral resources, such as mercury and uranium, have unique properties, and for these resources, no satisfactory substitutes can be found. Some of the other metals can be synthesized from related elements but only by prohibitively expensive methods. A number of strategic resources, however, can be synthesized from cheap, readily available materials at comparatively low cost.

After World War I, for example, Germany inventoried the resources it would need for another war. It soon became apparent that the country could be self-sufficient only if several of these resources were manufactured synthetically. Because of the shortage of crude oil, large synthetic oil plants were constructed to produce petroleum from coal, which Germany possessed in abundance. In anticipation that rubber shipments from Southeast Asia and Indonesia would be cut off, synthetic rubber plants were also built, to produce rubber from petrochemicals. Finally, the fertilizers needed for agriculture were to be produced synthetically using a process developed before World War I. In this process, nitrogen was extracted from the atmosphere.

The four strategic resources that would be in shortest supply in the United States were it to go to war are manganese, chromium, cobalt, and nickel. Manganese is a soft, silver-gray metal that is essential in the making of steel. Up to 7 kilograms of manganese are necessary for the production of each ton of iron or steel, and no satisfactory substitute has ever been found. Manganese removes undesired quantities of oxygen and sulfur from the iron during the steel-making process, yielding a hard, tough product suitable for bridge steel, projectiles, and armor plating. U.S. manganese deposits are small, low in grade, and expensive to work; 95 percent of its manganese is imported. The world's largest manganese producers are the Soviet Union, South Africa, and Brazil.

Chromium is a hard, silver-gray metal that is also essential in the making of steel and for which no satisfactory substitute has been found. Chromium makes steel resistant to corrosion and appears on the shiny, chromium-plated surfaces on automobiles. The chromium content of stainless steel varies from 12 to 30 percent. Chromium-steel alloys are also used in aircraft engines, military vehicles, and weapons. The United States has large, low-grade deposits of chromium ore in Montana, but they are expensive to process. Consequently, 90 percent of its chromium is imported, primarily from South Africa.

Cobalt is a silver-white metal that is also needed in steel making. The addition of small quantities of cobalt makes steel harder and heat-resistant. Consequently, cobalt steel has important applications in the manufacture of metal-cutting tools, jet engines, and rockets. Cobalt alloys are magnetic, and the magnetism is retained permanently; therefore, these alloys are used for the manufacture of magnets. The United States has a small cobalt production from low-grade ores in Missouri, but 90 percent of its cobalt is imported, primarily from the country of Zaire, in Africa.

Nickel is a nearly white metal that is another important alloying agent in the making of steel. Nickel steels do not corrode or rust, so large quantities of nickel are used in the manufacture of stainless steel. Nickel is also used in plating because of its shine, in coinage (as in familiar nickel coin), and for alloys that have important applications in the defense industry. The United States has very few high-grade nickel ore deposits, but there is a large, low-grade deposit in Minnesota. About 80 percent of its nickel is imported from Canada, the world's largest nickel producer.

Additional mineral resources that might be in short supply during wartime include platinum, titanium, and aluminum. Platinum resembles silver and is frequently used in jewelry because it does not tarnish and can be worked like silver and gold. It also has valuable chemical properties, because it resists corrosion and acts as a catalyst to speed chemical reactions. The United States imports 90 percent of its platinum, primarily from the Soviet Union and South Africa.

Titanium is a silver-gray metal used as an alloy. Because it imparts great strength, heat resistance, and resistance to corrosion, it is used in the construction of supersonic aircraft, jet engines, and space capsules. It is also used in the manufacture of white paint. Deposits of titanium ore are widespread, and the United States has adequate supplies; the cost of processing the ore is very high, however, because large amounts of electricity are required.

The same can be said for aluminum. Although aluminum is more abundant than iron in the earth's crust, workable deposits (known as bauxite) are restricted to tropical and subtropical regions, and large quantities of electricity are required to process aluminum. The major use for aluminum in the United States is in beverage cans, 56.5 billion of which were produced in 1983. Because most of the country's bauxite must be imported, and because of the high cost of energy, the U.S. government is encouraging a program of recycling aluminum cans. The importance of this program is that it not only reduces imports but also saves costly energy. In 1984, 18 percent of the United States' aluminum production came from recycled aluminum.

Methods of Study

Strategic resources can be studied in a variety of ways. The first is to identify which of the various earth resources are in shortest supply. That is done by analyzing production and usage figures for each of a nation's industrially important minerals in order to determine how much the nation relies on imports for each of these materials. When usage exceeds production, it is relying on imports. The greater the reliance on imports, the more strategic the resource becomes. In the late 1980's, for example, the United States imported about 95 percent of the manganese it used but only 30 percent of the iron. Clearly, manganese was a more strategic resource for the country than iron was.

A second way in which one can study strategic resources is to identify resources which are adequate at present but which may become scarce in the future. That is done by estimating reserves. A reserve is a supply of a mineral substance that still remains in the ground and is available to be extracted at some future time. Two types of reserve can be distinguished: proven reserves and undiscovered reserves. Proven reserves are reserves which have already been outlined by drilling or some other means; there is practically no risk of the desired substance's not being there. Undiscovered reserves, on the other hand, are reserves which are believed to be present on the basis of geologic studies but which are still inadequately explored.

The proven reserves of a mine, for example, are determined by estimating the extent of the ore body and then calculating the tonnage of ore-bearing rock that it contains. If the ore body contains 1 million tons of rock, and the rock averages 0.02 percent titanium, then the reserves of this mine are 200 tons of titanium. The titanium reserves of the entire country can be calculated by totaling the proven ore reserves of all of its titanium mines. If these reserves appear inadequate to meet the anticipated future demand, one knows that one is dealing with a resource that is currently available but that will soon be in short supply.

A third way of studying strategic resources is to begin a search for expanded supplies before current reserves are exhausted or before imports have become unavailable because of wartime conditions. Various methods have been employed for increasing the supply of a strategic resource. They include stockpiling, trade agreements (or territorial annexation, in extreme cases), manufacture of synthetics or the substitution of other substances, and the development of conservation or recycling programs.

Two additional avenues have also become available in the search for expanded supplies of strategic resources. One is the use of the plate tectonics theory. This theory proposes that the earth's surface is divided into a few large plates that are slowly moving with respect to one another. Intense geologic activity occurs at plate boundaries, and many mineral deposits are believed to have been formed by such activity. Much exploration for new deposits of strategic resources is being concentrated at plate boundaries. A second new avenue is the exploration of the deep-sea floor. Although manganese nodules were discovered on the deep-sea floor by the *Challenger* expedition in the late 1800's, it was not until the advent of manned submersibles and remote-controlled television cameras that it was realized that 15 percent or more of the ocean floor may be covered by such nodules. They have valuable amounts of iron, nickel, manganese, cobalt, and other strategically important substances. As exploration of the deep-sea floor continues, other supplies of strategic resources may be found there, as well.

Context

Because a nation's strategic resources are those that would be of critical importance in wartime, one would expect not to hear much about them in peacetime. They are substances which must be imported, however, and excessive imports lead to trade deficits. As a result, a government may resort to conservation measures in order to reduce such imports. A good example is the American program for recycling aluminum beverage cans. This program has two objectives: to reduce U.S. imports of costly aluminum ore and to conserve the large amounts of electricity needed to process aluminum ore.

In troubled times, such as during the 1973-1974 Arab oil embargo and the ensuing energy crisis, measures aimed at conserving strategic resources become very noticeable to the general public. To reduce oil consumption, Americans were asked to turn down their thermostats, the nationwide speed limit was reduced to 55 miles per hour, and automobile companies were told to improve the gas mileage of their cars, which led to a whole new generation of midsized cars. Futhermore, ripple effects caused by the oil shortage spread through the economy, triggering a recession, costing people their jobs, and setting off a stock market decline. Overseas, the value of the dollar declined against other currencies, and soon American tourists found themselves paying more for a hotel room or a meal.

In wartime, the need to conserve strategic resources may even result in rationing. This happened in the United States during World War II. Each driver was given a ration card entitling him or her to purchase a certain number of gallons of gasoline each week; drivers were placed in different categories depending on whether they drove for pleasure or to work.

At the international level, one can see how nations attempt to obtain needed supplies of strategic resources. Normally such resources are supplied by means of peaceful trade, and this trade creates jobs for many people. Sometimes a company even invests in the resources of a foreign country, which produces large dividends for the company stockholders. An example was the purchase, during the 1950's, of the oil rights to the Middle Eastern oil fields by seven oil companies: Exxon, Texaco, Gulf, Mobil, Chevron, Royal Dutch/Shell, and Anglo-Persian. At one time, these companies controlled 92 percent of the world's oil reserves outside the United States, Mexico, and the Soviet Union.

One can also see what a strong bargaining position a country with surplus strategic resources has. The rise to power of OPEC is a good example, as is the stubbornness of South Africa in the face of worldwide disapproval of its racial policies. What industrial nation wants to offend a country that is one of the world's largest producers of diamonds, gold, platinum, chromium, and manganese?

When all else fails, a strong country may even take forcible possession of a weaker one's strategic resources. Julius Caesar invaded Great Britain in the first century B.C. because Rome needed Britain's tin for the manufacture of bronze weapons. In the twentieth century, Germany has twice overrun France's province of Alsace-Lorraine in order to control the rich iron ore deposits there. Only the century had changed; the motives were the same.

Bibliography

Bartholomew, John C., ed. *The Times Atlas of the World*. New York: Times Books,

1980. A well-written overview entitled "Resources of the World" is followed by large, eight-color maps. The world mineral map shows the world distribution of metals and nonmetals and world geology. The world energy map shows the distribution of energy sources and their comparative consumption by nations. Excellent graphs. Suitable for high school readers.

Bramwell, M., ed. *The Rand McNally Atlas of the Oceans*. Skokie, Ill.: Rand McNally, 1977. A beautifully illustrated atlas with subsections on the various energy sources in the ocean, the continental shelves, manganese nodule deposits on the deep-sea floor, and offshore oil. Excellent color photographs, maps, and line drawings. Suitable for high school readers.

Craig, J. R., D. J. Vaughan, and B. J. Skinner. *Resources of the Earth*. Englewood Cliffs, N.J.: Prentice-Hall, 1988. A well-written text with numerous black-and-white photographs, color plates, tables, charts, maps, and line drawings. Chapter 2, entitled "Earth Resources Through History," contains excellent sections on strategic resources, resources and international conflict, and the reliance of the United States on imports. Suitable for college-level readers.

Jensen, M. L., and A. M. Bateman. *Economic Mineral Deposits*. 3d ed. New York: John Wiley & Sons, 1979. This outstanding economic geology text provides detailed information on metallic and nonmetallic mineral deposits and their modes of formation. Discusses the history of mineral use, the exploration and development of mineral properties, and the role of strategic minerals in international relations and war. For a college-level audience.

Klein, Cornelis, and C. S. Hurlbut, Jr. *Manual of Mineralogy*. 20th ed. New York: John Wiley & Sons, 1985. This well-known manual provides detailed descriptions of the various metallic and nonmetallic minerals, including their crystallography, physical properties, and chemical characteristics. There is also helpful information on the mode of formation of the various minerals, where they are found, and why they are useful. Summary tables are included.

Skinner, B. J. *Earth Resources*. 3d ed. Englewood Cliffs, N.J.: Prentice-Hall, 1986. This book provides an excellent overview of the earth's metallic, nonmetallic, and energy resources. Contains helpful line drawings, maps, tables, and charts; few photographs. Includes suggestions for further reading and a list of principal ore minerals and their production figures for 1982. Suitable for the interested layperson.

Tennissen, Anthony C. *The Nature of Earth Materials*. 2d ed. Englewood Cliffs, N.J.: Prentice-Hall, 1983. Contains detailed descriptions of 110 common minerals, with a black-and-white photograph of each. Chapter 7 includes helpful sections on the distribution of mineral deposits and the utilization of various earth materials. Suitable for college students.

Donald W. Lovejoy

Cross-References

RIVER BED FORMS

Type of earth science: Geology
Field of study: Sedimentology

Bed forms, produced by flows of water or air in natural environments and in artificial channels, are a distinctive aspect of the transport of granular sediment along a sediment bed. They have a strong effect on the magnitude of bottom friction felt by the flow. Because of their great variety as a function of flow conditions, bed forms are valuable in interpreting depositional conditions of ancient sedimentary deposits.

Principal terms

ANTIDUNE: an undulatory upstream-moving bed form produced in free-surface flow of water over a sand bed in a certain range of high flow speeds and shallow flow depths

BED CONFIGURATION: the overall geometry of a sediment bed molded by sediment transport by a flowing fluid

BED FORM: an individual geometrical element of a bed configuration

COMBINED FLOW: a flow of fluid with components of both unidirectional and oscillatory flow superposed on one another to produce a more complex pattern of fluid motion

CURRENT RIPPLE: a small bed form, oriented dominantly transverse to flow, produced at low to moderate flow speeds in unidirectional water flows

DUNE: a large bed form, oriented dominantly transverse to flow, produced at moderate to high flow speeds

FLUME: a laboratory open channel in which water is passed over a sediment bed to study the nature of the sediment movement

OSCILLATION RIPPLE: a small to large bed form, oriented dominantly transverse to flow, produced at low to moderate flow speeds in oscillatory water flows

OSCILLATORY FLOW: a flow of fluid with a regular back-and-forth pattern of motion

PLANE BED: a bed configuration without rugged bed forms produced in both unidirectional and oscillatory flows at high flow speeds

UNIDIRECTIONAL FLOW: a flow of fluid oriented everywhere and at all times in the same direction

Summary of the Phenomenon

A striking feature of the transport of loose granular sediment over a bed of the same material by a turbulent flow of fluid like air or water is that in a wide range of conditions of flow and sediment size, the bed is molded into topographic features, called bed forms, on a scale ranging from hundreds of times to even a million times larger than the grains themselves. Examples of such bed forms are sand ripples at one's feet at the seashore or on a dry river bed, sand dunes in the desert, and (less apparent to the casual observer) large underwater sand dunes in rivers and in the shallow ocean. The overall geometry of a sediment bed molded by a flow of fluid is called the bed configuration; bed forms are individual elements of this configuration. The term "bedform," written as one word, includes both the overall geometry and the individual elements of that geometry.

The enormous range of bed-form-producing flows, together with the complex dynamics of the response of the bed, makes for striking variety in the scale and geometry of bed forms. Scales span a range of five orders of magnitude, from a few centimeters to more than a thousand meters in spacing. Bed forms may appear as long ridges or circumscribed mounds, and their crests may be rounded or sharp. Most bed forms are irregular in detail, but elongated bed forms tend to show a more or less strong element of regularity in their overall arrangement, some even being perfectly regular and straight-crested. Elongated bed forms tend to be oriented transverse to flow, although flow-parallel forms are produced under certain conditions, and forms with no strongly preferred orientation are produced in some flows. Most bed forms are approximately wave-shaped and are often likened to waves, but they are waves only in a geometrical sense, not in a mechanical sense.

The most common bed forms are in sands (sediments with mean size lying between about 0.1 millimeter and 2 millimeters), but bed forms are produced in silts (sediments with mean size lying between about 4 micrometers and 0.1 millimeter) and gravels (sediment with mean size greater than 2 millimeters) as well. Bed forms produced by flows of air or water over mineral sediments in natural flow environments are of greatest interest to geologists, but a far wider range can be produced by flows of fluids with other densities and viscosities over sediments less dense or more dense than the common mineral sediments, which have densities mostly in the range 2.5-3.0 grams per cubic centimeter.

Bed forms are made by unidirectional flows of air or water, as in rivers and tidal currents and under sand-moving winds, and by oscillatory flows, as on the shallow sea floor beneath wind-generated surface waves, which cause the water at the bottom to move back and forth with a period the same as that of the waves and with horizontal excursion distances of a few centimeters to a few meters. Bed forms are also made by what are called combined flows: superpositions of unidirectional flows and oscillatory flows. Such combined-flow bed forms are not as well understood as those made by unidirectional and oscillatory flows, but they are common in the shallow ocean. Bed forms made under wind are called subaerial or eolian bed forms, and bed forms made under water are called subaqueous bed forms.

At first thought, it might seem that the natural mode of sediment transport would be over a planar bed surface. In certain ranges of flow, a planar transport surface is indeed the stable bed configuration; technically, such a plane bed is a bed configuration with no bed forms. In reality, plane-bed transport is the stable configuration only under certain conditions; rugged bed forms cover the transport surface over a wide range of conditions in both oscillatory and unidirectional flows. Why such bed forms develop at all on transport surfaces is still not well understood. In certain ranges of flow, the planar transport surface is unstable in the sense that small bed irregularities of the kind that can be built at random by the plane-bed sediment transport become amplified to grow eventually into bed forms rather than being smoothed out again. The physics behind this instability is complex and is still not clearly understood. An essential element of this complexity is that there is a strong interaction or feedback between the bed configuration and the flow: The flow molds the bed configuration, but the bed configuration in turn affects the nature of the flow.

In unidirectional flow, current ripples are formed in fine sands as soon as the current is strong enough to move sand, and they persist to moderate currents of about half a meter per second. In a vertical cross section parallel to the flow, these current ripples are triangular in shape, with downstream slopes about equal to the angle of repose of sand under water (about 30 degrees) and with gentler upstream slopes. In top or horizontal view, they are oriented mostly transverse to flow and are irregular in detail. Their spacings are 10-20 centimeters, and their heights are a few centimeters; this characteristic size changes little with flow strength or sediment size. With increasing unidirectional-flow speed, ripples give way to dunes, which are geometrically fairly similar to ripples but are of much larger scale—meters to thousands of meters in spacing and tens of centimeters to tens of meters in height, depending in a complex and poorly understood way on conditions of flow as well as sediment size. With further increase in flow speed to about a meter per second, dunes are replaced by a plane-bed configuration. The sequence of bed configurations with increasing unidirectional flow speed over coarse sands is different from that over fine sands: Transport is over a plane bed at flow strengths just above the threshold for sediment movement, and then dunes develop with further increase in flow strength. In sediments coarser than about 0.6 millimeter, current ripples are not formed in any range of flow speeds.

Current ripples and dunes move upstream or downstream at a speed far lower than the flow speed, by erosion of sediment on the upstream side of the bed form and deposition on the downstream side. When an individual ripple or dune can be watched carefully for a time, it is seen to change its size, shape, and speed irregularly, eventually to disappear by being absorbed into a neighboring bed form. Offsetting this loss of bed forms is the production of new ones by a kind of subdivision of one larger form into two smaller ones. In flows of water with a free upper surface, like rivers and tidal currents, undulatory bed forms called antidunes make their appearance at high flow speeds and shallow flow depths. Antidunes, so named because they tend to move slowly upstream by erosion of sediment on the downstream sides and deposition on the upstream sides, come about by a complex effect of standing surface waves (waves that move upstream about as fast as the flow is moving downstream) on the sediment bed.

In oscillatory flow, regular straight-crested bed forms called oscillation ripples, with sharp crests and broadly rounded troughs, are formed as soon as the sediment begins to be moved. At their smallest, their spacing is a few centimeters, but they grow in size to more than a meter in spacing as the period and amplitude of the oscillatory motion increases. In fine sands, these larger ripples become irregular and mound-shaped, but observations are not yet adequate for a detailed description. When the maximum flow speed during a single oscillation reaches about a meter per second, the bed forms are washed out to a plane-bed mode of transport. Combined flows produce a whole range of ripples intermediate between current ripples and oscillation ripples.

If the flow changes with time, as is the rule rather than the exception in natural flows, the bed configuration adjusts in response. Usually the bed configuration lags behind the change in the flow, with the result that the bed configuration is more or less out of equilibrium. Dunes formed by reversing flow in a tidal channel are a good example of such disequilibrium; commonly the weaker of the two flows (whether ebb or flood) modifies the shape of the dunes but does not reverse the asymmetry. Bed forms on a riverbed during passage of a flood also tend to lag behind changes in the flow.

Methods of Study

Bed forms can be observed and studied in natural flow environments and in laboratory tanks and channels. Each of these approaches has it advantages and disadvantages. In nature, observations on bed configurations are limited by various practical and technical difficulties. In laboratory tanks and channels, the bed forms can be studied much more easily, but for the most part water depths are unnaturally shallow.

A laboratory open channel in which a flow of water is passed over a sediment bed is called a flume. Flumes range from a few meters to more than a hundred meters long, from about ten centimeters to a few meters wide, and from several centimeters to about a meter deep. The water is usually recirculated from the downstream end to the upstream end to form a kind of endless river. The sediment may also be recirculated, or it may be fed at the upstream end and caught in a trap at the downstream end. In a flume, it is fairly easy to measure the profile of the bed configuration with a mechanical pointer gauge or with a sonic depth sounder, and the bed forms can be studied visually and photographed through the sidewalls and perhaps from the top. Time-lapse motion pictures of bed-form movement are also instructive. Oscillatory-flow bed forms can be studied either in long open tanks, in which water waves are passed over a sand bed to produce oscillatory flow at the bed, or in closed horizontal ducts, in which water is pushed back and forth in a regular oscillation between tanks at the ends of the duct.

In some natural flow environments, such as rivers and tidal currents, the geometry of the bed forms can be studied when they are exposed at low water. Observations of the bed forms when they are being molded by the flow, however, are more difficult. If the flow is not too strong, divers can make direct observations. Profiling of the bed geometry along lines or even across wide areas is usually possible by means of various sonar techniques, whereby the travel times of sound pulses reflected from the bed are converted to water depths. If the water is clear enough, bottom photographs of small areas can be taken. Current velocities can be measured with current meters anchored on the bed. Movement of large bed forms is difficult to measure because bed-form speeds are slow and usually no fixed reference points are available.

The status of observations on bed configurations leaves much to be desired. Even in laboratory channels and tanks, where the major outlines are by now fairly well known, there is much room for further work for two reasons: The narrowness of the flow tends to distort the three-dimensional aspects of the bed geometry, and little work has been done on bed forms in combined flows. There is a need for more observations on the geometry and movement of bed forms in natural flows as a function of flow strength, as well as on the effect of disequilibrium.

Context

Bed forms are ubiquitous in natural flow environments. They are most apparent to the casual eye in fields of sand dunes in deserts and in certain coastal environments where the wind molds available loose sand into dunes. They are widely present but less obvious in rivers and the shallow ocean. Apart from their intrinsic scientific interest as a widespread natural phenomenon, bed forms are of importance in both engineering and geology for various reasons. Large underwater bed forms many meters high in rivers and marine currents can be obstacles to navigation, and their movement can be a threat to submarine structures. Also, the inexorable movement of desert dunes or coastal dunes can bury roads and buildings.

The rugged topography of ripple and dune bed forms leads to a pattern of flow over each bed form in which the pressure on the upstream surface is relatively high and the pressure on the downstream surface is relatively low, much like an unstreamlined motor vehicle on the highway or a house in a strong wind. This pressure difference adds greatly to the force the flow exerts on the bed and, conversely, to the force the bed exerts on the moving flow. Hydraulic engineers have expended much effort on the effect of this resistance force on the depth a river assumes when it is given a particular rate of flow to carry. A river with a planar bed can pass a given flow rate at a shallower depth and greater velocity than can a river with a bed roughened by large dunes, which exert a large resistance force on the flow and make the velocity smaller and the depth greater.

Geologists have given attention to bed forms partly because of their effect on the geometry of the stratification that develops as a sediment bed is deposited while bed forms are active on the sediment surface. It is often possible to tell the kind of bed form that was present just by examining the stratification in a sedimentary rock like a sandstone. If the flow conditions responsible for making that kind of bed form are already known—from laboratory experiments or from observations in modern natural flow environments—the depositional conditions of that sedimentary rock (which may be geologically very ancient) can be interpreted. Such interpretations are one of the tools used in mapping the geometry of subsurface petroleum reservoirs in sedimentary rocks.

Bibliography

Allen, J. R. L. *Principles of Physical Sedimentology*. London: Allen & Unwin, 1985. A lucidly written introduction to the movement and deposition of sediment for sedimentology students at the college level and beyond. The chapter on bed forms is moderately mathematical, but there is some good descriptive material and illustrations of bed forms. The treatment of bed forms is concise but fairly comprehensive.

Collinson, J. D., and D. B. Thompson. *Sedimentary Structures*. London: Allen & Unwin, 1982. This book, written for beginning college-level students in sedimentology, presents a nonmathematical treatment of bed forms in the context of their sedimentological significance. Three chapters are devoted to bed forms and the sedimentary structures they produce. Numerous illustrations of the various kinds of bed forms.

Leeder, M. R. *Sedimentology: Process and Product*. London: Allen & Unwin, 1982. An introductory college-level text on sedimentology, with a well-illustrated and mostly nonmathematical chapter on bed forms. Suitable for high school readers who are willing to do some preparatory reading in the earlier parts of the book.

Middleton, G. V., and J. B. Southard. *Mechanics of Sediment Movement*. Tulsa, Okla.: Society of Economic Paleontologists and Mineralogists, 1984. This set of course notes, which has the content but not the format of an introductory textbook, is aimed at college-level students and beyond. Contains a long and mostly nonmathematical chapter on bed forms for sedimentologists, with material on both the observational characteristics and the basic hydrodynamics of bed forms. Emphasis on underwater bed forms. No photographs.

Reineck, H. E., and I. B. Singh. *Depositional Sedimentary Environments*. 2d ed. Berlin: Springer-Verlag, 1980. This almost entirely nonmathematical book, designed as a monograph on modern depositional environments for sedimentologists and marine geologists, has several long, nonmathematical, and extensively referenced sections on bed forms in a great variety of flow environments. Suitable for high school readers. Unusually well illustrated.

Vanoni, V. A., ed. *Sedimentation Engineering*. New York: American Society of Civil Engineers, 1975. This engineering reference manual, aimed at students and practicing engineers, deals with the fundamentals of sediment-transport mechanics from an applied standpoint. Parts of two chapters deal with bed forms, mainly in the context of rivers. The best and most authoritative source for information on the effect of bed forms on the behavior of rivers. Fairly heavily mathematical.

Yalin, M. S. *Mechanics of Sediment Transport*. 2d ed. Elmsford, N.Y.: Pergamon Press, 1977. This college-level textbook, designed for engineering students, devotes a long chapter to an unusually fundamental treatment of the mechanics of bed forms. Heavily mathematical, but with numerous qualitative insights into bed-form behavior. No illustrations.

John Brelsford Southard

Cross-References

RIVER FLOW

Type of earth science: Geology
Field of study: Sedimentology

Worldwide, rivers are the most important sources of water for cities and major industries. Hydroelectric power is a major source of electrical power, and transport of heavy, bulky goods by river barge is a vital link in most transportation systems. Understanding and predicting low, high, and average flows of rivers is therefore important to the people and industries that depend on them.

Principal terms

DISCHARGE: the total amount of water passing a point on a river per unit of time

EVAPOTRANSPIRATION: all water that is converted to water vapor by direct evaporation or passage through vegetation

HYDRAULIC GEOMETRY: a set of equations that relate river width, depth, and velocity to discharge

HYDROGRAPH: a plot recording the variation of stream discharge over time

HYDROLOGIC CYCLE: the circulation of water as a liquid and vapor from the oceans to the atmosphere and back to the oceans

HYDROLOGY: broadly, the science of water; the term is often used in the more restricted sense of flow in channels

RATING CURVE: a plot of river discharge in relation to elevation of the water surface; permits estimation of discharge from the water elevation

TURBULENT FLOW: the swirling flow that is typical of rivers, as opposed to smooth, laminar flow

Summary of the Phenomenon

There are two very different fundamental types of flow of water. Laminar flow is a smooth flow, in which two particles suspended in the water will follow parallel, nearly straight paths. Turbulent flow is a complex, swirling flow in which the paths of two suspended particles have no necessary relation to each other. Turbulent flow may have velocity components that are up or down from, sideways or upstream of the average flow direction, although the average flow direction is always in the downstream, or downslope, direction. Flow near the bottom and sides of a river or stream is always laminar, but the zone of laminar flow is very narrow. Turbulent flow dominates throughout the cross section of stream flow.

Because flowing water exerts a shear stress, or viscous shear, along the bottom and sides of the river, average flow velocity is least at the bottom and increases upward into the body of the river. Because of energy losses to surface waves, the average turbulent downstream velocity (hereafter referred to simply as velocity) at the river's surface is slightly below the maximum velocity. The maximum velocity occurs at about 0.6 of the river depth above the bottom of the river.

Because of viscous shear between flowing water and the bottom materials, the small (and sometimes large) sediment particles that make up most river bottoms are moved by the flowing water. Once in motion, small particles whose settling velocity is less than the upward component of turbulent flow move downstream with the water, settling out only in backwaters, such as the still water behind a dam, where flow velocities are very low. This continuously moving sediment is referred to as suspended load and is restricted, in most cases, to clay- and silt-sized material. Sand-sized and larger sediment grains are moved during periods of high flow velocity and dropped where, or when, flow velocity decreases. This coarse material is the "bed load." Bed-load transport normally occurs only near the river bed. It is the sediment in transport that does the work of the river: erosion and transport. Erosional features of river valleys—canyons, potholes, and many others—are produced by the "wet sandblast" of the suspended bed load, a process that is much more effective during periods of high flow velocity.

During periods of rainfall or snowmelt, direct precipitation into streams and runoff from adjacent land provides stream flow. Between periods of rainfall or snowmelt, stream flow comes from the slow seepage of groundwater into surface streams. Small streams, the smallest of which flow only during wet periods, join to form larger streams, which join to form rivers. Because rainfall or snowmelt occurs only occasionally in an area drained by a river (the river's drainage basin), the quantity of water flowing past any point on a river, or any point on any of its tributary streams, varies with time.

The quantity of water passing a point on the river is measured in cubic meters per second (or, in common North American and British practice, cubic feet per second) and is called the discharge. For a period of time after a rainfall or snowmelt event— for example, a flood—discharge increases at all points in the drainage basin. If the flood event occurs in only one part of the drainage basin, say the higher part of the basin with the smaller streams, the increase in discharge will occur first in the higher part of the basin and will occur in the larger streams lower in the basin at some later time.

If the discharge at a given point on a stream is measured continuously over a period of days and the discharge is plotted against time, with discharge on the vertical axis of the graph and time in days on the horizontal axis, the increase in discharge related to a storm or snowmelt (a flood) will appear as a hump in the discharge curve. A graph of discharge with time is called a hydrograph, and a hydrograph that shows a flood-related hump is a flood hydrograph. Flood hydrographs tend to be more pronounced—that is, the curve is higher and has steeper sides—on streams near the source of the flood water and longer and less pronounced—that is, lower and with more gently sloping sides—farther downstream. Putting it another way, the flood hydrograph attenuates, or dies out, downstream. The low, flat portion of the hydrograph that measures flow between flood events is called baseflow. Experience with flood hydrographs for a river enables hydrologists to predict the effect of future rainstorms and snowmelts of varying intensity and to predict low flow during prolonged dry periods.

An increase in discharge is accompanied by an increase in velocity. For rivers with sandy bottoms (sandy streambeds), the higher water velocity causes erosion, or scour, of the bottom; that is, the sand begins to move along the bottom with the water, and the river channel becomes deeper. The elevation of the water surface relative to some fixed point on the river bank also increases. As a rule, the banks are not vertical but sloping, and the increase in elevation of the water surface causes an increase in width. In summary, an increase in discharge is accompanied by increases in flow velocity, stream width, water surface elevation, and depth of channel (the last two items add up to an overall increase in depth). A reduction in discharge has just the opposite effect, including the deposition of new sand, arriving from upstream, in the channel as the velocity decreases.

In 1953, Luna Bergere Leopold and Thomas Maddock, Jr., introduced a concept that helps explain the relationships among the variables that change when discharge changes. The concept is called hydraulic geometry, and it is embodied in the following three equations: $w = aQ^b$, $d = bQ^f$, and $v = kQ^m$, where w is stream width, d is average depth of the stream, v is the flow velocity, and Q is discharge. The coefficients a, b, and k and the exponents b, f, and m are determined empirically—that is, by measurement in the field. Since the discharge is equal to the cross-sectional area of the stream (wd) times the flow velocity (that is, $wdv = Q$), $wdv = aQ^b \times bQ^f \times kQ^m = Q$. For this to be true, the product of a, b, and k must be 1 ($abk = 1$), and the sum of the exponents b, f, and m must also be 1 ($b + f + m = 1$). Many field studies have shown these equations to be good approximations of actual variation in width, depth, and velocity with variation in discharge.

The coefficients of the hydraulic geometry equations have little effect, relative to the powerful exponents, and are usually ignored. The exponents of the hydraulic geometry equations depend on the physical characteristics of the drainage basins and stream channels involved, but for a given point on a given stream, average values are $b = 0.1$, $f = 0.45$, and $m = 0.45$, which means that the increase in discharge during a flood event is expressed primarily in increases in depth and flow velocity.

The discharge of rivers increases downstream because of the larger length of stream receiving baseflow and the contribution from many tributaries, and hydraulic geometry equations may also be applied to downstream changes in discharge. Average values for the exponents in the downstream hydraulic geometry equations for width, depth, and velocity are $b = 0.5$, $f = 0.4$, and $m = 0.1$. This phenomenon is a paradox. Casual observation would suggest that small streams in the higher parts of the drainage basins flow faster than the large rivers in the lower parts of the drainage basins. Yet, appearances are deceptive: Water in the wider, deeper channels of the larger streams actually flows faster than does water in the smaller headwater streams.

When a flood flow exceeds the capacity of the river channel, the surface elevation of the river rises above the elevation of the river banks, and flooding of the surface adjacent to the stream occurs. This is what has generally been called a flood, or an overbank flood. Overbank floods do serious damage to homes, businesses, industrial facilities, and crops on the flooded areas, and much time and money are devoted to flood prevention. The principal method of flood prevention is the construction of levees, large earth embankments or concrete walls along the stream bank, at locations where the potential economic loss because of flooding justifies the expense of their construction and maintenance.

Methods of Study

Research on flow in rivers, or hydrology, almost invariably involves the determination of flow velocity and discharge. Because discharge (Q) equals stream width (w) times average depth (d) times average flow velocity (v), velocity and discharge are closely related. As implied by the world "average" in the preceding sentence, depth and velocity vary across the width of a river or stream. Velocity is lowest in the shallower parts of the river. Therefore, the cross section of the stream is divided into sections, and the discharge is taken as the sum of discharges of all the sections.

For a relatively small river, a rope or strong cord is stretched across the river and marked at regular intervals, typically 2 meters. The depth is measured at each marked point, and a current meter is used to measure the velocity at each point. The flow in rivers and streams is turbulent, and the current meter actually measures the average downstream component of velocity. Average downstream velocity varies with depth of the channel and also through the vertical section at any point on the stream, the lowest velocities occurring at the bottom and at the surface. Average velocity at any given vertical section of flow occurs at about 0.6 d above the bottom, which is where the current meter is positioned. Alternatively, two velocity measurements may be taken, at 0.2 and 0.8 d above the bottom, and averaged. The equation $Q = wdv$, where w is the interval at which measurements were taken, is computed for each section, or interval, across the stream; all the resultant discharges are summed to obtain the total discharge at the point on the stream, which is now called a station.

The process described above is laborious. If discharge at a station must be more or less continuously monitored, a quicker method is desirable, which is accomplished by developing a rating curve for the station. Discharge is measured in the manner described above at several different times, with as wide a range of discharges as practical. A staff gauge (a board mounted vertically in the stream and marked in units of length, usually feet in American and British practice) is erected at the station, and the level of the water surface, called the stage of the river, is determined each time the discharge is measured. The rating curve consists of a plot of stage against discharge. Once the rating curve has been determined, discharge is estimated from river stage by use of the rating curve. Because of the scour and fill of the river bottom that occur with each increase and decrease in discharge and velocity, the rating curve is not a straight line. Moreover, because the scour and fill may, over time, change the character of the river channel at the station, it is necessary actually to measure the discharge periodically to check the validity of the rating curve. If large changes in the channel occur, it is necessary to establish a new rating curve.

The U.S. Geological Survey maintains a large number of rating stations, or gauging stations, and periodically reports stream discharges. At most stations operated by the agency, the staff gauge is replaced by a vertical pipe driven in the streambed and perforated near the bed. Water is free to flow in and out of the pipe as river stage changes, but the water surface inside the pipe is not disturbed by surface waves. A cable with a weight at the end is attached to the float, and the cable is passed over a wheel near the top of the pipe. The float is free to move with the water surface inside the pipe and, as it moves, it turns the wheel. Sensitive instruments monitor the position of the wheel and therefore the river stage as well. In this way, the stage is periodically and automatically reported to a central office by telephone line or radio.

Context

All aspects of river flow—including the nature of flow (laminar and turbulent), flow velocity, quantity of flow, transport and deposition of sediment by flowing water, shaping of river channels by erosion and deposition, and their variation in time and space—constitute the scientific discipline of fluvial hydrology (river hydrology).

From a practical standpoint, the most important aspects of river flow are the quantity of flow, or discharge, and the velocity. Planning for water supply, treated waste disposal, flood control, river transportation, irrigation, and hydroelectric power requires knowledge of long- and short-term variation in discharge and flow velocity. As an example, the areas adjacent to rivers, the floodplains, are desirable sites for heavy industry because they are level, close to major supplies of water, and convenient to river transport. The drawback is that overbank flows, which flood these areas, occur every three years on average, with major floods occurring two or three times per century. One solution is to construct levees that prevent flooding of specific areas of the floodplain. Knowledge of river flow enables the levee designers to predict how high the levees must be and how they must be constructed to withstand the high flow velocities associated with high discharges.

Minimum flows also are of interest. Typically, low river flows occur at some season of the year, in the late summer and autumn in most of North America. If the low flow is inadequate to supply water for a major city, for example, reservoirs must be constructed. A knowledge of the expected degree and duration of low flow is required to determine what the capacity of the reservoirs must be.

Low flows are also critical in wastewater treatment. Although treated sewage is biologically clean, it has a high content of dissolved solids and, undiluted, is not suitable for reuse at downstream locations. The treated wastewater must be released into a river with a minimum discharge large enough to dilute it to an acceptable dissolved-solids content. If the expected minimum discharge of a given river is not adequate, the treatment plant must be relocated.

A very challenging problem arises in connection with the design of irrigation canals. Flow velocity in the canal must be high enough to prevent the settling, or deposition, of silt and clay in the irrigation water because this would block the canal, but the velocity must not be so high that the water will erode the banks of the canal. Methods of designing stable and efficient irrigation canals have been developed from study of erosion and deposition in natural rivers.

Every aspect of the management of water resources, a vital element in a complex industrial society, is dependent on knowledge of river flow. Intelligent planning for the multiple uses of rivers mentioned above requires knowledge of expected low, average, and high discharges and the expected timing of these events. River hydrology provides the basis for this planning.

Bibliography

Dingman, S. L. *Fluvial Hydrology*. New York: W. H. Freeman, 1984. A very clear development of all the equations that are essential to fluvial hydrology. For full understanding, a year of college calculus is necessary, but about 80 percent of the material can be mastered by a student with knowledge only of algebra and trigonometry. An excellent treatment of the subject, with many answered problems and a helpful annotated bibliography. The introductory chapters on units of measurement (dimensions), fundamentals of physical equations, and physical properties of water should be required reading for all science students.

Dunne, Thomas, and Luna B. Leopold. *Water in Environmental Planning*. San Francisco: W. H. Freeman, 1978. A thorough (818-page), essentially nonmathematical examination of the subject. Emphasis is on design to avoid environmental problems associated with water in all its manifestations. Many worked problems, most involving only basic mathematics.

Kindsvatter, C. E. *Selected Topics of Fluid Mechanics*. U.S. Geological Survey Water Supply Paper 1369-A. Washington, D.C.: Government Printing Office, 1958. Develops in an exceptionally clear way the fundamental concepts of fluid mechanics that underlie fluvial hydrology. Less than 10 percent of the material requires a knowledge of calculus. Many aspects of the approach are much superior to more recent texts.

Leopold, Luna B. *Water: A Primer*. San Francisco: W. H. Freeman, 1974. A brief (172-page), very readable introduction to the subject. Highly recommended for all newcomers to the field and most professionals.

Leopold, Luna B., M. G. Woolman, and J. P. Miller. *Fluvial Processes in Geomorphology*. San Francisco: W. H. Freeman, 1964. A lucid explanation of the fundamentals of the field by the originator of hydraulic geometry, written ten years after the first paper on the subject. Highly recommended for both beginners and professionals.

Manning, J. C. *Applied Principles of Hydrology*. Westerville, Ohio: Charles E. Merrill, 1987. An excellent short introduction to the principles of surface water and groundwater hydrology. Incorporates very little of the mathematics involved in the two fields, but the descriptions and illustrations of methods of making field measurements are clear and informative.

Richards, Keith. *Rivers, Form, and Process in Alluvial Channels*. London: Methuen, 1982. A college-level text requiring some familiarity with calculus for complete understanding. Its great strength is the very large number of research papers cited in the text. Conveys a sense of the quantity and type of research that has been done.

Robert E. Carver

Cross-References

Alluvial Systems, 31; Aquifers, 71; Deltas, 332; Drainage Basins, 384; Floodplains, 712; Floods, 719; The Geomorphology of Dry Climate Areas, 882; The Geomorphology of Wet Climate Areas, 890; The Hydrologic Cycle, 1102; Land-Use Planning, 1335; Precipitation, 2108; River Valleys, 2210; Sediment Transport and Deposition, 2290; Surface Water, 2504.

RIVER VALLEYS

Type of earth science: Geology
Field of study: Geomorphology

The valleys in which streams flow are produced by those streams through long-term erosion and deposition. The landforms produced by fluvial action are quite diverse, ranging from spectacular canyons to wide, gently sloping valleys. The patterns formed by stream networks are complex and generally reflect the bedrock geology and terrain characteristics.

Principal terms

AGGRADATION: the process by which a stream elevates its bed through deposition of sediment

BASE LEVEL: the theoretical vertical limit below which streams cannot cut their beds

FLUVIAL: of or related to streams and their actions

INTERFLUVE: an upland area between valleys

STREAM EQUILIBRIUM: a state in which a stream's erosive energy is balanced by its sediment load such that it is neither eroding nor building up its channel

UNDERFIT STREAM: a stream that is significantly smaller in proportion than the valley through which it flows

VALLEY: that part of the earth's surface where stream systems are established; it includes streams and adjacent slopes

Summary of the Phenomenon

River valleys consist of valley bottoms and the adjacent valley sides. Between valleys are undissected uplands known as interfluves. Valley floors may be quite narrow, as in the case of the Black Canyon of the Gunnison River, or they may be quite wide, as in the case of the Hwang Ho or the Brahmaputra. Similarly, valley sides may have very gentle to rolling slopes, or they may be nearly sheer, as in the case of the Arkansas River's Royal Gorge. In many areas, the interfluves are simply divides between adjacent valleys, but on tablelands such as the Colorado Plateau, they may be tens of kilometers wide in places.

River channels and river valleys are products of the streams that flow through them. As a stream erodes a channel for itself in newly uplifted terrain, it eventually carves a valley whose form is determined by the erosive power of the stream, by the structural integrity of the rock and debris of the valley walls, by the length of time that the stream has been operating on its surroundings, and by past environmental conditions. These past environmental conditions are attested by stream channel and valley profiles that have not entirely erased landforms produced during the most recent episodes of glaciation and climate change. The valley of the Mississippi

River, for example, is formed in the complex deposits of what was a much larger, more heavily laden glacial meltwater stream that existed only 15,000 years ago. River channels and valleys may be referred to as palimpsests, a term originally used to describe parchment manuscripts that had been partly scraped clean, then reused. On the fluvial (river-carved or river-deposited) landscape, previous landscape elements are seen, just as old words show through on a recycled piece of parchment.

In many parts of the world, streams are found flowing through valleys that appear to have been formed by a far larger stream. The valley width, amplitude of meanders, and caliber of coarse sediment are proportional to far larger stream courses. Such streams are said to be underfit, and the valleys are largely remnant features from times of wetter and cooler climates that accompanied glaciation, or the streams were glacial meltwater channels during deglaciation.

The fact that stream channels and valleys are not chance features on the landscape was first noted by British geologist John Playfair in 1802. Playfair suggested that instead of being isolated features on the landscape, streams are part of well-integrated networks. More important, these networks are finely adjusted to the landscape and to one another in such a way that tributaries almost always join the main trunk stream at the same level as that stream. Streams that must plunge over waterfalls to join a larger stream are quite rare. Such discordant streams are found primarily in recently glaciated terrain, where the stream-valley system has not yet become fully adjusted, such as in Yosemite Valley. This remarkable consistency of stream accordance is the strongest evidence indicating that streams carve their own valleys.

Streams develop into network patterns that are strongly influenced by bedrock structure. Where the bedrock is relatively uniform and without strong joints and faults, a dendritic pattern of drainage develops. In this pattern, a stream system is branched like a tree. On inclined plains such as the Atlantic coastal plain, the stream pattern is often parallel, with major streams flowing directly down the topographic slope to the sea. Inclined mountain systems such as the Sierra Nevada also produce parallel drainage. Where structural folding of the terrain has produced linear ridge and valley topography, main trunk streams occupy the linear valleys and are quite long, with short, steep tributaries feeding them off the flanks of the hills or mountains. In areas such as the Great Valley of Virginia, this type of pattern has developed and is known as trellis drainage. Volcanoes often produce a radial pattern of drainage; Mount Egmont, New Zealand, is often cited as an example.

The depth of a river valley is a function of the height of the land above base level, the length of time that has passed since the stream began to erode, the resistance of the bedrock to erosion, the load of sediment that the stream is carrying, and the spacing of adjacent streams. "Base level" refers to the theoretical lower limit to which a stream can cut. Ultimate base level for all streams is sea level, but local base level is significantly higher for many streams. Streams require a minimum slope to transport their sediment to the sea; this limits the depth to which a stream may cut. The upper section of the Hwang Ho near Tibet flows at elevations of more than 3,000 meters, but the river must still flow more than 4,000 kilometers to the sea. In order to carry its heavy load of sediment over that distance, the river must maintain its channel at a rather high elevation.

Valleys that are deep and relatively narrow are called canyons; those valleys that are especially narrow are called gorges. Streams require time to erode great canyons, although the rate of cutting can be quite rapid compared to most geologic processes. The process of downwearing of interfluves is far slower, so young (recently uplifted) landscapes produce the deepest canyons; as downcutting by the main stream ceases, upland weathering and erosion lowers the local relief. The deepest, narrowest canyons are eroded in strong, homogeneous rock such as granite and quartzite. The Royal Gorge of the Arkansas River and the Colca Gorge of Peru are excellent examples; both are cut in recently uplifted masses of resistant rock formations. The Colca Gorge is far narrower than is the Grand Canyon and, at more than 3,000 meters, it is nearly twice as deep.

As a mountain mass or tableland is uplifted, streams often develop that flow directly down the initial slope of the land; such streams are called consequent streams because their course is a direct consequence of the terrain slope. Because streams seek the path of least resistance, their courses often follow the outcrop pattern of weak rocks such as shale, producing what is known as a subsequent stream pattern. In many cases, however, streams seem to ignore the terrain and structural slope of the land entirely, flowing through mountains of quite resistant rock. An excellent example is the Black Canyon of the Gunnison River in Colorado, where the river carves a deep canyon through a high plateau, with its channel cut in resistant gneisses and igneous intrusives. What makes this so surprising is that much lower terrain, underlain by thick sequences of weak shale, lies only 3 kilometers to the west of the head of the gorge, which would seem to provide a much easier path to the sea. The reason for this course—and many other anomalous stream courses—is that the course of the Gunnison was established prior to the uplift of the plateau. As the land rose beneath the river, it maintained its position, carving an ever-deepening gorge in the rocks as they rose. Far older and more extensive is the anomalous course of the New River, which cuts directly across the structure of the Appalachians, flowing a great distance to the Ohio River rather than the shorter, more direct route to the Atlantic. Once again, this river is one that was established prior to the uplift of the land in which it is now entrenched, in this case the ancient Appalachians. Thus, the river is rather ironically named, considering that its course is older than the Appalachians.

At any given time, a stream may either erode or aggrade (build up) its bed. This vertical change in stream profile is determined by many factors internal to the stream, as well as outside environmental factors. Over geological time, the tendency of streams is to erode their beds deeper and deeper. Over shorter time intervals, however, a stream may reach a state of equilibrium between its erosive energy and the load of sediment that the stream is carrying. A delicate balance is maintained within the stream channel: If stream energy is increased by an increase in flood volume or frequency, for example, the stream is likely to respond by eroding its bed. Conversely, if stream power remains constant and the sediment load is significantly increased, the stream will respond by aggrading. This channel aggradation increases the channel slope, giving the stream more energy to transport the sediment load, and a new equilibrium is reached.

Methods of Study

River valleys are studied by means of several different techniques. The earliest studies were based entirely on field observations. Among the ancient natural scientists who speculated upon the origins of fluvial landforms were Aristotle and the Arab philosopher and physician Avicenna (c. A.D. 1000), who promoted the idea that river valleys could have been carved by running water. Near the end of the fifteenth century, Leonardo da Vinci advanced the understanding of landforms through his insightful observations and interpretations of the topography of southern Europe. Deductive studies advanced significantly during the eighteenth and nineteenth centuries as the concept of uniformitarianism began to take hold and the concept of deep geologic time began to gain acceptance. Uniformitarianism holds that the present is the key to the past, which means that processes occurring on the earth today are the same processes that have always occurred on the earth. Therefore, the erosion of the Grand Canyon or Tiger Leap Gorge on the Yangtze occurred as the result of the same fluvial processes that operate there currently. The most important corollary of the law of uniformitarianism is that vast amounts of time are required in order for great mountains to be uplifted, for valleys to be carved, and for uplands to be leveled.

As detailed topographic and geologic maps became available in the early twentieth century, deductive analysis of river valleys became much more precise. By comparing precise topographic cross sections of river valleys to the underlying geology, geomorphologists came to understand the importance of bedrock lithology in controlling valley wall slope and the importance of lithology and zones of rock weakness (joints and faults) in determining stream courses, network patterns, and stream spacing.

Stream gauges, which indicate the discharge of rivers, have been operating over large areas since the beginning of the twentieth century. Thus, a great wealth of information has become available concerning the manner in which streams erode and transport sediment. With gauge data concerning rates of runoff and sediment load, researchers are able to project over time the rates of regional denudation (lowering of the landscape by erosion). Results of such studies show that mountainous areas are being lowered at much faster rates than are piedmont and lowland areas, but the global average rate of denudation is on the order of a few centimeters per thousand years. From these same data, much has been learned about the relative importance of catastrophic floods and more frequent, low-magnitude runoff events.

Together with the compilation of up-to-date maps, the advent of low-altitude aerial photography has allowed researchers to study stream channel and valley alterations over relatively short time intervals. By comparing sequential high-resolution photographs, which are obtained about every ten years in the United States, it is possible to gain detailed knowledge of the magnitude and locations of such changes. In some cases, the changes are great enough to be detected from commercial satellite images, which provide repeat coverage as often as every fourteen days.

Laboratory studies are of increasing importance in studying river valleys. From simple stream tables to elaborate scaled physical models of river channels, such studies provide fluvial geomorphologists with an understanding of how streams operate and the nature of changes that will occur with environmental changes such as an increase in runoff, an increase in the caliber of sediment delivered to the stream, or the construction of a dam upstream. The results not only help in understanding basic fluvial processes but can aid greatly in management decisions as well.

River network formation and slope retreat are sometimes studied by observing the development of stream channels on recently denuded terrain such as construction sites. Although it is not possible to eliminate entirely the important role of geologic time in such an experiment, it is possible to gain insight into the nature of such processes by observing these fast-changing environments.

Computer simulation of stream network development and river valley processes has been utilized by a number of researchers. Computer modeling is based upon known physical properties of rock and soil materials, plus the laws of physics that govern flows of energy and materials. As models become more sophisticated, their ability to simulate and predict slow geologic processes in a short period of time will improve.

Context

Perhaps the greatest significance of river valleys proceeds from the importance of streams in sculpting the face of the earth. Fluvial erosion and valley formation are the most important processes by which uplifted masses of land are lowered over long periods of time. In order to gain an understanding of, and a true appreciation for, the "lay of the land," one must first understand the processes by which streams carve their valleys. It is no wonder, then, that students of landforms—from Aristotle to modern fluvial geomorphologists—have generally focused on streams and valleys.

Stream network patterns are almost always indicative of underlying geology, so reconnaissance geology often takes first aim at the stream channel network of an area. By understanding where and why stream channels have carved their valleys, one can learn much about the underlying geologic structure.

As future changes in climate—caused by carbon dioxide pollution and an attendant global greenhouse warming—are debated, substantial changes in stream flow will occur. One study suggested that a 10 percent reduction in precipitation in the Colorado River basin could result in a 50 percent reduction in stream flow of the

Colorado River. Such a change would be catastrophic in and of itself, but there would be significant changes in the behavior of the stream as well. Given a constant supply of sediment, the river would likely aggrade its bed, threatening streamside developments, irrigation diversions, and vegetation. Researchers believe that minor changes in discharge-sediment load relationships in Chaco Arroyo, Arizona, led to stream entrenchment that destroyed the advanced irrigation system built by the Anasazi people, leading to the abandonment of Chaco Canyon. An understanding of fluvial dynamics is essential to predicting such changes.

The oldest direct application of fluvial dynamics is the design of stable irrigation canals. The earliest civilizations using irrigation, such as the early Mesopotamian culture, discovered that canals had a tendency either to erode or to fill themselves with sediment if they were not carefully adjusted to take into account the volume of water flowing through the canal, the slope of the canal, the materials through which the canal was cut, and the sediment load of the water. More recently, it has become necessary to predict the changes in stream character below large man-made dams. Below Glen Canyon Dam, the Colorado River has been relieved of its heavy sediment load and has compensated by eroding the beaches along the river that are used for recreation.

Bibliography

Bloom, A. L. *Geomorphology: A Systematic Analysis of Late Cenozoic Landforms*. Englewood Cliffs, N.J.: Prentice-Hall, 1978. This book is intermediate in difficulty between the Butzer and Chorley geomorphology texts listed below. Chapters 8 through 12 cover the processes of fluvial landscape development thoroughly and evenly. The author does a good job of explaining the interrelations between valley form, structural control, and fluvial processes. Well illustrated and supported with numerous citations. Suitable for college-level readers.

Butzer, K. W. *Geomorphology from the Earth*. New York: Harper & Row, 1976. This geomorphology text is aimed at an introductory audience and does a good job of avoiding unnecessary jargon. Although not as thoroughly illustrated as some books on the subject, its level of presentation makes it accessible to a far larger audience than most. Suitable for advanced high school students and beyond.

Chorley, R. J., S. A. Schumm, and D. E. Sugden. *Geomorphology*. New York: Methuen, 1985. An advanced text in geomorphology that is best used as a reference. Provides detailed citations of the important scholarly works on each subject addressed and is quite thorough. Many diagrams, graphs, and line drawings supplement the material, but there are few photographs. Suitable for college students who have already gained some background in geomorphology.

Hunt, C. B. *Natural Regions of the United States and Canada*. San Francisco: W. H. Freeman, 1974. This book is primarily a physiography text, aimed at describing and explaining the pattern of landforms across North America. The author produced it in the light of "the general public's interest in the natural environment and the need for an authoritative account of it in language as nontechnical as possible." In both regards, the book is quite successful. Well illustrated with diagrams, line drawings, and photographs. Introductory chapters provide an explanation of the general phenomena, and the remaining chapters provide a very thorough, understandable coverage of the regional expression of landforms. Suitable for high school students and beyond.

Lutgens, F. K., and E. J. Tarbuck. *Essentials of Geology*. 2d ed. Westerville, Ohio: Charles E. Merrill, 1986. This short (310-page) physical geology text provides a brief introduction to all the major topics in the field. Its strengths are its full-color illustrations and its accessibility to the general reader. Suitable for anyone interested in the earth sciences.

McKnight, T. L. *Physical Geography: A Landscape Appreciation*. 2d ed. Englewood Cliffs, N.J.: Prentice-Hall, 1987. This physical geography text provides very thorough but understandable coverage of the concepts of stream networks, stream channel history, and fluvial dynamics. Richly illustrated with color diagrams and photographs. Suitable for high school students and beyond.

Skinner, Brian J., and Stephen C. Porter. *Physical Geology*. New York: John Wiley & Sons, 1987. A consistently excellent text in introductory physical geology, richly and generously illustrated in full color. Very thorough and quite extensive (more than seven hundred pages). Chapter 11, "Streams and Drainage Systems," is one of the best chapters. Suitable for advanced high school students and beyond.

Michael W. Mayfield

Cross-References

Aerial Photography, 17; Alluvial Systems, 31; Dams and Flood Control, 309; Drainage Basins, 384; Floodplains, 712; Floods, 719; Alpine Glaciers, 960; Grand Canyon, 988; The Hydrologic Cycle, 1102; Numerical Modeling, 1772; River Flow, 2203; Physical Properties of Rocks, 2225; Sediment Transport and Deposition, 2290; Weathering and Erosion, 2723.

ROCK MAGNETISM

Type of earth science: Geophysics
Field of study: Geomagnetism and paleomagnetism

Rock magnetism is the subdiscipline of geophysics that has to do with how rocks record the magnetic field, how reliable the recording process is, and what conditions can alter the recording and therefore raise the possibility of a false interpretation being rendered by geophysicists.

Principal terms

BASALT: a very common, dark-colored, fine-grained igneous rock

BLOCKING TEMPERATURE: the temperature at which a magnetic mineral becomes a permanent recorder of a magnetic field

CURIE TEMPERATURE: the temperature above which a permanently magnetized material loses its magnetization

DAUGHTER PRODUCT: an isotope that results from the decay of a radioactive parent isotope

DETRITAL REMANENT MAGNETIZATION: the magnetization that results when magnetic sediment grains in a sedimentary rock align with the magnetic field

FERROMAGNETIC MATERIAL: the type of magnetic material, such as iron or magnetite, that retains a magnetic field; also called permanent magnet

GRANITE: a low-density, light-colored, coarse-grained igneous rock

MAGNETITE: a magnetic iron oxide composed of three iron atoms and four oxygen atoms

RADIOACTIVITY: the spontaneous disintegration of a nucleus into a more stable isotope

THERMAL REMANENT MAGNETIZATION: the magnetization in igneous rock that results as magnetic minerals in a magma cool below their Curie temperature

Summary of the Phenomenon

The direct study of the earth's magnetic field is only four centuries old. This study involves the measurement of the field with scientific instruments and subsequent analysis of the resulting data. Four centuries is a very small fraction of the 4.6 billion years that the earth has existed; thus, direct study affords scientists very little understanding of the nature of the field over long periods of time. It is useful to know what happened to the earth's magnetic field in those billions of years before the present, because the field can be a source of information about conditions on the earth's surface and its interior. Magnetic minerals in rocks serve as recording devices, giving scientists clues regarding the nature of the ancient magnetic field.

A moving electric charge, such as an electron, produces a magnetic field that is the ultimate source of any larger magnetic field. An atom is composed of a nucleus, with its protons and neutrons, and the electrons that surround the nucleus. The protons do not move within the nucleus, and therefore they do not produce a magnetic field. The electrons, however, orbit the nucleus, and this movement produces a weak magnetic field. In addition, the electrons spin on their axes, and this activity also gives rise to a small magnetic field.

Because all atoms have electrons orbiting and spinning, one might think that all materials should have a permanent magnetic field, but the situation is more complicated. Strictly speaking, every material is magnetic, but there are different types of magnetism. Some materials are paramagnetic: When they are placed in an external magnetic field, the atoms align with the field. The atoms act as small compasses, orienting with the field, and the material is magnetized; the magnetic fields produced by the atom's electrons add to the intensity of the external field. When the external field is removed, however, the atom's orientation becomes randomized because of vibrations caused by heat, and the material is consequently demagnetized. Many materials, such as quartz, are paramagnetic and are not able to record the earth's magnetic field.

A much smaller number of minerals are ferromagnetic. There are various types of ferromagnetism, but the underlying principle is the same. In ferromagnetic materials, an external magnetic field again aligns the atoms parallel to the field, and the material is magnetized. When the field is removed, however, the atoms remain aligned, and the substance retains its magnetization; it is "permanently" magnetized. Actually, the substance can be demagnetized by heating or stress. Dropping a bar magnet on the floor or striking it with a hammer will demagnetize it slightly. The shock randomizes some of the atoms so that they cease to contribute to the overall magnetic field. The heating of a magnet above its Curie temperature also destroys its magnetization by randomizing the atoms and making the material paramagnetic. As the temperature drops below the Curie point, the material becomes slightly remagnetized, because the weak field of the earth aligns some of the atoms.

In ferromagnetic materials, atoms are not all aligned in one direction; rather, they are found in aligned groups, called domains. Under a microscope, the domains are barely visible. Within a particular domain, the atoms are aligned, but all the domains are not aligned in the same direction. A "permanent" magnetic material that is unmagnetized has all the domains randomly aligned, and the overall field cancels to zero. When placed in a magnetic field, some of the domains realign parallel to the direction of the field and stay aligned after the field is removed. It is these domains that give the material its overall magnetization. If a high enough magnetic field is applied, all the domains align with the field, and the magnetization has reached its saturation point; the strength of the material's magnetic field is at a maximum. One of the areas of research for physicists is the quest for materials that have high magnetic field strengths but with less material. Such materials are useful in making small, but powerful, electric motors.

Rocks are classified into three main groups: igneous, formed from crystallized molten rock; sedimentary, formed from weathered rock material; and metamorphic, produced when other rock is modified with heat, pressure, and fluids. Most magnetic minerals occur in igneous and sedimentary rocks.

Materials such as iron, cobalt, and nickel are ferromagnetic; for this reason they are used in making various permanent magnets. These metals are not found naturally on the earth's surface in the uncombined state, so they do not contribute to rocks' recording ability. Most of the minerals that make up rocks, such as quartz and clay, are not ferromagnetic. These minerals are useless as recorders, but many rocks contain magnetite or hematite, which are good recorders. These common magnetic minerals are oxides of iron.

Hematite is Fe_2O_3, which means that there are two iron atoms for every three oxygen atoms. Hematite is red in color, similar to rust on a piece of iron. Most reddish-brown hues in sedimentary rock are caused by hematite. This magnetic mineral is not a very strongly magnetized compound, but it is a very stable recorder in sedimentary rocks. Unfortunately, in many cases, its formation postdates that of the rock in which it occurs, so it does not necessarily record the magnetic field at the time of the rock's formation.

Magnetite (Fe_3O_4) has been known as lodestone for several millennia. It is a strongly magnetized iron compound that makes some igneous rocks very magnetic and supplies some of the recording ability of sedimentary rocks. The magnetite in rocks can record the field direction by one of several methods. In igneous rocks, magnetite crystals form as the magma cools. As the crystals grow, they align themselves with any magnetic field present. This process is called thermal remanent magnetization, or TRM. If the crystals are quite small or quite large, they cannot permanently record the field direction; after a short time the recording fades and becomes unreadable. The magnetism of such small grains is called superparamagnetism: They do align with a magnetic field, but they easily lose their orientation. The larger grains contain many magnetic domains that become misaligned over time so that the recording fades.

Grains the size of fine dust are good recorders. Unfortunately, not all igneous rocks have grains of the proper size. The size of the mineral crystal depends on the rate of cooling: When magma is cooled very slowly, large crystals are produced, while a rapid cooling results in smaller crystals. Granite is coarse-grained and thus is not the best recorder. The best igneous recorder is basalt, a black, fine-grained rock. Basalt can contain so much magnetite that a piece the size of a spool of thread acts like a bar magnet so that paper clips can be suspended from it. Basalt is fairly common on the surface of the earth, particularly in the ocean basins, where nothing but basalt underlies the sediment on the basin floor.

A useful magnetic recorder must provide information about how old it is. Basalt again fills this requirement, for its crystallization can be dated by measuring the amount of radioactive elements and their daughter products it contains. Clearly, basalt is an ideal source of information on the magnetic field. Unfortunately, it does not occur everywhere on the earth; moreover, as a recorder, it covers only times of eruptions of magma. Some other recorder must be used to fill in the blanks.

Sedimentary rock is formed from the products of the rock weathering that accumulate mostly in watery environments, such as rivers, lakes, and oceans. Clastic sedimentary rocks are formed from fragments of rock and mineral grains, such as grains of quartz in sandstone. Chemical sedimentary rock is derived from chemical weathering products, such as calcium carbonate or calcite, which is the major constituent of limestone. Most of the material in sedimentary rocks is not ferromagnetic, but there are a few grains of magnetite and other ferromagnetic compounds. As the grains fell through the water, they aligned with the magnetic field present at that time. When they hit the bottom, they retained the orientation, for the most part, and were subsequently covered by more sediment. This process is termed detrital remanent magnetization, or DRM.

An interesting aspect of DRM is the role that organisms play in its formation. The grains of magnetic minerals that fall through the water are oval-shaped, and when they strike the surface of the sediment they become misaligned with the field. Organisms such as worms disturb the sediment in a process known as bioturbation, which moves the sediment around and realigns the magnetic grains with the field. In the mid-1980's, it was discovered that certain varieties of bacteria have small grains of magnetite in their bodies. The bacteria use the grains like compasses to find their way down into the sediment on which they feed. The bacteria eventually die, and the magnetite grains become part of the sediment, aligned with the magnetic field; this phenomenon is known as biomagnetism.

The grain-size problem also occurs in DRM, given that sediment particle can be the size of a particle of clay, a boulder, or anything in between. Conglomerate, a rock composed of rounded pebbles and other large particles, is not a good recorder, nor is coarse sandstone. Finer sandstones, shales, siltstones, and mudstones are much better. Most chemical rocks, such as halite (common table salt), are poor recorders; limestone may or may not be good, depending on the conditions of formation.

The magnetization in sedimentary rocks is generally between one thousand and ten thousand times weaker than is the magnetization in a basalt. Very sensitive magnetometers are needed to measure the magnetic field in these specimens. To be useful in geomagnetic studies, sedimentary rocks must be dated, but this is a difficult task, as they cannot be dated using radioactive methods. By a complex method of determination, fossils can act as indicators of the age of the rock in which they are found. If igneous rock layers are located above and below the rock layer of interest, and if these igneous rock layers can be dated, an intermediate age can be assigned to the sedimentary layer.

Methods of Study

A magnetometer useful in the study of rock magnetism is the superconducting rock magnetometer, or SCM. Superconductivity is the phenomenon of a material's losing its resistance to electric current at low temperatures. Liquid helium is used to cool a portion of the magnetometer, composed of a cylinder of lead closed at one end. As the lead cools, it becomes superconducting, and if done in a region of low magnetic-field intensity, this low field is "trapped" inside the cylinder. Magnetic field sensors known as SQUIDS, or superconducting quantum interference devices, are very sensitive to low-intensity magnetic fields. The sample is lowered into the device, and its electronic display shows the intensity of the sample's magnetization. Such devices are useful in studying the rock magnetism of low-intensity sedimentary rocks.

The Curie temperature is important for establishing the thermal remanent magnetization for igneous rocks. A sample of a particular ferromagnetic material in a magnetic field is heated and the temperature is measured; the sample's Curie temperature is determined when the pull of the magnetic field on the sample weakens. The Curie point for various ferromagnetic materials is established by this method. Once that is done, the procedure is reversed. A sample of an unknown ferromagnetic material can be heated in a magnetic field to determine its Curie point, which can then be compared with the established table of values to identify the magnetic mineral. This method does not establish the exact composition of the material, but it does narrow down the possibilities, which is of value because other methods for determining composition are more expensive. In addition, it has been discovered that Curie temperature is not the only factor critical to the recording process. At the Curie point, the material is ferromagnetic but the recording ability is weak. The material has to cool through the blocking temperature for recording stability. Thereafter, magnetic minerals are magnetically stable for periods of billions of years.

Another area of study is the determination of the best grain size and shape for magnetic recording. Researchers experiment with different sizes and shapes of magnetic grains in magnetic fields of various strengths and directions and measure their responses to changes. It was found that crystals of magnetic materials such as magnetite develop features known as domains. These are areas where the atoms are aligned in one direction and produce the unified magnetic field for the domain. A small crystal has only one domain that can easily shift to another direction; therefore small crystals are poor recorders. If the crystal is quite large, it has many domains in which it is again easy to shift direction. Crystals with one large domain or several small domains are magnetically "hard" in that it is more difficult to shift the magnetic alignment. For magnetite, these are dust-sized particles, around 0.03 micron in diameter.

Other research reveals that the rock's recording of the field is not as "neat and clean" a process as portrayed in the previous paragraphs. Many events can lead to the alteration of the magnetic alignment. If the rock is heated above the Curie point and then cooled, the magnetic alignment is that of the field present at that time, and the old alignment is erased. The rock may be changed chemically, and old magnetic minerals may be destroyed and new ones produced. This process is referred to as chemical remanent magnetization, or CRM. These secondary magnetizations can be removed in some cases, and they can even provide more information on the rock's history. One method of magnetic cleaning or demagnetization involves subjecting the rock sample to an alternating magnetic field while other magnetic fields are reduced to zero. This "cleaning" will remove that portion of the mineral's magnetization that is magnetically "softer" than is the maximum alternating field. The magnetization above the level is unaffected and should represent the original magnetization. Heating a sample to a certain temperature is another method of demagnetization.

Context

The study of the earth's magnetic field history, and all the inferences about the earth drawn from that study, depends on the ability of rocks to record information about the magnetic field at the time of the rocks' formation. That ability, in turn, is dependent upon the magnetic characteristics of a few permanently magnetized minerals, such as magnetite.

The study of rock magnetism is rather esoteric; only a few individuals worldwide are involved in this subdiscipline of geomagnetism. Yet, such study has shown that rocks can faithfully record the history of the earth's magnetic field. This record is used to infer conditions on the earth hundreds of million years ago. Such studies have lent support to the idea that the continents have actually moved over the surface of the globe, and thus the theory of plate tectonics was born, with all its implications for the formation and location of petroleum and ore deposits, the origin of earthquakes and volcanoes, and the formation of mountain ranges such as the Himalaya. Such is an example of the odd twists and turns that science can take. Seemingly inconsequential findings can lead to a theory with great potential for making the earth and its workings much more understandable.

Bibliography

Cox, Allan, ed. *Plate Tectonics and Geomagnetic Reversals*. San Francisco: W. H. Freeman, 1973. Cox provides fascinating introductions to chapters that are composed of seminal papers concerning magnetic reversals and their contribution to the development of the theory of plate tectonics. Information on rock magnetism is scattered throughout the book in discussions on baked sediments, magnetization of basalt, magnetic intensity, and self-reversals in rocks. The papers are advanced for the average reader, but there are many graphs, diagrams, and figures that merit attention.

Glen, William. *The Road to Jaramillo: Critical Years of the Revolution in Earth Science*. Stanford, Calif.: Stanford University Press, 1982. This book gives a history of the plate tectonics revolution of the mid-1950's to the mid-1960's. Rock magnetism is specifically covered on pages 103-109. Other aspects of rock magnetism are discussed in various portions of the book, for example, those dealing with the magnetic minerals associated with rock magnetism and deep-sea core work. Of particular interest are the sections devoted to instruments used to measure rock magnetism.

Hargraves, R. B., and S. K. Banerjee. "Theory and Nature of Magnetism in Rocks." In *Annual Review of Earth and Planetary Sciences*, vol. 1, edited by F. Donath. Palo Alto, Calif.: Annual Reviews, 1973. The article covers the theories of the natural remanent magnetization of rocks (NRM). NRM is the combined magnetization of all magnetic minerals in a rock, such as those resulting from TRM. The various carriers of remanence are also covered, with a table that lists each mineral and its composition, crystal structure, magnetic structure, and other pertinent information. The paleomagnetic potential of rocks is also discussed. A few mathematical equations, but nothing too formidable. Numerous figures and a long list of references.

Lapedes, D. N., ed. *McGraw-Hill Encyclopedia of Geological Sciences*. New York: McGraw-Hill, 1978. Pages 704-708, under the heading "Rock Magnetism," provide concise descriptions of how rock magnetization occurs, the present field, magnetic reversals, secular variation, and apparent polar wandering. The text is very readable, with no mathematics and a fair number of graphs, tables, and figures.

O'Reilly, W. *Rock and Mineral Magnetism*. New York: Chapman and Hall, 1984. O'Reilly covers the atomic basis for magnetism, the magnetization process, the various remanent magnetizations such as TRM, the magnetic properties of minerals, and, finally, the applications of rock and mineral magnetism. Many tables, figures, and photographs of minerals. Some mathematics and chemistry are also included but should not be too difficult. References are included at the end of each chapter.

Stacey, F. D. *Physics of the Earth*. New York: John Wiley & Sons, 1977. Under section 9.1, "Magnetism of Rocks," the author provides a short, technical description of rock magnetism. Several figures show the various types of magnetic alignments. The domain structure of ferromagnetic materials is also discussed. Many other aspects of the earth's magnetic field are also covered at a technical level.

Tarling, D. H. *Paleomagnetism: Principles and Applications in Geology, Geophysics, and Archeology*. New York: Chapman and Hall, 1983. A very good resource on the subject of paleomagnetism, or the ancient magnetic field. Chapter 2 is devoted to the "physical basis" for the magnetization of material, with a discussion of the atomic level and the resulting magnetic domains. The various remanent magnetizations are covered in detail. Chapter 3 deals with the various magnetic minerals and their identification. The magnetization of the various rock types are covered in chapter 4. Chapter 5 discusses instruments used in paleomagnetic work. The remainder of the text deals with mathematical analysis used in paleomagnetic work and, finally, paleomagnetic applications.

Stephen J. Shulik

Cross-References

Earth's Age, 490; The Origin of Earth's Magnetic Field, 532; Secular Variation of Earth's Magnetic Field, 540; Earth's Magnetic Field at Present, 548; Geobiomagnetism, 811; Igneous Rocks: Basaltic, 1158; Crystallization of Magmas, 1420; Magnetic Reversals, 1439; Magnetic Stratigraphy, 1446; Oxides, 1976; Plate Tectonics, 2079; Polar Wander, 2101; Radioactive Decay, 2136.

MAGILL'S
SURVEY
OF
SCIENCE

ALPHABETICAL LIST

EARTH SCIENCE

CATEGORY LIST